THE ROUGH | KT-175-801

# Languedoc
# and Roussillon

There are more than two hundred Rough Guide titles
covering destinations from Alaska to Zimbabwe
and subjects from Acoustic Guitar to Travel Health

**Forthcoming travel guides include**
Devon & Cornwall • Malta • Tenerife
Thai Beaches and Islands • US Rockies • Vancouver

**Forthcoming reference guides include**
Cuban Music • 100 Essential Latin CDs • Personal Computers
Pregnancy & Birth • Trumpet & Trombone

**Rough Guides Online**
www.roughguides.com

## ROUGH GUIDE CREDITS

**Text editor:** Andrew Tomičić

**Series editor:** Mark Ellingham

**Editorial:** Martin Dunford, Jonathan Buckley, Jo Mead, Kate Berens, Amanda Tomlin, Ann-Marie Shaw, Paul Gray, Helena Smith, Judith Bamber, Orla Duane, Olivia Eccleshall, Ruth Blackmore, Geoff Howard, Claire Saunders, Gavin Thomas, Alexander Mark Rogers, Polly Thomas, Joe Staines, Richard Lim, Duncan Clark, Peter Buckley, Sam Thorne, Lucy Ratcliffe, Clifton Wilkinson, David Glen (UK); Andrew Rosenberg, Mary Beth Maioli, Stephen Timblin, Yuki Takagaki (US)

**Production:** Susanne Hillen, Andy Hilliard, Link Hall, Helen Ostick, Julia Bovis, Michelle Draycott, Katie Pringle, Robert Evers, Mike Hancock, Zoë Nobes

**Cartography:** Melissa Baker, Maxine Repath, Ed Wright, Katie Lloyd-Jones

**Picture research:** Louise Boulton, Sharon Martins

**Online:** Kelly Cross, Anja Mutić-Blessing, Jennifer Gold, Audra Epstein, Suzanne Welles (US)

**Finance:** John Fisher, Gary Singh, Edward Downey, Mark Hall, Tim Bill

**Marketing & Publicity:** Richard Trillo, Niki Smith, David Wearn, Chloë Roberts, Birgit Hartmann, Claire Southern (UK); Simon Carloss, David Wechsler, Kathleen Rushforth (US)

**Administration:** Tania Hummel, Demelza Dallow, Julie Sanderson

## ACKNOWLEDGEMENTS

Brian would like to thank Nuria Silleras Fernández, Elena Aznar, Peter Catlos, Robin Vose, Gîtes de France, Jean-François Pouget (CDT l'Hérault), Christian Rivière (OT Albi), Valérie Crouineau (CDT Ariège-Pyrénées), Myriam Journet-Fillaquier (CDT Aude), plus Jenny

Harris, Paul Brookes and D. Quadling for their letters. Thanks due also to Judith Bamber, Narelle Leffman and Kate Davis for Basics updates, Rob McKinlay for typesetting, The Map Studio, Romsey, Hants for cartography, and Susannah Wight for proofreading.

## PUBLISHING INFORMATION

This first edition published April 2001 by
  Rough Guides Ltd, 62–70 Shorts Gardens,
  London WC2H 9AH.
Distributed by the Penguin Group:
Penguin Books Ltd, 27 Wrights Lane, London W8 5TZ
Penguin Putnam, Inc. 375 Hudson Street, NY 10014,
  USA
Penguin Books Australia Ltd, 487 Maroondah Highway,
  PO Box 257, Ringwood, Victoria 3134, Australia
Penguin Books Canada Ltd, 10 Alcorn Avenue, Toronto,
  Ontario, Canada M4V 1E4
Penguin Books (NZ) Ltd, 182–190 Wairau Road,
  Auckland 10, New Zealand
Typeset in Linotron Univers and Century Old Style to an
  original design by Andrew Oliver.
Printed in England by Clays Ltd, St Ives PLC
Illustrations in Part One and Part Three by Edward Briant.

THE ROUGH GUIDE TO

# Languedoc
# and Roussillon

written and researched by

**Brian Catlos**

We set out to do something different when the first Rough Guide was published in 1982. Mark Ellingham, just out of university, was travelling in Greece. He brought along the popular guides of the day, but found they were all lacking in some way. They were either strong on ruins and museums but went on for pages without mentioning a beach or taverna. Or they were so conscious of the need to save money that they lost sight of Greece's cultural and historical significance. Also, none of the books told him anything about Greece's contemporary life – its politics, its culture, its people, and how they lived.

So with no job in prospect, Mark decided to write his own guidebook, one which aimed to provide practical information that was second to none, detailing the best beaches and the hottest clubs and restaurants, while also giving hard-hitting accounts of every sight, both famous and obscure, and providing up-to-the-minute information on contemporary culture. It was a guide that encouraged independent travellers to find the best of Greece, and was a great success, getting shortlisted for the Thomas Cook travel guide award,

and encouraging Mark, along with three friends, to expand the series.

The Rough Guide list grew rapidly and the letters flooded in, indicating a much broader readership than had been anticipated, but one which uniformly appreciated the Rough Guide mix of practical detail and humour, irreverence and enthusiasm. Things haven't changed. The same four friends who began the series are still the caretakers of the Rough Guide mission today: to provide the most reliable, up-to-date and entertaining information to independent-minded travellers of all ages, on all budgets.

We now publish more than 200 titles and have offices in London and New York. The travel guides are written and researched by a dedicated team of more than 100 authors, based in Britain, Europe, the USA and Australia. We have also created a unique series of phrasebooks to accompany the travel series, along with an acclaimed series of music guides, and a best-selling pocket guide to the Internet and World Wide Web. We also publish comprehensive travel information on our Web site:

**www.roughguides.com**

## HELP US UPDATE

We've gone to a lot of effort to ensure that the first edition of *The Rough Guide to Languedoc and Roussillon* is accurate and up to date. However, things change – places get "discovered", opening hours are notoriously fickle, restaurants and rooms raise prices or lower standards. If you feel we've got it wrong or left something out, we'd like to know, and if you can remember the address, the price, the time, the phone number, so much the better.

We'll credit all contributions, and send a copy of the next edition (or any other Rough Guide if you prefer) for the best letters. Please mark letters: "Rough Guide Languedoc and Roussillon Update" and send to:
Rough Guides, 62–70 Shorts Gardens, London WC2H 9AH, or Rough Guides, 4th Floor, 345 Hudson St, New York, NY 10014.
Or send email to: mail@roughguides.co.uk
Online updates about this book can be found on Rough Guides' Web site at **www.roughguides.com**

## THE AUTHOR

Born in Montréal in 1966, for the last sixteen years Brian Catlos has juggled university, travel and living abroad: as well as a student he's been, amongst other things, a motorbike despatch rider in London, hotel and coffeeshop runner in Amsterdam, tree-planter in northern Canada, and spent a year in the Middle East.

Having taken in all five continents on his travels and gained a PhD in Medieval Studies, Brian is now based mostly in Barcelona, where he lives with his lovely wife Núria. In addition to many academic articles and reviews, Brian has worked on *The Rough Guide to France* and *The Rough Guide to Barcelona*.

# CONTENTS

Introduction ix

# LIST OF MAPS

## MAP SYMBOLS

| | | | | | | |
|---|---|---|---|---|---|---|
| ▪▪▪▪ | International borders | P | Parking | 🗻 | Mountains |
| ▬▬▬ | Chapter division boundary | ⛷ | Ski station | ▲ | Peak |
| ═══ | Motorway | ♦ | Point of interest | ₥ | Spring |
| ═══ | Road | ⌁ | Lighthouse | ⌂ | Cave |
| ▥▥▥ | Steps | ⸸ | Church (regional maps) | Ⓗ | Hospital |
| ----- | Footpath | ⌂ | Abbey | ⓘ | Tourist office |
| ═══ | Waterway | ⌂ | Monastery | ⊠ | Post office |
| ─ ─ | Ferry route | ♜ | Castle | ■ | Building |
| ═■═ | Railway | ■ | Tower | ✚ | Church (town maps) |
| ✕✕✕ | ATM railway | ⸪ | Ruins | ⊞ | Cemetery |
| ✈ | Airport | 🏛 | Ancient site | ▒ | Park |
| ★ | Bus stop | ⊙ | Statue | ▒ | National park |
| Ⓜ | Metro stop | ⌂ | Refuge | ▒ | Forest |
| Ⓣ | Tram stop | ⤨ | Mountain pass | ▭ | Saltpan |

# INTRODUCTION

The Languedoc and Roussillon region is one of France's best-kept secrets. While Provence and the Côte d'Azur just across the Rhône have been living it up, attracting movie stars and the masses, its less pretentious neighbour has remained in comfortable obscurity. And so much the better for those in the know: a dramatically varied landscape, two distinct, proud cultures – Occitan and Catalan, a tradition of heresy and steadfast rebellion, and age-old customs all combine to make this a region deservedly unmatched in its romantic associations, at once epitomizing and contradicting everything that is France. Now shaking off centuries of sleepy neglect, Languedoc and Roussillon is emerging as one of the most enticing parts of the country, its remote villages and little-travelled byways affording a much-needed window onto a rural culture no longer found in northern France.

The **boundaries** of Languedoc have never been easy to fix. In its broadest – and original – sense, Languedoc includes the lands where the Occitan language (the *langue d'Oc*) was spoken in the Middle Ages, an area stretching along the Mediterranean from the foothills of the Pyrenees to the Italian Alps, and spreading north towards Savoy, through the Massif Central and west along the Atlantic coast, taking in even Bordeaux. Nowadays, for administrative purposes, it has been lumped together with its neighbour as the modern *région* of Languedoc-Roussillon, and trimmed down to the strip of coast running from Montpellier west to the border of Spain. But this latter, narrow definition of Languedoc is as inappropriate as the traditional one is vague. In defining Languedoc in this Guide, we've avoided artificial boundaries in favour of cultural and historical uniformity and the logistics of travel, so that the region covered butts up to neighbouring Provence at the Rhône, and stretches west and inland to include the medieval capital of Toulouse, as well as the lands of neighbouring Albi and Foix. Roussillon, Languedoc's accidental partner squashed in between the eastern Pyrenees and the Corbières hills, is also characterized by a particular linguistic heritage, derived in this case from a long history as part of the Catalan confederacy centred in Barcelona. Both regions have distinct cultures but, in addition to their border, share a common history of occupation, and of resistance and submission to the modern France of Paris and the north.

They also share a land renowned for its isolation, and immense diversity. On the far eastern edge, the Rhône disgorges into the swampy delta of the Camargue, the majority of which, east of the Petit Rhône, falls into adjacent Provence, leaving a small portion, the ranching territory of the **Petite Camargue** with its abundance of bird and wildlife, to Languedoc. A coastline of nearly unbroken **beach** bends west from here, punctuated by ancient fishing villages and their modern resort counterparts, while inland, beyond the band of the coastal plain, the land gradually rises, from scrubby hills to the cool, wooded highlands of **Haut Languedoc** and the forbidding peaks of the **Montagne Noir**. Great rivers, the Hérault, Orb and Aude, have carved their way down through the hills, leaving spectacular **gorges**, while vines and olive trees intersperse the rocks, giving way to a blanket of oak in the heights. West of Haut Languedoc the grain fields and vineyards extending from Toulouse to Albi are a world apart, while below it the **Canal du Midi**, a seventeenth-century waterway, bisects the region; south of its stately, cypress-lined banks the terrain rises again, first tentatively as the Corbières hills and the barren Pays de Sault, then surging skyward as the snow-capped **Pyrenees**. As the mountains draw close the coastline transforms into a series of rocky

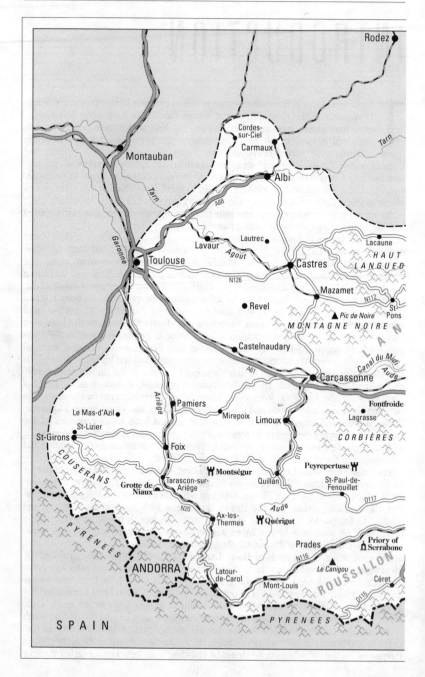

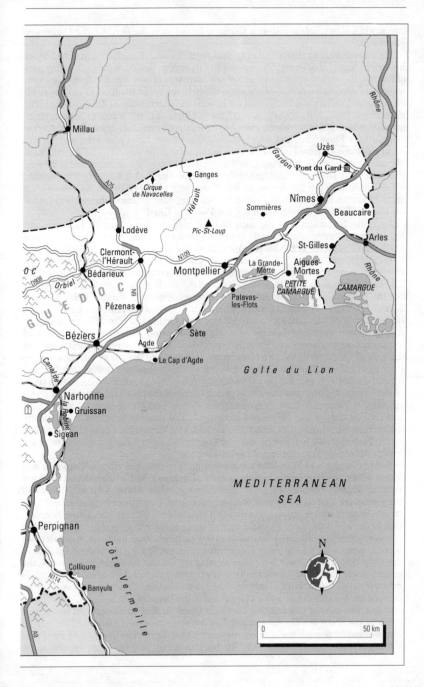

coves, while above, solitary **Mount Canigou** lords it over the deeply etched valleys of Roussillon.

The extraordinary geophysical range of Languedoc and Roussillon is matched by an **historical legacy** that lends the area much of its appeal. Settled as far back as any part of Europe, the region boasts evidence of our ancestors of over a half million years ago, while habitation in the Ariège valley some fifteen to thirty thousand years ago has yielded a rich and mysterious heritage of prehistoric **cave art**, some of the most engaging in southern Europe. As history dawned, the hill forts of Celtic tribes, or *oppida*, punctuated the broad Mediterranean plain – their scattered remnants are still visible today – while later Phoenician and Greek colonization on the coast paved the way for the eventual **Roman** expansion into the area in the second-century BC. The Romans built almost every town of importance in Languedoc today – the greatest being Nîmes, Narbonne and Toulouse – and linked them by roads such as the mighty Via Domitia, which sliced through the region to link Rome with southern Spain. An outstanding array of Roman monuments is the result, including Nîmes' **amphitheatre** and probably the world's most famous aqueduct, the **Pont du Gard**.

After the Romans it was the turn of local nobility, the counts of Toulouse and Barcelona respectively, to dominate Languedoc and Roussillon. Their wealth prompted a cultural renaissance in the Middle Ages, providing for the building of the sumptuously decorated and ubiquitous **Romanesque churches** and **monasteries** which still characterize the region, and engendering a mood of enlightenment as courtly troubadours and pilgrims en route to Santiago crossed the whole territory. Both left their mark, but the golden age wasn't to last, and in Languedoc popular dissatisfaction with the Church led to the following of a new – heretical – religion, Catharism, catalyst for the bloody series of wars known as the **Albigensian Crusades**. The military onslaught from the north and subsequent purge wrought destruction on the lands, leaving behind a record of events remembered with bitterness even now, and a string of spectacular and dramatically sited medieval fortresses, some restored like the *cité* of **Carcassonne** to their glory, others, like the Cathars' last redoubt at **Montségur**, left as desolate and romantic ruins. And as if this period wasn't unsettling enough, after three hundred years of submission to the crown and a brief period of prosperity based on dye manufacture – resulting in Toulouse's most opulent mansions – Languedoc rose up in rebellion again, this time as part of the **Huguenot** movement. The ensuing Religious Wars left the region scarred, repressed by autocratic rule and, with already poor Roussillon absorbed by the French crown too, marginalized and neglected. Even today it remains one of the least populated and poorest regions in the country.

But Languedoc and Roussillon are recovering. The principal cities of **Toulouse** and **Montpellier** are now bustling metropolises of industry and administration, injected with an alluring vibrancy by their university life, while towns such as Nîmes and Perpignan are managing to pull themselves out of a centuries-long slumber, their streets buzzing with people keen to savour a distinctive Mediterranean atmosphere and take in the new museums, art galleries and shops sprouting up across this part of the country. Away from the cities the mainstay is wine production, but tourism runs a close second. Languedoc's long sandy Mediterranean coast, lacking the overexploitation of the Cote d'Azur, has made it a prime destination for summer-time beach-goers, the coastal towns chock-full of facilities for every type of watersport imaginable. And this is only the tip of the **activities** iceberg. The Languedoc and Roussillon region is crisscrossed by an extensive network of long- and short-range hiking trails, or, if walking is too slow, you can opt to putt along the placid Canal du Midi in a converted barge, rent a *vélo* in just about any hamlet and pedal on the well-maintained bike trails, or chug up into the mountains on restored narrow-gauge train lines. The ranches of the Petite Camargue offer ample opportunity for horsemanship, and the high valleys of the

Pyrenees are peppered by ski resorts for the winter, while summer is the season for mule-trekking, canyoning and caving. Add to this a calendar packed with **festivals** ranging from local wine *fêtes* to the bullfights of Nîmes, from the traditional Catalan *sardana* dances of Roussillon to the cavalcades of horsemen and water-jousting revelry of Camarguaise celebrations and, in short, you have a variety which few parts of France, or indeed Europe, can match.

Diversity is also a feature of Languedoc and Roussillon's **cuisine**, which, though it shares in the finest Gallic culinary traditions, has in turn been infused by recent influences: immigration, both from Europe and abroad, has brought additional variety, with a strong Spanish influence complementing the already singular Catalan cookery of Roussillon, and Maghrebi and African newcomers adding a piquant element. In every village and town you'll find the solid, delicious *terroir* fare on which the region has subsisted for centuries: hearty cassoulet, foie gras, duck, a whole range of pork sausages and cheeses, fruits, nuts and olives from the sunbaked hills of Roussillon and Hérault, as well as truffles, mushrooms and other local products. Though it tends to get overshadowed by neighbouring regions, Languedoc and Roussillon is no slouch when it comes to **wine** either. Gaillac, from near Albi, is the oldest and most respected of the local *appellations*, but the eminently drinkable wines of the Corbières and Cabardès are also well reputed. Even if you're not a connoisseur you should take the opportunity to try out unique local vintages, such as Limoux's *blanquette* or the "sand wine" of the Petite Camargue.

## When to go

Languedoc and Roussillon is an exciting region to visit at any time of the year, all the more so because of its gentle **climate**. The weather is rarely extreme, although August temperatures can come close to sweltering, and mountain evenings remain cool all year round. Pack with this in mind, and bring along at least a jumper and raincoat, even if you're coming in the warmer months.

Many activities and events in the region are restricted by **season**. This doesn't apply so much if you're sticking to the major towns and architectural highlights – you're better off avoiding high-season accommodation prices and hassles, particularly in places like Carcassonne, Pézenas and Cordes, and entertainment and nightlife tend to be bet-

### AVERAGE DAILY MAXIMUM AND MINIMUM TEMPERATURES (°C) AND MONTHLY RAINFALL (MM)

| | Jan | Feb | March | April | May | June | July | Aug | Sept | Oct | Nov | Dec |
|---|---|---|---|---|---|---|---|---|---|---|---|---|
| **Montpellier** | | | | | | | | | | | | |
| Max | 10 | 12 | 15 | 17 | 21 | 25 | 28 | 27 | 24 | 20 | 15 | 11 |
| Min | 1 | 1 | 5 | 7 | 10 | 13 | 16 | 16 | 13 | 9 | 5 | 2 |
| Rain | 56 | 29 | 72 | 56 | 46 | 33 | 20 | 40 | 100 | 94 | 70 | 89 |
| **Toulouse** | | | | | | | | | | | | |
| Max | 8 | 11 | 13 | 16 | 20 | 25 | 27 | 27 | 24 | 18 | 12 | 9 |
| Min | 1 | 2 | 3 | 6 | 9 | 12 | 15 | 15 | 12 | 8 | 5 | 2 |
| Rain | 48 | 43 | 58 | 68 | 73 | 60 | 38 | 53 | 58 | 55 | 60 | 58 |

ter out of season too, but apart from that you've no major worries. Getting off the beaten track out of season, however, will need more careful planning, as many museums and monuments have very short hours from October to May, and restaurants and hotels frequently board up for the winter. Bus services are also liable to change; in summer months coastal services increase, while rural ones (often for school children) scale down. Likewise, most outdoor activities are limited by season: swimming and watersports are practical from late June to early September, canal boating from April to November, and skiing from December to April (sometimes longer depending on the weather). Other activities, like hiking, can be done year round, but bear in mind the potential both for high temperatures in summer and unpredictable weather in the mountains.

In addition, the **cultural and sporting calendar** may determine when you want to travel. You'll find colourful folk festivals and musical events taking place just about every month, but you might want to plan your visit to coincide with, say, a bullfight, in which case you should visit between Easter and September. Rugby leagues adjourn for the summer, while the coastal water-jousts are only held from June to September. Many towns have their local *fête* in late summer or early autumn, timed as often as not with the local harvest, and this time of year also sees a profusion of theatre and music festivals. Bastille Day (July 14) and Midsummer's Day (June 24) are major national celebrations, while Setmana Santa (Holy Week) in Roussillon, has a distinctly Catalan flavour.

All things considered the best month to visit is probably June, when the weather is warm but not hot and you've got the widest range of activities and events, without the crowds of July and August. Next best are the "shoulder" seasons of late spring (mid-April to May) and early autumn (Sept to mid-Oct) – particularly good if you plan on doing a lot of hiking or biking. But even if you do go in peak season, you can easily escape the crowds by wandering off the beaten path; you'll find that even a slight detour from a bustling town or city can bring you to a village where you'll find no shortage of accommodation, and a bit of peace.

# PART ONE

# THE

# BASICS

# GETTING THERE FROM BRITAIN

The quickest and most cost-effective way of reaching Languedoc and Roussillon from most parts of Britain is by air, though in the southeast of England this is now rivalled closely by the Channel Tunnel rail link, from where you can connect to the fast and efficient TGV services south from Lille and Paris. The standard rail- or road-and-sea routes are more affordable, but can be uncomfortable and tiring – and if you're just going for a short break, the journey time can significantly eat into your holiday.

## BY AIR

**Flying** can represent a considerable saving in time compared to other methods of getting to Languedoc and Roussillon: you can fly into Toulouse in less than two hours from London, for example. Direct flights from British regional airports also exist, and prices are not unfavourable compared with London fares. However, as often as not, if you live outside London, you'll find it pays to go to the capital and fly on to France from there: scheduled flights from London to Toulouse are available for as little as £120 and to Montpellier for around £140. To find the best deals you should shop around, ideally a month or so before you plan to leave.

Predictably, Air France and British Airways are the main carriers to France from Britain, offering **scheduled flights** and Apex fares which must be reserved one or two weeks in advance (depending on the route taken), and must include

one Saturday night. Your return date must be fixed when purchasing, and no subsequent changes are allowed. A couple of **low-cost airlines** also offer scheduled flights into the region – or hubs within easy striking distance of it – namely Ryanair and Buzz. There are no advance purchase conditions with these airlines, but obviously the earlier you book your seat the greater chance you have of taking advantage of special offers and availability.

**Air France** fly from Heathrow at least once daily direct to Toulouse, and to Paris Charles de Gaulle (from where you can make onward connections to Montpellier and Toulouse) around ten times daily; they also fly four times daily from London City (Mon–Fri) to Paris CDG, and daily from Manchester, Birmingham, Edinburgh and Glasgow. **British Airways** fly three times daily from Gatwick to Marseille, and once daily to Montpellier; they also fly to Paris CDG three times daily from Gatwick, eight times daily from Heathrow and at least once daily from Birmingham, Manchester, Newcastle, Aberdeen, Edinburgh and Glasgow.

There are a few direct flights into the region – mostly out of the London airports – with the new breed of low-cost airlines; these companies also offer a more frequent service into Paris, from where you could connect to internal flights or TGV trains south. **Ryanair** fly once daily out of Stansted to both Carcassonne and Nîmes; return fares can drop as low as £20, but generally they range, depending on season, from £60–150 for Carcassonne, and £45–125 for Nîmes, all exclusive of tax and subject to restrictions. **Buzz** fly daily from Stansted to Marseille, just over an hour east of Nîmes by train, for as little as £55 each way, and three times daily to Paris CDG – they also have winter-only deals into Toulouse.

A good place to look for **discount fares** from London to France is the classified travel sections of papers such as the *Independent* and the *Daily Telegraph* (Saturday editions), the *Observer*, *Sunday Times* and *Independent on Sunday*, where agents advertise special deals; if you're in London, check the back pages of the listings magazine *Time Out*, the *Evening Standard* or the free travel mag *TNT*, found outside main-line train stations. Independent travel specialists such as STA Travel and Campus Travel do deals for students and anyone under 26, or can simply sell a scheduled ticket at a discount price. Bear in mind that any travel agent can sell you a **package deal** with a tour operator (see p.8) and these can often offer exceptional bargain travel; sometimes it's possible to just buy the ticket for the **charter flight** – in theory supposed to be sold in conjunction with accommodation – at a discount. It's also worth keeping an eye on **Web sites** such as *www.lastminute.com*, *www.cheapflights.co.uk*, *www.deckchair.com* and *www.travelocity.com*,

which can offer some of the best discounted fares and last-minute deals available.

### BY TRAIN

The Channel Tunnel has slashed travelling time by **train** to France and has also led to a multitude of cut-rate deals on regular train and ferry or hovercraft fares via Calais, Boulogne and Dieppe. Crossing the Channel by sea and making onward connections to Languedoc and Roussillon by train can work out to be slightly cheaper than using the

---

## AIRLINES AND TRAVEL AGENTS IN BRITAIN

### AIRLINES

**Air France** ☎0845/084 5111,
*www.airfrance.fr.*
**British Airways** ☎0845/773 3377,
*www.britishairways.com.*
**British Midland** ☎0870/6070 555,
*www.britishmidland.co.uk.*

**Buzz** ☎0870/240 7070,
*www.buzzaway.com.*
**Ryanair** direct sales ☎0870/1569 569,
*www.ryanair.com.*

### TRAVEL AGENTS

**Campus Travel** (*www.campustravel.co.uk*), 52 Grosvenor Gardens, London SW1W 0AG (☎0870/240 1010). There are also branches in Birmingham (☎0121/414 1848); Brighton (☎01273/570 226); Bristol (☎0117/929 2494); Cambridge (☎01223/324 283); Edinburgh (☎0131/668 3303); Glasgow (☎0141/553 1818); Manchester (☎0161/273 1721); and Oxford (☎01865/242 067). Student/youth travel specialists, with branches also in YHA shops and on university campuses all over Britain.

**Flightbookers**, 177–178 Tottenham Court Rd, London W1P 0LX (☎020/7757 2000, *ebookers.com*); Gatwick Airport, South Terminal inside the British Rail Station (☎01293/568 300). Low fares on a wide selection of scheduled flights.

**North South Travel**, Moulsham Mill Centre, Parkway, Chelmsford, Essex CM2 7PX (☎01245/608 291). Friendly, competitive travel agency, offering discounted fares to most destinations – profits are used to support projects in the developing world, especially the promotion of sustainable tourism.

**STA Travel** (*www.statravel.co.uk*), London: 86 Old Brompton Rd, SW7 3LH; 117 Euston Rd, NW1 2SX; 38 Store St, WC1E 7BZ; and 11

Goodge St, W1P 2SX (☎020/7361 6161). There are also branches in Brighton (☎01273/728 282); Bristol (☎0117/929 4399); Cambridge (☎01223/366 966); Leeds (☎0113/244 9212); Liverpool (☎0151/707 1223); Manchester (☎0161/834 0668); Newcastle-upon-Tyne (☎0191/233 2111); Oxford (☎01865/792 800); Aberdeen (☎0122/465 8222); Edinburgh (☎0131/226 7747); and Glasgow (☎0141/338 6000); and on university campuses throughout Britain. Worldwide specialists in low-cost flights and tours for students and under-26s.

**Thomas Cook**, 45 Berkeley St, London W1X 5AE; and high streets across London and the UK (nationwide ☎0870/5666 222; Flights Direct ☎0870/5101 520, *www.tch.thomascook.com*). Long-established travel agency for package holidays and scheduled flights, with bureau de change (issuing Thomas Cook travellers cheques), own travel insurance and car rental.

**Trailfinders** (*www.trailfinders.com*), London: 1 Threadneedle St, EC2R 8JX (☎020/7628 7628); 215 Kensington High St, W6 6BD (☎020/7937 5400). There are also branches in Birmingham (☎0121/236 1234); Bristol (☎0117/929 9000); Manchester (☎0161/839 6969); Glasgow (☎0141/353 2224). One of the best-informed and most efficient agents for independent travellers.

Channel Tunnel, but you should note that it does take considerably longer, and is generally less convenient.

**Eurostar** operate high-speed passenger trains daily from London Waterloo to the continent via Ashford in Kent and the Channel Tunnel. There are nine trains daily direct to **Lille** (2hr) in northern France, from where you can connect at the same station with the high-speed **TGV network** to various stations in Languedoc and Roussillon (see p.31); there are two trains daily to Toulouse, a journey taking eight hours and costing £100–140, and three to Nîmes, which takes 5–6 hours and costs £80–105. There are also at least thirteen Eurostar trains daily from London to Paris-Gare du Nord (3hr).

Standard-class return **fares** from London to Lille range from £60 with the "Leisure Apex 14", which must be bought up to fourteen days before departure and must include a Saturday night, with fixed outward and return dates and no refunds. There are other cheap deals – such as the "Leisure Flexi", which can be purchased up to thirty minutes before departure for £110 – but for a high-season ticket with changeable departure and return times, bought close to your departure date, you're looking at £220. Youth-fare **concessions** are available on all the routes (student discounted tickets are only available from STA and USIT Campus Travel, not directly from Eurostar) – there are concessions also for over-60s, and for holders of an international rail pass.

You can also get **through-ticketing** – including the tube journey to Waterloo International – from other mainline stations in Britain; typical add-on prices for a return ticket to Lille from Edinburgh or Glasgow are £30, from Manchester £20 and Birmingham £10. However, there is still no sign of the promised direct high-speed Eurostar services from the north of England, Scotland and the Midlands, which means that add-on time to your journey is around four or six hours if you're travelling from the north of England or southern Scotland respectively.

**Tickets** can be bought directly over the phone from Eurostar, from most travel agents, from all main rail stations in Britain, and from the Waterloo International and Ashford ticket offices.

## TRAIN PASSES

If you plan to use the rail network to travel more widely than just in Languedoc and Roussillon,

---

### USEFUL TRAIN CONTACTS

**Campus Travel** (see box opposite).

**Eurolines**, 52 Grosvenor Gardens, London SW1W 0AU (bookings and enquiries ☎020 /7730 8235 or 01582/404 511, *www.gobycoach .com*). Tickets can also be purchased from any National Express agent (☎0870/5808 080).

**Eurostar**, Eurostar House, Waterloo Station, London SE1 8SE (☎0870/5186 186, *www .eurostar.com*).

**Eurotunnel**, Customer Services Centre, PO Box 300, Dept 302, Folkestone, Kent CT19 4QD (information and bookings ☎0870/5353 535, *www.eurotunnel.com*).

**Rail Europe**, 179 Piccadilly, London W1V 0BA (☎0870/584 8848, *www.raileurope.co.uk*).

---

there are several **train passes** you might consider buying before you leave.

The **Euro Domino Pass**, available from Rail Europe (SNCF) and USIT Campus offers unlimited rail travel through France for any three (£99), four (£119), five (£139), six (£159), seven (£178) or eight (£198) days within a calendar month; passengers under 25 pay £79, £95, £111, £127, £143 and £159 respectively. Children under 4 travel free, and those aged between 4 and 11 are charged half the adult price.

**InterRail** passes cover eight European "zones" and are available for either 22-day or one-month periods; you must have been resident in Europe for at least six months before you can buy the pass. The passes for those over 26 have now been extended to cover the same territory as for those under 26 and the only difference now is the price. France is in the zone including Belgium, the Netherlands and Luxembourg. A 22-day pass to travel this area is £159/229, a two-zone pass valid for a month is £209/279, a three-zone £229/309, and an all-zones pass £259/349. The pass is available from the same outlets as the Euro Domino (see above) and from STA Travel.

Note that InterRail passes do not include travel between Britain and the continent. Both the Euro Domino and InterRail passes entitle you to a discount on the Eurostar service, and on rail-ferry links to France.

## BY BUS

**Eurolines** run regular bus-ferry services from London Victoria to over sixty French cities. Prices

## SEA CROSSINGS

*The following services are ferry crossings, unless otherwise stated.*

| Route | Operator | Crossing Time | Frequency | One-Way Fares Small car + 2 adults | Foot passengers |
|---|---|---|---|---|---|
| **BRITTANY** | | | | | |
| Portsmouth–St-Malo | Brittany Ferries | 8hr 45min–11hr | 7 weekly | £97–203 | £24–47 |
| Poole–St-Malo (via Jersey and Guernsey) | Condor Ferries | 5hr 25min | 1 daily | £95–187 | £26 |
| Plymouth–Roscoff | Brittany Ferries | 6hr–7hr 30min | 2–12 weekly | £110–189 | £27–48 |
| Weymouth–St-Malo (via Jersey and Guernsey) | Condor Ferries | 5hr | May–Oct 1 daily | £95–187 | £27 |
| **NORMANDY** | | | | | |
| Newhaven–Dieppe (catamaran) | Hoverspeed | 2hr | 1–3 daily | £139–£195 | £28 |
| **CHERBOURG** | | | | | |
| Portsmouth–Cherbourg | P&O Portsmouth | 2hr 45min–7hr 30min | 1–7 daily | £95–178 | £20–41 |
| Poole–Cherbourg | Brittany Ferries | 4hr 15min–5hr 45min | 1–2 daily | £100–171 | £21–42 |
| Portsmouth–Caen | Brittany Ferries | 6hr | 2–3 daily | £80–185 | £19–43 |
| Portsmouth–Le Havre | P&O Portsmouth | 5hr 30min–7hr 30min | 2–3 daily | £95–178 | £20–41 |
| **PAS-DE-CALAIS** | | | | | |
| Folkestone–Boulogne (catamaran) | Hoverspeed | 55min | 4 daily | £115–155 | £24 |
| Dover–Calais | P&O Stena | 1hr 15min | 30–35 daily | £105–123 | £24 |
| Dover–Calais | Sea France | 1hr 30min | 15 daily | £118–163 | £15 |
| Dover–Calais (hovercraft) | Hoverspeed | 35min | 9–16 daily | £125–169 | £24 |
| **BELGIUM** | | | | | |
| Hull–Zeebrugge | P&O North Sea Ferries | 13hr 15min | 1 daily | £152–188 | £37–46 |

### RELEVANT FERRY COMPANIES IN BRITAIN

**Brittany Ferries** ☎0870/901 2400, *www.brittany-ferries.co.uk.*
**Condor Ferries** ☎01305/761551, *www.condorferries.co.uk.*
**Hoverspeed** ☎0870/524 0241, *www.hoverspeed.co.uk.*
**P&O North Sea Ferries** ☎01482/377177, *www.ponsf.com.*

**P&O Portsmouth** ☎0870/242 4999, *www.poportsmouth.com.*
**P&O Stena** ☎0870/600 0600, *www.posl.com.*
**Sea France** ☎0870/571 1711, *www.seafrance.com.*

are very much lower than for the same journey by train, with adult return fares at the time of writing £45 for Paris, £35 for Lille, and £89 each for Bordeaux and Toulouse, the journey time to Toulouse being roughly nineteen hours. Regional return fares from the rest of England and from Wales are available as are student and youth discounts. Again, prices are very much lower than for the same journey by train. As well as ordinary tickets on its scheduled coach services to an extensive list of European cities, Eurolines offers a pass for Europe-wide travel, for either thirty days (over-26s £245, youth pass and over-60s £195) or sixty days (£283/£227). **Tickets** are available directly from the company, from National Express agents and from most high-street travel agents.

## BY CAR: EUROTUNNEL AND MOTORAIL

It's a long drive south to Languedoc and Roussillon from the north coast of France, but if you do want to take your **car** with you, the most convenient way is to drive down to the **Channel Tunnel**, load your car on the train shuttle, and be whisked under the Channel in 35 minutes, arriving at Coquelles on the French side, near Calais. The Channel Tunnel entrance is off the M20 at junction 11A, just outside Folkestone, and the sole operator, **Eurotunnel**, offers a frequent, daily service. Because of the frequency of the service, you don't have to buy a ticket in advance (though this might be advisable in mid-summer and during other school holidays), but you must arrive at least thirty minutes before departure; the target loading time is just ten minutes. Inside the carriages, you can get out of your car to stretch your legs during the crossing. Tickets are available through Eurotunnel's Customer Service Centre, on the Internet or from your local travel agent. Fares are calculated per car, regardless of the number of passengers, and rates depend on the time of year, time of day and length of stay (the cheapest ticket is for a day-trip, followed by a five-day return); it's cheaper to travel between 10pm and 6am, while the highest fares are reserved for weekend departures and returns in July and August. As an example, a five-day trip at an off-peak time starts at £95 (passengers included) in the low season and goes up to £135 in the peak period.

If you don't want to drive far when you've reached France, you can take advantage of SNCF's **motorail**, which you can book through Rail Europe, putting your car on the train in either

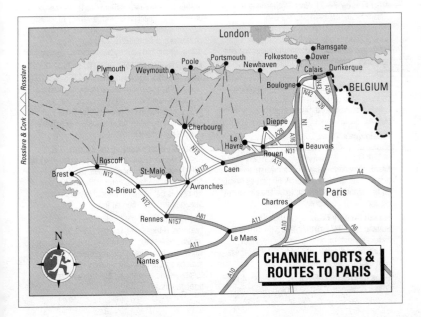

**CHANNEL PORTS & ROUTES TO PARIS**

Calais or Paris for Narbonne or Toulouse. This is a relatively expensive option though: for four people travelling from Calais to Toulouse, for example, the return price ranges from £560 to £980, dependent on the time of year.

## BY FERRY, HOVERCRAFT AND CATAMARAN

Though undoubtedly less convenient than travelling by plane or via the Channel Tunnel by train, **ferry, hovercraft and catamaran services** can work out to be much the cheapest way of getting to Languedoc and Roussillon, especially if you are travelling in a group, or are planning on hitching your way south through France. The most frequent crossings are between Dover and Calais, and Folkestone and Boulogne; while the services

out of Portsmouth to St-Malo, Cherbourg, Caen and Le Havre, are amongst the most competitively priced. If you're coming from the north of England or Scotland, you should consider the Hull–Zeebrugge (Belgium) overnight crossing with P&O North Sea Ferries.

Ferry **prices** are seasonal and, for motorists, depend on the size of your vehicle. The popular Dover–Calais routing costs from £105 one-way for a car and two adults. Note that return prices are substantially cheaper than one-way fares, but generally need to be booked in advance – details of routes, companies and current fares are given in the box on p.6. You can either contact the companies direct to reserve space in advance – essential in peak season if you're intending to drive – or any travel agent in the UK or France will

## TOUR OPERATORS AND VILLA AGENCIES IN THE UK

**Abercrombie & Kent**, Sloane Square House, Holbein Place, London SW1W 8NS (☎020/7730 9600, *www.abercrombiekent.co.uk*). Upmarket travel company providing "private travel arrangements for discerning travellers" – from finding that *châteaux* hideaway in the Pyrenees, to chartering a yacht for touring along the coast.

**Allez France**, 27–31 West St, Storrington, West Sussex RH20 4DZ (☎01903/742 345, *www.greatescapes.co.uk*). Self-drive and fly-drive accommodation packages (cottages, villas, hotels and caravans) throughout Languedoc and Roussillon. Also offers help organizing camping trips.

**Bike Tours**, Victoria Works, Lambridge Mews, Larkhall, Bath BA1 6QE (☎01225/310 859, *www.biketours.co.uk*). Biking trips throughout the region.

**Dominique's Villas**, 25 Thames House, 140 Battersea Park Rd, London SW11 4NB (☎020/7738 8772, *www.dominiquesvillas.com*). Small, upmarket agency with a diverse and tempting range of mostly older properties (some quite historic). Most are for large groups, sleeping six to eight or more.

**French Country Cruises**, 54 High St East, Rutland LE15 9PZ (☎01572/821 330). Offers a comprehensive range of cruises throughout France as well as offering boat rental for those who'd sooner go it alone.

**Gîtes de France Ltd**. The UK operation of this French Government letting service was taken

over in 1997 by Brittany Ferries (☎0870/901 2400, *www.brittany-ferries.co.uk*), although you can still deal directly with Gîtes de France (see p.40). Comprehensive list of houses, cottages and chalets throughout the south of France; ferry crossings extra.

**Holiday in France**, Model Farm, Rattlesden, Suffolk IP30 0SY (☎01449/737 664). Off-the-beaten-track specialists, with a variety of villas and some very attractive *chambres d'hôte* in *châteaux* and farmhouses. Also golf, horse-riding, skiing and boating holidays.

**Martin Randall Travel** (☎020/8742 3355, *www.martinrandall.com*). Small-group cultural tours led by experts on art, architecture, archeology and music. Tours are very specialized, and this is reflected in the price, but for those with specialist knowledge and interest, they may well prove a rewarding investment.

**Susie Madron's Cycling for Softies**, 2 & 4 Birch Polygon, Manchester M14 5HX (☎0161/248 8282, *www.cycling-for-softies.co.uk*). An easy-going cycle holiday operator. Although luggage transfer is not included in the deals, this can be arranged for an additional fee.

**Voyages Ilena**, 1 Old Garden House, The Lanterns, Bridge Lane, London SW11 3AD (☎020/7924 4440). Specializing in self-catering villas, this helpful and friendly agency can also arrange accommodation in luxury hotels; flights, fly-drives and tailor-made holidays can be arranged too.

do it for you. All ferry companies also offer foot passenger fares only, from £20 one-way; accompanying bicycles can usually be carried free, at least in the low season, and for a charge of around £5 one-way in mid- and high seasons.

The ferry companies will often offer **special deals** on three-, five- and ten-day returns, or discounts for regular users who own a property abroad. The tour operator **Eurodrive** (☎020/8324 4007, *www.eurodrive.co.uk*) can also arrange discounts on ferry crossings for people taking their cars across the Channel.

## PACKAGE TOURS

Any travel agent will be able to provide details of the many operators running **package tours** to Languedoc and Roussillon (see box opposite), which can be a competitively priced way of travelling. Some deals are straightforward travel-plus-hotel affairs, while others offer tandem

touring, air-and-rail packages and stays in country cottages. If your trip is geared around specific interests – like cycling or self-catering in the countryside – packages can work out much cheaper than the same arrangements made on arrival. Packages can also be a good idea if you are on a tight schedule, as these deals often include free transfers to your hotel and guided tours as well as flights and accommodation, leaving you more time to enjoy your holiday.

In addition to the addresses in the box opposite, bear in mind that most of the ferry companies (see p.6) also offer their own travel and accommodation deals. The **French Holiday Service** at 178 Piccadilly, London W1V 0AL (☎020/7355 4747), can book an especially large range. A complete list of package operators is available from the **French Government Tourist Office**, also at 178 Piccadilly, London W1V 0AL (☎0906/824 4123).

## GETTING THERE FROM IRELAND

By far the fastest – though often not the cheapest – way of getting to the south of France from Ireland is by plane. There are good deals out of the regional airports direct to the south of France as well as out of Dublin via Paris; you can also fly via Paris from Belfast, but the costs are generally much higher and the number of flights far fewer. It is also possible to sail to

northern France from Cork and Rosslare, and from there head south by car or train. However, the journey time is long (sea crossings are around 15hr) and the costs are not significantly lower than the flight deals out of the regional airports – but for families, or other groups travelling by car, and for those for whom cost is a bigger consideration than time, the ferries are an attractive option.

### BY AIR

By far the most convenient way to fly from the **Irish Republic** to Languedoc and Roussillon is with Go Holidays, who arrange charter flights in high season (April–Sept) from Shannon, Cork and Dublin to Toulouse, Montpellier and Marseille from IR£179/€227.28 return. Other options include flying with Aer Lingus, direct from Dublin and most other regional airports, to Paris CDG for around IR£199/€253, and continuing by air or overland from there; or with Ryanair, who have two flights daily from Dublin to Beauvais Tillé airport outside Paris for IR£97.50/€124.

In **Northern Ireland**, British Airways fly directly from Belfast City Airport to Paris CDG, but prices are generally much higher than taking a routing through London or Amsterdam – for example, Ryanair fly out of Derry Airport to London Stansted for around £60, from where you can pick up their onward flight to Nîmes. The French Holiday Service (see p.9) can arrange package deals including flights from Belfast.

## BY FERRY

The cheapest way of getting to France from Ireland – though far from the quickest – is by **ferry** from Cork or Rosslare outside Wexford to Cherbourg or Roscoff, in Brittany. From here you can head south by car or continue your journey by train – any of the ferry operators detailed in the box opposite should be able to arrange an

onward train ticket when you book your ferry crossing direct with them.

Ferry **prices** vary according to season and, for motorists, the size of their car; note that return prices are substantially cheaper but generally need to be booked in advance. Services are run by Brittany Ferries and Irish Ferries, and prices are around IR£140/€178 to IR£330/€419 for a small car and two adults one-way; P&O Irish Sea offer a slightly cheaper service for cars with no passengers. Foot passengers will pay between IR£45/€57 and IR£85/€108. Often ferry companies will offer special deals on return fares for a specified period, so check first. You can either contact the companies direct to reserve space in advance (essential at peak season if you're driving), or any competent travel agent at home can do it for you.

---

### AIRLINES, TRAVEL AGENTS AND TOUR OPERATORS IN IRELAND

#### AIRLINES

**Aer Lingus** Republic: ☎01/705 3333; Northern Ireland: ☎0845/973 7747; *www.aerlingus.ie*.

**British Airways** Republic: ☎1800/626 747; Northern Ireland: ☎0845/722 2111; *www.british-airways.com*.

**Ryanair** Republic: ☎01/609 7800; Northern Ireland ☎0870/156 9569; *www.ryanair.com*.

#### TRAVEL AGENTS

**Joe Walsh Tours**, 69 Upper O'Connell St, Dublin 2 (☎01/872 2555); 8–11 Baggot St, Dublin 2 (☎01/676 3053); 117 St Patrick St, Cork (☎021/277 959). Discounted flight agent.

**Thomas Cook**, 118 Grafton St, Dublin 2 (☎01/677 0469); 11 Donegall Place, Belfast (☎028/9055 0232 or 554 455). Package holiday and flight agent who can also arrange travellers cheques, insurance and car rental.

**Trailfinders**, 4–5 Dawson St, Dublin 2 (☎01/677 7888, *www.trailfinders.ie*). Competitive fares out of all Irish airports, as well as deals on hotels, insurance, tours and car rental.

**USIT** (*www.usitnow.ie*), 19 Aston Quay, Dublin 2 (☎01/602 1777 or 677 8117); Fountain Centre, College St, Belfast (☎028/9032 4073); plus branches in Cork, Galway, Limerick, Waterford and Derry. Student and youth specialists for flights and trains.

#### TOUR OPERATORS

**Go Holidays**, 28 North Great George St, Dublin 1 (☎01/874 4126). French holiday specialists offering city-breaks, fly-drive packages and charter flights to regional destinations.

**Irish Ferries**, 2–4 Merrion Row, Dublin 2 (☎1890/313 131, *www.irishferries.ie*). Self-drive self-catering package holidays – camping, mobile homes, apartments – to all coastal regions of France.

## FERRY ROUTES AND PRICES

| Route | Operator | Crossing Time | Frequency | One-Way Fares | |
|-------|----------|---------------|-----------|---------------|--|
| | | | | Small car + 2 adults | Foot passenger |
| Cork–Roscoff | Brittany Ferries | 14hr | April–Sept 1 weekly | IR£140–330/ €177.76–419 | IR£45–85/ €57.14–107.93 |
| Rosslare–Cherbourg | Irish Ferries | 16hr | March–Oct 2–3 weekly | IR£140–330/ €177.76–419 | IR£45–85/ €57.14–107.93 |
| Rosslare–Cherbourg | P&O Irish Sea | 18hr | 3 weekly | IR£110–260/ €139.67–330 | not allowed |
| Rosslare–Roscoff | Irish Ferries | 15hr | April–Sept 1–3 weekly | IR£140–330/ €177.76–149 | IR£45–85/ €57.14–107.93 |

### ADDRESSES IN IRELAND

**Brittany Ferries** Republic: ☎021/277801; Northern Ireland: 0870/536 0360; *www.birttany-ferries.com*.
**Irish Ferries** 24hr information: ☎1890/313131, *www.irishferries.ie*.

**P&O Irish Ferries** Republic: ☎1800/409049; Northern Ireland: 0870/598 0777; *www.poirishsea.com*.

## GETTING THERE FROM NORTH AMERICA

**Getting to Languedoc and Roussillon from North America is straightforward; there are direct flights from over thirty major cities to Paris, from where you can either take an internal flight to the region or transfer to France's excellent train network. Nearly a dozen different scheduled airlines operate flights to Paris, making it one of the cheapest destinations in Europe. If Languedoc and Roussillon is one stop on a longer European trip, a Eurail train pass may also be a useful option (see box on p.15).**

### SHOPPING FOR TICKETS

Barring special offers, the cheapest fare is usually an **Apex** ticket, although this will carry certain restrictions: you have to book – and pay – at least 21 days before departure, spend at least seven days abroad (maximum stay three months), and you tend to get penalized if you change your schedule. On transatlantic routes there are also winter **Super Apex** tickets, sometimes known as "Eurosavers" – slightly cheaper than an ordinary Apex, but limiting your stay to between 7 and 21 days. Some airlines also issue **Special Apex** tickets to people younger than 24, often extending the maximum stay to a year. Many airlines offer youth or student fares to **under-25s**; a passport or driving licence are sufficient proof of age, though these tickets are subject to availability and can have eccentric booking conditions. It's worth remembering that most cheap return fares involve spending at least one Saturday night

away and that many will only give a percentage refund if you need to cancel or alter your journey, so make sure you check the restrictions carefully before buying a ticket.

You can normally cut costs further by going through a specialist flight agent – either a **consolidator**, who buys up blocks of tickets from the airlines and sells them at a discount, or a **discount agent**, who deals in blocks of tickets offloaded by the airlines, and often offers special student and youth fares and a range of other travel-related services such as travel insurance, rail passes, car rental, tours and the like. Bear in mind, though, that penalties for changing your plans can be stiff, and that these companies make their money by dealing in bulk – don't expect them to answer lots of questions. Some agents specialize in **charter flights**, which may be cheaper than anything available on a scheduled flight, but again departure dates are fixed and withdrawal penalties are high (check the refund policy). If you travel a lot, **discount travel clubs** are another option – the annual membership fee may be worth it for benefits such as cut-price air tickets and car rental. It's also worth checking out **Web sites** such as *www.travelocity.com* for the latest worldwide dicounted air fares online.

A further possibility is to see if you can arrange a **courier flight**, although the hit-or-miss nature of these makes them most suitable for a single traveller who travels light and has a very flexible schedule. In return for shepherding a parcel through customs and possibly giving up your baggage allowance, you can expect to get a deeply discounted ticket. For more options, consult *Courier Bargains: How to Travel Worldwide for Next to Nothing* by Kelly Monaghan (US$17.50, postpaid, from The Intrepid Traveler, PO Box 438, New York, NY 10034). Flights are issued on a first-come, first-served basis, and there's no guarantee that the Paris route will be available at the time you want. Round-trip fares cost from around US$350, with last-minute specials as low as US$150 for flights booked within three days of departure.

Don't automatically assume that tickets purchased through a travel specialist will be the cheapest – once you get a quote, check with the airlines and you may turn up an even better deal. Be advised also that the pool of travel companies

## AIRLINES AND TRAVEL AGENTS IN NORTH AMERICA

### AIRLINES

**Air Canada** in US ☎1-800/776 3000; in Canada ☎1-800/555 1212; *www.aircanada.ca*.

**Air France** in US ☎1-800/237 2747; in Canada ☎1-800/667 2747; *www.airfrance.fr*.

**American Airlines** ☎1-800/433 7300, *www.aa.com*.

**AOM French Airlines** ☎1-800/892 9136, *www.aom.com*.

**Continental Airlines** ☎1-800/231 0856, *www.flycontinental.com*.

**Delta Airlines** ☎1-800/241 4141, *www.delta-air.com*.

**Iceland Air** ☎1-800/223 5500, *www.ice-landair.com*.

**Northwest Airlines** ☎1-800/225 2525, *www.nwa.com*.

**TWA** ☎1-800/892 4141, *www.twa.com*.

**United Airlines** ☎1-800/538 2929, *www.ual.com*.

**US Air** ☎1-800/622 1015, *www.usairways.com*.

### DISCOUNT TRAVEL AGENTS

**Air Brokers International**, 150 Post St, Suite 620, San Francisco, CA 94108 (☎1-800/883 3273, *www.airbrokers.com*). Consolidator.

**Air Courier Association**, 15000 W 6th Ave, Suite 203, Golden, CO 80401 (☎1-800/282 1202, *www.aircourier.com*). Courier-flight broker.

**Airhitch**, 2641 Broadway, New York, NY 10025 (☎1-800/326 2009 or 212/864 2000, *www.airhitch.org*). Standby-seat broker: for a set price, they guarantee to get you on a flight as close to your preferred destination as possible, within a week.

**Airtreks.com**, 442 Post St, Suite 400, San Francisco, CA 94102 (☎1-800/428 8735, *www.airtreks.com*). Travel company with a highly recommended interactive Web site.

**Council Travel**, 205 E 42nd St, New York, NY 10017 (☎1-800/226 8624, *www.counciltravel.com*). Nationwide US student travel organization with branches in (among others) San Francisco, Washington DC, Boston, Austin, Seattle, Chicago, Minneapolis.

**Flight Centre**, 3030 Granville St, Vancouver, BC V6H 3J9 (☎1-604/739 9539, *www.flightcentre.com*). Discount air fares from Canadian cities.

**Last Minute Travel Club**, 100 Sylvan Rd, Suite 600, Woburn, MA 01801 (☎1-800/LAST MIN). Travel club specializing in standby deals.

**New Frontiers/Nouvelles Frontières**, 12 E 33rd St, New York, NY 10016 (☎1-800/366 6387 or 514/526 8444, *www.newfrontiers.com*). French discount-travel firm; also markets charters to Paris and Lyon. Branches in New York, Montréal, Los Angeles, San Francisco and Québec City.

**STA Travel**, 10 Downing St, New York, NY 10014 (☎1-800/777 0112, *www.sta-travel.com*). Worldwide specialist in independent travel with branches in the Los Angeles, San Francisco and Boston areas.

**Travac**, 989 6th Ave, 16th Floor, New York, NY 10018 (☎1-800/872 8800, *www.thetravelsite.com*). Consolidator and charter broker; branches in New York and Orlando.

**Travel Avenue**, 10 S Riverside Plaza, Suite 1404, Chicago, IL 60606 (☎1-800/333 3335, *www.travelavenue.com*). Discount travel agent.

**Travel Cuts**, 187 College St, Toronto, ON M5T 1P7 (☎1-800/667-2887 or 416/979 2406, *www.travelcuts.com*). Canadian specialist student and discount travel organization with branches all over the country.

**Travelers Advantage**, 3033 S Parker Rd, Suite 1000, Aurora, CO 80014 (☎1-800/548 1116, *www.travelersadvantage.com*). Discount travel club.

**Worldtek Travel**, 111 Water St, New Haven, CT 06511 (☎1-800/243 1723, *www.worldtek.com*). Discount travel agency.

---

is swimming with sharks – exercise caution and never deal with a company that demands cash up front or refuses to accept payment by credit card.

Note that fares are heavily dependent on **season**, and are highest from around early June to the end of August; they drop during the "shoulder"

## TOUR OPERATORS IN NORTH AMERICA

**Abercrombie & Kent**, 1520 Kensington Rd, Oak Brook, IL (☎1-800/323 7308, *www.abercrombieandkent.com*). Deluxe hiking, biking, rail and canal journeys, including a luxury 6-night cruise in the Canal du Midi from Beziers to Carcassonne starting at US$2500.

**Back Door Travel**, 130 4th Ave North, Edmonds, WA 98020 (☎425/771 8303, *www.ricksteves.com*). Off-the-beaten-path, small-group travel with budget travel guru Rick Steves and his enthusiastic guides. Their fourteen-day "Best of Western France" tour goes from Rouen to Arles and costs $2300 for land only (air is separate).

**France Vacations**, 9841 Airport Boulevard, Suite 1120, Los Angeles, CA 90045 (☎1-800/332 5332, *www.francevacations.net*). Air, car, train, and accommodation services plus customized travel packages in Languedoc and Roussillon, and throughout France.

**The French Experience**, 370 Lexington Ave, # 812, New York, NY 10017 (☎1-800/28 FRANCE, *www.frenchexperince.com*). Accommodation and rental car packages throughout Languedoc and Roussillon.

**Globus and Cosmos Tourama**, 5301 S Federal Circle, Littleton, CO 80123-2980 (☎1-800/221 0090, *www.globusandcosmos.com*). Travel club

offering tours in the region and throughout France.

**Himalayan Travel**, 110 Prospect Street, Stamford, CT 06901 (☎1-800/225 2380, *www.gorp.com*). Hiking and cycling tours; their 12-day "The Way of St James" spends time in Languedoc and starts at US$1285.

**Holidaze Ski Tours**, 810 Belmar Plaza, Belmar, NJ 07719 (☎1-800/526 2827, *www.holidaze.com*). Ski specialist.

**Interhome**, 1990 NE 163rd St, N Miami Beach, FL 33162 (☎305/940 2299, *www.interhome.com*). Short-term house and villa rentals in Languedoc and Roussillon.

**Mountain Travel-Sobek**, 6420 Fiarmounte Avenue, El Cerrito, CA 94530 (☎1-800/228 2384, *www.mtsobek.com*). Outdoor adventure tours including a 9-day hiking tour in Southwest France starting at US$2390.

**Saga International Holidays**, 222 Berkeley St, Boston, MA 02116 (☎1-800/343 0273, *www.sagaholidays.com*). Specialist in group travel for 50s plus.

**Vacances en Campagne**, PO Box 299, Elkton, VA 22827 (☎1-800/327 6097, *www.britishtravel.com*). *Châteaux* and country houses for rent in Languedoc and Roussillon.

seasons (Sept–Oct & April–May) and you'll get the best deals during the low season (Nov–March, excluding Christmas). Note that Friday, Saturday and Sunday travel tends to carry a premium, and that one-way fares are generally slightly more than half the round-trip.

**Air passes**, coupons and discounts on further flights within Europe vary with airlines, but the basic rules are that they must be pre-booked with the main ticket, are valid for three months, and are available only with a return fare with the one airline – for example, you have to fly to France with KLM alone to be eligible for their airpass deals. Air France offers a Euroflyer for use in France and Europe at US$99 each flight (min 3, max 9). KLM's Passport to Europe uses coupons for single flights within Europe at US$100 each (min 4, max 12). Lufthansa's start at US$89 (max 12) during the low season up to US$159 in the high season per coupon. British Airways have a "One World: Visit Europe" program that offers

flights within Europe from US$92 to US$145 depending on the destination (min 2, max 12).

### FLIGHTS FROM THE USA

**Transatlantic fares** to France from the USA are very reasonable, thanks to intense competition. Any local travel agent should be able to access airlines' up-to-the-minute fares, although they may not have time to research all the possibilities, and you could call the airlines direct. The lowest discounted scheduled fares you're likely to get in low and high season flying midweek to Paris are US$448/966 from Chicago, US$468/876 from Houston, US$498/1116 from Los Angeles, US$368/866 from New York and US$408/635 from Washington DC.

Most airlines use Paris as the transatlantic gateway to France, though some charter carriers offer direct flights to Marseille in late spring to early autumn. Nearly a dozen different **scheduled airlines** operate flights to Paris. Air France has the most frequent and convenient service, but their fares tend to be on the expensive side. Other airlines offering non-stop services to Paris from a variety of US cities are United, daily from Chicago, San Francisco and Washington DC; Delta, daily from Cincinnati, Atlanta and New York; TWA, daily from New York and St Louis; and AOM French Airlines from Los Angeles three to five times a week, depending on the season. For the best fares, check the ads in Sunday newspaper travel sections and book with a discount agent or consolidator. It's also worth considering **charter flights**, which operate from late spring to early autumn. New Frontiers, a Canadian discount travel agency, has summer non-stop charters from Los Angeles to Paris on Corsair from US$800 round-trip.

### FLIGHTS FROM CANADA

The strong links between France and Québec's Francophone community ensure regular air services from **Canada to Paris**. The main route is

---

## EUROPEAN TRAIN PASSES FOR AMERICANS, AUSTRALIANS AND NEW ZEALANDERS

There are a number of European **train passes** that can only be purchased before leaving home, though consider carefully how much travelling you are going to be doing: these all-encompassing passes only really begin to pay for themselves if you intend to travel widely outside Languedoc and Roussillon.

The best-known and most flexible is the **Eurail Youthpass** (for under-26s), which costs US$388/A$733 for fifteen days, and there are also one-month and two-month versions; if you're 26 or over you'll have to buy a first-class **Eurail** pass, which costs US$554/A$1046 for the fifteen-day option. You stand a better chance of getting your money's worth out of a **Eurail Flexipass**, which is good for a certain number of travel days in a two-month period. This, too, comes in under-26/first-class versions: ten days for under-26s costs US$458/A$865, for over-26s US$654/A$1234; and for fifteen days US$599/A$1131 and US$862/A$1627.

A scaled-down version of the Flexipass, the **Europass** allows travel in France, Germany, Italy, Switzerland and Spain for US$233/A$440 and US$348/A$657 for five days in two months, on up to US$513/A$968 and US$728/A$1374 for fifteen days in two months; there are also cheaper three- and four-country combinations, as well as the option of adding adjacent "associate" countries.

In addition to the passes outlined above, you can buy a **more specific pass** valid for travel in France only. The **France Railpass** provides three days' unlimited travel in a one-month period for US$180/A$340 or, if travelling in groups of two or more, US$146/A$276 per person. Up to six additional days of travel may be purchased for US$30/A$57 per day. For under-26s, the **France Youthpass** provides four days of unlimited travel in a two-month period for US$164/A$310; up to six additional days may be purchased for US$20/A$38 per day. All passes must be purchased before departure and are available through travel agents or with rail specialists (see below).

In addition, the SNCF has a range of other reductions and passes, which can be purchased once in France: details of these can be found in "Getting around", p.32.

### RAIL CONTACTS IN NORTH AMERICA

**CIT Rail**, 15 W 44th St, 10th Floor, New York, NY 10036 (☎1-800/223 7987, www.fs-on-line.com). Eurail passes only.

**Rail Europe**, 226 Westchester Ave, White Plains, NY 10604 (☎1-800/438 7245, www.raileurope.com). Official Eurail pass agent in North America; also

sells the widest range of European regional and individual country passes.

**ScanTours**, 3439 Wade St, Los Angeles, CA 90066 (☎1-800/223 7226 or 310/636 4656, www.scantours.com). Eurail, and many other European country passes.

### RAIL CONTACTS IN AUSTRALIA AND NEW ZEALAND

**CIT World Travel**, see p.18.

**Rail Plus**, Level 3, 459 Little Collins St, Melbourne, Australia (☎03/9642 8644 or 1300/555 003, info@railplus.com.au); Level 2, 60

Parnell Rd, Auckland, New Zealand (☎09/303 2484).

**Thomas Cook**, see p.17.

Vancouver–Toronto–Montréal–Paris Charles de Gaulle, although most departures originate in Toronto.

Air France and Air Canada offer non-stop services to Paris from the major Canadian cities. There are also some excellent charter deals. Travel Cuts is a good source of general information on flights. The lowest discounted scheduled **fares** for midweek travel to Paris in low/high season will be around CDN$976/1316 from Montréal, CDN$976/1316 from Toronto, CDN$1360/1728 from Vancouver, and CDN$1008/1258 from Halifax on Iceland Air.

### PACKAGE TOURS

A tour is inevitably more confining than independent travel, but it can help you make the most of time if you're on a tight schedule; a tour can also ensure a worry-free first few days of a trip, and time to find your feet. Hundreds of tour operators specialize in travel to France, and many can put together very **flexible deals**, sometimes amounting to no more than a flight plus car or train pass and accommodation. If you're planning

to travel in moderate or luxury style, and especially if your trip is geared around special interests, such packages can work out cheaper than the same arrangements made on arrival.

Of greater interest are the **package-tour operators** that help you explore the country's unique points: many organize walking or cycling trips through the countryside, boat trips along canals, and any number of theme tours based around history, art, wine and so on. The box on p.14 mentions a few of the possibilities, and a travel agent will be able to point out others. Remember: bookings made through a travel agent cost no more than going through the tour operator.

Many **airlines** have reasonably priced packages including round-trip airfare, hotel, some sightseeing tours and, in the case of fly-drive packages, a rental car. Delta offers a seven-day fly-drive package to Paris starting at US$599 for New York departures. American Airlines offer a seven-day England–France fly-drive package, including Channel Tunnel crossing, from around US$900 per person for hotel, breakfast, rental car and Channel tickets.

## GETTING THERE FROM AUSTRALIA & NEW ZEALAND

Many people travelling to France from Australia and New Zealand will choose to travel via London although there are scheduled flights to Paris from Sydney, Melbourne, Brisbane, Cairns, Perth and

Auckland. Most airlines can add on a Paris (or any other major French destination) leg to any Australia/New Zealand–Europe ticket. Travelling time is around 22 hours via Asia and 30 hours via the USA – not counting time spent on stopovers. From Paris you can get onward connections to Toulouse or Montpellier.

Fares to France vary according to the **season** and the carrier. In general, low season lasts from mid-January to the end of February, and from the beginning of October to mid-November; high season is from mid-May to the end of August, and from the beginning of December to mid-January.

### SHOPPING FOR TICKETS

**Tickets** purchased direct from the airlines tend to be expensive; the **discount agents** listed in the box opposite offer much better deals, and have the latest information on limited special offers. Some of the best discounts are offered by companies such as Flight Centres, STA and

## AIRLINES, TRAVEL AGENTS AND TOUR OPERATORS IN AUSTRALIA AND NEW ZEALAND

### AIRLINES

**Air France** in Australia ☎02/9244 2100; in New Zealand ☎09/308 3352; *www.airfrance.fr.*

**British Airways** in Australia ☎02/8904 8800; in New Zealand ☎09/356 8690; *www.british-airways.com.*

**Cathay Pacific** in Australia ☎13/1747 or 02/9931 5500; in New Zealand ☎09/379 0861; *www.cathaypacific.com.*

**Garuda** in Australia ☎1300/365 330; in New Zealand ☎09/366 1855 or 1800/128 510.

**Japan Airlines** (JAL) in Australia ☎02/9272 1111; in New Zealand ☎09/379 9906; *www.japanair.com.*

**KLM** in Australia ☎1300/303 747; in New Zealand ☎09/302 1452; *www.klm.com.*

**Lauda Air** in Australia ☎02/9251 6155 or 1800/642 438, *www.lauda-air.com.*

**Lufthansa** in Australia ☎1300/655 727 or 02/9367 3887; in New Zealand ☎09/303 1529 or 008/945 220; *www.lufthansa.com.*

**Malaysian Airlines** in Australia ☎13/2627; in New Zealand ☎09/373 2741 or 008/657 472; *www.malaysiaair.com.*

**Olympic Airways** in Australia ☎02/9251 2044 or 1800 221 663, *www.olympic-airways.com.*

**Qantas** in Australia ☎13/1313; in New Zealand ☎09/357 8900 or 0800/808 767; *www.qantas.com.*

**Singapore Airlines** in Australia ☎02/9350 0262 or 13/1011; in New Zealand ☎09/303 2129 or 0800/808 909; *www.singaporeair.com.*

**Sri Lankan Airlines** in Australia ☎02/9244 2234; in New Zealand ☎09/308 3353.

**Thai Airways** in Australia ☎1300/651 960; in New Zealand ☎09/377 3886; *www.thaiair.com.*

**United Airlines** in Australia ☎13/1777; in New Zealand ☎09/379 3800; *www.ual.com.*

### TRAVEL AGENTS

*All the agents listed below offer competitive discounts on airfares as well as a good selection of packaged holidays and tours, and can also arrange car rental.*

**Budget Travel**, 16 Fort St, Auckland (☎09/366 0061 or 0800/808 040, *www.budgettravel.co.nz*); plus branches around the city.

**Flight Centre** (*www.flightcentre.com*) Australia: 82 Elizabeth St, Sydney (☎02/9235 3522); plus branches nationwide (for the nearest branch call ☎13/1600). New Zealand: 350 Queen St, Auckland (☎09/358 4310 or 0800/354 448); plus branches nationwide.

**Northern Gateway**, 22 Cavenagh St, Darwin (☎08/8941 1394, *oztravel@norgate.com.au*).

**STA Travel** (*www.statravel.com*) Australia: 855 George St, Sydney; 256 Flinders St, Melbourne; other offices in state capitals and major universities (for nearest branch call ☎13/1776; telesales ☎1300/360 960). New Zealand: 10 High St, Auckland (☎09/309 0458); other offices in major cities and university campuses (for nearest branch call ☎0800/874 773; telesales ☎09/366 6673). Fare discounts for students and those under 26, as well as student cards.

**Student Uni Travel**, 92 Pitt St, Sydney (☎02/9232 8444, *sydney@backpackers.net*); plus branches in Brisbane, Cairns, Darwin, Melbourne and Perth. Student/youth discounts and travel advice.

**Thomas Cook** Australia (*www.thomascook.com.au*): 175 Pitt St, Sydney (☎02/9231 2877); 257 Collins St, Melbourne (☎03/9282 0222); plus branches in other state capitals (for nearest branch call ☎13/1771; telesales ☎1800/801 002). New Zealand (*www.thomascook.co.nz*): 191 Queen St, Auckland (☎09/379 3920).

**Trailfinders** (*www.travel.com.au*), 8 Spring St, Sydney (☎02/9247 7666); 91 Elizabeth St, Brisbane (☎07/3229 0887); Hides Corner, Shield St, Cairns (☎07/4041 1199).

**Usit Beyond** (*www.usitbeyond.co.nz*), cnr Shortland St & Jean Batten Place, Auckland (☎09/379 4224 or 0800/788 336); plus branches in major cities. Student/youth travel specialists.

*. . .box continued from previous page*

## TOUR OPERATORS

**Adventure Specialists**, 69 Liverpool St, Sydney, (☎02/9261 2927 or toll-free 1800/634 465). Offer a good selection of adventure and specialists holidays in the region.

**Adventure World** Australia: 73 Walker St, North Sydney (☎02/9956 7766 or local call rate 1300/363, *www.adventureworld.com.au*); plus branches in Adelaide, Brisbane, Melbourne and Perth. New Zealand: 101 Great South Rd, Remuera, Auckland (☎09/524 5118, *www .adventureworld.co.nz*). Agents for a vast array of international adventure travel companies that operate small group tours in France.

**CIT**, 2/263 Clarence St, Sydney (☎02/9267 1255, *www.cittravel.com.au*); plus offices in Melbourne, Brisbane, Adelaide and Perth. Specialize in city tours and accommodation packages, plus bus and rail passes and car rental.

**European Travel Office** (ETO), 122 Rosslyn St, West Melbourne (☎03/9329 8844); Suite 410/368 Sussex St, Sydney (☎02/9267 7714); 407 Great South Rd, Auckland (☎09/525 3074). Offer a wide selection of tours and accommodation, from hotels to country inns, palaces and monasteries.

**France Unlimited**, 16 Goldsmith St, Elwood, Melbourne (☎03/9531 8787). All French travel arrangements, individually tailored holidays and guided walking and cycling holidays.

**French Cottages and Travel**, 674 High St, E Kew, Melbourne (☎03/9859 4944). International and domestic travel, independent tours and cottage rental throughout the region.

**French Travel Connection**, Level 6, 33 Chandos St, Sydney (☎02/9966 8600) Offers a good selection of country cottages in the region.

**Peregrine**, 258 Lonsdale St, Melbourne (☎03/9662 2700 or 1300 655 433, *www .peregrine.net.au*); plus offices in Brisbane, Sydney, Adelaide and Perth. Agents for Headwater's guided and independent walking and cycling trips through Languedoc.

**The Adventure Travel Company**, 164 Parnell Rd, Parnell, Auckland (☎09/379 9755, *advakl@hot .co.nz*). The NZ agent for Peregrine (see above).

**Travel Notions**, 136 Bridge Rd, Glebe, Sydney (☎02/9552 2852). Agents for the leisurely "Cycling for Softies" tours through the region.

---

Trailfinders (see box on p.17); they can also help with visas, travel insurance and tours. You might also want to have a look on the **Internet**: *www.travel.com.au* and *www.sydneytravel.com* offer discounted fares online.

If you intend to travel more widely outside Languedoc and Roussillon and have limited time, it's worth considering an **air pass**. Air passes, coupons and discounts on further flights within Europe vary with airlines, but the basic rules are that they must be pre-booked with the main ticket, are valid for three months, and are available only with a return fare with the one airline – for example, you have to fly to France with British Airways alone to be eligible for their air-pass deals. Air France offers a Euroflyer for use in France and Europe at A$200 each flight (minimum 3, maximum 9). British Airways have a zone system: around A$140 for each flight within France, A$210 each for single flights to and around Germany, Italy and Belgium, although you may originally have to travel via London, from where it will cost an extra A$170 to get to France (min 3, max 12).

If you're planning to visit Languedoc and Roussillon as part of an extensive European trip, it's also worth looking into a variety of **rail passes**. Details of passes on offer and rail contacts in Australia and New Zealand are given in the box on p.15.

Finally, if you're planning to travel in style, and especially if your visit is going to be geared around special interests, such as walking, cycling, art or wine, you may want to consider one of the **package tours** offered by the operators in the box above. Though these tours are inevitably more restrictive than independent travel, they may work out cheaper than making the same arrangements on arrival in France and can help you make the most of time if you're on a tight schedule.

## FLIGHTS FROM AUSTRALIA

Airfares **from east-coast gateways** are common rated, with Ansett and Qantas providing a shuttle service to the point of international departure. **From Perth and Darwin** they're around A$100–300 less via Asia, and A$400 more via the

USA. There's a host of airlines operating a service between major cities in Australia – with either a transfer or overnight stop in their home ports – to Paris.

Flights **via Southeast Asia**, with either a transfer or overnight stop in the airlines' home ports, are generally the cheaper option. The lowest fares are with Sri Lankan Airways and Garuda for A$1400 in the low season rising to A$2400 in the high season, while Alitalia/Qantas, Olympic Airways and JAL are A$1500 low season to A$2600 high season. Mid-range fares are with KLM, Malaysian Airlines, Lauda Air, Thai International, Air France (on to 87 destinations within France), Cathay Pacific and Lufthansa, all costing A$1600–2600. Qantas/Air France, British Airways and Singapore Airlines are higher still at A$1900–2800.

Generally flights to Paris are pricier **via the US**, with the best deals offered by United Airlines (via LA, Miami and Washington), from A$2100 to 3000; Canadian Airlines (via Toronto or Vancouver) are more expensive at A$2200 low season and A$3000 high season.

## FLIGHTS FROM NEW ZEALAND

**From New Zealand**, there is also a good range of airlines flying to Paris with either a transfer or overnight stop in their home ports. The best discounted deals to Paris from Auckland are **via Southeast Asia** with Garuda at NZ$1800 low season to NZ$2400 high season. Mid-range fares are with Japanese Airlines, Thai International, Malaysia Airlines, Cathay Pacific and Singapore Airlines, all costing NZ$2000–2400. Most of these airlines also include a **side-trip** within Europe in their fare.

As with Australia, flights **via the US** are more expensive, the best deals being with United Airlines (via LA, Miami and Washington) for NZ$2200 and NZ$3000. Fares with British Airways (via LA and London) and Canadian Airlines (via Vancouver or Toronto) cost NZ$2399 to NZ$3000.

## RED TAPE AND VISAS

Citizens of EU (European Union) countries can travel freely in France; and citizens of

Australia, Canada, the United States and New Zealand, among other countries, do not need any sort of visa to enter France, and can stay for up to ninety days. However, the situation can change and it is advisable to check with your embassy or consulate before departure. Note that the British Visitor's Passport is no longer available.

EU citizens (or other non-visa citizens) who **stay longer than three months** are officially supposed to apply for a **Carte de Séjour**, for which you'll have to show proof of income at least equal to the minimum wage (at least 6700F/€1025 per month). However, EU passports are rarely stamped, so there is no evidence of

---

### FRENCH EMBASSIES AND CONSULATES OVERSEAS

**BRITAIN**

**Embassy**: 58 Knightsbridge, London SW1X 7JT (☎020/7201 1004).

**IRELAND**

**Embassy**: 36 Ailesbury Road, Ballsbridge, Dublin 4 (☎01/260 1666).

**USA**

**Embassy**: 4101 Reservoir Rd NW, Washington DC 20007 (☎202/944 6195, *www.info-france-usa.org*).

**Consulates**: Prominence in Buckhead, Suite 1840, 3475 Piedmont Rd NE, Atlanta, GA 30305 (☎404/495 1660, *www.consulatfranceatlanta .org*); 31 St James Ave, Park Square Building, Suite 750, Boston, MA 02116 (☎617/542 7374, *www.franceboston.com*); 737 North Michigan Ave, Suite 2020, Chicago, IL 60611 (☎312/787 5360, *www.france-consulat.org/chicago*); 777 Post Oak Blvd, Suite 600, Houston, TX 77056 (☎713/572 2799, *www.consulatfrancehouston .org*); 10990 Wilshire Blvd, Suite 300, Los Angeles, CA 90024 (☎310/235 3200, *www .etats-unis.com/consulat-la*); One Biscayne Tower, 17th Floor, South Biscayne Blvd, Miami, FL 33131 (☎305/372 9799, *www.info-france-usa .org/miami*); 1340 Poydras St, Amoco Building, Suite 1710, New Orleans, LA 70112 (☎504/523 5772, *www.info-france-usa.org/nouvelle-orleans /index.html*); 934 Fifth Ave, New York, NY 10021

(☎212/606 3689, *www.franceconsulatny.org*); 540 Bush St, San Francisco, CA 94108 (☎415/397 4330, *www.accueil-sfo.org*).

**CANADA**

**Embassy**: 42 Sussex Drive, Ottawa, ON K1M 2C9 (☎613/789 1795, *www.amba-ottawa.fr*).

**Consulates**: 777 Main St, Suite 800, Moncton, NB E1C 1E9 (☎506/857 4191, *www.moncton .consulfrance.org*); 1 place Ville Marie Bureau 2601, Montréal, QC H3B 4S3 (☎514/878 4385, *www.montreal.consulatfrance.org*); 25 rue St-Louis, Québec, QC G1R 3Y8 (☎418/694 2294, *www.quebec.consulatfrance.org*); 130 Bloor St West, Suite 400, Toronto, ON M5S 1N5 (☎416/925 8044, *www.toronto.consulatfrance .org*); 1100–1130 West Pender St, Vancouver, BC V6E 4A4 (☎604/681 4345, *www.vancouver .consulatfrance.org*).

**AUSTRALIA**

**Consulates** (*www.france.net.au*): 492 St Kilda Rd, Melbourne, VIC 3001 (☎03/9820 0921); 31 Market St, Sydney, NSW 2000 (☎02/9261 5779.

**NEW ZEALAND**

**Embassy**: 34–42 Manners St, PO Box 11-343, Wellington (☎04/384 2555, *www.ambafrance .net.nz*).

how long you've been in the country. If your passport does get stamped, you can cross the border – to Spain, for example – and re-enter for another ninety days legitimately.

# COSTS, MONEY AND BANKS

Until the euro currency is introduced in 2002 (see box), the French unit of money is the the franc (abbreviated as F or sometimes FF), divided into 100 centimes. Francs come in notes of 500, 100, 50 and 20F, and there are coins of 20, 10, 5, 2 and 1F, and 50, 20, 10 and 5 centimes. During most of 2000, the exchange rate hovered around 11.10F to the pound, 7.60F to the US dollar, 5.10F to the Canadian dollar, 4.10F to the Australian dollar, and 3.40F to the New Zealand dollar. For the most up-to-date exchange rates, consult the useful **Currency Converter Web site** *www.oanda.com.*

## COSTS

Because of the relatively low **cost** of accommodation and eating out, at least by northern European standards, Languedoc and Roussillon may not seem an outrageously expensive place to visit, though this will depend on the relative strength of your own country's currency against the euro. When and where you go also makes a difference: hotel rates rise throughout the region in July and August, most dramatically in coastal resorts, but also in places which are major tourist attractions, like Carcassonne. More economical accommodation can sometimes be found in less visited areas, but increasing regulation has led many small-town hotels to close down, with those remaining deliberately aimed at tourists. For a reasonably comfortable existence, including a hotel room for two, a light restaurant lunch and a proper restaurant dinner plus moving around, café stops and museum visits, you need to allow at least 500F/€76.25 a day per person. But by counting the pennies, staying at cheap **hostels** (around 100F/€15.25 for bed and breakfast) or **camping** (from 30F/€4.58), and being strong-willed about

## THE EURO

France is one of twelve European Union countries who have changed over to a single currency, the **euro** (€). Although the transition period began on January 1, 1999, euro notes and coins are not scheduled to be issued until January 1, 2002, with francs remaining in place for **cash transactions**, at a **fixed rate** of 6.55957 francs to 1 euro, until they are officially withdrawn on February 28, 2002.

Even before euro cash appears in 2002, you can opt to pay in euros by **credit card** and you can get **travellers' cheques** in euros – you should not be charged commission for changing them in any of the twelve countries in the euro zone (also known as "Euroland"), nor for changing from any of the old Euroland currencies to any other (Italian lira to francs, for example).

All **prices** in this book are given in francs and the exact equivalent in euros. When the new currency takes over completely, prices are likely to be rounded off – and if decimalization in the UK is anything to go by, rounded up.

Euro notes will be issued in denominations of 5, 10, 20, 50, 100, 200 and 500 euros, and coins in denominations of 1, 2, 5, 10, 20 and 50 cents and 1 and 2 euros.

extra cups of coffee and doses of culture, you could manage on 250F/€38 a day, to include a cheap restaurant meal – less if your eating is limited to street snacks or market food.

For two or more people, **hotel accommodation** is nearly always cheaper and better value than hostels, which are only worth staying at if you're by yourself and want to meet other travellers. A sensible average estimate for a double room would be around 280F/€43, though perfectly adequate but simple doubles can be had from 190F/€29. Single-rated and -sized rooms are often available, beginning from 140F/€21 in a cheap hotel. **Breakfast** at hotels is normally an extra 30F/€4.50, for coffee, croissant and orange juice – about the same as you'd pay in a bar (where you'll normally find the coffee and ambience more agreeable). As for other **food**, you can spend as much or as little as you like. There are large numbers of reasonable **restaurants** with three- or four-course menus for between 65F/€10 and 120F/€18; the lunch-time or *midi* menu is nearly always cheaper. **Picnic fare**, obviously, is much less costly, especially when you buy in the markets and cheap supermarket chains, and take-away baguette sandwiches from cafés are not extortionate. **Wine** and **beer** are both very cheap in supermarkets; buying wine from the barrel at village co-op cellars will give you the best value for money. The mark-up on wine in restaurants is high, though the house wine in cheaper establishments is still very good value. **Drinks** in cafés and bars are what really make a hole in your pocket: black coffee, wine and draught lager are the cheapest drinks to order; glasses of tap water are free; and remember that it's cheaper to be at the bar than at a table.

**Transport** will inevitably be a large item of expenditure if you move around a lot. French trains are in any case good value, with many discounts available – two sample long-distance one-way fares are Paris to Toulouse, 445F/€67.86, and Paris to Montpellier, 379F/€57.80. Though prices vary enormously from one operator to another, buses are cheaper: a one-way bus ticket from Toulouse to Carcassonne for instance costs 63F/€9.61, compared with 94F/€14.34 for the same journey by train. Bicycles cost about 80F/€12 per day to rent. Petrol prices shot up in late 2000, and at the time of writing were around 7.70F/€1.17 a litre for unleaded (*sans plomb*), around 7.80F/€1.90 a litre for Super, and around 5.50F/€.84 a litre for diesel; there are 3.8 litres to

the US gallon. Most *autoroutes* have tolls: rates vary, but to give you an idea, travelling only by motorway from Calais to Montpellier would cost you around 379F/€57.80.

**Museums and monuments** can also prove a big wallet-eroder. Reduced admission is often available for those over 60 and under 18 (for which you'll need your passport as proof of age) and for students under 26 (for which you'll need an International Student Identity Card, or ISIC). Many museums and monuments are free for children under 12, and nearly always for kids under 4. Under-26s can also get a free **youth card**, or *Carte Jeune*, available in France from youth travel agencies like USIT and from main tourist offices (120F/€18.30; valid for a year), which entitles you to reductions in France and throughout Europe. Several towns operate a discount pass for their museums and monuments (detailed in the Guide).

## CHANGING MONEY

Standard **banking hours** are Monday to Friday 9am to 4pm or 5pm. Some close at midday (noon/12.30pm–2/2.30pm); some are open on Saturday 9am to noon. All are closed on Sunday and public holidays. They will have a notice on the door if they do currency exchange. **Rates and commission** vary from bank to bank, so it's worth shopping around; the usual procedure is a 1–2 percent commission on travellers' cheques and a flat rate charge on cash (a 30F/€4.58 charge for changing 200F/€30.50 is not uncommon). Be wary of banks claiming to charge no commission at all; often they are merely adjusting the exchange rate to their own advantage.

There are **money-exchange counters** (*bureaux de change*) at all the airports in the region and at the train stations of Toulouse and Montpellier, with usually one or two in town centres as well, often keeping much longer hours than the high-street banks. You'll also find **automatic exchange machines** at airports and train stations and outside many money exchange bureaux. They accept £10 and £20 notes as well as dollars and other European currency notes, but offer a very poor rate of exchange.

## TRAVELLERS' CHEQUES AND VISA TRAVEL MONEY

**Travellers' cheques** are one of the safest ways of carrying your money. Worldwide, they're available from almost any major bank (in most cases whether you have an account there or not), and from special American Express or Thomas Cook offices, usually for a service charge of 1 percent on the amount purchased. Banks may charge more to purchase, but check first with your own establishment as some offer cheques free of charge to customers meeting certain criteria. The most widely recognized brands of travellers' cheques are Visa, Thomas Cook and American Express, which most banks will change, and there are American Express and Thomas Cook offices in France; American Express travellers' cheques can also be cashed at post offices.

**French franc travellers' cheques** can be worthwhile: they may often be used as cash, and you should get the face value of the cheques when you change them, so commission is only paid on purchase. Banks being banks, however, this is not always the case.

The latest way of carrying your money abroad is with a **Visa TravelMoney Card**, a sort of electronic travellers' cheque. The temporary disposable debit card is "loaded up" with an amount between £100 and £5000 and can then be used (in conjunction with a PIN number) in any ATM carrying the Visa sign in France (and 112 other countries). When your funds are depleted, you simply throw the card away. It's recommended you buy at least a second card as back up in case your first is lost or stolen, though like travellers' cheques the cards can be replaced if such mishaps occur. Up to nine cards can be bought to access the same funds – useful for couples/families travelling together. Charges are 2 percent commission with a minimum charge of £3. The card is available from, among other places, Colombus Bank in the US and Thomas Cook in the UK. For further information, call Visa's 24hr toll-free customer services line on ☎1-410/581-9091 or check out their Web site at *www.visa.com*.

## CREDIT AND DEBIT CARDS

**Credit cards** are widely accepted; just watch for the window stickers. Visa – known as the *Carte Bleue* in France – is almost universally recognized; Access, Mastercard – sometimes called Eurocard – and American Express rank a bit lower. It's always worth checking, however, that restaurants and hotels will accept your card; some smaller ones don't. Be aware, also, that French cards have a smart chip, and machines may reject cards with a magnetic strip even if they are valid. If your card is refused because of this, you may be able to get them to confirm it by explaining the problem to the cashier or waiter in question: "Les cartes britanniques/américaines/canadiennes /australiennes/de Nouvelle Zealand ne sont pas cartes à puce, mais à piste magnétique. Ma carte est valable et je vous serais très reconnaissant(e) de demander la confirmation auprès de votre banque ou de votre centre de traitement."

You can also use credit cards for **cash advances** at banks and in ATMs. The charge tends to be higher – for example 4.1 percent instead of the 1.5 percent at home for Visa cards. The PIN number should be the same as you use at home but check with your credit card company before you leave. Also, because French credit cards are smart cards, some ATMs baulk at foreign plastic and tell you that your request for money has been denied. If that happens, just try another machine. All ATMs give you the choice of instructions in French or English. Post offices will give cash advances on Visa credit cards if you are having a problem using them in ATMs. **Debit cards** can also be used in ATMs or to pay for goods and services if they carry the appropriate

---

### LOSS OR THEFT OF CREDIT CARDS

**If your credit card is lost or stolen** you should ring your credit card company to cancel it. Some companies, like Diners' Club in the UK, allow you to reverse the charges; others will pay for the call if you're absolutely desperate. It is very important to cancel cards straight away as purchases can be made without the signature even being glanced at. If you don't have the relevant number to call, contact the French 24-hour lines below; they will speak English.

**Access, Mastercard, Eurocard**
☎01.45.67.53.53.
**Visa** ☎01.42.77.11.90.

**American Express** lost or stolen cards
☎01.47.77.72.00; lost or stolen travellers' cheques ☎08.00.90.86.00.
**Diners' Club** ☎01.49.06.17.50.

Visa symbol or there's an "edc" (European acceptance) sign. British cards are charged around 1 percent or a minimum of £1.50 when used in an ATM, so it makes sense not to take small sums out constantly, whereas North American cards tend to charge a flat rate of $1–2, making it the most economical and convenient method. You would not want the use of ATMs to be your sole source of money on a long trip far from home as a lost, stolen or malfunctioning card would leave you with nothing, so always have some spare currency or travellers' cheques as a backup.

## HEALTH AND INSURANCE

**Citizens of all EU and Scandinavian countries are entitled to take advantage of French health services under the same terms as residents, if they have the correct documentation. British citizens need form E111, available from post offices. North American and other non-EU citizens have to pay for most medical attention and are strongly advised to take out some form of travel insurance.**

Under the French Social Security system, every hospital visit, doctor's consultation and prescribed medicine incurs a charge. Although all employed French people are entitled to a refund of 70–75 percent of their medical and dental expenses, this can still leave a hefty shortfall, especially after a stay in hospital (accident victims even have to pay for the ambulance that takes them there).

The phone numbers and addresses of hospitals and the phone numbers for SOS Médecins (for emergency doctor call-out) are given in the "Listings" for all the main cities; the national number for **medical emergencies** is ☎15. You will also find the number for the local police sta-

tion, which can provide addresses of doctors on call, and for pharmacies open after hours. In smaller towns, to find a **doctor**, stop at any pharmacy and ask for an address, or look under "Médecins qualifiés" in the Yellow Pages of the phone directory. To qualify for Social Security refunds, make sure the doctor is a *médecin conventionné*. An average consultation fee would be between 150F/€22.88 and 180F/€27.45. You will be given a *Feuille de Soins* (Statement of Treatment) for later documentation of insurance claims. Prescriptions should be taken to a **pharmacie**, signalled by an illuminated green cross, where they must be paid for; the medicines will have little stickers (*vignettes*) attached to them, which you must remove and stick to your *Feuille de Soins*, together with the prescription itself. In addition to dispensing medicine, all pharmacies are equipped, and obliged, to give first-aid on request – though they will make a charge. When closed, they all display the address of the nearest open pharmacy, day or night. In serious emergencies you will always be admitted to the nearest **hospital** (*hôpital*), either under your own power or by ambulance, which even French citizens must pay for; many people instead call the *pompiers* (fire brigade), who are trained for such circumstances and whose number is ☎18.

### TRAVEL INSURANCE

A typical **travel insurance** policy usually provides cover for the loss of baggage, tickets and – up to a certain limit – cash or cheques, as well as cancellation or curtailment of your journey. Most of them exclude so-called **dangerous sports** unless an extra premium is paid. Read the small print and benefits tables of prospective policies carefully; coverage can vary wildly for roughly similar premiums. Many policies can be chopped and changed to exclude coverage you don't need

## ROUGH GUIDES TRAVEL INSURANCE

Rough Guides now offer their own **travel insurance**, customized for our readers by a leading UK broker and backed by a Lloyd's underwriter. It's available for anyone of any nationality travelling anywhere in the world. There are two main plans: **Essential**, for effective, no-frills cover, starting at £10 for two weeks; and **Premier** – more expensive but with more generous and extensive benefits. Each offer European or Worldwide cover, and can be supplemented with a "Hazardous Activities Premium" if you plan to indulge in sports considered dangerous, such as skiing, scuba-diving or trekking. Unlike many policies, the Rough Guides schemes are calculated by the day, so if you're travelling for 27 days rather than a month, that's all you pay for. You can alternatively take out annual **multitrip insurance**, which covers you for all your travel throughout the year (with a maximum of sixty days for any one trip).

For a **policy quote**, call the Rough Guides Insurance Line on UK freefone ☎0800/015 0906 or, if you're calling from outside Britain, on ☎(+44) 1243/621 046. Alternatively, get an online quote or buy an insurance policy at *www.roughguides.com/insurance*.

– for example, sickness and accident benefits can often be excluded or included at will. If you do take **medical coverage**, ascertain whether benefits will be paid as treatment proceeds or only after return home, and whether there is a 24-hour medical emergency number. When securing baggage cover, make sure that the per-article limit – typically under £500 equivalent – will cover your most valuable possession. If you need to make a claim, you should keep receipts for medicines and medical treatment, and in the event you have anything stolen, you must obtain an official statement from the police.

**British** bank and credit cards often have certain levels of medical or other insurance included and you may automatically get travel insurance if you use a major credit card to pay for your trip. If you have a good all-risks home insurance policy it may cover your possessions against loss or theft even when overseas. Many private medical schemes such as BUPA or PPP also offer coverage plans for abroad, including baggage loss, cancellation or curtailment and cash replacement as well as sickness or accident.

**Americans** and **Canadians** should also check that they're not already covered. Canadian provincial health plans usually provide partial cover for medical mishaps overseas. Holders of official student/teacher/youth cards are entitled to meagre accident coverage and hospital in-patient benefits. Students will often find that their student health coverage extends during the vacations and for one term beyond the date of last enrollment. Homeowners' or renters' insurance often covers theft or loss of documents, money and valuables while overseas, though conditions and maximum amounts vary from company to company.

# TRAVELLERS WITH DISABILITIES

France has no special reputation for providing facilities for disabled travellers. For people in wheelchairs, the haphazard parking habits and stepped village streets are serious obstacles, and public toilets with disabled access are rare. In the major cities and coastal resorts, however, ramps or other forms of access are gradually being added to hotels, museums and some theatres and concert halls. APF, the French paraplegic organization, which has an office in each *département* (we've given details of those in Toulouse and Montpellier, see below) will be the most reliable source of information on accommodation with disabled access and other facilities.

Public **transport** is certainly not wheelchair-friendly, and although many train stations now have ramps to enable wheelchair-users to board and descend from carriages, at others it is still up to the guards to carry the chair. The high-speed **TGVs** (including Eurostar) all have places for wheelchairs in the First Class saloon coach, which you must book in advance, though no higher fee is charged; on other trains, a wheelchair symbol within the timetable denotes whether that service offers special features, and you and your companion will again be upgraded to first class with no extra charge. The *Guide du Voyageur à Mobilité Réduite*, available free at main train stations, details all facilities. **Taxis** are obliged by law to carry you and to

## CONTACTS FOR TRAVELLERS WITH DISABILITIES

### FRANCE

**APF (Association des Paralysés de France)**, Head office, 17 bd Auguste-Blanqui, 75013 Paris (☎01.40.78.69.00, *orphanet.infobiogen.fr /associations/APF*); 116bis, rue des Amidonniers, Toulouse (☎05.62.30.64.00); 1620, rue St Priest, Parc Euromédecine, 34097 Montpellier (☎04.67.10.03.25). National organization providing useful information and lists of new and accessible accommodation. Their guide *Où Ferons-Nous Étape* is available at the office or by post to a French address.

**CNRH (Comité National Français de Liaison pour la Réadaptation des Handicapés)**, 236bis rue de Tolbiac, 75013 Paris (☎01.53.80.66.66); 91 rue de Fenouillet, 31200 Toulouse (☎05.61.13.48.00). Information service whose various useful guides include the *Guide Touristique pour les Personnes à Mobilitée Réduite*, available in English for 60F/€9.15.

### BRITAIN AND IRELAND

**Access Travel**, 6 The Hillock, Astley, Lancashire M29 7GW (☎01942/888 844, fax 891 811, *www .access.co.uk*). Tour operator that can arrange flights, transfer and accommodation. This is a small business, personally checking out places before recommendation. Established 1991; ATOL bonded.

**Disability Action Group**, 2 Annadale Ave, Belfast BT7 3JH (☎028/9049 1011). Offers

information about travel and access for disabled travellers abroad.

**Holiday Care**, 2nd floor, Imperial Building, Victoria Rd, Horley, Surrey RH6 7PZ (☎01293/774 535, fax 784 647, Minicom 01293/776 943, *www .holidaycare.org.uk*). Provides free lists of accessible accommodation throughout France. Information on financial help for holidays available.

**Irish Wheelchair Association**, Blackheath Drive, Clontarf, Dublin 3 (☎01/833 8241, fax 833 3873, *iwa@iol.ie*). Offers information about travel and access for disabled travellers abroad.

**RADAR** (Royal Association for Disability and Rehabilitation), 12 City Forum, 250 City Rd, London EC1V 8AF (☎020/7250 3222, Minicom ☎020/7250 4119). A good source of advice on holidays and travel abroad.

**Tripscope**, Alexandra House, Albany Rd, Brentford, Middlesex TW8 0NE (☎08457/585 641, fax 020/8580 7022, *www.justmobility.co.uk /tripscope*). This registered charity provides a phone-in travel information service offering free advice on transport for those with a mobility problem.

### USA

**Access First Travel**, 239 Commercial St, Malden, MA 02148 (☎1-800/557 2047). Offers up-to-date information for disabled travellers.

help you into the vehicle, also to carry your guide dog if you are blind. Specialist taxi services are available in some towns: these are detailed in the Ministry of Transport and Tourism's pamphlet *Guide des Transports à l'Usage des Personnes à Mobilité Réduite*, available at airports, main train stations and some tourist offices. The guide also gives some indication of the accessibility of urban public transport systems, and the availability of cars for rent with hand controls.

**Up-to-date information** about handicap accessibility, special programmes and discounts is best obtained from organizations at home before you leave or from the French disability organizations. The publication *Touristes Quand Même!*, produced by the CNRH (see box below), lists facilities throughout France but is not updated regularly. Some tourist offices have information but, again, it is not always very reliable. The

Holiday Care Service has an information sheet on accessible **accommodation** in France.

Most of the cross-Channel **ferry companies** offer good facilities, though up-to-date information about access is difficult to get hold of. **Eurostar**, having been established in the 1990s, offers an excellent deal for wheelchair users. There are two special spaces in the first class carriages for wheelchairs, with an accompanying seat for a companion. No advance bookings are necessary, though the limited spaces might make it wise to reserve ahead of time and also to arrange the special assistance which Eurostar offers at either end. As far as **airlines** go, British Airways has a better-than-average record for treatment of disabled passengers, and from North America, Virgin and Air Canada come out tops in terms of disability awareness (and seating arrangements) and might be worth contacting first for any information they can provide.

---

**Directions Unlimited**, 123 Green Lane, Bedford Hills, NY 10507 (☎1-800/533 5343). Tour operator specializing in customized tours for people with disabilities.

**Jewish Rehabilitation Hospital**, 3205 Place Alton Goldbloom, Chomedy Laval, PQ H7V 1R2 (☎450/688 9550, ext 226). Provides guidebooks and travel information.

**Mobility International USA**, PO Box 10767, Eugene, OR 97440 (☎541/343 1284 voice & TDD, *www.miusa.com*). Offers information and referral services, access guides, tours and exchange programmes. Annual membership $25 (includes quarterly newsletter).

**Society for the Advancement of Travel for the Handicapped** (SATH), 347 Fifth Ave, Suite 610, New York, NY 10016 (☎212/447 7284, *www.sath.org*). Non-profit-making travel industry referral service that passes queries on to its members as appropriate.

**Travel Information Service** (☎215/456 9600). Telephone-only information and referral service for disabled travellers.

**Wheels Up!**, PO Box 5197, Plant City, FL 33564-5197 (☎1-888/389 4335, *www.wheelsup.com*). Provides discounted airfare, tour and cruise prices for disabled travellers, as well as publishing a free monthly newsletter. Their Web site is comprehensive.

**CANADA**

**Twin Peaks Press**, Box 129, Vancouver, WA 98666 (☎360/694 2462 or 1-800/637 2256, *www.pacifier.com/twinpeak*). Publisher of the *Directory of Travel Agencies for the Disabled* ($19.95), listing more than 370 agencies worldwide; *Travel for the Disabled* ($19.95); the *Directory of Accessible Van Rentals* ($9.95); and *Wheelchair Vagabond* ($14.95), which is loaded with personal tips.

**AUSTRALIA**

**ACROD** (Australian Council for Rehabilitation of the Disabled), PO Box 60, Curtin, ACT 2605 (☎02/6282 4333); 24 Cabarita Rd, Cabarita, NSW 2137 (☎02/9743 2699). Provides lists of travel agencies and tour operators for people with disabilities.

**Barrier Free Travel**, 36 Wheatley St, North Bellingen, NSW 2454 (☎02/6655 1733). Independent consultant – draws up individual itineraries for people with disabilities for a fee.

**NEW ZEALAND**

**Disabled Persons Assembly**, PO Box 10, 138 The Terrace, Wellington (☎04/472 2626, *www.dpa.org.nz*). Provides details of tour operators and travel agencies for people with disabilities.

# INFORMATION AND MAPS

The French Government Tourist Office gives away large quantities of maps and glossy brochures for Languedoc and Roussillon, including lists of hotels and campsites. Some of these – like the maps of the inland waterways or footpaths, lists of festivals and so on – can be useful; others are just so much dead wood. For reviews of useful Web sites in France, see p.56.

## TOURIST OFFICES

In Languedoc and Roussillon itself you'll find a **tourist office** – usually an Office du Tourisme

(OT) but sometimes a Syndicat d'Initiative (SI) – in practically every town and many villages (addresses, contact details and opening hours are detailed in the Guide). For the practical purposes of visitors, there is little difference between them: SIs have wider responsibilities for encouraging business, while Offices du Tourisme deal exclusively with tourism; sometimes they share premises and call themselves an OTSI. In small villages where there is no OT or SI, the *mairie* (mayoral office), frequently located in the Hôtel de Ville (town hall), will offer a similar service.

### FRENCH GOVERNMENT TOURIST OFFICES

#### TOURIST OFFICES ABROAD

The official French Government Tourist Office, La Maison de France, is on the Web at *www.franceguide.com*.

**UK**
178 Piccadilly, London W1V 0AL (☎0891/244 123, 50p/min, fax 020/7493 6594).

**Ireland**
10 Suffolk St, Dublin 2 (☎01/679 0813, fax 679 0814).

**USA**
444 Madison Avenue, 16th floor, New York, NY 10022 (☎212/838 7800, fax 838 7855); 676 North Michigan Avenue, Suite 3360, Chicago, IL 60611-

2819 (☎312/751 7800, fax 337 6339); 9454 Wilshire Blvd, Suite 715, Beverly Hills, CA 90212-2967 (☎310/271 6665 or 310/272 2661, fax 276 2835).

**Canada**
1981 Avenue McGill College, Suite 490, Montréal, QUE H3A 2W9 (☎514/288 4264, fax 845 4868).

**Australia**
25 Bligh St, Level 22, Sydney, NSW 2000 (☎02/9231 5244, fax 9221 8682, *www.fgtousa.org*).

Note that **New Zealand** does not have a French Government Tourist Office.

#### REGIONAL AND DEPARTMENTAL TOURIST OFFICES

**Comité Régional du Tourisme Languedoc-Roussillon**: 20 rue de la République, 34000 Montpellier (☎04.67.22.81.00, fax 04.67.58.06.10, *www.cr-languedocroussillon.fr/tourisme*).

**Comité Départemental du Tourisme Aude**: Conseil General, 11855 Carcassonne (☎04.68.11.66.00, fax 04.68.11.66.01, *www.audetourisme.com*).

**Comité Départemental du Tourisme Gard**: 3 pl des Arènes, 30010 Nîmes (☎04.66.36.96.30, fax 04.66.36.13.14).

**Comité Départemental du Tourisme Hérault en Languedoc**: Maison du Tourisme, av des Moulins, BP 3067, 34043 Montpellier (☎04.67.67.71.71, fax 04.67.67.71.77, *www.herault-en-languedoc.com*).

**Comité Départemental du Tourisme Pyrénées-Orientales**: 7 quai de Lattre-de-Tassigny, BP 540, 66005 Perpignan (☎04.68.66.61.11, fax 04.68.67.06.10, *www.pyrenees-orientales.com*).

**Comité Régional du Tourisme du Midi-Pyrénées**: 54 bd de l'Embouchure, BP 2166, 31022 Toulouse (☎05.61.13.55.55, fax 05.61.47.17.16, *crt.midi-pyrenees@wanadoo.fr*).

**Comité Départemental du Tourisme Ariège-Pyrénées**: 31bis av de Général-de-Gaulle, BP 143, 09004 Foix (☎04.61.02.30.70, fax 04.61.65.17.34, *www.ariege.pyrenees.com*).

**Comité Départemental du Tourisme Tarn**: BP 225, 81006 Albi (☎05.63.77.32.10, fax 05.63.77.32.32, *www.resinfrance.com*).

From all these offices you can get specific local information, including listings of hotels and restaurants, leisure activities, car and bike rental, bus timetables, laundries and countless other things; many can also book accommodation for you. Most offices will provide a free town plan (though some places charge a nominal 5–10F/€0.76–1.53), if asked, and will have maps and local walking guides on sale. In mountain regions they display daily meteorological information and often share premises with the local hiking and climbing organizations. In the larger cities you can usually also pick up free *What's On* guides. The regional or departmental tourist offices also offer useful practical information (see box on p.28).

## MAPS

In addition to the various free leaflets – and the maps in this guide – the one extra map you'll probably want is a reasonable **road map** of Languedoc and Roussillon. The Michelin (*www.michelin-travel*

.com) yellow series (1:200,000 scale) is best for the motorist; maps 235 and 240 cover the entire area of the Guide. You can get the whole series in one large spiral-bound *Atlas Routier*. For a single map of Languedoc and Roussillon (except for the St-Girons area) try Euromap's Languedoc (1:300,000). A useful free map for car drivers, obtainable from filling stations and traffic information kiosks in France, is the Bison Futé map, showing alternative back routes to the congested main roads, clearly signposted on the ground by special green Bison Futé road signs.

If you're planning to **walk or cycle**, check the IGN (Institut Géographique National) maps – either green (1:100,000 and 1:50,000), or the more detailed blue (1:25,000) series. The IGN 1:100,000 series is the smallest scale available that has the contours marked – essential for cyclists, who tend to cycle off 1:25,000 maps in a couple of hours. Routes in the French Pyrenees are well covered by the twelve maps in the *Randonnées Pyrénées* series (1:50,000).

## MAP OUTLETS

### BRITAIN

**Bristol** Stanfords, 29 Corn Street, BS1 1HT (☎0117/929 9966, *www.stanfords.co.uk*).

**Cambridge** Heffers Map and Travel, 20 Trinity St, CB2 1TJ (☎01223/586 586, *www.heffers.co.uk*; mail order available).

**Glasgow** John Smith and Sons, 26 Colquhoun Ave, G52 4PJ (☎0141/221 7472, *www.johnsmith.co.uk*; mail order available).

**Inverness** James Thin Melven's Bookshop, 29 Union St, IV1 1QA (☎01463/233 500, *www.jthin.co.uk*; mail order available).

**London** Daunt Books, 83 Marylebone High St, W1M 3DE (☎020/7224 2295) and 193 Haverstock Hill, NW3 4QL (☎020/7794 4006); National Map Centre, 22–24 Caxton St, SW1H 0QU (☎020/7222 2466, *www.mapsnmc.co.uk*); Stanfords, 12–14 Long Acre, WC2E 9LP (☎020/7836 1321, *www.stanfords.co.uk*; maps by mail or phone order are available on this number and via email), and within the British Airways offices at 156 Regent St, W1R 5TA (☎020/7434 4744); The Travel Bookshop, 13–15 Blenheim Crescent, W11 2EE (☎020/7229 5260, *www.thetravelbookshop.co.uk*).

**Manchester** Waterstone's, 91 Deansgate, M3 2BW (☎0161/837 3000, *www.waterstonesbooks.co.uk*).

**Newcastle** Newcastle Map Centre, 55 Grey St, NE1 6EF (☎0191/261 5622, *www.newtraveller.com*).

**Oxford** Blackwell's Map and Travel Shop, 53 Broad St, OX1 3BQ (☎01865/792 792, *bookshop.blackwell.co.uk*).

### IRELAND

**Belfast** Waterstone's, Queens Bldg, 8 Royal Ave, Belfast BT1 1DA (☎028/9024 7355, *www.waterstonesbooks.co.uk*).

**Cork** Waterstone's, 69 Patrick St (☎021/276 522).

**Dublin** Easons Bookshop, 40 O'Connell St, 1 (☎01/873 3811; mail order available); Fred Hanna's Bookshop, 27–29 Nassau St, 2 (☎01/677 1255); Hodges Figgis Bookshop, 56–58 Dawson St, 2 (☎01/677 4754); Waterstone's, 7 Dawson St, 2 (☎01/679 1415).

### USA

Rand McNally has more than twenty stores across the US; call ☎1-800/333 0136 (ext 2111), or go to *www.randmcnally.com* for the address of your nearest store, or for **direct mail** maps.

*Box continues on next page. . .*

. . .box continued from previous page

**Chicago** Rand McNally, 444 N Michigan Ave, IL 60611 (☎312/321 1751).

**Corte Madera** Book Passage, 51 Tamal Vista Blvd, CA 94925 (☎415/927 0960, *www .bookpassage.com*).

**New York** The Complete Traveler Bookstore, 199 Madison Ave, NY 10016 (☎212/685 9007, *www.complete.traveller.com*); Rand McNally, 150 E 52nd St, NY 10022 (☎212/758 7488); Traveler's Choice Bookstore, 2 Wooster St, NY 10013 (☎212/941 1535, *tvlchoice@aol.com*).

**Palo Alto** Phileas Fogg's Books & Maps, #87 Stanford Shopping Center, CA 94304 (☎1-800/533 FOGG, *www.foggs.com*).

**San Francisco** The Complete Traveler Bookstore, 3207 Fillmore St, San Francisco, CA 94123 (☎415/923 1511, *www.complete .traveller.com*); Rand McNally, 595 Market St, CA 94105 (☎415/777 3131).

**Santa Barbara** Map Link Inc., 30 S La Patera Lane, Unit 5, CA 93117 (☎805/692 6777, *www.maplink.com*).

**Seattle** Elliott Bay Book Company, 101 S Main St, WA 98104 (☎206/624 6600, *www.elliottbaybook.com*).

**Washington** ADC Map and Travel Center, 1636 1st St NW, Washington DC 20006 (☎202/628 2608); Travel Books & Language Center, 4437 Wisconsin Ave, Washington DC 20016 (☎1-800/220 2665).

**White Plains** Forsyth Travel Library, 226 Westchester Ave, NY 10604 (☎1-800/367 7984; *www.forsyth.com*).

## CANADA

**Montréal** Ulysses Travel Bookshop, 4176 St-Denis, QUE H2W 2M5 (☎514/843 9447, *www.ulyssesguides.com*).

**Toronto** Open Air Books and Maps, 25 Toronto St, ON M5R 2C1 (☎416/363 0719).

**Vancouver** International Travel Maps and Books, 552 Seymour St, BC V6B 3J5 (☎604/687 3320, *www.itmb.com*).

## AUSTRALIA

**Adelaide** The Map Shop, 16a Peel St (☎08/8231 2033).

**Brisbane** Worldwide Maps and Guides, 187 George St (☎07/3221 4330).

**Melbourne** Map Land, 372 Little Burke St (☎03/9670 4383).

**Perth** Perth Map Centre, 884 Hay St (☎08/9322 5733).

**Sydney** Travel Bookshop, Shop 3, 175 Liverpool St, 2000 (☎02/9261 8200).

## NEW ZEALAND

**Auckland** Specialty Maps, 58 Albert St (☎09/307 2217).

**Christchurch** Mapworld, 173 Gloucester St (☎03/374 5399, *www.mapworld.co.nz*).

# GETTING AROUND

France has the most extensive train network in western Europe, and rail is the best way of moving between almost all of the major towns within Languedoc and Roussillon. The nationally owned French train company, the SNCF (Société Nationale des Chemins de Fer), runs fast, modern trains. In rural areas where branch lines have been closed, routes (such as Castres–Montpellier) are covered by buses operated solely by SNCF or in partnership with independent lines. It's an integrated service, with buses timetabled to meet trains and the same ticket covering both.

The private **bus** services that supplement the SNCF services are confusing and uncoordinated. Some areas, such as the coast or around larger centres like Toulouse, Albi and Castres, are quite well served, while the service in less populated regions, like the Corbières and parts of the Pyrenees and Haut Languedoc, is barely existent – often designed to carry the inhabitants of hamlets to and from weekly markets, and thus not very useful for travellers. Approximate journey times and frequencies can be found in the "Travel details" at the end of each chapter.

For a more private kind of independent transport, by **car** or **bicycle**, you'll need to be aware of a number of French road rules and peculiarities. **Hitching** is also an option, but is not easy and is becoming less and less popular. **Walking** (see p.36), on the extensive network of "GR" footpaths, is recommended, as are the more specialist realms of inland **boating** and **cross-country skiing** (see p.62), both of which have a high profile in Languedoc and Roussillon.

## TRAINS

The SNCF has pioneered one of the most efficient, comfortable and user-friendly railway systems in the world. Its staff are, with a few exceptions, courteous and helpful, and its trains – for the most part, fast, clean and frequent – continue, in spite of the closure of some rural lines, to cover much of Languedoc and Roussillon; a main rail corridor runs from Toulouse to Narbonne, where it joins the coastal line, linking Cerbère on the French border and Beaucaire (Tarascon) at the Rhône, while spur lines run up major river valleys – including the Tarn, Ariège and Conflent. For national train **information**, you can either phone ☎08.36.35.35.35 (2.23F/€0.34 per minute) or check on the Internet at *www.sncf.fr*.

Pride and joy of the system are the high-speed **TGVs** (*trains à grande vitesse*), capable of 300kph, and their offspring Eurostar. There are several stations connected to the TGV in Languedoc and Roussillon, among them Nîmes (journey time from Paris 4hr), Montpellier (4hr 30min), Narbonne (5hr), Béziers (4hr 45min), Perpignan (6hr) and Toulouse (4hr 30min). The only difference between TGV and other train fares is that you pay a compulsory reservation charge (from 20F/€3), plus a supplement on certain peak-hour trains. It is easiest to use the counter service for buying tickets, though if there are language problems or long queues the touch-screen computerized system available in most stations can be read in English and is a good way to check various fares and times – if need be; you can always press the red annulment button to cancel the transaction before committing yourself.

All tickets – but not passes (see below) – must be validated in the orange machines at station platform entrances, and it is an offence not to follow the instruction *Compostez votre billet* ("Validate your ticket"). Train journeys may be broken any time, anywhere, for as long as the ticket is valid (usually two months), but after a break of 24 hours you must validate your ticket again when you resume your journey.

After a spate of terrorist bombings in the late 1990s, most train stations closed their **luggage lockers** (*consignes automatiques*); these days a few have reopened, and larger stations have a staffed luggage check-in, usually with limited hours (*consignes* are noted in the Guide). Many stations also rent out **bicycles**, sometimes of rather doubtful reliability.

Regional rail **maps** and complete **timetables** are on sale at tobacconist shops (*tabacs*). Leaflet timetables for particular lines are available free at stations. *Autocar* or a bullet symbol at the top of a column means it's an SNCF bus service, on which rail tickets and passes are valid.

Aside from the regular lines there are a number of special tourist-oriented railways, including the spectaular *Train Jaune* which winds its way up through the Pyrenees, and the ATM train, which heads up into the hinterland of Narbonne. These are also detailed in the Guide.

### DISCOUNTS AND RAIL PASSES

There are several **passes** available offering unlimited travel on the French network; most must be bought before you leave for France and are detailed on p.5 and the box on p.15. In addition, the SNCF itself offers a whole range of discounted fares within France on standard rail prices on *période bleue* (blue period) and *période blanche* (white period) days, depending on exactly when you want to travel. A leaflet showing the blue, white (smaller discount) and red (peak) periods is given out at *gares SNCF*.

There is a range of **reductions** for which no pass is required. Any two people travelling together (*à deux*), or a small group of up to five people – whether a married couple, friends, family, whatever – are entitled to a 25 percent discount on return tickets on TGVs, subject to availability, or on other trains if they start their journey on a blue period day; the same reduction applies to a group of up to four people travelling with a child under 12, to under 26-year-olds, over-60s, and for anyone who books a return journey of at least 200km in distance, including a Saturday night away (this latter is called the *séjour*).

There is a range of other train passes, which can be purchased through most travel agents in France or from main *gares* SNCF and are valid for one year. Over-60s can get the **Carte Senior**, which costs 285F/€43.46 for unlimited travel. It offers up to 50 percent off tickets on TGVs, subject to availability, or other journeys starting in blue periods, a 25 percent reduction on white period journeys, as well as a 30 percent reduction on through international journeys involving most countries in western and central Europe. The same percentage reductions are available for under-26s with a **Carte 12–25** pass, which costs 270F/€41.18. Under-12s can obtain the same advantages for themselves and up to four

travelling companions of any age by purchasing the **Enfant Plus Carte** (350F/€53.38).

## BUSES

The most convenient **bus services** are those run as an extension of rail links by SNCF, which always run to and from the SNCF station and access areas formerly served by rail. In addition to SNCF buses, private, municipal and *départemental* buses can be useful for mid- to long-distance journeys. The most frustrating thing about them is the multiplicity of services and the difficulty in obtaining departure information other than at bus stops and stations. In Toulouse, city buses can be used to access outlying villages, and in Montpellier the network goes as far out as the coast. Some *départements*, like the Hérault and the Tarn, have rural bus networks; their roadside stops usually have a copy of the schedule attached to the sign or shelter. Private operators cover much of rural Languedoc and Roussillon too – unfortunately, their routes miss some of the more interesting and less inhabited areas, and the **timetable** is constructed to suit working, market and school hours – all often dauntingly early. All buses are, generally speaking, cheaper and slower than trains.

Larger towns usually have a **gare routière** (bus station), often next to the gare SNCF. However, the private bus companies don't always work together and you'll frequently find them leaving from an array of different points (the local tourist office will usually help locate them).

## DRIVING

**Driving** in Languedoc and Roussillon can be a real pleasure. **Autoroutes** in the region run through the same corridors as the main rail lines: connecting Toulouse and Narbonne, and from here, running north and south along the Mediterranean coast. If you are in a hurry, it is well worth paying the toll (see below) for their use, as the free national routes, which also follow this corridor, tend to be heavily travelled by both local drivers and long-distance truckers. By *autoroute*, in good traffic conditions, you can reach Nîmes from Toulouse in a matter of hours. Away from the main arteries, the older main roads or **routes nationales** (marked N9 or RN230, for example, on signs and maps) are generally uncongested and, passing through the centres of the towns along the way, make for a more scenic, if slower, drive than the *autoroutes*. Smaller **routes départementales** (marked with a D) should not be shunned. Although they are occasionally in relatively poor condition, you can often travel for kilometres across country, seeing few other cars, on a road as broad and well maintained as a major road in Britain.

The most challenging part of driving in Languedoc and Roussillon is likely to be entering large cities for the first time. Specific directions are given for each city in the Guide, but as a general rule of thumb you can usually reach the centre by following signs for the tourist office. That said, parking is likely to be problematic, so you may instead want to follow the indications for the gare SNCF, which will have some pay parking and most likely be in walking distance of the centre.

Of course, there are times when it is wiser not to drive: **congestion** is a major problem on the *Autoroute Méditerranéen* in summer, particularly in the first and last few days of July and August, when holiday periods tend to begin or end, and the same goes for roads of all categories along the coast on summer weekends, when the going is frustratingly slow. The high cost of **fuel** can also be a discouraging factor; you'll find the cheapest gas (*essence*) or diesel fuel (*gasoil*) at out-of-town superstores. Four-star is *super*, unleaded is *sans plomb*.

In addition, there is a charge for the use of the *autoroutes* themselves (payable at the frequent **toll gates** or *péages*). To give you an idea of the costs involved, the toll from Calais to Montpellier, taking in three different toll gates, would cost you around 379F/€57.80, while the trip from Montpellier to Toulouse would come to 104F/€15.85.

The costs of driving can, however, be amortized if your car carries a full complement of passengers, and the extra mobility and carrying capacity make it much easier to camp. But, practical considerations aside, the great gain is the freedom to explore places that would otherwise remain inaccessible, in particular the sparsely populated upland of Haut Languedoc, the Hérault and the Pyrenees.

All the major car manufacturers have garages and service stations in Languedoc and Roussillon, which can help if you run into **mechanical difficulties**. You can find them in the Yellow Pages of the phone book under "Garages d'automobiles". For breakdowns, look under "Dépannages". If you have an accident or break-in, you should make a report to the local police (and keep a copy) in order to make an insurance claim. Many car insurance policies cover taking your car to Europe; check with your insurer while planning your trip. However, you're advised to take out extra cover for motoring assistance in case your car breaks down, costing around £45 for seven days. Look into the RAC's European Motoring Assistance (☎0800/550055, *www.rac.co.uk*); the AA's Five-Star Europe cover (☎0800/444500, *www.theaa.co.uk*); or Europ Assistance (☎0645/947000). In the US, contact the American Automobile Association (☎1-800/222 4357, *www.aaa.com*); in Canada, the Canadian Automobile Association (☎1-800/267 8713, *www.caa.ca*); in Australia, the Australian Automobile Association (☎02 /6247 7311, *www.aaa.asn.au*); and in New Zealand, the New Zealand Automobile Association (☎09/377 4660, *www.nzaa.co.nz*).

## RULES OF THE ROAD

British, Irish, Australian, Canadian, New Zealand and US **driving licences** are valid in France, though an International Driver's Licence makes life easier if you get a police officer unwilling to peruse a document in English. If the vehicle is rented, its registration document (*carte grise*) and the insurance papers must be carried. GB stickers are, by law, meant to be displayed, and a Green Card, though not a legal requirement, might save some hassle. If your car is right-hand drive, you must have your headlight dip adjusted to the right before you go – it's a legal requirement – and as a courtesy change or paint them to yellow or stick on black glare deflectors. Remember also that you have to be eighteen years of age to drive in France, regardless of whether you hold a licence in your own country.

The law of *priorité à droite* – **giving way** to traffic coming from your right, even when it is coming from a minor road – is being phased out as it is a major cause of accidents. It still applies in built-up areas, so you still have to be vigilant in

---

**ROAD INFORMATION**

For information on traffic and road conditions on *autoroutes* throughout France, ring the multilingual service, Autoroutel (☎08.36.68.10.77) or consult their Web site *www.autoroutes.fr*. Traffic information for non-motorway routes can be obtained 24 hours per day at ☎01.56.96.33.33.

towns, keeping a lookout along the roadside for the yellow diamond on a white background that gives you right of way – until you see the same sign with an oblique black slash, which indicates vehicles emerging from the right have right of way. At roundabouts the *priorité à droite* law no longer applies. *Stop* signs mean stop completely; *Cédez le passage* means "Give way". Other signs warning of potential dangers are *déviation* (diversion), *gravillons* (loose chippings), *nids de poules* (potholes) and *chaussée déformée* (uneven surface).

**Fines** of up to 2500F/€381.25 for driving violations are exacted on the spot, and only cash is accepted. The fines for exceeding the speed limit by 1–30kph (1–18mph) range from 900F/€137 to 5000F/€763. Speed limits are: 130kph (80mph) on *autoroutes*; 110kph (68mph) on dual carriageways; 90kph (56mph) on other roads; and 50kph (37mph) in towns. The town limit is constant, but in wet weather, and for drivers with less than two-years' experience, the three road limits are 110kph (68mph), 100kph (62mph), and 80kph (50mph) respectively. Random breath tests are common, and the legal blood alcohol limit (0.05 percent alcohol) is lower than in the UK and North America; fines range from 900F/€137 to 30,000F/€4575.

## CAR RENTAL

**Car rental** in France costs upwards of 2000F /€305 a week (from around 290F/€44.23 a day), but can be cheaper if arranged before you leave home. You'll find the big firms – Hertz, Avis, Europcar and Budget – at airports and in most big cities, with addresses detailed throughout the Guide. Rental from airports normally includes a surcharge. Local firms can be cheaper but you need to check the small print and be sure of where the car can be returned to. It's normal to pay an indemnity of around 1000F/€152 against any damage to the car – they will take your credit card number rather than cash. You should return the car with a full tank of fuel. Extras are often pressed on you, like medical cover, which you may already have from travel insurance. The cost of car rental includes the basic legally necessary car insurance. North Americans and Australians in particular should be forewarned that it is very difficult to arrange the hire of a car with **automatic** transmission; if you can't drive a manual you should try to book an automatic well in advance, possibly before you leave home, and be prepared to pay a much higher price for it.

## CAR RENTAL AGENCIES

### BRITAIN AND IRELAND

**Autos Abroad** (in the UK ☎020/7287 6000, *www.autosabroad.co.uk*).

**Avis** (in Britain ☎0870/606 0100; Northern Ireland ☎0870/5900 500; Irish Republic ☎01/874 5844; *www.avis.com*).

**Budget** (in the UK ☎0800/181181; Irish Republic ☎0800/973159; *www.budgetrentacar.com*).

**Europcar** (in the UK ☎0845/7222 525; Irish Republic ☎01/874 5844; *www.europcar.com*).

**Hertz** (in Britain ☎0870/844 8844; Northern Ireland ☎0870/5996 699; Irish Republic ☎01/676 7476; *www.hertz.com*).

**Holiday Autos** (in Britain ☎0870/400 0011; Northern Ireland ☎0870/5300 400; Irish Republic ☎01/872 9366; *www.kemwel.com*).

**National Car Rental** (in the UK ☎01895/233 300, *www.nationalcar.com*).

**Thrifty** (in the UK ☎01494/442 110, *www.thrifty.com*).

### USA AND CANADA

**Auto Europe** (☎1-800/223 5555).

**Avis** (☎1-800/331 1084).

**Budget** (☎1-800/527 0700).

**Europe by Car** (☎1-800/223 1516, *www.europebycar.com*).

**Hertz** (in US ☎1-800/654 3001; in Canada ☎1-800/263 0600).

**Holiday Autos** (☎1-800/422 7737).

**National** (☎1-800/CAR RENT).

**Thrifty** (☎1-800/367 2277).

### AUSTRALIA AND NEW ZEALAND

**Avis** (in Australia ☎13/6333; in New Zealand ☎09/526 5231 or 0800/655 111).

**Budget** (in Australia ☎1300/362 848; in New Zealand ☎0800/ 652 227 or 09/375 2270).

**Fly and Drive Holidays** New Zealand ☎09/529 3709.

**Hertz** (in Australia ☎1800/550 067; in New Zealand ☎09/309 0989 or 0800/655 955).

**Renault Eurodrive** Australia ☎02/9299 3344.

Most rental companies will only deal with people over 25 unless an extra insurance premium, typically around 130–150F/€20–23 per day, is paid (but you still must be over 21 and have driven for at least one year). OTU Voyage (Paris office ☎01.40.29.12.12), the student travel agency, can arrange car rental for young drivers, with prices beginning at 459F/€70 for three days, insurance extra.

## MOPED AND MOTORBIKE RENTAL

**Mopeds** and scooters are relatively easy to find; outside the mountainous areas everyone from young kids to grandmas seems to ride them, and although they're not built for any kind of long-distance travel, they're ideal for shooting around town and nearby. Places that rent out bicycles will often also rent out mopeds; you can expect to pay 175F/€26.69 a day for a 50cc Suzuki. No licence is needed for 50cc and under bikes, but for anything larger you'll need a valid **motorbike** licence. Rental prices are around 220F/€33.55 a day for an 80cc motorbike, 300F/€45.75 for a 125cc; also expect to leave a hefty deposit by cash or credit card – 6000F/€900 is not unusual – which you may lose in the event of damage or theft. Crash helmets are now compulsory on all mopeds and motorbikes.

### HITCHING

If you're intent on **hitching**, you'll have to rely almost exclusively on car drivers, as lorries very rarely give lifts. Even so, it won't be easy. Looking as clean, ordinary and respectable as possible makes a very big difference, as conversations with French drivers soon make clear. Experience also suggests that hitching the less-frequented D roads is much quicker. In mountain areas a rucksack and hiking gear will help procure a lift from fellow aficionados.

**Autoroutes** are a special case. Hitching on the *autoroute* itself is strictly illegal, but you can make excellent time going from one service station to another and, if you get stuck, at least there's food, drink, shelter and washing facilities at most service stations. It helps to have the *Guide des Autoroutes*, published by Michelin, which shows all the rest stops, service stations, tollbooths (*péages*), exits, etc. Remember to get out at the service station before your driver leaves the *autoroute*. The tollbooths are a second best (and legal) option; ordinary approach roads can be disastrous.

For long-distance rides, or for a greater sense of safety, you might consider using the national **hitching organization**, Allostop Provoya, 8 rue Rochambeau (on square Montholon), 17009 Paris (Mon–Fri 9am–7.30pm, Sat 9am–1pm & 2–6pm; ☎01.53.20.42.42, fax 01.53.20.42.44, *pcb .ecritel.fr/allostop/welcome*; Mᵒ Cadet/ Poissonnière); reservations are normally made through the Paris number, or via the Internet, but there is also a local branch in Montpellier, detailed in the Guide. The cost comprises a registration fee (30F/€4.58 for a journey less than 200km, 50F/€7.63 if less than 400km, 60F/€9.15 if less than 500km and a maximum of 70F/€10.68 if more than 500km, or you can buy a 180F/€27.45 membership card which is good for eight trips over two years), plus a charge of 22 centimes for every kilometre of the journey.

### BICYCLES

**Bicycles** (*vélos*) have high status in France. All the car ferries carry them for nothing; the SNCF makes minimal charges; and the French respect cyclists – both as traffic and, when you stop off at a restaurant or hotel, as customers. In addition, municipalities like Toulouse and Montpellier, and their respective *départements* – Haute Garonne and L'Hérault – are actively promoting cycling, not only with city paths, but comprehensive networks linking rural areas (frequently utilizing disused roadways and rail rights of way). These days more and more cyclists are using **mountain bikes**, which the French call VTTs (*vélos tout terrain*), even for touring holidays, although it's much less effort, and much quicker, to cycle long distances and carry luggage on a traditionally styled touring or racing bike.

Restaurants and hotels along the way are nearly always obliging about looking after your bike, even to the point of allowing it into your room. Most large towns have well-stocked retail and **repair shops**, where parts are normally cheaper than in Britain or the US. However, if you're using a foreign-made bike which doesn't have standard metric wheels, it's a good idea to carry spare tyres. Inner tubes are not a problem, as they adapt to either size, though make sure you get the right valves.

The **train** network runs various schemes for cyclists, all of them covered by the free leaflet *Guide du Train et du Vélo*, available from most stations. Trains marked with a bicycle in the timetable allow you to take a bike as free accompanied luggage. Otherwise, you have to send your bike parcelled up as registered luggage for a fee of 150F/€22.88. Although it may well arrive in less time, the SNCF won't guarantee delivery in under five days; and you do hear stories of bicycles disappearing altogether.

**Ferries** either take bikes free or charge a maximum of £5 one way. British Airways and Air France both take bikes free – you may have to box them though, and you should contact the airlines first. **Eurostar** allow you to take your bicycle as part of your baggage allowance provided it is dismantled and stored in a special bike bag, and the dimensions don't exceed 120cm by 90cm. Otherwise it needs to be sent on unaccompanied, with a guaranteed arrival of 24 hours (you can register it up to ten days in advance; book through Esprit Europe ☎0800/186 186); the fee is £20 one-way.

Bikes – usually mountain bikes – are often available to **rent** from campsites, hostels and *gîtes d'étapes*, as well as from specialist cycle shops and some tourist offices for around 80F/€12.20 per day; these machines are likely to be more reliable, though more expensive, than those of the SNCF. The bikes are often not insured, however, and you will be presented with the bill for its replacement if it's stolen or damaged. Check whether your travel insurance policy covers you for this if you intend to rent a bike.

As for **maps**, a minimum requirement is the IGN 1:100,000 series – the smallest scale that carries contours. In the UK, the Cyclists' Touring Club, Cotterell House, 68 Meadrow, Godalming, Surrey GU7 3HS (☎01483/417 217, fax 01483/426 994, *cycling@ctc.org.uk*), will suggest routes and supply advice for members (£25 p.a. or £12.50 for unemployed). They run a particularly good insurance scheme. Companies running specialist bike touring holidays are listed on pp.8, 14 and 17.

## WALKING

Long-distance **walkers** are well served in Languedoc and Roussillon by an extensive network of marked footpaths, including long-distance routes, known as *sentiers de grande randonnée* or, more commonly, **GRs** (see also p.29). They're fully signposted and equipped with campsites and rest huts along the way. Some of the main routes in the region are the GR10, which runs the length of the Pyrenees, the GRs 7 and 36, which wind their way down from Haut Languedoc through the Corbières, and GR653 which follows the medieval Arles–Jaca pilgrimage route (*le chemin de St-Jacques*) to Santiago in Spain. Other routes are composites, like the "Sentier Cathar", which utilizes various GRs and ARs (local paths) to link Cathar sites between Perpignan and Foix.

### A CYCLING VOCABULARY

| | | | |
|---|---|---|---|
| to adjust | *régler* | loose | *déserré* |
| axle | *l'axe* | to lower | *baisser* |
| ball-bearing | *le roulement à billes* | mudguard | *le garde-boue* |
| battery | *la pile* | pannier | *le pannier* |
| bent | *tordu* | pedal | *le pédale* |
| bicycle | *le vélo* | pump | *la pompe* |
| bottom bracket | *le logement du pédalier* | puncture | *la crevaison* |
| brake cable | *le cable* | rack | *le porte-bagages* |
| brakes | *les freins* | to raise | *remonter* |
| broken | *cassé* | to repair | *réparer* |
| bulb | *l'ampoule* | saddle | *la selle* |
| chain | *la chaîne* | to screw | *visser/serrer* |
| cotter pin | *la clavette* | spanner | *la clef* |
| to deflate | *dégonfler* | spoke | *le rayon* |
| derailleur | *le dérailleur* | to straighten | *redresser* |
| frame | *le cadre* | stuck | *coincé* |
| gears | *les vitesses* | tight | *serré* |
| grease | *la graisse* | toe clips | *les cale-pieds* |
| handlebars | *le guidon* | tyre | *le pneu* |
| to inflate | *gonfler* | wheel | *la roue* |
| inner tube | *la chambre à air* | | |

Each path is described in a *Topoguide* (available in Britain from Stanfords, see p.29), which gives a detailed account of the route (in French), including maps, campsites, refuge huts, sources of provisions, etc. In addition, many tourist offices can provide guides to their local footpaths, especially in popular hiking areas, where they often share premises with professional mountain guides and hike leaders. The latter organize climbing and walking expeditions for all levels of experience. Topoguides are produced by the principal French walkers' organization, the Fédération Française de la Randonnée Pédestre, 14 rue Riquet, 75019 Paris (℡01.44.89.93.93, fax 01.40.35.85.67, *asp.ffrp .asso.fr/accueil.asp*). The main climbing organization is the Club Alpin Français, 24 ave de Laumière, 75019 Paris (℡01.53.72.87.00, fax 01.42.03.55.60, *www.clubalpin.com*); most of the major towns in the Guide have a branch office, the most useful being the CAF de TOULOUSE, 3 rue de l'Orient, 31000 Toulouse (Mon 2–5pm, Tues–Fri 9am–noon & 2–7pm; ℡05.61.63.74.42, fax 05.61.63.96.60, *www.chez .com/caftoulouse*). In the Pyrenees, CIMES offers similar services and has its own network of refuges. Contact CIMES-Pyrenees at 1 rue Maye-Lane, BP 2, 65420 Ibos (℡05.62.90.09.92, fax 05.62.90.67.61, *www.cimes-pyrenees.com*).

## INLAND WATERWAYS

Languedoc is home to one of France's most famous inland waterways, the **Canal du Midi**, which leads from Toulouse (where it hooks up with the River Garonne) to Agde and Sète, passing Carcassonne and Béziers en route. A spur, the **Canal de la Robine**, passes Narbonne before reaching the sea at Gruissan and Port-Nouvelle. From Sète, you can enter the **Canal de Rhône à Sète**, which heads east, passing St-Gilles and Beaucaire, until it reaches the Rhône. Subsidiary canals branch out through the flatlands of the Petit Camargue, and penetrate the extensive Rhône delta. For information on maximum dimensions, documentation, regulations and so forth, ask at a French Government Tourist Office for their booklet *Boating on the Waterways*, or contact Voies Navigables de France, 175 rue Ludovic Boutleux, 62408 Bethune (℡03.21.63.24.24, fax 03.21.63.24.42, *www.vnf.fr*), which has information on boating in Languedoc and Roussillon, and lists of French firms that rent out boats (we've recommended various places in the Guide).

# ACCOMMODATION

At most times of the year, you can turn up in any town in Languedoc and Roussillon and find a room, or a place in a campsite. Booking a couple of nights in advance can be reassuring, however, as it saves you the effort of trudging round and ensures that you know what you'll be paying. In most towns, you'll be able to get a double for around 180–260F/€27–40, or a single for around 150–180F/€23–27. We've detailed a selection of hotels in most of the destinations listed in the Guide, and given a price code for each (see box); as a general rule the areas around train stations have the highest density of cheap hotels. Phone numbers as well as addresses are given in the Guide, and the "Language" section at the back (see pp.378–82) should help you make a reservation call, though many hoteliers and campsite managers – and almost all hostel managers – speak some English. We've also included fax numbers, in case you want to fax through booking requests before you leave home, and, where possible, Web sites or email addresses.

Problems arise mainly between mid-July and the end of August, when the French take their own vacations en masse. The first weekend of August is the busiest time of all. During this period, hotel and hostel accommodation can be hard to come by, particularly in the coastal resorts, and you may find yourself falling back on local tourist offices for help and ideas. Some tourist offices offer a **booking service** but they cannot guarantee rooms at a particular price. All tourist offices can provide lists of hotels, the various hostels or the organizations such as CROUS (see p.41) to contact, details of campsites, and bed-and-breakfast possibilities. With **campsites**, you can be more relaxed about finding an empty space, unless you're touring with a caravan or camper van or looking for a place on the Mediterranean coast or upper Ariège valley.

## HOTELS

Most French **hotels** are **graded** from zero to five stars. The price more or less corresponds to the number of stars, though the system is a little haphazard, having more to do with ratios of bathrooms-per-guest than genuine quality, and non-classified and single-star hotels are often very good. What you get for your money varies enormously between establishments. For under 180F/€27, the bed is likely to be old and floppy, there won't be soundproofing and showers will be communal. However, you should have your own toilet, bidet and washbasin (*lavabo*), partitioned off from the rest of the room in an area referred to as a *cabinet de toilette*: this allows some privacy if you're travelling with a friend and means that you can wash in the sink to s[...]

## ACCOMMODATION PRICE CODES

All the hotels and guesthouses listed in this book have been price-coded according to the following scale, and though costs will rise slightly overall with the life of this edition, the relative comparisons should at least remain valid. The prices quoted are for the **cheapest available double room in high season**, although remember that many of the cheap places will have more expensive rooms with en-suite facilities.

① Under 160F/€24
② 160–220F/€24–34
③ 220–300F/€34–46

④ 300–400F/€46–61
⑤ 400–500F/€61–76
⑥ 500–600F/€76–91

⑦ 600–700F/€91–107
⑧ 700–800F/€107–122
⑨ Over 800F/€122

money. The shared showers down the hall are not usually free – they cost between 15F/€2.29 and 20F/€3.05 per shower (*douche*). If you plan to shower every day and there is more than one of you, it's worth adding up what the ultimate cost will be – you might be better off moving to a more expensive room with its own shower. Over 250F/€38 will get you a room with its own bath or shower though not necessarily a toilet (*WC*), and, though the décor may not be anything to write home about, comfortable furniture. If wandering dark halls late at night in search of a toilet is not your idea of fun, ask for a bathroom (*salle de bain*) which will get you both a toilet and a shower in a separate room; these occasionally have bath tubs (*bain*) too. This type of room will be had for around 300F/€46, and may also come with a TV. At more than 450F/€70, you should expect a higher standard of fittings and something approaching luxury. Hotels with one star or above have a telephone in the rooms, though some phones can only receive calls.

Big cities have a good variety of cheap establishments; in small towns or villages where the choice is limited, you may not be so lucky. The modern and cheesy resorts which have sprung up along the Languedoc coast have inordinately high July and August prices. If you are staying more than three days in a hotel it's often possible to negotiate a lower price, particularly out of season.

**Breakfast** is not normally included and can add 20–35F/€3–5.25 per person to a bill – though there is no obligation to take it and you will nearly always do better at a café. The cost of eating **dinner** in a hotel's restaurant can be a more important factor to bear in mind when picking a place to stay. Officially, it is illegal for hotels to insist on your taking meals, but they often do in places heavily dependent on seasonal tourism. But this is not always such a bad thing, especially in times of economic recession, and you can get a real bargain. **Single rooms** are only marginally cheaper than doubles, so sharing always slashes costs. Most hotels willingly provide rooms with **extra beds**, for three or more people, at good discounts.

Note that many family-run hotels are closed every year for two or three weeks some time between May and September – where possible we've detailed this in the text. In addition, some hotels in smaller towns and villages close for one or two nights a week, usually Sunday or Monday – if in doubt, ring first to check.

A very useful option, especially if it's late at night, are the **motel chains**. In contrast to the downtown hotels which often offer doubtful value (worn-out mattresses, dust, noise, etc) you can count on a decent and reliable standard in the chains even if they are without much charm. Among the cheapest is the one-star **Formule 1** chain, well signposted on the outskirts of most big towns. They are characterless, but provide rooms for up to three people from 140F/€21.35. With a Visa, Mastercard, Eurocard or American Express credit card, you can let yourself into a room at any hour of the day or night. Addresses are most easily available on Minitel – 3615 or 3616 Formule 1 – but the hotels are not difficult to find as long as you're travelling by car, and a brochure with full details can be picked up at any one of them. Other cheap chains include 1<sup>er</sup> Classe, Etap Hôtel and Balladins; they tend to be grouped together near *autoroute* exits. More comfortable but still affordable chain hotels are **Campanile** (*www.campanile.fr*), **Ibis** (*www.ibis.fr*) and **Clarine** (*www.clarine.fr*), which all have en-suite rooms with cable TV and direct dial phones from 270–320F/€41–49. All three of these hotel chains can be reached by Internet and will accept reservations by email. They will also send a complete list of their locations in France by email request within a few days.

Aside from the chains, there a number of **hotel federations** in France. The biggest of these is **Logis de France**, an association of over 3000 hotels nationwide. They have a central reservation number (☎01.45.84.83.84, fax 01.45.83.59.66) and Web site (*www.logis-de-france.fr*), which you can contact to obtain their free yearly guide (or write to 88 av d'Italie, 75013 Paris).

Several cities in Languedoc and Roussillon participate in the "**Bonne Weekend en Ville**" programme, whereby you book through the local tourist office and get two nights for the price of one (Oct–May only) at participating hotels, as well as an array of discount coupons and special deals. Participating towns include Albi, Carcassonne, Nîmes and Toulouse, but the list is growing, so it is worth enquiring about when you are making arrangements to stay in larger towns.

## BED AND BREAKFAST AND RENTED ACCOMMODATION

In country areas, in addition to standard hotels, you will come across *chambres d'hôtes* and *fermes auberges*, **bed-and-breakfast accommodation** in someone's house or farm. These vary in standard and are rarely a cheap option, usually costing the equivalent of a two-star hotel. However, if you're lucky, they may be good sources of traditional home cooking and French company. The brown leaflets available in tourist offices list most of them.

If you are planning to stay a week or more in any one place it might be worth considering **renting a house**. You can do this by checking adverts from the innumerable private owners in, for example, British Sunday newspapers (*Observer* and *Sunday Times*, mainly), or trying one of the numerous holiday firms that market accommodation/travel packages (see the boxes on pp.8, 14 and 18 for a brief selection of these).

Alternatively you could contact **Gîtes de France**, 59 rue St-Lazare, Paris 75009 (Mon–Sat 10am–6.30pm; ☎01.49.70.75.75, *www .gites-de-france.fr*), a government-funded agency which promotes and manages a range of bed-and-breakfast and self-catering accommodation in France, the latter usually consisting of a self-contained country cottage, known as a **gîte rural** or **gîte de séjour**. Further details can be found in their two very useful national guides – *Chambres et Tables d'Hôtes* (120F/€18.30) and *Chambres d'Hôtes de Prestige et Gîtes de Charme*

(120F/€18.30) – which are also sometimes on sale in bookstores and tourist offices. The national guides, however, are not exhaustive; complete listings (with photos) are available in the guides (60F/€9.12) distributed by departmental Gîtes de France offices – you can either contact the main office for a complete list, or pick up copies from local and departmental tourist offices.

## YOUTH HOSTELS, FOYERS AND STUDENT ACCOMMODATION

At between 60F/€9.15 and 120F/€18.30 per night for a dormitory bed, and generally breakfast thrown in, **hostels** – *auberges de jeunesse* – are invaluable for single travellers on a budget. For hostels, **per-person prices** of dorm beds are given throughout the Guide. Many of the modern hostels now also offer rooms for couples, with en-suite showers, but they don't necessarily work out cheaper than hotels – particularly if you've had to pay a bus fare out to the edge of town to reach them. However, many hostels are beautifully sited, and they allow you to cut costs by preparing your own food in their kitchens, or eating in their cheap canteens. Normally, to stay at FUAJ or LFAJ hostels (see below) you must be a member of Hostelling International (HI) or the International Youth Hostel Federation (IYHF). Head offices and membership fees, which differ from country to

## HOSTELLING ASSOCIATIONS

**France** Fédération Unie des Auberges de Jeunesse (FUAJ), 27 rue Pajol, 75018 Paris (☎01.44.89.87.27, fax 01.44.89.87.10, *www.fuaj.org*); Ligue Française pour les Auberges de Jeunesse (LFAJ), 38 bd Raspail, 75007 Paris (☎01.45.48.69.84, fax 01.45.44.57.47); Union des Centres de Recontres Internationales de France (UCRIF), 27 rue Turbigo, 75002 Paris (☎01.40.26.57.64, fax 01.40.26.58.20, *ucrif@aol.com*).

**England and Wales** Youth Hostel Association, Trevelyan House, 8 St Stephen's Hill, St Albans, Herts AL1 2DY (☎0870/870 8808, *www.yha.org.uk*); London membership desk and booking office: 14 Southampton St, London WC2 7HY (☎020/7836 8541). Annual membership £12.

**Scotland** Scottish Youth Hostel Association, 7 Glebe Crescent, Stirling FK8 2JA (☎01786/451 181, *www.syha.org.uk*). Annual membership £6.

**Ireland** Republic: 61 Mountjoy St, Dublin 7 (☎01/830 4555, *www.irelandyha.org*); annual membership IR£10/€12.70. Northern Ireland: 22 Donegal Rd, Belfast BT12 5JN (☎028/9031 5435, *www.hini.org.uk*); annual membership £8.

**USA** Hostelling International, 733 15th St NW, Suite 840, PO Box 37613, Washington DC 20005 (☎202/783 6161, fax 202/783 6171, *www.hiayh.org*).

**Canada** Hostelling International/Canadian Hostelling Association, Room 400, 205 Catherine St, Ottawa, ON K2P 1C3 (☎1-800/663 5777 or 613/237 7884, fax 613/237 7868).

**Australia** Youth Hostel Association of Australia, 422 Kent St, Sydney (☎02/9261 1111, *www.yha.com.au*).

**New Zealand** Youth Hostels Association of New Zealand, 173 Gloucester St, Christchurch (☎03/379 9970, *www.yha.co.nz*).

country, are listed in the box opposite. If you don't join up before you leave home, you can purchase a **membership card** in relevant French hostels for 100F/€15.25.

Slightly confusingly, there are three rival French **hostelling associations** (see box opposite): the main two being the Fédération Unie des Auberges de Jeunesse (FUAJ; 180 hostels), which has its hostels detailed in the *International Handbook*, and the Ligue Française pour les Auberges de Jeunesse (LFAJ; 100 hostels). The third organization is the Union des Centres de Recontres Internationales de France (UCRIF), with 60 hostels in France; membership is not required.

A few large towns provide a more luxurious standard of hostel accommodation in Foyers des Jeunes Travailleurs/Travailleuses, **residential hostels** for young workers and students, where you can usually get a private room for around 60F/€9.15. They normally have a good cafeteria or canteen.

At the height of summer (usually July & Aug only), there's also the possibility of staying in **student accommodation** in university towns and cities. The main organization to contact for this is CROUS, Académie de Paris, 39 av Georges-Bernanos, Paris 75005 (☎01.40.51.36.00, *www.crous.fr*). Prices are similar to the official hostels, from around 70F/€10.68 per person, and you don't need membership.

### GÎTES D'ÉTAPE AND REFUGES

In the countryside, another hostel-style alternative exists: **gîtes d'étape**. *Gîtes d'étape* are often run by the local village or municipality (whose mayor will probably be in charge of the key) and are less formal than hostels. They provide bunk beds and primitive kitchen and washing facilities

from around 40F/€6.10, and they are are marked on the large-scale IGN walkers' maps and listed in the individual GR *Topoguides*. In addition, mountain areas are well supplied with **refuge huts**, mostly run by the Club Alpin Français (CAF), but also by CIMES (in the Pyrenees). Many are open in summer only. They are the only available shelter once you are above the villages. Costs are from around 60F/€9.15 for the night, less if you're a member of a climbing organization affiliated to the CAF. Meals – invariably four courses – cost around 80F/€12.20, which is not unreasonable when you consider that all supplies have to be brought up by mule or helicopter.

More information can be found in the guides *Gîtes d'Étapes et Sejours* (60F/€9.12), published by Gîtes de France (see above), and *Gîtes d'Étape et Refuges*, published by Guides La Cadole, available in French book shops for 110F/€16.78.

### CAMPING

Practically every village and town in France has at least one **campsite** to cater for the thousands of people who spend their holiday under canvas – camping is a very big deal in France. The cheapest – at around 25–35F/€3.80–5.30 per person per night – is usually the *Camping municipal*, run by the local municipality. In season or whenever they're officially open, they are always clean and have plenty of hot water; often they are situated in prime local positions. Out of season, those that stay open often don't bother to collect the overnight charge.

If you're planning to do a lot of camping, an **international camping carnet** is a good investment. The carnet serves as useful identification, covers you for third party insurance when camping, and helps you get ten percent reductions at

---

### DEPARTMENTAL OFFICES OF GÎTES DE FRANCE

**Ariège**: 31bis av Général-de-Gaulle, BP 143, 09004 Foix (☎05.61.02.30.89, fax 05.61.65.17.34, *gites-de-france.ariege@wanadoo.fr*).

**Aude**: 78 rue Barbacane, 11000 Carcassonne (☎04.68.11.40.70, fax 04.68.11.40.72).

**Gard**: CDT 3 pl des Arènes, BP 59, 30007 Nîmes (☎04.66.27.94.94, fax 04.66.27.94.95).

**Haute-Garonne**: 14 rue Bayard, BP 845, 31015 Toulouse (☎05.61.99.70.60, fax 05.61.99.41.22).

**Hérault**: Maison de Tourisme, 1977 av des Moulins, BP 3070, 34034 Montpellier (☎04.67.67.62.62, fax 04.67.67.71.69, *www.gites-de-france-herault.asso.fr*).

**Pyrénées-Orientales**: 30 rue Pierre-Bretonneau, 66017 Perpignan (☎04.68.55.60.95, fax 04.68.50.68.44).

**Tarn**: Maison des Agriculteurs, La Milliasolle, BP 89, 81003 Albi (☎05.63.48.83.01, fax 05.63.48.83.12).

campsites listed in the CCI information booklet that comes with your carnet. It is available in the UK from the AA or the RAC or the Carefree Travel Service (☎01203/422024), who also book inspected camping sites in Europe and arrange ferry crossings; in the US from Family Campers and RVers (FCRV), 4804 Transit Rd, Building 2, Depew, NY 14043 (☎1-800/245 9755); and in Canada from FCRV, 51 W 22nd St, Hamilton, ON LC9 4N5 (☎1-800/245 9755).

On the coast around the beach towns, there are **superior categories** of campsite where you'll pay prices similar to those of a hotel for the facilities – bars, restaurants and sometimes swimming pools. These have rather more permanent status than the *Campings municipaux*, with people often spending a whole holiday in the one base. If you plan to do the same, and particularly if you have a caravan, camper or a big tent, it's wise to book ahead – reckon on paying at least 35F/€5.34 a head with a tent, 40F/€6.10 with a camper van. Inland, *camping à la ferme* – on somebody's farm – is another possibility (generally without facilities). Lists of sites are detailed

in the Tourist Board's *Accueil à la Campagne* booklet.

A number of companies in the UK also specialize in selling **camping holidays**, including Allez France (see box, p.8), Canvas Holidays (☎08709/022 022, *www.canvasholidays.com*) and Sunsites (☎01606/787 555, *www.sunsites.co.uk*). Twelve nights' camping at Argelès, near Perpignan, with Sunsites, for example, costs from £862 for two adults, with up to four children under 18 free, which includes the price of the Channel ferry.

Lastly, a word of **caution**: never camp rough (*camping sauvage*, as the French call it) on anyone's land without first asking permission. If the dogs don't get you, the guns might – farmers have been known to shoot before asking questions. On the other hand, a politely phrased request for permission will as often as not get positive results. Camping on public land is not officially permitted, but is widely practised by the French, and if you are discreet you will likely not meet with problems. On beaches, it's best to camp out only where other people are doing so.

## EATING AND DRINKING

Languedoc and Roussillon – a traditionally poor and marginalized area – is not famed for the elaborate *haute cuisine* which typifies French cookery in the popular imagination. The food of this overwhelmingly rural region tends to be simple, and little family restaurants serving classic peasant (*terroir*)

dishes based on local produce – and where the bill is less than 100F/€15 – are still common enough here that your chief challenge, should you stay in a single locale for any length of time, will be fighting culinary ennui. That said, as you cross the region you'll find that the huge diversity of the landscape has contributed to a correspondingly wide range in local specialities – immediately obvious when you visit town and village produce markets – and in all but the most out of the way hamlet you'll be able to find relief in a more adventurous (and expensive) *gastronomique* restaurant. Due to its relative isolation Languedoc and Roussillon has thankfully also fared better than many regions in escaping the processed, boil-in-the-bag and ready-to-microwave productions – known in France as *mal-bouffe* ("bad grub") of the global food industry.

In the rarefied world of **haute cuisine**, where the top chefs are national celebrities, a battle is currently raging between traditionalists, determined to preserve the purity of French cuisine, and those who experiment with different flavours from around the world to create novel combinations. At this level, French food is still brilliant – in both camps – and the good news is that prices are continuing to come down. Many gourmet palaces offer weekday lunch-time menus where you can sample culinary genius for around 290F/€44.

Languedoc and Roussillon is also a great place for **foreign cuisine**, in particular North African, Caribbean (known as *Antillais*) and Asiatic. Moroccan, Thai or Vietnamese restaurants are not necessarily cheap options but they are usually good value for money. Chinese restaurants tend, on the other hand, to be inexpensive but disappointing.

On the whole, **vegetarians** can expect a somewhat lean time in Languedoc and Roussillon; *rurale cuisine* is relentlessly meat-based, and in some traditional farming villages even understanding the concept of vegetarianism can be a mighty stretch. A few cities have specifically vegetarian restaurants (detailed in the text), but elsewhere you'll have to hope you find a sympathetic restaurant (crêperies and pizzerias can be good standbys). Sometimes they're willing to replace a meat dish on the *menu fixe* with an omelette; other times you'll have to pick your way through the *carte*. Remember the phrase "Je suis végétarien(ne); il y a quelques plats sans viande?" (I'm a vegetarian; are there any non-meat dishes?). **Vegans**, however, should probably forget all about eating in French restaurants and stick to self-catering.

## BREAKFAST AND SNACKS

A croissant, *pain au chocolat* (a square-shaped chocolate-filled light pastry) or a sandwich in a bar or café, with hot chocolate or coffee, is generally the best way to eat **breakfast** – at a fraction of the cost charged by most hotels. (The days when hotels gave you mounds of croissants or brioches for breakfast seem to be long gone; now it's virtually always bread, jam and a jug of coffee or tea for about 30F/€4.50.) Croissants and sometimes hard-boiled eggs are displayed on bar counters until around 9.30am or 10am. If you stand – cheaper than sitting down – you just help yourself to these with your coffee; the waiter keeps an eye on how many you've eaten and bills you accordingly.

At **lunch time**, and sometimes in the evening, you may find cafés offering a *plat du jour* (chef's daily special) at between 40F/€6.10 and 75F/€11.44, or *formules*, a limited or no-choice menu. *Croques-monsieur* or *croques-madame* (variations on the toasted-cheese sandwich) are on sale at cafés, brasseries and many street stands, along with *frites* (potato fries), crêpes, *galettes* (wholewheat pancakes), *gauffres* (waffles), *glaces* (ice creams) and all kinds of fresh-filled baguettes (these very filling sandwiches usually cost between 18F/€2.75 and 28F/€4.27 to take away). For variety, there are Tunisian snacks like *brik à l'œuf* (a fried pastry with an egg inside), *merguez* (spicy North African sausage), Greek souvlaki (kebabs) and Middle Eastern falafel (deep-fried chickpea balls in flat bread with salad). Wine bars are good for regional sausages and cheese, usually served with brown bread (*pain de campagne*).

**Crêpes**, or pancakes with fillings, served up at ubiquitous crêperies, are popular lunch-time food. The savoury buckwheat variety (often called *galettes*) provide the main course; the sweet white-flour ones are dessert. They taste nice enough, but are usually poor value in comparison with a restaurant meal; you need at least three, normally at over 30F/€4.58 each, to feel full. **Pizzerias**, usually *au feu du bois* (wood-fire-baked), are also very common. They are somewhat better value than crêperies, but quality and quantity vary greatly – look before you leap into the nearest empty seats.

For **picnics**, the local outdoor market or supermarket will provide you with almost everything you need from tomatoes and avocados to cheese and pâté. Cooked meat, prepared snacks, ready-made dishes and assorted salads can be bought at *charcuteries* (delicatessens), which you'll find everywhere – even in small villages, though the same things are cheaper at supermarket counters. You purchase by weight, or you can ask for *une tranche* (a slice), *une barquette* (a carton) or *une part* (a portion).

**Salons de thé**, which open from mid-morning to late evening, serve brunches, salads, quiches, and the like, as well as gateaux, ice cream and a wide selection of teas. They tend to be a good deal pricier than cafés or brasseries – you're paying for the posh surroundings. As bars are to men in France, *salons de thé* are to women, and they generally have a more female ambience and clientele. For cakes and pastries to take away, you'll find impressive arrays at every boulangerie-pâtisserie.

## MEALS

There's no difference between **restaurants** (or *auberges* or *relais* as they sometimes call themselves) and **brasseries** in terms of quality or price range. The distinction is that brasseries, which resemble cafés, serve quicker meals at most hours of the day, while restaurants tend to stick to the traditional meal times of noon to 2pm, and 7pm to 9.30pm or 10.30pm. After 9pm or so, restaurants often serve only à la carte meals (single dishes chosen from the menu) – invariably more expensive than eating the set *menu fixe*. In touristy areas in high season, and for all the more upmarket places, it's wise to make reservations – easily done on the same day. In small towns it may be impossible to get anything other than a bar sandwich after 10pm or even earlier; in major cities, town centre brasseries will serve until 11pm or midnight and one or two may stay open all night.

When hunting for places to eat, avoid places that are half empty at peak time, use your nose and regard long menus with suspicion. Don't forget that **hotel restaurants** are open to non-residents, and are often very good value. In many small towns and villages, you'll find the only restaurants are in hotels. Since restaurants change hands frequently and have their ups and downs, it's also worth asking people you meet (locals, not fellow tourists) for recommendations. This is the conversational equivalent of commenting on the weather in Britain and will usually elicit strong views and sound advice.

**Prices**, and what you get for them, are posted outside. Normally there's a choice between one or more *menus fixes*, where the number of courses has already been determined and the choice is limited, and choosing individually from the *carte* (menu). **Menus fixes** are normally the cheapest option. At the bottom end of the price range, they revolve around standard dishes such as steak and chips (*steak frites*), chicken and chips (*poulet frites*) and various concoctions involving innards. But further up the scale they can be much the best-value way of sampling regional specialities, sometimes running to five or more courses. If you're simply not that hungry, just go for the *plat du jour*.

Going **à la carte** offers greater choice and, in the better restaurants, unlimited access to the chef's specialities – though you'll pay for the privilege. A simple and perfectly legitimate tactic is to have just one course instead of the expected three or four. You can share dishes or go for several starters – a useful strategy for vegetarians. There's no minimum charge.

In the French **sequence of courses**, any salad (sometimes vegetables, too) comes separate from the main dish, and cheese precedes a dessert. You will be offered coffee, which is always extra, to finish off the meal.

Service compris or s.c. means the **service charge** is included. Service non compris, s.n.c. or servis en sus means that it isn't and you need to calculate an additional 15 percent. **Wine** (vin) or a **drink** (boisson) is occasionally included (*compris*) in the cost of a menu fixe. When ordering house wine, the cheapest option, ask for un quart (0.25 litre), un demi-litre (0.5 litre) or une carafe (1 litre). If you're worried about the cost ask for vin ordinaire or the vin de table. In the Guide the lowest price menu or the range of menus is given; where average à la carte prices are given it assumes you'll have three courses and half a bottle of wine.

The French are much better disposed towards **children** in restaurants than other nationalities, not simply by offering reduced-price children's menus but in creating an atmosphere – even in otherwise fairly snooty establishments – that positively welcomes kids; some even have in-house games and toys for them to occupy themselves with. It is regarded as self-evident that large family groups should be able to eat out together.

A rather murkier area is that of **dogs** in the dining room; it can be quite a shock in a provincial hotel to realize that the majority of your fellow diners are attempting to keep dogs concealed beneath their tables.

## REGIONAL SPECIALITIES

Languedoc and Roussillon is an extremely varied and exciting area for cuisine. In the east, around Nîmes and in the **Gard**, the influence of Provençal cuisine is strongly felt – especially in the use of the herbs that spring up throughout the *garrigues* – while the *manades* (ranches) of the **Camargue** ensure that beef plays a notable role, especially

## CHEESES OF LANGUEDOC AND ROUSSILLON

You can find the great **cheeses** from all over France in Languedoc and Roussillon, but it is still worth hunting out local specialities. Many cheese-makers have successfully protected their products by AOC (*appellation d'origine controlée*) laws similar to those for wines, which means that the subtle differences between French local cheeses have not been overwhelmed by the industrialized uniformity that has plagued other countries. Although just about everything is available in supermarkets, farm-produced cheese will have to be hunted down in speciality shops (a *fromagerie*, or a regional produce outlet) and country markets.

Throughout the sheep-producing areas of the region, locally elaborated cheeses can be picked up at country markets, or at times directly from the farms themselves. The milk which produces the famous Roquefort cheese comes exclusively from Haut Languedoc's sheep (specifically, an ancient breed of Lacaune), while a few noteworthy cheese varieties in Languedoc and Roussillon itself include **Pélardon des Cévennes**, a flavourful goats' (*chèvre*) milk cheese recently developed at St Hippolyte-du-Fort; the creamy but acidic **Pélardon des Corbières**, an older variant of the Cévennes version, round in shape and coated in natural mould, best served after about a week; and **Le Pérail**, a white *fromage de brébis* (sheep) from the Gard, whose taste transforms as it ages – from a subtle freshness when first produced to a sharp tanginess when aged a fortnight.

in sausage and in the wine-marinated *brandade de la Gardienne*. Other prominent ingredients include truffles, gathered in the scrubby woodland of the northern fringe around **Uzès**, olives, cultivated in low hills rising up from the coastal plains and yielding reasonable oil, and rice, which is grown locally in the Camargue. The fair sunny climate also favours vegetables and fruit, including asparagus, but more notably peaches and apricots (especially around St-Gilles).

As can be expected, fish and seafood abound in the **coastal cuisine** of Languedoc, whether in brothy *coquillages*, the garlicky *bourride* of Sète, or baked or barbecued. Tuna, anchovy and sardine dominate, but the range of fish used is very broad. The shallow *étangs* are home to large-scale mussel and oyster farming, of which Mèze and Leucate are the main centres. In the uplands of the **Hérault**, the transition to cooler higher terrain is marked by an increase in sheep-based dishes (using both meat and cheese), although fruits such as figs also mark local cookery. Tripe (*tripoux*) is another staple along the whole inland strip of Languedoc.

The highland and forest ingredients are all the more accentuated in **Haut Languedoc**, where seasonal delicacies such as the ubiquitous mushrooms of late summer add variety. Some of the finest mutton comes from the Cabardés district, on the southern slopes of the Montagne Noire. Further northeast, the cereal lands of the **Tarn** are notable for high-quality foie gras and land snails (*escargots*), while Lautrec is an undisputed garlic capital, famed for its pink version. Duck (*canard*), popular throughout France, is also a staple in the zone stretching from Toulouse to Albi, and you are likely to encounter it in the form of a *confit* (a jellied conserve). The Tarn also falls heavily under the culinary influence of the **Aude**, whose staple, cassoulet, a bean stew originating in Castelnaudary, has colonized the whole of Languedoc. Carcassonne marks something of a midpoint, between the wheat and bean fields which spread west to Toulouse, and the east, which is known for its olives. The city, and the lands along the Aude, are home to some of the region's most interesting sweets, ranging from the rosemary-tinged honey of the Corbières hills, to the nougat of Limoux, and candied chestnuts, a tradional late-autumn treat. The cuisine of the Aude, and its neighbour, **Ariège**, are transformed as the landscape rises towards the Pyrenees. While the foothills produce excellent beef, sheep and goats come to play an increasing role as the terrain climbs, appearing in well-reputed cheeses and supplementing or replacing pork in the ubiquitous sausage (*saucisson*).

**Roussillon** represents something of a shift, with its marked Catalan base and Spanish influence – immediately noticeable in the strong influence of olive oil. The region's dry and grilled pork sausages (in Catalan *embutits* and *botifares*) are particularly worth trying, and a countryside staple is the hearty pork-based *ollada* soup. Special occasions are celebrated with a *cargolada* – an

## A FOOD GLOSSARY

### BASIC TERMS

| | | | | | | | |
|---|---|---|---|---|---|---|---|
| *l'addition* | bill/check | *cuit* | cooked | *moutarde* | mustard | *sucre* | sugar |
| *beurre* | butter | *emballé* | wrapped | *œuf* | egg | *sucré* | sweet |
| *bouteille* | bottle | *à emporter* | takeaway | *offert* | free | *table* | table |
| *chauffé* | heated | *fourchette* | fork | *pain* | bread | *verre* | glass |
| *couteau* | knife | *fumé* | smoked | *poivre* | pepper | *vinaigre* | vinegar |
| *cru* | raw | *huile* | oil | *salé* | salted/spicy | | |
| *cuillère* | spoon | *lait* | milk | *sel* | salt | | |

### SNACKS

| | | | |
|---|---|---|---|
| **un sandwich/ une baguette** | **a sandwich** | *pain bagnat* | bread roll with egg, olives, salad, tuna, anchovies and olive oil |
| *au jambon* | with ham | | |
| *au fromage* | with cheese | *panini* | toasted Italian sandwich |
| *au saucisson* | with sausage | *tartine* | buttered bread or open |
| *à l'ail* | with garlic | | sandwich |
| *au poivre* | with pepper | | |
| *au pâté (de campagne)* | with pâté (country style) | **œufs** | **eggs** |
| *croque-monsieur* | grilled cheese and ham sandwich | *au plat* | fried |
| | | *à la coque* | boiled |
| | | *durs* | hard-boiled |
| *croque-madame* | grilled cheese and bacon, sausage, egg or chicken sandwich | *brouillés* | scrambled |
| | | **omelette** | **omelette** |
| | | *nature* | plain |
| | | *aux fines herbes* | with herbs |
| | | *au fromage* | with cheese |

### PASTA (*PÂTES*), PANCAKES (*CRÊPES*) AND FLANS (*TARTES*)

| | | | |
|---|---|---|---|
| *nouilles* | noodles | *socca* | thin chickpea-flour pancake |
| *pâtes fraîches* | fresh pasta | *panisse* | thick chickpea-flour pancake |
| *raviolis* | pasta parcels of meat or chard – a Provençal, not Italian, invention | *pissaladière* | tart of fried onions with anchovies and black olives |
| *crêpe au sucre/ aux œufs* | pancake with sugar/ eggs | *tarte flambée* | thin pizza-like pastry topped with onion, cream and bacon or other combinations |
| *galette* | buckwheat pancake | | |

### SOUPS (*SOUPES*)

| | | | |
|---|---|---|---|
| *baudroie* | fish soup with vegetables, garlic and herbs | *pistou* | parmesan, basil and garlic paste added to soup |
| *bisque* | shellfish soup | *potée auvergnate* | cabbage and meat soup |
| *bouillabaisse* | soup with five fish and other bits to dip | *potage* | thick vegetable soup |
| | | *rouille* | red pepper, garlic and saffron mayonnaise served with fish soup |
| *bouillon* | broth or stock | | |
| *bourride* | thick fish soup | | |
| *consommé* | clear soup | *soupe à l'oignon* | onion soup with rich cheese topping |
| *garbure* | potato, cabbage and meat soup | *velouté* | thick soup, usually fish or poultry |

## STARTERS (*HORS D'ŒUVRES*)

| | | | |
|---|---|---|---|
| assiette anglaise | plate of cold meats | hors d'œuvres | combination of the above |
| crudités | raw vegetables with dressings | ...variés | ...plus smoked or marinated fish |

## FISH (*POISSON*), SEAFOOD (*FRUITS DE MER*) AND SHELLFISH (*CRUSTACES* OR *COQUILLAGES*)

| | | | | | |
|---|---|---|---|---|---|
| aiglefin | small haddock or fresh cod | crevettes grises | shrimp | maquereau | mackerel |
| anchois | anchovies | crevettes roses | prawns | merlan | whiting |
| anguilles | eels | daurade | sea bream | moules | mussels |
| barbue | brill | éperlan | smelt or whitebait | (marinière) | (with shallots in white wine sauce) |
| baudroie | monkfish or anglerfish | escargots | snails | | |
| bigourneau | periwinkle | favou(ille) | tiny crab | oursin | sea urchin |
| brème | bream | flétan | halibut | palourdes | clams |
| bulot | whelk | friture | assorted fried fish | poissons de roche | fish from shore-line rocks |
| cabillaud | cod | gambas | king prawns | praires | small clams |
| calmar | squid | hareng | herring | raie | skate |
| carrelet | plaice | homard | lobster | rouget | red mullet |
| claire | type of oyster | huîtres | oysters | saumon | salmon |
| colin | hake | langouste | spiny lobster | sole | sole |
| congre | conger eel | langoustines | saltwater crayfish (scampi) | thon | tuna |
| coques | cockles | | | truite | trout |
| coquilles St-Jacques | scallops | limande | lemon sole | turbot | turbot |
| crabe | crab | lotte de mer | monkfish | violet | sea squirt |
| | | loup de mer | sea bass | | |

## FISH DISHES AND TERMS

| | | | | | |
|---|---|---|---|---|---|
| aïoli | garlic mayonnaise served with salt cod and other fish | friture | deep-fried small fish | mousse/mousseline | mousse |
| | | fumé | smoked | pané | breaded |
| anchoïade | anchovy paste or sauce | fumet | fish stock | poutargue | mullet roe paste |
| | | gigot de mer | large fish baked whole | raïto | red wine, olive, caper, garlic and shallot sauce |
| arête | fish bone | grillé | grilled | | |
| assiette de pêcheur | assorted fish | hollandaise | butter and vinegar sauce | quenelles | light dumplings |
| beignet | fritter | à la meunière | in a butter, lemon and parsley sauce | thermidor | lobster grilled in its shell with cream sauce |
| darne | fillet or steak | | | | |
| la douzaine | a dozen | | | | |
| frit | fried | | | | |

## MEAT (*VIANDE*) AND POULTRY (*VOLAILLE*)

| | | | | | |
|---|---|---|---|---|---|
| agneau (de pré-salé) | lamb (grazed on salt marshes) | boudin noir | black pudding | faux filet | sirloin steak |
| | | caille | quail | foie | liver |
| andouille, andouillette | tripe sausage | canard | duck | foie gras | (duck/goose) liver |
| bifteck | steak | caneton | duckling | gigot (d'agneau) | leg (of lamb) |
| bœuf | beef | contrefilet | sirloin roast | grenouilles (cuisses de) | frogs (legs) |
| boudin blanc | sausage of white meats | coquelet | cockerel | grillade | grilled meat |
| | | dinde, dindon | turkey | | |
| | | entrecôte | rib steak | | |

*box continues on next page...*

...box continued from previous page

| | | | | | |
|---|---|---|---|---|---|
| hâchis | chopped meat or mince hamburger | mouton | mutton | rognons | kidneys |
| | | museau de veau | calf's muzzle | rognons blancs | testicles |
| langue | tongue | oie | goose | sanglier | wild boar |
| lapin, | rabbit, | onglet | cut of beef | steak | steak |
| lapereau | young rabbit | os | bone | tête de veau | calf's head (in jelly) |
| lard, | bacon, | poitrine | breast | tournedos | thick slices of fillet |
| lardons | diced bacon | porc | pork | tripes | tripe |
| lièvre | hare | poulet | chicken | tripoux | mutton tripe |
| merguez | spicy, red sausage | poussin | baby chicken | veau | veal |
| | | ris | sweetbreads | venaison | venison |

## MEAT AND POULTRY DISHES AND TERMS

| | |
|---|---|
| aïado | roast shoulder of lamb stuffed with garlic and other ingredients |
| aile | wing |
| au feu de bois | cooked over wood fire |
| au four | baked |
| baeckoffe | Alsatian hotpot of pork, mutton & beef baked with potato layers |
| blanquette, daube, estouffade, hochepôt, navarin, ragoût | types of stew |
| blanquette de veau | veal in cream and mushroom sauce |
| bœuf bourguignon | beef stew with Burgundy, onions and mushrooms |
| canard à l'orange | roast duck with an orange and wine sauce |
| canard périgourdin | roast duck with prunes, pâté de foie gras and truffles |
| carré | best end of neck, chop or cutlet |
| cassoulet | casserole of beans and meat |
| choucroute | pickled cabbage with peppercorns, sausages, bacon and salami |
| civit | game stew |
| confit | meat preserve |
| coq au vin | chicken cooked until it falls off the bone with wine, onions and mushrooms |
| côte | chop, cutlet or rib |
| cou | neck |
| cuisse | thigh or leg |
| en croûte | in pastry |
| épaule | shoulder |
| farci | stuffed |
| garni | with vegetables |
| gésier | gizzard |
| grillé | grilled |
| magret de canard | duck breast |
| marmite | casserole |
| médaillon | round piece |
| mijoté | stewed |
| pavé | thick slice |

| | |
|---|---|
| pieds et paques | mutton or pork tripe and trotters |
| poêlé | pan-fried |
| poulet de Bresse | chicken from Bresse – the best |
| râble | saddle |
| rôti | roast |
| sauté | lightly cooked in butter |
| steak au poivre (vert/rouge) | steak in a black (green/red) peppercorn sauce |
| steak tartare | raw chopped beef, topped with a raw egg yolk |
| tagine | North African casserole |
| tournedos rossini | beef fillet with foie gras and truffles |
| viennoise | fried in egg and breadcrumbs |

### terms for steaks

| | |
|---|---|
| bleu | almost raw |
| saignant | rare |
| à point | medium |
| bien cuit | well done |
| très bien cuit | very well done |
| brochette | kebab |

### garnishes and sauces

| | |
|---|---|
| américaine | white wine, cognac and tomato |
| arlésienne | with tomatoes, onions, aubergines, potatoes and rice |
| au porto | in port |
| auvergnat | with cabbage, sausage and bacon |
| béarnaise | sauce of egg yolks, white wine, shallots and vinegar |
| beurre blanc | sauce of white wine and shallots, with butter |
| bonne femme | with mushroom, bacon, potato and onions |
| bordelaise | in a red wine, shallot and bone-marrow sauce |
| boulangère | baked with potatoes and onions |
| bourgeoise | with carrots, onions, bacon, celery and braised lettuce |
| chasseur | white wine, mushrooms and shallots |

| | | | |
|---|---|---|---|
| *châtelaine* | with artichoke hearts and chestnut purée | *périgourdine* | with foie gras and possibly truffles |
| *diable* | strong mustard seasoning | *piquante* | gherkins or capers, vinegar and shallots |
| *forestière* | with bacon and mushroom | *provençale* | tomatoes, garlic, olive oil and herbs |
| *fricassée* | rich, creamy sauce | | |
| *mornay* | cheese sauce | *savoyarde* | with gruyère cheese |
| *pays d'auge* | cream and cider | *véronique* | grapes, wine and cream |

## VEGETABLES (*LÉGUMES*), HERBS (*HERBES*) AND SPICES (*ÉPICES*)

| | | | | | |
|---|---|---|---|---|---|
| *ail* | garlic | *cornichon* | gherkin | *pâte* | pasta or pastry |
| *anis* | aniseed | *echalotes* | shallots | *persil* | parsley |
| *artichaut* | artichoke | *endive* | chicory | *petits pois* | peas |
| *asperge* | asparagus | *épinard* | spinach | *piment* | pimento |
| *avocat* | avocado | *estragon* | tarragon | *pois chiche* | chick peas |
| *basilic* | basil | *fenouil* | fennel | *pois* | |
| *betterave* | beetroot | *férigoule* | thyme (in Provençal) | *mange-tout* | snow peas |
| *blette/bette* | Swiss chard | *fèves* | broad beans | *pignons* | pine nuts |
| *cannelle* | cinnamon | *flageolets* | white beans | *poireau* | leek |
| *capre* | caper | *gingembre* | ginger | *poivron* | sweet pepper |
| *cardon* | cardoon, a beet related to artichoke | *haricots (verts, rouges, beurres)* | beans (French/ string, kidney, butter) | *(vert, rouge)* | (green, red) |
| | | | | *pommes de* | |
| *carotte* | carrot | *laurier* | bay leaf | *terre* | potatoes |
| *céleri* | celery | *lentilles* | lentils | *primeurs* | spring vegetables |
| *champignon,* | types of | *maïs* | corn | *radis* | radish |
| *cèpe,* | mushrooms | *menthe* | mint | *riz* | rice |
| *chanterelle* | | *moutarde* | mustard | *safran* | saffron |
| *chou (rouge)* | (red) cabbage | *oignon* | onion | *salade verte* | green salad |
| *choufleur* | cauliflower | *panais* | parsnip | *sarrasin* | buckwheat |
| *concombre* | cucumber | *pélandron* | type of string bean | *tomate* | tomato |
| | | | | *truffes* | truffles |

## VEGETABLE DISHES AND TERMS

| | | | | | |
|---|---|---|---|---|---|
| *alicot* | puréed potato with cheese | *gratiné* | browned with cheese or butter | *petits farcis* | stuffed tomatoes, aubergines, courgettes and peppers |
| *allumettes* | very thin chips | *à la grecque* | cooked in oil and lemon | | |
| *à l'anglaise* | boiled | | | | |
| *beignet* | fritter | *jardinière* | with mixed diced vegetables | *pimenté* | peppery hot |
| *biologique* | organic | | | *piquant* | spicy |
| *duxelles* | fried mushrooms and shallots with cream | *mousseline* | mashed potato with cream and eggs | *pistou* | ground basil, olive oil, garlic and parmesan |
| *farci* | stuffed | *à la* | sautéed in butter | *râpée* | grated or shredded |
| *feuille* | leaf | *parisienne* | (potatoes); with white wine sauce & shallots | *sauté* | lightly fried in butter |
| *fines herbes* | mixture of tarragon, parsley & chives | | | *à la vapeur* | steamed |
| | | *parmentier* | with potatoes | *en verdure* | garnished with green vegetables |

## FRUIT (*FRUIT*) AND NUTS (*NOIX*)

| | | | | | |
|---|---|---|---|---|---|
| *abricot* | apricot | *banane* | banana | *cassis* | blackcurrant |
| *acajou* | cashew nut | *brugnon,* | | *cérise* | cherry |
| *amande* | almond | *nectarine* | nectarine | *citron* | lemon |
| *ananas* | pineapple | *cacahouète* | peanut | *citron vert* | lime |

*box continues on next page. . .*

*. . . box continued from previous page*

| | | | | | | |
|---|---|---|---|---|---|
| datte | date | mangue | mango | pastèque | watermelon |
| figue | fig | marron | chestnut | pêche | peach |
| fraise | strawberry | melon | melon | pistache | pistachio |
| (de bois) | (wild) | mirabelle | small yellow plum | poire | pear |
| framboise | raspberry | myrtille | bilberry | pomme | apple |
| fruit de la | | noisette | hazelnut | prune | plum |
| passion | passion fruit | noix | nuts | pruneau | prune |
| grenade | pomegranate | orange | orange | raisin | grape |
| groseille | redcurrant | pamplemousse | grapefruit | reine-claude | greengage |

## FRUIT DISHES AND TERMS

| | | | |
|---|---|---|---|
| agrumes | citrus fruits | flambé | set aflame in alcohol |
| beignet | fritter | fougasse | bread flavoured with orange-flower water or almonds (can be savoury) |
| compôte | stewed fruit | | |
| coulis | sauce of puréed fruit | | |
| crème de marrons | chestnut purée | frappé | iced |

## DESSERTS (*DESSERTS OR ENTREMETS*) AND PASTRIES (*PÂTISSERIE*)

| | | | |
|---|---|---|---|
| bombe | moulded ice-cream dessert | marrons Mont Banc | chestnut purée and cream on a rum-soaked sponge cake |
| brioche | sweet, high-yeast breakfast roll | | |
| calisson | almond sweet | mousse au chocolat | chocolate mousse |
| charlotte | custard and fruit in lining of almond fingers | omelette norvégienne | baked alaska |
| chichi | doughnut shaped in a stick | palmier | caramelized puff pastry |
| clafoutis | heavy custard and fruit tart | parfait | frozen mousse, sometimes ice cream |
| crème Chantilly | vanilla-flavoured and sweetened whipped cream | | |
| crème fraîche | sour cream | petit-suisse | a smooth mixture of cream and curds |
| crème pâtissière | thick, eggy pastry-filling | | |
| crêpe suzette | thin pancake with orange juice and liqueur | petits fours | bite-sized cakes/pastries |
| | | poires belle hélène | pears and ice cream in chocolate sauce |
| fromage blanc | cream cheese | tarte tatin | upside-down apple tart |
| gaufre | waffle | tarte tropezienne | sponge cake filled with custard cream topped with nuts |
| glace | ice cream | | |
| Ile flottante/ œufs à la neige | soft meringues floating on custard | tiramisu | mascarpone cheese, chocolate and cream |
| macaron | macaroon | | |
| madeleine | small sponge cake | yaourt, yogourt | yoghurt |

## DESSERT DISHES AND TERMS

| | | | |
|---|---|---|---|
| barquette | small boat-shaped flan | pâte | pastry or dough |
| bavarois | refers to the mould, could be a mousse or custard | sablé | shortbread biscuit |
| | | savarin | a filled, ring-shaped cake |
| coupe | a serving of ice cream | tarte | tart |
| crêpe | pancake | tartelette | small tart |
| gênoise | rich sponge cake | | |

elaborate dish of grilled land snails. Moving towards the milder climes of the coast, fruit makes a dramatic reappearance, in the cherries of Cèret, as well as almonds, peaches and pears.

The coastal hills are swathed in olive trees, while seaside villages like Collioure and Port-Vendres have long survived from fishing. The Spanish influence of the twentieth century has also helped to popularize southern Spanish dishes such as paella and the ubiquitous tapas.

## DRINKING

Wherever you can eat you can invariably drink, and vice versa. **Drinking** is done at a leisurely pace whether it's a prelude to food (*apéritif*), a sequel (*digestif*), or the accompaniment, and cafés are the standard places to do it. Every bar or café has to display its full price list, usually without the fifteen percent service charge added, with the cheapest drinks at the bar (*au comptoir*), and progressively increasing prices for sitting at a table inside (*la salle*), or outside (*la terrasse*). You pay when you leave, and it's perfectly acceptable to sit for hours over just one cup of coffee.

**Wine** (*vin*) is drunk at just about every meal or social occasion. Red is *rouge*, white *blanc* and rosé *rosé*. *Vin de table* or *vin ordinaire* – table wine – is generally drinkable and always cheap, although it may be disguised and priced-up as the house wine, or *cuvée*. The price of AOC (*appellation d'origine contrôlée*) wines can vary from 10F/€1.53 to 100F/€15.25 and over, and that's the vineyard price. You can buy a very decent bottle of wine for 20F/€3.05 or 30F/€4.58, and 60F/€9.15 and over will buy you something really nice. By the time restaurants have added their considerable mark-up, however, wine can constitute an alarming proportion of the bill.

The basic **wine terms** are: *brut*, very dry; *sec*, dry; *demi-sec*, sweet; *doux*, very sweet; *mousseux*, sparkling; *méthode champenoise*, mature and sparkling. There are grape varieties as well, but the complexities of the subject take up volumes. A glass of wine is simply *un rouge*, *un rosé* or *un blanc*. You may have the choice of *un ballon* (round glass) or a smaller glass (*un verre*). *Un pichet* (a pitcher) is normally a quarter-litre. A glass of wine in a bar will cost around 30F/€5.58.

The best way to **buy bottles** of wine is directly from the producers (*vignerons*), either at vineyards, at Maisons or Syndicats du Vin (representing a group of wine-producers), or at Coopératifs Vinicoles (wine-producer co-ops). At all these places you can sample the wines first. It's best to make clear at the start how much you want to buy (if it's only one or two bottles) and you will not be popular if you drink several glasses and then leave without making a purchase. The most economical option is to buy *en vrac*, which you can also do at some wine shops (*caves*), taking an easily obtainable plastic five- or ten-litre container (usually sold

on the premises) and getting it filled straight from the barrel. In cities supermarkets are the best places to buy your wine, and their prices often beat those of the *vignerons*.

Familiar light Belgian and German brands, plus French brands from Alsace, account for most of the **beer** you'll find. Draught beer (*à la pression*) – usually Kronenbourg – is the cheapest drink you can have next to coffee and wine; ask for *un pression* or *un demi* (0.33 litre). A *demi* costs around 17F/€2.59. For a wider choice of draught and bottled beer you need to go to the special beer-drinking establishments or English-style pubs found in most city centres and resorts. A small bottle at one of these places will cost at least twice as much as a *demi* in a café. In supermarkets, however, bottled or canned beer is exceptionally cheap.

**Strong alcohol** is consumed from as early as 5am as a pre-work fortifier, and then at any time through the day according to circumstance, though the national reputation for drunkenness has lost much of its truth. Brandies and the dozens of *eaux de vie* (spirits) and liqueurs are always available. *Pastis* – the generic name of aniseed drinks such as Pernod or Ricard and a favourite throughout Languedoc – is served diluted with water and ice (*glaçons*). It's very refreshing and not expensive. Among less familiar names, try Poire William (pear brandy), or Marc (a spirit distilled from grape pulp). Measures are generous, but they don't come cheap: the same applies for imported spirits like whisky (*Scotch*). Two drinks designed to stimulate the appetite – *un apéritif* – are Pineau (cognac and grape juice) and Kir (white wine with a dash of Cassis – blackcurrant liquor – or with champagne instead of wine for a Kir Royal). **Cocktails** are served at most late-night bars, discos and music places, as well as at upmarket hotel bars and at every seaside promenade café; they usually cost at least 45F/€6.86.

On the **soft drink** front, you can buy cartons of unsweetened fruit juice in supermarkets, although in the cafés the bottled (sweetened) nectars such as apricot (*jus d'abricot*) and blackcurrant (*cassis*) still hold sway. You can also get fresh orange or lemon juice (*orange/citron pressé*), at a price. A *citron pressé* is a refreshing choice for the extremely thirsty on a hot day – the lemon juice is served in the bottom of a long ice-filled glass, with a jug of water and a sugar bowl to sweeten it to your taste. Other drinks to try are syrups (*sirops*) of mint, grenadine or other flavours mixed with

## WINES OF LANGUEDOC AND ROUSSILLON

In Languedoc and Roussillon good economical **wines** can be found in the *vins de pays* category (also known as *vins d'Oc* in these parts). Quality wines are denoted by the *appellation d'origine contrôlée* (AOC), which strictly controls quality and the amount of wine that a particular area, whether several hundred square kilometres or just two, may produce. Within each *appellation* there is enormous diversity generated by the different types of soil, the lie of the land, the type of grape grown – there are over forty varieties grown in Languedoc and Roussillon – the ability of the wine to age, and the individual skills of the wine-grower.

Aside from the uplands of the Pyrenees and Haut Languedoc, the grape is grown more or less throughout the region, with cultivation most concentrated along the windswept coast. The southernmost wines are those of the **Côtes de Roussillon**, classified in three distinct AOCs which produce fruity and exciting reds – reminscent of the Catalan vintages grown on the far side of the Pyrenees. Some of the best **Muscat**, which is not a regional *appellation* but a type of sweet wine, obtained by adding alcohol during the fermentation process (thus preventing the yeast from consuming all of the sugar), also comes from Roussillon, of which the most famous is the **Byrrh of Thuir**. Just north of Perpignan lie the *domaines* of **Fitou**, a recent AOC (1948) which combines characteristics of the heavy, robust vintages yielded by the neighbouring Corbières region's hill and littoral; **Corbières** wines are one of the great AOCs of Languedoc, as varied as the terrain which stretches along the Aude and the hillsides on its southern bank.

Closer to the water, but sheltered from the strong coastal winds by the mountain which separates Narbonne and Gruissan, the **Clape** AOC produces robust and flavourful reds. The vineyards of the coastal plain stretching from Bézier to near Nîmes and inland along the Hérault valley were grouped together some twenty years ago as the AOC **Côteaux de Languedoc**, which produces a solid if unexceptional range of reds, whites and rosés. On the other hand, the vintages of the **Costières de Nîmes**, which spread south and east of the city to the marshes of the Camargue, produce well-regarded reds, known for their strength and subtlety. Lastly, **Listel**, a rosé, is one of the best of the *vins du sable*, the "sand wines" of the Camarguais coast, which originated around Aigues-Mortes and Grau-du-Roi.

But the coast does not exercise a monopoly on fine wines in Languedoc and Roussillon. The foothills of Haut Languedoc, stretching west from Narbonne as far as the Montagne Noire, are home to the full-bodied reds of the **Cabardès**, and the honey-tinted whites and fruity reds of the **Minervois**. South of Carcassonne, you'll find **Blanquette de Limoux**, the Aude's most famous *appellation*: a sparkling white elaborated since at least the mid-sixteenth century. Curiously, one of Languedoc's most venerable and well-reputed vintages comes from far inland, in the district around **Gaillac**, the transitional zone between the Atlantic and Mediterranean climatic systems where cool ocean-borne winds take the edge off the harsh southern weather. First established as an AOC over a thousand years ago, it is best known for its whites, but also produces excellent reds and rosés.

water. The standard fizzy drinks of lemonade (*limonade*), Coke (*coca*) and so forth are all available. Bottles of **mineral water** (*eau minérale*) and spring water (*eau de source*) – either sparkling (*gazeuse*) or still (*eau plate*) – abound, from the big brand names to the most obscure spa product. But there's not much wrong with the tap water (*l'eau de robinet*) which will always be brought free to your table if you ask for it.

**Coffee** is invariably espresso – small, black and very strong. *Un café* or *un express* is the regular; *un crème* is with milk; *un grand café* or *un grand crème* are large cups. In the morning you could also ask for *un café au lait* – espresso in a large cup or bowl filled up with hot milk. *Un déca* is decaffeinated, now widely available. Ordinary **tea** (*thé*) is Lipton's nine times out of ten and is normally served black, and you can usually have a slice of lemon (*limon*) with it if you want; to have milk with it, ask for *un peu de lait frais* (some fresh milk). *Chocolat chaud* – **hot chocolate** – unlike tea, lives up to the high standards of French food and drink and can be had in any café. After eating, **herb teas** (*infusions* or *tisanes*), served in every *salon de thé*, can be soothing. The more common ones are *verveine* (verbena), *tilleul* (lime blossom), *menthe* (mint) and *camomille* (camomile).

COMMUNICATIONS, THE INTERNET AND THE MEDIA/53

## COMMUNICATIONS, THE INTERNET AND THE MEDIA

You should have no problem keeping in contact with people at home while you are in France. The country has an efficient postal system and you can have letters and packages sent general delivery to any of the official branches. The Internet is widely accessible, and is gradually displacing the now-primitive Minitel telnet system which France pioneered. Should you need to use the phone, you can use cheap pre-paid phone cards or access home-country operators via free numbers.

French **newspapers** (not to mention **radio** and **television**) will be of less interest if you are not a reader (or speaker) of French. There are some local English-language magazines, but you will probably find yourself reaching for an international edition of a British or American newspaper or an international news magazine to keep up on current events. These are available in the larger cities and tourist centres, though they can get to be an expensive habit.

### MAIL

French **post offices** (*bureaux de poste* or *PTTs*) – look for bright yellow La Poste signs – are generally open 9am to 7pm Monday to Friday, and 9am to noon on Saturday. However, don't depend on these hours: in smaller towns and villages offices may close earlier and for lunch.

You can receive mail at the central post offices of most towns. It should be addressed (preferably with the surname first and in capitals) "**Poste Restante**, Poste Centrale", followed by the name

of the town and its postcode, detailed in the Guide for all the main cities. To collect your mail you need a passport or other convincing ID and there may be a charge of around a couple of francs. You should ask for all your names to be checked, as filing systems are not brilliant.

For sending letters, remember that you can buy **stamps** (*timbres*) with less queueing from *tabacs*. Standard letters (20g or less) and postcards within France and to European Union countries cost 3F/€0.46, to North America 4.40F/€0.67 and to Australia and New Zealand 5.20F/€0.79. Inside many post offices you will find a row of yellow-coloured *guichet automatiques* – automatic ticket machines with instructions available in English with which you can weigh packages and buy the appropriate stamps; sticky labels and tape are also dispensed. A machine can change notes into change, so there is no need to queue for counter service. If you're sending parcels abroad, you can try to check prices on the *guichet* if available or in various leaflets available: small post offices don't often send foreign mail and may need reminding, for example, of the reductions for printed papers and books.

You can also use Minitel (see below) at post offices, change money, make photocopies, send faxes and make phone calls. To post your letter on the street, look for the bright yellow **postboxes**.

### PHONES AND FAXES

You can make domestic and international **phone calls** from any telephone box (*cabine*) and can receive calls where there's a blue logo of a ringing bell. A 50-unit (40.60F/€6.19) and 120-unit (97.50F/€14.87) phone card (called a *télécarte*) is essential, since coin boxes are being phased out. **Phone cards** are available from *tabacs* and newsagents as well as post offices, tourist offices and some train station ticket offices. You can also use **credit cards** in many call boxes. Coin-only boxes still exist in cafés, bars, hotel foyers and rural areas; they take 50 centimes, 1F, 5F or 10F pieces; put the money in after lifting up the receiver and before dialling. You can keep adding more coins once you are connected. Local calls are costed in France at 0.813F/€0.123 for 3 minutes (1F/€0.15 minimum); long-distance calls within France cost up to 2.44F/€0.37 for 3 minutes depending on the distance. Off-peak charges apply on weekdays between 7pm and 8am and after noon on Saturday until 8am Monday.

For calls within France – local or long-distance – simply dial all ten digits of the number. Numbers beginning with ☎08.00 are free numbers; those beginning with ☎08.36 are premium-rate (from 2.23F/€0.34 per minute), and those beginning with 06 are mobile and therefore also expensive to call. The major international calling codes are given in the box below; remember to omit the initial zero of the local area code from the subscriber's number.

**Cheap rates** operate between 7pm and 8am Monday to Friday, from midnight to 8am and noon to midnight on Saturday, and all day Sunday. From a private phone, a call to the UK (*Royaume-Uni*) will cost between 1.64F/€0.25 and 2.47F/€0.38 per minute, from a public phone 2.17–2.57F /€0.33–0.39; to Ireland 1.95–2.97F/€0.30–0.45 per minute or 2.85–3.52F/€0.45–0.54; to US (*États-Unis*) and Canada 1.95–2.97F/€0.30–0.45 per minute or 2.85–3.52F/€0.45–0.54; to Australia and New Zealand 4.31–6.55F/€0.66–1 per minute or 7.99–10.16F/€1.23–1.55. By far the most convenient way of making international calls is to use a **calling card**, opening an account before you leave home; calls will be billed monthly to your credit card, to your phone bill if you are already a customer or to your home address. However, the rates per minute of these cards are many times higher than the cost of calling from a public phone in France, with flat rates only. The best value is offered by Interglobe (☎020/7972 0800; 50p/min to the UK), followed by AT&T (☎0500/626262; $US1.50/min to the UK), then Cable and Wireless Calling Card (☎0500/100505; 68p/min to the UK), and Swiftcall Global Card (☎0800/7691444; 70p/min to the UK). British Telecom's BT Charge Card (☎0800/345600 or 0800/345144) offers the worst value with calls from France to the UK charged at 90p per minute. But since all of these cards are free to obtain, it's certainly worth getting one at least for emergencies. You dial a free number (make sure you have with you the relevant number for France), your account number and then the number you wish to call. The drawback is that the free number is often engaged and you have to dial a great many digits. If you need to make many foreign calls from France, several companies offer cheap-rated

## TELEPHONES

### IDD CODES

**From France** dial ☎00 + IDD code + area code minus first 0 + subscriber number.
Britain ☎44    Ireland ☎353    USA and Canada ☎1    Australia ☎61    New Zealand ☎64
**From Britain** to France: dial ☎00 33 + nine digit number (leaving out the first 0).
**From the USA and Canada** to France: dial ☎011 33 + nine digit number (leaving out the first 0).
**From Australia** to France: dial ☎011 33 + nine digit number (leaving out the first 0).
**From New Zealand** to France: dial ☎0044 33 + nine digit number (leaving out the first 0).
**Within France**: telephone numbers have **ten digits**; the first eight digits are preceded by by 01 for the Paris and Île de France area, 04 for the région of Languedoc Roussillon, and 05 for the région of Midi-Pyrénées. Even when you are within the same area, you must dial all ten digits.

### USEFUL NUMBERS WITHIN LANGUEDOC AND ROUSSILLON

**Weather** ☎08.36.68.02 + the number of the department: Ariège, 09; Aude, 11; Haute-Garonne, 31; Hérault, 34; Pyrénées-Orientales, 66; Tarn, 81.

**Traffic and road conditions** ☎08.36.68.20.00.

**Telegrams by phone** Internal ☎36.55; external ☎08.00.33.44.11 – all languages.

**Time** ☎36.99.

**International operator** For Canada and the US ☎00 33 11; for all other countries ☎00 33 followed by the country code.

**International directory assistance** For Canada and the US ☎00 33 12 11; for all other countries ☎00 33 12 followed by the country code.

**French operator** ☎13 to signal a fault.

**French directory assistance** ☎12.

phone cards, such as the bargain-basement store Tati who sell a 50F/€7.62 or 100F/€15.24 **Intercall Carte Téléphone** (☎08.00.51.79.43) for calling overseas which you can use in a public or private telephone; a 50F/€7.62 card gives you, for example, 15 minutes to Australia, 32 minutes to Canada or the US and 49 minutes to the UK. These rates work out much cheaper than using France Telecom from a public phone.

To avoid payment altogether, you can, of course, make a reverse charge or **collect call** – known in French as *téléphoner en PCV* – by contacting the international operator (see box opposite). You can also do this through the operator in the UK, by dialling the Home Direct number ☎08.00.89.00.33; to get an English-speaking operator for North America, dial ☎00.00.11.

Some British **mobile phones**, as long as they're digital, will work in France. Getting a mobile phone in France is – in principle – simply a matter of visiting a phone boutique (for instance, a France Telecom store) with identification, proof of address and proof of ability to pay. This involves setting up a French bank account, which will entitle you to the *bona fide* certificate known as an RIB (*Relève d'Identité Bancaire*); to obtain this you will need to provide a copy of a utility bill with your name on it, not necessarily a problem since banks are prepared to accept foreign utility bills.

**Faxes** can be sent from all main post offices and many photocopy stores: the official French word is *télécopie*, but people use the word fax. A typical rate for sending a fax within France is 25F/€3.81 for the first and 6F/€0.92 for subsequent pages.

## MINITEL

Many French phone subscribers have **Minitel**, a dinosaurial online computer that's been around since the early 1980s, which allows access through the phone lines to directories, databases, chat lines, etc. You will also find it in post offices. Most organizations, from sports federations to government institutions to gay groups, have a code consisting of numbers and letters, which you can call up for information, to leave messages, make reservations, etc. You dial the number on the phone, wait for a fax-type tone, then type the letters on the keyboard, and finally press *Connexion Fin* (the same key ends the connection). If you're at all computer-literate and can understand basic keyboard terms in French

(*retour* – return, *envoi* – enter, etc), you shouldn't find them hard to use. Be warned that most services cost more than phone rates. Directory enquiries (☎12) are free.

### EMAIL AND THE INTERNET

**Email** is the cheapest and most hassle-free way of staying in touch with home while in France. Practically every reasonable-sized town has a **cybercafé** or connection point of some sort, and in less populated areas, the need is being filled by post offices, many of which now have rather expensive public Internet terminals, which are operated with a prepaid card (50F/€7.63 for the first hour). In addition France Telecom has street-side Internet kiosks in major cities. We have given details of cybercafés and other Internet access points in the Guide so you can stay online while travelling. Prices range from 15F/€2.29 to 60F/€9.15 per hour, so it can be worth shopping around. It's easy to open a free email account to use while you're away with Hotmail or Yahoo: head for *www.hotmail.com* or *www.yahoo.com* to find out how.

The existence of Minitel and the relatively low level of personal computer ownership in France contributed to the rather slow adoption of the **Internet** here, but in recent years the situation has changed and France as a nation has come fully online. Information about practically every aspect of French culture and travel can now be picked up on the Internet: government agencies are now online, including even some of the smallest local tourist offices; in the cultural sphere even the most obscure and esoteric associations have discovered the importance of getting their message out over the Web; and the hotel and restaurant businesses have come to realize that the Net is a key to foreign markets. You'll find Web sites which deal with practically every aspect of life in Languedoc and Roussillon, from Cathars to cookery. On the down side, many or most of these pages do not have **English-language** versions, although they are gradually coming to be seen as indispensible in all but the most locally focused sites. As anywhere on the Net, persistent combing of links pages and use of search engines (among the best are *www.google.com* and *www.dogpile.com*, and the French *www.enfin.com*) will almost certainly get you the information you are looking for.

**Web sites** or, in the case of accommodation and tourist offices email addresses (if there's no

## FRANCE ON THE NET

### TOURISM AND RECREATION SITES

*www.tourist-office.org*
Handy database of France's municipal and local tourist offices arranged by *région* and *département*. Town listings have practical and cultural information and links to local Web sites.

*www.franceguide.com*
The official site of the French Government Tourist Office, with news, information on local festivals and useful links. Has a good English-language version.

*www.cr-languedocroussillon.fr*
Languedoc-Roussillon´s official Web site, with links to activities, accommodation, gastronomy and culture. One of the best starting points, but limited to the boundaries of the modern administrative *région*.

*www.monuments-france.fr*
Information on over 200 national monuments and museums – many in Languedoc and Roussillon – including news on special events.

*www.fr-holidaystore.co.uk*
France Holiday Store is a useful site for planning with tour operators – everything from cycling to canal cruising, fly-drive and short breaks and skiing. Property search with over 1000 places listed with photos-plus-brochure searches and regional and tourist info.

*www.francesport.com*
Links page for French national sports associations, both professional sports and participatory outdoor activities. Everything from hiking to handball.

*www.little-france.com*
Roussillonaise weekly webzine with information on culture, tourism, art, politics and economy.

*www.pyrenees-online.fr*
The homepage of Pyrénées-Online, with information on accommodation, sights, recreational activities and regional specialities.

*www.cr-mip.fr*
Guide to festivals in the Midi-Pyrénées région, with information dates, venues, and admission prices as well as links to Web pages of participating cultural and arts groups.

*www.europe-today.com/france/active.htm*
English-language master-site for outdoor activities in Languedoc and Roussillon. Features contact details for a variety of sports and pursuits, from canyoning to parachuting.

### NEWS AND INFORMATION SITES

*www.gksoft.com/govt*
Gateway to English-language listings of all French government Web sites, including embassies, departmental and regional tourist boards, political parties, municipalities and media.

*www.radio-france.fr*
Radio France's official page has national and international news coverage, current affairs, as well as music, culture and the latest in French sports. French language only.

---

Web site available), are given where available throughout the Guide, and as a supplement to this you'll find below a list of some of the most useful and important French Web sites in the box above.

## NEWSPAPERS AND MAGAZINES

**English-language newspapers**, such as *The Times*, the *Washington Post*, *New York Times* and the *International Herald Tribune*, are on sale the same day in some of the region's larger cities, like Toulouse, Montpellier and Nîmes, and the day after publication at resorts. Of the **French daily papers**, *Le Monde* is the most intellectual; it is widely respected, but somewhat austere, making no concessions to such frivolities as photographs. *Libération*, founded by Jean-Paul Sartre in the 1960s, is moderately left-wing, independent and more colloquial, with good, if choosy, coverage,

while rigorous left-wing criticism of the French government comes from *L'Humanité*, the Communist Party paper. The other nationals are all firmly right-wing in their politics: *Le Figaro* is the most respected. The top-selling national is *L'Équipe*, which is dedicated to sports coverage, while *Paris-Turf* focuses on horse-racing. The widest circulations are enjoyed by the **regional dailies**: in Languedoc-Roussillon this is the *Midi-Libre* – though for travellers, this, like the rest of the regionals, is mainly of interest for its listings.

**Weeklies** of the *Newsweek/Time* model include the wide-ranging and socialist-inclined *Le Nouvel Observateur*, its right-wing counterpart *L'Express* and the boringly centrist *L'Évenement de Jeudi* and the newcomer with a bite, *Marianne*. The best investigative journalism is to be found in the weekly satirical paper *Le Canard*

*www.lemonde.fr*
The French-language Web version of one of France's most reputable daily newspapers. Includes national and international news, culture and sports.

*www.france2.fr/cyber*
France TV 2's daily Web page has the latest on news, weather, and road conditions as well as listings and reviews of cultural events. Also has a youth section.

*www.jobvillage.com*
English-language site for those looking for work in Languedoc and Roussillon. Emphasis is on the food and hospitality industries.

## ARTS AND CULTURE SITES

*web.culture.fr*
French Ministry of Culture's page, with information on everything from monuments to exhibitions and also comprehensive lists of links to organizations related to the whole gamut of artistic media.

*www.bpi.fr*
Home page of the Bibliothèque Pompidou, with good links to media and a very comprehensive list of arts and humanities pages for France.

*www.revue-spectacle.com*
Arts page, set up by a group of newspapers and radio stations in cooperation with the Ministry of Culture. Covers theatre, dance and mime events and is updated monthly. No English version presently, but a link to the Babelfish translation page.

*www.ladanse.com*
Multilingual site with comprehensive information on French and international dance including news, links and a database of artists and companies.

*www.cathares.org.com*
Everything you wanted to know about Cathars but were afraid to ask. A French-only site featuring information on culture, history and historical sites, as well as regular updates on related events and exhibitions.

*www.multimania.com/music/Languedoc-Roussillon.html*
Regularly updated site for concert listings across Languedoc and Roussillon. Links provide information about venues and artists, including reviews, interviews and bios. French-language only.

*www.philagora.net/cuisine/lang-doc.htm*
A French-only site dedicated to the cuisine of Languedoc, and featuring weekly recipes, information regarding food-oriented events and festivals, and links to other culinary sites.

*www.multimania.com/simorre/oc/presoc.htm*
English-language Web site ideal if you want to learn more about Occitan langauge. Links to the history and literature (including works in translation), as well information on grammar and a short tutorial.

*perso.wanadoo.fr/joseph.riera/menu.htm*
French-language page dedicated to the history and culture of "French Catalonia" – Roussillon – with detailed explanations of history, customs and language.

---

Enchaîné. *Charlie Hebdo* is a sort of *Private Eye* or *Spy Magazine* equivalent. There is also *Paris-Match* for gossip about stars and the royal families. **Monthlies** include the young and trendy – and cheap – *Nova*, which has excellent listings of cultural events, and *Actuel*, which is good for current events. There are, of course, the French versions of *Vogue*, *Elle* (weekly) and *Marie-Claire*, and the relentlessly urban *Biba*, for women's fashion and lifestyle.

Moral **censorship** of the press is rare. On the newsstands you'll find pornography of every shade, as well as covers featuring drugs, sex, blasphemy and bizarre forms of grossness alongside knitting patterns and DIY. You'll also find French **comics** (*bandes dessinées*), which often indulge such adult interests: wildly and wonderfully illustrated, they are considered to be quite

an artform and whole museums are devoted to them.

Some of the huge numbers of homeless people in France (*les sans-logement*) make a bit of money by selling magazines on the streets which combine culture, humour and self-help with social and political issues. Costing 10F/€1.53, the most well known of these is *L'Itinerant*.

### TV AND RADIO

**French TV** has six channels: three public (France 2, Arte/La Cinquième and FR3); one subscription (Canal Plus – with some unencrypted programmes); and two commercial open broadcasts (TF1 and M6). In addition there are the **cable** networks, which include France Infos, CNN, the BBC World Service, BBC Prime, MTV, Planète, which specializes in documentaries, Paris Première (lots of French-dubbed films), and Canal Jimmy (*Friends* and the like in French). There are two music channels: the American MTV and the French-run MCM, where you can get a real education on French rap.

**Arte/La Cinquième** is a joint Franco-German cultural venture that transmits simultaneously in French and German: offerings include highbrow programmes, daily documentaries, art criticism, serious French and German movies and complete operas. During the day (6am–7pm), La Cinquième uses the frequency to broadcast educational programmes. **Canal Plus** is the main **movie channel** (and funder of the French film industry), with repeats of foreign films usually shown at least

once in the original language. **FR3** screens a fair selection of serious movies, with its *Cinéma de Minuit* slot late on Sunday nights good for foreign, undubbed films. The main French **news broadcasts** are at 8.30pm on Arte and at 8pm on F2 and TF1.

If you've got a **radio**, you can tune in to English-language news on the BBC World Service on 648kHz AM or 198kHz long wave from midnight to 5am (and Radio 4 during the day). The Voice of America transmits on 90.5, 98.8 and 102.4 FM. For radio **news in French**, there's the state-run France Inter (87.8 FM), Europe 1 (104.7 FM) and round-the-clock news on France Infos (105.5 FM).

# OPENING HOURS, PUBLIC HOLIDAYS AND FESTIVALS

**Basic hours of business are 8am or 9am to noon or 1pm, and 2pm or 3pm to 6.30pm or 7.30pm. In big city centres shops and other businesses stay open throughout the day, and in July and August most tourist offices and museums are open without interruption. Otherwise almost everything closes for a couple of hours at midday, or even longer in the south. Small food shops often don't reopen till halfway through the afternoon, closing around 7.30pm or 8pm just before the evening meal.**

The standard **closing days** are Sunday and/or Monday, with shops taking turns to close with their neighbours; many food shops such as

*boulangeries* (bakeries) that open on Sunday will do so in the morning only. In small towns you'll find everything except the odd boulangerie shut on both days. This includes **banks**, which in cities are usually open Monday to Friday (often Tuesday to Friday in small towns) from 9am to 4pm or 5pm, making it all too easy to find yourself dependent on hotels for money-changing at poor rates and high commission. Restaurants and cafés also often close on a Sunday or Monday.

**Museums** tend to open between 9am and 10am, close for lunch at noon until 2pm or 3pm, and then run through to 5pm or 6pm, although in the big cities they will stay open all day. **Closing days** are usually Tuesday or Monday, sometimes both. **Admission charges** can be very off-putting, though many state-owned museums have one day of the week (often Sun) when they're free or half-price, and you can often get reductions if you're a full-time student (with ISIC card), under 26 or over 60. **Cathedrals** are almost always open all day every day, with charges only for the crypt, treasuries or cloister and little fuss about how you're dressed. **Church** opening hours are often more restricted; on Sunday mornings (or at other times which you'll see posted up on the door) you may have to attend Mass to take a look. In small towns and villages, however, getting the key is not difficult – ask anyone nearby or seek out the priest, whose house is known as the *presbytère*.

## PUBLIC HOLIDAYS

There are thirteen national holidays (*jours fériés*), when most shops and businesses (though not necessarily restaurants), and some museums, are closed. May in particular is a big month for holidays: as well as May Day and Victory Day, Ascension Day normally falls then, as sometimes does Pentecost.

**January 1** New Year's Day

**Easter Sunday**

**Easter Monday**

**Ascension Day** (forty days after Easter)

**Pentecost** or Whitsun (seventh Sunday after Easter, plus the Monday)

**May 1** May Day/Labour Day

**May 8** Victory in Europe Day

**July 14** Bastille Day

**August 15** Assumption of the Virgin Mary

**November 1** All Saints' Day

**November 11** 1918 Armistice Day

**December 25** Christmas Day

## FESTIVALS

It's hard to beat the experience of arriving in some small French village, expecting no more than a bed for the night, to discover the streets decked out with flags and streamers, a band playing in the square and the entire population out celebrating the feast of their patron saint. Apart from Bastille Day (July 14) and the Assumption of the Virgin Mary (August 15), there are many traditional folk **festivals** still thriving in Languedoc and Roussillon.

Celebrations of local patron saints are concentrated in summer months and are the occasion for fireworks, dancing and *pétanque* competitions. These are particularly colourful in the fishing ports of the Languedoc coast, where saints' effigies are paraded down to the sea and events include water-borne jousting competitions. In wine country, there are inevitably festivals coinciding with the grape harvest, and in other regions with that of the dominant local product. Throughout the Languedocian plain – notably from Béziers and east and in certain towns of the Pyrenees – *tauromachie* (see p.60), which involves Spanish-style *corridas* (bullfights) or indigenous *courses camarguaises*, occurs regularly throughout the summer, and at other big holidays, such as Pentecost and the pre-Lenten carnival. The most important and interesting festivals are outlined at the beginning of each chapter of the Guide.

## SPORTS AND OUTDOOR ACTIVITIES

**Languedoc and Roussillon offers a wide range of sports – both spectator and participatory. Although you can watch local teams play big league sports such as football, you'll find that locally popular games like rugby are more worthwhile to seek out. You also have the choice of a variety of outdoor activities, including hiking, cycling and skiing, and water-borne diversions such as rafting and sailing.**

### SPECTATOR SPORTS

As well as rugby, the outdoor spectacle of **bull-fighting**, or more properly, *tauromachie*, is incredibly popular across the region, both in Spanish and indigenous styles. **Water-jousting** (see p.263), a coastal tradition which pits boat-borne jousting teams against each other in an effort to unseat their opponents, has its home at Sète, but is practised along the length of the coast. **Pétanque**, or *boules*, is a game which you will see played in towns and villages throughout the region, and which you can play yourself if you purchase a set (available at sports shops and large department stores).

### Football and rugby

Languedoc and Roussillon are not the best places in France for **football**, and the only cities in the region which have a team in the First Division are Toulouse, whose club were clinging tenuously to the bottom, eighteenth place, at the time of writing, and Montpellier, who were faring better

(although their finest moment was when they took the French Cup in 1990).

**Rugby** is the field game of choice in the region, and virtually every town of any size boasts a team. Top teams in the region include Toulouse, Narbonne, Perpignan, Nîmes and Castres, and these teams have traditionally provided the core of the French national side.

Rugby originated in 1832, in England, and although it arrived in France not long after it only really caught on in the Occitan south – perhaps as an unconscious means of marking a difference from the northern French. Post-game camaraderie is a big part of the whole experience, and you'll find yourself caught up in the cheerful spirit of things whether you see a major team like Stade Toulousain in action, or a small town match with teams of the level of Albi or Pamiers.

### Tauromachie

Bulls have been raised in eastern Languedoc since time immemorial, and in the last centuries **tauromachie** – "the art of the bull" (see box on p.214) – has come to play an important role in the culture of the whole region. While the people of the Petite Carmargue ranch lands see it as a measure of virility, Occitan patriots are attracted to it as a custom which has no equivalent in the north of France.

Two distinct types of *tauromachie* are practised in Languedoc and Roussillon, the better known of which is the Iberian-style **corrida**. This event, which can be seen at the *ferias* of Nîmes, St-Gilles, Béziers as well as smaller towns across Languedoc, and in Céret in Roussillon is a highly ritualized ceremony. In a typical afternoon, three matadors dispose of six bulls, each of which will face a number of torments, including being poked by horseback *picadores*, and pricked with spears by running *banderilleros*, before a series of choreographed passes is executed by the matador and the bull is killed. Crowds are extremely vocal; poor matadors are subjected to catcalls and shouts, while a successful performance is awarded with loud ovations.

The French **course**, which has its origin in the medieval *jeu taurin* ("bull-baiting") is quite distinct from the *corrida*. Less expensive and elaborate, it is more common in village *fêtes*, such as at Uzès or Aigues-Morte, and usually involves the bulls (or cows) being led into a ring and fitted with a rosette of ribbon and colourful tassels suspended between their horns. For fifteen minutes *raseteurs* provoke the bull into charging and attempt to snatch the rosette or tassels without getting trampled or gored. When all is complete, the bulls are herded out nervous, but otherwise unharmed, back to their pen. Unlike the ceremonial Spanish version, the *course* is more of a sport, with a stronger element of competition among the human participants.

Today *tauromachie* is more popular than ever; the *ferias* of Nîmes draw thousands of enthusiasts from all over France and the rest of Europe and are universally acknowledged as southern France's liveliest and most colourful festivities. But *tauromachie* has taken firm root even in the smallest of villages far from the *manades* of the plains. Even if they can afford no more than an *encierro*, villagers pool their money in order to pay for some sort of taurine display, without which no *fête* would be seen as complete. On the other hand, urban culture has prompted a low-level reaction against these activities, and has resulted, for instance, in the disappearance of *tauromachie* in Toulouse.

## Pétanque

Once the preserve of sweatered old men in berets, recently **pétanque**, or *boules*, has seen a surge in popularity and a broadening of appeal to include more young people and women. The game is similar to English bowls. Two equally numbered teams (from one to three persons) find a space of hard, compact ground and throw a *cochonnet* (jack) a few metres (technically 6 to 10). A small circle is then marked on the ground to show the limit of the area in which the throwers must stand (hence *pétanque* from the Provençal "pied tanqués" or "feet together"). They then proceed in turns to launch a total of three balls (two in a 6-person match), each with the object of having their metal *boules* closest to the *cochonnet* at the end of the exchange. A point is gained for each ball that is closer than the nearest ball of the opposing team. The jack is then thrown again and play continues until one side scores 13. *Pétanque* matches invariably draw a crowd of onlookers, and you will not be considered rude if you stop to observe. The best times to watch are during village *fêtes*, which invariably include a tournament, drawing out the best players in the village.

## OUTDOOR ACTIVITIES

**Hiking** is undoubtedly the way to get the most out of a visit to the region. Well-marked and maintained GR paths, signposted with their distinctive yellow and red bars, span the region, punctuated by *gîtes*, refuges and campsites along the way. The highest concentration of paths (and the best hiking scenery) is found in the Pyrenees and its foothills, where you will find and extensive network of yellow and red marked GRP (*grand randonées du pays*) paths as well as HRP (*haute route des Pyrénées*) routes. In addition local AR footpaths abound, and in virtually every village you'll find an information board with a map outlining local itineraries of varying length and difficulty.

**Biking** is the next best option, and the cities of the south have been remarkably quick to adapt to two-wheeled transport, particularly Toulouse and Montpellier. Around Montpellier, Agde and Narbonne extensive networks of bike paths, often using decommissioned roads, link the coastal villages and the cities. In the countryside disused rail lines, such as the Gijou Valley trail (see p.192), have been set up as bicycle (VTT) routes, and canal towpaths make it possible to cross the region with ease. Traffic off the main roads is surprisingly light, and with the exception of the coastal plain you will find the biggest challenge to be the hillyness of the terrain.

While **horse-riding** is not practical as a means of transport, it is an excellent way of enjoying the countryside. Practically every town, and many farms have equestrian centres where you can ride unaccompanied or with a guide on local trails. In the Pyrenees **mules** provide a more practical alternative. Local tourist offices can give you information on riding centres or you can contact the regional equestrian tourism organization ATECREL, 14 rue des Logis, 34140 Loupian (☎04.67.43.82.50), or the Fédération Française d'Équitation (DNTE), 30 av d'Iéna, 75116 Paris (☎01.53.67.44.44, fax 01.53.67.44.22, *dnte @magic.fr*). For mule-trekking, contact the Fédération Nationale Ânes et Randonnées, Broissieux, 73340 Bellecombe-en-Bauges, (☎04.79.63.84.01).

There are a number of **ski stations** in the Eastern Pyrenees, and although they cannot offer anything to compare to the great resorts of the French Alps, you will be able to find some decent downhill skiing if you visit between November and

April. Cross-country skiing, or *ski de fond*, is also a possibility, and the broad massifs of the Cerdagne and Ariège are particularly well suited to it. The relatively low altitude of some resorts is partially off-set by the extensive use of snow-making machines. The most important and better-known resorts, among them Font-Romeu, Formiguères and Porté-Puymorens, are detailed in the Guide, and regional and departmental tourist offices – in this case Ariège and Pyrénées-Orientales (see p.28) – will also have information.

While you are exploring the hilly uplands of the Languedoc and Roussillon, you ought to sample also the thrill of **rafting** down one of the region's many dramatic rivers. This sport has exploded in recent years, and you will scarcely pass a gorge which is not capped by a rafting outfit at its upper end. The biggest concentration is in the upper Hérault south of Ganges, but good opportunities can be found on the Orbiel, west of Lamalou, and on the Ariège around Tarascon. More placid paddling can by done by **canoe**, notably on the calmer stretches of water of the Aude and Gardon, and at the Pont du Gard.

Most of the seaside towns have been fully developed as resorts, and have facilities for the whole gamut of **watersports**: in summer months you'll find everything from jet-skis and sail-boards to houseboats and yachts for rent. If you are specifically looking for beachside activities, Le-Grau-du-Roi has the best range of facilities, while La Grande-Motte, runs a close second.

## TROUBLE AND THE POLICE

**Petty theft is endemic in all the major cities and along the coast. Drivers, particularly with foreign number plates or in rental cars with Parisian registration, face a high risk of break-ins. Vehicles are rarely stolen, but car radios and luggage make tempting targets.**

It obviously makes sense to take the normal **precautions**: not flashing wads of notes or travellers' cheques around; carrying your bag or wallet securely; never letting cameras and other valuables out of your sight; and parking your car overnight in an attended garage or within sight of a police station. But the best security is having a good insurance policy, keeping a separate record of cheque numbers, credit card numbers and the phone numbers for cancelling them (see p.23), and the relevant details of all your valuables.

If you need to **report a theft**, go along to the *commissariat de police* (addresses are given in the Guide for the major cities), where they will fill out a *constat de vol*. The first thing they'll ask for is your passport, and vehicle documents if relevant. Although the police are not always as co-operative as they might be, it is their duty to assist you if you've lost your passport or all your money.

If you have an **accident** while driving, you have officially to fill in and sign a *constat à l'aimable* (jointly agreed statement); car insurers are supposed to give you this with the policy, though in practice few seem to have heard of it. For **non-criminal driving offences** such as speeding, the police can impose an on-the-spot fine.

---

### EMERGENCY NUMBERS

**Fire brigade** (*pompiers*) ☎18.
**Medical emergencies** ☎15.
**Police** ☎17.
**Rape crisis** (*SOS Viol*) ☎08.00.05.95.95.
**AIDS information** (SIDA Info Service) ☎08.00.84.08.00.
All these numbers are free.

People caught smuggling or possessing **drugs**, even a few grams of marijuana, are liable to find themselves in jail, and consulates will not be sympathetic. This is not to say that hard-drug consumption isn't a visible activity: there are scores of kids dealing in *poudre* (heroin) in the big French cities and the authorities seem unable to do much about it. As a rule, people are no more nor less paranoid about cannabis busts than they are in the UK or North America.

Should you be **arrested** on any charge, you have the right to contact your consulate (addresses are given on p.20).

## THE POLICE

The two main types of **police** – the Police Nationale and the Gendarmerie Nationale – are for all practical purposes indistinguishable. The CRS (Compagnies Républicaines de Sécurité), on the other hand, are an entirely different proposition. They are a mobile force of paramilitary heavies, used to guard sensitive embassies, "control" demonstrations, and generally intimidate the populace on those occasions when the public authorities judge that it is stepping out of line. Armed with guns, CS gas and truncheons, they have earned themselves a reputation for brutality over the years, particularly at those moments when the tensions inherent in the long civil war of French politics have reached boiling point. You can be stopped anywhere in France and asked to produce ID. If it happens to you, it's not worth being difficult or facetious. Lastly, in the Pyrenees, you may come across specialized **mountaineering sections** of the police force. They are unfailingly helpful, friendly and approachable, providing rescue services and guidance.

---

### RACISM IN FRANCE

**Racist attitudes** in the populace and the police are rife. A survey on French attitudes to race, commissioned by the French government and published in June 1998, resulted in 38 percent of the population declaring themselves racist, double the figures for similar surveys in Britain and Germany, and the **Front National**, a neo-fascist, racist party, headed by **Jean-Marie Le Pen**, won fifteen percent of the vote in the last parliamentary elections. Support for the party was highest in Provence and the Côte d'Azur although in Languedoc and Roussillon Perpignan´s *mairie* and several seats in the Hérault *département*'s council also went to the far right. The Front National's alliance with conservatives led to changes in educational, cultural and sporting programmes to suit its policies, the party's fundamental priority being the withdrawal of benefits to immigrants who have not yet been granted French citizenship.

However, the mood in France altered after the 1998 World Cup victory of its multicultural team and Le Pen was forced to modify some of his racist statements. Since then the party has fractured and lost popularity (with it and the splinter group rated at about nine percent), so the next round of elections may change the current unpleasant state of affairs.

It will take a long time for the warm glow created by the World Cup to transform France into a racially tolerant country, and for the moment being black, particularly if you are Arab or look as if you might be, makes your chances of avoiding unpleasantness very low. Hotels claiming to be booked up, police demanding your papers, and abuse from ordinary people is horribly frequent. In addition, even entering the country can be difficult. Changes in passport regulations have put an end to outright refusal to let some British holiday-makers in, but customs and immigration officers can still be obstructive and malicious. In North African-dominated areas of cities, identity checks by the police are very common and not pleasant. The clampdown on illegal immigration (and much tougher laws) have resulted in a significant increase in police stop-and-search operations. Carrying your passport at all times is a good idea.

If you suffer a **racial assault**, you're likely to get a much more sympathetic hearing from your consulate than from the police. There are many anti-racism organizations which will offer support (though they may not have English-speakers): Mouvement contre le Racisme et pour l'Amitié entre les Peuples (MRAP) and SOS Racism have offices in most big cities.

# GAY AND LESBIAN FRANCE

France is more liberal on homosexuality than most other European countries. The legal age of consent is sixteen. In Languedoc gay communities thrive in larger centres, such as Toulouse and Montpellier, and some beach towns, like Palavas, though lesbian life is rather less upfront. Addresses are listed in the Guide, and you'll find details of groups and publications for the whole region in the box below.

In general, the French consider sexuality to be a private matter and homophobic assaults are very rare. On the whole, gays tend to be discreet outside specific gay venues, parades and certain coastal resorts (like Palavas). Toulouse has the reputation for being a city with a vibrant gay and lesbian culture, although there is no notable gay "ghetto" as such. Montpellier, traditionally politically left-wing and socially liberal, officially embraces gay culture, supporting many events in the city.

Hedonistic lifestyles have changed, here as elsewhere, since the advent of **AIDS** (SIDA in French). The resulting homophobia, though not as extreme as in most parts of the world, has nevertheless increased the suffering among gay men. Lesbian organizations fight alongside gays on the general issue of anti-homosexuality, while also lobbying for womens' rights.

## GAY AND LESBIAN CONTACTS AND INFORMATION

**ARCL** (Les Archives, Recherches et Cultures Lesbiennes), based at the Maison des Femmes (☎01.46.28.54.94, *www.mrap.asso.fr*). ARCL publish a biannual directory of lesbian, gay and feminist addresses in France, *L'Annuaire* (70F/€10.68), and organize frequent meetings around campaigning, artistic and intellectual issues.

**Centre Gai et Lesbienne Toulouse**, 4 rue de Belfort (☎05.61.62.30.62). Open for phone calls and visits Mon–Fri 5–8pm, Sat 3–8pm, and on Sunday the *Café Positif*, a great place for meeting people, is open from 3 to 7pm.

**Minitel**. 36.15 GAY is the Minitel number to dial for information on groups, contacts, messages, etc.

### GAY AND LESBIAN MEDIA

**Fréquence Gaie (FG)**, 98.2 FM. 24-hour gay and lesbian radio station with music, news, chats, information on groups and events, etc.

**Guide Gai Pied**. The most comprehensive gay guide to France, published annually and carrying a good selection of lesbian and gay addresses, with an English section (79F/€12.05); available in newsagents and bookshops in France. You can look at their Web site at *www.gaipied.fr*.

**Lesbia**. The most widely available lesbian publication, available from most newsagents. Each monthly issue features a wide range of articles, listings, reviews, lonely hearts and contacts.

**Spartacus International Gay Guide**. Guidebook in English focusing mainly on gay travel in Europe with an extensive section on France. Geared mostly towards males but with some info for lesbians. Available around the world at travel and gay book shops.

# WORK AND STUDY

**Specialists aside, most Britons, North Americans, Australians and Kiwis who manage to survive for long periods of time in France do it on luck, brazenness and willingness to live in pretty basic conditions. In the cities, bar work, club work, freelance translating or teaching English, software fixing, data processing and typing or working as an au pair are some of the ways people scrape by; in the countryside, the options come down to seasonal fruit- or grape-picking (*vendange*), teaching English, busking or DIY oddjobbing. Remember that unemployment in France is very high, and particularly so in traditionally depressed Languedoc and Roussillon, where it hovers around 23 percent.**

Anyone staying in France for over three months must have a *carte de séjour* (see p.20), or residency permit – citizens of the EU are entitled to one automatically. France has a **minimum wage** (the SMIC – Salaire Minimum Interprofessional de Croissance), indexed to the cost of living; it's currently around 40F/€6.10 an hour (for a maximum 169-hour month). Employers, though, are likely to pay lower wages to temporary foreign workers who don't have easy legal resources, and make them work longer hours. By law, however, all EU nationals are entitled to exactly the same pay, conditions and trade union rights as French nationals.

If you're looking for something secure, it's important to plan well in advance. A few books which might be worth consulting are *Work Your Way Around the World* by Susan Griffiths (Vacation Work), *A Year Between* and *Working Holidays* (both Central Bureau) and *Living and Working in France* by Victoria Pybus, published by Vacation Work 1998. **In France**, check out the "Offres d'Emploi" (Job Offers) in *Le Monde*, *Le Figaro* and the *International Herald Tribune*; and try the youth information agency CIDJ (Centre d'Information et de Documentation Jeunesse), 101 quai Branly, 17015 Paris, or CIJ (Centre d'Information Jeunesse) offices in other main cities, which sometimes have temporary jobs for foreigners. The national employment agency, ANPE (Agence Nationale pour l'Emploi), with offices all over France, advertises temporary jobs in all fields and, in theory, offers a whole range of services to job seekers open to all EU citizens, but is not renowned for its helpfulness to foreigners. Non-EU citizens will have to show a work permit to apply for any of their jobs. Vac-Job, 46 av Réné-Coty, 17014 Paris (☎01.43.20.70.51), publishes the annual *Emplois d'Été en France* (*Summer Jobs in France*), which may be useful.

Finding a job in a **French language school** is also best done in advance. In Britain, jobs are often advertised in the *Guardian*'s "Education" section (every Tues), or in the weekly *Times Educational Supplement*. Late summer is usually the best time. You don't need fluent French to get a post, but a degree and a TEFL (Teaching English as a Foreign Language) qualification are normally required. The month-long TEFL course currently costs £944. The annual *ELT Guide* (£12.95) gives a thorough breakdown of TEFL courses available; the booklet is produced by EFL Ltd, 1 Malet St, London WC1E 7JA (☎020/7255 1969, fax 7255 1972), and the same company publishes the monthly *ELT Gazette* which is filled with job advertisements (subscription for 12 issues £25.50). Vacation Work, 9 Park End St, Oxford OX1 1HJ (☎01865/241 978, fax 790 885) publishes the useful *Teaching English Abroad* (£10.99 plus £1.50 post and packaging) while the British Council's Web site (*www.britcoun.org/english /engvacs.htm*) has a list of English-teaching vacancies. If you apply for jobs from home, most schools will fix up the necessary papers for you. It's just feasible to find a teaching job when you're in France, but you may have to accept

## FRENCH BUREAUCRACY: A WARNING

French officialdom and bureaucracy can damage your health. That Gallic shrug and "Ce n'est pas possible" is not the result of training programmes in making life difficult for foreigners: it drives most French citizens mad as well. Sorting out social security, long-stay visas, job contracts, bank accounts, tenancy agreements, university enrolment or any other financial, legal or state matter, requires serious commitment. Your reserves of patience, diligence, energy (both physical and mental) and equanimity in the face of bloody-mindedness and Catch-22s, will be tested to the full. Expect to spend days repeatedly visiting the same office and considerable sums on official translations of every imaginable document.

semi-official status and no job security. For the addresses of schools, look under "Écoles de Langues" in the "Professions" directory of the local phone book. Offering **private lessons** (via university notice boards or classified ads), you'll have lots of competition, and it's hard to reach the people who can afford it, but it's always worth a try.

Some people find jobs **selling magazines** on the street and **leafleting** by asking people already doing it for the agency address. The American/Irish/British **bars and restaurants** in the main cities and resorts sometimes have vacancies. You'll need to speak French, look smart and be prepared to work very long hours. Obviously, the better your French, the better your chances are of finding work.

**Au pair** work is usually arranged through one of a dozen agencies, listed in Vacation Work's guide (see p.65). In Britain, the *Lady* is the magazine for classified adverts for such jobs, arranged privately. As initial numbers to ring, try Avalon Au Pairs (☎01344/778 246, *www.city2000.com /avalonaupairs/top*) in Britain, the American Institute for Foreign Study (☎203/869 9090, *www.aifs.com*) in the US, or Accueil Familial des Jeunes Étrangers (☎01.42.22.50.34; 690F /€105.23 joining fee) in Paris. These have positions for female au pairs only and will fill you in on the general terms and conditions (never very generous); you shouldn't get paid less than 1650F/€252 a month (on top of board and lodging and some sort of travel pass). It is wise to have an escape route (like a ticket home) in case you find the conditions intolerable and your employers insufferable. It may be better to apply once in France, where you can at least meet the family first and check things out.

Temporary jobs in the **travel industry** revolve around courier work – supervising and working on bus tours or summer campsites. You'll need good French (and maybe even another language) and

should write to as many tour operators as you can, preferably in early spring. In Britain, ads occasionally appear in the *Guardian's* "Media" section (every Mon) while travel magazines like the very reliable *Wanderlust* (every two months; £2.80) have a Job Shop section which often advertises job opportunities with tour companies. Getting work as a courier on a campsite is slightly easier. It usually involves putting up tents at the beginning of the season, taking them down again at the end, and general maintenance and troubleshooting work in the months between; Canvas Holidays (☎01383/644 018) are worth approaching. The British company PGL Young Adventure Ltd, Alton Court, Penyard Lane, Ross-on-Wye HR9 (☎01989/764 211, *www.pgl.co.uk*) runs several children's activity centres in France, employing people proficient in watersports or with youthwork experience, and offers general catering, domestic and driving work, between May and September every year; you should apply before April.

An offbeat possibility if you want to discover rural life is being a **working guest** on an organic farm. The period can be anything from a week to a couple of months and the work may involve cheese-making, market gardening, beekeeping, wine-producing and building. For details of the scheme and a list of French addresses, you can write to Willing Workers on Organic Farms (WWOOF), 19 Bradford Rd, Lewes BN7 1RB, in the UK; WWOOF W Tree, Buchan, VIC 3885 (*www. earthlink.com.au/wwoof*) in Australia; or WWOOF RR2, Carlson Rd, S18 C9, Nelson, British Columbia VIL 5P5 in Canada, enclosing an self-addressed envelope.

## CLAIMING BENEFIT

Any British or EU citizen who has been signing on for **jobseeker's allowance** for a minimum period of four to six weeks at home, and intends to continue doing so in France, needs a letter of introduction from their own Social Security office, plus an E303 certificate of authorization (be sure to give them plenty of warning to prepare this). You must register within seven days with the ANPE (Agence Nationale pour l'Emploi), whose offices are listed under "Administration du Travail et de l'Emploi" in the Yellow Pages or ANPE in the White Pages.

It's possible to claim benefit for up to three months while you look for work, but it can often take that amount of time for the paperwork to be processed (also see warning opposite).

Pensioners can arrange for their **pensions** to be paid in France, but not, unfortunately, to receive French state pensions.

## STUDYING IN FRANCE

It's relatively easy to be a **student** in Languedoc and Roussillon. Foreigners pay no more than French nationals to enrol for a course, and the only problem then is to support yourself. Your *carte de séjour* and – if you're an EU citizen – social security will be assured, and you'll be eligible for subsidized accommodation, meals and all the student reductions. In general, French universities are much less formal than British ones and many people perfect their fluency in the language while studying. There are strict entry requirements, including an exam in French, for undergraduate degrees, but not for postgraduate courses. For full **details and prospectuses**, contact the Cultural Service of any French embassy or consulate (see p.20). In Britain, the embassy will refer you to the French Institute, 17 Queensbury Place, London SW7 2DT (☎020/7838 2148), a cultural centre which has a cinema and a library where you can go to pick up a list of language courses in France (library hours Tues–Fri noon–7pm & Sat noon–6pm); otherwise send a letter requesting the list accompanied by a self-addressed envelope. The embassies and consulates can also give details of **language courses** at French universities and colleges, which are often combined with lectures on French "civilization" and usually very costly. You'll find ads for lesser language courses advertised all over the place. Nîmes has the region's newest university, but the best places to study in Languedoc are undoubtedly Toulouse and Montpellier – both have been reputable university towns since the 1300s, and have huge student populations. In Roussillon, you can study in Perpignan, as well as the summer university for Catalan studies in Céret. There are French-language academies through the two regions.

It's also worth noting that if you're a full-time non-EU student in France (see p.65), you can get a non-EU **work permit** for the following summer so long as your visa is still valid.

# DIRECTORY

**BEACHES** Beaches are public property within 5m of the high-tide mark, so you can kick sand past private villas. Under a different law, however, you can't camp.

**CAMERAS AND FILM** Film is considerably cheaper in North America than France – or Britain – so stock up before travelling. If you're bringing a video camcorder, make sure any tapes you purchase in France will be compatible. Again, American videotape prices are way below French prices.

**CHILDREN AND BABIES** Kids are generally welcome everywhere, and in most bars and restaurants, though French children seem to be much better trained at a younger age in restaurant etiquette. Hotels charge by the room, with a small supplement for an additional bed or cot, and family-run places will usually babysit or offer a listening service while you eat or go out. Especially in the seaside towns, most restaurants have children's menus or will cook simpler food on request. You'll have no difficulty finding disposable nappies (*couches à jeter*), but nearly all baby foods have added sugar and salt, and French milk powders are very rich indeed. SNCF charge nothing on trains and buses for under-4s, and half-fare for 4–11s (see p.32 for other reductions). In most museums children under 4 are free and it's usually half-price for under-18s, while entry to many monuments is free for under-12s. Most local tourist offices have details of specific activities for children – in particular, many resorts supervise "clubs" for children on the beach. And almost every town down to small ones has a children's playground with a good selection of activities. Most parks have a children's play area; unfortunately the majority of parks are gravelled rather than grassed and when there are lawns they are often out of bounds (*pelouse interdite*), so sprawling horizontally with toddlers and napping babies is usually not an option. Something to beware of – not that you can do much about it – is the difficulty of negotiating a child's buggy over the large cobbles that cover many of the older streets in town centres.

**CONTRACEPTIVES** Condoms (*préservatifs* or *capotes*) are available at all pharmacies, as well as from many clubs and street dispensers (10F/€1.50 for 3–4 condoms) in larger cities. You can also get spermicidal cream and jelly (*dose contraceptive*), plus the suppositories (*ovules, suppositoires*) and (with a prescription) the Pill (*la pillule*), a diaphragm (*le diaphragme*) or IUD (*le sterilet*). Test sticks (*tests réactifs*) for the Persona monitor (only available in Europe) are readily available in pharmacies for 95F/€14.49 per packet.

**ELECTRICITY** This is almost always 220V, using plugs with two round pins. If you haven't bought the appropriate transformer before leaving home, the best place in France to find the right one is the electrical section of a department store, where someone is also more likely to speak English; cost is around 60F/€9.15.

**FISHING** You get fishing rights by becoming a member of an authorized fishing club – tourist offices have details.

**LAUNDRY** Laundries are common in French towns, and some are listed in the Guide – elsewhere look in the phone book under "Laveries Automatiques". They are often unattended, so come pre-armed with small change. Machines are normally graded into 5kg, 8kg or 10kg wash sizes, and the smallest costs around 12F/€1.80 for a load, though some laundries only have bigger machines and charge around 20F/€3. If you're doing your own washing in hotels, keep quantities small as most forbid doing any laundry in your room.

**PEDESTRIANS** French drivers pay no heed to pedestrian/zebra crossings marked with horizontal white stripes on roads. It is very dangerous to step out onto one and assume drivers will stop as in Australia and Britain. Take just as great care as you would crossing at any other point. Also be careful at traffic lights: check cars are not still speeding towards you even when the green man is showing.

**SWIMMING POOLS** Swimming pools (*piscines*) are well signposted in most French towns and reasonably priced, usually around 16F/€2.44 for a swim. Tourist offices have their addresses. You may be requested to wear a bathing cap, whether you are male or female, so come prepared.

**TIME** France is one hour ahead of the UK, six hours ahead of Eastern Standard Time, and nine hours ahead of Pacific Standard Time. This also applies during daylight savings seasons, which are observed in France (as in most of Europe) from the end of March through to the end of September.

**TOILETS** Ask for *les toilettes* or look for signs for the WC (pronounced "vay say"); when reading the details of facilities outside hotels, don't confuse *lavabo*, which means wash-basin, with lavatory. Usually found downstairs along with the phone, French toilets in bars are still often of the hole-in-the-ground squatting variety, and tend to lack toilet paper. Standards of cleanliness are often not high, and men shouldn't expect much privacy in the urinal, which often won't have a door. Both bar and restaurant toilets are usually free, as are toilets in museums, though toilets in railway stations and department stores are commonly staffed by attendants who will expect a bit of spare change. Some have coin-operated locks, so always keep 50 centimes and one and two franc pieces handy for these and for the frequent Tardis-like public toilets found on the streets. These beige-coloured boxes have automatic doors which open when you insert coins to the value of two francs, and are cleaned automatically once you exit. Children under 10 aren't allowed in on their own.

# PART TWO

## THE

# GUIDE

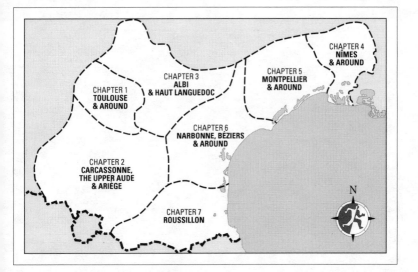

CHAPTER 1
**TOULOUSE
& AROUND**

CHAPTER 3
**ALBI
& HAUT LANGUEDOC**

CHAPTER 5
**MONTPELLIER
& AROUND**

CHAPTER 4
**NÎMES
& AROUND**

CHAPTER 6
**NARBONNE, BÉZIERS
& AROUND**

CHAPTER 2
**CARCASSONNE,
THE UPPER AUDE
& ARIÈGE**

CHAPTER 7
**ROUSSILLON**

N

# CHAPTER ONE

# TOULOUSE AND AROUND

S et midway between the cool shores of the Atlantic and the sun-baked
Mediterranean coast, **Toulouse** and its surrounding area forms the gateway to Languedoc. The city itself is a dynamo, undoubtedly the liveliest
and most interesting on this side of the Rhône, and the neighbouring countryside, though not especially dramatic, is a land of distinctive culture and cuisine.
Among the gently undulating wheatfields – the **Lauragais**, heartland of
Toulouse's traditional agricultural prosperity – you'll find little-known but colourful towns like **Lavaur** and **Revel**. Scattered between these is an array of villages
and castles whose ancient stones have witnessed both the success of the region's
famous dye trade, and the violence and terror of Crusades and Wars of Religion.
**Castelnaudary**, birthplace of the famous Languedocian staple cassoulet and
largest town in Toulouse's environs, not only contains a number of unique historical buildings, but is also the main inland port of the **Canal du Midi**, an engineering marvel which stretches from Toulouse to the sea and is one of the
emblems of the Southwest.

Toulouse is a major rail centre, with regular trains in all directions; these are
complemented by SNCF and local buses, the former following several east–west
routes across the Lauragais and the latter fanning out from Toulouse. Moving
north to south across the area is more difficult, although the quiet roads make for
good, if uphill, biking.

## Toulouse

Although it falls into the modern administrative *région* of Midi-Pyrénées,
**TOULOUSE** has a long tradition as the capital of Languedoc, while a solid industrial base, notably as the centre for French aeronautics, helps maintain it as the
sixth largest city in the nation. It's a lively, cheerful place, with a vibrant arts community and a distinct Mediterranean look – as the sun edges towards the horizon,
the hallmark pink brick buildings soak up the soft light and glow with a muted
luminescence (hence its old nickname, *La Ville Rose*). For the traveller, the city has
a lot to offer: aside from excellent medieval churches and mansions, and first-rate
galleries, its cultural programme is an almost constant succession of **festivals** (see
box on p.76); in addition, it's the most cosmopolitan city in the Southwest, with a
vigorous nightlife fuelled by the massive student population of its famous university, and a range of immigrant cultures reflected in a variety of restaurants.

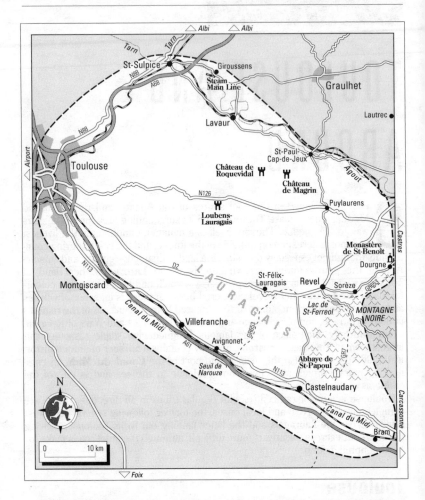

It's hard not to enjoy Toulouse, whether you are merely sitting in one of its multitude of outdoor cafés, strolling through its ancient streets, or taking in some of the best museums west of the Rhône. A stay here is the easiest way to introduce yourself to southwest France, and you could easily spend a week exploring, but if you are short of time, the two sights which should not be missed are the Romanesque **Basilique de St-Sernin** and the **Les Abattoirs** modern art gallery.

## Some history

Originally located a bit further upstream on the Garonne from the present city-centre, Toulouse (then called Tolosa) was moved to the plain which it currently occupies when the Romans took it over in 120 BC. With the disintegration of the empire the city briefly became the capital of the Visigoths in 414 AD, but when their centre of power shifted to Spain, the Franks moved in and gained control in

628. Under their feudal agrarian regime the town stagnated until the eleventh century, when the local **counts** (who were almost without exception named Raymond) began to encourage the nascent carpentry and leather industries. A century later a city council, or **Capitolo**, was set up to handle administration and justice and the wealthiest townsfolk – merchants and landholders – served as its members (the *capitoules*); the resulting convergence between their economic interests and political power allowed the city to flourish. Meanwhile, the counts – for all intents and purposes independent sovereigns – began to extend their influence over the other major families of the south, including the Trencavels (see p.117). By the late twelfth century they effectively controlled all of Languedoc, and adopted the surname of "St-Gillies", in honour of one of their favourite fiefs.

Both the counts and the city prospered until the reign of Raymond VI, by which time Cathar beliefs, considered heretical by the Church, had taken firm root in the region (see p.138). Raymond may or may not have been a Cathar himself, but was in any case content to let his subjects choose their religious beliefs, thus provoking the ire of the papacy and providing the northern French aristocracy with a justification for war against him. When their knights stormed into Languedoc on a campaign of religious and political conquest – the **Albigensian Crusade** – Toulouse fell to the forces, led by the cruel Simon de Montfort. Raymond, with the help of Catalan allies, recovered it in 1217, but it fell definitively under the power of the French Crown in 1271. One of the consequences of the Catholic takeover was the foundation of Toulouse's **university** early in the thirteenth century, which the strong presence of the Dominican Order helped make into the second most important theological centre in France after Paris.

Despite suffering grievously from a series of plagues, the city's prosperity soared with the booming woad **dye** industry in the 1400s (see box on p.99), and in the sixteenth century it became the official capital of Languedoc, although it later suffered – along with the whole of the south – as a result of the Wars of Religion, and as a consequence of the failed **revolt** against Cardinal Richelieu led by Henri de Montmorency (1595–1632), Governor of Languedoc. The Revolution of 1789, which the city fervently supported, heralded a new age of affluence as industry recovered and the Canal du Midi provided better market access for the agricultural hinterland. The good times were interrupted only by the Napoleonic Wars, during which the English general, Wellington, pursued the retreating Soult to the city in 1814; the French field marshal broke through the near encirclement, dealing the English a minor defeat before escaping towards the Montagne Noire.

German-occupied in World War II, Toulouse passed through the war more or less unscathed, and today the city is best known for its thriving **aerospace** industry, along with electronics and related hi-tech manufacturing. Home to Airbus Industries, the principal manufacturer of commercial airliners in Europe, this is where the successful A340 and A440 crafts, the first "fly-by-wire" (entirely electronically controlled) planes are assembled, and where plans are being made to launch a new two-level super-liner, bigger even than Boeing's largest Jumbo.

# Arrival, information and city transport

Toulouse's **airport** (*www.toulouse.aeroport.fr*) is located some 6km northwest of the centre in the suburb of Blagnac. As you'd expect it has better services than many regional airports, with banking and exchange facilities (including an automatic exchange dispenser), car rental offices (all the major companies), and a

## FESTIVALS IN AND AROUND TOULOUSE

Toulouse and the surrounding area isn't the best place to look for folk- or traditional festivals – for these you're better off heading for the uplands of Languedoc or the Pyrenees to the south. Toulouse's strength is the arts – its splendid galleries and museums are complemented by a series of music, dance and art festivals which bring in top-notch names from around the world. Where we haven't given contact details enquire at the tourist office (see below).

### February
**Feb 17** Dourgne: Fête Médiéval du Romarin. A one-day medieval pageant ostensibly to celebrate the herb rosemary, the symbol of the village, but in reality a typical but entertaining *terroir fête*, including music, dancing, sports competitions and, of course, a market of crafts and local produce.
**Feb and March** Toulouse: Festival Toulouse Bahia Danse. Acclaimed dance festival held annually since 1989, which in recent years has placed heavy emphasis on its international flavour, drawing groups from as far a field as South America and Asia. For programme information and list of venues contact Collectif Chorégraphes Midi-Pyrénées (CHOC; ☎05.61.39.17.39), or the tourist office.

### March
**Mid-March** Toulouse: Festival Irlandais. A festival of Irish music, theatre and dance leading up to the St

Patrick's Day festivities and featuring highly rated Irish performers. For information contact TILT, 27 rue Ste-Blanche, 31200 Toulouse (☎05.61.13. 20.08).
**Mid-March** Toulouse: Rencontres Cinémas d'Amérique Latine (☎05.62. 30.25.35, *arcalt@easynet.fr*). Long-running Toulousain eight-day film festival, with both feature-length and short productions ranging from documentary and drama to the experimental. Also colloquia and exhibitions, held in various venues around town.

**May** Toulouse: Hep, un Livre! A month-long book exhibition put on by seventy publishing houses from the Midi-Pyrénées region. Held in the place du Capitole.

### June and July
**Last week of June to start of July** Toulouse: Garonne! Le Festival (☎05. 61.25.96.93, *www.festival.garonne.org*).

small selection of shops and travel agencies, although it lacks a left luggage facility. A **shuttle bus** runs to the centre (every 20min; journey time 20min; 23F/€3.36; ticket can be bought from driver), making various stops in town, including the Compan-Caffarelli, place Jeanne d'Arc (near St-Sernin), place Jean-Jaurès (near place Wilson) and the *gare routière*. A taxi to the centre will normally cost around 100F/€15.25. **Trains** arrive at the grand old **Gare Matabiau** on boulevard Pierre-Sémard along the banks of the Canal du Midi – a twenty-minute walk northeast of the old town. The large station has a good café, but the left-luggage facility is still closed for security reasons. Any of the city buses which stop here will take you down to the boulevard Strasbourg (the ring road around the old town), while bus #2 will carry on through old Toulouse, passing rue de Metz and the Grand Rond; the place du Capitole is just two stops away from Matabiau on the metro. **Buses** pull in at the modern **gare routière** right beside the gare SNCF, which has an excellent information desk (Mon–Sat 7am–8pm). **Driving** into town, follow directions for the "Centre" and you will wind up on the A61 ring road – from this take

Massive festival of theatre, art, film and dance, attracting international artists. It has a different theme each year, and many exhibitions continue on into September.

**Throughout June and July** Toulouse: Festival Déodat-de-Séverac (☎05.61.83.01.83). Wednesday- and Thursday-night concert series at the church of St-Pierre-des-Cuisines, featuring works of or inspired by the celebrated nineteenth-century St-Félix-born composer.

**Throughout July** Toulouse: Musique d'Été. Eclectic programme of concerts held in the Couvent des Jacobins, Notre-Dame-de-la-Daurade and Zénith on Tuesday and Thursday nights, featuring a diversity of styles – from classical, to gospel and Flamenco.

**Throughout September** Toulouse: Piano aux Jacobins. Nightly recitals in the cloister of the Jacobins by pianists from around the world. For programme details, contact the Piano aux Jacobins, 61 rue de la Pomme, 31000 Toulouse (☎05.61.22.40.05).

**October**
**Throughout Oct** Toulouse: les Orgues (☎05.61.53.81.16, *www.toulouse-les-orgues .org*). Using some of the city's finest

antique organs, this music and choral series features Saturday and Sunday night concerts in the city's famous churches.

**Mid-Oct** Toulouse: Cinespaña (☎05.61. 12.12.20, *www.cine-espagne.com*). The city's newest festival (since 1999) brings in Spanish directors and actors for twelve days of screenings and awards.

**Mid-Oct to mid-Nov** Toulouse: Marionettissimo (☎05.61.49.63.41). Sixteen marionette companies from around the world are invited to the city to put on various puppet shows, not all of which are composed with children in mind.

**End-Oct** Toulouse: Jazz sur Son 31 (☎05.24.45.05.92). The world-class jazz festival of the Haute-Garonne *département* brings in the biggest and best names in jazz, blues and salsa. Past performers include Miles Davis, Chick Coréa and Sonny Rollins. Programme available early September.

**December**
**Dec 1–10** Toulouse: Sequence Court-Métrage (☎05.62.49.37.48). Ten-day programme and competition of short films. Screenings at various venues.

any one of exits 14–17 or 21–30. There are plenty of car parks, as well as metered street parking and free parking in place St-Sernin in the centre, place St-Auban east of the centre, and les allées Jules-Guesde south of the centre. For contact details regarding departures from Toulouse see "Listings", p.98.

The main **tourist office** (May–Sept Mon–Sat 9am–7pm, Sun 10am–1pm & 2–6.30pm; Oct–April Mon–Fri 9am–6pm, Sat 9am–12.30pm & 2–6pm, Sun 10am–12.30pm & 2–5pm; ☎05.61.11.02.22, fax 05.61.22.03.63, *www.Mairie-Toulouse.fr*) is housed in a restored medieval tower in place Charles-de-Gaulle, directly behind the Capitol building (metro Capitole). This large and efficient office can help make hotel reservations, sells tickets to many festivals and events, and organizes walking tours of the city.

The narrow streets of the old town necessarily make **walking** the best way to see Toulouse, and the Guide that follows has been written with this in mind. **Cycling** is also an option should you want to give your feet a break; you can rent both bikes and scooters at Rev'moto, 14 boulevard de la Gare (☎05.62.47.07.08), and the tourist office distributes a map of bike paths, although these are general-ly confined to the new part of the city. Additionally, there's a comprehensive bus and metro network, which covers Toulouse and outlying villages. Although more are planned, for the time being there is just one **metro** line, running from the northeast (via Gare Matabiau) to the new university campus in the southwest; for visitors it comes in handy for getting from the *gares* to the main hotel districts (metro Jean-Jaurès or Capitole), or over the river to see the Les Abattoirs (metro Cyprien-République). With the exception of getting to outlying sights, like the Cité de l'Espace or the campsite, Toulouse's **bus** network won't be of much use – it's also quite elaborate, so you'd do well to pick up a transport map, available at the SEMVAT **information office**, 7 place Esquirol (☎05.62.11.26.11; metro Esquirol), or at the tourist office and metro stations. **Tickets** serving both bus and metro are available from bus drivers, as well as at metro stations and tobac-conists; a single costs 8F/€1.22, a return 15F/€2.29, and you can also buy a day-pass for 34F/€5.18 or a ten-trip ticket for 64F/€9.76. The only problem with the city's public transport network is that it shuts down very early (by 9pm), and even the nightbus network, whose hub is the *gare*, winds up around midnight. If time is short and you want to see the highlights, **taxis** offer a special "taxi touristique" tariff: 150F/€22.88 for a one-hour circuit and 300F/€45.96 for a two-hour circuit of the town, for up to three people (see "Listings", p.98).

## Accommodation

Unless you are planning on staying in Toulouse for a lengthy period you will be more or less confined to choosing among the city's **hotels** – and there's no short-age of them, in every bracket of price and comfort. You'll find a whole cluster of establishments right around the station, which range from inexpensive to moder-ate, but have the disadvantage of being in a zone which is rather nondescript and far from the centre. Closer in, there are cheap options around place de Belfort, which is also a sort of red-light district. In the old town, the hotels concentrated around place Victor Hugo (just up from the Capitole and place Wilson) are an easy bet, again covering the gamut of possibilities.

There is no youth hostel as such, but there are a number of **accommodation centres**, primarily designed for students but also useful for visitors who plan on staying for more than a few days. Their facilities vary considerably: some provide dorm accommodation, others private rooms or self-catered shared suites. The local youth information centre, the CRIJ (Centre Régional d'Information de Jeunesse), 17 rue de Metz (Mon–Sat 10am–1pm & 2–7pm; ☎05.61.21.20.20) and the Club UNESCO Midi-Pyrénées, forum des Arènes (☎05.62.13.62.13, fax

---

### ACCOMMODATION PRICE CODES

All the hotels and guesthouses listed in this book have been price-coded according to the following scale. The prices quoted are for the cheapest available double room in high season.

| | | |
|---|---|---|
| ① Under 160F/€24 | ④ 300–400F/€46–61 | ⑦ 600–700F/€91–107 |
| ② 160–220F/€24–34 | ⑤ 400–500F/€61–76 | ⑧ 700–800F/€107–122 |
| ③ 220–300F/€34–46 | ⑥ 500–600F/€76–91 | ⑨ Over 800F/€122 |

05.62.13.62.14) can inform you about current availability. The only **campsite** close enough in to be of use is the well-outfitted *Camping de Rupé*, just a few kilometres north from the centre on chemin du Pont du Rupé (☎05.61.70.07.35; bus #59 from place Jeanne-d'Arc to "Rupé").

## Cheap hotels

**des Ambassadeurs**, 68 rue Bayard (☎05.61.62.65.84, fax 05.61.62.97.38). Very friendly little hotel run by a young couple, just down from the station. Its rooms all have TV, en-suite bath and phone – a surprisingly good deal given the price. ②.

**des Arts**, 1bis rue Cantegril (☎05.61.23.36.21, fax 05.61.12.22.37). On a corner diagonally opposite the Augustins museum, this is a top choice in the lower price range, with large, quirky rooms (some with a fireplace) in a superb old building. ①.

**Beausejour**, 4 rue Caffarelli (☎ & fax 05.61.62.77.59). Basic, but dirt cheap and with a great copper-balconied facade. This is the best of the hotels in this slightly dodgy but engagingly gritty neighbourhood around place de Belfort. ①.

**de la Bourse**, 11 rue Clemence-Isaure (☎05.61.21.55.86). Basic and a bit run-down, but a comfortable hotel tucked away in a small street in a quiet part of the old town. Run by a friendly older couple, and well located for the sights. ①.

**La Camarguais**, 9 bd de Bonrepos (☎05.61.62.58.09). Basic, clean and friendly, all rooms at this small hotel have shower, TV and phone. ②.

**Le Chartreuse**, 4bis bd Bonrepos (☎05.61.62.93.39, fax 05.61.62.58.17). Efficiently modern if soulless choice, right by the station. Great value, considering the amenities: each room has a private shower, toilet and TV. ②.

**Le Clochez de Rodez**, 14 pl de Jeanne-d'Arc (☎05.61.62.42.92, fax 05.61.62.68.99). Freshly decorated, comfortable and central, with secure parking. Despite its size, it exudes a very personal hospitality. Wheelchair accessible. ②.

**du Palais**, 4 allées Paul-Feuga (☎05.62.26.56.57, fax 05.62.26.47.87). An old, but friendly and well-kept one-star hotel located on the southern edge of the old town by the Pont St-Michel, with a decent restaurant and lively sports bar. Good access to the sights, but in a less frequented corner of the city. Reception closed Sun. ②.

**Wilson Square**, 12 rue d'Austerlitz (☎05.61.21.67.57, fax 05.61.21.16.23, *hotwilson@aol.com*). Clean and well-kept place at the top end of Austerlitz, with TV, AC and a lift. Also has a great *pâtisserie* on street level. ②.

## Moderate hotels

**Albert 1er**, 8 rue Rivals (☎05.61.21.17.91, fax 05.61.21.09.64). Set in a quiet side street just off the Capitole and close to the central market in place Victor-Hugo. A small, comfortable and good-value establishment. ③.

**Athénée**, 13bis rue de Matabiau (☎05.61.63.10.63, fax 05.61.63.87.80). This well-renovated hotel offers all mod cons, including TV, garage parking and a cocktail bar, amidst a carefully chosen contemporary décor. Quiet, despite its location between the station and the old town. Wheelchair accessible. ⑤.

**des Beaux-Arts**, 1 pl du pont-Neuf (☎05.34.45.42.42, fax 05.34.45.42.43, *hba@internetclub.fr*). Located in a 150-year-old building, this hotel's contemporary but refined interior contrasts well with its ageing facade, making for solid, old-world elegance. Each room is individually decorated and some have views of the Garonne. ⑤.

**Castellane**, 17 rue Castellane (☎05.61.62.18.82, fax 05.61.62.58.04). A cheerful new hotel with a wide selection of room types and sizes – most of which are bright and quiet. One of the few wheelchair-accessible hotels in this price range. ⑤.

**François 1er**, 4 rue d'Austerlitz (☎05.61.21.54.52, fax 05.61.22.88.25). Small but basic hotel near the main market. Clean and friendly, and makes up in price and location what it lacks in extras. Rooms have TV. Closed part Aug. ③.

**Grand Balcon**, 8 rue Romiguières (☎05.61.21.48.08, fax 05.61.21.59.98). Just off place du Capitole, this ageing classic was frequented by the aviation pioneers, such as St-Exupéry, who first established Toulouse as a capital of manned flight. It's now rather run-down, but definitely a good bargain, and smack in the centre of things. Closed most of Aug. ③.

**Ours Blanc**, 25 pl de Victor-Hugo (☎05.61.21.62.40, fax 05.61.23.62.34). Right by the covered market and steps from the Capitole, this welcoming hotel is one of the city's better bargains. The entire building has recently been renovated and each room has TV, air conditioning and telephone, as well as a private bath. ④.

**Phoenicia**, 7 bd Bonrepos (☎05.61.63.81.63, fax 05.61.63.02.06, *hotelphoenicia@visiopub.fr*). Weird retro-décor but good service and facilities in this three-star place just down from the *gares*. The staff are friendly, and it has a small cocktail bar on the main floor. ④.

**St-Sernin**, 2 rue St-Bernard (☎05.61.21.73.08, fax 05.61.22.24.96). Well-renovated old hotel in one of the best districts of the old town, around the basilica – close to all the action, but far enough away to provide peace in the evening. ④.

**Terminus**, 13 bd Bonrepos (☎05.61.62.44.78, fax 05.61.63.18.06). This old three-star stationside hotel has large, renovated rooms that make it worth the price, and there are special room prices for off-season weekends. Parking and buffet breakfast available (42F/€6.41), the only drawback being that the hotel is rather far from the sights. ④.

### Expensive hotels

**Grand Hôtel Capoul**, 13 pl Wilson (☎05.61.10.70.70, fax 05.61.21.96.70, *grand-hotel-capoul-sa@wanadoo.fr*). The best of the hotels on place Wilson, the *Capoul* combines elegance with warmth and contemporary design; it has all of the conveniences and amenities you'd expect and the staff are attendant, professional and friendly. ⑦.

**Grand Hôtel de l'Opéra**, 1 pl du Capitole (☎05.61.21.82.66, fax 05.61.23.41.04, *www.grand-hotel-opera.com*). The *grand dame* of Toulouse's hotels presides over the place du Capitole in the guise of a seventeenth-century convent. The rich décor, peppered with antiques and artwork, underlines the atmosphere of sophistication. Also has a fitness centre for working off that second helping of foie gras. ⑧.

**Mermoz**, 50 rue de Matabiau (☎05.61.63.04.04, fax 05.61.63.15.64). Immaculate, comfortable rooms in this 1930s Art Deco-style hotel close to the station. Also has wheelchair access and a parking garage. ⑥.

# The City

Toulouse's **old town**, straddling a curve in the River Garonne and hedged by a busy, roughly hexagon-shaped ring road (which marks the course of its former defensive walls), is where you'll find most of the city's points of interest. Its heart is the majestically broad **place du Capitole**, the town hall square near the northeastern edge, from which crooked streets radiate out, web-like, to a series of *places*. East from the place du Capitole is primarily a business district, where you'll find a great deal of the city's offices, hotels and restaurants. To the north, the area around the wonderful **Basilique de St-Sernin**, with the nearby archeological museum, forms the university quarter, while west of the Capitole towards the river lies the bulk of medieval Toulouse – major sights here include the Dominicans' **Les Jacobins** complex, plus a number of noteworthy churches: St-Pierre-des-Cuisines, Notre-Dame-de-la-Dalbade and Notre-Dame-de-la-Daurade. It is also home to most of the city's majestic Renaissance-era **hôtels particuliers** (private mansions), some of which, like the magnificent **Hôtel d'Assézat**, are now open as museums, but most simply worth seeing for their striking and varied facades. The city's shopping district, focused on rue d'Alsace-Lorraine and rue St-Rome, stretches south to intersect with rue de Metz, south of which again, after

### TOULOUSE MUSEUMS

The normal entrance fee for Toulouse's historical museums is 12F/€1.83, except for the first Sunday of each month, when it's free. You can also buy museum **passeports** for three or six visits (30F/€4.57 and 50F/€7.62 respectively) to the following museums: the Augustins, the Musée St-Raymond, the Musée Paul-Dupuy, the Musée Georges-Labit and the Jacobins.

the cathedral, a further series of *places* leads down to the formal gardens, the **Grand Rond** and **Jardin des Plantes** at the southeast corner of the old town. Beyond this, you'll find the town's canal port and a couple of small museums. Across the Garonne to the west, the neighbourhood of **St-Cyprien** is of interest for its comprehensive modern-art gallery, **Les Abattoirs**, while the only reason to visit the **suburbs** is to see two modern exhibitions revolving around the city's aeronautical tradition.

## Place du Capitole and place Wilson

**Place du Capitole**, the sweeping plaza containing Toulouse's historical seat of government, the **Capitole**, forms the administrative and civic hub of the city. Apart from when it fills up with market stalls on Wednesday and Sunday mornings, the *place* is a magnet for rollerbladers and host to a constant surge of pedestrian traffic –great for people-watching. Prettiest at sunset, when permeated by a pink glow reflected off the huge Capitole's brick, the square is best appreciated from one of the bank of cafés which line its western side – the perfect spot from which to contemplate the Neoclassical symmetry and elegance of the building's 130-metre-long facade. Deriving its name from the twelfth-century administration of the city (p.75), the palace dates back to the sixteenth century, although the frontage you see today was raised in the mid-eighteenth. In addition to its function as the centre of municipal government, it serves as home to its most prestigious opera and ballet venue (see p.97). There's not much to see in its cavernous seventeenth-century **foyer** (daily 9am–7pm; free), aside from a gallery of paintings extolling the glories of France and celebrating the execution of revolt-leader Montmorency, which took place in the square, but you can stroll through to place Charles-de-Gaulle on the other side of the palace. Sadly, this small patch of green, presided over by Viollet-le-Duc's (see p.123) restored late-medieval *donjon* – the only remnant of the original Capitole and now the tourist office – has become a haven for local junkies. Continuing east from here, along rue-la-Fayette, brings you to the oblong **place Wilson**, which, rimmed by modern, expensive hotels, retains a certain grandeur despite the traffic. Directly north of place Wilson is the lively triangle of streets centred on the town's main **indoor market** (Tues–Sun 6am–noon) in place Victor-Hugo. The market sells local agricultural produce, meat and fish, and the surrounding area is home to an array of cheapie hotels and restaurants, as well as some great places to pick up regional culinary goodies – look out for the Ducs de Gascogne delicatessen at 1 rue du Remparts Villeneuve, and the Chocolatier de Bayonne, next door. **Rue d'Alsace Lorraine**, the western boundary of the triangle, is Toulouse's principal shopping street, its towering nineteenth-century apartments for the most part converted into shops and office space. Nevertheless, the magnificent facades, with their monumental doorways, elaborately carved cornices and wrought-iron balconies still exude *fin-de-siècle* elegance.

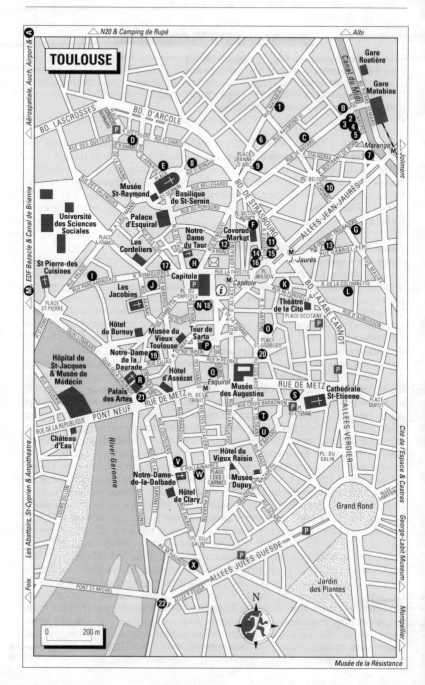

| ACCOMMODATION | | | | RESTAURANTS | | | |
|---|---|---|---|---|---|---|---|
| Albert 1er | 12 | François 1er | 15 | Asia Fast Food | B | Le Damas | W |
| des Ambassadeurs | 3 | Grand Balcon | 17 | Auberge Louis XIII | P | Flor au Lilles | V |
| des Arts | 20 | Grand Hôtel Capoul | 16 | La Bascule | X | Au Gascon | J |
| Athénée | 6 | Grand Hôtel de l'Opéra | 18 | Le Bistrot des Vins | S | Les Jardins de l'Ópera | N |
| Beausejour | 10 | Mermoz | 1 | Au Chat Deng | R | Maharaj | H |
| des Beaux-Arts | 21 | Ours Blanc | 14 | Le Chateaubriand | I | Michel Sarran | M |
| de la Bourse | 19 | du Palais | 22 | Chez Atilla | F | Au Pois Gourmand | A |
| La Camarguais | 4 | Phoenicia | 5 | Chez Émile | O | Saveurs Bio | K |
| Castellane | 13 | St-Sernin | 8 | Chez Fazoul | T | Le Sept Place St-Sernin | E |
| Le Chartreuse | 7 | Terminus | 2 | Le Colombier | C | Shun | G |
| Le Clochez de Rodez | 9 | Wilson Square | 11 | Cosi Fan Tutte | U | Taverna El Casa Manolo | D |
| | | | | La Crêperie du Moulleau | Q | Le Ver Luisant | L |

## North to the Basilique de St-Sernin and beyond

Leading north out of place du Capitole, rue de Taur is a street full of lively studenty cafés and shops, a reminder that Toulouse has long been a university city. Just along from the *place* is the church of **Notre-Dame du Taur**, the original resting place of St-Sernin, boasting a turreted facade; further up the street, you'll pass the sprawling sixteenth-century Palace d'Esquiral, now home to the city's main cinema and a meeting place for student literary groups.

This is just steps from the **Basilique de St-Sernin** (daily 8.30am–6.15pm; free), which, with its wedding-cake bell tower – an emblem of Toulouse – is arguably southern France's greatest Romanesque church and the largest of its style in Western Europe. Begun in 1080 to hold the remains of the city's first bishop, who was killed by the Romans in 250 AD – dragged to death by a bull (hence the name of the approaching street) – the church was an important stop on the pilgrimage to Santiago de Compostela. Despite the fact that the present building was not completed until the fourteenth century it has almost no Gothic elements, and it's this stylistic purity, combined with the sheer size of the construction, that makes it such a singular monument. The most striking feature of its exterior is the early twelfth-century **Miégeville door**, whose restrained but expressive biblical sculptures mark it as a product of the pivotal era in the evolution of medieval art. Inside, the uniform simplicity of the cavernous nave is impressive; the plain marble altar, which is still used today, was consecrated by Urban II in 1096. But the real attraction is the church's incredible collection of **reliquaries** (daily 10am–6pm; 10F/€1.53), which it amassed over the years under the patronage of kings and with the financial help gained through donations of Santiago-bound pilgrims. Set into the walls and chapels of the ambulatory and stored in the crypt below the altar, reposing in carved and gilded boxes, body parts of all of the major saints can be found here, including those of James the Greater, whose thirteenth-century painted effigy is decked out in pilgrim's garb. The crypt also contains some very good examples of fourteenth-century polychrome saints' **statues**.

On the other side of place St-Sernin, which is unfortunately used as a car park, is the small **Musée St-Raymond** (daily: June–Sept 10am–7pm; Oct–May 10am–6pm; 12F/€1.83), which holds the city's archeological finds. The best part of this collection is the prehistoric and Bronze Age section on the first floor, which includes not only the usual arrowheads and brooches, but a decent range of pre-Roman jewellery, weapons, and even chariot wheels. The Roman religious sculpture and third-century portraiture is also worth a mention. In the basement you'll find the remains of part of the city wall as well as the excavations of Roman and medieval cemeteries.

North from the *place*, up rue Gatien-Arnoult, there's a small but lively **African quarter** – Maghreb, in particular – you might want to venture into; the shops and restaurants of rue Trois Pilliers exude wafts of mint and parsley. Narrow rue Gramat, just before Trois Pilliers, is also worth a look – after a long campaign to convince the city, local artists were permitted in July 2000 to decorate the walls, cheering up the previously decrepit street with a series of colourful murals. From here, the concrete blight of Place Bernard marks the end of the old town and a dull zone of low-rent apartments and university buildings. It's better to turn back and follow a series of quiet neighbourhood squares: des Tiercerettes, St-Julien and Peyrou, each of which has a couple of small café-restaurants. From place du Peyrou, rue des Lois will take you back to the Capitole.

## Les Jacobins and west

The most colourful part of Toulouse's old town is found in the labyrinth of streets radiating west and south from the place du Capitole, and dominated by the former Dominican headquarters, known as **Les Jacobins** (daily 7am–7pm; 20F/€3.05, cloister only 14F/€2.14), tucked away off rue Lakanal. This was the first ever convent of St Dominic's Order of Preachers (the Dominicans), founded here in 1215 to combat the Cathar heresy. From its humble beginnings the Order quickly grew in power, soon taking charge over the Church's Holy Inquisition and exercising, for a time, a near monopoly over the bishoprics and universities of the medieval Latin West – this building is, in fact, Toulouse's original university, home of the Theology Faculty which the Dominicans established in order to strengthen Catholic orthodoxy. The cavernous **interior** of the church (free entry), through which you enter the complex, contains a single file of seven enormous supporting columns, from which a web of delicate interlacing ribs fan out across the vaulted ceiling. These ribs, still bearing their original painted pattern of red and black bands, contrast beautifully with the cream-coloured brick they support. In a modest gilt box under the grey marble altar in the centre of the nave rest the remains of **St Thomas Aquinas** (1225–74), the great Dominican philosopher who strove to introduce the thoughts of Aristotle into Catholic theology – there's still a pilgrimage here on his feast day (Jan 28). Leaving the church, you enter a low Gothic **cloister**, which, with its stubby and unadorned columns, is as sober in style as the Order that built it. In fact, the cloister isn't original, but the structures along its north side are – including the large **chapterhouse**, which also preserves its wall decoration, and the fourteenth-century **chapel of St-Antonin**, whose walls are graced by richly detailed period paintings. The old **refectory**, also accessed from the cloister, now houses high-quality temporary art exhibitions of a decidedly secular character.

From the north end of rue Lakanal, following rue Pargaminières will take you to the placid little **place St-Pierre** on the banks of the Garonne. There are a couple of small pubs here and, on its northern side, **St-Pierre-des-Cuisines** (Mon 10am–noon), an ancient church reputed to be the oldest building in southwest France, constructed over an interesting Gallo-Roman necropolis, accessed via the church's **crypt** (guided tour daily 11am; 12F/€1.83). The church was recently converted into a 400-seat concert hall.

Just west of the *place*, the languid **Canal de Brienne** leads away from the river through a nineteenth-century industrial area, where newly erected student apartment buildings abut old warehouses and cigarette factories. The River Garonne has been exploited for industrial purposes since grain mills were first set up here in the twelfth century. They became a symbol of the city's prosperity, which was at this time based on local wheat production, and achieved such renown that the sixteenth-century satirist Rabelais cited them as the most powerful in the world. In 1890 the **EDF Bazacle** (Mon–Fri 10am–noon & 2–6pm, Sat & Sun 2–7pm; free), a generating plant that powers up Toulouse to this day, was built on the banks at the former site of the mills, about a ten-minute walk from St-Pierre. It is an interesting complex, where you can see both the modern and the original turbines churning away, have a look at the cascading fish ladder, and take in local and international art exhibits, displayed in the station's main foyer (free).

Back at place St-Pierre, an old ironwork bridge still decked out with gaslight fixtures leads south over the Garonne. This is the most direct route to the Les Abattoirs art gallery in St-Cyprien (see p.90) – you can see the mammoth cupola of the St-Joseph hospital ahead. If you prefer to stay on this side of the river, your best bet is to climb down to the riverside promenade Henri-Martin, whose grassy verge will take you down towards the place de la Daurade.

## Place de la Daurade and around

A rare green space in the old town, **place de la Daurade** makes a great spot to take a break and loll by the riverside, or, should you wish to get on the river, is also the point from where boats depart on cruises (see "Listings", p.97). Across the Garonne you can see Toulouse's medieval hospital, the Hôtel-Dieu St-Jacques, with the stub of the old bridge still poking out from its walls, while on the flood banks above the square you'll find the city's oddest church, **Notre-Dame-de-la-Daurade** (opening times vary), a curious compound of disparate architectural styles. The church started out as a pagan temple and was then converted to Christian worship in the fifth century, but today's building, with its weighty Neoclassical facade, dates from the eighteenth. Entering the church through the modern parish hall tacked incongruously on the north side, you'll be met by a hive of painted Baroque busyness, with fields of trompe l'oeil held back by armies of cherubs, all presided over by a massive array of organ pipes. At the centre of it all sits the *Vierge noire*, a black Madonna reputedly empowered to cure ailments and bring good fortune to the unborn child, and still the object of popular pilgrimage even today, a fact attested to by the many devotional plaques fixed around the entrance. Next door, on quai de la Daurade, you'll find the **Palais des Artes**, now sadly abandoned except when used for temporary exhibitions (free), but possessing a typically nineteenth-century facade, which vainly attempts to immortalize a series of forgotten French artists.

Back in place de la Daurade, the *Café des Artistes* (see p.95) makes a handy refreshment stop before heading back up towards the Capitole. If you take this route keep an eye out for the sixteenth-century **Hôtel de Burnuy**, one of Toulouse's famed *hôtels particuliers* (see box on p.86), at the beginning of rue Gambetta. Although now incorporated into a school, you can still poke your head inside to have a look at its two luxurious courtyards. This was the home of Jean de Burnuy, the town's wealthiest woad merchant, who was, literally, rich enough to afford a king's ransom; he stood his fortune as security to pay for François I's release from captivity at the hands of the Hapsburgs, against whom he had fought in vain for the title of Holy Roman Emperor. Even when the palace is closed, its 1504 **facade** will draw your attention – the square windows are complemented by delicate Gothic details, while its cherub-topped main entrance completes the

## TOULOUSE MANSIONS

One of the hallmarks of Toulouse is its multitude of luxurious private mansions or **hôtels particuliers**, which are scattered throughout the old town. Built for the most part in the fifteenth and sixteenth centuries, they are testament to the tremendous prosperity which the town enjoyed at that time as a result of the *pastel* dye industry, which turned the local merchants and bankers into veritable princes (see box on p.99). The earliest mansions have some sections of timber and daub, but the majority are constructed from local brick, which – ageing badly – detracts somewhat from their majesty. This, however, is superseded by some wonderful **masonry**, the mansions' splendour tending to reside in their stone doorways and window frames, which were embellished with carved figures, statues, coats of arms and floral designs. Stone was relatively expensive here, so more masonry was a sign of greater wealth – indeed, the most opulent buildings have facades constructed entirely from stone. In later examples, you'll find Renaissance flourishes, imported from Italy to lighten the solid – but perhaps rather plain and chunky – medieval building style, and which can be distinguished by a movement towards greater symmetry and complexity of carving. Some of these "mature" *hôtels* have graceful **turrets**, built to reflect the status of the owner; only the chartered elite – those who were wealthy enough to serve as *capitoules* – could add a tower. The heady times of mansion-building, however, were not to last, and in the late sixteenth century declining *pastel* production precipitated the end of the woad-lords, and their magnificent homes fell into a gradual decay. Today they serve a variety of functions, including apartments, schools and museums.

strange stylistic mix. Stepping back from the building, you'll see its slender tower rising high above the street.

### Rue St-Rome and the Hôtel d'Assézat

A number of less grand but still intriguing sights can be found along the pedestrian promenade which heads straight south from the place du Capitole. This route starts with **rue St-Rome**, a busy shopping street lined with clothing stores and sandwich stands. The second street on the right after the *place* leads to the sixteenth-century **Hôtel du May**, built by a regent dean of the university's medical faculty, and now home to the **Musée du Vieux Toulouse** (June–Sept Mon–Sat 2–6pm; 12F/€1.83). One of the town's least ornate *hôtels* – with only a simple door decoration to boast – it is proof that even then academics were underpaid. Nor is the museum itself particularly stimulating, as its collection consists of items of purely local interest: ceramics, paintings of local grandees and nineteenth-century knick-knacks.

Back on rue St-Rome, opposite rue de Muy, you'll see an old Neoclassical bank building, dating from 1734, and behind it, at no. 4 rue Jules-Chalande you'll find another courtyard, whose small tower marks it as the home of a former *capitoule*. Rue Chalande itself leads into an eminently explorable warren of narrow streets punctuated by tiny, and wonderfully serene *places* – most of which have some sort of bar and a number of shops. Back on St-Rome, you can look down rue Tripière, where an old timber-and-brick **mansion** is studded with stone decorations in the form of rabbits (guided tours every 30min Wed 2.30–6pm; free). A little further south, rue St-Rome turns into rue des Changes, dominated by the three-storey **Tour de Sarta**, another former palace. The length of this old street is lined by

place Rouaix, bounded to the northeast by the town's impressive eighteenth-century Chamber of Commerce building. On the far side of this, you'll be back in place Esquirol, right at the Musée des Augustins.

## The Musée des Augustins

The former home of the city's powerful canons of the Augustinian Order now houses what was, until the opening of Les Abattoirs, Toulouse's largest and most important museum, the **Musée des Augustins** (Mon & Thurs–Sun 10am–6pm, Wed 10am–9pm; *www.augustins.org*; 12F/€1.83). Unless you are an aficionado of medieval sculpture, which dominates the collection, you may be surprised by the reputation the museum enjoys – but even if you are not, the quality of work here is undeniable and the building itself is well worth a look. An externally featureless fourteenth-century brick precinct, covering an area almost as big as the place du Capitole and dominated by a strikingly huge bell tower, the monastery was founded in 1309 on the authority of Pope Clement V and is a fine example of southern French Gothic style, with an extensive cloister and large chapterhouse surviving from the original construction. Its smaller Neoclassical cloister dates from the seventeenth century, and it also has an apparently medieval refectory, though this is, in fact, one of Viollet-le-Duc's dubious nineteenth-century reconstructions.

The museum's **collection** consists of two disparate sections: superb medieval sculpture and less remarkable eighteenth- and nineteenth-century painting. The former is made up of stone carvings – found in the course of excavations for the museum itself and from the ruins of local churches and cloisters – of exceptional quality, thanks to the wealth of the city's twelfth-century counts. The complex was only restored to its original size in the last thirty years, and in the course of these works, more medieval treasures were discovered and added to the displays. The main floor consists of a series of rooms and chapels opening out on to the cloister; these contain a substantial part of the sculpture collection, with pieces not just from France, but from as far afield as northern England. The star attraction here is the forest of Romanesque **columns** on the bottom floor of the refectory, found just off the cloister on the west side. Rescued from the ruins of the town's various churches, these were crafted by a school of Toulouse sculptors that throve under the patronage of the counts in the first half of the twelfth century, and their consummate skill is evident in the impressively carved capitals. Moving through the refectory, you can follow the development of the Toulouse school, as the elaborate vegetal forms of the 1120s to 1140s give way to busy narrative scenes in increasingly high relief as the century progresses and draws to a close. The last examples, many taken from the cathedral's destroyed cloister, are the most spectacular – wonderfully carved scenes centred around episodes such as the death of John the Baptist. From the refectory, a monumental staircase leads to the upper floor, which, along with the stifling third storey, contains a collection of largely unimpressive **paintings**, amassed by city counsellors of the post-Revolution period. On your way out, back on the ground floor, you'll walk past a series of grounded gargoyles set upright on the floor and apparently yawning, unimpressed by their surroundings.

From the museum head north up rue des Arts to place St-Georges, now packed with restaurants and either continue up the elegant rue St-Antoine, a narrower version of rue d'Alsace-Lorraine, to place Wilson or head northwest up rue de la Pomme to arrive back at the Capitole.

## St-Cyprien and Les Abattoirs

Although the old neighbourhood of **St-Cyprien** was also enclosed within the medieval city's defensive walls, its location on the west bank of the Garonne meant that it became marginalized. Home to tanners and butchers, professionals banned from the main town for sanitary reasons, since the Middle Ages it was also the home of Toulouse's hospitals, where the sick were kept in semi-quarantine. Thus, on this side of the river, you won't find the grand mansions of *capitouls* and merchants, but nondescript streets containing fairly ordinary houses. That said, you should not leave Toulouse without setting foot in St-Cyprien, if only to visit the splendid new modern art gallery, Les Abattoirs; and once you cross over there's a clutch of smaller museums which are also worth a look. Coming from the station or the old town, you can get to St-Cyprien by bus (#1 or #14) and metro ("St-Cyprien République" stop), but the best way to get there is to walk, which at the most leisurely pace should not take more than fifteen minutes.

Crossing the Pont Neuf at the western end of rue de Metz brings you over to the broad grassy bank of the Prairies des Filtres. On the left side of the bridge you'll see the **Château d'Eau** (Mon & Wed–Sun 2–7pm; 15F/€2.29), a former pumphouse, now a small photographic museum holding good quality monthly exhibitions. On the north side of the bridge is the old **hospital of St-Jacques**. Modern hospitals grew out of the hospices which cared for pilgrims en route to shrines like the Holy Land or Santiago, and which eventually took over the care of sick people in general. Toulouse, being on the pilgrim route and the site of a major university, was a pioneer in medieval medicine. In the plague-ridden centuries preceding the Revolution, the most contagious patients arrived at the hospital directly by boat, so as not to infect the town. Today, these buildings house the administrative offices for Toulouse's centralized medical services, as well as a small **Musée de Médécin** (Mon–Fri 5–7pm, Sat & Sun 1–7pm; free) with collections of surgical instruments and pharmaceutical equipment. Further along the riverbank you'll see the huge dome of the sixteenth-century **hospital of St-Joseph de la Grave**, which is still a working hospital. Hard-core philatelists will want to head over to the Centre Municipal de l'Affiche, a small **stamp museum** and resource centre (Mon–Fri 10am–noon & 2–6pm; free), nearby at 58 allée Charles-de-Fitte.

The main reason for visiting St-Cyprien – indeed a good reason for visiting Toulouse itself – is to see the contemporary art gallery, **Les Abattoirs** (Tues–Sun noon–8pm; 20F/€3 and 20–50F/€3–7.60 for special exhibitions; *www .lesabattoirs.org*) at 76 allées Charles-de-Fitte, the avenue which marks the precinct of the city's former western wall, just behind the great cupola dominating the river's left bank. This splendid new venue, opened in July 2000, is not only one of France's best contemporary art museums, but also an inspired piece of urban regeneration. The massive brick complex was constructed in 1828, and functioned as an abattoir until 1989, when environmental concerns forced it to close. The space itself is massive, with huge chambers perfectly suited to display even the largest canvases. Comprising over 2000 works by 130 artists, the collection covers everything from painting to multimedia exhibits. Most European and American schools are well represented, with the major post-war French movements, including Support-Surface, Art Brut and Figuration Libre, plus Italian and Spanish works, a particular strength. The most striking piece is undoubtedly Picasso's massive 14m-by-20m theatre backdrop, *The Stripping of the Minotaur in the Harlequin Suit*, painted in 1936 for Romain Rolland's *Le 14 Juillet* and towering over the lower gallery. Other avant-garde works which stand out are the untitled canvases of Tàpies and Barceló, Bettencourt's provocative mosaic *The Conversion of St Paul*, and a large collection of Dubuffet's paintings. The collection is so large and varied however – more unusual exhibits include a sculpture made up of transparent pipes into which you drop coins – that whatever your tastes you're unlikely to come away disappointed. The complex also includes libraries and a resource centre, interactive terminals on which you can manipulate digital images, and a fantastic children's play area. Behind the museum, the grassy Jardin Raymond IV stretches out towards the river, along an impressive section of the city's fourteenth-century **walls**.

## South of the old town

If you have the time and energy, the area south of the old town is also worth exploring. The district is marked off from old Toulouse by the wide Allées Jules-Guesde, the southernmost stretch of the former walls and site of an **antiques market** from Thursday to Sunday. On its northern side is the grassy Jardin Royal, while at its eastern end, a roundabout encircles the surprisingly tranquil **Grand Rond**, with its pretty flower-rimmed fountain (a favourite for wedding photographs). The town's main park, the formally styled **Jardin des Plantes** (daily 7.45am–dusk), can be entered through a large arch off Jules-Guesde. The park itself is a lively place, complete with kids' rides, ice-cream stands and an ersatz mountain and waterfall. At its southern end you'll find the **Monument à la Résistance** (Mon–Fri 10am–noon & 2–5pm; free), where you can enter a solemn stone commemorative chapel.

If this theme interests you, continue down allée des Demoiselles opposite the park; among the fading glory of the Art Deco mansions you'll come across plaques marking the spots where Resistance fighters were shot dead by the Germans in the street fighting of 1944. Finally, at no. 52, you'll arrive at the **Musée de la Résistance et de la Déportation** (Mon–Fri 2–6pm, Sat 2–5pm; free). Founded to mark the fiftieth anniversary of the liberation of Toulouse on June 19, 1944, this resource centre and museum commemorates through photos, artefacts and dioramas the life of the maquis, the plight of those living under occupation, and the crimes of the occupiers, including the massacre of the Forest of Bouconne. A ten-minute walk up the rue du Japon, just outside the museum's doors, you'll find something much more uplifting: the tiny mansion belonging to the traveller and collector, Georges Labit. This nineteenth-century pavilion is pure Orientalist fantasy, a Gilbert and Sullivanesque vision of the East, but the **museum** (Mon & Wed–Sun: July & Aug 10am–6pm; Sept–June 10am–5pm; 12F/€1.83) inside holds a small but incredibly varied collection of Asiatica, including Chinese artefacts going back to the tenth century, temple carvings from Northern India and two complete Samurai suits of armour. Just a stone's throw away, a canalside path leads up to the remains of old Canal du Midi port, **Port St-Saveur**, now being refitted as a modern pleasure port. From here it's a short walk north along boulevard Monplaisir back to the Grand Rond; incidentally, the towpath running parallel forms the first leg of the canalside bike and walking route from Toulouse to the Seuil de Naurouze (see p.112).

## The suburbs

A number of specific sights may tempt you to leave old Toulouse and its immediate environs and head for the suburbs. First among these is the **Cité de l'Espace** (daily: July & Aug 9.30am–7pm; Sept–June 9.30am–6pm; *www.cite-espace.com*; 69F/€10.52, children 49F/€7.47), east of the city centre by exit 17 of the *periphérique est* ring road. This is a massive high-tech science centre, with scores of exhibits on the theme of space and its exploration, including satellite communications, space probes, a real Ariadne rocket and, best of all, the opportunity to walk inside a mock-up of the MIR space station – fascinating, but absolutely chilling. Many of the exhibits are interactive and, though it's a bit on the pricey side, you could easily spend a half day here, especially if you've got children in tow. Unfortunately, getting there by public transport is a nuisance; the closest bus lines (#16 and #19, from place Esquirol and Gare Matabiau respectively) leave you a good twenty-minute walk north of the park.

Only slightly more down to earth is the tour of **Aérospatiale**'s assembly plant. In 1970 Toulouse became home to the French branch of the European conglomerate Airbus Industries, which manufactures passenger jets. The planes are assembled, painted and tested in a vast hanger, L'Usine Clément Ader, before taking their maiden flights from next-door Blagnac airport. After a brief bus tour round the site and a short PR film, you climb high above the eerily quiet assembly bays where just one hundred people churn out five planes a week, ably assisted by scores of computerized robots. **Guided tours** (Mon–Sat; 55F/€8.39) last approximately ninety minutes and must be booked well in advance (July & Aug contact the tourist office, Sept–June ring ☎05.61.18.06.01). The huge factory is in Colomiers, near the airport – the closest bus route is #64 (from metro Arènes), and the bus driver will direct you to the site.

The last attraction consists of the scant remains of Roman Toulouse's **amphitheatre**, constructed in the first century and used through to the end of the fourth. On site, you can also see vestiges of Roman baths and visit a small archeological centre. The site is about halfway to the airport, 5km downstream from the centre on the Garonne, on avenue des Arènes-Romaines and can be reached by buses #66 (from metro St-Cyprien to "Cautarets") or #70 (from place Jeanne-d'Arc to "Purpan").

# Eating and drinking

There's no shortage of good **eating** options in Toulouse. The city's ethnic mix has engendered a culinary cosmopolitanism, and for French cooking you'll find a multitude of choices in every category of style and price. Toulouse is also a city which loves its **cafés** and **bars** – not surprisingly, given that the population swells by almost a quarter with the annual inundation of university students. The establishments listed below are only a fraction of what's out there – whichever part of town you find yourself in, you're never far from a drink or a meal.

### Restaurants

There are several good areas for **restaurants**. Rue de la Colombette in the St-Aubin district, just across boulevard Carnot, has some attractive and fashionable choices. The area surrounding St-Sernin is particularly good: just north, place Arnaud-Bernard and the tiny adjacent place des Tiercerettes have attractive options; between the basilica and place Bernard there's a compact knot of Arabic and Maghrebi restaurants; and rue du Taur has a number of Vietnamese places and sandwich bars. Should you feel stuck to choose, you can always head south of place Wilson to place St-Georges, where you'll find a gaggle of typical terraced eateries.

If you're on a tight budget you can pick up **picnic supplies** in the Monoprix department store at 39 rue d'Alsace-Lorraine, or head from place du Capitole down rue St-Rome, where there's a string of inexpensive and good kebab and sandwich stands. The best lunch-time bargain is in the covered **market** on place Victor-Hugo (closed Mon), whose upper floor has a group of very cheap food counters.

## *CHEAP*

**Asia Fast Food**, 4 rue Bayard. If you want a quick bite on the way to the station, drop in to this cheerful, self-service cafeteria at the southern end of rue Bayard. Chinese, Vietnamese and Thai dishes at budget prices. Open till midnight.

**Auberge Louis XIII**, 1 rue Tripière (☎05.61.21.23.97). Good, uncomplicated home cooking with local dishes in generous portions, and a nice courtyard in the summer. Menus at 52F/€7.93, 70F/€10.68 and 86F/€13.12. Closed Sat & Sun.

**Le Bistrot des Vins**, 5 rue Riguepels (☎05.61.25.20.41). Situated on the north side of the cathedral, with modern décor inside, and pavement tables outside. An attractive, informal place with excellent grilled meats and a *plat du jour* at around 50F/€7.63, with, as the name suggests, a huge selection of wines. Closed Sun & Mon.

**Le Chateaubriand**, 42 rue Pargaminières. Named after the politician rather than the steak, this casual little restaurant serves an excellent cassoulet, made with flavourful *haricots Tarbais*, and scrumptious home-made desserts. Lunch menus from 50F/€7.63, or 100F/€15.25 for dinner. Closed Aug, Sat lunch & Sun.

**Chez Atilla**, in the market at pl Victor-Hugo. The best of the market restaurants, this no-nonsense lunch-time establishment is also one of Toulouse's best options for seafood – their Spanish zarzuela stew is a fish-lover's dream. Menus from 58F/€8.85. Closed Mon & part Aug.

**Le Colombier**, 14 rue Bayard (☎05.61.62.40.05). Cassoulet's the thing in this elegant restaurant, but there are other regional delights, such as *gésiers* ("gizzards") and foie gras, as well as seafood and game. Menus from 75F/€11.44. Closed Sat lunch & Sun.

**La Crêperie du Moulleau**, 11 rue de la Bourse. Good selection of generous-sized salads, main courses and dessert crêpes and other light fare for under 50F/€7.63.

**Le Damas**, 32 rue Pollainaires (☎05.61.55.01.40). Great Syrian/Moroccan restaurant with gold and red furnishings throughout. Wide selection of dishes, ranging from Moroccan-style *tajine* to home-made Syrian *kibbah* meatballs, and good vegetarian *plat* at 70F/€10.68.

**Maharaj**, 21 pl du Capitole. Good quality, but unsurprising, northern Indian cuisine in this busy place on the Capitole. Lunch-time specials from 59F/€9 and a ten percent discount for students.

**Taverna El Casa Manolo**, 24 rue de 3 Piliers(☎05.61.23.85.06). Lively Spanish *taverna* hidden away amongst the couscous places north of St-Sernin. Tapas for 30–40F/€4.58–6.10 and a massive two-person paella at 170F/€25.93. Closed Sun–Tues.

**Le Ver Luisant**, 41 rue de la Colombette (☎05.61.63.06.73). A bar and simple restaurant frequented by the arty set. The good food – mostly regional but with some cosmopolitan touches – is copious and the atmosphere fun. *Plat du jour* 35F/€5.34 at lunch time, or 80–150F/€12.20–22.88 for an evening meal. Closed Sat lunch & Sun.

## *MODERATE*

**La Bascule**, 14 av Maurice-Hauriou (☎05.61.52.09.51). A Toulouse institution. Its chromy interior is pure Art Deco and the food well preprared and presented. The menu includes regional dishes like cassoulet, *foie de canard* and oysters from the Bay of Arcachon. Menus from around 120F/€18.30. Closed Sun eve & Mon eve.

**Au Chat Deng**, 37 rue Peyrolières. Small, hip bistro with cool blue décor across from the *Petit Voisin* bar. The selection is not overly imaginative, with a sold southern French base and occasional Italian incursions (usually in the form of pasta). Menus from 85F/€12.96, but considerably more à la carte. Closed Sun.

**Chez Fazoul**, 2 rue Tolosane (☎05.61.53.72.09). Welcoming restaurant serving local dishes in its pleasant, brick-walled dining room. Menus, featuring all the usual suspects: steak, cassoulet, *confits* and *cépes*, at 65–170F/€9.91–25.43. Closed Sun.

**Cosi Fan Tutte**, 8 rue Mage (☎05.61.53.07.24). Great stylish Italian place with a richly garish red décor. Ordering à la carte is considerably more expensive than the 70F/€10.68 daily specials.

**Flor au Lilles**, 2 rue H.-de-Grosse. Cosy little *terroir* restaurant, housed in a small but atmospheric old building, complete with wooden beams, by the entrance to the Dalbade church. One of the two tiny dining areas has a fireplace. Evening menu from 145F/€22.11.

**Au Gascon**, 9 rue des Jacobins (☎05.61.21.67.16). Popular restaurant on the corner of rue Mirepoix serving hearty Gascon fare, with duck featuring strongly. Good portions and reasonable prices mean you need to get here early, or book ahead. Menus from 59F/€9 at lunch time, or 128F/€19.52 in the evenings. Oct–May closed Sun lunch time.

**Saveurs Bio**, 22 rue Maurice-Fonvielle (☎05.61.12.15.15). Toulouse's best vegetarian place, offering everything from spinach quiche to alfalfa salads, and with various set meals for under 100F/€15.25. Closed Sat eve & Sun.

**Le Sept Place St-Sernin**, 7 pl St-Sernin (☎05.62.30.05.30). A small house behind the basilica conceals a lively and cheerful restaurant which serves inventive and original cuisine with a constantly changing *carte*, followed by dazzling desserts. Menus from 95–195F/€14.49–29.74. Closed Sun.

**Shun**, 35 rue Bachelier (☎05.61.99.39.20). Surprisingly well priced Japanese restaurant at the north end of the St-Aubin district. Basic menus at 80F/€12.20 but plan on spending more. Closed Mon.

### *EXPENSIVE*

**Chez Émile**, 13 pl St-Georges (☎05.61.21.05.56). One of Toulouse's best, and well situated on this busy oblong square. Regional cuisine downstairs and seafood upstairs, at 105–250F/€16.01–38.13 on the menu. Closed Sun & Mon.

**Les Jardins de l'Ópera**, 1 pl du Capitole (☎05.61.23.07.76). The *Grand Hôtel*'s restaurant is Toulouse's best and most luxurious. If you fancy a splurge this is the place to do it – the food is outstanding – but you will pay for it: a basic menu starts at 220F/€33.55. Closed Sun & part Aug.

**Michel Sarran**, 21 bd Armand-Duportal (☎05.61.12.32.32). Justifiably renowned *gastronomique* restaurant, a fifteen-minute walk from the place du Capitole (follow rue des Lois and rue des Salenques to the end, and turn left). Imaginative dishes with a strong Mediterranean streak are served with style and warmth. Menus from 240F/€36.60. Closed part Aug.

**Au Pois Gourmand**, 3 rue Émile Heybrard (☎05.61.31.95.95) Great location in a riverside nineteenth-century house. The quality French cuisine does not come cheap here (lunch 130F/€19.83, dinner from 185F/€28.21), but is of a predictably high standard, and the *carte* presents a pleasant departure from purely regional dishes. Bus #66 or #14 from metro St-Cyprien-République. Closed Sat lunch & Sun.

## Cafés and bars

Many establishments cater to a mellow coffee and beer clientele during the day and put on the music after 10pm. Regular daytime café-lounging can be pursued around the popular student/arty hangout of place Arnaud-Bernard, while place du Capitole is the early evening meeting-place. Place St-Georges has been somewhat inundated by restaurant terraces but remains another option, while the more elegant terraces of place Wilson are good if you don't mind the traffic.

**Bagdam Café**, 4 rue de la Croix (☎05.61.99.03.62). Catering for women only, with readings, music and drama as well as coffee, drinks and food. Tues–Sat from 7pm. Closed mid-Aug to mid-Sept.

**Bapz**, 13 rue de la Bourse. English-style bakery and tearoom – definitely not your typical "caff", with good breakfasts and snacks. Smart service (and prices).

**Bibent**, 5 pl du Capitole. On the south side of the square, this is Toulouse's most distinguished café, with exuberant plasterwork, marble tables and cascading chandeliers.

**Le Café des Artistes**, pl de la Daurade. Lively, young café overlooking the Garonne. A perfect spot to watch the sun set on warm summer evenings, as floodlights pick out the brick buildings along the quays.

**Le Donjon Bar**, 2 rue du Poids de l'Huile. Tiny bar on the south side of the Capitole building. Impossibly crowded but great fun for watching rugby or having a drink. Open until 2am. Closed Sun.

**Dubliners Irish Pub**, 15 av Crampel. Toulouse's biggest Irish pub. Few surprises. Open until 2am. Closed Sun.

**Le Florida**, 12 pl du Capitole. Relaxed café with a nicely retro air. One of the most pleasant places to hang out on the central square.

**The Frog and Rosbif**, 14 rue de l'Industrie. Stop by this friendly British pub, just off bd Lazare-Carnot, for a pint of Darktagnan stout, or one of their other excellent home-brews. Quiz nights, football and fish and chips draw a surprisingly international crowd. Open until 2am, Sat until 4am. Closed part Aug.

**Bar Gambetta**, 39 rue Gambetta. Quirky place with a long bar and a vaguely 1950s feel, just off the place du Capitole. Closed Sun.

**Jour de Fête**, 43 rue de Taur. Funky tearoom and brasserie with a small street-side patio. Friendly service and a young studenty crowd. Open until 2am Fri & Sat.

**Bar du Matin**, 16 pl des Carmes. Great old street-corner bar in the finest beer, peanuts and pastis tradition. A friendly and deservedly popular place. Closed Sun.

**Au Père Louis**, 45 rue des Tourneurs (☎05.61.21.33.45). A lively, old-fashioned bar with *chansons* and music some nights. Open till 10pm. Closed Sun.

**St-Philipe**, 19 rue Arnaud-Bernard. Just off of place Bernard to the north of the St-Sernin, on the edge of the Maghribi neighbourhood, this bar attracts a mixed crowd of locals, students and business people. There's a pool table, *foozball* and video games to keep you busy over your beer.

**Le Scot'tea**, 35 rue du Taur. Easy-going café-bar-brasserie which attracts a young, laid-back crowd. Friendly place and you can amuse yourself reading or with their collection of board games.

**Le Thé l'Ollier**, 10 rue Perchapinte. This chilled café makes the perfect break from antique-shopping around the cathedral, or if you just fancy a read to the relaxing sound of the fountain in the *place*. Also does light snacks.

**Au Trait d'Union**, 12 rue des Gestes. Funky tea-house and art gallery down a small street just off the place du Capitole. Closed Sun & Mon.

# Nightlife

The annual influx of university students ensures that the city's **nightlife** is active, sustaining a whole range of **music-bars** and **clubs**; if the French are not famous for exuberant partying, Toulouse helps belie the stereotype. Things slow down from July to September, when the academic year breaks, but even in the summer you will have no trouble keeping yourself drinking and dancing as late as you like. Unfortunately some of the city's best venues lie in the suburbs, which basically condemns you to paying for a taxi. However, as the list below shows, there's no shortage of options closer to the old town. Entrance fees to discos and clubs may be charged depending on the night and event, but generally in these places you're expected to buy a rather expensive drink (40–50F/€6–7.50), while at venues which are essentially bars you can enter free of charge.

## Music-bars and clubs

**L'Ambassade**, 22 bd de la Gare. Downbeat club where funk and soul rule. Live jazz on Sunday nights. Open until 2am, Sat 5am. Closed Sun.

**Arc en Ciel**, 34 rue Teinturiers. One of Toulouse's best small venues for live rock music. Tues–Sat 9pm–2am.

**Le Bikini**, 55 chemin des Ètroits, rte de Lacroix-Falgarde. On the city's southern outskirts, this is *the* hangout of Toulouse rockers, and a prime venue for live gigs. Typical entry charge is 20F/€3.05, including free drink. Open Thurs–Sun.

**Bodega-Bodega**, 1 rue Gabriel-Péri. The old *Telegraph* newspaper building makes a superb venue for this bar-restaurant, with its hugely popular disco after 10pm. Daily until 2am, Sat 4am.

**Café Classico**, 37 rue des Filatiers. Trendy, designer-ish establishment that's a café by day and music-bar by night. House, hip-hop and jungle. Daily until 1am, Sat 4am.

**Le Chat d'Oc**, 7 rue de Metz. Hip bar near the Garonne. Attracts a mixed crowd which gets younger as the night progress. Nightly *animations* include DJs and occasional live acts, with themes from grunge to Goth. Open until 2am, Sat 5am. Closed Sun.

**Erich Coffie**, 9 rue Joseph-Vié. Just west of the river in the quartier St-Cyprien, this is one of the city's liveliest and most enjoyable music-bars, with an eclectic music policy. There's food available and live bands most evenings. Open Tues–Sat from 10pm.

**Le Griot**, 3 rue Amélie. Massive super-bar and concert hall, with dance floors, videos, pool room and restaurant. Happy hours 7–8pm & 10–11pm. Daily until 2am.

**Le Klub**, 2bis rue Delpech. Large club with two dance floors and a changing repertoire. Open until 5am, closed Mon. No admission fee.

**Hey Joe**, pl Héralcès. Popular disco with theme nights on Thursdays. Men pay 50F/€7.63, women get in free; happy hour is from midnight to 1am. Daily 11pm–5am.

**José – fait jeter les Watts**, 11 pl des Puits Clos. Popular with the grunge set this bar has a good patio by day and DJs by night. Open until 2am, closed Sun.

**Le Petit Voisin**, 37 rue Peyrolières. A neighbourhood place, just like the name, "the little neighbour", says. Laid back during the day when workers and businessmen stop for a drink, and livelier at night, when it fills with a student crowd. Open until 2am, Sat 4am. Closed Sun & mid-Aug.

**Puerto Habana**, 12 port St-Etienne. Toulouse's hottest salsa venue, in a superb setting beside the Canal du Midi. Also has an excellent restaurant and a house band Thurs–Sat. Mon–Fri until 2am, Sat till 5am.

**Le Rex**, 15 av Honoré-Serres. Located in an old converted cinema building, just north of the old town, this bar/concert hall usually features ska and punk acts. Opening hours vary so check with the local entertainment magazines for concerts and events.

**Theleme, l'Abbaye**, 41 rue Paradoux. Friendly bohemian refuge where customers and staff play guitar or piano in impromptu recitals. Fine wines and a few light snacks are on offer. Occasional literary nights. Open till midnight, closed Tues.

**L'Ubu**, 16 rue St-Rome. Long-standing pillar of the city's dance scene, that remains as popular as ever. Mon–Sat 11pm till dawn.

# Entertainment and festivals

Drinking and dancing aside, there's still plenty to do in Toulouse. Several **cinemas** regularly offer v.o. showings, including ABC, 13 rue St-Bernard

(☎05.61.29.81.00), Cinémathèque, 68 rue de Taur (☎05.62.30.30.10), and Utopia, 24 rue Montardy (☎05.61.23.66.20). The city also has an extremely vibrant **theatre** culture. The official Théâtre de la Cité, 1 rue Pierre-Baudis (☎05.34.45.05.05, *www.tnt-cite.com*) is home to the Théâtre National de Toulouse Midi-Pyrénées, which has a narrative theatre programme livened up by occasional dance performances, while the workshop Nouveau Théâtre Jules-Julien (6 av des Écoles-Jules-Juliens; ☎05.61.25.79.92) has a reputation for staging provocative drama, with a particular emphasis on Absurdist productions. The large venue Odyssud (4 av du Parc Blagnac; ☎05.61.71.75.15; bus #66) features both theatre and **opera**, but the place to head for exclusively for the latter, as well as **ballet** and **contemporary dance** performances, is the Théâtre du Capitole, housed in the Capitole building (☎05.61.63.13.13, *www.theatre-du-capitole.org*), a highly acclaimed venue where you can also hear recitals and chamber music. **Classical music** fans also have the Orchestre National du Capitole, with its base in the Halle aux Grains in place Dupuy (☎05.61.99.78.00, *www.onct .mairie-toulouse.fr*). The city's biggest **rock music** venue, with 9000 seats, is Zénith at 11 avenue Raymond Badiou (☎05.62.74.49.49; metro Arènes), which features both French and foreign groups, including visiting jazz and blues performers, while for something a little less energetic Cave-Poesie (71 rue de Taur; ☎05.61.23.62.00) is home to various **literary workshops** and gatherings of a decidedly bohemian spirit.

Toulouse's **festivals** calendar is packed out, with a virtually back-to-back programme of artistic, musical or literary events throughout the year. For a full rundown of these see the box on p.76. To get the most up-to-date **information** on the latest cultural events check the weekly magazines *Toulouse Hebdo* (3F/€0.46) or *Flash* (6F/€0.92), which have detailed concert and event listings and are available in newsstands, or Books and Mermaides' monthly *Doings in Toulouse*, an English-language info-mag (4.50F/€0.69). The monthly *Ramdam* (12F/€1.83) has listings for the whole region of Midi-Pyrénées.

## Listings

**Airlines** Air France (☎08.02.80.28.02); American Airlines (☎05.61.12.62.02); British Airways (☎08.02.80.29.02); Continental (☎05.61.99.12.76); Ryanair (☎04.68.71.96.65).

**Airport** Aéroport Toulouse-Blagnac (☎05.61.42.44.00, *www.toulouse.airport.fr*); for shuttle bus infirmation (☎05.34.60.64.00).

**Banks and exchange** Most major French banks have offices and ATMs around the place du Capitole. The Banque de France is at 4 rue Deville (Mon–Fri 9am–12.20pm & 1.20–3.30pm). For bureaux de change Banque Populaire Toulouse Pyrénées has an office at the airport (Mon–Fri 8am–7pm, Sat 10am–noon & 1.30–6pm) and C2E Capitole Exchange is in the centre at 30 rue du Taur (June–Aug Mon–Sat 9am–7pm; Sept–May Mon–Sat 9am–12.30pm & 2–6pm).

**Bike rental** Serious cyclists planning a longer trip may want to contact the Association Vélo, 2 rue de la Daurade, 31000 Toulouse (☎05.61.11.87.09, *www.multimania.com/velotlse*).

**Boat trips** Various outfits offer tours on the Garonne and the canals du Midi and de Brienne. Le Capitole has several daily departures for a ninety-minute journey on the Garonne (departs pl de la Daurade; reserve at the tourist office; 50F/€7.63). The Cap d'Ambre has one daily departure (Jan–Oct 2.30pm; 80F/€12.20) for a ninety-minute cruise on the Brienne and Garonne, leaving from the Porte de l'Embouchure (bus #16 or #70 to "Ponts Jumeaux"; must call first to reserve on ☎05.61.71.45.95). Alternatively you can rent an electric boat and buzz around yourself: Société AQUALUB (☎06.86.71.33.46) has its fleet moored at Port St-Saveur, southeast from the Grand Rond at the end of allée des Soupirs.

**Books** The best general bookstores are Castéla, on place du Capitole, and FNAC, at 16 allées F-Roosevelt. Toulouse Presse, 60 rue Bayard, stocks a good range of IGN maps and guides while Ombres-Blanches on 50 rue Gambetta is another good choice for travel literature. For English-language books, Books and Mermaides, 3 rue Mirepoix, specializes in secondhand tomes and will exchange, while The Bookshop, 17 rue Lakanal, stocks new titles. There are book markets on Thursday mornings in place Arnaud-Bernard, and all day Saturday in place St-Etienne.

**Bus departures** *Gare routière* (information booth Mon–Fri 8.30am–4pm; ☎05.61.61.67.67) beside the gare SNCF.

**Car rental** A2L, 81 bd Déodat-de-Séverac (☎05.61.59.33.99); Avis, gare SNCF (☎05.61.63.71.71); Budget, 49 rue Bayard (☎05.61.63.18.18); Europcar, 15 bd Bonrepos (☎05.61.62.52.89); Hertz, gare SNCF (☎05.61.62.94.12).

**Consulates** Britain, c/o Lucas Aerospace, 20 chemin de la Porte (☎05.61.15.02.02); Canada, 30 bd de Strasbourg (☎05.61.99.30.16); USA, 25 allées Jean-Jaurés (☎05.34.31.36.50).

**Gay and lesbian** For information contact the gay and lesbian students' group Jules et Julies (Comité des Étudiants, Université du Mirail, 5 Allée Machado, 31058) or Gais et Lesbiennes en Marche (☎06.11.87.38.81, *gelem@altern.org*).

**Hospitals** There are two major hospitals, both outside the A61 ring road: CHR Ranguiel, chemin du Vallon (☎05.61.32.25.33) to the south, and CHR Purpan, pl du Dr Baylac (☎05.61.77.22.33) to the west.

**Internet access** Cybermedia, 10 rue de la Colombette (Mon 2–8pm, Tues–Sat 10am–8pm; ☎05.62.73.40.37), or @fterbug, 12 pl St-Sernin (Mon–Fri noon–2am, Sat noon–5am, Sun 2–10pm; *afterbug@free.fr*). Aside from these, the CRIJ office at 17 rue de Metz has a free terminal, and you can also get online at the main post office, and at Telecom France kiosks at 11 rue Alsace-Lorraine and 18 place Wilson.

**Language courses** Alliance Française, 9 pl du Capitole (☎05.34.45.26.10), and Maison de l'Europe, 21 pl St-Sernin (☎05.61.54.11.6930) both run French-language courses.

**Laundry** Lavomat, 20 rue Arnaud-Bernard (daily 7am–10pm), and Lavaria Auto, 7 rue Mirepoix (daily 7am–9pm).

**Markets** Antiques in place St-Sernin and allées Jules-Guesde (Thurs–Sun 8am–4pm). Produce and clothes in place du Capitole (Wed & Sun 8am–1pm). There is also a mammoth food and clothing market on Sundays and Mondays along boulevard Strasbourg (beware if driving). And more produce markets at places des Carmes, St-Cyprien and Victor-Hugo (all Tues–Sun).

**Pharmacy** There are pharmacies in the place du Capital and dotted throughout the city. The Pharmacie de Nuit, 17 rue de Remusat is open until 8pm.

**Police** 23 bd de l'Embouchure (☎05.61.12.77.77).

**Rugby** Toulouse is a centre of excellence for French rugby – many players in the national team hail from these parts. You can see their first-rate Stade Toulousain team in action at their stadium at 114 rue de Troenes (☎05.61.57.05.05; bus #16 to "Stade").

**Swimming** There are several public pools in town. Alfred Nakache is open year-round (allées Paul-Bienes; ☎05.61.22.31.35).

**Taxis** Allo Association Taxi (05.62.16.26.16); Capitole (☎05.34.25.02.50); Taxi Radio Toulousain (☎05.61.42.38.38). For taxis to the airport call ☎05.61.30.02.54.

**Train departures** Tickets can be bought at the gare SNCF, or at the SEMVAT building, 7 pl Esquirol (Mon–Fri 2–6pm). Information on ☎05.61.10.11.04.

**Travel agencies** USIT Voyages (*www.usitconnect.fr*) has branches at 16 rue Pierre-Paul Riquet (☎05.61.99.38.47) and 5 rue de Lois (☎05.61.11.52.42); Nouvelles Frontières is in 2 pl St-Sernin (☎08.03.33.33.33).

# Around Toulouse

Predominantly flat, and ribbed by a multitude of small streams, the hinterland fanning out to the north and east of Toulouse has long been the source of the city's wealth. The woad boom of the fifteenth and sixteenth centuries may have powered its prosperous golden age, but the cereal farming carried out in this immensely fertile region has been Toulouse's traditional financial mainstay. Field after field of wheat dominates the rolling landscape, cut across by narrow bands of wood, and dotted by the church steeples of modest, introverted hamlets – havens of determined rural existence where elderly farmers speak French with a permanently round Occitan accent. The region is hedged to the north by the River Agout and to the west by the rising peaks of the Montagne Noire (see Chapter 3), but is most notable for its southern boundary, the remarkable waterway of the Canal du Midi.

The northern stretch of the region, known as the *pays de Cocagne* (see box below) is dominated by **Lavaur**, with its beautifully preserved old town, which was once a stalwart Cathar centre. On either side of this, a series of quiet hamlets, **St-Sulpice**, **Giroussens**, **St-Paul** and **Damiette** line the Agout, crossing it with narrow old trestle bridges. The easternmost town in the area, sitting on the edge of the Parc du Haut Languedoc, is the old *bastide* of **Revel**, with its medieval covered marketplace. Just south of here, at **St-Ferreol**, you'll find part of the incredible catchment system of the Canal du Midi, while just to the northeast,

## THE WOAD TO RICHES

From the mid-fifteenth to the mid-sixteenth century Toulouse and Albi experienced an unprecedented wave of prosperity, based on the humble **woad** plant (*Isatis tinctoria* or in French, *pastel*). When craftsmen in Albi discovered that the innocuous weed, which was used for medicinal purposes across the Mediterranean, yielded a rich blue dye, they knew they were on to a good thing; blue was one of the colours for clothing most in demand by the growing middle class, and up to that point it could only be produced from rare and expensive raw materials. With capital from Toulouse, intensive woad cultivation operations were set up across the Lauragais, which had ideal soil and climate conditions for the plant. Once the woad had been harvested, the process of dye production lasted approximately four months, during which the leaves were picked, crushed and rolled into balls (*coques*) and left to ferment for two weeks, whereafter the sticky dye could be pressed out and rolled into balls (*cocagnes*). Demand from textile manufacturers across Europe brought staggering wealth to the region, which became know in common parlance as the **pays de Cocagne** (a play on words, also meaning "the land of plenty"). The woad merchants, many of whom became *capitoules* of Toulouse, erected fine mansions, the *hôtels particuliers*, which even today bear witness to their former wealth. By the late sixteenth century, however, *pastel* began to be superseded by cheaper indigo-based dyes brought over to Europe from the Indies, and production went into decline – the violent upheavals of the Wars of Religion, ravaging fields and interrupting transport, provided the final blow, and the dye, along with the incredible affluence it generated, became a thing of the past.

**Sorèze** and **Dourgne** embody the past and present of the monastic traditions of the Benedictines and their heirs. The flat Lauragais district stretches southwest of Revel: **St-Félix** is its prettiest town, but **Castelnaudary** – the area's capital – contains a surprising number of monuments and mansions. More significantly, it is also the main town on this stretch of the **Canal du Midi**, the engineering marvel constructed in the seventeenth century to link the Mediterranean and the Atlantic, and now a favourite with boating enthusiasts and cyclists.

## Lavaur and around

Thirty-seven kilometres east of Toulouse, **LAVAUR** is the biggest town on the Agout west of Castres, and the traditional capital of the surrounding *pays de Cocagne*. It's also a key town in the history of Catharism, the twelfth-century heretical movement (see box on p.138). Seat of a Cathar bishop, the "citadel of Satan" – as it was known to Catholic forces – was besieged twice by the northern French aristocracy. It resisted in 1181, but when the violent leader of the papal military, Simon de Montfort, arrived in March 1211, he meant business. After nearly two months of encirclement the walls were breached, and the town taken – with bloody consequences: Guiraude de Laurac, widow of the town's lord and leader of the defence, was thrown down a well and pelted with stones; her brother, along with nearly a hundred knights, was put to the sword; and some four hundred Cathars were burnt at the stake. Despite such brutality the heresy persisted, prompting the papacy and crown to establish a series of religious foundations here, starting with a Dominican house to run the local Inquisition and finally, in the fourteenth century, a cathedral. In the sixteenth century the town was a Huguenot hotbed, pitting itself once more against the Catholic establishment and the seigniorial powers of the North. Nevertheless it prospered, profiting first from the lucrative woad industry and, later, silk manufacture. Today Lavaur is an attractive if quiet rural centre, surrounded by the wheat fields of the Agout valley.

The town's main landmark, the brick-built former **cathedral** of St-Alain, stands on a wide plaza above the river. The present structure was built in 1254, replacing that destroyed by the Crusaders, and although the interior has been given a hideous nineteenth-century remodelling, the exterior does hold a few surprises. These include a wooden door on the south side, which survives from the original pre-Crusade building, a highly stylized fifteenth-century doorway and an incredible mechanical clock, perched high above the ground in one of its two towers. This *jacquemart* – a clock which strikes using a mechanical figure in the form of a soldier wielding a hammer – dates back to 1523. Looking across the river from the plaza, you'll be treated to a vista of old mansions set in the fields along its banks, while heading southwest from the cathedral entrance a series of signs leads you on a pleasant stroll past the highlights of the town. Chief among these is the fourteenth-century **church of St-François**, dedicated to St Francis of Assisi, founder of the Franciscans, the first group established to preach against heretics and the Dominicans' great rivals, who also came here to rehabilitate the Cathar population. Set in the town's old main street, the Grand Rue, this church has weathered the centuries, losing its cloister and other appendages to Huguenots and revolutionaries. Nevertheless the graceful simplicity of its single nave and surviving columns make it worth a look. In the adjoining **garden** keep an eye out for the old dovecote, one of the first along the route des Colombiers (see p.102). Nearby, the **church of the Cordeliers**, built in the years immediately following the Crusade, also merits a visit for its elegant Gothic interior. As you walk around the town you'll find that there are quite a number of timber-and-brick houses, many dating from the fourteenth to sixteenth centuries; there may be no major sights in Lavaur, but the narrow old streets make for a pleasantly atmospheric whole. Finishing up, the circuit through the old town leads back towards the cathedral, passing the eighteenth-century Neoclassical *mairie*, which houses the local historical and archeological museum, the Musée du Pays Vaurais, under indefinite renovation at the time of writing.

## Practicalities

Trains and buses stop at Lavaur's **gare SNCF**, located northeast of the old quarter on the place de Stalingrad. From here it's a fifteen-minute walk to the **tourist office** (Mon & Sun 3–6.30pm, Tues–Sat 9.30am–noon & 2.30–6.30pm; ☎05.63.58.02.00), which is housed in a small turret on the riverside quai Tour de Rondes. Decent **hotels** include the comfortable if unremarkable *le Terminus* (☎05.63.58.31.14, fax 05.63.58.15.11; ③) by the station, and the basic *Central*, 7 rue d'Alsace-Lorraine (☎05.63.58.04.16; ①–②), but the best place to stay is the **chambres d'hôtes** *Taverne de la Dame du Plô*, 5 rue du Père Colin (☎05.63.41.38.77; ③), an ancient house located just a short walk from the old cathedral with four small but cosy rooms. It also has a great bar, worth a stop whether you're staying there or not. For eating, the best choice is the **restaurant** of the *Terminus* (closed Sat), a very friendly place serving up inventive *terroir*-based food; you can eat well here for under 100F/€15.25. You'll also find a clutch of places in the elongated square stretching up from the tourist office, the most interesting of which is *Bistro Azurro* (closed Sun), a Basque restaurant where you can get a half-chicken lunch with wine for only 45F/€6.86. Lavaur's **country market** is on Saturday morning throughout the old town, and there's a **horse-fair** held on the third Saturday of each month near the *gare*.

## Giroussens and St-Sulpice

Some fifteen kilometres northwest of Lavaur, the ancient village of **GIROUSSENS** huddles on the slope of a high ridge. For thousands of years and right up to the present day, this town has been a centre of pottery production, as the shops which line the road through town reveal. Aside from an attractive thirteenth-century **church**, there's little to draw you here, but if you are walking, cycling or driving by, it makes a good place to spend the night. Just across the river on the south bank of the Agout, you'll find the hamlet of **St-Lieux-lès-Lavaur**, site of a much-touted **steam train** (mid-July to Aug daily 2.30–6.30pm; Easter to mid-July & Sept–Oct Sun & school holidays only same times; subject to cancellation if less than ten tickets sold; 25F/€3.81), which runs a one-hour return trip eastwards along the river valley, the highpoint of which is the crossing over a twenty-metre-high viaduct. Beware, however, that the management frequently substitutes a regular diesel model for the trip. Also in St-Lieux is the **Jardin des Martels** (daily 10am–7pm; 35F/€5.34), a botanical garden with thousands of varieties of flowers and plants, as well as a petting zoo. The train and garden make a good combination if you are travelling with children.

The best place to **stay** or **eat** in Giroussens is *L'Échaguette* (☎05.63.41.63.65, fax 05.63.41.63.13; ③–④), in the lower part of the village. This beautiful thirteenth-century building has several well-furnished rooms and a small, intimate dining room, with delicious *terroir*-based menus (under 100F/€15.25 at lunch and from 120F/€18.30 at dinner).

You're only likely to make a stop in tiny **ST-SULPICE**, 8km further west, if changing buses or trains en route to Toulouse or Albi from Lavaur or the Montagne Noire. The village is quite plain, apart from an attractive old suspension **bridge** over the Agout, which flows into the Tarn just west of town. There's also a mildly interesting fourteenth-century **church** just south of the old bridge, whose crenellated facade shows it originally served as part of the town's defences. On one of the doors you can see a depiction of Moses descending from Mount Sinai bearing the Ten Commandments and sprouting ram's horns. The origin of this curious motif, recurrent in Catholic art, is an error on the part of St Jerome, who translated the Bible into its popular Latin version, the *Vulgate*, in the fourth century. Led astray by the Hebrew text (in which vowels are not written) he confused two adjectives – the original read that Moses returned from his interview with God "radiant", but Jerome read it as "horned". Medieval artists, faithfully following scripture, dutifully depicted the Patriarch sprouting horns.

The **tourist office** is at Parc Georges-Spenale (Tues–Sat 3–7pm; ☎05.63.41.89.50). To **stay** the night, you can choose between the *Hôtel Le Relais Fleuri* (☎05.63.41.80.20; ③), and several **chambres d'hôtes**, two of which are *Le Cambou* (☎05.63.41.82.66; ②) and *Le Pepil* (☎05.63.41.62.84; ③). There's also a **campsite** in town, *Borio-Blanco* (☎05.63.41.89.55), which is open all year. If you are looking for a **meal**, head out on the RN88 to *L'Auberge du Pointe* (☎05.63.41.80.14; closed Tues eve, Wed off-season & part Oct), one of the best *gastronomique* restaurants on this stretch of the Tarn, where you can enjoy subtle and elaborate menus for 100–200F/€15.25–30.50.

## The route des Colombiers, St-Paul-Cap-de-Joux and Damiette

If you are cycling or driving from Lavaur, you should take the time to explore the **route des Colombiers**, a loose circuit of approximately 20km which you can start on the southern bank of the Agout heading east out of the town. *Colombiers*, elaborate and varied dovecotes, have been constructed here among the farm fields since the Middle Ages to house the pigeons which formed a valuable part of the rural economy, providing food and fertilizer. The tourist office in Lavaur has a map with detailed directions to all of the dovecotes as well as some explanatory text. If you don't want to do the whole circuit, which leads about 10km east before looping back, you'll pass a good number of dovecotes by taking the small riverside road from Lavaur towards St-Paul (follow signs for "Flamarens"), but there are also plenty to see right along the main D112 highway which runs between Lavaur and Castres. Ten kilometres after the river road and the main road meet you'll come to a bridge over the Agout, abutted on the south side by **ST-PAUL-CAP-DE-JOUX** and on the north by **DAMIETTE**. These two sleepy little towns don't hold any attractions themselves but are the closest places to the castles of Magrin and Roquevidal to the southwest, and make a possible meal stop if you are cutting south by car through the *pays de Cocagne* towards Revel and the Canal du Midi. St-Paul has a small **tourist office** in avenue de Strasbourg (mid-June to mid-Sept Mon–Sat 10am–noon & 2–6pm; mid-Sept to mid-June Tues 10am–12.30pm & 4.30–6.30pm; ☎05.63.70.52.10), which can give you information for the whole of the valley downstream of Castres. Unfortunately, the old *Hotel Central*, on rue Jeanne d'Arc opposite the church, no longer rents rooms, but you can still get a light meal here (menu 75F/€11.44). Damiette has a **gare SNCF** on the Toulouse–Revel line and a **campsite** (mid-June to mid-Sept; ☎05.63.70.66.07, *bernard.belin@wanadoo.fr*).

If you have transport, and you would like to visit less frequented sights of the region, ten kilometres down the twisting D40 road from St-Paul you'll come to the **Château-Musée de Magrin** (mid-July to Aug daily 10.30am–noon & 3–6pm; Sept to mid-July Sun 3–6pm; 23F/€3.51 for entry or 38F/€5.80 for guided tour). Largely ruined, this castle dates to before the Albigensian Crusade, although most of what survives is from the Renaissance. Included in the visit is a museum of woad, which has displays, reconstructions and models illustrating the techniques of dye manufacture. A few more kilometres along to the west you'll find the **Château de Roquevidal** (Aug Sun 3–7pm; 20F/€3.05) a square thirteenth-century keep, remodelled as a manor house in the late fourteenth century. Its collection of antique furniture and knick-knacks, complemented by old typewriters and printing presses, is anything but exceptional, but makes for a pleasant stop if you happen to be driving through.

If you head south from St-Paul towards Revel, there isn't much to detain you along the way. The old town of **Puylaurens**, once a centre of local Huguenot learning, is not worth stopping in, despite the profusion of tourist brochures which may tempt you otherwise. Midway between Puylaurens and Toulouse the hamlet of **Loubens-Lauragais** is still dominated by its old seigniorial **castle** (July, Sept & Oct Sun 2.30–6.30pm, Aug Thurs–Sun 2.30–6.30pm; 35F/€5.34), most of whose present structure dates from the sixteenth century. The setting is idyllic, with stately white geese lolling in the pond by its gate, while inside you'll find a collection of antique furniture (including some good Aubusson tapestries) amassed by the family that has lived here for 22 generations.

## Revel and around

Situated at the westernmost point of the long Montagne Noire massif, **REVEL** is a tiny but busy district capital, which serves as a regional bus hub – this is where you catch the bus to Sorèze and Dourgne – and a good base for exploring the surrounding area. It was founded as a *bastide* in 1232 by Philip IV, and the deliberate plan of the town is reflected in its octagonal layout and regular streets – indeed, Revel's original charter prescribed a uniformity which even regulated the size of the houses which could be built. Today, it is still dominated by the immense market which covers the entirety of the town's central square. The market was built soon after the town was founded, its rows of stout pillars supporting a single-gabled roof, converging at a stone-constructed tower. Revel was the principal market town for the farmland of the region before becoming a centre for furniture manufacture in the nineteenth century, taking advantage of the wooded slopes of the Montagne Noire to its east. There's nothing much to see or do here, but if you are changing buses or hiking out of the hills it is a good place to spend a comfortable night and get your laundry done. At any rate, you should take a walk around the compact old town and look at the many medieval houses which remain. The local workshops still turn out exceptionally crafted wooden furniture, and if you are interested in how it used to be done check out the **Conservatoire des Métiers du Bois**, the "Woodworkers Conservatory", at 13 rue Jean Moulin (Wed–Sun 2–6.30pm; 15F/€2.29). Here you can see a collection of old tools, observe as furniture is made according to traditional techniques and, naturally, make a purchase.

One of the main reasons why you may pass through Revel is to make your way up to the **Lac de St-Ferreol**, an artificial reservoir created in 1672 with the completion of a massive 780-metre-long dam. This was part of the incredible Canal du Midi project (see p.110), and took some 7000 workers five years of hard labour to construct. It was here that run-off from the Montagne Noire was collected to feed the canal, flowing down the Rigole de Canal du Midi to Naurouze, some 25km to the southwest. Nowadays it is a popular weekend spot. The woods make for easy walking, and you can **swim** or **sail** on the lake. A variant of the **hiking** trail GR7 swings by the reservoir, linking up with the G653 west at the Rigole, and passing close to Castelnaudary to the south.

Also worth a stop, particularly if you're travelling between Revel and Toulouse, is the tiny picturesque hill-top hamlet of **St-Félix-Lauragais** – birthplace of the composer Déodat-de-Séverac (1872–1921) – which dominates the flatlands stretching west towards the capital of Midi-Pyrénées. Nothing remains of the time when the town was a meeting place for Cathar clergy, but it does retain a fine wooden **market** with a small stone tower, a curious Gothic-style **church** tucked away amongst the buildings of the main street, and a profusion of timber-frame houses.

## Practicalities

**Buses** passing through **Revel** stop on the place de la République, on the main road just north of the town's covered market, where there is a small SNCF bus ticket office (Tues–Fri 9am–noon & 1.30–6.30pm, Sat 9am–noon; ☎05.61.83.53.73). The **tourist office** (July–Sept Mon–Fri 9.30am–7.30pm, Sat 9am–6.30pm, Sun 10am–12.30pm & 3–6pm; Oct–June Mon–Fri 9.30am–12.30pm & 2.30–6.30pm; ☎05.61.83.50.06, fax 05.62.18.06.21, *www.revel-lauragais.com*), located in the tower in the market's centre, can give you information about neighbouring towns (including Sorèze and Dourgne) too. The best of the **hotels** here, set in a refined old nineteenth-century mansion, is the *Auberge du Midi* at 34 boulevard Gambetta, just north of the market (☎05.61.83.50.50, fax 05.61.83.34.74; ③). Close by, at 7 rue de Taur, you'll find the *Commanderie Hôtel* (☎05.63.46.61.24; ③), a good second choice, with an old timber-frame facade and a remodelled interior. For **eating**, the *Auberge* also has the town's best restaurant choice (menus from 90–180F/€13.73–27.45) and there are a number of places on the market square to get a drink or a light meal, including *Le Progress*, which has a daily 50F/€7.63 *plat du jour*, and the *Café des Arcades*, for sandwiches and drinks. Across the square, the old *Hôtel du Centre* no longer offers accommodation, but still has an atmospheric old hotel **bar**. For a chance to see the old covered *halles* in use try and catch the Saturday morning **market**.

**Lac de St-Ferreol** has a profusion of **hotels** and **campsites**, most of them clumped along the northwest corner, where the road from Revel meets the lake. Two of the better places to stay are the *Hôtellerie du Lac* (turn right coming from Revel; ☎05.62.18.70.80, fax 05.62.18.71.13; ④), which also has multiroom suites with kitchenettes, and *La Renaissance* (☎05.61.83.51.50, fax 05.61.83.19.90, *www.logis-de-france.fr*; closed Nov–March; ④), right at the main intersection. The *Hôtellerie* also has a decent **restaurant** (menus 85–190F/€12.96–28.98), while next door at *Chez Nany* (June–Sept) you can enjoy a less expensive meal (50–75F/€7.63–11.44) on a broad terrace with good views of the lake. The campsites around the lake tend towards the deluxe multifacility type, and the closest to the water is *En Salvan* (☎05.61.83.55.95; April–Oct). You can rent **bikes** and **sail-**

**boats** through Le Biouvac (☎05.61.27.53.94), in rue des 4 Vents, behind the *Hôtellerie*.

The excellent **hotel-restaurant** *Auberge du Poids Public* (☎05.61.83.00.20, fax 05.61.83.96.21; closed Jan; ③ or half-pensions from 320F/€48.80 per person) is reason enough to visit and stay in **St-Félix**. Located in an large old house beside the town's public weigh-bridge, the hotel has been restored and decorated in warm luxury, while the restaurant is widely praised for its gastronomic creations (menus 180–350F/€27.45–53.83) based on regional themes (try the rabbit and pigeon dishes) and served up with fine Gaillac vintages; you'll need to book ahead if you plan to stay or eat.

# Sorèze and Dourgne

Taking the D85, the scenic route from Revel to Castres, you'll pass through two small villages, which, with few attractions themselves, are worthy of a visit only if you happen to be driving, walking or biking through, or if you wish to use them as bases for exploring the western reaches of the Montagne Noire. This is cattle-grazing land, an idyllic expanse of rolling green pasture with the wooded ridge of the mountains rising up sharply along the south side of the road. Narrow forest roads twist and turn up into the hills, converging in the shadow of Mount Alric (813m) before arriving at Arfons (see p.200).

**SORÈZE**, just 6km east of Revel, is an ancient town which grew around a monastery founded in 758 by Pepin the Short, forerunner of Charlemagne. The only remaining vestige of the once huge religious complex is the curious octagonal **bell tower**, dating from the fifteenth century and located near to where the mountain road winds out of town. The other sight worth a stop is the old Dominican **convent-school**, which was converted into a military academy in the eighteenth century and can be visited on a free but unremarkable hour-long guided tour through the building (July & Aug daily 10.30am, 3pm & 5pm; May–June & Sept–Oct Mon–Fri same times; Nov–April Mon–Fri 10.30am, 2pm & 5pm). The convent is also presently home to a **hotel-restaurant**, the *Abbaye-École* (☎05.63.74.44.80; ③–④) which has great old timber-beamed rooms – the restaurant has menus from 70–190F (€10.68–28.98). Less luxurious accommodation can be found in two **gîtes**, *Le Moulin du Chapître* (☎05.63.74.18.18; ①) and *La Rivière* (☎05.63.74.10.94 or 05.63.48.83.01; ①), both on the outskirts of town, or at the municipal **campsite**, *Les Vigariès* (July & Aug; ☎05.63.74.18.06). You can also eat or get a drink at the *Pub St-Martin*, in a restored and appropriately rustic stables building in the old town centre (4 rue St-Martin; ☎05.63.74.18.71). The town has a **tourist office** (daily 10am–noon & 2–6pm; ☎05.63.74.16.28) in the main square, place Dom-Device, but this will be of less use – in the summer at any rate – than the **Maison du Parc** (July & Aug daily 9am–noon & 2–6pm; ☎05.63.74.16.28), which is on the main road at the west end of town. It is here that you'll find the most up-to-date information on exploring the Parc Naturel de Haut Languedoc, which begins in the hills above the town.

Just a few kilometres beyond Sorèze lies the even smaller village of **DOURGNE**, still marked on the east side by the crumbling walls of an ancient abbey. Today the town's monastic tradition is as alive as ever, revived in the nineteenth century with the founding of two Benedictine communities just up the road at **En Calcat**. The larger of the two is the **Monastère de St-Benoît**, which you can visit and sit in on any of the five daily services to hear a chanted mass;

the smaller convent of **Ste-Scholastique** is the home of nuns who pass the time in devotion and weaving. Although the town is quite pretty, with its old streets and arcaded houses, the only other sight is a rather unexceptional sixteenth-century church. If you are hungry, stop in at the **restaurant**, *Hôtellerie de la Montagne Noire* at 15 place des Promenades, which serves up hearty *terroir*-inspired food (menus from 95F/€14.49). The *Hôtellerie* also operates as a small **hotel** (☎05.63.50.31.12; ②), aside from which there are two **chambres d'hôtes**, run by Rose Pauthe (☎05.63.50.31.30; ②) and Agnès Kovacs (☎05.63.50.12.97; ③) respectively, as well as a tiny one-star municipal **campsite** (☎05.63.50.31.20). The **tourist office** (July & Aug 8.30am–12.30pm & 1.30–6.30pm; ☎05.63.74.27.19, fax 05.63.50.15.13) can be found in the centre of the village, on place Jean-Bugies.

# Castelnaudary

The biggest stop on the Canal du Midi between Carcassonne and Toulouse, **CASTELNAUDARY** holds the honour of being the legendary birthplace of that most Occitan of dishes, cassoulet, and is also the capital of the Lauragais region, the flat grain-producing hinterland of Toulouse. With its wide **Grand Bassin**, or reservoir, the town is the major pleasure port on the Canal, and a great place to start a waterborne trip towards the Mediterranean. Like the surrounding region, Castelnaudary's past is intimately linked with Cathar history – the town endured no less than three sieges during the Albigensian campaigns, and was also the birthplace of Pierre de Castelnau, the papal legate whose murder prompted Pope Innocent III to proclaim the Crusade. When the Inquisition arrived here in 1235, the grey-robed Dominicans' efforts to root out heretics were thwarted by the solidarity of the townsfolk, who refused to implicate their fellows. It was also just outside of town that the last dream of Languedocian independence died, with the capture in 1632 of the rebellious Henri, Duke de Montmorency, who was borne away to Toulouse and executed on orders of Cardinal Richelieu.

---

### CASSOULET

One of the great pillars of Southern French *terroir* ("country" or "local") cuisine is the humble **cassoulet**. A simple but tasty baked dish, made up of white beans and garlic cooked with bits of pork and sausage, cassoulet is a staple you'll find just about everywhere between the peaks of the Pyrenees and the banks of the Rhône. Legend has it that the dish originated in Castelnaudary in the mid-fourteenth century, when the Black Prince Edward besieged the town during the course of the Hundred Years War. The defenders, gathering their last provisions, which amounted to some beans and scraps of meat, not only managed to concoct a culinary triumph under extreme duress but, thus fortified, put the English troops (whose own inferior syrupy brown baked-bean diet could not compete) to flight. Today the "original" recipe is safeguarded by the amusingly solemn Confraternity of the Grand Cousselet, a collective of local chefs who occasionally dress up in distinctive medieval-style robes for culinary events and fairs. You'll have plenty of chances to eat cassoulet in Languedoc and Roussillon, but be warned, local wisdom (and common sense) says that it is a dish best avoided in the summer.

## Arrival, information and accommodation

Trains arrive at Castelnaudary's **gare SNCF** (☎04.68.94.41.55), located on the south side of the Canal du Midi. At the end of the avenue de la Gare, the road running directly from the station, you should turn right onto Avenue Arnaut-Vidal, which will lead you over the river and straight to the place de la République, at the centre of town. The **gare routière**, on the other hand, is on the north side of town, on avenue Frédéric-Mistral. Following this street as it veers right (now called rue de 11 Novembre) also takes you to the central *place*, and the town's **tourist office** (mid-July to mid-Sept Mon–Sat 9.30am–12.30pm & 2.30–7pm, Sun 9.30am–12.30pm & 3–7pm; mid-Sept to mid-July Mon–Sat 9.30am–12.30pm & 2–6.30pm; ☎04.68.23.05.73, fax 04.68.23.61.40, *castelnaudary@fnotsi.net*). To connect to the **Internet** check at the main **post office**, 18 cours de la République, whose pay terminal should be up and running. **Bicycles** can be rented at Trigano Cycles (☎04.68.23.09.77), in St-Martin-Lalande, 4km east on the RN113.

There are several **hotels** to choose from in town, the best of which is the friendly, canalside *Hôtel du Canal* (☎04.68.94.05.05, fax 04.68.94.05.06; ②–③), at 2 avenue Arnaut-Vidal – a comfortable place with all mod cons (including satellite television) and a parking garage. The second choice is the *Hôtel du Centre et du Lauragais* (☎04.68.23.25.95, fax 04.68.94.01.66; closed Jan to mid-Feb; ②–③) a converted nineteenth-century house, centrally located at 31 cours de la République, close by the post office. Other decent options include the three-star *Hôtel de France*, at 2 avenue Frédéric-Mistral (☎04.68.23.10.18, fax 04.68.94.04.64, *hdf@cassoulet.com*; ③), and the simple but welcoming *Grand Hôtel Fourcade* (☎04.68.23.02.08, fax 04.68.94.10.67, *www.logis-de-france.fr*; closed part Jan & Sept, April Mon & Sun; ①–②), at 14 rue des Carmes, near the covered market. The municipal **campsite**, *La Giraille* (mid-June to mid-Sept; ☎04.68.23.11.23) can be found west of town, a twenty-minute walk along avenue Georges-Pompidou from the bridge at the foot of cours de la République.

## The Town

Although Castelnaudary's main attraction is its canal port (see below), there are quite a number of interesting things to see in the town itself. The first you are likely to encounter is the **halle aux grains**, the former cereal market. It's a handsome building with a plain but dignified arcaded front on the west side of place de la République, and now houses the tourist office, as well as acting as a venue for occasional theatre and dance productions. Heading uphill from the *halle* along allée du Cassieu you can follow the main road west to the thirteenth-century **church of St-François**, inside which you'll find a well-crafted statue of the Virgin and Child, dating from the same period. If you continue another 800m further (turning up towards the cemetery on the impasse Claude-Chappe), you'll come to the curious **Tour Chappe**. This tower (currently being renovated) was once part of the immense semaphore network which covered much of France. Napoleon used the system extensively, and on a clear day messages could be passed from Strasbourg to Paris in just over three hours, using over 180 of these signal stations. The network was a huge success, but the introduction of the electric telegraph in 1859 rendered it immediately obsolete.

Alternatively, you can continue straight uphill from the *halles* to rue de Château; this will take you to the old **Moulin de Cugarel** (Sun 2–6pm; 5F/€0.88), the last of the town's wind-powered grain mills. With the building of the canal du Midi farmers suddenly had access to markets as far afield as

Toulouse and the Mediterranean, and so no less than 32 mills were built to process the wheat which they brought to be sold. The *moulin* is an attractive stone structure, and its superb grinding mechanism was fully restored in 1962. Below the mill the heart of the old town makes a rough trapezoid, marked off by place de Verdun and rue Goufferand on the east and west, and Grand Rue and rue de Dunkerque on the north and south. **Place de Verdun** was the medieval town's main square. Ringed by handsome mansion facades, including that of the Hôtel Dupuy on its north side, the *place* is home to the town's main covered *halle*, as well as the site of the colourful Monday market originally instituted on June 1268 by order of Alphonse de Poitiers, Count of Toulouse, who wanted to spark the town's economy. Following Grand Rue from the marketplace will lead you past two more attractive seventeenth-century **mansions**, the Hôtel de Laudun-Courtiade at no. 26, and the Hôtel Latapie, on the corner of rue de la Terrasse. Turning the corner you'll soon reach the southern-Gothic-style collegiate **church of St-Michel**, built in the fourteenth century. Its exterior is notable for its beautiful steeple, towering 55m above the neighbouring place de St-Just, as well as two fine doorways on the north side, but the interior, clinically white, has little to recommend it. Rue du College, which continues from St-Michel, leads on into place Auriol, at the far end of which you'll be able to ascend to the **Présidial**. This sombre stone building was raised on the site of the town's castle in 1585, when Henri III made the town capital of the Lauragais. First serving as a courthouse and later a prison, it now holds a rather dull **museum of pottery** (Mon 3–6.30pm, Tues–Sat 10am–12.30pm & 3–6.30pm, Sun 3–6.30pm; 15F/€2.29.

Finally, there are two more points of interest in the old town, both along rue de l'Hôpital, north of place Auriol. The first of these is the chapel of **Notre-Dame-de-Pité**, founded in the eleventh century and a popular stop on the medieval pilgrimage route of Compostela. The dazzling interior of the chapel, which was reworked in the sixteenth century (and which you can peek at through the grills), contains a feast of gilt wooden low-relief panels depicting angels and Biblical scenes in the most outrageously flamboyant Baroque style – an effect which you'll either consider the height of good taste or the depths of bad. Further along you'll reach the **Apothicairerie** (book first with tourist office; 10F/€1.53), a pre-Revolution pharmacy, which has sat on this spot for over two centuries. Nearly two hundred porcelain phials line the shelves, labelled with the kinds of ingredients that make you glad you didn't get sick in the eighteenth century. If you time yourself to arrive here towards lunch or dinner and you still have an appetite after contemplating jars which once held pickled lizard, Castelnaudary's best restaurant, *Le Tirou* (see below) is just a short walk beyond the old apothecary.

### The Grand Bassin

Castelnaudary's biggest draw is the section of the **Canal du Midi** which runs through the town and is punctuated by the broad **Grand Bassin**. This roughly oblong pool, some seven hectares in area, is the largest reservoir along the length of the navigable canal. Constructed as a port, where barges could turn around, get repaired, and load up with the grain harvested in the Lauragais, it now serves as a **pleasure port** and point of embarkation for tours and trips along the inland waterways of the Midi and Languedoc. To the west, the Grand Bassin empties into the Petit Bassin, marked by the two road bridges over the canal, before narrowing to wind its way towards Toulouse. On the east side, a remarkable series of six locks, the **Écluse des St-Roch** lowers barges and boats bound for the

Mediterranean. If you want to rent a boat for a few hours or a few weeks, take a tour, or simply take in the variety of modern and historical craft which you can find on the canal, this is the place to do it (see the Canal du Midi "Practicalities").

## Eating and drinking

If you're looking for cassoulet and other *terroir* treats in Castelnaudary there is no shortage of **restaurants** to choose from. The best, and most expensive, is undoubtedly Le Tirou (☎04.68.94.15.95), on the east end of town at 90 avenue Monseigneur de Langle. This old stone house has a pleasant garden and an excellent *terroir carte* (expect to pay 200–300F/€30.50–45.75). Of the hotel restaurants, the best is that of the *Centre et Lauragais*, whose traditional Midi dining room is closer to the centre and less expensive than *Le Tirou* (menus from 100F/€15.25), while *La Belle Époque* (☎04.68.23.39.72; closed Tue eve & Wed), at 55 rue Général-Dejean, is a great place to taste the famous *cassoulet* (basic menu 60F/€9.15). If you're tired of beans and foie gras, there are several international options in town, including the quality Chinese and Vietnamese cooking of *Le Dragon* (☎04.68.23.33.61) at 22 rue Soumet, by the market, to the Italian pizza and seafood of *Le Gondolier* at 10 rue Maréchal-Foch (closed Mon eve & Tues; menus for under 100F/€15.25), and the local kebab joint, *Agadir*, at 9 Grand Rue. You can also pick up cassoulet and other regional delicacies "to go" from the town's well-reputed *traiteurs* and *conservateurs*, artisanal butchers and confectioners. There are a number of them in the old town, including Le Regal, at 30 rue Dunkerque, Escudier, at no. 9, and Au Gourmet Chaurien at 38 cours de la République.

## Near Castelnaudary

If you happen to be in Castelnaudary on April 30 or at Christmas you can get a glimpse of the closed world of France's notorious **Foreign Legion**, whose base, 2km southeast of town on the D33, opens its doors to the public on these two occasions. Another short excursion, 8km east on the D113, is to the **abbey of St-Papoul** (April–June & Sept–Oct 10am–noon & 2–6pm; July & Aug 10am–7pm; 20F/€3.05 guided tour in French, reduction with "Carte Intersite" pass – see p.127), set on the edge of the Lauragais plain. Founded in the eighth century by Pepin the Short, it went on to huge success after 1317 when its abbot was elevated to the status of bishop. The church itself is impressive, with some sections dating back to the twelfth century, while the **cloister** has some fine carved capitals executed by the master-craftsman, the anonymous "Master of Cabestany". This twelfth-century masonry genius, whose speciality was human figures in high relief, worked as far afield as Tuscany and Catalonia, but many of his works can be found in a wide band of territory stretching from Castelnaudary to the sea.

# Along the Canal du Midi from Toulouse to Carcassonne

The Canal du Midi runs a roughly straight path through the wheat-producing lands of the Lauragais, clearing the compact suburbs of Toulouse and steering its tree-lined course east, parallel to the Hers River, towards its highest point, at the Seuil (or "threshold") de Naurouze. From here it descends to the basin at Castelnaudary, as the Montagne Noire, the source of the canal's water, comes into view to the north. From the Grand Bassin, the waterway cuts eastwards across the plain, bridging the 32km to **Carcassonne**, where it begins to adapt to the contours of the Aude valley, and start in earnest its descent towards the sea (see

### THE CANAL DU MIDI

The **Canal du Midi** runs for some 240km from the River Garonne at Toulouse, via Castelnaudary, Carcassonne and Béziers, to the Mediterranean at Agde or Sète, and via its subsidiary, the **Canal de la Robine**, to Narbonne, entering the sea at Gruissan. The waterway was the brainchild of Pierre-Paul Riquet, a minor noble and the holder of the lucrative salt-tax concession for Languedoc (the *gabelle* – a tax levied on the sale of salt – was one of the royal treasury's most lucrative sources of income), who succeeded in firing the imagination of Louis XIV (and more importantly, his first minister, Colbert) with the idea of linking the Atlantic and the Mediterranean via the Garonne (in reality the connection wasn't actually to happen until long after the principal stretch had been finished).

The main canal, begun in 1667, took fourteen years to complete using tens of thousands of workers. At the start, an engineering problem automatically presented itself: how to feed the canal with water when the Mediterranean was obviously at sea level, the Garonne at 132m above sea level, and, in the middle, the Col (or Seuil) de Naurouze at 201m. Riquet's solution was to build a system of dams and reservoirs at St-Ferréol, Lampy and on the Alzeau in the Montagne Noire, channelling run-off water from the heights down to Naurouze. He spent the whole of his fortune on the canal (sacrificing even his daughters' dowries) and, sadly, died just six months before its inauguration in 1681. But the waterway, built to accommodate barges of up to 30m in length, was a success and sparked a wave of prosperity along its course, thanks to the access it provided local farmers, manufacturers and raw material industries to foreign markets (via the Mediterranean). Traffic increased steadily until 1856, when it carried 111,000 metric tonnes of material as well as one million passengers, and the official link-up to the Garonne and the Atlantic opened. The next year the Sète–Bordeaux railway came into being and, rail transport being faster and more cost-effective, traffic on the canal dropped to all but nothing almost immediately.

In the last ten years or so, however, the canal has been revived as a course for pleasure craft, and it's not difficult to see why. It remains a marvel of engineering and beauty, incorporating no fewer than 99 locks (*écluses*) and 130 bridges. The various topographical challenges were met with imagination, including the

Chapter 6). The towns along the route are not especially notable, but afford you a glimpse of rural France at its most antiquated and peaceful.

The first town of any size which you'll pass is the old *bastide* of **Montgiscard**, some 10km from the port of Toulouse. There's not much to see here, but if you are tempted to stop, take a look at the medieval church, part of which was remodelled by the same architect who designed Toulouse's Hôtel d'Assèzat. Next along you'll come to **Ayguesvives** and **Montesquieu-Lauragais**, both of which have impressive nineteenth-century *châteaux*. Eighteen kilometres out from Toulouse you'll reach the **écluse de Négra**, which is where you leave the canal to reach Villefranche, and was once the first post-stop on the way to Agde – several of the old canal-side buildings survive. Just to the east, **Avignonet-Lauragais** was once a wealthy woad town, and is notable for being the place where, in 1242, the Cathars holed up in Montségur launched an attack on and massacred a contingent of the Dominican Inquisition; the resulting counterattack brought about the destruction of Montségur castle and the mass execution of its garrison and population (see p.139). Today the town has a fourteenth-century church with a fine retable dating from 1632. The last stop before reaching Naurouze is the

construction of canal **tunnels** and **bridges**, the latter allowing water to cross valleys and gullies, suspended in the air. No less beautiful are the stone foot and road bridges, most of which date back to the first era of construction. The graceful oval **lock-basins**, built in that shape for more strength, are guarded by uniform *maisons d'éclusier*, where the controls of the mechanism are housed; and, as along any major route, inns and restaurants punctuate the canal's course. Even the double file of trees which lines most of the waterway's length, giving it a distinctive "Midi" look, serves a technical as well as an aesthetic purpose: to shade the water and impede its loss through evaporation.

Unsurprisingly, the canal was designated a UNESCO World Heritage Site in 1996, ensuring its conservation. You can follow it by road, and many sections have foot or bicycle paths, but the best way to travel it (and an ideal way to spend a family or group vacation) is, of course, **by boat**. It's a gentle, restful chug down a tunnel of greenery enhanced in spring by the bloom of yellow iris and wild gladioli, with occasional glimpses of a world beyond: a distant smudge of hills, the pinnacles of Carcassonne. There are outfits in all of the major ports which **rent houseboats and barges** – most of which will also rent bikes as an extra, which is perfect for exploring the sights along the waterway – and if you prefer to be driven rather than drive, there are many cruises too. All of the companies listed in the Guide keep their fleets well maintained, so price may be your major concern when shopping around. The Canal du Midi is navigable from March to November, but the high season of July and August is best avoided – boat availability declines, prices rise, and the canal gets quite crowded. Navigation itself is straightforward (literally!) and an orientation session by the boat rental company is all you need to get you on your way – no licence is required. Generally, **locks** are open daily from 8am to 12.30pm and 1.30pm to 7.30pm, but closed on major holidays. There's no charge for passage, and you can count on about a quarter of an hour for a basin to fill or empty. With a maximum permitted speed of 6km per hour you're not going to break any records, and you should not count on being able to travel more than 250km in a week of cruising. Canal **information** can be found at the port offices of Voies Navigables de France, the government organization in charge of inland waterways – we've given the details of these in the relevant parts of the Guide.

modern **Port-Lauragais**, built specifically for pleasure boating. There's a **restaurant** here, as well as an **information centre** (daily 10am–6pm; ☎05.61.27.14.63) which houses permanent and temporary exhibitions on the building of the canal. **Naurouze**, the highest point on the canal's path, is where the Rigole, or feeder canal, arrives bearing the water gathered on the slopes of the Montagne Noire; it has long been a point of transit, as the vestiges of Roman road here testify. The area around the canal junction has been set up as a **picnic area** and **park** (unfortunately, with no toilets), and nearby you'll find a rather sombre monument to the Canal's founder, Pierre-Paul Riquet. Incidentally, this is also the site where Soult signed his surrender to Wellington in 1814. From Naurouze it's another 12km to Castelnaudary (see p.106).

The only place of any interest between Castelnaudary and Carcassonne is **BRAM**, an ancient village in which the houses are arranged in tight concentric circles around the church, which dates back to the thirteenth century. Bram's villagers resisted the Albigensian Crusaders in 1210, and when the town eventually fell to the Catholic forces, the inhabitants came to a grizzly end. Simon de Montfort ordered a hundred prisoners to be blinded and mutilated – the refugees

---

**BIKING AND HIKING**

If you are not prepared to invest the time and money in renting a boat, the easiest part of the canal's route along which to **bike** or **hike** is the initial – paved – stretch from **Toulouse to the Seuil de Naurouze**, following a path from Port St-Saveur (see p.91). The surrounding farmland, which gradually ascends the further you go, doesn't make for the most spectacular of backdrops, but the canal – its tree-lined placidity interrupted only by the "putt-putt" of passing boats – is beautiful in its own right. The total distance along the paved path is 50km, which can be biked in about five hours and walked in under twenty. If you decide on the latter course of action you need not commit yourself to going the whole way – you can stop at Villefranche-Lauragais at the 30km-mark to catch a bus back or onwards, or spend the night at *En Jonty* (☎05.61.81.57.35; ③), a **chambres d'hôtes** near the centre of Avignonet. From Port-Lauragais, a further 12km on from Villefranche, you have the option of continuing the rest of the journey to Naurouze on a boat cruise (see "Practicalities"). The paved path ends at Écluse Ocean, shortly after the port, and a gravel towpath (fine for mountain bikes) continues on to Carcassonne; should you wish to continue beyond Castelnaudary and on to Bram, you'll find *chambres d'hôte* at *Domaine de Pigne* (☎04.68.11.40.70, fax 04.68.11.40.72; ③) on the outskirts of the village.

---

carrying their amputated body parts were then sent to the as yet unsurrendered fortress of Cabaret, led by the only villager with an eye remaining.

## Practicalities

The head office of Voies Navigables de France is at 2 Port St-Étienne in Toulouse (☎05.61.36.24.24, fax 05.61.54.66.50, *www.vnf.fr*); they also have English-speaking port offices at Carcassonne (☎06.84.81.96.20), Castelnaudary (☎06.84.81.96.23) and Port St-Saveur (☎06.84.81.96.21). There is also a small **tourist office** at Villefranche, in place Général-de-Gaulle (☎04.61.27.20.94).

If you are interested in **renting a boat** in Toulouse contact Société AQUALUB (☎06.86.71.33.46). In Castelnaudary the biggest boat rental company is Crown Blue Line, Le Grand Bassin, BP1201, 11492 Castelnaudary (☎04.68.94.52.72, fax 04.68.94.52.73, *boathols@crown-blueline.com*) – their fleet (as do most) consists mostly of modern craft, so if you are hoping for a more authentic-looking barge, you may have to shop around and book well ahead. At Carcassonne you can rent from Nautic (☎04.68.71.88.95, fax 04.67.94.05.91), while Locaboat (☎03.86.91.72.72, *www.locaboat.com*) rents out *pénichettes*. At any of these firms expect to pay between 5250F/€800 and 10,000F/€1525 per week, depending on season, for a three- to five-person boat.

In case you don't feel like navigating yourself, Le St Roch, in Castelnaudary's Grand Bassin (☎04.68.23.49.40), organizes canal tours lasting from thirty minutes to two hours (20–55F/€3.05–8.39 per person), while Croisières Cathy (☎06.09.33.15.96), also in Castelnaudary, has half- and full-day programmes with optional on-board meals. You must book in advance: full-day cruises, which depart at 9am, cost 175–320F/€26.69–48.80 depending on whether you have the meal; and half-day tours, leaving at 11.30am, cost 100F/€15.25. Additionally, just west of Naurouze at Port-Laugarais, the *Lucie* runs a thirty-minute circuit to the Seuil and back (daily April–Sept; 20F/€3.05), as well as other longer itineraries whenever ten or more passengers assemble.

## travel details

### TRAINS

**Toulouse** to: Albi (12 daily; 1hr 13min); Avignonet (3–5 daily; 38min); Ax-les-Thermes (5–10 daily; 2hr); Béziers (10 daily; 2hr–3hr 20min); Bram (9 daily; 1hr 5min); Carcassonne (9 daily; 1hr); Carmaux (10 daily; 1hr 46min); Castelnaudary (9 daily; 37min); Castres (4–8 daily; 1hr 8min); Cordes (6 daily; 1hr 12min); Damiette (2 daily; 50min); Foix (5–10 daily; 1hr); Gaillac (12 daily; 48min); l'Hospitalet (2–6 daily; 2 hr 30min); Lavaur (4–8 daily; 30min); Lisle (12 daily; 38min); Mazamet (4–8 daily; 1hr 28min); Montpellier (8 daily; 2hr 55min); Narbonne (12 daily; 1hr 18min–2hr 50min); Nîmes (8 daily; 3hr 22min); Paris (12 daily; 5hr 7min–7hr 10min); Rabastens (12 daily; 30min); St-Sulpice (12 daily; 22min); Tarascon (5–10 daily; 1hr 15min); and Villefranche (3–5 daily; 32min).

**Castelnaudary** to: Carcassonne (9 daily; 25 min); Toulouse (9 daily; 37min).

**Lavaur** to: Castres (4–8 daily; 25min); St-Sulpice (4–8 daily; 15min).

**St-Sulpice** to: Albi (12 daily; 1hr 50min); Castres (4–8 daily; 40min); Cordes (6 daily, 50 min); Gaillac (12 daily; 24min); Lavaur (4–8 daily; 1hr 8min); Toulouse (12 daily; 22min).

### BUSES

**Toulouse** to: Albi (6 daily; 1hr 40min); Lavelanet (1–3 daily; 2hr 25min); Mas-d'Azil (2 daily; 1hr 50min); Mirepoix (1–3 daily; 2hr); Pamiers (1–3 daily; 1hr 30min); Revel (6–8 daily; 1hr 10min); St-Félix-de-Lauragais (4 daily; 1hr); St-Sulpice (6 daily; 30min).

**Castelnaudary** to: Alet-les-Bains (1 weekly; 1 hr 55min); Axat (1 weekly; 1hr 50min); Bram (Mon–Sat 1 or 2 daily; 30min); Carcassonne (Mon–Sat 2–4 daily; 1hr 10min); Limoux (Mon–Fri 1 daily; 55min); Quillan (1 weekly; 1hr 30min); and Revel (Mon–Fri 2 daily; 24min).

**Lavaur** to: Castres (2 daily; 45min); Damiette (2 daily; 14min).

**Revel** to: Castelnaudary (Mon–Fri 2 daily; 24min); Castres (8 daily; 1hr); St-Félix (4 daily; 20min); Toulouse (6–8 daily; 1hr 10min).

**St-Sulpice** to: Albi (6 daily; 1hr 20min); Gaillac (6 daily; 50min); Toulouse (6 daily; 20min).

# CHAPTER TWO

# CARCASSONNE, THE UPPER AUDE AND ARIÈGE

The citadel of **Carcassonne** is quintessential Languedoc: a medieval fortress with the foothills of the Pyrenees rising off to the south, the peaks of the Montagne Noire looming to the north, and the languid waters of the Canal du Midi gliding past towards the Mediterranean. Although it fell to Catholic forces early in the Crusade, Carcassonne was held to be the epicentre of the Cathar heresy: the castles which form a far-flung ring in the Corbières and the Pyrenean slopes to the south were referred to as its "sons". The land fanning southwest of the city rises in a series of ridges and plains, cut through by two rivers. The first, the **Aude**, runs north to Carcassonne, skirting the highlands of the **pays de Sault** on its way down from the mountains; journeying up this valley and into the *pays*, a region littered with narrow gorges and high passes, is like flipping through the pages of Cathar history – from the site of their greatest fortified city to the ruins of their last redoubt, **Montségur**. The second, flowing down from Andorra to Toulouse, gives its name to the *département* – **Ariège** – constituting the remainder of the chapter. **Foix**, once the thriving capital of a proudly independent county, sits at the centre of the *département*, guarding the course of the rapid river itself, as it twists through the northern slopes of the Pyrenees past **Tarascon-sur-Ariège** and an incredible array of **prehistoric caves** – justification alone for a trip to the region – and the skiing and hiking country around the spa of **Ax-les-Thermes**. The plain northeast of Foix was the haunt of troubadours and men of religion, be they Cathar *parfaits* (see p.138) or the Inquisitors sent to hunt them, but was reduced to a ruin in the Wars of Religion – its ancient, near-abandoned villages with their arcaded squares and crumbling walls offer the only faded record of the district's rich past. At the southwestern limits of the *département*, the **Couserans**, snowcapped peaks ranged in breathtaking cirques, form a virtually impenetrable barrier to Spain beyond.

Today, the Aude valley – with the exception of ever-popular Carcassonne – and the Ariège *département* are two of the least developed regions in the French Southwest. Isolated by difficult terrain, and afflicted for generations by the

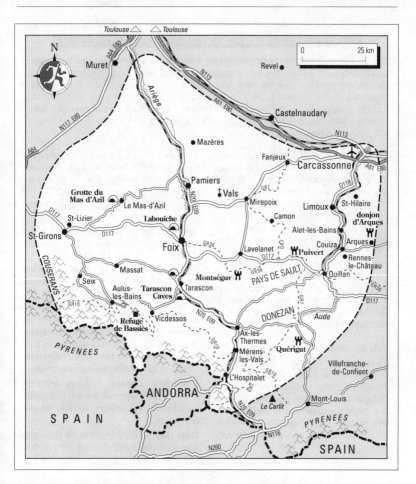

emigration of youth to better prospects in the northern cities, there is little economic base here apart from farming and herding. In recent years, tourism has rescued the area from its relentless decline, and to a certain extent, the construction of ski resorts, spas and local museums has served to improve the region's prospects. But these recent initiatives, if they have stimulated the local economy, have not detracted from the essential flavour of the area – a refuge of mountain tradition.

As you'd expect, the region is not the best for **public transport**. There's a good rail service running up the Ariège valley, from Toulouse to beyond the Col de Puylorens (and hooking up with the Tech service of Roussillon), while the other line, from Carcassonne to Quillan, has considerably less service. Bus services, even between larger towns, are infrequent, and you should consult the "Travel Details" section before planning a route.

## FESTIVALS IN CARCASSONNE AND THE ARIÈGE

July and August are the best months for **festivals** in the Ariège. The lively *fêtes locaux* invariably feature live music and dancing, and are a good opportunity to pick up country produce; several have colourful (if not always accurate) medieval re-enactments. The biggest festival is Carcassonne's Bastille Day, but bear in mind that the town packs out for the event, with parked cars lining the Route National for several kilometres from the *cité*. Limoux's Carnaval is also a unique event, worth planning for if you will be in the area.

**Mid-Jan to March** Limoux: Carnaval. An extended Lenten celebration featuring vividly costumed dancers in the old town squares. Three sets of performances (11am, 4pm & 10pm) on Saturdays and Sundays.

**May** St-Lizier: Festival d'Art Sacrée (☎05.61.96.77.77). A month-long celebration of religious artistic expression, with a heavy emphasis on the medieval. Concerts ranging from Gregorian chant to choral music are performed in the cathedral, alongside art exhibitions and performances of dramatic works.

### July to August

**Throughout July** Carcassonne: Festival de la Cité (☎04.68.25.33.16). Month-long festival of dance, music and theatre with nightly performances in the castle's amphitheatre. Highpoint is the Bastille Day (July 14) celebration, which culminates in a giant fireworks display.

**First two weeks** Tarascon: Résistances (*www.capmedia.fr/resistances*). Festival of new, cutting-edge film, with a predominantly French programme.

**Second week** St-Girons: Festival RITE (☎05.61.96.26.60, *assoc.wanadoo.fr/sigurd/bethmalais*). International festival of traditional song and dance, presided over by a group dedicated to preserving the rich culture of the Couserans area, but also featuring music and dance groups from as far afield as South America and Africa.

**Second weekend** Seix: Fête de la Transhumance. Three-day celebration timed for the traditional passing of the sheep herds. Market with traditional products and crafts and various events.

**Late July** Limoux: Folklore festival. Five-day international festival featuring traditional storytelling, theatre, dance and music.

**Late July** Quillan: Festival du Folklore International. Held over six days at the

# Carcassonne

Your first view of **CARCASSONNE**, its fairy-tale citadel perched high above the grassy verges of the River Aude, is likely to be a memorable one. The famous **cité**, slated as a UNESCO World Heritage site in 1997, enjoys must-see status on any trip through southwest France, and if it has suffered through the ages – beaten, burnt and dismantled – you'd never guess from looking at it. Aside from the walled town, with its castle and basilica, there's the medieval lower town, or **ville basse**, set on the far side of the Aude. Together, the two complement each other: the first is outstandingly beautiful, while the latter is lively, with a sprinkling of good services. Good transportation links by bus, rail, canal and air also make Carcassonne an ideal base for exploring the surrounding areas: the uplands of the

end of July, this international festival features storytelling and theatre with an impressive repertoire of groups from as far afield as East Asia and South America.

**Late July** Ax-les-Thermes: Spectacles de Grands Chemins (☎05.61.64.38.00). A festival of street theatre featuring over twenty French companies, held over three days.

**Last weekend** Tarascon: Festival de l'Art et de la Culture latino-americaine (☎05.61.05.94.94). Music, dance and food from Central and South America.

**July & Aug** Foix: Journées Médiévales Gaston Phébus (☎05.61.02.88.26). One week in mid-July and one week in mid-August. Medieval market and re-enactments in honour of the town's hero.

**July & Aug** Mirepoix: Fêtes Médiévales. Third weekend of July and the second weekend of August. Medieval pageantry, market and fair in the arcaded squares around the cathedral.

**August**

**Early Aug** Mirepoix: Festival de la Marionette (☎05.61.68.20.72). Four-day festival of puppetry along with a large craft and produce market.

**First two weeks** Carcassonne: Spectacle Médiéval (☎04.68.71.35.35,

*www.terredhistoire.com*). Medieval costumes and pageantry and a theatrical re-enactment with a different theme each year.

**First two weeks** St-Lizier: Festival de Musique (☎05.61.96.67.89). Nightly classical concerts, ranging from Mozart to Paganini to classical guitar works, performed in the cathedral by international artists. The *fête locale*, including markets, music and a weekend-long Gallo-Roman festival, is also held at this time.

**September**

**First two weeks** Foix: Fêtes de Foix. The town's yearly festival, with produce markets, music and a medieval theme, centred on the illustrious figure of Gaston Fébus.

**Mid-Sept** Mirepoix: Grand Fête de St-Maurice. Held over four days, a lively festival with market and some costumed events.

**Sept 21** Vicdessos: St-Matthieu. Transhumant livestock fair, formalized by the Count de Foix in 1313. Nowadays, the tradition continues with a lively market and celebration.

**Dec 17** Carcassonne: Marche au Gras. Lively Christmas market featuring produce and regional crafts.

Ariège and the Aude covered later in the chapter, and to the north, the ominous Montagne Noire (Chapter 3).

Carcassonne was settled as far back as the sixth-century BC, passing through the hands of Romans and Visigoths before its golden age under the great Languedocian family, the **Trencavels**. This family, which had various holdings in Languedoc, became vassals of the Counts of Toulouse (the "St-Gilles" family) in 1163, and used Carcassonne as their principal residence, ensuring the town a prosperous economic base. As a consequence of the Crusade against the Cathar heretics, the town was besieged and taken in 1209, eventually passing on to the notorious Simon de Montfort, who made it **"capital"** of the extensive territories he was taking over from local nobility. After the feared warrior died outside the walls of Toulouse in 1218, the Trencavel Raymond-Roger VII briefly recovered the town, only to see it pass to royal control in 1229. Some twenty years later, King

## THE LEGEND OF DAME CARCAS

The origin of Carcassonne's strange sounding name has given rise to a number of interesting stories, the most enduring and popular of which is that of **Dame Carcas**. This legend asserts that when the town was under Muslim control in the early Middle Ages, the Emperor Charlemagne arrived to lay siege, knowing that if his army attacked for long enough, eventually the town would run short of food. However, just when defeat looked inevitable, Carcas, the Muslim ruler's wife, ordered a pig to be force fed with the last of the town's precious grain and tossed over the battlements.Whenthe pig hit the ground it immediately split open, and Charlemagne's troops, seeing the contents, despaired, believing that the town must have abundant supplies. They lifted the siege and retreated, and as the town's church bells pealed in celebration, the townsfolk cried "Carcas, sonne!" ("Ring, Carcas!"). It's a great story, but pure fantasy of course. A Muslim ruler, for whom pork would have been considered unclean, would never have kept pigs within the confines of his fortress, and in the early ninth century the locals spoke something more akin to Latin than modern French. Nevertheless it is decidedly more poetic than the truth, which is that the town's name derives from two Occitan roots: *carac*, for "rock" (after the spur on which it is built), and *sonne*, for "wood" (for the forests which surrounded it).

Louis IX laid out the *ville basse*, a *bastide* which would serve as a regional market and increase the town's wealth, on the far banks of the river. Carcassonne thus prospered until the **Black Prince** invaded during the course of the Hundred Years' War and, frustrated by his inability to seize the strong citadel, burnt the *ville basse* to the ground in 1355. Despite this setback, the town's citizens rallied and rebuilt the lower town, and for the rest of the Middle Ages Carcassonne enjoyed a healthy economy, profiting handsomely from its location – perfect for a market – on the frontier of the old French kingdom. With the annexation of Roussillon in 1659 all of this changed, the border shifted south, and Carcassonne entered a period of stagnation, during which time the citadel was abandoned and eventually quarried for its stones. This is how it remained until it was rediscovered in the nineteenth century by **Viollet-le-Duc**, whose visionary fifty-year restoration project rescued it from obscurity.

Today Carcassonne continues to flourish largely because of that vision, which brings in thousands of visitors every year – despite the fact that the citadel is the only sight as such, and there is essentially very little to do here, it is nevertheless a great place to spend a relaxing few days. Additionally the *cité* has become something of a symbol of medieval France; its yearly **pageants** and spectacular Bastille Day celebrations (see p.116), featuring the second largest fireworks display in France, keep the streets full of both French and foreign tourists, though its role as the administrative capital of the *département* ensures that the town is more than merely a money-making exercise too.

## Arrival, information and accommodation

Carcassonne's **airport** is just west of town; there's a small **information** booth (Mon–Fri 10am–6pm), a bank with exchange services, several shops, and car rental offices in the arrivals hall. A **navette** service (hourly; 15min; 10F/€1.53) leaves from outside the terminal and stops in town at the gare SNCF, place Gambetta and the *cité*. The **gare SNCF** (☎08.36.35.35.35) is on the north side of the *ville basse*, just over the Canal du Midi from boulevard Omer Sarraut. From the station you can catch the *navette* described above, or simply follow the ring road around to place Gambetta and the main **tourist office** at 15 boulevard Camille Pelletan (July & Aug daily 9am–6pm; Sept–June Mon–Sat 9am–12.15pm & 2–6.30pm; ☎04.68.10.24.30, fax 04.68.10.24.38, *www.tourisme.fr/carcassonne*); if you don't wish to stop in the lower town there's a second tourist office (daily 9am–6pm; ☎04.68.10.24.36) in the *cité* itself, just inside the main entrance. Carcassonne has no *gare routière* as such; **buses** arrive along the broad boulevard de Varsovie on the west side of the *ville basse*, a ten-minute walk from the tourist office. If you're arriving **by car**, you can park up by the *cité*, where the mandatory car park charges a 20F/€3.05 fee, but there are cheaper options ringing the *ville basse*, as well as free or metered street parking.

Place Gambetta is the **local transport** hub; all city buses and *navettes* leave from here – a free *navette* to the *cité* and campsite departs from near the Caisse d'Epargne bank (daily, every 20min: 8am–noon & 2–8pm). Local transport information, including maps, can be picked up at the tourist offices, or you can contact Carcassonne's urban transport company (☎04.68.47.82.82). You can rent **bikes** at Decathalon, ZI La Bouriette, near the *autoroute* interchange (bus #1 or #3; ☎04.68.10.22.40), and scooters at MacDonald's, 15 boulevard Omer Sarraut (no reservations), across from the gare SNCF.

Although your first impulse may be to get a room in the *cité*, beware that if you are hoping to pass the evenings in a medieval idyll you will most likely be disappointed. There is little **accommodation** here and it is expensive; furthermore, the citadel is very busy – verging on lunacy in high season. You'll end up more satisfied with a room along the slopes down towards the riverbank, or in the *ville basse* (from where you get the view of the *cité*). Be warned, also, that Bastille Day (July 14) is very big here; hotels book up a year in advance and traffic jams clog approaches to the town for kilometres in every direction.

## Hotels

**de la Cité**, place de l'Église (☎04.68.71.98.71, fax 04.68.71.50.15; see map p.121). If you can afford it, this luxurious hotel with its beautiful enclosed courtyard will separate you from the maddening crowds of the *cité*. The price matches the opulence. Closed Dec to mid-Jan. ⑨.

**Le Donjon**, 2 rue du Comte Roger (☎04.68.11.23.00, fax 04.68.25.06.60, *hotel.donjon.best. western@wanadoo.fr*; see map p.121). The other *cité* hotel is surprisingly affordable for what you get: a thoroughly renovated hotel with well-equipped rooms. Just a stone's throw from the *donjon*, with everything you need to stay comfy. ⑤.

---

### ACCOMMODATION PRICE CODES

All the hotels and guesthouses listed in this book have been price-coded according to the following scale. The prices quoted are for the cheapest available double room in high season.

| | | |
|---|---|---|
| ① Under 160F/€24 | ④ 300–400F/€46–61 | ⑦ 600–700F/€91–107 |
| ② 160–220F/€24–34 | ⑤ 400–500F/€61–76 | ⑧ 700–800F/€107–122 |
| ③ 220–300F/€34–46 | ⑥ 500–600F/€76–91 | ⑨ Over 800F/€122 |

**Éspace Cité**, 132 rue Trivalle (☎04.68.25.24.24, fax 04.68.25.17.17, *www.interhotel.com*; see map opposite). What this hotel lacks in charm it tries hard to make up for with amenities such as air conditioning, TV, and garage parking. Just downhill from the main gate to the *cité*; wheelchair accessible. ②.

**Grand Hôtel Terminus**, 2 av de Maréchal Joffré (☎04.68.25.25.00, fax 04.68.75.53.09; see map p.124). Fading steam-age luxury in this station-side hotel, which has a splendid *fin-de-siècle* facade. Also has a good bar, lifts and TV in the rooms. Closed Dec–Feb. ④.

**Montmorency**, 2 rue Camille St-Saëns (☎04.68.11.96.70, fax 04.68.11.96.79; see map opposite). Like the *Éspace*, this establishment provides a good range of services and is well located for those only interested in visiting the citadel, as it is just one street north of the *cité*. Wheelchair accessible and swimming pool. ④.

**Montségur**, 27 allée d'Iéna (☎04.68.25.31.41, fax 04.68.47.13.22; *www.logis-de-france.fr*; see map p.124). Comfortable rooms in this impressive-looking nineteenth-century townhouse. Located a 15min walk west of the cathedral, off boulevard Barbès, it is not the closest hotel to the *cité*, but it's competitively priced. Closed late-Dec to late-Jan. ④.

**du Pont Vieux**, 32 rue Trivalle (☎04.68.25.24.99, fax 04.68.47.62.71; see map opposite). Perhaps the best all-round choice in town this "olde worlde" hotel is on a lively, atmospheric little street which winds up from the medieval bridge towards the *cité*; TV, parking and pets are welcome. ③.

**de la Poste**, 21 rue de Verdun (☎04.68.25.12.18; see map p.124). A basic no-frills option with a great location on the main street of the *ville basse*. The rooms are small but well kept, and the hotel has few amenities or facilities, apart from a small bar. ②.

**Relais du Square**, 51 rue du Pont Vieux (☎04.68.72.31.72, fax 04.68.25.21.88; see map p.124). Budget choice which is slightly run-down but in a great location. Basic, with no en-suite bathrooms, but serviceable. Closed Sun Dec–March. ②.

**St Joseph**, 81 rue de la Liberté (☎04.68.71.96.89, fax 04.68.71.36.28; see map p.124). Another good deal in the *ville basse*, down a quiet sidestreet not far from the station. You get TV, a lift and car park at one-star prices. ①–②.

## Hostels and campsite

**Camping de la Cité**, rte St-Hilaire (☎04.68.25.11.17, fax 04.68.47.33.13). Exceptional ground with good shady sites, some bungalows and a shop. Tucked off among parkland to the south of town it can be reached by local bus #8 or by foot (about a 20min walk) from the *cité*. If you point your tent the right way you get a sterling view of the citadel poking up over the trees.

**HI hostel**, rue Trencavel (☎04.68.25.23.16, fax 04.68.71.14.84, *carcassonne@fual.rog*; see map opposite). Excellent, modern hostel in the heart of the citadel. Its dorms (75F/€11.44) and rooms are clean and bright, there's a large patio for respite from the crowds outside, plus a bar. Membership (available on site) required in summer. Sheet rental 17F/€2.59. Open Feb to mid-Dec.

**Notre Dame de l'Abbaye**, 103 rue Trivalle (☎04.68.25.16.65, fax 04.68.72.71.74; see map opposite). A second choice for hostel-style accommodation. Great location in a beautiful street, comfortable dorms (70F/€10.68) and sheet rental available (15F/€2.29).

# The Town

Carcassonne's layout can be a bit confusing initially. The town is divided into three main parts, the oldest of which is the **cité** – the compact, walled citadel perched on a hill on the east bank of the Aude. Descending from here you pass through the medieval suburb of La Barbacane and cross the river to arrive at the **ville basse**, formally known as La Bastide de St-Louis – a typical grid of thirteenth-century streets, ringed by a one-way system where there was once a wall. Splayed out around this is the **new town**, a nondescript series of suburbs which hold nothing of interest for the visitor.

## The Cité

By the time you reach the walls of Carcassonne's ancient citadel, you'll be tingling with anticipation. Although you can enter through the **Porte d'Aude**, on the citadel's western side (and closer to the *ville basse*), a more visually impressive and evocative option is to head to the main **Port Narbonnaise**, where the local *navettes* and main car park are found – on the far side of the *cité*. From whichever direction you approach, though, its stout ramparts and conical towers piercing the sky, present one of the South of France's most striking images – straight out of a medieval fantasy. And that is partly what it is – a piece of imaginative reconstruction by the eighteenth-century restorer Viollet-le-Duc, whose spirit for the medieval inspired him to invent inaccurate features like the towers and arrow-slits, which the original medieval fortress lacked. In fact, so much of Carcassonne is fabrication that it only squeaked by in its application for UNESCO status.

CARCASSONNE: CITÉ

**ACCOMMODATION**

| | |
|---|---|
| Camping de la Cité | 8 |
| de la Cité | 7 |
| Le Donjon | 6 |
| Espace Cité | 2 |
| HI hostel | 5 |
| Montmorency | 4 |
| Notre Dame de l'Abbaye | 1 |
| du Pont Vieux | 3 |

**RESTAURANTS**

| | |
|---|---|
| Auberge du Dame Carcas | B |
| Le Barbacane | C |
| Le Fontaine du Soleil | D |
| Tête de l'Art | A |

Nevertheless, as you cross over the moat, passing the wide grassy verges between the thick double walls, you do feel as though you're entering another world. Following the rue Cros Mayrevieille, with its phalanxes of souvenir shops and ice-cream stands, will lead you to the entrance to the twelfth-century **Château Comtal** (daily: June–Sept 9.30am–7.30pm; April, May & Oct 9.30am–6pm; Nov–March 9.30am–5pm; 70–90min guided tour only; 35F/€5.34), the castle where Count Raymond Roger Trencavel made his last stand against the northern knights, and surrendered, in 1209. Although you can wander around the *cité* for free, the ticket office for the Château Comtal is just inside the Porte Narbonnaise, on the left-hand side, and the mandatory guided tours of the *château* begin in the main castle courtyard (at the end of the street), from where the guides lead you through the scanty remains of the now open-roofed keep. The tour continues southwards along a section of the citadel's three kilometres of walls and through three of its 31 towers (some of whose Roman foundations can be discerned) before arriving at the modern **amphitheatre**, built on the side of the fortress's former abbey-church and used since 1908 for theatre, dance and musical performances. Take care along the walls, as stairways can be slippery and the inadequate railings are no match for curious children. The ruins themselves are anything but spectacular – Carcasssonne is best when looked at from outside – but the views from the walls are good, and the guides' frank account of the history of the town is lively and informative.

The tour ends at place St-Nazaire, behind the **basilica** of the same name (daily 9–11.45am & 1.45–6pm), a late eleventh-century church that was originally Romanesque, but underwent major Gothic and neo-Gothic remodellings, first in the thirteenth century and then again in the nineteenth, by Viollet-le-Duc. As you follow the building round to the entrance in place Pierre Pont look up to see a stunning series of **gargoyles** along the eaves, as well as amusingly carved heads above the door. Inside, the church's plain nave betrays its pre-Gothic origins – the choir and rosette window are thirteenth-century additions – and at the southern end you'll find the tomb where Simon de Montfort lay until his body was transferred to his family's main fief at Montfort l'Amaury near Paris.

There's not a great deal else to see or do in the *cité* apart from wander the narrow, crooked streets, and absorb the convincingly medieval ambience. From behind the basilica, follow the walls east along rue Plô. At no. 3 there's the small **Musée de l'École** (Feb–Nov 10am–6pm; 20F/€3.05), a reconstruction of a *fin-de-siècle* classroom, and slightly further along you'll pass a little park at place du Petit Puits, with its old well – a good place to pause and soak up the atmosphere – before eventually reaching the restaurant-clogged **place Marcou**. The small section of town on the far north of rue Cros Mayrevielle is somewhat less developed and provides a bit of respite from the teeming masses of visitors. Here you can visit a **torture museum** in rue du Grand Puits (daily 9.30am–4.30pm; 40F/€6.10), with mock-ups, models and some genuine instruments of pain dating from the Middle Ages to the French Revolution.

Before finishing up your visit of the *cité*, you should also take the time to walk around the grassy **lices**, a narrow space some 1100m in length, created with the building of the second set of walls in 1200s, and divided into two sections. The **lower lices** run from the Porte Narbonnaise to the Porte de l'Aude around the northern perimeter of the citadel; starting out from the former, you'll notice a section of brick-and-stone-constructed wall dating back to the end of the period of Roman occupation. Walking along the slightly longer

## VIOLLET-LE-DUC

It can be something of a disappointment to discover that so many of the buildings of medieval France which can be seen today are, are in fact, reconstructions, reassembled or repaired in the nineteenth century. Up until then, the Middle Ages was considered to be a period of "Gothic" barbarism best forgotten but in the early 1800s European intellectuals began to look back at the medieval era as the time when their own nations were born, and all over western Europe, projects were undertaken to recover its neglected art and architecture. In France the major figure in this movement was Eugène Emmanuel **Viollet-le-Duc**, the prolific restorer extraordinaire who left his – sometimes fantastical – mark all over France, but particularly in Languedoc and Roussillon.

Born in Paris in 1814, Viollet-le-Duc studied art history at the Sorbonne before embarking on an extended tour of France and Italy in his early twenties. On his return to Paris, he assisted in the renovation of the glorious stained glass and stone-carved interior of the **Ste Chapelle**; it was here that he found his calling and made his reputation, and in the years that followed he was inundated with contracts to restore buildings such as Narbonne's Hôtel de Ville (see p.285) and the basilica of St-Nazaire in Carcassonne – accomplished works which served to further his renown. By 1853, when Louis-Napoleon, prince-president of the Second Republic, had given him overall supervision of the restoration of all of France's medieval buildings, Viollet-le-Duc had already begun the massive reconstruction of Carcassonne's walled **cité** – a project which would take fifty years to complete and which he would not live to see finished. After drawing up the restoration plans, he returned to his old university to butt heads with critics and colleagues and dabble as a professor of Art History but, finally disillusioned with the criticisms his theories provoked, he left, returning to his work and writing, eventually dying in his adopted home of Switzerland in 1879.

Viollet-le-Duc's idiosyncratic **theory** of restoration dictated that buildings shouldn't necessarily be returned to their exact previous state, but rather modified according to their essential underlying architectural principles (as he saw them, naturally). As a result, the elaborate restorations – in which he sometimes started from nothing more than a pile of stones – are reflections of Viollet-le-Duc's imagination, and bear little or no relation in design or form to their originals. Works such as the Ste Chapelle, which were taken on early in his career and not under his direct supervision, tend to be more faithful, but with later renovations he was more or less given free rein. In Carcassonne's *cité* for example he not only made "improvements", such as adding arrow-slits and crenellation to the walls, but adopted features which are aesthetically pleasing but, quite simply, inaccurate: the pointed roofs on the towers are German-style as opposed to the flat Languedocian version. In this way he created France's medieval heritage almost single-handedly – a heritage which reflects historical reality as much as Sir Walter Scott's *Ivanhoe* or Cecil B. deMille films, but which now forms a focus for French national and Occitan regional identity, as well as the foundation for the booming tourist industry of the twentieth century. Whatever you think about Viollet-le-Duc's easy attitude to verisimilitude, as you travel around Languedoc and Roussillon, bear in mind that – for better or worse – almost all the great medieval monuments here have "benefited" to some degree from his endeavours.

southern circuit of the **upper lices** gives you good views of the elaborate towers added to the citadel's defences under Philip III in the late thirteenth century. Once a space for medieval archery practice and other military excercises, the *lices* now provide a favourite route for horsedrawn *calêches*, and a great place to have a picnic.

Outside the Porte Narbonnaise, on the chemin des Anglaises, you'll find the **Musée Mémoires du Moyen Âge** (Museum of Memories of the Middle Ages; daily 10am–6pm; 25F/€3.81), a collection of dioramas depicting battalions of medieval soldiers hacking and slashing at each other, but all around various parts of Viollet-le-Duc's nineteenth-century version of the *cité* – strictly for kids. A fifteen-minute walk south at Colline de Pech Mary you'll find **Les Aigles de la Cité**, which runs exciting 45-minute-long live **falconry** shows (July & Aug daily 3–6pm; April–June & Sept–Oct Mon–Sat 3pm, Sun 3pm & 4.30pm; *www.atarax-ie.fr/aigles*; 40F/€6.10).

## The Ville Basse

When you leave the *cité*, instead of backtracking through the main gates and past the car park, a better option is to take the gate at the end of rue Notre Dame, off place du Grand Puits, and cut down to rue Trivalle, a world away from the touristy scrum in the fortress above. This leads to the picturesque fourteenth-century **pont vieux**, adorned on its far side by the small and simple Gothic structure of the twelfth-century Notre Dame de la Santé **chapel**. The riverbanks on the *cité* side have been kept free of building and make a nice grassy spot to relax or have a picnic.

Just up from the bridge you reach the southeastern edge of the **ville basse** at place Gambetta, which, despite the traffic, has an airy feel, as well as some attractive nineteenth-century facades. On the northwest corner, keep an eye out for the impressive Art Deco facade of the Groupe Scolaire Jean-Jaurès. Here, by the tourist office, rue Verdun (formerly Grand Rue), will take you straight into the grid of the thirteenth-century *bastide*. Just along, in an eighteenth-century *hôtel*, you'll find the **Musée des Beaux-Arts** (mid-June to mid-Sept Wed–Sun 10am–noon & 2–6pm; mid-Sept to mid-June Tues–Sat same times; free), which, aside from its large but unremarkable collection of eighteenth-century landscapes, sometimes hosts interesting temporary exhibitions. Further along you'll arrive at place Carnot, the heart of the old *ville basse* – a wide square with shops, cafés and bars as well as a good morning **market** (Tues, Thurs & Sat mornings). At the far end of rue Verdun, at no. 53, the **Musée des Mémoires** (Tues–Fri 2–5.30pm, Sat 9.30am–noon & 2–5.30pm; free) pays homage to local-born surrealist poet Joë Bousquet (1857–1950). Left paraplegic by battle wounds received at Vailly in 1918, Bousquet lived out the rest of his life bedridden in this house in Carcassonne, comforted by opium and producing dark and mystical poetical reflections which attracted the attention of the interwar intelligentsia. Near the fourteenth-century cathedral of St-Michel you'll find the most substantial remains of the town's once stout defences; the **Porte des Jacobins**, a medieval gate which was widened and remodelled in Neoclassical style in 1778, is in good shape, while beside it lie the remains of the old ramparts. Otherwise, keep an eye out for some of the impressive old private *hôtels* which can be found in the *ville basse*, especially along rue Verdun, such as Hôtel Burlat, at no. 81, the former home of an eighteenth-century treasurer of France.

If you're heading back to the *cité*, the unpleasant walk along the modern road bridge east of place Gambetta will give you a great view of the citadel and the *pont vieux*. On the other side, cut across to the old bridge and follow rue de la Barbacane up past the church of St-Ginier. From here you can get to the Porte de l'Aude, walking between the double walls to re-enter the *cité*.

## Eating, drinking and nightlife

You'll never have a problem getting something **to eat** in Carcassonne, whether in the *cité*, where every other facade seems to belong to a bistro, or in the *ville basse*, which has a good selection of simple and upper-crust establishments. If you don't feel like choosing from the restaurants listed below, head for the mass of indistinguishable patios on place Marcou, all of which have *menus* in the 70F/€10.68 range. For something lighter rue Cros Mayrevieille at the entrance to the *cité* is crammed with *crêpe* and sandwich stands, while there are traditional café-bars in and around the *bastide*'s place Carnot.

For a small city, Carcassonne does quite well as far as **nightlife** goes, with a good selection of late-night **bars** (normally open until 2am, sometimes 4am or 5am at weekends). *Le Bar*, 32 boulevard Omer Sarraut, livens up later with a mixed gay/straight crowd, while nearby, *Le Flanaghan*, at no. 21, is the town's obligatory Irish-style watering hole. At 49 avenue Henri Goût, *La Fiesta Bodega* (a rather pricey Spanish-Mexican restaurant by day) stays open late as a lively tapas bar. Tiny rue de l'Aigle d'Or, just off place Carnot, is the centre for local hipsters, with bars like *Le Conti*, at no. 16, which has two dance floors and a predominantly Latin beat (daily till 5am), or the rockish *Le Note*, at no. 18

(Tues–Sat till 2am). In the *cité* itself, *Bar au Vin*, in rue Plô, is the best place for a drink – a post-show favourite for visiting actors and musicians. For **dancing**, try *La Bulle* (closed Mon & Tues), just below the *cité* at 115 rue Barbacane, or *La Rapière*, a house-sound disco popular with under-25s, just outside the main gates.

## Restaurants

**Auberge du Dame Carcas**, 3 pl du Château (☎04.68.71.23.23; see map p.121). Large restaurant with several dining rooms, serving up excellent-quality traditional and regional cuisine, including roast meats cooked over an open fire. With menus from 85F/€12.96 this is one of the best-value places in town, so call ahead. Closed Sun eve, Mon lunch & Feb.

**Le Bangkok**, 6 rue Denisse (see map p.124). Carcassonne's Thai option, with hospitable English-speaking staff. Expect to spend 50F/€7.63 and upwards. Closed Sun eve & Mon.

**Le Barbacane**, pl de l'Église (☎04.68.71.98.71; see map p.121). The most elegant (and expensive) of the three restaurants operated by the *Hotel de la Cité*. Adventurous *gastronomique* cuisine with four-star service. You'll pay upwards of 400F/€61.

**La Bérbére**, 2 rue Denisse (see map p.124). A friendly Moroccan restaurant and *salon du thé* just off the place Carnot. All the usual suspects: couscous, *tajine*, and deadly sweet *baklawa*. 55F/€8.39 menu. Closed Sun & Mon.

**La Divine Comédie**, 29 bd Jean-Jaurès (☎04.68.72.30.36; see map p.124). If you can take the garish red interior, this *fin-de-siècle* eccentricity is Carcassonne's best Italian restaurant, with decent pasta, as well as traditional cassoulet and *confit du canard*, and a lively clientele. Menus from 80F/€12.20. Closed Sun & late-Dec to early Jan.

**l'Écurie**, 43 bd Barbès (☎04.68.72.04.04; see map p.124). This place, offering elegant dining in a converted eighteenth-century stable, is popular with gays and lesbians. Menus from 140F/€21.35, offering local cuisine as well as dishes with adventurous touches such as mackerel brochettes in thyme sauce. Closed Sun eve.

**Le Fontaine du Soleil**, 32 rue de Plô (see map p.121). One of the best deals in the *cité*: small, friendly and cheap with good local, home-style cookery. You can eat well here for about 60F/€9.15 in a quiet little interior patio. Closed Jan.

**Le Jardin de la Tour**, 11 rue Porte d'Aude (☎04.68.25.71.24; see map p.124). Just outside the citadel's Porte d'Aude, this is a good option for local and Mediterranean cuisine, with a small garden dining area. Expect to pay 80–110F/€12.20–16.78. Closed Sun eve, Mon & Nov.

**Le Petit Couvert**, 18 rue de l'Aigle d'Or (see map p.124). Snappy and cheerily decorated little restaurant with good cheap menus based around combinations of salads and simple meat dishes (from 65F/€9.91) and a small street-side terrace. Also "light" options for vegetarians. Closed Sun, Mon & March.

**Le Quai Bellevue**, 2 rue des 3 Couronnes (☎04.68.25.05.60; see map p.124). Good regional cuisine served at this riverside patio, which offers excellent views of the medieval bridge and the walls of the *cité*. Expect to spend about 70F/€10.68. Closed Oct–April.

**Tête de l'Art**, 37bis rue Trivalle (☎04.68.71.23.11; see map p.121). Located on the atmospheric thoroughfare which connects the old bridge and the *cité*, with an unassuming exterior girded by a tiny sidewalk patio, and an interior festooned with the contemporary painting and sculpture. Excellent *terroir* fare from 75F/€11.44.

# Listings

**Airlines** Air Liberté (☎08.03.80.58.05); Ryanair (☎04.68.71.96.65).

**Airport information** ☎04.68.71.96.46.

**Banks** Most major French banks, plus ATMs, are represented. Try, for example, Caisse d'Epargne, 5 bd Camille Pelletan, which also has a 24-hr automatic change machine, or Crédit Agricole, 8 pl Carnot; after 5pm use the post office (Mon–Sat till 7pm).

**Bus departures** Various bus lines operate from Carcassonne, departing from along bd de Varsovie. Tickets can be bought on the buses, from the "Depêche" newsstand on the south-east corner of pl Carnot, or from Verdi Voyages, 1 av Maréchal-Joffre (☎04.68.25.09.06, fax 04.68.47.66.44). For times and destinations, enquire at Verdi Voyages or the tourist office.

**Car rental** Avis, 52 rue Antoine Marty (☎04.68.25.05.84); Budget, 5 bd Omer Sarraut (☎04.68.72.31.31); Europcar, 7 bd Omer Sarraut (☎04.68.25.05.09); Garage la Bouriette, 58 bd Denis Papin (☎04.68.47.80.00); Location Occitan de Véhicules, 36 av Franklin Roosevelt (☎04.68.11.74.10). All of these companies, except for Garage la Bouriette, also have offices at the airport.

**Hospital** Centre Hospitalier Général, rte de St-Hilaire (☎04.68.24.24.24), on the south side of town.

**Internet access** Alert Rouge, 73 rue de Verdun (Mon–Fri 10am–1am, Sat 2pm–3am, Sun 2–7pm; ☎04.68.25.20.39, *alert_rouge.cbhouse.fr*).

**Laundry** Hallwash, 18 pl Carnot.

**Lost property** 13 rue Jean Bringer (☎04.68.10.27.00).

**Pharmacy** There several in rue Verdun: try Pharmacie Serin at no. 56; after 8pm enquire at the police station.

**Police** 4 bd Barbès (☎04.68.77.49.00).

**Swimming pool** Grazailles, rue du Moulin de la Seigne (☎04.68.47.81.83) is the one municipal pool open year-round (bus #2 or #3).

**Taxi** Radio Taxi ☎04.68.71.50.50.

# The upper Aude valley

The River Aude, whose course can be followed due south from Carcassonne, is like a highway of Catharism – the majority of the most famous sights and ruins associated with the heretical sect lie along its path as it ascends into the Pyrenees. The river's lower regions hold fewer attractions but are consequently less visited, making quiet towns like **Limoux** and **Alet-les-Bains** good places to get away from the summer crowds, but as the valley winds its way up to the modern service centre of **Quillan** more and more relics of the area's history reveal themselves. This is most obvious in the appearance of the so-called "Cathar castles" (many of which, in reality, postdate the Crusade), which form a rough chain stretching from Foix in the west, passing Quillan, and on to the Fenouillèdes to the east. South of Quillan, the valley narrows into a series of gorges as you begin the climb into the mountains, eventually reaching the isolated **Donezan** region. This upper portion of the river, skirting the southeastern edge of the highlands of the pays de Sault, has a good network of trails and *gîtes*, stretching out over varied terrain – a great area for **hiking**. From Quillan, you can connect to Foix and

---

### THE CARTE INTERSITE PASS

If you are planning on visiting a few of the Cathar sites in the region, you might consider purchasing a "**Carte Intersite**" pass. For 20F/€3.05, this ticket, valid for a year (and available at participating sites and local tourist offices), gives you reductions on the entry price to selected castles and monuments of the Aude *département*, including the castles of Arques, Carcassonne, Lastours, Minerve, Montségur, Peyreperteuse, Puilaurens, Puivert, Quéribus, Termes and Villerouge, plus the abbey of Lagrasse. Total savings, if you visit all the sites, is 65F/€9.91.

access the caves along the River Ariège, while a network of hiking trails leads over the Donezan, southwest towards Tarascon and southeast to the Têt valley of Roussillon.

# Limoux and around

Famous for its sparkling white *blanquette* ("little white") wine, **LIMOUX** is the first major town you will arrive at as you follow the course of the Aude upstream from Carcassonne. There's little else to write home about here, apart from the Lenten Carnival **festival**, held from January through to March, which features displays of masked dancers and live music in the town's main place de la République.

Limoux has dominated this neck of the woods since the Middle Ages and the same **bridge** which spans the Aude today brought prosperity in the form of merchants and traders as far back as the fourteenth century, when the town was rebounding from the repression it suffered as a consequence of its Cathar tendencies. At this time the town, like many of the "new towns" of the era, was governed by a board of consuls rather than by a feudal lord, and was wealthy enough to construct a formidable set of **defensive walls**, part of which can still be seen along the riverside. But these did not prove strong enough to keep out either the Black Death or the Black Prince, and a century and a half later Calvinism arrived, bringing religious strife, quickly followed by a poverty from which it never quite recovered.

Today, Limoux is quiet and has something of an air of neglected decay, but at least provides an opportunity to stretch your legs on the way towards the Pyrenees. The heart of the town is the **place de la République**, a wide square with some fine old stone arcading, a number of timber-frame houses, and the requisite café and restaurant patios. Just down rue St-Martin, the town's main **church** has some top-notch stained-glass windows and remarkably restrained sixteenth- and seventeenth-century décor in the side chapels. Behind it the canalized Aude separates the old town from the newer districts. Heading away from the river from place de la République, the quiet streets lead past a hideous nineteenth-century market and on to promenade de Tivoli, the Carcassonne–Quillan highway. Here, you'll find the small **Musée Petiet** (June–Aug Mon–Fri 9.30am–noon & 2–6pm, Sat & Sun 10am–noon & 2–5pm; Sept–May Mon–Sat 9.30am–noon & 4–6pm; 15F/€2.29) in the same building as the tourist office. Its collection of paintings, dominated by local nineteenth-century pointillism and allegory, contains some works of surprising quality. Just in case you'd forgotten you were in Cathar-country, **Catha-rama** (daily: July & Aug 10.30am–7pm; Sept–June 2–7pm; 25F/€3.81), across the street from the museum, will remind you, with a cheesy thirty-minute audiovisual show in four languages, emotionally recounting the repression of the religious movement, now a pillar of regional identity. Alternatively, if you're more interested in the local *blanquette* wine, head to the *domaine* Caves Sieur d'Arques (Mon–Sat 10–11am & 3–5pm; free) on avenue de Mauzac, 1km west on avenue Charles de Gaulle from the main roundabout. Here you can learn about the history of the vintage, as well as sample and buy some to take home.

If you have a car or bike, you may want to follow the winding D104 from Carcassonne to Limoux rather than the main D118, stopping at **ST-HILAIRE**, where you can visit the **abbey-church** (daily 9am–noon & 2–6.30pm; 20F/€3.05) of the same name; the ancient cloister's delicate double columns and carved corbels are particularly fine, and it contains a number of interesting tombs.

## Practicalities

Trains arrive at Limoux's **gare SNCF**, located on the east bank of the river, a good twenty-minute walk from the old town, while **buses** (☎04.68.31.09.64) stop outside the cinema on allées de Marronniers, in the old town. The **tourist office** (July & Aug Mon–Fri 9.30am–noon & 2–6pm, Sat & Sun 10am–noon & 2–5pm; Sept–June Mon–Sat 9.30–noon & 4–6pm; ☎04.68.31.11.82, fax 04.68.31.87.14, *limoux@fnotsi.net*) is on promenade de Tivoli, just south of the main roundabout. There is little reason to spend the night in Limoux, but should you feel obliged, the best two choices are the splendid and stately *Modern & Pigeon* (☎04.68.31.00.25, fax 04.68.31.12.43, *modpig@chezcom*; closed Wed; ④) in place Général Leclerc, and the humbler *Des Arcades* (☎04.68.31.02.57, fax 04.68.31.66.42, *www.logis-de-france.fr*; ③), south of the church at 96 rue St-Martin. Both are comfortable and have amenities such as television and parking. The municipal **campsite** (☎04.68.31.13.63; mid-May to Sept) is on the east bank of the river, south of the old bridge. Limoux's **market** is held on Fridays, and if you want to rent a **bike**, contact Cycles Taillefer (☎04.68.31.02.01).

**Restaurants** range from the expensive but excellent dining room of the *Modern & Pigeon* (closed Sat lunch & Mon), which has elaborate menus starting at 150F/€22.90, to the *Grand Café* at 25 place de la République, where you can enjoy a menu inside or on the sunny terrace for only 59F/€9. Otherwise, *Maison de la Blanquette*, at 46bis promenade du Tivoli, is a good place to wash down regional cuisine with the bubbly white (from 78F/€11.90), or there's *l'Hibiscus* (closed Mon), Limoux's *gastronomique* restaurant at the edge of town en route to St-Polycarpe (75F/€11.44 and up).

# Alet-les-Bains

Sixteen kilometres further upstream, **ALET-LES-BAINS** is a better place than Limoux to make a stop. This ancient little village still owes its modest prosperity to the **hot springs** which bubble out of the ground on the north side of town, and which were first harnessed for curative purposes by the Romans. From the ninth century the town flourished as the site of a Benedictine abbey, and from the fourteenth as a bishopric, before declining into obscurity with the Wars of Religion. Today it is largely overlooked, a fact which helps to preserve an atmosphere of antiquity in the village, but which is also a shame, given that the quiet streets conceal some surprising relics. An old seventeenth-century **bridge** still connects Alet with the Limoux–Quillan highway, and just across it loom the ruins of the **abbey of Notre-Dame** (daily: July & Aug 9am–7pm; Feb–June & Sept 10am–1pm & 2–6pm; Oct–Jan 9.30am–12.30pm & 1.30–5.30pm; 15F/€2.29), destroyed in 1577 during the religious wars and plundered to strengthen the town's walls. From here, the narrow rue de Séminaire leads back to the town's **square**, boxed in by timbered houses and the stone **Maison de Consuls**, the medieval home of the town council. Following the narrow and evocative rue de la Cadène north from the square will take you through a gate and on to a few **Roman relics**, including a scrap of ancient road. South from the square, sleepy rue de la Rose leads to another gate and a long section of twelfth-century walls. Just inside the gates, to the west, you'll find several tiny **medieval houses**, which, 800 years ago, housed merchants' families.

## Practicalities

**Buses** passing between Limoux and Quillan will drop you on the main road by the old bridge, from where it's a short walk to the town's **tourist office** (daily: July & Aug 9am–7pm; Sept–June 10am–1pm & 2–6pm; ☎04.68.69.93.56, *alet-les-bains@fnotsi.net*) in rue Nicolas Pavillon, beside the ruined abbey. Staying in Alet-les-Bains is made all the more worthwhile by its excellent **hotel**, the *Hostellerie de l'Évêché* (☎04.68.69.90.25, fax 04.68.69.21.4, *www.logis-de-france.fr*; closed Oct–April; ③), in a wooded garden just over the old bridge. If this is full, there are **chambres d'hôtes** at the friendly, English-run *Maison Val d'Aleth* (☎04.68.69.90.40, fax 04.68.69.94.60, *maison.valdaleth@wanadoo.fr*; ②) on the same street. The town's **campsite** is situated on the riverbank, further along rue Nicolas Pavillon. There are two good **restaurants** in town: *l'Évêché*'s dining-room (closed Sun; menus from 100F/€15.25), which serves high-quality regional cuisine, and *Auberge de la Main d'Argent* (closed Tues; menu from 80F/€12.20), located in a seventeenth-century house in the central place de la République.

# Rennes-le-Château and Arques

There is little to detain you along the road from Alet-les-Bains to Quillan, but if you have time, it is worthwhile leaving the course of the Aude at **Couiza** for detours to the ancient abbey-town of Rennes, and the castle at Arques, east of the main highway.

**RENNES-LE-CHÂTEAU** (not to be confused with the nearby spa town of Rennes-les-Bains) is found at the end of a 4km-long neck-twisting mountain road winding up from Couiza, with impressive vistas over the Aude valley. It was here that the mysterious Béranger Saunière, Rennes' parish priest, died in 1917 after having lived a life of luxury for nearly thirty years, which included building himself a private villa, conservatory and library. The town's **church** is full of veiled symbols and secret codes, which, some say, indicate that Saunière had discovered the lost treasure of Solomon, brought here by the Visigoths in the fifth century. Unlikely as this may be, the fact that the fortunes of the priest changed precisely when he was conducting discreet "historical" excavations in the church's ruins, leaves no doubt he discovered a substantial buried treasure. Strange events continue to surround the village, the latest being the discovery of aerial photos, dating back to 1967, which allegedly reveal the image of a Virgin and child in a nearby field. Aside from the church, garishly redecorated by Saunière, the town's attractions include a small **museum** (daily: May–Sept 10am–7pm; Oct–April 10am–6pm; 25F/€3.81), whose most interesting piece is the late-Visigothic-era base which once supported the church's main altar, and within which it is believed Saunière discovered the ancient parchments which led him to the treasure. Also worth a look is the lavish **estate** (same hours and ticket as museum) of the priest, including his villa "Béthania", and a fortified tower which he built to house his office and library.

To reach the **donjon d'Arques** follow the D613 as it winds slowly uphill from Couiza eastwards along the course of the Orbieu. Coming into view 10km later, the perfectly preserved square **keep** (daily: July & Aug 10am–7pm; April–June & Sept–Oct 10.30am–6pm; March & Nov 11am–5pm; 25F/€3.81) is unmistakable as it rises 25m above the surrounding fields. Both the remains of the walled perimeter and the tower of this so-called Cathar castle date from after the famous Crusade, but it is without doubt the most beautiful of the region's *château*. The

Maison Carrée, Nîmes

Place de la Comédie, Montpellier

Building facades, Toulouse

A Camarguais festival

Basilique de St-Sernin, Toulouse

Sculpted balcony support, Toulouse

Minerve, viewed from across the River Cesse

Les Arènes, Nîmes

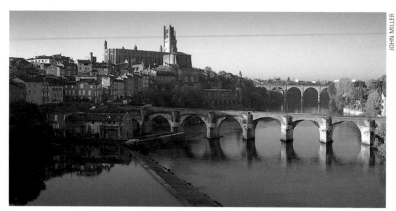

Albi, viewed from across the River Tarn

La Cirque de Navacelles

Harbour, La Grande-Motte

central *donjon*, which dates back to the thirteenth century, is extremely well preserved, with graceful Gothic vaulting sustaining two of its great chambers and a number of ogival (pointed-arched) windows dating from the period of its original construction. The third-floor hall is dominated by an impressively huge fireplace, while the walls, which were constructed in the following century, are breached by a simple gate and buttressed by a square guard tower on the southwest corner. Outside, there's a group of beehives clustered just to the side of the entrance, where you can buy fresh honey. The village of **ARQUES** is about 1500m east of the castle – a nondescript little hamlet, which has a fourteenth-century church, some contemporary buildings, and a small and dull exhibit on Catharism held in the **Maison de Déodat Roché** (same hours and ticket as the castle). From Arques the road continues (no public transport) through ever more untamed and isolated terrain towards the castles at Termes and Villerouge-Termenès (see pp.294 & 293), and the abbey-town of Lagrasse (see p.295). Returning to Couiza and following the Aude towards Quillan, you'll run the gauntlet of a series of dubious museums, none of which are particularly worth the effort to see.

## Practicalities

If you have no transport, you can reach Rennes and Arques by **taxi** from Cuiza (☎04.68.74.25.36), although, if you are up to it, the strenuous walk to Rennes is enjoyable. Cycling to Arques is another option – Aul Fil de l'Aude (☎04.68.74.16.69) in Couiza rents **bikes**. You can **stay** comfortably either in the former priest's estate at Rennes, the *Domaine de l'Abbé Saunière* (☎04.68.74.31.66; closed Nov–March; ②), or at Couiza in the *Château des Ducs* (☎04.68.74.04.20, fax 04.68.74.14.65; ③). For further information, contact the **tourist office** in Rennes (daily: mid-June to mid-Sept 10am–7pm; mid-Sept to mid-June 10am–5.30pm; ☎04.68.74.72.68, fax 04.68.74.72.76). There are good *terroir* **restaurants** in the area, the best being the *Château des Ducs de Joyeuse* (closed Sun & Mon eve, Jan & Feb; menu from 90F/€13.73) in Couiza, which sometimes has a dinner-theatre show, *Jardins de l'Abbé* (☎04.68.74.31.16; closed Sun & Mon lunch & Nov–April; from 90F/€13.73) in Rennes and *Auberge du Moulin d'Arques* (closed Sun & Mon, Jan–March; from 75F/€11.44) in Arques.

# Quillan

Clustered on the west bank of the Aude about halfway along its course, **QUILLAN** is a half-heartedly industrialized place with a number of services, its main attraction being its proximity to the pays de Sault (see p.133), plus the river itself, a sturdy torrent running right past the town providing ample canoeing and rafting possibilities (see below). The only monument of interest is the ruined **castle**, on the east bank of the Aude just across the *pont vieux*. Built on the site of a Visigothic fortress, it was burned by the Huguenots in 1575 during the course of the Religious Wars and partly dismantled in the eighteenth century, but the remnants are still worth a scramble.

The **gare SNCF** and **gare routière** are both central, on boulevard Charles-de-Gaulle. The **tourist office** occupies a prominent kiosk beside the train station (summer Mon–Sat 8am–noon & 2–7pm, Sun 9am–noon; ☎04.68.20.07.78), and can help with Grotte de l'Aguzou reservations (see p.132) among other things. Opposite, you'll find the least expensive **hotel** in town, *Le Terminus*, at no. 45 (☎ & fax 04.68.20.93.33; ③) – indeed all accommodation is on this same, noisy street, which doubles as the D117; you won't get much more peace and quiet, but you will get more comfort for scarcely more money at the *Cartier*, at no. 31 (☎04.68.20.05.14, fax 04.68.20.22.57; ③) or the *Canal* at no. 36 (☎04.68.20.08.62, fax 04.68.20.08.27.96; ③). All have attached **restaurants**, though the *Canal's* shuts on Sunday. The Centre International de Séjour Sports et Nature, located in the *mairie*, runs a **gîte d'étape** (☎04.68.20.33.69; ①), while *La Sapinette* at 21 rue René-Delpech, off boulevard Jean Bourrel, is the closest **campsite**. Centre de Séjour Sports Nature de la Forge (☎04.68.20.23.79), at the southern edge of town en route to Axat, organizes **canoeing** and **rafting**, as well as climbing and canyoning trips – it also has a gîte (①). You can rent **bikes** from Cycles Benassis (☎04.68.20.18.91).

# South from Quillan

The road **south from Quillan** is a fabulous approach to the eastern peaks of the Pyrenees. Coursing down from the Capcir plateau, the Aude has cut successively through granite, gneiss and schist, and finally soft limestone, carving spectacular **caves** (*grottes*) and ever deeper **gorges** along the way. Public transport here is limited to a summer **bus** service (3 weekly) to Quérigut, 44km south of Quillan. There's a map of the region on pp.134–135.

### Défilé de Pierre-Lys and Axat

Gorge country begins almost immediately after you leave Quillan heading south, with rock overhangs blasted as necessary to allow passage. The narrowest bit is the cliff-lined **Défilé de Pierre-Lys**, 8km to the south, where climbers can usually be seen swinging above the road. Four kilometres beyond the *défilé*, there's a **campsite**, *Le Moulin du Pont d'Aliès* (April–Nov), plus canteen, at the eponymous crossroads, the junction where the D117 highway peels off east towards the Fenouillèdes.

Continuing south 1km beyond the crossroads on the D618 brings you to **AXAT**, where an old bridge, under which rafters often put in, links the through-road district with the east-bank quarter. There's just one **hotel** here, the adequate *Hôtel de la Poste* (☎04.68.20.59.20; closed part Sept; ③), at 16 route National, the main street.

### Grotte de l'Aguzou

If you have sufficient time to spend in this region, try to visit the **Grotte de l'Aguzou**, 15km southwest of Axat towards the upstream end of the Gorges de l'Aude. The guided tour (300F/€45.75 full day, 180F/€27.45 half-day) of this magnificent complex is as close as a non-speleologist can get to the real thing and is very popular, so book well in advance (contact Philippe Moreno, ☎04.68.20.45.38, *grotte.aguzou@wanadoo.fr*). Equipped with overalls, helmet and lamp, groups of four to ten people are taken into the unlit cave system at 9am, to be conducted through the *grandes salles* of stalactites, stalagmites, columns and draperies, some of which are 20m high. Lunch (you bring your own) is taken 600m underground, and then it's on to the so-called "gardens of crystals" – loads of them in a fantastic array of forms and shapes, some growing from the rock in long, thin needles, or like pine cones dusted by hoar frost, and others clear and convoluted like a Venetian glass-blower's accident.

The best place to **stay** for an early start is the designated *camping sauvage* area by the river, 300m from the cave entrance. There's also a *gîte d'étape* (☎04.68.20 .37.07; ①) just over 3km west at Fontanès-de-Sault.

## The Donezan

In the twelfth century the **Donezan** region, and its then-capital Usson – in the southern neck of the Gorges de l'Aude – became a sort of forerunner to Andorra: separated from the rest of Ariège by the **Col de Pailhères** (2001m), it was granted special financial privileges on account of its inaccessibility. Today **USSON**, like the rest of this remote region of seven villages, houses barely enough people to function as a *canton*; the spa of Usson-les-Bains 1km downstream is boarded up and for sale, while the dry-stone walls around the fields are as dilapidated as the **château** (July & Aug daily 10am–1pm & 3–7pm; Sept–Nov Sat & Sun 10am–1pm & 3–7pm; 20F/€3.05), the first place of safety for the four Cathars who escaped the massacre at Montségur (see p.139). Dating back to at least the eleventh century, the castle, between the thirteenth and sixteenth centuries, marked the eastern boundary of the possessions of the Counts of Foix, once champions of the Cathars and resolutely hostile to the French Crown.

Just above Usson, 3km along the D25 to Ax-les-Thermes, **MIJANÈS** is an immensely attractive stone-built village, where you may **stay and eat** year-round at the simple but perfectly adequate *Relais de Pailhères* (☎04.68.20.46.97; ②), with well-sized, wooden-floor rooms. This is the only such facility between Quillan and Quérigut, with people coming from some distance away to patronize it, so reservations are advisable at weekends. When there's good snow the nearby **ski station** of Mijanès-Latrabe (☎05.61.20.41.37) opens – not a frequent occurrence, as the four drag-lifts rise to only 2060m.

These days, **QUÉRIGUT**, 7km south of Usson, is the capital of the region. It stands at the head of a slope of neglected terraces, notable only for the stump of the **Château de Donezan**, the last stronghold of the Cathar leadership, who held out here for eleven years after the fall of Montségur. Quérigut makes a good walking base for jaunts southwest through the forest; **accommodation** is either at the ageing *Hôtel le Donezan* (☎04.68.20.42.40, fax 04.68.20.47.06; ②), uphill from the church opposite the fountain (which also has the only **restaurant**), or at the *Auberge du Cabanas* **gîte** (☎04.68.20.47.03; ①). There is also a **campsite**, *Le Bousquet*, down by the stream below the village. Usson and Quérigut can be reached in about an hour on Monday, Wednesday and Friday afternoons by Petit Charles **bus** from Quillan, making the return trip the same day.

# The Pays de Sault

The magnificent **PAYS DE SAULT** – the upland area more or less bounded by the rivers Aude and Ariège and, to the north, the main road from Quillan to Foix – is pure Cathar territory, as evinced by its most famous sight, the cliff-top stronghold of **Montségur**. For visitors it also offers some of Languedoc's most outstanding scenery; the vast highlands are composed primarily of limestone, and thus riddled with caves and ravines like the spectacular **Gorges de la Frau**. Above ground, the region's agricultural methods seem to have changed little since Cathar times – pesticides have yet to infiltrate the region's ecosystem, so the silhouettes of birds of prey are seldom out of the sky.

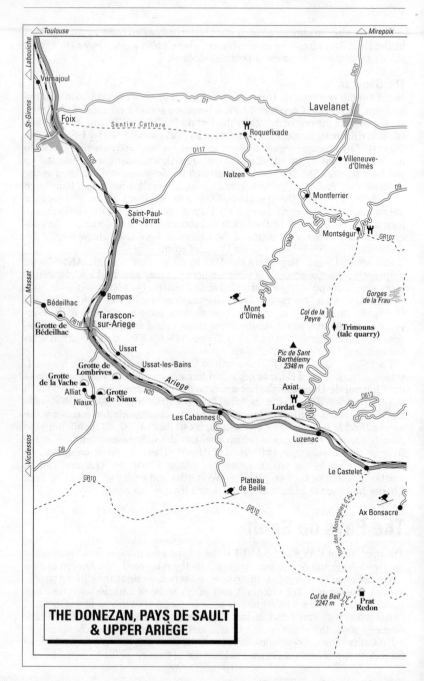

**THE DONEZAN, PAYS DE SAULT & UPPER ARIÈGE**

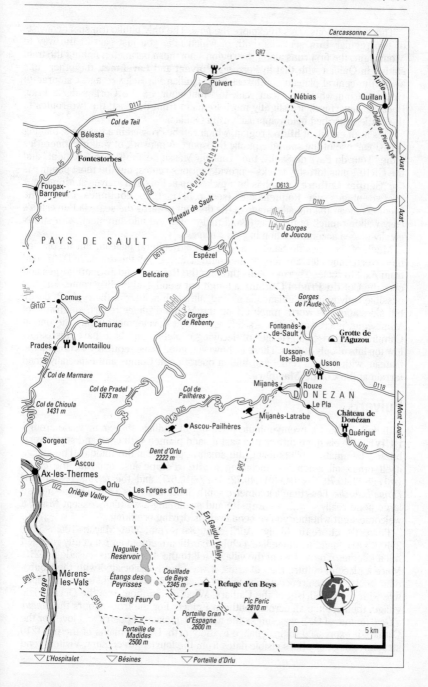

There are various ways to explore the *pays*. The only public transport consists of two regular **bus** services, both of which take you just part of the way to Montségur: the first runs along the region's northern perimeter, linking the train station in Quillan with that in Foix, via **Puivert** and **Lavelanet**; the other runs along the central plateau southwest from Quillan via Belcaire and Camurac to **Comus**, from where you can walk to Montségur via the Gorges de la Frau. Because departures are slightly more frequent from the east, the two routes to the castle described below approach from Quillan.

This is an excellent **hiking** region, which can be crossed in a few days, making occasional use of the sporadic public transport. A network of walking itineraries – the "Tour du Pays de Sault", the "Tour du Massif de Tabe", the "Piémont" and the GR107, plus forestry tracks – provide various routes, but the most popular is the **"Sentier Cathare"**, which is best picked up at Foix and arrives at Montségur in two stages via Roquefixade (see p.141), then continues on to the Mediterranean (taking advantage of the descent towards the sea) via Puivert; it's easy walking much of the year (avoid mid-winter and mid-summer), with strategically placed accommodation in *gîtes d'étape*.

Much of the Pays de Sault is a spacious agricultural plateau, but it contains more vertiginous terrain, too. At the southeastern edge, the dramatic D107 road from Axat to Ax-les-Thermes runs through the **Rebenty** and **Joucou** gorges and over the **Col du Pradel** (1673m), a tough but wonderful **cycling** route. Another possible activity in the uplands is **skiing**, although neither of the region's downhill ski stations is worth much effort: the Monts d'Olmes resort, southwest of Montségur, is crowned with a seedy apartment development, while the one at Camurac comprises a "village" of decaying chalets – and both have impossibly low top-lifts of only 1940m. There is, however, good **cross-country skiing** on the plateau, with a small rental and tuition operation at Comus and especially good terrain at the **Col de Marmare**.

# Puivert

Although it's just a twenty-minute drive out of Quillan, the countryside around **PUIVERT** feels quite different, a vast upland planted with corn and sunflowers, buzzed by amateur pilots using the small airport near the middle. The village itself offers all amenities, including a **gîte d'étape** just opposite the castle (☎04.68.11.40.70, fax 04.68.11.40.72; 70F/€10.68), and the *terroir* **restaurant** *Dame Blanche*. Less than a kilometre south of the village is a small lake – more a large pond really – with a **campsite** and swimming area (daily except Mon), a welcome sight whether you've been cycling, driving or hiking.

Puivert's **château** (daily: April–Sept 8am–7pm; Oct–March 10am–5pm; 25F/€3.81), standing alone like a child's cardboard cutout atop a gently rounded hill a kilometre or so east of the village, fell to the Albigensian Crusade in 1210. More a place of culture than of arms, it was closely associated with the troubadour poets, whose preoccupation with themes of romance might seem incompatible with the asceticism of the Cathars. What united them was the Occitan language, then spoken all across southern France. For the troubadours the *langue d'Oc* ("tongue of Oc") was simply the natural language of poetry and love; for the Cathars it expressed their defiance of the North. Little remains of the pre-1210 structure; most of what's visible dates from the fourteenth century. Visitors tend to focus on the various floors of the *donjon*; the chapel features vigil seats at the north and south windows, a wall font and rib-vaulting on the ceiling, culminating in a keystone embossed with images of the Virgin and St George. The highest chamber is dubbed the "musicians' room" after its eight *culs-de-lamps* or torch sockets at the termini of more rib-vaulting, each sculpted in the form of a figure playing a different period instrument. Back down in the village a small **museum** (daily July & Aug 10am–7pm; April–June & Sept 10am–noon & 2–6pm; March, Oct & Nov 10am–noon & 2–5pm; 25F/€3.81) holds displays of local traditional crafts as well as a collection of reproductions of medieval instruments copied from the castle's sculptures.

# Northern approaches to Montségur

From Puivert the road heads west over the Col de Teil, the Pyrenean watershed: east of it, rivers flow to the Mediterranean, while on the west they empty into the Atlantic. You can walk from Puivert to Montségur along the "Sentier Cathare", a long but not difficult day of some 25km, mostly through dense fir forests.

### Bélesta and Fougax-Barrineuf
A better place to begin the walk, however, is 11km west at **BÉLESTA**, the next stop on the bus route. It's a far more manageable village than Lavelanet (see below), and if you get stranded there's **accommodation** at the somewhat pricey *Le Troubador*, on the through road (☎05.61.01.60.57; ③), a cheaper no-name *Café-Hotel* diagonally across from the *mairie* on the main square (②) and **camping** on the east side of the village at *Le Val d'Amour* (June–Sept). Attractions begin almost immediately on the way south: some 1500m out of Bélesta, the route to Montségur passes Fontestorbes, an artesian spring (*source intermittente*) under a rock overhang that in summer spurts water for six-minute periods evenly separated by 32-minute pauses (in winter the water flows continuously). From the *source* you can continue directly to Montségur by walking along various marked GRs – roughly a three-hour trip, or taking a longer detour via the Gorges de la Frau, 8km south (see p.140).

The most direct approaches pass through the double village of **FOUGAX-BARRINEUF**, 2km southwest, which offers a fine **restaurant**, *Les Cinque Fours*, occupying an old bone-comb factory (formerly an important local industry, established by Protestants between the sixteenth and eighteenth centuries). The portions aren't huge, but they suffice, and the 85F menu is quite adequate as a four-course lunch.

### Lavelanet
**LAVELANET**, 8km west of Bélesta along the Quillan–Foix road, has little to offer other than its onward bus connections, its **tourist office** (July & Aug Mon–Sat 9am–noon & 2–7pm, Sun 9am–noon; Sept–June Mon–Sat 9am–noon & 2–7pm; ☎05.61.01.22.20, fax 05.61.03.06.69, *lavelanet.tourisme@wanadoo.fr*) on the central *rond point* and the clean, modern **campsite** *Camping de Lavelanet* (April–Sept; ☎05.61.01.55.54) southwest of the centre. There's no excuse for getting stuck here, and if you do the only **hotels**, the *Parc* (☎05.61.03.04.05, fax 05.61.03.08.66, *www.logis-de-france.fr*; ④), on the road out to Bélesta, and the *Espagne*, on the road to Foix (☎05.61.01.00.78; ②), are hardly enticing.

## CATHARISM AND THE ALBIGENSIAN CRUSADE

The origins of **Catharism** seem to lie in **Manichaeism**, a dualistic Persian doctrine popular in the late Roman Empire and founded on the concept of the material world as an invasion of the realm of Light by the powers of Darkness. It later found practical expression in Europe among the Bogomils of the Balkan peninsula, with whom the Crusaders who journeyed overland to Palestine in the 1090s came into contact. By the twelfth century a modified version of this principle, most likely brought west by the returning Crusaders, had taken hold in the south of France. Those practising Catharism came to be known popularly as **Albigeois** (or Albigenses) due to the fact that the earliest attempts by the Catholic Church to counter the heresy took place in Lombers, near Albi, in 1165.

According to Cathar thinking, God reigned over the spiritual world, the Devil created all matter, and Christ was God's messenger, through whom human souls could be united with the Divine and attain immortality. The belief posed a number of problems for the Roman Catholic Church. Firstly, Cathars denied the doctrine of the Virgin Birth, and insisted that the Catholic faithful, in worshipping any Creator (of matter), were in fact worshipping the Devil. They were **immaterialists** by definition – ascetism was seen as the only route to redemption – and thus had no need for the sumptuous buildings and trappings favoured by the Church, and they were also purportedly **pacifists**, who condemned the Crusades. Additionally, the austere spirituality of their leaders – the *parfaits* and *parfaites* (lay adherents were known simply as *bons hommes* and *bonnes femmes*) – was a constant rebuke to the dissolute clergy of the Church, while their contact with the population answered to the needs of the common folk, ignored by corrupted Catholic institutions. And on top of all this, their conviction that they were exempt from feudal vows of allegiance made them politically attractive to independent-minded local nobility – and politically dangerous to greater powers.

After his election in 1198, **Pope Innocent III** began to put pressure on the Occitan nobility, under whose protection the Cathars lived, to return to the fold. A meeting was arranged whereat **Raymond VI of Toulouse**, who had been excommunicated for protecting his Cathar subjects, was to meet the papal legate Pierre de Castelnou to reconcile differences. Instead, an argument broke out, and the meeting ended with Pierre dead by a swordstroke of one of Raymond's men. Innocent felt that the time for compromise had passed, and launched what is now referred to as the **Albigensian Crusade** against the Cathars, which initially found ready support among various factions, including the predatory Northern French nobility – whose greatest figure was the seasoned crusader **Simon de Montfort**. But the first big impetus was given by the powerful monastic orders – in particular – the Cistercians, whose leader, the abbot of Cîteaux, Bernard de Clairvaux, rallied knights from across northern Europe to the fight.

In 1209 an army led by the archbishop of Narbonne and the new legate **Arnaud Amaury**, invaded Languedoc, with a heavy contingent of English mercenaries in its ranks. Nîmes and western Languedoc yielded without struggle, but at Béziers local Catholics refused to release the handful of Cathars who lived within their midst. The city was duly besieged and its entire population – a figure put by some authorities at twenty thousand – was massacred. When asked how the Catholic citizens were to be distinguished from the heretics, Amaury replied: "Kill them all, God will recognize His own." Shortly after, Simon de Montfort took over military command and proceeded to Carcassonne, which fell only after protracted resistance and was handed over to the leader. Intent on making himself lord of all Languedoc, de Montfort pursued a relentless campaign against Raymond VI and the other Occitan noble families – his atrocities aimed at generating terror among his enemies. In short order Raymond and his son were forced to flee to the English court of King John, the elder Raymond's brother-in-law. When the two Raymonds eventually returned from exile they resumed battle with de Montfort at Toulouse, which their arch-foe was besieging – a campaign that cost him his life in June 1218. Their success was fairly short-lived; although the younger Raymond, who succeeded his father in 1222, managed to regain lost territory and reorganize the Cathar communities, a new scorched-earth campaign unleashed in 1226 brought him to his knees by 1229. Raymond VII had to submit to public flagellation, the razing of Toulouse's walls, the loss of his possessions beyond the Rhône and the marriage of his only daughter to the younger brother of the Parisian king Louis IX.

In 1231, as part of the mop-up operation, Pope Gregory IX authorized Dominican friars to root out all heretics in Languedoc, laying the foundation for the later infamous **Inquisition**. The Dominican Order had been founded in 1215 by Domingo de Guzmán – the future St Dominic himself having come specially from Castille to the Cathar heartland to counter the growing heresy. Leaving violent coercion to others, his preferred strategies were strenuous disputations with Cathar theologians and imitation of their austere habits – even before his order had been approved by the pope, he had founded a convent at Prouille (near Fanjeux – see p.143) to receive Cathar women who recanted their beliefs. However, when persuasion failed, the Dominicans would hand obstinate or unrepentant heretics over to the secular authorities – who would kill them.

Despite the military victories of the Crown and the work of the Dominicans, Catharism continued to persist openly in the inaccessible foothills of the Pyrenees. But the fate of the Cathars was sealed when, in 1242, a group of sixty knights from Montségur, led by **Pierre-Roger de Mirepoix**, went to Avignonet and assassinated eleven inquisitors. The retaliatory assault on **Montségur**, by a force of almost ten thousand men, began in May 1243, and continued through the winter – the first time in the Albigensian Crusades that the fighting was not suspended when the weather turned. In March 1244, de Mirepoix, despairing of relief, agreed terms: the two hundred or so non-Cathar soldiers within the citadel would be allowed to go, but after fifteen days' truce the Cathars themselves were to abjure their faith or submit to whatever fate the victors devised for them. On the night of March 15, in contravention of the terms, four Cathars climbed down the cliffs, escaped over the Col de la Peyre and recovered the Cathar "treasure" from a cave where it had been hidden the previous Christmas; what happened to it is a mystery, giving rise to a confusion of romantic legends, one of which identifies the treasure as the Holy Grail, and the Cathars themselves as the Knights of the Round Table. On March 16 Montségur surrendered, and the 225 surviving Cathar civilians who refused to abjure their beliefs were burned on a mass pyre, those who could not walk being thrown on with their stretchers.

In effect, Catharism ceased to exist as a significant force in France after the massacre at Montségur, though two of the four escapees later appeared in Lombardy to support a refugee Cathar community established there. Quéribus and Puilaurens – the final Cathar holdouts – came under royal control between 1255 and 1258. When Raymond VII's daughter died childless in 1271, all of Languedoc passed to the French Crown, and in the years that followed, Catharism persisted mainly as an underground network or, more openly, in the rural villages of the French, Aragonese and Catalan Pyrenees. But it didn't last. The last Cathar *parfait*, Guillaume de Bélibaste, was burned at the stake in Pamiers in 1321, and in 1412 an isolated community of Cathars was discovered in the village of Montaillou (see p.140) and prosecuted by an inquisition led by the Bishop of Foix.

## The southern approach to Montségur via Comus

From Monday to Friday there are two late-afternoon buses daily from Quillan to Comus, about 40km southwest. You may, however, want to alight slightly earlier at Camurac, 3km short of Comus, and walk the rest of the way via **MONTAILLOU** village, a detour which takes about two hours. Montaillou subscribed to the Cathar heresy long after the fall of Montségur, until the Inquisition, directed by the bishop of Pamiers, set to work here during the 1320s. The records compiled by the inquisitors were so precise that author Emmanuel Le Roy Ladurie was able to recreate every aspect of the villagers' lives from them, from the minutiae of domestic economics to the details of their sexual habits, in his book about the village, *Montaillou*. Fewer than twenty people live here permanently now, all of them descendants of the Cathars, as you can see by comparing their surnames with those on the headstones in the ancient graveyard. **CAMURAC** can offer **accommodation** at the economical *Auberge du Pays de Sault* (☎04.68.20.32.09; ②) as well as *Camping les Sapins*.

**COMUS** isn't a lot bigger than Montaillou, but does have an excellent **gîte d'étape** (☎04.68.20.33.69 ①) attached to the Centre École Pleine Nature, which specializes in **caving**, the limestone hereabouts being peppered with two hundred known caves. Montségur is 13km away, through the **Gorges de la Frau**. From Comus take the recently designated GR107, formerly the GR7B, which drops down as a mule track between fields to a wide gorge that suddenly becomes a *défilé*, where thousand-metre-high cliffs admit the sun only during the early afternoon. When the gorge widens again, you meet the dead end of the D5 coming south from Bélesta and Fougax-Barrineuf. There are two ways of continuing to Montségur: either along the Sentier Cathare westwards, wrapped in tree shade alongside a stream (turn off at the first farm, 45min along the D5), or via a bridle trail beginning about an hour along the tarmac, offering higher, more open ground. Either way, walking time from Comus is four hours.

## Montségur

The ruined castle of **MONTSÉGUR** lives up to the promise of its distant view, its plain stone walls poised emphatically above the straggling, namesake village on a 1207-metre-high *pog* (a local variant on the Occitan *puèg*, or "hill"). The original fortifications were built by Guillaume "Short-Nose", duke of Aquitaine, but between 1204 and 1232 it was reconstructed as a bastion of the Cathars under the direction of Guilhabert de Castres, leader of the sect. Drastically eroded into naked vertical faces and gullies, the *pog* would have been a formidable defence. Only on the western side is it possible to walk up to the summit (about 30min), through what is now called the *prat dels cremats*, where the surviving Cathars were burned to death after the castle fell (a stone memorial pays tribute to them); see the box on p.138.

The beauty of **the site** (daily: May–Aug 9am–7.30pm; April & Sept 9am–5.30pm; March & Oct 10am–5pm; Feb & Nov 10am–4pm; Dec 10am–4pm, closed Mon; 22F/€3.36) is what hits you first, since the original walls were reduced by half after the siege, and all internal structures are gone except the simple keep, now open to the sky. Then you begin to wonder how that last Cathar community of five hundred people could have held out so long in such a small space. Even given that some lived in now-vanished houses at the foot of the walls on the north and west faces, there was still a garrison of two hundred to be accommodated, together with the *faydits* – local aristocrats dispossessed by the crusade against Catharism. What's left of the castle takes no more than a few minutes to explore – rather disappointingly, you're no longer allowed to climb up on the walls, merely to traverse the keep to visit the west *donjon* – but it isn't so much what you see at Montségur that makes the trip unforgettable, as what your imagination can recreate from its remnants.

Down in the village, 1km below, a one-room **archeological museum** (daily: May–Sept 10am–noon & 2–5.30pm; March, April, Oct & Nov 1–5.30pm; Feb 2–5.30pm; Dec 2–5pm, closed Mon; free) displays artefacts excavated since the 1950s from the original village up beside the walls, from both pre- and post-Cathar periods – mostly food bones, personal effects, tools and surviving fragments of houses.

### Practicalities

Despite its small size, tourist numbers at Montségur village have prompted a **tourist office** (July–Sept daily 10am–1pm & 2–6pm; ☎ & fax 05.61.03.03.03, *www .citaenet.com/montsegur*), of most use for information on the precise route of the GR107. If you'd like to stay the night – and the beautiful scenery certainly encourages the notion – there are a couple of **hotels**: the old-fashioned *Couquet* (☎05.61.01.10.28; ①), a rambling country pension of wood-furnished rooms with washbasins; and the adjacent, en-suite *Costes* (☎05.61.01.10.24, fax 05.61.03.06.28, *www.logis-de-france.fr*; ②), just uphill, which also manages the nearby **gîte d'étape** (April to mid-Nov; ☎05.61.01.10.24; ①). The closest **campsite** (tents only) is the *Point Acceuil Jeunes* (☎05.61.01.10.27), at the lower end of the village on the Bélesta side. Both hotels have attached and reasonably priced **restaurants** serving nourishing food: the *Couquet* represents great value with four large home-made courses for well under 100F/€15.25; the *Costes* is fancier, featuring game and *Ariègeois* specialities for well over that figure. There's also *Le Bufadou*, which offers a three-course vegetarian menu for under 100F/€15.25.

# Roquefixade

Approximately 8km west of Lavelanet, the village of Nalzen is the best point along the D117 for access to **ROQUEFIXADE**, westernmost of the Cathar castles and last stop on the "Sentier Cathare" before Foix. A two-kilometre side road leads up to the eponymous village, rebuilt after the Albigensian Crusade as a *bastide*. From the high end of the village it's a twenty-minute climb to the unenclosed castle (free), which takes its name (originally *roca fissada*) from the vast natural fissures augmenting its defences. Perched at the western end of a long ridge, it's bigger than it appears from below but utterly ruinous; your main reward is the view over the valley below with its clustered villages, and south – weather permitting – to the high Pyrenean ridge. A **gîte d'étape** (☎05.61.03 .01.36, *roquefixade@mail.dotcom.fr*; ①) stands by the base of the path up to the castle, and their outdoor seating is a good place for a drink after the climb; however, they only have twelve places, so let them know in good time if you wish to stay. Alternative accommodation if they're full is the small inn, *Relais des Pogs* (☎05.61.01.14.50; ②).

# Mirepoix and the lower Ariège valley

The lower part of the Ariège valley winds a leisurely course through a broad, rolling upland, whose rich dairy and wheat farms set it apart from the dry, vine-dominated scrub of most of Languedoc and Roussillon. The plain adjacent to this part of the river, centred on **Mirepoix**, was, like its southern counterpart the pays de Sault, a land of Cathars and castles; today it is home to a series of surprising and unique medieval **monuments**. Along the river proper you'll pass through unprepossessing **Pamiers** to **Foix**. Head of Ariège, France's smallest *département*, Foix was once the capital of a proudly independent principality, whose ambitions of independence were as strong and as fruitless as those of Toulouse county – today the only testament to this is the town's strikingly poised castle.

## Mirepoix and around

The village of **MIREPOIX**, tucked away amongst the undulating hills of the Hers Valley, is one of the region's best kept secrets. And little wonder, as its only transport connection is made up of four daily buses running each way between Pamiers to the west and Lavelanet to the south. Without a car it would take a solid day's cycling to cover the 48km from Carcassonne, or a lengthy 30-kilometre trek along the GR7 from Villepinte (near Castelnaudary), via Fanjeux.

Mirepoix was a Cathar stronghold which paid dearly for its heresy, suffering a massacre at the hands of the Catholic Crusaders; but this in fact was only the beginning of its misfortunes, as a generation later it was all but destroyed by a flood. The present town dates back to 1290, when the noble Jean de Lévis laid out a new *bastide* in a safer location. At the centre of the village sits the broad place Général-Leclerc (or place de Couverts), arguably the most beautiful town **square** east of the Ariège. Almost the entire perimeter is rimmed by broad arcades supported by stout old beams, above which rise two storeys of pastel timber-frame houses. Although the *place* as a whole is beautiful, its star attraction is the fourteenth-century **Maison des Consuls** (now a hotel, see below) in the centre of the north side, at no. 6. This old council-house, courthouse and prison dates back to the fourteenth century and is decorated by nearly 150 **wooden heads**, carved out in high relief of the ends of the beams supporting the second storey. Each carving is individual, the portraits ranging across the gamut of medieval social classes and professions and on to include exotic and foreign peoples (including some very early portrayals of black Africans), as well as demons, monsters, animals and assorted grotesques. They make a singular masterwork.

By passing through an attractive nineteenth-century wrought-iron **market hall** on the south side of the square, you arrive at another arcaded *place*, Philip de Lévis – not as stunning as its larger counterpart, but also impressive. In the middle stands the fourteenth-century **cathedral of St-Maurice** (Mon–Sat 9am–noon & 2–6pm), whose broad single nave is the widest of any Gothic-style church in France. Local lore attributes the absence of supporting columns to the clergy's desire to monitor parishioners, checking that they were not carrying out forbidden Cathar practices, but this is doubtful given that the cathedral was not consecrated until 1509. The interior itself has suffered a rather excessive Baroque renovation, but the massive pipe organ and large carved gallery are impressive.

Aside from a small thirteenth-century **gate** and a section of the old town wall a few metres west of place Leclerc, all of the town's sights are grouped around the two squares. There is little enough to do, but the beauty of the town makes it the perfect spot to relax on a terrace, have a drink and soak up the atmosphere. On Monday mornings both of the *places* fill with the **market** stalls of local farmers – an excellent opportunity to prepare a picnic lunch.

## Practicalities

**Buses** passing through Mirepoix stop within sight of the cathedral, and it is a short walk from there to the **tourist office** (Mon–Sat 9am–noon & 2–6pm; ☎05.61.68.83.76, fax 05.61.68.89.48), located in the only modern building on place Leclerc. There are two **hotels** to choose from here, but unless you are on a very strict budget, there is no excuse for passing up a night in the gorgeous *Maison des Consuls* (☎05.61.68.81.81, fax 05.61.68.81.15; ⑤–⑦); the *Commerce*, in cours Docteur Chabaud (☎05.61.68.10.29, fax 05.61.68.20.29; closed Jan & part Oct; ④), pleasant and well maintained though it is, simply cannot compete in style. Nearby is the municipal **campsite** (mid-June to mid-Sept; ☎05.61 .68.84.90). Mirepoix sustains a number of **restaurants**, the best of which are the *Porte d'Aval* (☎05.61.68.19.19; closed Mon) on cours Maréchal de Mirepoix, and *La Flambée* (☎05.61.68.16.59; closed Sun eve & Mon) at 27 rue Porte d'Amont, both of which are in the 80F/€12.20-and-up range and specialize in cassoulet and dishes based on locally raised beef. On the main square, *Le Cantegril* (closed Wed out of season) at no. 25 has cassoulet and foie gras (from 69F/€10.52), and *Café-Créme* (closed Tues) at no. 32, is the good economy choice (menus from 49F/€7.47). Further, at the east end of the same *place*, there are two surprisingly hip-looking **cafés**: the stylish *Castignolles*, and *Atmospher*, which brings in a younger crowd.

## Fanjeux

Halfway between Mirepoix and Carcassonne, tiny **FANJEUX** is a town which has fallen from medieval glory into virtual obscurity. Once the capital of Occitan troubadours, it was here that the *jocs florals* ("floral games"), a competition of Occitan poetry and song in which the winners were awarded gilded flowers for their efforts, were first held in 1324 (see p.374). In 1206, St Dominic de Gúzman passed through town and, contemplating the horizon from the town's belvedere, saw a series of miraculous fireballs. Inspired by this divine meteorological phenomenon he founded a convent at nearby Prouille, the precursor of his communities of preaching friars, the Dominicans. Nowadays, not even the buses stop in Fanjeux; the streets are quiet, and the various vestiges of its medieval splendour, the old Dominican headquarters and the town's church, moulder away unvisited, except by groups of nuns on field trips. If you are intent on exploring the town, there is an **information office** (Mon–Fri 10.30am–12.30pm & 3–7pm, *fanjeux-bram-montreal@fnotsi.net*) in the *mairie* which may be able to get you access to the monuments (the tourist office on the main road below the old town is closed for the moment). And if you are passing through on the GR7, you might want to stay the night in any of a number of sporadically open **chambres d'hôtes**, including the Dominican convent (☎04.68.24.70.16), or grab a meal in the town's **restaurant**, *La Table Cathare* (closed Sun & Mon), leaving town on the road to Mirepoix.

## South to Camon

The hamlet of **CAMON**, 13km southeast of Mirepoix along the GR7, is a better stop, and one which can be visited on a one-day walking trek. Taking up the trail by the small bridge across the River Hers just east of Mirepoix's main round-about, you'll walk along the well-marked trail over gentle, hilly farmland for 8km, until you reach **Lagarde**. There is a dramatic-looking ruin here, an ancient **château** (private and closed to visitors) whose empty window frames set in broken walls romantically frame the blue sky behind. Continuing along for 3km the trail merges into a paved country lane, arriving at Camon shortly thereafter. This tiny settlement, founded by Charlemagne himself, is still dominated by its **abbey-castle** and surrounded by parts of its two sets of walls (fourteenth- and sixteenth-century). The castle is private and operates as a luxurious bed-and-breakfast, but its richly appointed sixteenth-century interior can also be taken in as part of a guided tour (arranged by the tourist office; 30F/€4.58). The small **tourist office** on Grand Rue (Mon–Fri 9am–noon & 2–5pm; ☎05.61.68.88.26, fax 05.61.68.12.07, *mairie.camon@worldonline.fr*) can also get you into the town's unexceptional fourteenth-century church. If you want to **stay** the night, *L'Abbaye-Château* (☎04.61.68.28.28, fax 04.61.68.81.56; ⑦) is the obvious choice if you can afford it; if you can't you should at least enjoy a drink in its *salon du thé*, *La Tartine*. There are two **chambres d'hôtes** in the village, *Le Clos du Dormeur* (☎05.61.68.18.84; ②) and *La Besse* (☎05.61.68.13.11; ②), which also operates a **campsite**. *La Bergerie*, an old farm 1km west of town towards Mirepoix, has a rustic **restaurant** which serves *terroir* cuisine (closed Wed; menus from 70F/€10.68). If you continue south from Camons on the GR7, keep an eye out for the *cabanes*, sturdy little stone shepherds huts, hidden amongst the growth.

## Vals

Perhaps the most interesting sight in the vicinity of Mirepoix is the church at **Vals**, 12km west of town on the north bank of the Hers. Vals itself is little more than a cluster of a half-dozen farmhouses – a dusty hamlet, with no services, and where you are as likely to encounter a cow as a human walking along its streets. The small and incredibly ancient **subterranean church** (daily 9am–6pm; free), once a stopping-point on the pilgrims' route to Compostela, is built on a rocky spur. Entering through a hobbit-sized doorway you climb a staircase carved in the living rock, passing through a pseudo-crypt of pre-Roman origin before reaching the church itself. When you enter, grope for the light switch to the left of the door to illuminate the curious three-chambered vertical structure; in the arches of some of its windows you'll find well-preserved late eleventh and early twelfth-century frescoes of saints and angels, which recall the styles of painted churches of the Pyrenees. Lacking bicycle or car, you can reach Vals by getting off the Pamiers–Mirepoix bus at the turn-off from the D40 (just east of Les Pujols) and walking the remaining 4km.

# Pamiers and the Grotte du Mas d'Azil

**PAMIERS** is a disappointment. The town is loaded with history but suffered so gravely in the Wars of Religion that there is virtually nothing left to see here. Founded by returning Crusaders – who named it after the ancient desert trading post of Apamea in Syria – Pamiers later played the role of headquarters for the anti-Cathar Crusaders. In 1321, the Inquisition burned the last Cathar *parfait* Guillaume Bélibaste here. Now, of the town's vanished medieval glory only a scattering of old bell towers survive, poking above the rooftops in the tight knot of streets on the east bank of the Ariège, which make up Pamier's bland old town. The only reason you should be tempted to stop here is to use the town as a jumping-off point to head east to Mirepoix or west to Mas d'Azil and St-Girons.

Trains and buses stop at Pamiers' **gare SNCF**, just east of the old town, and a short walk from the **tourist office** (July & Aug Mon–Sat 8.30am–noon & 2–6pm; Sept–June Mon–Fri 8.30am–noon & 2–5pm; ☎05.61.67.52.52, fax 05.61.67.22.40) on boulevard Delcassé, at the southeastern corner of the ring road. If you do want to stay here, head for the *Hôtel de France* on 5 cours du Rambaud (☎05.61.60.20.88, fax 05.61.67.29.48, *www.interhotel.com*; closed late Dec & early Jan; ④), a welcoming, old-style hotel. The alternatives are *Le Roi Gourmand* (☎05.61.60.12.12, fax 05.61.60.16.66, *www.logis-de-france.fr*, ④), an adequate two-star number opposite the train station, and *Hôtel de la Paix*, in place Albert Tournier (☎05.61.67.12.71, fax 05.61.60.61.02, *www.logis-de-france.fr*; ②). Each of these hotels has a **restaurant** (the *de la Paix* being the cheapest with a 49F/€7.47 menu), and there are other places scattered about the town, but nothing outstanding.

**Bikes** can be rented from Cycles Passion (☎05.61.60.14.05) and Cycle Portet (☎05.61.67.04.12). You will also find a number of **laundries** here, and you can use the terminal in the town's post office to get on the **Internet**.

## The cave and village of Mas d'Azil

The swathe of land which sweeps northwest of Pamiers towards the banks of the Garonne and Toulouse holds virtually nothing of interest, its flat landscape peppered by farming hamlets and populated largely by cattle. There is, however, a good **bike route** (if you're in good shape) across the western spur of the low Plantaurel mountains to the **Grotte du Mas d'Azil**, and on to St-Girons – you can also drive it. Pick this up by crossing the Ariège west of Pamiers' old town on the D110 (direction St-Victor); 7km later you'll hook up with the main D119. Thereafter, the road climbs steeply before dipping into the valleys of the Lèze and Arize. At Sabaret a gruelling series of hairpin curves ascends to the village of **MAS D'AZIL**, whose massive cavern is not only noteworthy for being the most northerly and largest of the great Pyrenean prehistoric *grottes* (see p.157), it is also Europe's only **drive-through cave**. The gaping maw (some 50m in height) opens up just to the south of the town, swallowing the D119 road whole, before disgorging it several hundred metres later. Once a lair of the giant cave-bears which populated the south of France in the days of the great mammals, and, roughly 30,000 years ago, a home for our own humble ancestors, historically the cave has provided refuge for a whole series of endangered species, including early Christians, Cathars and Huguenots. Indeed, it was here and in the village that a group of the last of these made a valiant and desperate stand in 1625, fending off a Catholic army which outnumbered them fifteen to one. If you're interested in seeing more than simply what passes by your window, other sections of the cave are accessible by foot (July–Sept daily 10am–noon & 2–6pm; May & June Mon–Sat 2–6pm, Sun 10am–noon & 2–6pm; April Mon–Fri 2–6pm, Sat & Sun

10am–noon & 2–6pm; March, Oct & Nov Sun 2–6pm; 40F/€6.10, including museum entry), and you can stroll through galleries littered and decorated with the vestiges of its former inhabitants. The village itself, which lost its fortifications to a spiteful Richelieu, has a small **museum** (same hours as the cave; 30F/€4.58) by the church, with prehistoric knick-knacks collected from the cavern and a section on the local glass-making tradition. The same building houses the local **tourist office** (April–Sept daily 10am–1pm & 2–6pm; ☎05.61.69.97.22). The only **hotel** in the hamlet is the family-run *Hôtel Gardet* (☎05.61.69.90.05; closed mid-Nov to mid-March; ②), and there is a municipal **campsite** (mid-June to mid-Sept) only a twenty-minute walk away. The best place to eat is *Le Jardin de Cadettou* (☎05.61.69.95.23; closed Sat lunch time, Sun eve & Mon), a homely **restaurant** with excellent menus of regional cuisine from 80F/€12.20. A less expensive option is the *Hôtel Gardet*, whose family-run dining room has menus from 60F/€9.15.

Emerging from the cave in the blinking sunlight the road meanders through attractively forested uplands before meeting the main highway at Lescure, just 8km east of St-Girons (see p.151).

# Foix and around

**FOIX**, 18km upstream from Pamiers, has few specific sights itself but is the most agreeable base in the valley, with connections by train and bus into the mountains. It has a good range of services, and is surprisingly lively for a relatively small town. What's more, people tend to hurry past, so that although Foix is located in the midst of the greatest concentration of prehistoric caves in France, it is never overwhelmed by visitors and retains an appealing intimacy and freshness.

## Arrival, information and accommodation

The **gare SNCF** sits on the right bank of the Ariège, a ten-minute walk north of the centre; most **buses** stop on the central cours Gabriel-Fauré, near the Resistance monument, although some will drop you off behind the post office. The **tourist office** at 45 cours Gabriel-Fauré (July & Aug Mon–Sat 9am–7pm, Sun 10am–12.30pm & 3–6pm; June & Sept Mon–Sat 9am–noon & 2–6pm, Sun 10am–12.30pm; Oct–May Mon–Sat 9am–noon & 2–6pm; ☎05.61.65.12.12) can be reached from the train station by walking south along the east bank of the Ariège and then crossing the Pont-Neuf.

Most **accommodation** is found in the old town, on the west bank of the Ariège, though little of it is inspiring. If you have the means, the quietest and most comfortable option is the three-star *Hôtel Lons*, 6 place Duthil, near the Pont Vieux (☎05.61.65.52.44, fax 05.61.02.68.18, *www.logis-de-france.fr*; ⑤). *La Barbacane*, 1 avenue de Lerida (☎05.61.65.50.44, fax 04.61.65.50.44; ④) occupies the next rank down, but suffers from traffic noise. The *Eychenne*, 11 rue Nöel-Peyrevidal (☎05.61.65.00.04, fax 05.61.65.56.63; ②) is the only real cheapie, with decent enough rooms but a nocturnally lively bar on the ground floor; across the street at no. 16 is the friendly **youth hostel** *Auberge Léo Lagrange* (☎05.61.65.09.04; 80F/€12.20), which has one- to four-person rooms. The municipal **campsite**, *Lac de Labarre* (May–Oct; ☎05.61.65.11.58), is 4km up the N20 towards Toulouse.

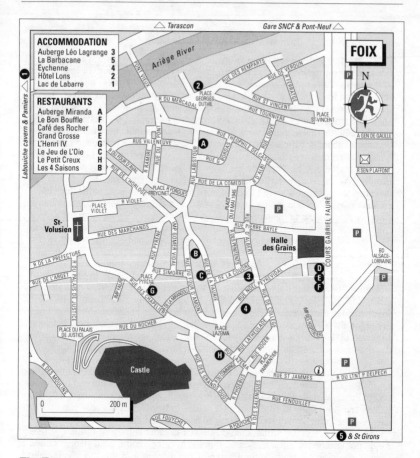

## The Town

Foix has a well preserved **old town** of narrow alleys, wedged in the triangle between the Ariège and the Arget rivers. A few of the overhanging houses here date from the fourteenth to sixteenth centuries, and especially attractive are **place Pyrène** and **place St-Vincent** with their fountains, though many junctions in the old quarter sport some sort of water-quirk. All lanes seem to lead eventually to the conspicuously large **church of St-Volusien** in the north of the old town, originally Romanesque but almost completely reconstructed after being razed during the Wars of Religion. Its eponymous square, along with the Halles des Grains just off cours Gabriel-Fauré, hosts lively Wednesday and Friday **markets** – farm produce and plants at the *place*, and meat, cheese, savouries and pastries at the metal-roofed *halles*, which on other days is a prime drinking venue.

Presiding over the old town is Foix's grey hill-top **castle**, not so much a single fortification as three magnificent, dissimilar towers from different eras: a slender

## GASTON FÉBUS

Foix's greatest hero, a towering figure in the history of the central Pyrenees, is **Gaston Fébus** (or Phébus, in French), Count of Foix and Viscount of Béarn (just to the west). Although ultimately frustrated in his plans, Fébus is a local legend, revered as a leader who fought hard for regional independence and whose character epitomizes the ideals of chivalry associated with the Middle Ages. Soldier and poet, Fébus was born in 1331 and died sixty years later, but the details of his life are difficult to disentangle; with his dashing, aristocratic image he naturally became a subject for the songs of troubadours, while Gaston himself, a relentless self-promoter, did everything he could to encourage and embroider tales of his valour and prowess – he even invited Jean Froissart, the great chronicler of the Hundred Years' War, to write his biography. His own surname, Fébus, was his invention too, derived from the Occitan word for sun and celebrating his long, golden hair. What is certain is that he was known as a dauntless soldier, and in battle could be found leading his men with the cry *Fébus avan* ("Fébus forward"). As a ruler he was very much the image of medieval nobility – he had no time for the legislative councils of town dwellers, which he abolished, and set himself up as the highest judicial authority in his realms.

Fébus' great ambition was to create an autonomous kingdom in the Pyrenees, adding by conquest the western regions of Bigorre and Soule to the lands of Nébouzan, Béarn and Foix (including all the upper Ariège valley), which he had inherited. This goal was made impossible by the continuing Hundred Years' War, which divided the loyalties of his subjects: in the west lived Gascons who were loyal to the English Crown, and in particular the Black Prince, who ruled them between 1362 and 1371 – while to the east lay Languedoc, subject to the French king. These divisions exacerbated the feuding of the leading knightly families in his realms, and gave greater purpose to the neighbouring nobles against whom he was pitted. In 1362 he did manage to inflict a crushing defeat on his Gascon archenemies, the English-allied Armagnacs, but despite successes such as this, in the end he had to accept the unworkability of his plan. His dreams of dynastic dominance were dealt a final, crushing blow in 1380, when he is said to have killed his only son on discovering the latter's role in a conspiracy to assassinate him.

Thereafter, determined that should his own dreams fail, those of his enemies would not succeed, Gaston dedicated himself to campaigning for a strong, united France, pledging his lands to the Crown by inheritance. But this too was initially thwarted, with the d'Albret family, one of Gaston's rivals, gaining the throne of Béarn and keeping it out of French control until 1589. Nevertheless, Gaston Fébus' ideals and endeavours have come to represent all that is romantic about the medieval era and, in Foix especially, he is celebrated with festivals in July and August and remembered fondly for *l'hypocras*, a spiced wine drink which he invented and is enjoyed in the region to this day.

twelfth-century turret, a bulky square fourteenth-century keep and a broad and rounded fifteenth-century tower – dramatic when viewed from any angle. From 1012 the castle on this site was the seat of the counts of Foix, whose association with the Cathar faith led to its being besieged four times by Simon de Montfort, who failed to break the fort's resistance. One of these counts, Roger-Bernard II "Le Grand", was a determined opponent of the Albigensian Crusade, but perhaps made his most lasting contribution to history by marrying Ermensende of

Castellbó early in the thirteenth century, thereby linking the fortunes of Foix and Andorra. Although the dynasty ended illustriously with Huguenot king Henri III of Foix-Béarn and Navarre, who annexed what had become a Pyrenean mini-state to the Crown on becoming Henri IV of France in 1589, the biggest name in Foix is that of the fair-haired knight whose features can be seen on postcards all over town – Gaston III, known as Gaston Fébus (see box opposite).

The best aspect of a castle **visit** (daily: July & Aug 9.30am–6.30pm; May, June & Sept 9.45am–noon & 2–6pm; Oct–April Wed–Sun 10.30am–noon & 2–5.30pm; 25F/€3.81) is the opportunity to clamber up worn stairs in the southern and central towers for startling views up the valley. The interior houses the rather listless **Musée d'Ariège** (irregular guided visits only), a time-waster which consists of four rooms with dull exhibits ranging from prehistoric to medieval times.

### Eating, drinking and nightlife

The best area for **eating** is rue de la Faurie, the old blacksmiths' bazaar at the centre of the old town, where the best of several establishments is *Les 4 Saisons* at no. 11, whose gimmick is to bring to your table a hotplate – a *pierrade* – on which you cook fish and meat pieces yourself; they also do a wide range of crêpes. *Le Jeu de L'Oie* (closed Sat noon & Sun in winter) nearby at no. 17 is also worth trying for more traditional fare, while *Auberge Miranda* (closed Mon) at 36 rue Labistour (the continuation of Faurie) is an old-fashioned bar with *plats du jour*. Food at *L'Henri IV* on place Pyrène is nothing extraordinary, but the outdoor seating is a good way to take in the square and the castle; the nearby *Le Petit Creux* at 9 rue Lazéma has a limited but well-executed menu which guarantees pavement-table crowds at lunch time. At any of these places you can expect to pay 70–90F/€10.68–13.73 for a menu.

There is a row of café-restaurants which double as night-time **music-bars** on the west side of the cours Gabriel Fauré, on either side of the old market hall. *Café des Rocher*, *Grand Grosse* and *Le Bon Bouffe* all have decent if unspectacular dinner menus for 65F/€9.91, and stay open for drinking. Later on, you can head to the **disco** *Le Crysco Club* (Wed–Sat 10pm–3am) at 3 cours Irénée Cros, on the far side of the *pont vieux* over the Ariège.

### Listings

**Bike rental** Intersport (☎05.61.65.00.41) and Sport Xpert (☎05.61.65.00.41) both rent bikes, and the tourist office distributes a booklet of local routes, *Randonée journée et raids à étapes*, for 20F/€3.05.

**Car rental** ADA, 59 avenue du Général Leclerc (☎05.61.68.38.38), Europcar ZA, Foix Sud (☎05.61.65.15.99) and Hertz ZA Foix Sud (☎05.61.02.32.74) have offices in or near town.

**Internet access** To get online head to the friendly Bureau de Information Jeunesse (Mon 1–5pm, Tues–Fri 10am–5pm; closed Aug) on rue Roger (off rue de College, behind the tourist office) or to the pay-terminal at the post office on the same street.

**Laundry** There's a coin-operated launderette (daily 7am–9pm) on place Lazéma.

**Swimming pools** There are indoor and outdoor swimming pools at place du Champs du Mars, behind the main post office (15F/€2.29 admission).

**Watersports** The narrow Lac Labarre reservoir, just north of town, has the usual gamut of waterside facilities; ASPTT (☎05.61.02.62.99) rents kayaks and canoes, and organizes rafting trips.

## West of Foix

Heading west from Foix, the main road, the D117, climbs rapidly to the **col de Bouich** (599m) before descending through the Aujole and Baup valleys to arrive at St-Girons and St-Lizier, near the western limit of the *département*. On this particular road, there's little to detain you, although you might stop at **La Bastide de Serou**, just under halfway, to have a drink in the square outside its old market building. Just past the village, a treacherous forest road provides cuts up towards Mas d'Azil (see p.145).

If however you take the Vernajoul road from the town centre, which eventually links up with the D117, you'll come to the subterranean **river-cavern of Labouiche** some 3km northwest of Foix (July & Aug Mon–Sat 9.30am–5.30pm, Sun 10–11.45am & 2–5.15pm; June & Sept Mon–Sat 10–11.15am & 12–5.15pm, Sun 10–11.45am & 2–5.15pm; April, May, Oct & Nov Mon–Sat 2–5.15pm, Sun 10–11.45am & 2–5.15pm, usually a 15min wait; 44F/€6.71), claimed to be the longest such navigable cave in western Europe. It appears never to have been inhabited by humans, and indeed the water levels in winter are so high as to block access completely. The same amusement-park atmosphere prevails here as at Lombrives (see p.159): twelve-person boatloads travel for 75 minutes in opposite directions along the 1500m of galleries open to the public. Entry is either via the natural entrance, or an artificial one bored at the upstream end, on either side of the ticket office – you're told which to assemble at. Highlights of the cavern are the **waterfall** at the upstream end of the river and a small chamber full of formations below the artificial entry; these and other oddities along the way are described by the guides, who do their best to keep up a witty patter while hauling the crafts via ceiling-mounted cables.

There are also two unusual English-run **chambres d'hôtes** off the road between Foix and St-Girons. At Rimont, 34km from Foix, there is – a rarity in France – excellent and reasonably priced vegan (not even eggs) accommodation, at *Le Gurrat*, Suzanne Morris and Tervor Warman's working organic farm (☎05.61.96.37.03; ③), while at Lescure, 4km further on, Pyrenean Field Study Services (☎ & fax 05.61.96.37.67; ③) do accompanied walks and tours to discover the wildlife and flora of the mountain and forest.

# The Couserans

Southwest of Foix, the peaks and the northern slopes of the Pyrenees shelter a series of high river valleys known collectively as the **Couserans**. As the Garbet, Salat, Arac and Alet rivers drain off of the high glaciers they flow down through a country traditionally as poor and isolated as it is majestically beautiful. Cattle-farming, herding and forest industries were the original means for the meagre population of this area, while later, mineral exploitation and spa development brought tenuous fits of humble prosperity, and sustains the area today. The two towns which dominate this region, **St-Girons** and **St-Lizier**, are worth a visit if only to appreciate a subtle cultural shift offered by the mid-Pyrenees – the westernmost zone of Occitan influence coloured by contacts with Navarre, the Basque country, and the flatlands of Gascony; the most immediate manifestation of the change is the merciful disappearance of cassoulet from *terroir* menus. If you have the time, energy and perseverance, exploring the highlands to the south will lead you through some of the most remote and splendid scenery, and distinctive culture, the Pyrenees has to offer.

Given the area's isolation and poverty, it should come as no surprise that there is little by way of public transport in the region. There are bus links from Toulouse and Foix to St-Girons, and a regular service up into the Couserans, but unless you have a car, to do any real exploring you'll have to resort to hiking – cycling in these hills is strictly for the dedicated.

## St-Girons and St-Lizier

The two complementary villages of St-Girons and St-Lizier, 45km west of Foix along the D117, and separated from each other by only 1500m of riverbank, to all intents and purposes form a single unit. The former is the administrative and commercial centre, which, with good transport links to Toulouse and a range of services, is most useful as a base for exploring the mountains. The latter, which was the capital of the Couserans until the role was ceded to St-Girons, is where you'll find the sights.

Apart from its long association with making cigarette papers, the most striking thing about **ST-GIRONS** is its pavements, made of a local dark-grey marble veined with white, and with finely chiselled gullies to carry away the rainwater. And although there are no other memorable sights, it's a far from unpleasant place, with a couple of decent **festivals**: folklore in mid-July, and theatre in early August. The simplest centre for orientation is the **Pont-Vieux**. Straight ahead on the right bank of the River Salat, the bridge points you into the old commercial centre of the town, with some marvellously old-fashioned shops, their fronts and fittings unchanged for generations. To the right is the typically provincial **place des Poilus**, its cachet largely due to the faded elegance of the *Grand Hôtel de France* and the equally old-fashioned *Hôtel de l'Union*, opposite, where you can still stay (see below). The *Grand Café de l'Union* on the square is a splendidly balconied period café that faces the *mairie*. Beside it, along the river bank, a wide gravelled *allée* of plane trees, the **Champ de Mars**, provides the site for a big general market on the second and fourth Mondays of every month, and for a regular produce market every Saturday morning.

St-Girons' older and prettier sibling, **ST-LIZIER**, occupies a little hillock, still partially enclosed by walls and towers built under the Romans in the third and fourth centuries. Strolling along its narrow streets, keep an eye out for the carved facades of its numerous fifteenth-century palaces, particularly around the places de l'Église and des Entends, and on the rues des Nobles and d'Horloge. Of special note is the late seventeenth-century **bishop's palace**, from the terrace of which you get a great view over the Couserans rising to the south, with the snowcapped peaks of the Pyrenees as a backdrop. Inside, the **museum** (July & Aug Mon & Wed–Sun 10am–12.30pm & 2–6.30pm; May, June & Sept same days 10am–12.30pm & 2–6pm; Oct–April Sun 2–5pm; 25F/€3.81) contains an uninspiring collection of local handicrafts, bric-a-brac, and household items.

The main attraction here is the **cathedral of St-Lizier** (daily 10am–3pm; free) an eleventh-century structure built on Roman foundations, with a magnificent array of Romanesque frescoes on the walls and ceiling of its twelfth-century apse;

the figure of Christ, in the pose of *pantocrator* ("Lord of all") presides over angels, apostles and various other figures who descend in hierarchy towards the floor. The adjacent **cloister** is particularly noteworthy for the carvings of its capitals – in addition to the usual floral motifs and monsters are extraordinary narrative scenes illustrating the highlights of the Old and New Testament. Over the five centuries after its founding the church was completed piecemeal, with sections added on in a strange higgledy-piggledy manner, and though there hardly seems to be a right angle in the floor plan, somehow it all holds together. Apart from the building itself, the church's **treasury** is host to a stunning sixteenth-century reliquary bust of St Lizier, as well as other pieces dating back to the eleventh century. The town's other cathedral, Notre-Dame-de-Sède, has long been closed for renovations.

## Practicalities

**Buses** arriving from Toulouse and the Couserans arrive in St-Girons on the left bank of the river at place des Capots. There's a **tourist office** here, in the central place Alphonse-Seintein (July & Aug Mon–Sat 9am–7pm, Sun 10am–1pm; Sept–June Mon–Sat 9am–noon & 2–6pm; ☎05.61.96.26.60, fax 05.61.96.26.69, *otCouserans@wanadoo.fr*), and another one up in St-Lizier (same hours as St-Girons; ☎05.61.96.77.77, fax 05.61.96.08.01, *www.ariege.com/st.lizier*). With both atmosphere and comfort, the best **accommodation** in the area is St-Lizier's *Hôtel de la Tour* (☎05.61.66.38.02, fax 05.61.66.38.02; ③) in a remodelled old building down by the riverbank. Otherwise *La Clarière* (☎05.61.66.66.66, fax 05.34.14.30.30; ②), on the south side of St-Girons, comes a close second (very close, if you factor in the pool), and the *Hôtel de Union* (☎05.61.66.09.12, fax 05.61.04.81.73; ①–④), on allée Champs de Mars, has some cheaper rooms. If you look like a hiker, the St-Lizier tourist office will arrange a berth in the hamlet's pilgrim **hostel** for a single night (①), and the nearby **campsite** *Parc des Palettes* (☎05.61.66.06.79), is open from March to September and rents out bungalows.

The *de la Tour* and *La Clarière* both have **restaurants** (menus from 89F/€13.57; closed Sun eve), the first with a strong *terroir* streak, and the second somewhat more adventurous. For lighter fare, head to *Allo Pizza* on rue Villefranche, or *Chez Alain et Dominique* at 8 place Jena Jaurès; expect to spend 50–80F/€7.63–12.20 at either. Vegetarians will be grateful for *La Végé'table* at 13 rue Joseph Pujol (menus 35–55F/€5.34–8.39; closed Sun & Mon out of season).

**Bikes** can be rented at Moto Relais (☎05.61.04.87.67) or Horizon Vertical (☎05.61.96.08.22) in St-Girons and Garage Carbonne (☎05.61.66.31.00) in St-Lizier. Also, while here you can check your email at the **Internet** terminal in the St-Girons post office.

# Over the Couserans to Tarascon

Looping back from St-Girons to Tarascon (see p.155) in the Ariège valley provides an opportunity to take in the stunning terrain of the **COUSERANS**, which buttress some of the highest peaks in the Pyrenees and, culturally, remains a unique and independent zone, quite different from Languedocian Foix. Gascon is still spoken here, and if you have the good fortune to visit during local festivities, you'll be treated to the area's singular costume and music: men wearing white embroidered jackets (reminiscent of traditional Greek styles) and red *baretos* (hats) sport curious wooden shoes with high (up to 30cm) pointed toes, while women wear long dresses draped with colourful scarves; the clarinet-like *hautbois*, accompanied by drums, supplies the sounds for traditional dances. The villages in the region are likewise distinctive, built low in stone and timber to resist the high mountain clime. The Couserans has traditionally been a difficult area to access and even more so to govern, the proud mountain people resentful of any infringement on their liberties or threat to their way of life. As late as the nineteenth century, the villagers waged a guerrilla war against the French government – the so-called Guerre des demoiselles ("war of the girls"), when they dressed up as women in a surprise attack on local property owners, government foresters and police.

The magnificent landscape is accessible by road and trail and, if you have time, there are a number of rewarding circuits. Most of the villages of the Couserans have tourist offices, but hours can be irregular and confirmation is best made at the office in St-Girons, which has information and **walking** itineraries for the whole region. You may also want to contact the Ariège tourist board for **information** (CDT Ariége Pyrénées, 31bis avenue du Général de Gaulle, BP 143, 09004 Foix; ☎05.61.02.30.70, fax 05.61.65.17.34, *www.ariegepyrenees.com*). There are two main **routes** which traverse the Couserans from west to east, only one of which is partially accessible by public transport from St-Girons (a single bus route climbing from St-Girons to Aulus-les-Bains), and both of which are very demanding drives.

## Via Massat

Starting out by following the Salat south of St-Girons, and winding upstream through the dramatic **Gorges de Riabouto** will bring you to the confluence of the Arac and Riabouto. Here, you can take the most direct of the two routes to Tarascon by heading due east to the village of **MASSAT**. As you approach, the fifteenth-century bell tower of its church rises 60m above the village in a marvellous Pyrenean tableau. There is a **tourist office** here (☎05.61.96.92.76, fax 05.61.96.99.44) and good shops and services, and if you decide to stay, the *Auberge du Gypaète Barbu* in place de l'Église (☎05.61.04.89.92; closed part Jan, part June; ②), also does decent food. Continuing east the road climbs in a seemingly endless succession of hair-raising bends until you reach the 1250m-high Col de Port. On the left rise the wooded slopes of the **Montagnes de l'Arize**, while on your right the barren **Pic de Trois Seigneurs** (2199m) scratches the clouds. A steep 18-kilometre descent then brings you to Tarascon, passing the Parc Pyrénéen de l'Art Préhistorique (see p.156) at the entrance to the town.

## Via Seix and Aulus-les-Bains

From the mouth of the Riabouto gorge, the bus will take you further up the Salat to **SEIX**, where the peaks of the **cirque** at the valley's head come into view. This market town, still lorded over by a fifteenth-century castle and with a distinctive church tower, provides another opportunity to stock up on supplies, and is a good base if you plan to do some hiking in the region; you can get up-to-date information at the village **tourist office** (☎05.61.96.52.90) in the town centre – if **mountain biking** is your thing, enquire about the circuit just south of town. There are two **hotels** in town, the *Auberge des Deux Rivières* (☎ & fax 05.61.66.83.57; ②), and the *Auberge du Haut Salat* (☎05.61.66.88.03; ②), both with restaurants. There is also a gîte, *Pyrénées Anes* (☎05.61.66.82.15, *pyrenees.anes@free.fr*; ①). La Marmotte (☎05.61.66.91.60) rents **bikes**, and the local Crédit Agricole bank handles currency **exchange**.

From Seix, the bus line continues up the Alet river to its terminus **AULUS-LES-BAINS**, a spa-village and adjunct to the mediocre and poorly snowed ski-station of **Guzet-Neige** (☎05.61.96.00.11), separated from Spain's Vall de Cardós by a 10-kilometre-wide mountain wall, and lying among moist and fragrant meadows ringed by dramatic peaks. The most remote point of the traditionally poor Couserans, Aulus was once famous for its bear trainers, who toured the wealthier lowlands. The classic walk here involves heading south along the GR10 to the **Cascade d'Ars** waterfall, a round trip of about five hours. Aulus' **tourist office** on allée des Thermes (☎05.61.96.00.01, fax 05.61.96.03.36) can provide detailed information regarding hikes, as well as accommodation options. Thanks to the therapeutic industry which keeps the town busy from May to November, and the skiing which brings people in winter there are a number of places to eat and stay. In Aulus, the best deal for **accommodation** is the *Hôtel de France* (☎05.61.96.00.90, fax 05.61.96.03.29; closed Nov; ②) which has comfortable rooms and an excellent and affordable **restaurant** (from 60F/€9.15). A more expensive and attractive choice is the *Hôtel les Ousaillès* (☎05.61.96.03.68, fax 05.61.96.03.70; ④), while the cheapest digs are at the **gîte** (☎05.61.96.94.67; ①). For light meals, the tearoom and bar *Les Fontanalia* (weekends only in winter) can fix you up with snacks from 12–45F/€1.83–6.86. The nearest **campsite** to Aulus is *Le Couledous* (☎05.61.96.02.26; year round) in a holiday complex neighbouring the town.

From Aulus, a narrow mountain road and the GR10 wind separate paths along the northern fringe of the **Pic Rouge de Bassiès** (2676m), weaving in and out of the tree line. Looking back, you'll see the high-walled crenellated cirque formed by the peak and its nearest neighbour, the Pic des Trois Comtes; the drama of the cirque's heights is underscored by wedges of snow lying beneath the sheerest faces, while below, the steep slopes are luxuriant with beech. The road rises to the east, then the north, skirting the small Étang de Lers and passing herds of grey cows grazing the alpine meadow, to arrive at the pass, the **Port de Lers** (1517m). Eventually passing the waterfall, the **cascade d'Arbu**, some 3km beyond, you begin a sharp descent towards Vicdessos. The GR10, on the other hand, continues due east to the Port de Saleix (1794m) where it meets two other paths. The main trail takes a right, arriving 2km later at the CIMES **refuge**, *de Bassies* (☎05.61.64.89.98; meals available June–Sept; ①), and then, passing a series of reservoirs, it branches east, crossing the **Pic du Far** and descending to Auzat and Vicdessos – in total some 16km of often demanding trail. In the final leg of the hike, keep an eye out for the squat stone shepherds' shelters, or *orris*, hidden among the underbrush – some as much as 700 years old.

There is little to detain you in **VICDESSOS**, the capital of a remote and poor *canton*, and nearby **AUZAT** is remarkable chiefly for the large and ugly aluminium factory which dominates it. It is however at these villages that the footpath and road route converge again, and where the main road descends the river valley, passing the grotte de Niaux (see p.157), shortly before entering **Tarascon**. If the journey has tired you, you may want to take a **room** or **meal** at the homely *Hôtel Henri Hivert* (☎05.61.65.88.17; ②) in Vicdessos. Alternatively the farmhouse, *Les Marmousets* (☎05.61.64.81.62; ②), between

Auzat and Vicdessos, has two *chambres d'hôtes*, and the local **campsite** (☎05.61.64.82.22) also rents bungalows off-season. The town is also the head-quarters of the departmental association of *accompagnateurs*, which can set you up with a reliable **guide** (1 rte de la Prade ☎05.61.64.83.96) for hikes up into the Couserans.

# The upper Ariège valley

South of Foix, the **upper Ariège** narrows rapidly, and forest slopes rise sharply on either side as the riverbed twists and cuts down through gneiss and schist of the Pyrenean foothills towards **Tarascon**. This is caveman country, and it is along this part of the river that you will find in thick concentration many of France's best and most famous prehistorically inhabited **caves**, decorated by the hand-prints, etchings and animal figures left by our ancestors up to a quarter of a million years ago. This, along with the beauty of the countryside, has made the upper Ariège an extremely popular destination, especially for French tourists. High season, particularly August, is mayhem, and if you're hoping to see the renowned cave art you should plan (and reserve) as far ahead as possible. Further up in the hills towards the Spanish and Andorran frontiers, the high peaks of the Pyrenees loom ever closer. Here, around **Ax-les-Thermes**, there is breathtaking mountain scenery and great **walking** to be had. There's a map of the region on pp.134–135.

## Tarascon-sur-Ariège and the caves

A small, utilitarian mining and metallurgy centre with traffic roaring past on the bypass highway, **TARASCON-SUR-ARIÈGE** has nothing about it to suggest that this is the heart of one of the most fascinating areas in Europe. Yet any account of the emergence of the human species must include the **caves** around the town, which taken as a group constitute an unequalled display of prehistoric painting and artefacts. The *grottes* served as shelters – and, arguably, as places of worship – for early humans, later coming in handy as hideouts for religious dissidents during the Christian era, and their high concentration in the Ariège is due to the limestone which constitutes the hillsides here – permeable rock ideally suited to the millennial work of cavern-creation. There are four main sites, all accessible in a single day if you have your own transport.

Tarascon itself is more rewarding than first impressions imply, and worth an hour's stroll. From the east bank of the Ariège, where riverside cafés provide pleasant vantage points, a narrow pedestrian lane leads up, past craft shops and even narrower alleys, to the old quarter. Here the church of St-Michel presides over a partly arcaded square, and various surviving bits of the medieval walls, razed in 1632, crop up here and there: the **Tour St-Michel**, and the **Porte d'Espagne** with a fountain inside. From the gate, the short hike past walled orchards up to the **Tour du Castella**, now a clock tower, is worthwhile for the views over the five valleys which converge here. Tarascon is the sight of two lively livestock **fairs**, on May 8 and September 30, timed for the passing of the transhumant herds. A regular **market** is held on Wednesday morning in the place de l'Horte, and Saturday morning in the place de l'Ayroule.

---

### PYRENEAN CAVE ART

The **painted caves** of the Pyrenees are known to have been created by nomadic and semi-nomadic communities of *Homo sapiens* during the Late Paleolithic period, between 10,000 and 35,000 years ago. Almost everything else about them is conjecture.

The big historical names in the evaluation of cave art are the French prehistoric anthropologists **Abbé Breuil** (1877–1961), **André Leroi-Gourhan** (1911–86) and the latter's colleague **Annette Laming-Emperaire**. Abbé Breuil began his career working on the caves of the Dordogne, but dedicated years of study to the western and central Pyrenees, arriving at the theory that cave art served a **magical function**, to ensure "that the game should be plentiful, that it should increase and that sufficient should be killed". The frequency with which ibex, wild boar, reindeer and bison appear on the walls makes this notion attractive, but there are objections to it, the most obvious being that the animal remains found in the caves show that the species depicted were not the main food supply. Moreover, although some of the animals are marked by symbols that might be arrows, over ninety percent of them are not. And finally, the Late Paleolithic period seems to have been a time of plenty, when hunters would have needed no magical assistance.

Leroi-Gourhan's and Laming-Emperaire's main contention is that cave art was arranged in a **specific layout**, much like the decorative schemes of frescoed Christian churches. From examination of 865 subjects in 62 caves they noted, for example, that hands were depicted only at the entrance to caves or in the centre, and that mammoths and bison were confined to the centre. More controversially, they went on to suggest that the arrangement had a sexual polarity, with bison symbolizing the female element, and horses the male. Some people have raised the objection that the weak illumination available to the cave-dwellers – since they had only grease and a wick perhaps, or wooden torches – would not have allowed them to see the cave decorations as a unity. A problem is also posed by the way successive outlines were superimposed to the extent that they became indecipherable, even though suitable areas of blank rock were available to either side. Nevertheless, most experts agree that there is some

---

If you haven't managed to make reservations at the caverns, you can still experience the Neolithic era, albeit vicariously, at the **Parc Pyrénéen de l'Art Préhistorique** (daily: July & Aug 10am–6.30pm; April–June, Sept & Oct 10am–6pm; 65F/€9.91), just 5km outside Tarascon (take the N20 north towards Toulouse, you'll see it signposted at the junction for St-Girons). This rambling park contains nature trails, and prehistoric-related exhibits including replica bison and reproductions of some of the more important and inaccessible cave art – a good alternative to the real thing, if you have children along.

## Practicalities

Buses and trains call frequently from nearby Ax-les-Thermes and Foix, on the line from Toulouse to Latour-de-Carol; the **gare SNCF**, which also serves as the bus stop, is on the left bank of the Ariège, in the northern half of town. The **tourist office** (July & Aug daily 9am–7pm; Sept–June Mon–Sat 9am–6pm; ☎05.61.05.94.94, fax 05.61.05.57.79, *pays.de.tarascon@wanadoo.fr*) is inside the multipurpose hall known as the Espace François Mitterand, on avenue des

sort of pattern: bison and horses, for example, are thirty times more likely to occur in the central area than are deer, a statistic impossible to dismiss as coincidence.

The most cogent refutation of the above theories was published in five years ago as *Les Chamanes de la Prehistoire* (Editions Seuil) by Jean Clottes, a French prehistorian and cave-art expert, and David Lewis-Williams, a South African archeologist specializing in the art and beliefs of the Kalahari Bushmen, one of the last surviving hunter-gatherer societies with strong parallels to European Paleolithic culture. They propose that many of the images may have been executed by **shamans** in a trance or other altered state, and that "the paintings and engravings do not represent real animals that are hunted for food in an actual landscape; rather they are visions drawn from the subterranean world of spirits because of their supernatural powers and ability to help the shamans."

The caves will doubtless continue to stimulate speculation. From the accumulation of rubbish on the cave floors – sometimes nearly 4m deep – and from the apparent stylistic development of the paintings, it would seem that habitation in these caves was quite stable, and it is possible that painting was the responsibility of one person within the community. Furthermore, the similarities between decorative work in caves hundreds of kilometres apart would seem to indicate that there was interaction between groups all along the range.

A great many decorated caves of the Pyrenees are closed to the general public, an essential precaution if they are to be preserved; application through a caving organization might gain access to some of these. The most spectacular examples, though, are open to all. After the Tarascon group, the major Pyrenean cave is **Gargas**, with its vast array of hand prints in red and black, many with apparently mutilated fingers. Whatever the uncertainties about its significance and the ways in which it was made, Pyrenean cave art offers an extraordinary aesthetic experience, marvellously conjuring shape and movement from the most basic natural materials, and even, in places, exploiting the very contours of the rock. Niaux itself contains an excellent example of such artistic opportunism: one of the bison carved on the clay floor is formed around holes caused by dripping water, which now function as an eye and wound marks.

Pyrénées in the centre. Quietest and most attractive of the **hotels** is the *Confort* on the riverside quai Armand-Sylvestre (☎ & fax 05.61.05.61.90; ③), with some rooms facing a courtyard. For more comfort, with the quieter rooms facing the river, try the *Hostellerie de la Poste*, 200m north on the main through road (☎05.61.05.60.41, fax 05.61.5.70.59, *pays.de.tarascon@wanadoo.fr*; ③). If these are full, your third choice will be the somewhat noisy *La Bellevue*, between the two at 7 place Jean-Jaurès (☎05.61.05.60.45, fax 05.61.05.10.41; ②). There are two **campsites**: *La Bernière*, near the junction of the road to Bédeilhac, and the municipal *Pré Lombard*, upstream from town on the right bank. All of the hotels have attached **restaurants**, with the best food and service at *Hostellerie de la Poste,* which offers a reasonably priced Gascon menu featuring *auzinat*, a rich hotpot of cabbage, potato, sausage, game and other goodies.

## Grotte de Niaux

Unquestionably the finest of the Pyrenean caves is the **Grotte de Niaux**, 2km southwest of Tarascon. Rivals like Lascaux in the Dordogne and Altamira in Spain are now closed or very nearly so, but the only restriction on access to Niaux is the mandatory **reservation** (call ☎05.61.05.88.37) for places on the twenty-person 45-minute **guided tour** (daily: July to early Sept 8.30–11.30am & 1.30–5.15pm; early Sept to end Sept 10–11.30am & 1.30–5.15pm; Oct–June visits at 11am, 3pm & 4.30pm; 60F/€9.15).

The contemporary entrance to Niaux is a tunnel created in 1968 near the low and narrow natural opening under an enormous rock overhang. Using torches for illumination, you penetrate 900m (from a total 4km of galleries) to see just some of the famous black outlines of horse and bison, minimally shaded yet capturing every nuance. Analysis has established that these drawings, and those of the ibex and stag in the recess further back, were produced around 10,800 BC with a "crayon" made of bison fat and manganese oxide. A line of footprints left by the artists can be seen in a part of the cave that was opened up in 1970, while their primitive form of writing is represented by the dots and bunches of lines on the wall of the main cavity.

**NIAUX** village itself, between the cave and Tarascon, has a small, private **Musée Pyrénéen** (daily: July & Aug 9am–8pm; Sept–June 10am–noon & 2–6pm; 35F/€5.34) which displays a splendid collection of tools, furnishings, archival photos and impedimenta illustrating the vanished traditions of the Ariège. Exhibits also explain local Pyrenean architecture, with its use of *lauzes* (stone slabs), *ardoise* (slate) and occasionally *chaume* (thatch) for roofing. About halfway between Niaux and Tarascon, keep your eye peeled also for the picturesque remains of a medieval smelting works by the riverside.

## Grotte de la Vache

The **Grotte de la Vache** (July & Aug daily 10am–5.30pm; Easter–June & Sept Mon & Wed–Sun 3–4.30pm; other times by arrangement – ring ☎05.61.05.95.06; 45F/€6.86) at Alliat is well worth the couple of kilometres' journey across the valley from Niaux, south on the road to Vicdessos; a path, beginning some 150m before the Niaux museum, slightly shortcuts the road. Excavations here over two decades sifted through the detritus of ten thousand years of habitation, beginning between 15,000 and 12,500 BC and ending in the Bronze Age. Around 30,000 fragments of flint tools were unearthed and over 6000 complete tools, mainly for engraving in rock; some pieces are displayed in the cave.

## Grotte de Bédeilhac

To reach the **Grotte de Bédeilhac** (July & Aug daily 10am–5.30pm; Easter–June & Sept to mid-Dec Mon–Sat 2.15–5pm; mid-Dec to Easter Mon–Sat 2.30–4.30pm & Sun 3pm; ☎05.61.05.95.06; 50F/€7.63) above the eponymous village, you have to return to Tarascon and cover 5km along the D618 towards Saurat. This cave, a hollow in the ridge of Soudour, contains examples of every known technique of Paleolithic art, including polychrome painting (now faded to monochrome). The imposing entrance yawns 35m wide by 20m high, making it easy to understand how the Germans managed to adapt the cavern as an aircraft hangar during World War II. Although the art within is not as immediately powerful as that at Niaux, diversity compensates: low reliefs in mud, paintings of bison, deer and ibex, and stalagmites used to model figures.

In the village below, **beds** are provided by the *Relais d'Étape* (☎05.61.05.15.56; ①) and **meals** by the adjacent *Auberge de la Grotte*, on the through road next to the *mairie* and the post office.

## Grottes de Lombrives

The **Grotte de Lombrives** (July & Aug daily 10am–7pm; June & Sept daily tours at 10am, 10.45am & 2–5.30pm; Easter–May & Oct to early Nov Sat & Sun tours at 10am, 10.45am & 2.30pm, plus May Mon–Fri 2–5.30pm; or by appointment, ☎05.61.05.98.40; 40F/€6.10), 3km south of Tarascon along the N20, near Ussat-les-Bains, could only disappoint if you've already seen Niaux, Vache and Bédeilhac. The access by underground train gives it something of an amusement-park feel – as do the nocturnal *spéctacles* regularly staged here in July and August – but the stalagmite formations are superb, and the sheer size of the complex is impressive. It is, in fact, the largest cavern in the EU open to tourists, and would take five days' walking to see it in its entirety. For groups of eight or more, you can arrange for three- or five-hour walk-throughs by ringing the number above. Lombrives was inhabited around 4000 BC, but all the material found here now rests in museums such as that at Foix. Its later history is embellished by legends of the last Cathars walled up inside in 1328, and of 250 soldiers subsequently disappearing without trace, the victims of cave-dwelling bandits. For a more serious visit, you can book on one of the "Visites longue durées caractère spéléologique", which are run from June to September.

# Ax-les-Thermes and around

**AX-LES-THERMES**, 26km southeast of Tarascon on the main N20 road, is an unobjectionable spa resort with little specifically to see – owing to numerous disastrous fires in centuries past – other than a lively Monday market along the river promenade, but it makes the most convenient centre for skiing or walking in the Ariège region. **Hikes** can be routed in circuits, permitting use of the town as a base, and several **ski resorts**, both downhill and nordic, are scattered in all directions within a convenient distance.

Ax dates back to at least Roman times, while the commercial exploitation of its hot springs goes back to the thirteenth century; the smell of sulphur that early

---

### SKIING AROUND AX-LES-THERMES

The nearest **ski station** to Ax is **Ax-Bonascre** (☎05.61.64.20.64), 8km south up the D820; in winter there are ski-bus services from the town centre. Bonascre itself is a hideous knot of high-rises, but once you get into the *télécabine* and up to the **Plateau du Saquet**, with the beautiful Andorran frontier peaks as a backdrop, it's a different matter. The snow record here is good, there are 55km of pistes (some over 3km long) and the top lift is at 2305m. An alternative station is to be found 13km east of Ax at **Ascou-Pailhères** (☎05.61.64.60.60), which has 10km of downhill runs and a top station of 2020m. It's a pretty drive up to the station, and though it only has one black piste, it's quite a challenging one.

Three valleys west of Bonascre, the **Plateau de Beille** is a likely area for **cross-country skiing**. The 55km of pistes range in length from one to twenty kilometres, at an altitude of just under 2000m – which should ensure adequate snow. You reach the plateau by taking the "route Forestière" (an unpaved "forest road") from the village of Les Cabannes, 15km north of Ax along the main N20 road. You can also get good cross-country skiing to the north of Ax around the **Col de Chioula** (1431m).

twentieth-century travellers complained about has gone, but the ambience of a spa remains. Four *thermes* still exist, all of them part of the central *Hôtel Royal Thermal*, and in total there are more than forty sources, producing a volume of water in excess of 600,000 litres per day, at temperatures hotter than 70°C in a few cases. The town itself is small and pleasant enough, but there's little to see once you've wandered a couple of streets in the quarter to the right of the N20, which forms the main street. Rue de l'École and rue de la Boucarie retain a few medieval buildings, and above place du Breilh, the **church of St-Vincent** is of architectural interest for its Romanesque tower. Just across the road you can join the locals and dangle your feet for free in the **Bassin des Ladres**, a pool of hot sulphurous water which is all that remains of the hospital founded in 1260 by St Louis for soldiers wounded in the Crusades.

## Practicalities

The **gare SNCF** is on the northwest side of town, just off the main avenue Delcassé; **buses** stop in the town centre. You'll pass two-star **hotels** as you walk into the centre, first the *Hôtel de France* (☎05.61.64.20.30, fax 05.61.64.60.97, *www.logis-de-france.fr*, ④) followed by *Les Pyrénées* (☎05.61.64.21.01; ④), before arriving at the central place du Breilh, home to the **tourist office** (July & Aug daily 9am–1pm & 2–7pm; May, June, Sept & Oct Mon–Sat 9am–noon & 2–7pm, Sun 9am–noon & 2–6pm; Nov Mon–Sat 9am–noon & 2–6pm; Dec–April daily 9am–noon & 2–6pm; ☎05.61.64.60.60, *www.vallees-ax.com*) and another old-fashioned two-star hotel, the *La Paix* (☎05.61.64.22.61; ②). Other convenient, quiet and recommendable accommodation includes the friendly *La Terrasse*, 7 rue Marcaillou (☎05.61.64.20.33; ④), which attracts many skiers and has a restaurant; and *Pension Barat-Aliot* near the Hôtel de Ville below place du Marché (☎05.61.64.22.01; ②), also with attached restaurant. The municipal **campsite**, *Malazéou* (☎05.61.64.22.21; open year-round), is beside the Ariège, 500m from the train station. Ax Sports, near *La Paix*, will replace any lost or worn-out mountaineering and ski gear.

Other than the hotel dining rooms and restaurants, **eating** prospects aren't brilliant in Ax – thus the preponderance of half-board offers at the hotels. Exceptions include the pizzeria opposite the *Hôtel de France* on the main road, and the *Terminus Bar* near the station. For **snacks** on the hoof, there are numerous cheap *boulangeries* and over-the-counter pizza places in rue de l'Horloge, leading off the place du Marché. More atmospheric venues for a **drink** are the old *Grand Café*, beside *Les Pyrénées*, and *Brasserie Le Club* on place Roussel.

## The Oriège valley

Extending east from Ax, the damp, leafy **Oriège valley** allows access to both the Carlit peaks for hikers (see p.162) and the **Réserve Nationale d'Orlu**, created south of the road in 1975 to benefit a growing herd of isards as well as roe deer, golden eagles and lammergeiers. Under the shadow of the distinctive Dent d'Orlu, beloved of technical climbers, the D22 road heads up the valley to **ORLU**, where there's camping at the *Municipal* (☎05.61.64.30.09) and a popular *gîte d'étape* aimed at walkers, the *Relais Montagnard* (☎05.61.64.61.88; ④). A path from **Les Forges d'Orlu** further up the valley permits a link-up with the "Tour des Montagnes d'Ax" (see below), via a climb from near the power station to the dam at Naguille.

At a popular picnic area some 8km beyond Orlu, the asphalt ends and a jeep track, from which all private cars are banned, climbs south into the *réserve* through the En Gaudu valley, before meeting the GR7 below the Étang d'en Beys, with its refuge. If you're approaching the Carlit via the Oriège, it's well worth splashing out for a taxi to the picnic grounds: the walk in is tedious and steep, with little chance of a lift in either direction.

### Walks near Ax-les-Thermes
With an office next door to the tourist office in Ax, the Bureau des Guides et Accompagnateurs Montagne des Vallées d'Ax (☎05.61.64.31.51) maintains a list of seventeen brief **walks** around the town, ranging in length from twenty minutes to seven hours, though most of these prove rather short and over-generously timed; it also keeps information on all the mountain huts and refuges, climbing courses and weather forecasts. To fill a day properly, take the suggested itinerary to the attractive village of **SORGEAT** and link this hike with other sections.

Among the long-distance hikes in the area, the five-day, four-night **Tour des Montagnes d'Ax** is most recommended, since it covers a variety of terrain, including parts of the Carlit. You can begin at **Le Castelet**, on the main road 5km northwest of Ax, climbing south for a day to hook up with the GR10 at the **Col de Beil** (2247m); the closest crude shelter is at **Prat Redon**. The route then heads eastwards to cross the Ariège valley at Mérens-les-Vals, your second overnight stop, from where you stick with the GR10, and later the GR7, all the way to the *Refuge d'en Beys* – the refuge (☎05.61.64.24.24; ①) will be your third night out, after a very long day unless you spend the night at the refuge *Les Bésines* (☎05.61.05.22.44; meals available June–Sept; ①) at the junction of the two trails. From the refuge, you've a shorter day up to the gentle **Couillade de Beys** (2345m), then past the easterly Étang des Peyrisses and the Naguille dam before the descent to the floor of the Oriège valley.

## Mérens and L'Hospitalet

The reputation of **MÉRENS-LES-VALS**, 8km south of Ax along the N20, rests on the stocky frame of the **Mérenguais horse**, a breed which – partly on the strength of the Niaux cave paintings (see p.157) – is considered the closest thing in western Europe to the wild horse of prehistory. Nowadays there are more specimens outside the mountains of Mérens than in them, but the village remains a place of pilgrimage for horse lovers. Mérens itself, though, is unexceptional, one part clustered on the main road, the other spread out on the slopes to the east around a Romanesque church. The village straddles the GR10, which accounts for the attractively restored **gîte d'étape** in the upper village (☎05.61.64.32.50; ①), a congenial place to base yourself for a few days' walking, serving excellent food – luckily enough, since there are no other hotels or restaurants open in the town at present, though there is a **campsite** just off the main road, near the river.

Mérens makes a good base for **walks**, short or long. A popular one-day circuit involves following the GR10, and then a local path, southwest up the Mourgouillou valley, where Mérenguais horses still graze, to the **Étang de Couart**, and then dropping back down to the train station at L'Hospitalet by using the **HRP** (the Haute Route des Pyrénées, a trail which traverses the whole range). Alternatively, heading southeast, the GR10 offers a more appealing, if more strenuous introduction to the **Carlit range** than the HRP from L'Hospitalet (see below), but be warned that both French and translated *topoguides* sketch the route on the wrong bank of the River Nabre.

## L'Hospitalet

Ten kilometres further south from Mérens is **L'HOSPITALET-PRÈS-L'ANDORRE**, whose sole interest – in the absence of any monumental or natural attraction – is as a route convergence: the HRP goes through here, as do buses to and from adjacent Andorra, and trains south into the Cerdagne and north to Toulouse. There are basic and unremarkable two one-star **hotels** – the *Puymorens* (☎05.61.64.23.03; ③) and *Le Sisca* (☎05.61.64.23.02; ②), plus a **gîte** (☎ & fax 05.61.05.23.19, *gitedetape.lhospitalet@libertysurf.fr*), and a **campsite**. Heading into the Carlit Massif, the **HRP** gets you quickly to grips with the mountains, offering the shortest approach from the west as it climbs unusually gently to the dam and pair of refuges at Bésines, where you link up with the GR10. Heading south of L'Hospitalet, a 7km-long road tunnel pierces the Col de Puymorens (1915m), reducing the road distance to Latour-de-Carol to only 20km.

## travel details

### TRAINS

*In the Aude and Ariège valleys, some scheduled trains may be substituted by SNCF buses.*

**Carcassonne** to: Alet-les-Bains (4–6 daily; 50min); Castelnaudary (6–8 daily; 25min); Limoux (4–6 daily; 35min); Montpellier (4 daily; 1hr 30min); Nîmes (6 daily; 2hr 5min); Perpignan (5 daily; 1hr 30min); Quillan (3–4 daily; 55min); Toulouse (5 daily; 45min).

**Foix** to: Ax-les-Thermes (6–7 daily; 45min); L'Hospitalet (4 daily; 1hr 10min–1hr 30min); Latour-de-Carol (5 daily; 2hr); Pamiers (11 daily; 15–25min); Tarascon-sur-Ariège (6–7 daily; 20min); Toulouse (11 daily; 1hr).

**L'Hospitalet-près-l'Andorre** to: Ax-les-Thermes (5 daily; 20min); Latour-de-Carol (5 daily; 25min); Tarascon-sur-Ariège (4 daily; 1hr); Toulouse (4 daily; 2hr–2hr 20min).

**Latour-de-Carol** to: Ax-les-Thermes (5 daily; 55min); Bourg-Madame (5 daily; 15min); Foix (4 daily; 1hr 30min–1hr 40min); L'Hospitalet-près-l'Andorre (5 daily; 25min); Mont-Louis (5 daily; 1hr 20min); Puigcerdà (4 daily; 7min); Tarascon-sur-Ariège (4 daily; 1hr 15min–1hr 25min); Toulouse (4 daily; 2hr 30min–2hr 45min); Villefranche-de-Conflent (4 daily; 2hr 25min–2hr 55min).

**Limoux** to: Carcassonne (4–6 daily; 35min); Quillan (3–4 daily; 55min).

**Pamiers** to: Ax-les-Thermes (6–7 daily; 1hr 10min); Foix (11 daily; 15–25min); Latour-de-Carol (5 daily; 2hr 20min); Toulouse (11 daily; 40min).

**Quillan** to: Carcassonne (3–4 daily; 55min); Limoux (3–4 daily; 55min).

**Tarascon-sur-Ariège** to: Foix (4 daily; 20min); Toulouse (4 daily; 1hr 45min).

### BUSES

**Axat** to: Castelnaudary (1 daily; 1hr 50min); Limoux (1 daily; 50min).

**Ax-les-Thermes** to: Foix (2–6 daily; 1hr); Pas de la Casa (2 daily; 45min); Tarascon-sur-Ariège (2 daily; 30min).

**Caracassone** to: Albi (1 daily; 2hr); Axat (1 daily; 1hr 45min); Castelnaudary (4–6 daily; 45min); Castres (8 daily; 1hr 50min); Quillan (4 daily; 1hr 15min).

**Comus** to: Quillan (2 daily Mon–Fri; 1hr 5min).

**Foix** to: Lavelanet (Mon–Sat 1–2 daily; 35min); Mirepoix (Mon–Sat 1 daily; 1hr 30min); Pamiers (4–6 daily; 25min); Quillan (Mon–Sat 1 daily; 2hr); St-Girons (4 daily; 45min).

**L'Hospitalet-près-l'Andorre** (SNCF bus) to: Andorra la Vella (2 daily; 1hr 30min–1hr 40min); Pas de la Casa (2 daily; 25–30min).

**Latour-de-Carol** to: Font-Romeu (4 daily; 50min); Perpignan (2–4 daily; 3hr 5min).

**Lavelanet** to: Foix (Mon–Sat 4–6 daily; 50min); Mirepoix (2 daily; 40min); Quillan (Mon–Sat 2 daily; 1hr); Toulouse (2–6 daily; 2hr 20min).

**Limoux** to: Castelnaudary (3 daily; 35min).

**Mas d'Azil** to: Toulouse (2 daily; 1hr 55min).

**Mirepoix** to: Lavelanet (2 daily; 40min); Pamiers (2 daily; 30min).

**Quillan** to: Axat (2 daily; 20min); Comus (1–2 daily; 1hr 5min); Perpignan (2 daily; 1hr 30min); Quérigut (3 weekly in summer; 1hr 30min).

**St-Girons** to Aulus-les-Bains (1–2 daily; 1hr 15min); Seix (3 daily; 30min); Toulouse (2–3 daily; 2hr 30min).

**Tarascon-sur-Ariège** to: Vicdessos/Auzat (2 daily during school year, otherwise 1–2 weekly; 30min).

# CHAPTER THREE

# ALBI AND HAUT LANGUEDOC

T**arn**, the *département* to the east of Toulouse, consists of two contrasting zones. The northwest is wine country: the rolling landscape on the banks of the river after which the *département* is named is punctuated by towns which grew up on the modest prosperity of the grape and other products of the soil, including garlic and woad. The southeast, on the other hand, is a rugged upland where herding and wool have sustained a precarious living for the villagers of the high valleys as far back as can be recalled. Today the Tarn is not the most of dynamic of regions – it has fallen victim to the rural depopulation which typifies much of southern France, with the result that there is almost no industry. Nevertheless, there's much to see here and though, like Toulouse, it falls outside the modern administrative *région* of Languedoc-Roussillon, it is culturally and historically inseparable from the Occitan coastal lands.

In the northwest, **Albi**, the Tarn's principal town, was ruled for centuries by the counts of Toulouse, and its name is synonymous with the Cathar sect with which modern *languedociens* still proudly identify. The undulating lowlands which surround the town are defined by the flow of the Tarn: to the east, descending from the Grandes Causses, it follows a rapid, rocky course, cutting down through forested hills and meandering dramatically around **Ambialet**; north of the capital, gritty **Carmaux** sits atop a coal-rich landscape, scarred by the centuries-long search for the black stuff; to the west, the stunningly preserved medieval citadel of **Cordes** marks the transition to the Aveyron valley; and finally, passing Albi, the Tarn flows west toward **Gaillac** and one of the most praised wine regions of the south of France, veering south, past the ancient *bastides* of **Lisle** and **Rabastens**, before being met by the tributary Agout. The region's interior, south of Albi, has a scattering of sleepy old towns set amidst fields of corn and wheat; moving away from the river past Graulhet and Réalmont, the land becomes more hilly, and here you'll find **Lautrec**, the most beautiful town of the Albigeois.

To the southeast **Haut Languedoc** ("Upper Languedoc"), a wild hinterland of rocky hills, has a history of religious and political non-conformity befitting its mountain character – once a remote hotbed of Protestant Huguenots, it presents a wilderness surprising for an area so close to the bustle of the coast. At its base lies **Castres**, Albi's poorer cousin, a lively little provincial town, birthplace of the socialist hero Jean Jaurès and home to an important collection of Spanish art. In

## FESTIVALS IN ALBI AND HAUT LANGUEDOC

As elsewhere in Languedoc and Roussillon, most towns have their local *fêtes* between June and August, here featuring dances, fireworks and *pétanque* competitions. Some of the more exceptional ones are listed below; where we haven't given a number for information contact the town's tourist office.

**Feb–March** Albi: Carnaval. Held from the last Sunday in February to the first Sun in March, Albi's traditional French Lenten festival coincides with "Rebonds", a festival of sculpture, modern dance and contemporary music.

**Mid-May** Gaillac: Wine contest. Held over four days this competition is one of the two most important dates on the Gaillac calendar, when the new year's vintages are debuted and judged.

**June–July** Albi: Open-air theatre festival. Nightly performances of mostly French works, covering everything from the classics of Molière to avant-garde, at the Palace de la Berbie (9.45pm), running from the last week of June through to mid-July.

### July

**Early July** Albi: Jazz festival. Held over one week this festival draws French and international musicians alike, playing in a range of venues, both indoor and outdoor.

**Mid-July** Cordes: Fêtes du Grand Fauconnier. This four-day medieval festival converts the town into a costumed extravaganza, complete with exhibitions on medieval crafts and falconry. Daily admission to the old town is 25F/€3.81.

**Last two weeks** Castres: Goya festival. Nightly performances of classical music, theatre and opera, all performed on an outdoor stage in the place 1er du Mai. Brings in symphonies and companies from around France and western Europe.

### August

**First three weeks** Castres: Couleurs du Monde. Free World music performances held nightly in the place 1er du Mai, and featuring performers from Africa, the Caribbean, Latin America and across Europe. Information on ☎05.63.71.59.84.

**First weekend** Gaillac: Fête du vin. Gaillac's second wine festival is timed to coincide with the beginning of the grape harvest season, with wine contests and tastings, as well as concerts and cultural events.

**Mid-Aug** Rabastens: Grande Cavalcade. Typical village *fête* held for two days and featuring dancing, fireworks, and a parade through the town centre.

### November

**Mid-Nov** Albi: Les Œillades. A one-week festival of new French feature films (with some entries from Belgium and Quebec) with an emphasis on young film-makers. Plenty of seminars and prizes are awarded for the films, actors and directors. Held at Ciné-forum, 104 av Colonel-Teyssier (☎05.63.38.25.17, *www.oeillades.com*).

**Nov 23** Albi: Ste Cécile Day. Feast of the patron saint of the cathedral, with a special mass held, and a market in the adjacent square.

the uplands, most of which have been incorporated into the **Parc Naturel Régional de Haut Languedoc**, dark woods and high pasture are interspersed by a series of seemingly forgotten villages, including Lacaune, La Salvetat and St-

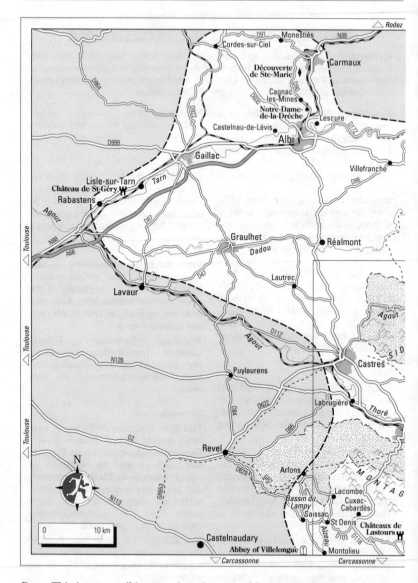

Pons. This is easy walking terrain, crisscrossed by *grand randonnées* and local trails like the Gijou Valley Railway Path. Further south the **Montagne Noire**, rising south of **Mazamet**, presents an even more isolated and untamed landscape, guarded on its southern side the ruined fortress of **Saissac** and the Cathar castles of **Lastours**. Chilling out in Castres is a good option, especially given its

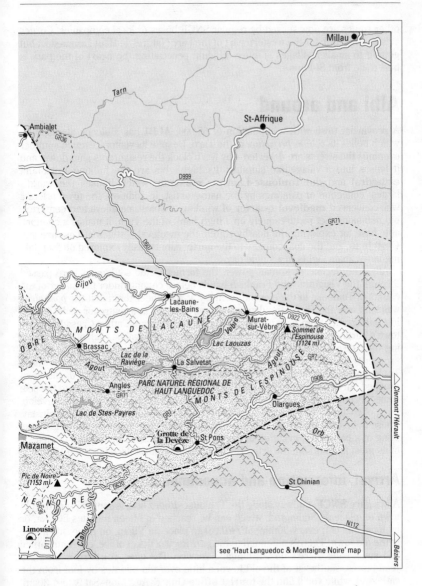

see 'Haut Languedoc & Montaigne Noire' map

museums and amenities, while the rest of the region presents a rugged country-side, ideal for rambling or back-road motoring.

Despite its general isolation, the area of Albi and Haut Languedoc is well served by public transport. The main Toulouse–Rodez rail line follows the course of the Tarn up to Albi and Carmaux, with branch-offs to Cordes and Mazamet, while other routes are now served by regular SNCF buses or local companies. Cordes acts as a bus hub for the western part of the Parc Naturel de Haut Languedoc, but getting to smaller villages is more difficult; penetrating the heart of the park is best done from St-Pons.

# Albi and around

A provincial town with a population of 65,000, **ALBI** has a sleepy atmosphere which belies its role as *préfecture* of the Tarn. Despite its visitors, even in summer evenings the streets are deserted – by ten o'clock the restaurants shut down, and it lapses into a village-like slumber. Its highlights are the hulking brick-built **cathedral** and the **Toulouse-Lautrec museum**, which houses the world's largest collection of paintings by the native artist. In addition, the town offers a well-conserved **medieval quarter** of winding cobblestone alleys and centuries-old mansions. Set picturesquely on a high bank of the Tarn, it makes a comfortable base for exploring the nearby sights: the medieval vestiges of **Lescure** and **Castelnau**, and the coal country to the north. Albi is easily explored on foot, taking in the main sights in a single day.

After the decline of Roman power, the former Celtic settlement here passed through the Visigothic and Frankish hands before coming under the power of the counts of Toulouse in the eleventh century. It was under them that the *pont vieux* was built over the Tarn, stimulating the town's growth as a centre for trade, attracting immigrants from as far away as the Rhine. The anti-Cathar Crusade let the town's burghers and bishops play the counts and kings against each other, increasing their own autonomy, and under the rule of the bishops, Albi rode a wave of prosperity from the 1300s onwards, based on the same woad trade that powered Toulouse (see box on p.99). But when demand for the dye declined, the town dropped out of history, and by the 1700s the adventurous were turning to the sea, some becoming renowned navigators. Industrialization came with the development of coalfields to the north; glass-working and textiles becoming the mainstay. These industries persist in Albi, on a modest scale, and today the town is something of a backwater, living on under the shadows of its cathedral and the legacy of its most famous son, the artist Henri-Toulouse Lautrec (see box on p.172).

## Arrival, information and accommodation

Albi's **gare SNCF**, midway along the Toulouse–Rodez line, is southwest of the old town on place de Stalingrad, which can be reached in fifteen minutes by foot, or by local bus (#1; every 30min; 5F/€0.08) to place du Vigan, on the eastern side of the old town. There's not much to the *gare* itself: a ticket office, car rental office and small café; there's no left luggage service. The **gare routière** is on place Jean-Jaurès, southeast of the old town, a little over ten minutes by foot from the cathedral, while you'll find the **tourist office** (July & Aug Mon–Sat 9am–7.30pm, Sun 10.30am–1pm & 3.30–6.30pm; Sept–June Mon–Sat 9am–noon & 2–6pm, Sun 10.30am–12.30pm & 3.30–5.30pm; ☎05.63.49.48.80, fax 05.63.49.48.98, *www.mairie-albi.fr*) housed in the Palace de la Berbie, beside the cathedral – it will change money when banks are closed.

Given its size, Albi offers a surprisingly wide selection of **hotels**, and even those located near the train station are only a short walk from the historical centre; rock-bottom budget places though are scarce. There's only one **HI hostel** in town, the *Auberge de Jeunesse*, at 15 rue République (reception Mon–Fri 6–9pm, Sat & Sun 8–9pm; ☎05.63.54.53.65; 65F/€9.91), a members-only place fifteen minutes' walk east from the old town, which has a café, plus laundry and kitchen facilities, no curfews and rents sheets (15F/€2.29). The two-star **campsite**, *Camping de Caussels*, is a thirty-minute walk east of the centre in Parc de Caussels (Easter–Oct; ☎05.63.60.37.06; Albibus #5 to "Camping" from place Jean-Jaurès).

### Hotels

**Georges V**, 29 av Maréchal-Joffre (☎05.63.54.24.16, fax 05.63.54.69.59, *hotel.georgev @ilink.fr*). Located by the train station, a small eighty-year-old hotel in a converted house. Each room is individually decorated in modern pastel tones, and there's a garden for breakfasts. You'll need to book ahead. ③.

**Hostellerie de Vigan**, 16 pl du Vigan (☎05.63.54.01.23, fax 05.63.47.05.42, *www.france-resa .com*). Near the *gare routière*, this modern building is rather more functional than charming, with big but bland rooms. Comfortable, clean and quiet though, and it has all the amenities. ③.

**Hostellerie St-Antoine**, 17 rue St-Antoine (☎05.63.54.04.04, fax 05.62.47.10.47, *stantoine @ilink.fr*). Classy establishment at the top of the high end of this price bracket, founded in 1734 and run by the same family for five generations. The sumptuous rooms are appointed with antique furnishings, but the hotel also has modern facilities such as parking and air conditioning. ⑥.

**Mercure les Bastides**, 41 rue Porta (☎05.63.47.66.66, fax 05.63.46.18.40, *mercure.albi @wanadoo.fr*). A luxury establishment in a restored eighteenth-century mill building, with modern facilities and décor, and a highly rated and well-priced restaurant. Try for one of the riverside rooms, which have spectacular views over the river to the cathedral. ⑤.

**Régence**, 27 av Maréchal-Joffre (☎05.63.54.01.42, fax 05.63.54.80.48). Next door to, and a virtual replica of the *George V*, and a fine second choice when that hotel is full. ③.

**St-Clair**, 8 rue St-Claire (☎05.63.54.25.66, fax 05.63.47.27.58). In a converted old brick-and-timber house in the heart of the old town only 50m from the cathedral, this friendly establishment is clean and well maintained. Also has parking. ③.

**Le Vieil-Alby**, 25 rue Toulouse-Lautrec (☎05.63.54.15.69, fax 05.63.54.96.75, *www.logis-de-france.fr*). Comfortable and quiet, this hotel, set in another renovated medieval house in the centre, is possibly the best deal in town. It also has a great restaurant (closed Sun eve & Mon) and very friendly management. ③.

## The Town

All of Albi's sights are within or adjacent to the compact limits of the once-walled **old town**, whose northern boundary is formed by the steep banks of the Tarn,

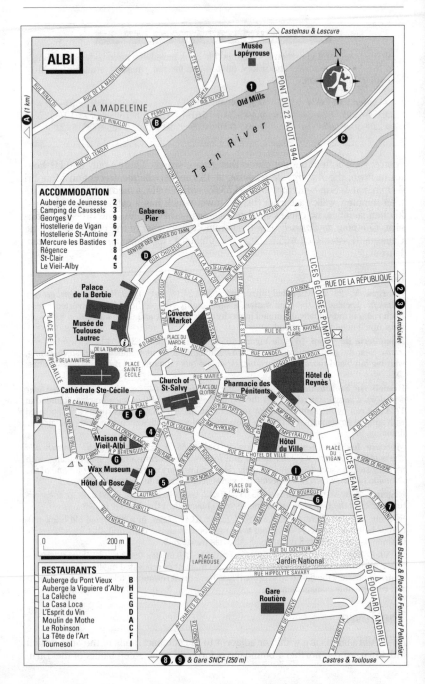

△ Castelnau & Lescure

**ALBI**

N

Musée
Lapéyrouse

① Old Mills

LA MADELEINE

*Tarn River*

**ACCOMMODATION**

| | |
|---|---|
| Auberge de Jeunesse | 2 |
| Camping de Caussels | 3 |
| Georges V | 9 |
| Hostellerie de Vigan | 6 |
| Hostellerie St-Antoine | 7 |
| Mercure les Bastides | 1 |
| Régence | 8 |
| St-Clair | 4 |
| Le Vieil-Alby | 5 |

Gabares
Pier

Palace
de la Berbie

Musée de
Toulouse-
Lautrec

Covered
Market

Cathédrale Ste-Cécile

Church of
St-Salvy

Pharmacie des
Pénitents

Hôtel de
Reynès

Maison de
Vieil-Albi

Hôtel
du Ville

Wax Museum

Hôtel du Bosc

PLACE DU
PALAIS

Jardin National

0          200 m

**RESTAURANTS**

| | |
|---|---|
| Auberge du Pont Vieux | B |
| Auberge la Viguiere d'Alby | H |
| La Calèche | E G |
| La Casa Loca | D |
| L'Esprit du Vin | G |
| Moulin de Mothe | D |
| Le Robinson | A |
| La Tête de l'Art | C F |
| Tournesol | I |

Gare
Routière

▽ ⑧, ⑨ & Gare SNCF (250 m)

Castres & Toulouse ▽

and which is now completely surrounded by the sprawl of the new town. Across the river, the eighteenth-century suburb of **La Madeleine** is also worth a look, primarily for the spectacular views of the Tarn which it affords, with medieval Albi perched above.

## The Cathédrale Ste-Cécile

The rounded arches and towers and red-brick construction of the **Cathédrale Ste-Cécile** (June–Sept daily 8.30am–7pm; Oct–May Mon–Sat 9am–noon & 2.30–6.30pm, Sun 8.30am–7pm; free) dominate Albi, evoking a mix of the Middle Ages and Art Deco that makes it without doubt the most curious medieval cathedral you are likely to see. Financed by the proceeds of the Inquisition, the first bricks were laid in 1282, some fifty years after the Cathar defeat, but the 30-metre-wide nave and 78-metre-tall tower were not completed for more than a century after. The cathedral's clean lines, narrow windows and hulking mass reflect its role as a bastion of militant Catholicism in a region plagued by heresy, but two alterations spoil its unity: a gaudy and incongruous sixteenth-century stone porch, and a Baroque frenzy of trompe l'oeil festooned about the interior. In better harmony with the structure are the fifteenth-century **statues** of saints and biblical figures which decorate the rood screen to the right of the entrance, while the west wall is dominated by a giant contemporary **mural** of the Last Judgement – sadly marred by the later construction of a chapel – replete with nasty devils carrying off teeth-gnashing souls to the inferno. To the immediate right of the entrance, a doorway leads to the **choir** (5F/€0.80), consisting of wooden stalls backed by elaborately carved stonework and more statuary, similar to that of the nave. The **treasury** (20F/€3.05), reached by a spiral staircase on the north wall, is disappointingly small. If you can, catch the **organ recitals** held in the cathedral in July and August (Wed 5pm & Sun 4pm; free), or the tourist office's night-time **tours** in English (June–Sept daily 9.30pm; 28F/€4.27).

## The Palace de la Berbie and the Musée de Toulouse-Lautrec

Next to the cathedral, the matching brick-built **Palace de la Berbie** ("bishop", in local parlance), the fortified redoubt of Albi's lord-bishops, squats over the slow-passing Tarn. This complex began as a simple keep in the thirteenth century, but was elaborated in succeeding centuries by its wealthy owners, who strengthened its fortifications, linked it to the cathedral and laid out a classical garden. Today the palace houses the **Musée de Toulouse-Lautrec** (April–Sept daily 10am–noon & 2–6pm; Oct–March Wed–Sun 10am–noon & 2–5pm; 24F/€3.66), the most important public collection of the painter's work, and the only part of the palace interior which is open to the public. Conceived and endowed by the artist's mother and opened in 1922, it is comprehensive (boasting both his first and last works) – a must for any fan of the diminutive Albigeois. His famous depictions of the entertainers and prostitutes of *fin-de-siècle* Paris, such as the candidly matter-of-fact *In the Salon in Moulin Street*, or the erotic *Woman Disrobing*, are complemented by many **posters** and lesser-known works inspired by his family life in the local countryside. Off in a corner up a spiral stairway, you'll find a sumptuous thirteenth-century **chapel**, with a beautiful ceiling of gold-painted stars on a blue background – once the audience chamber of the bishops. The topmost of the museum's three storeys houses works by other modern French artists, including Brayer, Gauguin and Matisse.

## HENRI TOULOUSE-LAUTREC

Perhaps the most famous of Languedoc's artists is the painter and illustrator **Henri Toulouse-Lautrec**. Born into the venerable family of the Viscounts of Toulouse-Lautrec in 1864, Henri was deprived of a traditional aristocratic upbringing due to a congenital bone condition; his frailty kept him out of school, and after two falls at his home in Albi resulted in broken legs, any hope of pursuing a "normal" life ended. He thus turned to painting, and his earliest works, scenes from his family's milieu such as *Artilleryman Saddling a Horse*, and portraits – particularly of his mother – showed great promise. With the support of his family and the encouragement of their friend, the painter René Princeteau, Henri moved to Paris to study under Bonnat and Cormon, two successful conservative artists. Settled in bohemian Montmartre and accompanied by his friend and fellow student **Vincent Van Gogh**, he came under the spell both of the Impressionists and the seedy underside of the city, and it was here that his own vivid style began to flourish. Seduced by the subversive Parisian **nightclubs**, he began to convey their dynamism in charcoal sketches like *Gin-Cocktail* and *Chocolate Dancing*, which were published in popular newspapers and magazines. By the early 1890s he was renowned as an illustrator, doing colourful line-drawn adverts, posters for the famous **Moulin-Rouge** cabaret, and covers for magazines like *La Revue Blanch* so that by 1894, when he began his series of sketches and paintings on Paris **brothels**, including *In the Sitting Room at Moulins Street* and *The Two Girlfriends*, he was already successful.

Henri's disabilities did not prevent him from living life to the full: he travelled widely, drank copiously and, of course, patronized with gusto the brothels he depicted (he was known to Parisian prostitutes as the "teapot", owing to his rotund figure and excessive endowment). In the end his vices aggravated his already fragile state, and by 1899 he was seeking treatment for **alcoholism**. In September 1901, at the age of 37, he died in a family castle near Bordeaux. What compelled Lautrec's dissolute lifestyle is uncertain – it wasn't his family relations, as he remained close to his parents throughout his life – but his contribution to the artistic world is unquestionable; with a unique illustrative style – a peculiar outgrowth of Impressionism – he not only influenced successive movements such as the Fauvists, but set the precedent for innovative poster design – to this day his Moulin Rouge adverts remain some of the most reproduced pictures in the world.

The palace also has a partly covered gallery (free) with a shady outdoor **café** providing views of the old bridge and the far river bank, as well as access to the garden; you enter it from the place de l'Archevêché, on the east side of the complex.

### The old town and La Madeleine

Albi's **old town** is a chaotic jumble of narrow streets spreading east and south of the cathedral-palace complex. From the square by the tourist office, you'll see the red-brick spire of the much mistreated **church of St-Salvy**, which marks the old town's centre. While the interior of the building is nothing special, its simple Romanesque **cloister** can be entered from the streets to either side (daily: mid-June to mid-Sept 8am–noon & 2.30–6.30pm; mid-Sept to mid-June 8.30am–noon & 2–5.45pm; free) – a great place to read or just take a break. Just east in rue Timbal sits the sixteenth-century brick-and-timber "**Pharmacie des Pénitents**", once a wealthy merchant's mansion and now a pharmacy, with playfully carved faces on its wooden beams, while across the street lies the rather more austere and plain Renaissance and Gothic **Hôtel de Reynès** (courtyard open Mon–Fri 8am–noon & 1.30–5.30pm; free). To the south a hulking Renaissance mansion, now housing the **Hôtel du Ville**, holds a huge, timbered council chamber within its regal interior (Mon–Fri 8am–noon & 1.30–5.30pm; free). West from the town hall, the narrow cobbled streets overhung with balconies of medieval houses evoke the age when the bishops and woad merchants held sway. Here you'll find the medieval **Maison de Vieil Albi** (Mon–Sat 3–7pm; 5F/€0.76), a museum displaying items of local interest, including memorabilia of the young Toulouse-Lautrec, but – more interestingly – a period town-house interior. Close by are the artist's childhood home, the **Hôtel du Bosc** (no entry), and a laughably shabby **wax museum** (June–Sept Tues–Sun 10am–6pm; 20F/€3.05).

Across the river from the main body of the old town lies the eighteenth-century suburb of **La Madeleine**, best reached by the oft-rebuilt eleventh-century *pont vieux* to the east of the bishops' palace. Before you cross over, however, you might want to explore the banks of the Tarn, where under the shadow of the palace walls, *gabares* (traditional river boats) depart downriver for half-hour **excursions** (mid-June to mid-Sept 10am–7pm; 22F/€3.36). La Madeleine is a compact knot of residential houses, with a number of disused eighteenth-century mill buildings clustered along the riverbank on its eastern side. Part of the mill complex, back from the river, holds the **Musée Lapéyrouse** (April–Sept Mon & Wed–Sun 9am–noon & 2–6pm; Oct–March same days 10am–noon & 2–5pm; 15F/€2.29), named in honour of the adventurous navigator (1741–88) who fought the British in New France before embarking on a scientific voyage to South America, Japan, Siberia and the East Indies, where he perished in a shipwreck. The museum reviews the admiral's career in a lively display of personal and period artefacts, maps and dioramas.

# Eating, drinking and nightlife

Culinary variety is not a high priority in Albi and most of the **restaurants** specialize in local *terroir* ("country cooking"), with the usual dishes – cassoulet, foie gras and duck, accompanied by fine Gaillac wine. You can also get *lou tastou*, tapas-sized portions which permit you to sample a variety of dishes without breaking the bank. Pizzas and *briques*, quick and cheap, can be found on the place du Vigan. Numerous **cafés** and **bars** lining place de l'Archevêché and place du Vigan have terraces for a daytime drink, including *Café de la Poste* on the north side of the latter, which has a good selection of Belgian beers, while others offer night-time **music** (predominantly Latin), including *Ô Caliente* (nightly till 2am) opposite the Palace de la Berbie and *Les Gargouilles* (weekends till 2am) in the place de l'Archevêché. *Le Shamrock*, 57 avenue Charles de Gaulle is an Irish-style option.

## Restaurants

**Auberge du Pont Vieux**, 98 rue Porta (☎05.63.77.61.73; closed Tues). On the north bank of the Tarn, this popular establishment serves traditional Albigeois cuisine and offers both a vaulted dining room and a riverside terrace. *Terroir* menus go from 99F/€15.10.

**Auberge la Viguiere d'Alby**, 7 rue Toulouse-Lautrec (☎05.63.54.76.44). The Chatellains' family-run establishment offers *lou tastou* and solid Tarn cuisine. In the garden "César," a twenty-year-old tortoise, will happily help to finish your plate. Several evening menu options for under 100F/€15.25.

**La Calèche**, 8 rue de la Piale (☎05.63.54.15.52). Comfy dining room built under the supporting vaults of the cathedral, and a wide range of lunch and dinner menus, including cassoulets, *escargots*, excellent salads, and Moroccan dishes (starting from 59F/€9.00 & 85F/€13.57). The service is fast and professional, yet friendly.

**La Casa Loca**, rue Puech Bérenguier (☎05.63.47.26.00; closed Sat noon & Sun). A cosy and informal little place, featuring genuine Spanish food, with tapas (from 14F/€2.14 each) and, of course, paella (from 50F/€7.63), all made by ex-pat Spaniards.

**L'Esprit du Vin**, 11 quai Choiseul (☎05.63.54.60.44; closed mid-Feb to May). Under the shadow of la Berbie, it scores on both décor and quality with imaginative *gastronomique* cuisine, balancing sweet and savoury with variations on themes of duck, lamb and fish as well as excellent home-made desserts. Menus from 100F/€15.25.

**Mercure les Bastides**, 41 rue Porta (☎05.63.47.66.66; closed Sat & Sun noon & late Dec). A luxurious, but nevertheless affordable restaurant in the hotel of the same, with fine views of the old town across the river. Match this with quality food and good service and you have a winner. Lunch menus from 100F/€15.2.

**Moulin de Mothe**, rue de Lamothe (☎05.63.60.38.15; closed Sun noon). Albi's well-established home of excellent Tarnais fare, located on the Madeleine side, a pleasant 1km stroll west from the *pont vieux*. Dishes include heartwarming *pot au feu* stews, first-rate foie gras, and roast pigeon in a delicate fruit and nut sauce, with menus from 140–380F/€21.35–57.95.

**Le Robinson**, 142 rue Edouard-Branly (☎05.63.46.15.69). Reached by a footpath from the new bridge and set in a riverbank park, this converted house in a garden definitely gets an "A" for atmosphere, and the food and service are acceptable, if unexceptional (menus from 60–150F/€9.15–22.88).

**La Tête de l'Art**, 7 rue de la Piale (☎05.63.38.44.75). Decidedly unrestrained atmosphere and wacky décor makes for a pleasant change from its more formal rivals. Menus consisting of plentiful portions start at 100F/€15.25.

**Tournesol**, rue de l'Ort-en-Salvy, off place du Vigan (☎05.63.38.44.60; closed Sat eve, Sun & Mon) Albi's herbivorous option; expect to pay 75F/€11.44 for a variety of salads, quiches, and other organic options.

## Listings

**Banks** Most of the major French banks have branches in the old town offering currency exchange and ATMs. After bank hours, change money at the tourist office.

**Bike rental** Rey Sport, 39 rue Soult (☎05.63.47.24.22).

**Bus information** ☎05.63.53.31.28.

**Car rental** Avis, rte de Toulouse (☎05.63.54.76.54); Budget, rue Albert 1er (☎05.63.47 .97.00); Europcar, 67 rue Maillot (☎05.63.48.88.33); Hertz, av François Mitterand (☎05.63.54.17.34); and Lavail, rte d'Albi (☎05.63.71.93.34).

**Hospital** Centre Hospitalier, bd Général Sibille (☎05.63.47.47.47), southwest of the old town.

**Internet access** Le Darllo Cybercafé, 10 av de Gaulle (Mon–Sat 10am–2am).

**Laundry** 10 rue Emile Grand (daily 8.30am–8pm).

**Police** Police Municipal, Hôtel du Police, 11 Licés Georges-Pompidou.

**Shopping and markets** Flea market in the Halle de Castelviel (Sat 8am–noon), just west of the cathedral, and produce markets in the place Ste-Cécile and the place du Marché (Tues–Sun 8am–noon). Organic foods are sold in the Jardin National (Tues 5–7pm) and at Aliments Naturels, 1 rue Puech Bérenguier (☎05.63.54.44.86).

**Taxi** Albi Taxi Occitan ☎05.63.54.19.82.

**Train information** ☎05.63.53.32.68.

# Around Albi

Albi makes a good base for a number of easy excursions, most of which are well served by public transport (either Tarnbus, or private firms). On the north bank of the Tarn, 6km west of Albi, tiny **Castelnau-de-Lévis** boasts the ruins of a hill-top **castle** (free entry) founded after the Albigensian Crusade by a rehabilitated Raymond VII of Toulouse. Little remains apart from a single slender tower, but climbing its 198 steps provides breathtaking views of Albi and the plains of the *pays du cocagne*. Another vantage point from which to take in the panorama of Albi is the nineteenth-century octagonal sanctuary of **Notre-Dame-de-la-Drèche**, set on a rise 6km north of town. Founded by returning missionaries, the working church has a small museum recalling their efforts overseas (Mon–Sat 9.30–12.15pm & 4–6pm; free); the grassy grounds outside the church are a popular picnic spot, and make an ideal rest stop for those returning by foot or bike from Cagnac (see p.177). A visit to the sanctuary can also be combined with a trip to **Lescure**, on the northeast edge of Albi, whose draw is the must-see eleventh-century **chapel** of St-Michel (hours vary). Founded by the monks from Gaillac and presently used as a space for photographic and artistic exhibitions, the ancient church boasts a striking Romanesque doorway and is festooned inside and out with carvings of gargoyles, animals and biblical scenes. Die-hard Toulouse-Lautrec fans will want to trek 45km north to **Château de Bosc** (daily 9am–7pm; 30F/€4.58), the family's principal estate, easily accessible from Albi by car or train to Naucelle-Gare, and then 3km southeast (follow signs for "Bosc").

# Ambialet

Following the twisting and rocky bed of the Tarn 21km east from Albi you reach **AMBIALET** (on the GR36), a mandatory stop on the way to Millau and not unworthy of exploration in its own right. Here the river doubles back in a dramatic oxbow, leaving a spit of land only 25m across at its narrowest point – a truly striking location. First mentioned in 924 AD, Ambialet belonged to Toulouse until it was seized by Simon de Montfort during the Albigensian Crusade. Over the following centuries it suffered in the Hundred Years' War and Wars of Religion; by the nineteenth it lay abandoned and even today it exudes a certain sleepy desolation. The main sight here is the austere Romanesque **church** (daily 7.15am–10pm; free) – still used by the resident monks; perched on the top of the hill it provides an impressive panorama of the town below. You reach it by climbing up a path from the "old town", which sits at the narrowest part of the river's meander (the "new town" is above the road tunnel), and can return either the same way or by following the road behind the monastery for 2km. The countryside south of Ambialet is agricultural land – high plains deeply etched by winding rivers. Apart from pleasant scenery, there is little of interest until you reach the Monts de Lacaune of the Parc du Haut Languedoc (see p.189), some 35km south.

**Buses** stop in the car park on the south bank, near which you'll find Ambialet's summer **tourist office** (July & Aug 10am–noon & 2–6pm). On the north bank, the village's only **hotel**, the well-appointed *du Pont* (☎05.63.55.32.07, fax 05.63.55.37.21, *www.logis-de-france.fr*; closed Jan–Feb; ④), has been run by the same family for almost two centuries. Its **restaurant** (open daily) offers menus from 100F–280F/€15.25–42.70. Ambialet also offers three **campsites** (May to mid-Sept), all clustered along the riverbank near the bridge: the municipal site (☎05.63.55.32.93), the *Pont de Couris* (☎05.63.55.32.25) and the *La Moulinquié* (☎05.63.56.43.53), which also has two *gîtes*. **Bikes** can be rented at the hotel, while **kayaks** and **canoes** can be rented near the bridge on the same side of the river, and at other locales along the length of the river on the way to Albi. Wednesday's "country" **market** is strictly a tourist affair.

# Carmaux and around

Lying 16km north of Albi, down-to-earth **CARMAUX** owes its minor wealth to the thirty-square-kilometre coalfield over which it sits, and its few visitors are drawn by the relics of the defunct mining industry around the town: the open pit of **St-Marie**, and the museum of **Cagnac**. These sights can be taken in by car, bicycle, or even by foot, and combined with a visit to the church of Notre-Dame-de-la-Drèche, make a good day's outing from Albi. The countryside hereabouts is flat, scarred by excavation, and not particularly welcoming, but it improves as you head west towards Cordes, passing through **Monestiés**, home to a well-preserved ensemble of late medieval statues. If you're reliant on public transport, you'll have to catch one of the frequent buses which follow the old highway to see the mining sites; there's no public transport link between Carmaux and Monesties.

Carmaux's **coal** vein has been used since the twelfth century, but mining on a grand scale didn't begin until the 1700s, when the local squire, Georges Solages, received a royal licence to exploit the deposit. Late in the nineteenth century, the massive coalface at nearby Cagnac was discovered and became the focus of a boom. By the end of that century though, brutal conditions prompted miners, supported by Jean Jaurès, to unionize; in the half-century that followed the mines enjoyed their greatest period of production. In the 1970s things began to wind down, and the last mine, the great open pit, closed in 1997.

Carmaux itself offers little to visitors aside from a refreshing roughness – a relief after the pretensions of one too many polished-up *bastides*. In fact, the only attraction is the deceptively named **Musée de Château**, the former Solages estate 1km west of the centre, now housing a **museum** of mining and glass-working (French-only guided visits: Mon–Fri 9.30am–noon & 2.30–4.30pm, Sun 3–5pm; 20F/€3.05). With its unremarkable and run-down appearance the mansion is an eyesore, unfortunately not redeemed by the subterranean exhibition, which, dominated by examples of local glass products and over-technical displays on coal mining, is insubstantial and dull.

## Practicalities

Carmaux's **gare SNCF**, on the Albi–Rodez line, sits on the west side of the town centre. Turning left out of the station, boulevard Malroux leads north 100m to avenue Jean-Jaurès, the main street; at the junction turn right and you'll arrive three minutes later at the *place* of the same name, the town's centre. Two streets beyond lies place Gambetta, where same kiosk serves as **gare routière** and **tourist office** (Mon–Fri 10am–noon & 2–6pm, Sat 10am–noon; ☎05.63.76.76.67, fax 05.6336.84.51). Of the town's **hotels**, the *Terminus* (☎05.63.76.50.28, fax 05.63.76.80.27, *www.logis-de-france.fr*; closed Sat, mid-Aug & late Dec; ③), across from the train station on avenue Jean-Jaurès, is the best option. On the other hand, *La Gambetta* (closed Sun ; ☎05.63.76.51.21; ①), opposite the tourist office, is clean and does a three-course lunch for only 58F/€8.85. The **campsite** (May–Oct) is beside the museum. *La Mouette* (closed Sun & Mon eves & mid-Feb; ☎05.63.36.79.90), the town's best **restaurant**, is on place Jean-Jaurès, and offers original and varied menus featuring grilled meats and *confits* starting at 57F/€8.69 for lunch. **Bikes** can be rented from Patrick Gelac (☎05.63.56.05.64) on boulevard Augustin-Malroux, near the station.

## Cagnac-les-Mines

With the land sloping down towards Albi, it makes the most sense to start a trip through the once coal-filled landscape to Cagnac from Carmaux. Just 2km south of town, at Blayes-les-Mines, you'll come upon the abandoned *découverte*, or **open pit**, of Ste-Marie, marked by the silent hulks of rusting machinery parked along its rim. Further along the D90 you'll pass the **Cité du Homps**, a little industrial suburb of single storey wooden huts, built for the Polish miners who immigrated in the Fifties, until you reach the **Musée Mine de Cagnac** (Mon–Sat 10.30am, 11.30am & 2.30–4.30pm, Sun 10.30am, 11.30 & 3–5pm; 32F/€4.88), a vivid recreation of the world of the coal mine, and undoubtedly the region's most original museum. This consists of a claustrophobic ninety-minute guided tour through 350m of galleries, excavated by out-of-work miners, and over a century of mining history, as you're shown different types of tunnels and machinery, a broad coal face, and the miners' day quarters. There's a **picnic** area with a pond beside the museum, and in Cagnac village, a kilometre further along, you'll find a couple of simple **café-bars**. From the village, the D90 begins a rapid descent, reaching Notre-Dame-de-la-Drèche (see p.175) after 3km, before continuing on to Albi.

## Monestiés

Some 8km west of Carmaux is the rather run-of-the-mill village of **MONESTIÉS**, remarkable only for a much-touted set of fifteenth-century religious **statues** housed its **Chapelle St-Jacques** (daily: April–Oct 9am–noon & 2.30–6.30pm; Nov–March 2.30–5pm & Sun 9am–noon; 15F/€2.29). The stone carvings on display are a set of four works representing together a group of figures in Christ's tomb, the Crucifixion, and a pietà – they are well executed and preserved, but most likely only fans of late medieval art will feel that the admission price is justified. The town is also home to the small **Bajén-Vega Museum** (daily 10am–noon & 2.30–6.30pm; 15F/€2.29), with works by the two unexceptional local twentieth-century artists after whom it is named, housed in the same building as the **tourist office** (same hours; ☎05.63.76.22.78, fax 05.63.76.12.77). The only **hotel** is the intermittently open *L'Orée des Bois* (☎05.63.76.11.72, *www.logis-de-france.fr*; ③), opposite the *chapelle*, but there is a basic riverside municipal **campsite** off the road to Cordes. *Auberge Occitane* (closed late-Aug to Sept & Wed), on the main street, is friendly and serves two-course **meals** from 45F/€6.86; the grocery store (☎05.63.76.11.51) rents **bikes**.

# Cordes-sur-Ciel

**CORDES-SUR-CIEL**, 27km northwest of Albi and just west of Monestiés, is the most spectacularly preserved of the Albigeois fortified planned towns, or *bastides*.

Dramatically situated on a steep hill, the origin of the town's surname *sur-ciel* ("in the sky") can be appreciated on mornings when fog cloaks the foot of the hill and the medieval *cité* pokes through, apparently suspended in the clouds. No single sight brings people to Cordes; rather, the town as a whole, girded by several concentric medieval walls and endowed with a score of old houses, is something of an open-air museum and artisanal centre. It can be seen in an afternoon, but if you can afford the relatively expensive hotels, it makes for an atmospheric place to spend a night or two.

Founded in 1222 by Count Raymond VII of Toulouse at the height of the war against his Cathar subjects, Cordes provided a durable and defiant stronghold against Simon de Montfort's attacks. Its forename comes from the **leatherworking** industry (a craft associated with Córdoba, in Spain) which supported, and enriched the town, bringing rapid growth; in the 1200s alone the walls had to be enlarged no less than seven times. Things took a downturn, however, with the arrival of the plague in the 1400s. Although Cordes later recovered, and had a notable lace industry in the nineteenth century, its real renaissance did not come until the 1970s, when hippies, including the **craftsmen** and **artisans** whose wood, metalwork and other studios now cram the upper town, arrived to put Cordes back on the map, attracted by the place's beauty and abandon.

## The Town

The existentialist writer Albert Camus said, "The traveller, who from the terrace of Cordes regards the summer's night, knows that he has no need to go further, and that if he allows it, day after day, the beauty here will raise him out of any solitude." This gives you some idea of the town's allure, and hard though it may be to achieve such a placid state when the streets are packed during summer days, in the evening or out of season Cordes' romance returns. To watch the sun rise from the ramparts is worth getting up for, and with every other building a medieval mansion, walking the town before the crowds arrive is a delight. Its layout is simple: the old citadel – the "**upper town**" – runs along and down the sides of the long and narrow ridge which juts up from the plain, while the modern "**lower town**" consists of a clump of streets at the foot of the old town's eastern tip. The best route to the upper town is the knee-cracking Grand Rue Basse ascending from the lower tourist office (see below), although at busy times, it is more pleasant to take one of the picturesque but less crowded side streets. Alternatively, a *navette* ("minibus"; July & Aug; 15F/€2.29) makes frequent trips from outside the tourist office. Along the way a series of medieval **gates** leads to the compact upper town.

Entering the last of the fortified entryways, you'll reach the **Musée Charles-Portal** (July & Aug daily 11am–noon & 3–6pm; Sept–June Mon–Sat same times, Sun 3–6pm; 15F/€2.29), housing a display on the medieval wells which riddle the town, and which were used in time of siege for water supply or to store grain. Further along on Grande Rue, the elegant and symmetrical arcaded face of the fourteenth-century **Maison du Grand Fauconnier** conceals the **Musée Yves Brayer** (same times and price as the Charles-Portal), which has one room filled with works by the local figurative painter, and another with a French-only audio presentation explaining the town's lace-making tradition – hardly worth the stop. Across the street squats the ancient covered market, where you can peer down one of the town's famously deep wells. Continuing along Grand Rue, you'll see the **Maison de Grand Veneur** ("House of the Great Hunter") – whose otherwise plain stone facade is festooned with amusingly sculpted and extremely well-preserved medieval caricatures of beasts and hunters. A few doors down is the similarly impressively carved frontage of Raymond of Toulouse's old palace, now home to the hotel *Grand Ecuyer* (named after the finely sculpted horse figure) while, just beyond, the contemporary **Porte des Ormeaux** ("Gate of the Birds") takes you out of the old town.

There are more than forty **boutiques** in Cordes (marked on the official map), including some which are thinly disguised as "museums". If you would like to shop for leatherwork, metal and handicraft items and price is not an issue, you could easily spend an afternoon or two (and a considerable sum) here. Many of the stores double as workshops, so even window-shopping is quite interesting. One of the better deals is *Le Petit Bois*, in the place de l'Eglise, which has ingenious toys and gifts.

## Practicalities

**Trains** stop 5km to the west of Cordes at **Vindrac** (☎05.63.56.05.64), where SNCF passengers can also rent **bikes**, otherwise you can content yourself to a pleasant hour-long walk. **Buses** stop near the lower-town summer-only **tourist office** (July & Aug Mon–Sat 9am–noon & 2–6.30pm & Sun 3–5pm), while the main tourist office (year-round same hours; ☎05.63.56.00.52, fax 05.63.56.19.52, *www.cordes-sur-ciel.org*) is in the heart of the *cité*. If you're driving, **parking** can be a challenge – in the summer months the area a few metres east of the lower tourist office soon fills up and cars line the roads leading into town. Don't be tempted to drive into the old town. The best **hotel** in town is the *Grand Ecuyer* (☎05.63.53.79.50, fax 05.63.53.79.51, *grand.ecuyer@thuries.fr*; closed Oct–Easter; ⑤), housed in Raymond's former palace. Across from the Charles-Porte museum, *Hôtel de la Cité*, is a lower-priced alternative offering the same medieval trappings (closed Nov to mid-April; ☎05.63.56.03.53, fax 05.63.56.02.47; ③), while *Hôtel de la Bride*, on the *place* of the same name (closed Jan; ☎05.63.56.04.02; ③), is the cheapest option – rather basic, but well kept. There's also a **campsite** (open April–Sept; ☎ & fax 05.63.56.11.10) 1km southeast on the Gaillac road. The best **restaurants** are in the town's hotels, including that in the *Grand Ecuyer*, which is known for its lamb and truffles (menus 170–470F/€25.93–71.68). Much simpler, the scruffy but friendly *Hôtel de la Bride* has menus from 75F/€11.44. Aside from these, other options include the creperie *La Factorie* (closed Jan & Dec) at 53 Grand Rue and, next door, *Le Grand Veneur* (closed Dec), which serves sixty brands of Belgian **beer** and decent **pizzas** (from 68F/€10.37) in its hokey "salle médiéval". **Nightlife**, such as there is in Cordes, consists of occasional live music (jazz, blues, rock or Latin) shows put on by passing bands at the *Le Ménestral* bar/pizzeria on the main road opposite the lower town's tourist office.

# Gaillac and around

Twenty-three kilometres west of Albi along the Tarn, **GAILLAC**, located at the heart of the wine region bearing its name, is a town built on the grape. It has a climate ideal for viticulture, and its inhabitants started putting corks in bottles more than 2500 years ago. But the industry really took off in the eighth century with the founding of the Benedictine abbey of St Michel – as part of their rule, monks are given a healthy daily ration of wine which, along with that needed for mass, ensured a high demand for the local product. In the tenth century the entrepreneurial order decided to guarantee the quality of their vintage by laying down the rules as to which wines could quality as Gaillacoises – and thus one of France's most famous AOCs was born. Today, Gaillac continues to live off the deserved reputation of its wine, but the commercial success of such a class-conscious product has led the simple town to adopt certain arrogant pretensions unmerited by its provincial reality. The chief reason for staying here longer than a few hours is to use the town as a base for exploring the old *bastide*-villages of **Lisle** and **Rabastens**, further downstream.

## The Town

Gaillac, with its compact medieval core, sits on the north side of the river. The focal point of the old town, though not its geographic centre – set as it is by the old bridge over the Tarn – is the ponderous **abbey-church of St-Michel**, constructed in the eleventh century, and impressively large for its era. The interior is unadorned, apart from a fourteenth-century painted Virgin and Child near the main altar. The uninspiring **Musée des Arts et Traditions Populaires** (July & Aug Mon & Wed–Sun 10am–noon & 2–6pm; Sept–June Fri–Sun same times; 15F/€2.29), adjacent to the church, is dedicated to wine-making, with a twenty-minute French-only audiovisual show, displays of old grape presses, barrels, tools and bottles, although its chief attraction is its location in the old monastery cellars. The real business in Gaillac goes on down in the **Maison de Vins de Gaillac** (daily 10am–noon & 2–7pm; free) in the same complex, where you can sample – and are encouraged to buy – local vintages.

The old town spreading out to the north and east of the abbey-church retains a number of brick-and-timber houses worth seeking out, while a few minutes' walk northwest from place Lapérouse across the old Pont Château-de-Homps sits the **natural history museum** (daily 10am–noon & 2–6pm; 15F/€2.29), with a collection of specimen cases stacked with the usual stuffed birds, dead bugs and sea creatures. Behind the monastery, off place Eugénie de Guérin, lies the medieval *faubourg*, whose twisting lanes lack grand monuments but are loaded with atmosphere. On its eastern side, shady **Parc Foucaud** surrounds a surprisingly good **Musée des Beaux-Arts** (daily 10am–noon & 2–6pm; 15F/€2.29). The nineteenth- and twentieth-century Impressionist works of local artists Raymond Tournon and Henri Loubat deserve a look, and some of the contemporary art rises well above the quality of a provincial museum.

## Practicalities

Gaillac's **gare SNCF** (☎05.63.57.00.23), which is also where **buses** stop, is off to the north of the old town, a good twenty-minute walk from the wine centre and the snooty **tourist office** (July & Aug Mon & Wed–Sun 10am–noon & 2–6pm; Sept–June Fri–Sun same times; ☎05.63.57.14.65, fax 05.63.57.61.37) at the heart of things. **Accommodation** is plentiful and relatively cheap, with the best digs at *La Verrerie* (☎05.63.57.32.77, fax 05.63.57.32.27, *www.logis-de-france.fr*, ④), a converted glass factory in rue de l'Egalité. A good budget choice is the cosy *Hôtel du Parc* (☎05.63.57.02.07; ①; menu from 60F/€9.15), and Lucile Pinon (8 place St-Michel; ☎05.63.57.61.48, fax 05.63.41.06.56; ③) has **chambres d'hôtes** in her comfortable seventeenth-century *faubourg* house. The municipal **campsite** (June to mid-Sept; ☎05.63.57.18.30) is nicely situated along the river, under the shadow of the abbey.

The best **restaurant** in town is *Les Sarments* at 27 rue Cabrol (☎05.63.57.62.61; closed Sun eve & Mon; menus from 125F/€19.06), a *gastronomique* place tucked away in a medieval cellar in the *faubourg*. But the much cheaper *Aux Charmes Gaillacois*, on rue Denfert-Rochereau near the train station, offers inexpensive and abundant four-course menus which include wine and home-made desserts (from 62F/€9.46).

## Lisle-sur-Tarn and Rabastens

Only a ten-minute ride (7km) south on one of the frequent buses or trains from Gaillac, **LISLE-SUR-TARN** is a tranquil twelfth-century *bastide* known for its *pountets*, the overhead covered passages which connect many of its brick-built medieval houses. There is little to detain you here apart from a stroll through the town and a relaxed drink in arcaded place Saissac, at its centre. The small local **museum** (same hours as tourist office; free) is tucked away to the southeast of the square and contains works by the native designer Raymond Lafage (who studied under Michelangelo). To the east, a street descends to the riverside and a point which long ago was the town's pier – an evocative spot. By the modern bridge just downstream sits the town's strikingly bold fourteenth-century brick **church**.

Lisle's **tourist office** (May–Oct daily 10am–noon & 2–6pm; Nov–April Tues–Fri 2–6pm, Sat & Sun 10am–noon & 3.30–5.30pm; ☎05.63.40.31.85, fax 05.63.33.36.18) is on the east side of place Saissac. *Le Princinor* (☎05.63.33.35.44, fax 05.63.33.89.84; ③), on the road to Rabastens, is the town's only **hotel**; don't be fooled by its box-like exterior, the rooms are comfortable and the menu (95–160F/€14.49–24.40) has a distinctly northern French flavour. The tiny one-star **campsite** (July–Sept; ☎05.63.33.35.18) near the *Princinor* is another option. Méridiac on avenue d'Albi (☎05.63.33.38.96) rents **bikes**.

**RABASTENS**, the next village downriver on the Tarn, can be reached easily by bicycle or foot and is a better choice than Lisle for an overnight stop. On weekend evenings the streets fill with young people, giving it a vivacity surprising for its size and making it a welcome contrast to the sleepier villages of the Albigeois. Still guarded by vestiges of its brick ramparts, Rabastens was born in the time of the fifth-century barbarian invasions, when it served as a refuge for the inhabitants of a huge Gallo-roman villa. A walk through town is complemented by a visit to the twelfth-century **Notre-Dame du Bourg**, worth visiting for its fourteenth-century **frescoes** and a chapel dedicated to St James, donated by the Archbishop of Santiago, grateful for the wealth which the pilgrimage route was bringing his diocese. The **Musée du Rabastinois** (mid-April to Oct Mon–Sat 10–noon & 2–6pm, Sun 2–6pm; Nov to mid-April Sat & Sun only 2–6pm; free) is just down the street and contains pieces from the Gallo-Roman and medieval periods. Halfway between Lisle and Rabastens sits the impressive **Château de St-Géry** (July & Aug daily 2–6pm; Sept–June Sun 2–6pm; 25F/€3.81), whose surviving buildings date from the 1300–1700s, and boast furnished Louis XV and XVI salons and a bedroom where Richelieu once slept.

**Buses** from Lisle pass through the centre of Rabastens, but the **gare SNCF** is located just across the river in Couferoul – about a ten-minute walk from the centre. The **tourist office** (mid-Feb to Nov Tues–Sat 10am–noon & 2–6pm, Sun 2–6pm; ☎05.63.40.65.65), at 2 rue Amadée-Clausade, is by the old bridge and the church. The best **hotel** in Rabastens is the *Hostellerie du Pré-Vert* (closed Sun, Mon & Jan; ☎05.63.33.70.51, fax 05.63.33.82.58, *www.logis-de-france.fr*; ③), an eighteenth-century mansion on the promenade des Licés, but budget travellers should head for the *Río Tinto* (closed Sun; ☎05.63.33.57.17; ②) on place St-Michel. The one-star **campsite**, *Les Auzerals* (May–Aug; ☎05.63.33.70.36), is situated 3km northwest of town, on a small lake. As far as food and drink goes, any of the bistros and **restaurants** on the main promenade will provide solid Tarnaise sustenance, but for something different head to the *Río Tinto*, which has authentic Andalucian ambience and menus from 59F/€9.00, including wine.

# Graulhet, Réalmont and Lautrec

The undulating wheat lands stretching southeast from Gaillac towards Castres are dominated by three small *bastides*. Of these, **Graulhet** and **Réalmont** are better served by transport (both falling on the Albi–Toulouse line) but are less interesting – unless you have a car, they do not merit including in your itinerary. **Lautrec**, on the other hand, picturesquely set on a windmill-capped spur, is a nice place to spend an afternoon or evening, but can only be accessed from Albi either via Graulhet or Castres.

### Graulhet

One of the possible bus routes from Albi to Lautrec involves a change in **GRAULHET**, located 16km southeast of Gaillac and 30km northwest of Castres, on the Dadou river, and the transfer is about the only reason you would want to stop here – it is a grim, unsmiling town, whose unremarkable old quarter has been allowed to decay into a shambles. The town's name is derived from *groule*, the Occitan word for leather, which has been the source of the town's meagre prosperity since the Middle Ages – as early as the twelfth century raw hides from the pasture lands of the Montagne Noire were brought here to be tanned and finished. **Buses** stop in place du Jourdain, across the river from the main road, below the old quarter capping the low rise on the north side of the square. The **tourist office** (Mon–Sat 9am–noon & 2–6pm; ☎ & fax 05.63.34.75.09) on place Foch has maps of the town's paltry highlights. If you do need to **stay** here, *Le Grandgousier* (☎05.63.34.50.32, fax 05.63.34.25.57, *www.logis-de-france.fr*; ③), also in place du Jourdain, has reasonable rooms and a **restaurant** (from 90F/€13.73). Finer dining can be found at *La Rigaudié* (☎05.63.34.50.07; closed Sat & Sun eves, Aug & late Dec), 2km east of town out on the St-Julien-du-Puy road, and with an excellent fish menu (145F/€22.11).

### Réalmont

Seventeen kilometres east of Graulhet, **RÉALMONT** is one of the "royal *bastides*" founded by the twelfth-century Capetian kings to weaken the power of the local nobility. Today, only a few vestiges of its medieval past – the arcades of the main square and the grid of streets typical of medieval "new towns" – survive. The town's **church**, dating from the sixteenth century, is unremarkable. Wednesday morning is the best time to stop in here; the country **market** has local produce at excellent prices – a great opportunity to stock up for a picnic. The **tourist office** (Mon–Sat 10am–12.30pm & 2.30–6pm, closed hols; ☎05.63.45.52.05) is in rue Cabroult, behind the charming but slightly decayed *Hôtel Noël*. This is the town's only **hotel** (closed Sun eve & Mon; ☎05.63.55.52.80, fax 05.63.55.69.91, *www.logis-de-france.fr*; ②) and has been run by the Granier family for six generations.

There is also a basic **campsite** 2km away on the Graulhet road (May–Sept; ☎05.63.55.50.41). The best **restaurant** is *Les Routiers* (☎05.63.55.65.44; closed Sun) on boulevard Armengaud, which serves up massive menus (from 60F/€9.15), including dessert and wine.

### Lautrec

The most picturesque of the towns between Albi and Castres, **LAUTREC** is located on a minor road 15km southeast of Graulhet. The vanes of the windmill still churn on top of the hill where the castle once stood, and the hamlet gathered around it is a warren of steep, twisting streets, interspersed by little arcaded squares. It was here that a marriage alliance of 1196 established the family of the Counts of Toulouse-Lautrec (the artist Henri's forebears). Nowadays the town prides itself on its pungent pink **garlic**, first brought by Spanish merchants in the eighteenth century. Celebrated with a festival (Aug 6), 4000 tonnes of the stuff are harvested here every year, but smaller quantities can be purchased at the town's Friday **market**.

Entering the old town through rue Mercadiel, where the main road passes on the north side, the *mairie* is just on the left, in a building which also houses the tourist office and the two-room **archeological museum** (mid-Feb to Dec Wed–Sat 9.30am–12.30pm & 3–6pm, Sun 3–6pm; 10F/€1.53). The latter is a fairly humble affair, with a display on local medieval burial customs and information on the scores of wells which perforate the old town and, as at Cordes, served primarily for grain storage. Continuing from the museum to the first crossroads, you can descend on the left towards Lautrec's remaining twelfth-century **gate**, or continue to the fourteenth-century collegial **church**, now a Baroque monstrosity inside. To get to the functioning seventeenth-century **windmill** perched above the town (July & Aug daily 3–7pm; Sept–June Sun 3–6pm; 10F/€1.53) climb the street to the right immediately before the church. Entering the mill on a windy day, the sight and sound of the large, rapidly spinning wooden mechanisms is exhilarating. The hill top also offers a superb panoramic **view** towards the south.

There is no **hotel** here, but a number of **gîtes** in or near the town can put you up. The **tourist office** (☎05.63.75.31.40, fax 05.63.75.32.90, *perso.wanadoo.fr /crea-fm*) has a complete list, but the most homely of the lot are *La Pergola*, 5 rue St-Esprit, below the windmill (☎05.63.75.89.77; ③), Bridget Audouy's house in rue d'Église (☎05.63.75.95.11; ④), and Alain Routier's house in place du Monument (☎05.63.75.98.77; ③) – the last two proprietors speak English. The two best **restaurants** are *La Pergola* (May to mid-Sept, closed Thurs; from 100F/€15.25) which serves home-made food made with garden-grown ingredients, and *Le Champ d'Allium* at 4 route de Castres (closed Sun eve & Mon, and lunch time except July & Aug; ☎05.63.70.05.24), where widely praised gastronomic experimentation is the order of the day (menus from 130F/€19.83).

# Castres and around

Southeast of Lautrec the rolling agricultural landscape comes to an abrupt end as the land begins to rise and you approach Haut Languedoc, a highland ridged by peaks rising up to 1100m. **CASTRES**, on the western edge of the uplands, 42km south of Albi, began some two thousand years ago as a Roman military base (as its name, from the word for "camp" or "fort" recalls). An important Benedictine monastery was built here in the seventh century but, like the Roman town, its traces have all but vanished. In the twelfth century Castres was swept up in the Cathar movement, and it was here that the first Albigensian **martyrs** were burned at the stake in 1209. The ever-rebellious population took up the Protestant banner four centuries later, and the town became an important centre of **Huguenot** administration. Today, still supported by the textile industry which boomed in the eighteenth century, Castres is a town with energy – worth visiting in its own right and an ideal point of access to the northern and western parts of the Parc Naturel Régional de Haut Languedoc (see p.189). Boasting a colourful medieval core and a pleasantly diverse populace, it is also enlivened by two summer **music festivals**. In addition, it has a couple of good museums: one dedicated to Castres' native son, the nineteenth-century socialist Jean Jaurès, and the other to Spanish art. The Sidorbe, a granite massif to the east famed for its peculiar rock formations, makes an easy excursion.

## Arrival, information and accommodation

Castres' **gare SNCF**, avenue Albert 1er, lies west of the old town, which can be reached by bus #7 ("Arcades" stop; 5F/€0.80) or a 25-minute walk, and the **gare routière** on place Soult lies on the far eastern edge of the centre – a short walk west from the river. The **tourist office**, at 3 rue Milhau-Ducommun (April–Oct Mon–Sat 8.30am–7pm, Sun 10am–noon & 2–6pm; Nov–March Mon–Sat 8.30am–12.30pm & 1.30–6.30pm, Sun 2–6pm; ☎05.63.62.63.62, fax 05.63.62.63.60), sits along the riverbank in the old town, by the *pont vieux*; in summer it offers a **"Passe culturel de l'été"** (25F/€3.81), which includes admission to the town's three museums and is valid for one month.

Castres has two marvellous seventeenth-century mansions converted into luxurious but affordable **hotels**; the more deluxe is the *Renaissance* at 17 rue Victor Hugo (☎05.63.59.30.42, fax 05.63.72.11.57; ④), while close behind is the *L'Europe*, just up the same street at no. 5 (☎05.63.59.00.33, fax 05.63.59.21.38; ③). Otherwise, the *Rivière*, 10 quai Tourcaudière (☎05.63.59.04.53, fax 05.63.59.61.97; ③), has pleasant views over the Agout and helpful staff, and the very friendly and clean *Le Périgord*, 22 rue Zola (☎05.63.59.04.74; ①) is a bargain, with a *bain complet* in every room, and great half- and full-pension plans. The three-star **campsite** at Parc Gourjade (April–Sept; ☎05.63.59.72.30, fax 05.63.50.88.91) also has bungalows – you can reach the park, which has walking trails and water-sports facilities, by buses #3, #6 or #7 (direction Borde-Basse) or by the Miredames river-boat (see "Listings").

## The Town

Don't let yourself be fooled by the drab suburbs which surround it; Castres' **old town**, spilling just over the River Agout to the east, and whose rough square outline reflects its Roman layout, is a delight. The brightly painted riverside **dyers' houses** are the town's hallmark, while the impressive sixteenth-century mansions hidden among its narrow streets make the medieval quarter a pleasure to stroll through. At its centre, café-girded **place Jean-Jaurès** is home to a bustling produce market four days a week, while just south of the square, the unprepossessing **Cathédrale St-Benoît**, constructed in 1677, stands on the site of the old monastery church. It's a squat and not especially noteworthy Baroque building, although the marble saints' statues around the choir are worth a look.

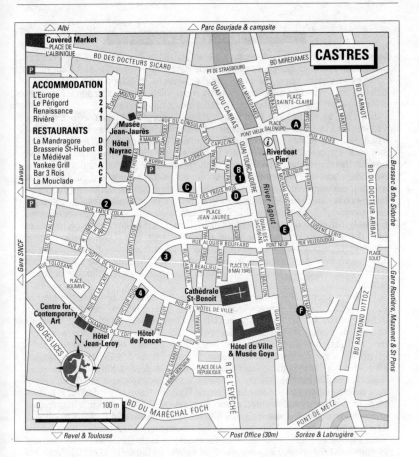

Across the street, the **Hôtel de Ville** reposes within the former bishops'
palace, a dour, hulking square edifice, whose grey sobriety is contrasted by the
bright formal gardens, the **Jardins de l'Évêché**, which stretch out on its southern side. The town hall shares the building with Castres' foremost museum, the
**Musée Goya** (Aug daily 9am–noon & 2–6pm; Sept–July Tues–Sun same times;
20F/€3.50), which was established a century ago by private donation, and now
holds the biggest collection of Spanish paintings in France apart from the Louvre.
Dominating its largest salon, the core of the exhibition is, as you'd expect, taken
up by the artist after whom it is named, but the paintings here are not the dark,
sinister visions for which **Francisco Goya** is most famous, but rather his portraiture, including his *Self-portrait with Glasses*, and politically inspired works like
*The Junta of the Philippines Presided over by Ferdinand VII*. A separate room features several series of his satirical pen-and-ink cartoons, depicting vices and
virtues, and popular adages, as well as series on bullfighting and war. Other
rooms contain numerous pieces by other seventeenth-century Iberian masters –
including **Velázquez**'s *Portrait of Philip IV*, **Murillo**'s *Virgin with Rosary* and

## JEAN-JAURÈS

**Jean Jaurès**, the nineteenth-century labour activist, politician and martyr, is a figure whose presence travellers can scarcely escape in Languedoc and Roussillon. Nearly every town has at least one street or square – usually a main one – and a building or two named after this **socialist hero**, whose tireless struggle for workers' rights and international peace eventually cost him his life.

Born in Castres in 1859, Jean Jaurès showed exceptional promise as a student and was sent by scholarship to complete his studies in Paris. When these were finished, rather than stay in the capital he returned to his home *département* of Tarn and took a post teaching philosophy in **Albi**'s *lycée* (high school), and giving lectures at the University of Toulouse. But the miserable conditions under which his **working-class** neighbours toiled drew him out of the academy; their dangerous working environment, underpayment, and near-total lack of rights and representation could have been lifted straight from the pages of **Emile Zola**'s contemporary *Germinal*. Jean ran for political office and at the young age of 26 was elected a deputy (or legislative representative) of Tarn. One of his first projects was to help the glass-workers at Albi found the collectively run V.O.A. bottle factory, which still operates today. Continuing in politics and the cause of social justice, in 1893, as socialist deputy for **Carmaux**, he supported the miners' struggle for better working conditions (see p.176), and his renown as a social reformer began to spread.

However, Jaurès desire for reform went beyond simply improving the lives of those around him. Five years later he joined other liberals, including Zola, in defence of the Jewish army captain, **Alfred Dreyfus**, convicted on (unfounded) charges of espionage. National feelings of resentment against Dreyfus were running high, but despite this Jaurès persisted in his defence of the underdog, and – eventually – got him pardoned. The patriotically charged issue temporarily cost Jaurès his popularity, but he was soon back on the stage, founding the Communist daily *l'Humanité* in 1904 (still one of France's major newspapers) and the following year helping found the socialist SFIO party. With the dawn of World War I, however, Jaurès' internationalist brand of socialism revealed itself again in an outspoken and unpopular **pacifist** stand – and led to his **assassination** in Paris by a nationalist extremist in July 1914. On his death he was martyred, the perfect hero for the Tarn – a local politician who improved the quality of life in this underdeveloped and marginalized region, and who wasn't afraid to take on the political establishment of Paris in order to defend higher justice.

**Zurburán**'s *Carthusian Martyr*. Flemish-influenced medieval paintings by fifteenth-century Catalan and Spanish artists round out the collection. There are also displays of old coins, royal seals and assorted archeological knick-knacks, as well as a room dedicated to the local war-time Resistance. An adjacent gallery (separate admission) houses temporary exhibits of impressive quality.

Heading west from the Goya Museum along rue Chambre de l'Edit takes you past three palatial residences dating from the sixteenth and seventeenth centuries. On rue Guy, first street on the right, the seventeenth-century **Hôtel de Poncet** stands out, with its classically inspired Renaissance facade, caryatid columns supporting an elegant Ionic-columned loggia. Further along rue de l'Edit you'll find the earlier **Hôtel Jean-Leroy**, notable for its stately carved casement windows and topped by a defensive tower. Next door to that, **Hôtel de Viviès**, built along the now-vanished city walls, was once the seat of the town's Huguenot judicial court and now houses the small **Centre for Contemporary Art** (July & Aug daily 10am–noon & 2–6pm; Sept–June Tues–Fri & 3–6pm Sat & Mon 3–6pm; 5F/€0.76, Sept–June free), home to temporary exhibitions of local and international modern works. Castres' shopping district stretches north from here, on the far side of which, in rue Thomas, you'll find Castres' grandest *hôtel particulier*, the **Hôtel de Nayrac**, built in the brick-and-stone style of the Toulouse mansions, with three sober facades boxing in a broad symmetrical courtyard. Just beyond is the **Musée Jean-Jaurès** (July & Aug daily 9am–noon & 2–6pm; Jan–June Tues–Sun 9am–noon & 2–6pm; Sept–Dec Tues–Sun 9am–noon & 2–5pm; 10F/€1.52) which pays homage to the life of Castres' favourite son (see box), recounting the martyred activist's career with newspaper reports, memorabilia and contemporary artefacts.

Over on the far side of the river, the scruffier east bank of the Agout is home to a number of interesting little restaurants and cafés, and although it lacks historical buildings the neighbourhood's proletariat feel is refreshing. The sparsely adorned medieval **fountain** in place Fagerie, just north of the pont Neuf, is also worth seeking out, if only for the "undiscovered" atmosphere of the square in which it sits.

## Eating, drinking and nightlife

For its size, Castres has an impressive range of **restaurants**. Of the hotel options, the best is *l'Europe*, which features well-executed *terroir* fare with excellent service (menus for 60–115F/€9.15–17.54, plus a lunch special for 49F/€7.47). *La Mandragore*, 1 rue Malpas (closed Sun & Mon lunch; ☎05.63.59.51.27) is praised both for its *gastronomique* cuisine and selection of wines – menus here range from 75–240F/€11.44–36.60, while for a no-nonsense quality **brasserie**, try the *St-Hubert* beside the *Rivière* (meals from 90F/€13.73) or *Le Médiéval* (closed Sun & Mon; ☎05.63.51.13.78) at 44 rue Milhau-Ducommun, whose eleventh-century dining room sits poised above the Agout, and has a funky pseudo-medieval décor (menus from 110F/€16.78). Along rue Fuzies, which runs east from the bridge by the tourist office, you'll find a number of cheaper but no less interesting options: in addition to a selection of kebab stands and Chinese places the *Yankee Grill* (closed Sun noon) offers Tex-Mex à la carte from 60F/€9.15. The jazzy *Bar 3 Rois*, in the street of the same name, also has a small upstairs dining room. For lighter food fare, *La Mouclade*, at 6 rue d'Empare, is a small mussels bar whose multiply-pierced owners do up the delicious bivalves fifteen different ways – afterwards you can get a pint at the very un-Irish *Moran's Pub* a few doors down at no. 18 – and a good café is *Saveurs du Temps*, 4 rue Fuzies. Aside from this, any of the **bars** around place Jean-Jaurès will do for a coffee or drink, and *Glacier* (on the south side) sometimes has live music. Late-night diversion is provided by the rock **club** *One-Two-Two* (after 11pm), through the graffitied door (no sign) in passage Henri IV.

## Listings

**Banks** There are several banks with ATMs in the old town, including Crédit Agricole in pl Jean-Jaurès.

**Bike rental** You can rent bikes from Etablissements Tabarly, 38 pl Soult (☎05.63.35.38.09), and the gare SNCF.

**Boat trips** The Miredames river-boat does a 45-min round trip down the Agout (May, June & Sept 2pm, 3.20pm, 4.40pm & 6pm; July & Aug additional departure at 10.30am; 25F/€3.81), leaving from the pier outside the tourist office.

**Bus information** ☎05.63.35.37.31.

**Car rental** Ada, 32 av Charles de Gaulle (☎05.63.51.10.26); Avis, rte de Toulouse (☎05.63.72.82.21); Budget, rue Albert 1er (☎05.63.71.31.28); Europcar, 67 rue Maillot (☎05.63.72.24.69); Hertz, av François Mitterand (☎05.63.59.01.14); and Lavail, route d'Albi (☎05.63.71.93.34).

**Hospital** Centre Hospitalier, pl Alsace-Lorraine, just south of the Hôtel de Ville (☎05.63.71.15.15).

**Internet access** Cyberspace, 31 rue Fuziers (Mon–Sat 2–9pm; ☎05.63.62.00.80).

**Laundry** Lavanderie Express, 8–9 rue Fuziers (daily till 9pm).

**Market** Tue, Thurs, Fri & Sat in pl Jean-Jaurès and pl l'Albinique.

**Police** 2 av Charles de Gaulle (☎17 or ☎05.63.35.40.10).

**Taxis** ☎05.63.71.55.55.

**Train information** ☎05.63.59.37.03.

# Around Castres

There are a number of interesting day-trip destinations in the immediate vicinity of Castres. Just to the east lies the hundred-square-kilometre granite plateau known as the **Sidorbe**. This oft-promoted area is known for the boulders which litter it, either eroded into evocative shapes or balancing precariously. Many are found within a 3km radius of Lacrouzette, including the rock-strewn waterfall, **Saut de la Truite**, and while some of the formations are truly remarkable, others are really rather lame – the **Trois Fromages** ("Three Cheeses"), for example, merely comprises a group of three roundish boulders set on top of each other. South of these groups lies the **Peyro Clabado**, an 800-tonne boulder perched on a smaller stone, and the **Rochers de Sept-Faux**, two giant stones balanced in such a way that upper one, 900 tonnes in mass, can be rocked simply by pushing on it. The wooded paths which lead to the sites are well maintained and make for pleasant walking, although on weekends they crowd with families and pensioners. Bring sufficient water or be prepared to pay over the odds at the cafés and drinks stands near the trails. All the sights of the region are easily accessed by **bus** from Castres, and **accommodation** can be found in nondescript Lacrouzette, at *l'Auberge du Crémaussel* (closed Sun eve, Wed all year, Jan & winter weekends; ☎05.63.50.61.33; ③), which also has a restaurant (menus from 90F/€13.73, including wine). For something more unique, head for the *chambres d'hôtes* of the luxurious fourteenth- to sixteenth-century castle in **Burlats** (☎05.63.35.29.20, fax 05.63.51.14.69; ④). Nearby **St-Salvy** also has a great lunch or dinner stop: *Le Clos du Roc* (closed Wed eve, Sun eve & part Feb; ☎05.63.50.57.23; menus from 60F/€9.15; call ahead), located in a converted barn, has excellent cuisine at economical prices.

South of Castres on the way to Mazamet, you may pass through **LABRU-GIÈRE**, a quaint "round village", laid out in concentric circles around the village church. Dating back to the Middle Ages, the town owes its notoriety to the 1484 **witch trial** of Péronne Bachère. Accused of making a pact with the Devil, casting spells, and killing a neighbour with magic powder, she confessed all when interrogated and was burnt at a nearby crossroads. The parchment which recorded her trial can be seen today in a display at the *mairie* on the town's main square.

# The Parc du Haut Languedoc

The southeastern half of the *département* of the Tarn is dominated by the mountain-ridged highlands of Upper Languedoc. In this region of isolated hamlets the scant population has traditionally subsisted on herding and agriculture, supplemented nowadays by a growing outdoor recreation industry. Long a backwoods of proudly self-sufficient Calvinist Huguenots, these hills later proved a fertile recruiting ground for anti-German resistance after the occupation of Vichy France. The zone is dominated by the sprawling **PARC NATUREL RÉGIONAL DU HAUT LANGUEDOC**, an imprecisely bounded region which, in the near thirty years since its establishment, has grown to encompass additional territory almost yearly. Its designation as a park is primarily administrative, which can lead to confusion – the boundaries aren't well marked, and there's no change in the landscape or villages which distinguishes the parkland from the surrounding area. That said, a good approximation is to define the park more or less by the mountains which cross it: the **Monts de Lacaune** in the north, the **Monts de l'Espinouse** to the east, and the north face of the Montagne Noire range (see p.197), tacked onto the park's southwest. The man-made **lakes** which punctuate the highland near **La Salvetat, Fraïsse** and **Anglès** are the focus of a thriving tourist industry: each is ringed by campsites and boat-rental outfits which do a brisk trade in the summer months. Although public transport across the park is poor, it serves **hikers** well, crisscrossed by a network of footpaths: *grand* and *petit randonnées*, and local routes, such as the **Gijou Valley Railway** linking Lacaune, Vabre and Brassac. Native wildlife, which still includes some wild boar and deer, is less frequently encountered as the park becomes more popular – although you might see the ancient breed of mouflon sheep if you cross the Monts de l'Espinouse – and despite straddling the border of the Atlantic and Mediterranean climatic zones, the bulk of the park lies in the cooler, humid northern zone, where the flora is dominated by forests of sturdy oak and chestnut. Detailed park **information** can be obtained at the **Maison du Parc** offices in **St-Pons**, the "capital" of the park, and Murat; local tourist offices sell a guide to fifteen **bicycle** itineraries in the area.

## Lacaune-les-Bains and around

Poised on the northern edge of the park, slate-roofed **LACAUNE-LES-BAINS** lies east from Castres, at a distance of either 67km along the tortuous Agout and Gijou Valley road, or 46km along the mountainous route which passes through Brassac. At 885m, it sits just below the source of the Gijou river in the **Monts de Lacaune**, whose sheep are the exclusive source of milk for the famous blue cheese of Roquefort. The town was a curative spa (specializing in urinary tract ailments) in the Middle Ages, a role commemorated by a fourteenth-century iron **fountain** in the town centre known as "Les Pisseurs", featuring four tiny but impressively endowed male figures peeing into a pool below. Beside the fountain, in place du Friggoul, is the **Musée de Vieux Lacaune** (June–Sept Wed–Sun 10am–noon & 2–6pm; Oct–May by appointment only; ☎05.63.37.25.38; free), which offers an unexceptional look at local nineteenth-century rural life. In similar vein, you can also visit the **Filature Ramond**, a wool workshop from the same era, where you can see the various tools and machines used (Mon, Tues & Fri

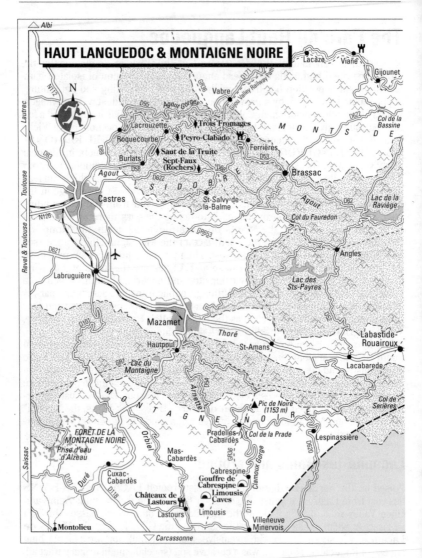

△ Albi

## HAUT LANGUEDOC & MONTAIGNE NOIRE

Lacaze  Viane

Gijounet

N

GR36

Vabre

Agout Gorges

D55

Lacrouzette

Roquecourbe

Burlats

D58

Lacrouzette

Trois Fromages

Peyro-Clabado

Saut de la Truite

Sept-Faux
(Rochers)

S I D O B R E

D622

Castres

N126

St-Salvy-de-
la-Balme

Ferrières

D53

Brassac

Agout

Col du Fauredon

GR653

M  O  N  T  S    D  E

Col de la
Bassine

Lac de la
Ravièae

Labruguière

D621

Mazamet

Hautpoul

Lac du
Montaigne

GR7

M  O  N  T  A  G  N  E

Orbiel

FORÊT DE LA
MONTAIGNE NOIRE

Prise d'eau
d'Alzeau

Saissac

Cuxac-
Cabardès

Duré

D118

Montolieu

Mas-
Cabardès

Châteaux de
Lastours

Lastours

Thoré

St-Amans

Arnette

Pic de Noire
(1153 m)

N  O  I  R  E

Pradelles-
Cabardès

Col de la Prade

Cabrespine

Gouffre de
Cabrespine

Limousis

Limousis
Caves

Villeneuve-
Minervois

Angles

Lac des
Sts-Payres

Labastide-
Rouairoux

Lacabarede

Col de
Serières

GR36

Clamoux Gorge

D112

D620

▽ Carcassonne

11am–noon & 1.30–4pm; 10F/€1.53, must be booked through the tourist office).
Aside from taking in the surroundings there is little to do in Lacaune, apart from
enjoying the Sunday morning local **market** and a larger regional **fair** on the 21st
of each month. The town has good bus connections, but the best way to leave is
along the old Gijou Valley Trail, a narrow-gauge railway line heading west
towards Castres, which has been converted to a foot and bike path (see below).

**Buses** trundle through Lavaur stopping at place de la République, on the far
side of which is a small **tourist office** (July & Aug Mon–Sat 10am–noon & 2–6pm,

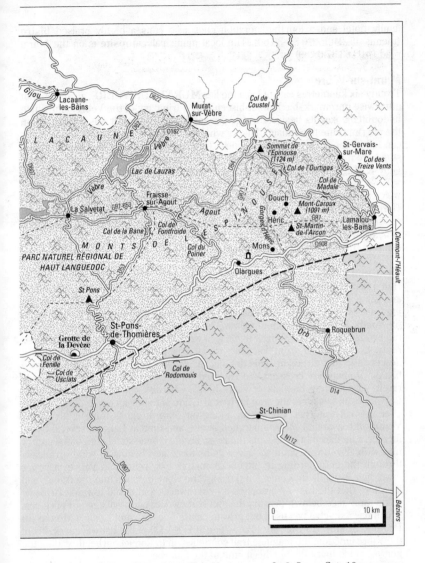

Sun 10am–noon; Sept–June Mon–Fri 10am–noon & 2–5pm, Sat 10am–noon; ☎05.63.37.04.98, fax 05.63.37.03.01), which has detailed information on walks in the area. **Bikes** can be rented at Terral, 15 rue République (☎05.63.37.04.12). If you want to **stay** the night, the *Central Hôtel Fuzies* (closed Jan, Fri eve & Sun Nov–March; ☎05.63.37.02.03, fax 05.63.37.10.98, *hotelfusies@grand-sud.com*; ④) on rue de la République offers all the three-star amenities. More attractive and cheaper is the *Calas* (☎05.63.37.03.28, fax 05.63.37.09.19, *www.logis-de-france.fr*; ③), tucked away in the place de la Vierge – Claude Calas, the owner of this small family hotel and a fourth-generation chef, also runs a highly praised **bistro** (menus 45–240F/€6.86–36.60). The local municipal **campsite** is on the Murat road (☎05.63.37.03.59).

## Murat-sur-Vèbre

Twenty-six kilometres east of Lacaune lies **MURAT-SUR-VÈBRE**, an ancient but otherwise unremarkable hamlet bisected by a tributary of the Vèbre, and which undoubtedly saw its heaviest traffic passing through when it was a way-stop on the pilgrim route to Santiago. Hikers who want to relive a bit of the Middle Ages can follow the "chemin de St-Jacques" (now the GR653) east to Castres. If you stop here it will most likely be to pick up information from the **Maison du Parc** (July & Aug Mon–Sat 10am–noon & 2–6pm; Sept–June 10am–noon & 2–5pm; ☎05.63.37.45.76), an annex to the local tourist office (same hours; ☎05.63.37.47.47). Should you decide to stay, the only **hotel**, the rather basic *Durand* (☎05.63.37.41.91; ②), has a reasonable but unexceptional **restaurant** (closed Fri eve & Sat out of season), and there's also a **campsite**, *Les Adrets* (☎05.63.37.41.16; June–Sept). Those who want to make Murat a temporary base can rent **bikes** from the tourist office.

## The Gijou Valley Railway Path

Half a century ago locomotives still threaded the tortuously meandering Agout and Gijou valleys, steaming up the cliff-hanging **narrow gauge railway** connecting Castres with Vabre and Lacaune to the east, and branching off to Brassac to the south, 16km up the Agout valley. The trains have long disappeared, but the rail-bed has been brought back to life as a well set out **hiking** and **biking** trail – a route best travelled from Lacaune westwards for the simple reason that it descends in that direction. This defunct railway winds along steep and forested banks, dramatically crossing the riverbed on ancient trestle bridges and only rarely passing tiny hamlets of slate-shingled houses and solitary farmsteads. Leaving from Lacaune, the trail arrives at **Gijounet** after a couple of hours, just after a small waterfall. Continuing along for 5km, it skirts the slightly larger **Viane**, with a ruined *château* perched above, and then at **Lacaze**, several hours further, a medieval bridge spans the river, beside a once-stately fifteenth-century **mansion**. From this point the river gains force and begins to wind erratically through the cliffs girding it; fifteen kilometres now remain to **Vabre**, a larger town, but distinctly unscenic. On the way, the Gijou empties into the Agout, and it is here that the railway branches off southwards and uphill towards **Brassac** 16km away (see below), passing the still fiercely Huguenot village of **Ferrières**, which has a much advertised but private **castle** (closed), and a paltry **Musée du Protestantisme** (July & Aug 11am–7pm; 10F/€1.53) at the halfway mark. From the Vabre junction, the mainline trail continues on to Roquecourbe, threading the gorges which mark the northern limit of the Sidorbe.

There are few opportunities to pick up supplies en route – Lacaze, with a **store** and **café**, is the first good spot to refuel – but for those who plan on making the journey over a night or two, each of the villages along the line has a very basic and free **campsite**. Vabre has a number of services, including a **tourist office** in the *mairie* (Mon–Fri 10am–noon & 2–5pm; ☎05.63.50.48.75). A short walk 2km east of town on the Berlou river, the Clarensons' comfortable **farm/gîte**, *Le Mouline* (☎05.63.50.41.91, fax 05.63.50.49.77) has several cabins for four to eight people, with a four-person cabin at 1400F per week.

## THE HUGUENOTS OF HAUT LANGUEDOC

The rugged and isolated hills of Haut Languedoc remain a bastion of France's much mistreated but stubborn Protestant community, or **Huguenots**. During the sixteenth century, Protestantism, like Catharism before it, exercised a strong attraction on the inhabitants of Languedoc – in an age when political and religious obedience were perceived as parallel the people of the south felt exploited, on the one hand by an absolutist monarchy in Paris and on the other by a Church which manifested itself most visibly as a tax-collector.

The new faith arrived in the Haut Languedoc close on the heels of Martin Luther's defiance of Church authority in 1519 – the first Protestant was burned in Toulouse only eight years later. The Huguenot movement – named after an obscure Swiss political event – however, tended to follow the Frenchman **John Calvin**'s teachings, which had a more politically revolutionary message: his principle of "Inferior Magistrates" dictated that people were morally justified in disobeying and deposing an unfit ruler. The established order was clearly under threat from the dangerous new religion, and when the Crown and Church attempted to eradicate it, arresting Reforming theologians and preachers and impounding French-language versions of the Bible, the people of the south, backed by the equally dissatisfied local nobility, retaliated, and the long and bloody **Wars of Religion** ensued. The nobility, already divided into factions, used the theological conflict as justification for open warfare: the princely house of Guise and their allies championed Catholicism, while the rival Bourbons took up the Protestant flag. After a prolonged series of military campaigns and massacres the wars ended, or rather paused for while, with a compromise when the formerly Protestant Henry IV passed the **Edict of Nantes** in 1598, recognizing limited Huguenot rights. Castres became a "protected zone" for Protestants, and eventually home to one of the four courts of the land empowered to mediate legal disputes between Catholics and Huguenots. Almost a century later however, this uneasy accommodation ended when the supreme autocrat Louis XIV outlawed Calvinism again in 1685, and set in motion a harsh period of **repression** in Haut Languedoc. Soldiers were billeted in suspected Protestant homes, and possession of the Bible in French (instead of the official Latin) became a criminal offence. Huguenots reacted by escaping into exile or going underground, like the community in Ferrières, who hid bibles in secret wall-compartments or women's bonnets, and held clandestine services in the forest. Eventually many villages fled en masse to the even more isolated Cévennes to the east, out of reach of royal officials and the army. Many returned only in 1787, when the **Edict of Toleration** finally established Protestant liberties; with the foundation of the secular revolutionary government two years later, Catholicism ceased to be an official measure of "Frenchness". Although Protestantism declined as a result of centuries of persecution, today nearly every hamlet in the highlands and every sizeable town in Languedoc has a Huguenot church (or *temple*), and country folk of Haut Languedoc still recall the stalwart independence of their ancestors with pride.

## Brassac

**BRASSAC**, lying some 20km southwest of Lacaune, is undoubtedly the most attractive town on the west side of the park. Here the Agout, girded by nineteenth-century textile plants and the towers of a small medieval **castle**, is crossed by a picture-postcard twelfth-century **bridge**. Something of a focal point for the even smaller hamlets of the countryside, Brassac has some decent amenities: its

**stores** and **ATMs** recommend it as a possible base for exploring the western sector of the park. The former stage-post, the *Café de Paris* (☎05.63.74.00.31; ②) offers **accommodation**, and has a **restaurant** (closed Sun Sept–June) which serves menus from 68F/€10.37. Across the street, the *Centre* (☎05.63.74.00.14; ②), with a little **bar**, also offers rooms and food (65F/€9.91). You'll find the basic municipal **campsite** (☎05.63.74.09.11) just to the north of the village.

# The Plateau des Lacs

Sandwiched between the mountains of Lacaune and l'Espinouse, and stretching from Murat in the northeast almost as far as Mazamet to the southwest, the rambling upland of the park, the **Plateau des Lacs**, is punctuated by three large, artificial lakes along the Vèbre and Agout rivers, which converge here. **LA SALVETAT-SUR-AGOUT**, smack in the middle of the uplands, is the hub of the plateau, and the terminus of the Béziers–St-Pons bus line. The attractive little town has not been spoiled by the souvenir shops which dot its centre, and when the daily hubbub subsides, the tangled knot of streets which makes up the old town evokes the eleventh century, when La Salvetat was founded. There is nothing in particular to look for within the village, but two historical relics lie just outside of town: the twelfth-century Romanesque **chapel** (July & Aug daily 3–7pm), which contains a "black Virgin"– a Romanesque statue discoloured by time – and the stone bridge next to it, used by medieval pilgrims on the way to Santiago. The town is a short walk from the ten-kilometre-long **Lac de la Raviège**, which has been extensively developed as a holiday spot – here you'll find **beaches**, and plenty of **canoe**, **sail** and **motorboat** rental outlets. Those wishing to explore the surrounding area on foot can purchase a booklet with twelve well-laid-out *petits randonnées* for 5F/€0.76 at the tourist office.

La Salvetat's **tourist office** (Mon–Fri 9am–noon & 2–6pm, Sat & Sun 10am–noon & 2–5pm, Sept–June closed Sun; ☎ & fax 04.67.97.64.44) can help find furnished flats and cottages, but otherwise the English-owned *La Pergola* (☎04.67.97.60.57, fax 04.67.97.56.76; ①), just off the main road by the *place* where the **buses** from St-Pons stop, has inexpensive **rooms** and serves generous portions of home cooking (for guests only) in its restaurant. There's also a cosy **B&B** in the centre, on rue de Poterie (May–Oct; ☎04.67.97.65.13, fax 04.67.97.50.97; ②) and the *chambres d'hôtes*, *La Moutousse* (☎04.67.97.61.63; ②), in an old farm 4km out of town on the GR653. **Bikes** can be rented at the shop on place de Compostela. There are no fewer than four **campsites** within walking distance; the nearest is *La Blannquière* (May–Aug; ☎04.67.97.61.29) on allée St-Etienne de Cavall just north of the centre, while down by the lake you'll find the small *Calcia* (☎04.67.97.63.45). Of the several **restaurants** in town, none merits special mention, apart from *la Ficelle* (☎04.67.97.56.01), on the route de Lacaune, which is open all year.

## Fraïsse-sur-Agout and Lac de Lauzas

Although **FRAÏSSE-SUR-AGOUT**, 10km east of La Salvetat by road (D14) or trail (GR71), is only 2km south of **Lac de Lauzas** as the crow flies, the winding of the road which crosses the intervening hills clocks in at nearly 10km. This hamlet set at a hilly crossroads has become rather touristy in summer, but still retains its bucolic air thanks to its diminutive size and the isolated beauty of its surroundings. From the ancient bridge over the Agout, a short trail leads southwards uphill for 2km to the **Prat d'Alaric** and a traditional working **farm museum** (July 20 to Aug Tues–Sun 2.30–7pm; free). Lac de Lauzas to the north is purely of interest to those who are looking for developed waterside **camping**, with the gamut of activities which this implies. Fraïsse has a **tourist office** (July & Aug daily 10am–12.30pm & 2–5pm; May, June & Sept Sat & Sun 10am–12.30pm & 2–5pm; ☎04.67.97.53.81), and you can **stay** at the basic but comfortable *Campotel* (☎04.67.69.64.29; ②) by the riverside or the small *Auberge de l'Espinouse* (☎04.67.97.56.14; March–Oct; ③). Lac de Lauzas' main **campsite** is *Rieu Montagné* (mid-June to mid-Sept; ☎05.63.37.15.42) on the north side of the lake.

## Anglès

Some 16km south from Brassac on the St-Pons road, **ANGLÈS**, a collection of houses which are home to no more than a handful of families, is only likely to be of interest to hikers following the GR71 west from La Salvetat or the GR653 east from the Sidorbe, although the hamlet is served by regular buses from Mazamet. Although in Julius Caesar's time it served as a border post guarding the frontier against the Gallic barbarians, its oldest presently surviving monument is a small twelfth-century **gate**. The village is about 5km from **Lac des Sts-Peyres**, on the westernmost edge of the plateau, which remains undeveloped for tourism and is a good spot for a bit of peace and quiet. Anglès' seasonal **tourist office** (July & Aug 10am–noon & 4–6pm; ☎05.63.74.59.13) is adjoined by two **hotels**, of which *Auberge de la Souque* (March–Nov; ☎05.63.70.98.53; ②) is the most economical. The other, *Le Manoir de Boutaric* (☎ & fax 05.63.70.96.06, *www.logis-de-france.fr*; ③), just south of town, is a two-star rural affair with a **campsite** (April–Oct). The *Manoir*'s **restaurant** is open in July and August only; the rest of the year you can eat at *Aux Épis*, in Anglès itself, where you can get a hearty meal for about 80F/€12.

# St-Pons-de-Thomières and around

Deep in the folds of the Jaur valley, 52km from Castres and 35km due east on the N112 from Mazamet, sits **ST-PONS-DE-THOMIÈRES**, the park's principal information centre, separated from the Plateau des Lacs to the north by a high ridge, the western spur of the Monts de l'Espinouse (see below). It is also a transport hub for the park, with two main **bus** lines, the Béziers–La Salvetat and Castres–Montpellier, intersecting here. This ancient town's curious compound name originates with local count Raymond Pons, who founded a monastery (hence, the "St" part of the name) across the river, north of the hamlet of Thomières in 936. St-Pons' old quarter is worth a walk around – on the edge of it, on the north side of the modern road, is poised the twelfth-century **cathedral**, with its incongruous, slapped-on seventeenth-century facade, around the back of which you can still see the statues on the medieval tympana, faces chipped off by iconoclastic Huguenots in the sixteenth century. The bulk of the old town, however, lies south of the main road on both sides of the Jaur, which is crossed by a medieval **bridge**. Amidst the ancient alleys the square fourteenth-century defensive tower, the **Tour de la Évêché**, pokes above the rooftops. To the west of the old town, the **Musée de la Préhistoire** (mid-June to Oct daily 10am–noon & 2.30–6pm; Nov to mid-June Wed, Sat & Sun 10am–noon & 2–5pm; 20F/€3.05) has information on the area's menhirs as well as an exhibition of local Flintstonian relics, and also arranges speleological **safaris** in the neighbouring Ponderatz cave complex (☎05.67.97.22.61; check for availability of English-speaking guides). Cave fans will also want to check out the **Grotte de Devèze**, 5km west of St-Pons on the N112, and its **Musée Français de la Spéléologie** (July & Aug daily 10am–6pm; April–June & Sept daily 2–5pm; otherwise call to book; ☎04.67.97.03.24; 38F/€5.80). Opened in 1932, the cave contains a variety of rockforms, including an impressive stone cascade and several calcite "draperies".

**Buses** pull up near the main crossroads of St-Pons, on the south side of which is the town's **tourist office** (July & Aug daily 9am–7.30pm; Sept–June Mon–Fri 10am–noon & 2.30–6pm, Sat 10am–noon; ☎04.67.97.06.65, fax 04.67.97.29.65); the central information office for the park, the **Maison du Parc**, is also located nearby – beside the cathedral, at 13 rue du Cloître (Mon–Fri 8am–noon & 1.30–6pm; ☎04.67.97.38.22). If you're looking for a **hotel**, the best is *Le Somail* (☎04.67.97.00.12; ②) near the tourist office, which also has a reasonably priced dining room (menu from 60F/€9.15). The municipal **campsite** (☎04.67.97.06.65) is open in summer only.

# Olargues and around

From St-Pons, the Jaur river snakes northeast, skirting the **Monts de l'Espinouse** looming over the north bank to arrive at **OLARGUES**. Approached from the west, this hamlet presents an impressive vista: a high and gracefully arched medieval **bridge** backed by the steep hill where its castle once stood. From a covered staircase just west of the parking area along the main street, a ten-minute climb through the steep medieval alleys leads up to the lonely **clocktower**, the only remaining vestige of the eleventh-century fortress. Nearby, the Romanesque **priory** of St-Julien makes a good hike or a short drive, its shady wooded surroundings providing a great picnic spot and wonderful **views** of the Jaur Valley; take the Bédariuex road east for 2.5km and climb steeply on the left up the narrow signposted road a further 1500m.

### The Monts de l'Espinouse

Olargues is a natural place to begin a circuit of the **Monts de l'Espinouse**, an area whose isolated beauty is preserved in part by its inaccessibility; there's no public transport here. From the village the D14 switchbacks steeply up past slate-covered hamlets clinging to near perpendicular slopes until you reach the central pass of the **Col de Fontfroide** (971m). Here, **trails** (including the main GR7-71) crisscross the barren hillsides, and a sombre **monument** commemorates the German occupation. Turning east on the lonely D53 the forest gets thicker (a picnic paradise) as you approach the 1124m **summit** (sommet de l'Espinouse). A few kilometres later, rounding the Col de l'Ourtigas, the country opens up dramatically into a series of broad gorges, the vibrant green landscape contrasted with dull grey rock. Continuing on for 4km, you come to the turn off for **Douch**, after which the road descends to **Lamalous-les-Bains**. Douch is a good place to pick up the GR7 trail to reach either **Mont Caroux** (1091m; 2hr round trip) or the **Gorges d'Héric**, which you access via the tiny stone hamlet of Héric, 2km west of Douch. The deep and narrow gully of sparkling red granite shaded by thickly covering oak descends rapidly to the River Orb, 6km below, and the beauty of the gorge accounts for its popularity with day-trippers. Those who don't fancy the trek to the gorge may take the *petit train* which ascends from the main road near **Mons** (1 hour round trip; daily, times vary: mid-June to mid-Sept all day; Easter to mid-June & mid-Sept to mid-Nov afternoons only; 35F/€5.34).

## Practicalities

Olargues' summer-only **tourist office** (July & Aug daily 10.30am–12.30pm & 4.30–8pm; ☎04.67.97.71.26, fax 04.67.97.78.93) is on the main road. The **hotel** *Laissac* (closed Nov–March; ☎04.67.97.71.26; ②) can put you up, but a better deal is Pauline Giles' homely *Les Quatr' Farceurs* in rue de la Comporte (☎ & fax 04.67.97.81.33, *lqf@libertysurf.fr*, ②), which also serves huge meals with free-flowing wine for 90F/€13.73. There is a municipal **campsite** (mid-April to mid-Sept) and **bikes** can be rented from Oxygène (☎04.67.97.87.00). Walking the Gorges d'Héric or westwards through the mountains you'll find **gîtes** both in Douch (☎04.67.95.21.41; ①), and Héric (☎04.67.97.80.43; ②).

# Mazamet and the Montagne Noire

The highlands of Haut Languedoc are bounded on their southwest side by the deep valley of the River Thoré, which empties into the Agout just west of Castres. A separate massif, the **MONTAGNE NOIRE**, stretches in a narrow 50km band along the south side of the river course and westwards to Revel (see p.103), its highest peak, the **Pic de Noire** (1153m), located more or less at the centre of the range. The two sides of the Montagne Noire present a stark contrast: the north face, which has been incorporated into the Parc du Haut Languedoc, is thickly covered in a mixed forest of oak, beech and spruce, while the south presents a scrubby Mediterranean landscape of brush and vine. This whole district has tra-ditionally been even poorer and more isolated than Haut Languedoc proper: near-subsistence farming and herding continue to be the only activities through most of the zone, now that the mining of Salsigne and cloth industry of **Mazamet**, which boomed in the nineteenth century, have been reduced to shadows of their former selves. The Montagne Noire's chief attraction is its isolated wilderness, even more extreme than that to the north; you'll find that the outdoor facilities which have sprung up in the main body of the park are lacking here. South of Mazamet, the closest service town to the range, the ruin of medieval **Hautpoul** is a popular stop. There are two direct routes over the mountains: the first starts at Hautpoul before continuing on to the Pic de Noire and Carcassonne via the **Clamoux Gorges**; the second, ten kilometres west and roughly parallel to this route, follows the dark and evocative Orbiel valley down to the Cathar castles of **Lastours**. Further west still, on the far side of the main Mazamet–Carcassonne road, you can skirt the massif to medieval **Saissac**, a good base from which either to ascend to the forests around Arfons, or descend via **Montolieu** – known for its book shops – past the ruined abbey at **Villelongue** and on into the open country around Carcassonne. Public transport in this neck of the woods is more or less non-existent, the only regular service being the Mazamet–Carcassonne bus.

## Mazamet and around

Lying 17km southeast of Castres, **MAZAMET** is a pale imitation of that town, owing its meagre prosperity to the cloth industry. Its only allure is as a place to recharge your batteries – and even in this case Castres is a better choice. The town's single sight is the **Musée Mémoire de la Terre** (June–Sept daily 2.30–6.30pm; 20F/€3.05) in the old Fuzier-family mansion – an unimpressive exhibition consisting mainly of a fifteen-minute French-language slide show lamenting the fate of the Cathars. More interesting is a short trip to **Hautpoul**, the precursor of Mazamet, a Cathar redoubt perched on a hillside above, and which was all but levelled by the unstoppable de Montfort in 1212. The trip up to the village follows the serpentine **Route des Usines**, climbing the bed of the Arnette, where windowless relics of hulking nineteenth-century factories hunch at every hairpin. Now consisting of nothing more than one winding street and the sparse vestiges of the **castle**, Hautpoul is lorded over by the **Maison du Bois** (July & Aug daily 10am–noon & 2–6pm; June & Sept daily 2–6pm; April, May & Oct–Dec Sat & Sun 2–6pm; free), an artisanal operation churning out wooden toys. Despite having relatively little to offer, Hautpoul is a popular spot for excursions, in part because of the strong Cathar connection. But even if you aren't a Cathar fan, you'll still enjoy the hamlet's breathtaking setting, with views over the seemingly endless forested hills. If you have neither a car nor the desire to walk up to the hamlet, take one of the tourist office's **organized trips** (regular departures March–Oct; 25F/€3.81).

## Practicalities

Mazamet's **gare SNCF** (☎05.63.61.19.00) is located just off the Castres road, a fifteen-minute walk from the town centre; **buses** stop here or 300m further south on avenue Rouvière, by the post office. The **tourist office** (Mon–Sat 9am–noon & 1.30–7pm; ☎05.63.61.27.07, fax 05.63.98.24.16) is further south on the cours René Reille, where you can park. Inexpensive **hotels** are plentiful in Mazamet; the cheapest is the basic and ageing *Le Nord* at 4 place Olombel (☎05.63.61.00.53, fax 05.63.61.57.74; closed part June; ②), while the other two options – *Le Boulevard*, 24 boulevard Soult (☎05.63.61.16.08, fax 05.63.98.44.86, *www.logis-de-france.fr*; ②), and *Le Jourdon* at 7 avenue Albert Rouvière (closed Sun eve; ☎05.63.61.56.93, fax 05.63.61.83.38; ③) – offer a higher comfort level. The three-star **campsite** *La Lauze* (☎05.63.61.24.69; May–Sept) lies some 5km east of town. Once again, the hotel **restaurants** are the best bet for food here – *Le Boulevard* has a good-value 68F/€10.37 menu with wine included, but *Le Jourdan* beats it on quality at only a slightly higher price.

## St-Amans-Soult and the Thoré valley

Climbing east from Mazamet, the **Thoré valley** still retains its long-established role as a transport link between Castres and the Mediterranean coastlands, now the N112. Not far east of Mazamet you reach **ST-AMANS-SOULT**, a nondescript town which changed its name in honour of its native son, Field Marshal **Nicolas Soult** (1769–1851), nemesis of Wellington in the Peninsular War. The warrior's sombre and monolithic tomb is hardly worth stopping to see, but not so his palatial estate, **Château de Soult-Berg** (June–Sept Wed & Sun 3–5pm; 30F/€4.58), set amidst a wooded park. The richly furnished rooms here are immaculately preserved, and the mansion's rich library reflects the eighteenth-century ideal of the Renaissance man: aristocratic, learned and soldierly. From here the highway continues on, passing through tiny **Labastides** and eventually reaching St-Pons.

St-Amans and Labastides will be of interest to hikers in need of supplies or yearning for a hotel. The former is crossed by the **GR36** on its way to the Pic de Noire, and the latter by the **GR7**, descending from the Monts de l'Espinouse. In

St-Amans the only **hotel** is the *Hostellerie des Cèdres* (☎05.63.98.36.72, fax 05.63 .98.26.18, *www.logis-de-france.fr*; ③), while 1.5km north of Labastides, *La Bouriotte* offers comfortable **farm accommodation** and plentiful home-cooked food (☎05.63.98.07.64; ③). Both St-Amans (☎05.63.98.87.31) and Labastides (☎05.63.98.49.74) have **campsites**.

## South via the Pic de Noire

If you are heading towards Carcassonne from Mazamet, and you have your own transport, there are a couple of interesting routes which you can take across the Montagne Noire. To cross via the **Pic de Noire**, continue up the Arnette, past the turn-off to Hautpoul, for 3km, until you reach a junction from which the massive transmission tower crowning the summit should be in easy view. An arm-wrenching series of switchbacks then takes you to the flat and barren mountain top around the antenna's base, and a breathtaking combination of cool, thin air and sweeping panorama. From the peak, the tortuous road descends several kilo-metres to the hamlet of **Pradelles-Cabardés**, with its medieval **church**, before threading through the steep and forested cliffs of the **Clamoux gorges**, where, after 12km, you'll pass the turn-off for the **Gouffre de Cabrespine** (daily: July & Aug 10am–7pm; March–June & Sept–Nov 10am–noon & 2–6pm; 42F/€6.41), a huge vertical subterranean cavern with a main chamber 250m in height. The route continues to **Villeneuve-Minervois**, a quiet little town with some traces of medieval buildings, including the remains of its **castle**. Services along this route are minimal and you should plan to complete it before nightfall. In Pradelles there is a basic **campsite** on a nearby reservoir, and a **café** which also serves simple meals, while in Villeneuve the **restaurant** *Au Chanoine Gourmand* (menu from 50F/€7.63) also has **rooms** (☎04.68.26.15.69; ②).

## South via the Orbiel valley

An alternative route across the Montagne Noire, which you pick up by turning east off the D118 just after Lac du Montagne, is via the **Orbiel valley**, and south to the castles at **Lastours**. Descending the valley, the blanket of iridescent green forest threatens to swallow the steep and narrow stone-buttressed road, and the continuous series of hairpin curves makes the 11km to Mas-Cabardés seem at least twice as long. Driving here is an effort, however, which the scenery makes worthwhile, and when you pass the romantically ruined church of St-Pierre-de-Vals you are just outside **Mas-Cabardés**, a village which makes a good spot to stretch your legs before the tortuous second leg of the trip. While here check to see if the medieval **church**, crowned by a fifteenth-century bell tower, is open; if it is, step inside and check out the fourteenth-century statuary within. From Mas-Cabardés, as you approach Lastours, the road bends sharply, and the old textile mill which serves as the entrance to the grounds of the **Châteaux de Lastours** (July & Aug daily 9am–8pm; April–June, Sept & Oct daily 10am–5pm; Feb, March, Nov & Dec Sat & Sun 10am–5pm; 20F/€3.05) looms on the right. A cluster of four separate forts, perched dramatically on the points of the rocky hill dominating the river-bend, these are the northernmost of the Cathar castles, although in fact, only two of them, eleventh-century Cabaret and twelfth-century Surdespines, date from the era of the Crusade. When Simon de Montfort had conquered Minerve to the east and Termes to the south, the survivors took refuge in these forts, which were the redoubt of the Cathar-protecting lord, Pierre-Roger Cabaret. Efforts to besiege them proved vain and de Montfort only took the castles in 1211, when Pierre-Roger surrendered in exchange for pardon. Two more castles were built in the fourteenth century. A path climbs the steep and scrubby hill, and leads from one small castle to the next – an exhilarating walk which takes about two hours. The *châteaux* are quite ruined, and really their location is more evocative than their remains, so if you don't want to climb, you can drive to the look-out point (same ticket), set on a ridge to the west, which affords the best perspectives. Before continuing south, cut over 5km on the D111 to **Limousis**, whose **cave complex** (daily: July & Aug 10am–6pm; April–June 10am–noon & 2–6pm; Sept 10am–noon & 2pm–5pm late-March & Oct 2–5pm; 38F/€5.80) boasts impressive calcite formations, including the largest known cluster of the crystalline mineral, Aragonite. The lively English-speaking guides also make the visit enjoyable. Although there are simple **restaurants** in Mas-Cabardès and Lastours, you'll enjoy the trip more by packing a picnic lunch before departing and finishing up in Carcassonne or another substantial town. This said, the basic **campsite** beside the belvedere at Lastours is recommendable for its location overlooking the castles.

## Saissac and around

By traversing the Montagne Noire and heading west along its lower slopes you'll arrive at **SAISSAC**, an ancient hamlet whose steeply sloping lanes lead downhill from the main road to a large ruined fortress looking out towards Carcassonne – the medieval walls and towers can be clearly made out in the distance. Although little remains of the fifteenth-century **castle** (free entry), which can be reached from the road in about ten minutes, the hollow ruin is evocative – and a great place for viewing sunsets. Up on the road itself, a solitary tower surviving from the town's now-vanished walls holds a dull **museum** (mid-June to mid-Sept daily 10am–12.30pm & 2.30–6.30pm; mid-Sept to mid-June Sun 3–6pm; 15F/€2.29) containing an exhibition of tools used in local crafts and agriculture.

If you are leaving Saissac by car, you can easily reach the **Bassin du Lampy**, the smallest of the Park du Haut Languedoc's reservoirs, and a quiet place to have a swim, 5km up the D4 (picked up just west of Saissac). From the reservoir, the road continues north, through ever-thickening forest, to **Arfons**. Set among a series of grassy clearings, this little hamlet has an enchantingly forgotten air and is a great place to buy freshly picked mountain produce, including splendid wild mushrooms in late summer. South of Arfons a turn-off to the east leads towards Lacombe, following a narrow path through the **Forêt de la Montagne Noire**, lush, dark and green woods which make for another prime picnicking zone. In the heart of the *forêt*, at the hamlet of La Galaube, a path leads south for twenty minutes to the **Prise d'eau d'Alzeau**, the uppermost reservoir of the Canal du Midi's catchment system. The easy-to-follow trail to the site, where a statue to the visionary engineer stands, is a good way to get a feel for the forest of this region.

Saissac's **tourist office** is in the same tower as the museum (July & Aug daily 10am–12.30pm & 2–6.30pm, ☎04.68.24.47.80, *saissac@fnotsi.net*). Its only **hotel**, *Montagne Noire* (☎04.68.24.46.36, fax 04.68.24.46.20; ②), is nothing special, and it's certainly better to eat in the town below at *Au Beau Site* (closed Sat & Sun Sept–June; ☎04.68.24.40.37), which also has good views and menus from 80F/€12.20. The L'Ambinets run a comfy two-room **gîte** to the east at **St-Denis**

(☎04.68.26.42.13 ②), and they also rent **bikes**. At the Bassin du Lampy, the *Domaine du Lampy-Neuf* (☎04.68.24.46.07; ③) offers deluxe **chambres d'hôtes** and *gîte* dorms (①), while *La Galaube* (☎04.68.26.51.23; closed mid-Sept to mid-Jan ②) – by the *prise* has simpler rooms and an inexpensive year-round restaurant. You'll find basic **campsites** at the reservoir and at Arfons (ask at the bakery). The *bassin* also has a snack-bar, while Arfons has a bar and **restaurant**.

## Montolieu and Villelongue

A short drive south of Saissac, **MONTOLIEU** has striven to make a mark over the last decade as a "town of books", – a contrived (and pale) imitation of England's famous Hay-on-Wye. One shop, the aptly titled English Bookshop in rue de la Mairie, specializes in English-language titles, while several of the rest concentrate on New Age and occult books. You can also visit the **Conservatoire des Arts et Métiers du Livre** (daily 10am–noon & 2–6pm; free) at the north end of the village, with a collection of old presses and book-binding tools. West of Montolieu, tucked away in a wooded vale down a seemingly endless country lane, lie the ruins of the twelfth-century Cistercian **Abbey of Villelongue** (May–Oct daily 10am–noon & 2–6.30pm; 20F/€3.05) – worth driving to if only for their picturesque location on the banks of the Vernassonne. The remains of the abbey include the thirteenth-century vaulted cellar, a fourteenth-century Gothic cloister and the ruins of the abbey-church, now surrounded by a garden. In Montolieu you can **stay** at the very funky *Café du Livres*, two streets south of the town's church (☎04.68.24.81.17; call ahead; ①), but greater luxury can be enjoyed at the *Château de Villeneuve* (☎04.68.24.84.08, *lacalle@wanadoo.fr*; ③), a wine *domaine* just north of town. At Villelongue, the former monastery also offers **rooms** (④), but these are rather Spartan and monkish given the price.

## travel details

### TRAINS

**Albi** to: Carmaux (10 daily; 20min); Gaillac (6 daily; 40min); Naucelle (10 daily; 1hr); Toulouse (6 daily; 1hr 30min).

**Castres** to: Labrugière (3–6 daily; 7min); Mazamet (3–6 daily; 15min); Toulouse (4–8 daily; 1hr 8min).

**Gaillac** to: Lisle-sur-Tarn (12 daily; 35min); Rabastens (12 daily; 45min); St-Sulpice (12 daily; 50min); Toulouse (12 daily; 1hr 5min); Vindrac (for Cordes; 6 daily; 20min).

**Mazamet** to: Castres (9 daily; 12min); Labrugière (9 daily; 9min); Lavaur (9 daily; 55min); St-Paul/Damiette (9 daily; 40min); St-Sulpice (9 daily; 1hr 5min); Toulouse (9 daily; 1hr 30min).

### BUSES

**Albi** to: Ambialet (3 daily; 1hr 15min); Carcassonne (1 daily; 2hr); Carmaux (5 daily; 30min); Castres (6–8 daily; 1hr 15min); Cordes (3 daily; 35min); Gaillac (6 daily; 20min); Graulhet (2 daily; 40min); Lacaune (1 daily; 1hr 30min); Lisle (6 daily; 40min); Mazamet (1 daily; 1hr 45min); Naucelles (3 daily; 55min); Rabastens (6 daily; 50min); Réalmont (6–8 daily; 20min); St-Sulpice (6 daily; 1hr 5min); Toulouse (6 daily; 1hr 40min).

**Castres** to: Bédarieux (2 daily; 2hr); Béziers (2 daily; 2hr 30min); Brassac (4 daily; 50min); Carcassonne (8 daily; 2hr); Labrugière (2 daily; 15min); Lautrec (4–8 daily; 30min); Lavaur (11 daily; 55min); Mazamet (2 daily; 25min); Montpellier (2 daily; 2hr 30min); Olargues (2 daily; 1hr 45min); Revel (8 daily; 1hr); St-Pons (2 daily; 1hr 30min); the Sidorbe (frequent; 20min).

**Carmaux** to: Albi (5 daily; 30min).

**Gaillac** to: Albi (6 daily; 20min); Graulhet (4 daily; 20min); Lisle (4–8 daily; 10min); Rabastens (4–8 daily; 20min).

**Graulhet** to: Albi (2 daily; 40min); Gaillac (4 daily; 20min); Lautrec (4 daily; 30min).

**Mazamet** to: Anglès (2 daily; 20min); Labastide (2 daily; 35min); Labrugière (2 daily; 10min); Lacabarède (2 daily; 30min); La Salvetat (2 daily; 45min); Lavaur (2 daily; 1hr 10min); St-Amans (2 daily; 20min); St-Paul (2 daily; 55min); St-Pons (4 daily; 45min); St-Sulpice (2 daily; 1hr 30min); Toulouse (2 daily; 2hr).

**St-Pons** to: Bédarieux (5 daily; 1hr 20min); Béziers (5 daily; 1hr 20min); Lamalou-les-Bains (5 daily; 55min); La Salvetat (3 daily; 45min); Montpellier (1 daily; 2hr 20min); Olargues (5 daily; 25min).

# CHAPTER FOUR

# NÎMES AND AROUND

**N**îmes is Languedoc's most revitalized city, on the way up after an 1800-year slump following its decline as an imperial settlement. Chock-full of the region's most impressive Roman monuments, and a showroom for its most exciting new architecture, it's a busy little place, embodying an intriguing combination of ancient glory and modern style. The lands around the city comprise the southern half of **Gard**, the easternmost *département* of Languedoc-Roussillon – hemmed in on the east by the mighty Rhône river and on the west by the River Vidourle. On the Mediterranean coast, the **Petite Camargue**, the western section of the Rhône delta, rises tentatively out of the sea. This is desolate and windswept country, dominated by bull and horse farms near the seaside, and vineyards closer inland. As you move away from the sea, the sand dunes gradually give way to the hills known as the **Garrigues**, around Nîmes itself and to the north. These in turn are cut through by the deep gorge of the Gardon river – on the far bank of which runs the band of flatland once dominated by the ducal castle of **Uzès**. Vineyards cover the river valley, but in the scrub-covered hills stunted holm oaks compete with hardy thistles, lavender and thyme.

Although the numerous and majestic **Roman ruins** of the southern Gard, including Nîmes' **Les Arènes** and the magnificent **Pont du Gard**, attest to the area's prosperity in Roman times, this corner of the south has for centuries been something of a poorer cousin of neighbouring Provence – relegated to secondary status as the house of Toulouse collapsed in the wake of the Albigensian Crusade. This traditional economic marginalization is reflected in the faded glory of the former medieval port towns of **Beaucaire** and **St-Gilles**, although further south recent revival has drawn developers to the **beaches** and **pleasure ports** of the Carmarguaise coast. To the west, the gentle Vidourle is still spanned by **Roman bridges** and dotted by all but forgotten hamlets.

The weather in the Gard tends to extremes: hot summers and mild winters, punctuated by violent rainstorms in autumn and the merciless buffeting of the cold mistral wind in spring. The best season to visit is undoubtedly summer, but if you want to see Nîmes and the Gard at their most traditional, try to visit during the local **festivals**, which invariably entail *tauromachie* – bullfighting and horsemanship, both Camarguais and Spanish-style.

Getting around in the southern Gard presents some difficulties if you're reliant on **public transport**, and want to get off the main routes. Nîmes is the hub, with good train and bus services to most of the region's towns, services to the coast becoming more frequent in summer. Crossing between the various routes from Nîmes, or accessing out-of-the-way areas like the Petite Camargue or the Garrigues, however, is more inconvenient. That said, the flattish-terrain makes for relatively easy biking and walking, and as elsewhere in the south, local drivers are generally helpful when it comes to hitching.

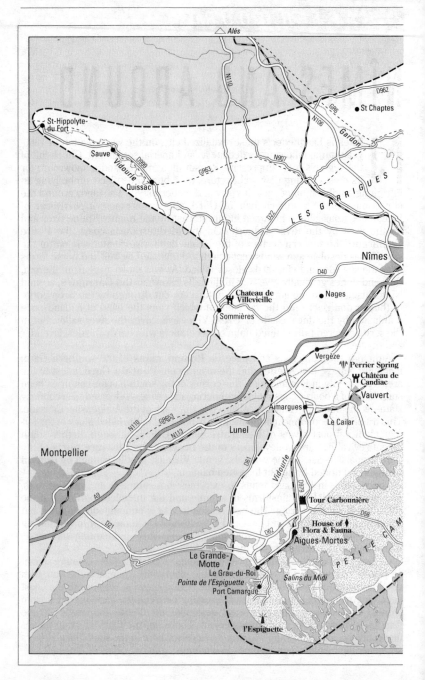

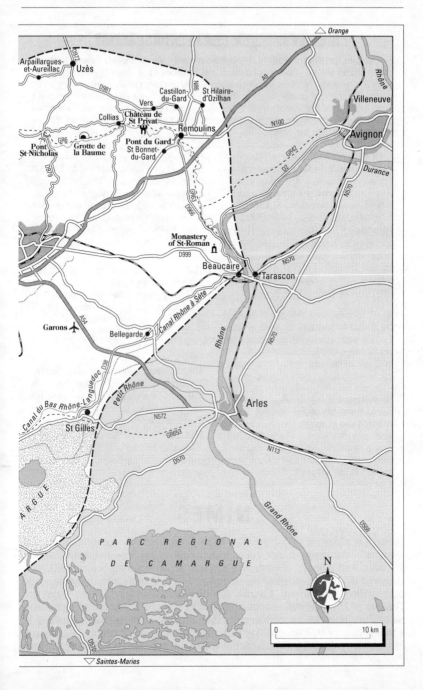

## FESTIVALS IN AND AROUND NÎMES

Festivals in the *département* of the Gard have a decidedly bullish flavour to them. In the bigger places – Nîmes, Beaucaire and St-Gilles – full-blown Spanish-style *corridas* are held for the most important occasions, but otherwise, nearly every small town will somehow involve bulls in their celebrations. Aside from these there are a number of fairs and events which commemorate the area's medieval past or its regional products. Where no specific information number is given, contact the relevant tourist office for details.

### February and March

**Fourth week before Easter** Nîmes: Feria de Primavera. The local celebration for pre-Lenten Carnaval, and the first of Nîmes' famed *ferias*, a street festival including music, and *tauromachie*.

**Late-March** St-Gilles: Carnaval. Held for one week and similar to Nîmes', but on a much smaller scale and with emphasis on the traditions of the Camarguaise cowboy culture: horsemanship, *courses camarguaises* and *corridas*.

**April** Sommières: Medieval festival. On the first weekend in April, a street festival with costumed merchants and performers, markets, music and cookery, all revolving loosely around a medieval theme.

**May** Nîmes: Feria de Pentecôte. The city's most important festival, and a frenzied rite of Spring, held on the fifth weekend after Easter. The festival has a heavy emphasis on bullfighting, along with music, dancing and a large street market in the old town.

### June

**Early June** Beaucaire: Fête du Drac. A three-day medieval festival, held in conjunction with neighbouring Tarascon, and celebrating the legend of the river beast, La Tarasque, a child-eating amphibious monster of local medieval folklore. Admission charge of 50F/€7.63 per day.

**Mid-June** Le Grau-du-Roi: Fisherman's festival. Along with the traditional *courses camarguaises*, water-jousting competitions are held in the harbour and canals in this four-day celebration of Le Grau's traditional industry.

### July

**Throughout July** Nîmes: Les Jeudis. Thursday nights. Street market with live music running the gamut of styles and nationalities in nearly every square (and many restaurants).

**Mid-July** Nîmes: Mosaïques Gitanes. A four-day festival of Romany ("Gypsy") culture including music, dancing and an outdoor market.

# NÎMES

**NÎMES** is a city inextricably linked to its Roman past. Its location on the Via Domitia – the main chariot route from Spain to Rome – helped make it a favourite with a series of emperors of the first and second centuries AD, who endowed it with the outstanding collection of monuments which dominate the place today; the **Maison Carrée**, the **amphitheatre** (or "Arènes") and the **Temple of Diana** are all testament to the city's bright, if short-lived, splendour. Since then, over the last eighteen hundred years, Nîmes has had something of a tough time of it, having to vie with neighbouring rivals Arles, Avignon and Montpellier (see p.244), which each in their time stole the city's limelight. From

**Mid-July** St-Gilles: Fête de la pêche et de l'abricot. A one-week harvest festival, celebrating two of the area's major agricultural products, peaches and abricots, with emphasis also on ranch culture and *tauromachie*.

**Mid-July** Sauve: African festival (☎04.66.77.59.96). Yearly four-day festival which brings in performers of traditional and modern music from across Africa. Concerts held in the town's Théâtre de Verdure. Admission 50F/€7.63.

**Mid-July to mid-Aug** Uzès: Autres Rivages. A world-music festival featuring primarily African groups. Performances are held in sites of architectural and archeological interest in the countryside around town.

**Fourth week** Beaucaire: Estivals. A summer festival with a medieval emphasis including market, parades, fireworks and bullfights. Daily admission 50F/€7.63.

**Throughout July & Aug** Les Beaux Quais du Vendredi. Friday-night open-air concerts, featuring live acts ranging from blues to World music, plus a lively canal-side street market.

**August**

**Throughout Aug** Aigues-Mortes: Les Nuits d'Encens (☎04.66.73.91.23). The town's "Nights of Incense" offer an eclectic musical programme, with styles from around the world and across the ages – from European chamber music to medieval Hispano-Arabic sounds. Nightly performances at 10pm in the courtyard of the Logis du Gouverneur.

**Early Aug** Quissac: Les Vidourlades (☎04.66.77.15.13, *www.vidourlades.com*). A three-day World music festival with a Spanish and North African bent. Nightly performances are held in the medieval ruins atop the town's hill.

**Late Aug** Aigues-Mortes: Fête de St-Louis. Held on the closest weekend to August 25, a medieval pageant and reconstruction of St Louis' departure for the Crusades, celebrating the day when the saint-king set out to fight the Muslims.

**September**

**Third week** Nîmes: Feria des Vendages. The third great *feria* in Nîmes, celebrating the wine harvest. Another *tauromachie* extravaganza, with live open-air concerts, parades and a market.

**October**

**Mid-Oct** Aigues-Mortes: Fête local. A three-day annual party featuring Gardois *tauromachie* performed alongside the medieval walls of the old town.

1983 on however, a succession of two flamboyant mayors have promoted the city within and without, engaging in a series of audacious building projects (including a retractable cover for the Roman amphitheatre), sponsoring concerts and festivals and drawing in artists and musicians. Their efforts have succeeded, kindling a spark that not even the massive mudslide of 1988, which covered the city in two and a half metres of muck and claimed the lives of seven people, could extinguish. Nowadays, crowds come not only to see the shrines of the Caesars and the dusted-off **mansions** of the cloth-making bourgeoisie, but a collection of some of the most provocative contemporary urban architecture in a city which is redefining itself. Nîmes also has two surprisingly good **art galleries**, and hosts some of the South of France's most colourful **festivals** – February's Carnaval, and the *ferias* of Pentecost and September, when the arena fills with **bullfighting** aficionados and the bars and restaurants are packed late into the night with noisy revellers.

## Some history

**Nemausus** had been a Roman colony since 40 BC, but didn't really take off until Augustus Caesar (then, Octavian) defeated Mark Antony and Cleopatra at Actium in 31 BC, bringing Egypt under his power. As a reward, he settled his veterans here, laying out a Roman grid-plan city and endowing it with powerful fortifications. In honour of their victory in Egypt, his soldiers adopted the ensign of a crocodile (the Nile) chained to a palm tree, which subsequently became the city's **symbol**. As the town grew, water demand outstripped the resources of its sacred spring and, under Claudius, a 50km-long canal, of which the Pont du Gard (see p.225) is part, was constructed to supply water. A century later, the city was at its zenith, enjoying the special patronage of the emperor Antoninus Pius, whose mother's family hailed from these parts. From that glorious era, however, things went rapidly downhill. Within a decade of Antoninus' death, the Roman Empire spun into a temporary political crisis, and by the time things had corrected, Christianity had replaced paganism in the Empire and Christian Arles had supplanted polytheistic Nîmes as the local capital.

With the Roman decline, Nîmes was to suffer conquest by Germanic "barbarians". For 250 years the town was held by the Visigoths, in turn displaced by Muslims who came up from Spain in about 724. Only seven years later the Muslims were forced out, and for the next four hundred years the town was incorporated into a series of rapidly dissolving principalities including West Francia, Aquitaine and Septimania. In 1185, it came under the control of the **Counts of Toulouse**, under whom the town briefly flirted with Catharism; the sight of de Montfort's powerful army, however, was enough to make it "repent" and return to the Catholic fold. Nîmes was absorbed by the French crown in 1226, but by this time little was left of the glorious Roman city – only two clusters of houses huddled around the cathedral and amphitheatre.

After three sleepy centuries as a poor market town, Nîmes began to discover a new vocation as a textile centre – until the **Wars of Religion** wracked the place. Calvinist preachers found eager ears in Nîmes' new prosperous class of cloth-makers, to the extent that local Huguenots destroyed the eleventh-century cathedral and, on St Michael's Day of 1567, massacred some two hundred clergy. Following their repression in the wake of the Wars, Protestants from Nîmes as well as exiles from Haut Languedoc rose up together in the Camisard rebellion, brutally suppressed by royal forces in 1704, following its leader's defection to the Catholic forces at Nîmes. Many Protestants fled, while others persevered, having to disguise their faith. After the Revolution, religious issues were laid aside and still predominantly Protestant Nîmes got back down to making money, which it did by spinning silk and **cotton**. The town's product became so successful that the cotton cloth "de Nîmes" (or denim) went west, where in 1848 an American, Levi Strauss, hit upon the idea of attaching small red labels to pants made out of the material. Recent history is dominated by mayors Jean Bousquet and Alain Clary, who embarked on a daring policy of reconstruction, including drawing leading avant-garde architects to the city, and opening its first university.

# Arrival, information and accommodation

Garons **airport**, which also serves Arles, has few facilities, basically limited to an ATM and car rental desks. Located 10km south of Nîmes along the D42, just outside St-Gilles, from here the trip to the city can be made by *navette* (2–4 daily; ☎04.66.29.27.29; "Gambetta" or "Imperator" stop; 28F/€4.27). By taxi, the trip will cost at least 60F/€9.15. Nîmes' **gare SNCF** and **gare routière** are both located at the end of avenue Feuchères, about a ten-minute walk south of the old town – the gare SNCF has **left luggage** lockers and a **tourist office** (July & Aug Mon–Sat 9.30am–12.30pm & 2–6pm, Sun 9.30am–12.30pm & 1.30–3.30pm; Sept–June Mon–Fri 9.30am–12.30pm & 2–6pm; ☎04.66.84.18.13), which can help with hotel reservations. Arriving **by car** on the A9 take either exit and follow signs for the centre (north of the autoroute); there are underground parking spaces on the ring road, and street parking is also legal, if difficult. The **main tourist office** (July & Aug Mon–Fri 8am–8pm, Sat 9am–7pm, Sun 10am–6pm; Sept–June Mon–Sat 9am–7pm, Sun 10am–6pm; ☎04.66.58.38.00, fax 04.66.58.38.01, *www.ot-nimes.fr*) is about a twenty-minute walk from the *gares* at 6 rue Auguste, and can also be reached by bus #8 ("Antonin").

Unless you're staying at the campsite, hostel or one of the far-flung motels, you'll most likely have no use for Nîmes' city transport system. The **bus** network's hub is avenue Feuchères, through which all the main lines pass, the most useful of which, line #8, circles the city centre. Transport **maps** are available from tourist offices, and single **tickets** (6F/€0.92) can be bought from the drivers. If you want to cycle around Nîmes the youth hostel (see below), gare SNCF and campsite **rent bikes** to guests, and there's also Cycles Rebour, at 38 rue Hôtel Dieu (☎04.66.76.24.32). Alternatively, TRAN **taxis** (see "Listings") charge 150F/€22.88 for a one-hour tour of Nîmes for a maximum of six people.

**Accommodation** options in Nîmes are plentiful, although rock-bottom budget places aren't so easy to come by. You can reserve many hotels in the city through a **central reservation** office (☎04.66.36.96.30, fax 04.66.67.65.25, *slagard@aol.com*), and should book ahead as far ahead as possible for visits during any of the city's celebrations. Bear in mind too that Nîmes participates in the "Bonne Weekend en Ville" program (see Basics, p.39); contact the tourist office for details. Nîmes' comfortable **HI hostel** (☎04.66.23.25.04, fax 04.66.23.84.27; July & Aug membership required; Sept–June 11pm curfew; 65F/€9.91), which also has camping facilities, is on Chemin de la Cigale, 2km northwest of the centre (take bus #2 to "Stade"). The

## ACCOMMODATION PRICE CODES

All the hotels and guesthouses listed in this book have been price-coded according to the following scale. The prices quoted are for the cheapest available double room in high season.

① Under 160F/€24     ④ 300–400F/€46–61     ⑦ 600–700F/€91–107
② 160–220F/€24–34     ⑤ 400–500F/€61–76     ⑧ 700–800F/€107–122
③ 220–300F/€34–46     ⑥ 500–600F/€76–91     ⑨ Over 800F/€122

municipal **campsite** (☎04.66.38.09.21; open year-round) is further out, on the route de Générac, 5km south of the centre, beyond the A9 autoroute (bus #D: "La Bastide" stop).

# Hotels

With the exception of the *Imperator*, none of the city's hotels offer anything unique, but all of the establishments listed below are solid possibilities. Most of the cheaper **hotels** are located between the Arènes and the train station. At *feria* times, you may have to resort to the cluster of motels around the Nîmes-Ouest exit of the A9, which include the *Holiday Inn* (☎04.66.29.86.87; ⑤), *Mercure* (☎04.66.70.48.00; ⑤), *Novotel* (☎04.66.84.60.20; ⑤) and *Mas de Galoffre* (☎04.66.38.15.36; ②).

**Atria**, 5 bl de Prague (☎04.66.76.56.56, fax 04.66.76.26.36). Just south of the old town, this modern building is somewhat of a monstrosity compared with Nîmes' other hotels, but it has all the mod cons – at a price. ⑥.

**Audrans Terminus**, 23 av Feuchères (☎04.66.67.66.20, fax 04.66.76.22.30). Right by the train station, this is a well-decorated and lively hotel, with attentive staff. Amenities include cable TV. ③.

**La Baume**, 21 rue Nationale (☎04.66.76.28.42, fax 04.66.67.28.45). Located in a former mansion, tastefully decorated, with friendly and professional service, this hotel is at the high end of this bracket, but worth it. ④.

**Cat**, 22 bd Amiral-Courbet (☎04.66.67.22.85, fax 04.66.21.57.51). A traveller's favourite for both comfort and price, this hotel is clean, and the rooms all have TV. Garage parking is extra. ②.

**Central**, 2 pl du Château (☎04.66.67.27.75, fax 04.66.21.77.79). Just behind the temple and the Porte d'Auguste, with English-speaking management, this is a small but cosy hotel which also has secure parking. ④.

**Le France**, 4 bl des Arènes (☎04.66.67.23.05, fax 04.66.67.76.93). Cheapest of the cheap and a bit noisy, but right in the middle of things. The rooms are basic and in need of renovation, but if budget is your priority you'll be happy enough here. ①.

**Imperator Concorde**, quai de la Fontaine (☎04.66.21.90.30, fax 04.66.67.70.25). Nîmes' best and most prestigious hotel, with top service and amenities in an atmosphere-loaded *fin-de-siècle* mansion with a stately garden. Prices quadruple during *ferias*. ⑤.

**Lisita**, 2bis bd des Arènes (☎04.66.67.66.20, fax 04.66.76.22.30). Long-establised place, and one of the funkier digs in town; the Spanish flavour is popular not only with travellers but with visiting bullfighters. Rooms have air conditioning and TV. ③.

**de la Maison Carrée**, 14 rue de la Maison Carrée (☎04.66.67.32.89, fax 04.66.76.22.57). Right by the famous temple, this small hotel has a cheery décor and a great rooftop breakfast terrace. Extras include air-conditioning and TV. ②.

**de Provence**, 5/7 square de la Couronne (☎04.66.76.04.92, fax 04.66.36.77.99). Well located near the train and bus stations and the amphitheatre. Rooms have cable TV, and garage parking is extra. ②.

**Royal**, 3 bd Alphonse-Daudet (☎04.66.67.28.36, fax 04.66.21.68.97). Near the *Imperator*, the *Royal* has a cool Spanish-style décor which also draws in passing *toreros*. The rooms are individually decorated with a distinctly Iberian flavour, and the place exudes a certain cool chic. This is also home to the *Bodeguita* tapas bar. ④.

**du Temple**, 1 rue de l'Amphithéâtre (☎04.66.67.28.51, fax 04.66.67.07.79; closed Jan). A quiet hotel in an eighteenth-century house, its slight state of neglect only adding to the atmosphere of faded elegance. TV and parking available. ②.

# The City

The heart of Nîmes' is the compact warren of pedestrian streets which make up the city's **old town**, a triangle hemmed in by the boulevards Gambetta on the north, Amiral Courbet on the southeast, and Victor Hugo on the southwest. Ironically, Nîmes oldest remains – its **Roman monuments** – lie for the most part on the edge or outside of the old town, and the route described below is a looping

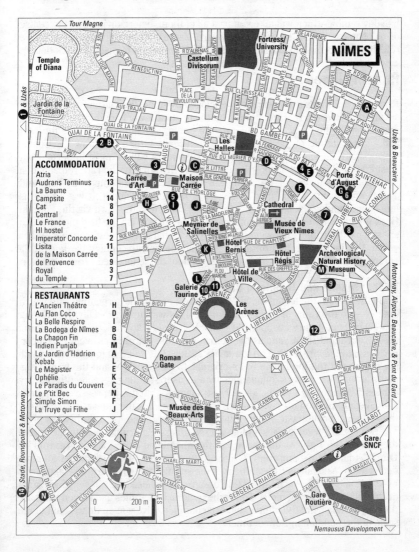

**ACCOMMODATION**

| | |
|---|---|
| Atria | 12 |
| Audrans Terminus | 13 |
| La Baume | 4 |
| Campsite | 14 |
| Cat | 8 |
| Central | 6 |
| Le France | 10 |
| HI hostel | 1 |
| Imperator Concorde | 2 |
| Lisita | 11 |
| de la Maison Carrée | 5 |
| de Provence | 9 |
| Royal | 3 |
| du Temple | 7 |

**RESTAURANTS**

| | |
|---|---|
| L'Ancien Théâtre | H |
| Au Flan Coco | D |
| La Belle Respire | I |
| La Bodega de Nîmes | B |
| Le Chapon Fin | G |
| Indien Punjab | M |
| Le Jardin d'Hadrien | A |
| Kebab | L |
| Le Magister | E |
| Ophélie | K |
| Le Paradis du Couvent | C |
| Le P'tit Bec | N |
| Simple Simon | F |
| La Truye qui Filhe | J |

---

**DISCOUNT PASSES**

If you plan on visiting more than one of the Roman sights, you might consider buying a "Billet Global", a combined ticket allowing entry to Les Arènes and the Tour Magne for 45F/€6.86, or the "Forfait 3 Jours" which gets you in to all of Nîmes' monuments and museums for 60F/€9.15, valid for three days. Both are available at the Tour Magne and Les Arènes.

---

half-day ramble which will take you past all of them, before diving into the centre of old Nîmes. Dotted around the city are also a number of **museums**; we've referred to these in the Roman Nîmes circuit if you want to make a quick detour.

# Roman Nîmes

**Roman Nîmes** was a sprawling city enclosed by some 7km of thick walls (which survived as late as 1786), reinforced by thirty stout towers and pierced by seven monumental gates. Tucked away north of boulevard Gambetta, beside the cold and sinister facade of the town's eighteenth-century **fortress** (now the Centre Universitaire du Vauban; Oct–June; free) sits one of Nîmes' most important but least known Roman artefacts – the **castellum divisorum**, the rare remains of a first-century waterworks (the only similar ones are at Pompeii in Italy and Tiermes in Spain), which mark the start of the Roman circuit. It was from this innocuous-looking open basin that the water carried to the town via the Pont du Gard was distributed to the various parts of the Roman city by lead pipes, which are still partly visible. Following the quiet residential streets west from here takes you to the **Jardin de la Fontaine**, a formal eighteenth-century garden with a complex series of fountains and pools, at the foot of the forested **Mont Cavalier**.

## La Tour Magne and Temple of Diana

From the *place* at the foot of the hill, follow the signs up the serpentine path which takes you to the ruins of the **Tour Magne**. This **watchtower** (daily: July & Aug 9am–7pm; Sept–June 9am–5pm; 15F/€2.29), based on an earlier Celtic structure, dates from about 15 BC, and as the Roman settlement grew, was eventually incorporated into the city walls. The tower has suffered its share of indignities, including the loss of the top fifteen of its original 45-metre height and the frantic diggings around the tower's foundations by a treasure-hunting seventeenth-century gardener deluded by a prediction of Nostradamus – but it is impressive even in its ruined state. Broken off and eroded, the tower evokes the romantic etchings of the nineteenth-century travellers who marvelled at it, and it is still the best place from which to survey Nîmes and its surroundings. Returning back to the foot of the hill, to the right of the Jardin sit the shambolic ruins of the "**Temple of Diana**" (daily 8am–8pm; free). Originating as a *nymphaeum*, a sacred fountain dedicated to Nemausus (the goddess of the spring), the structure was taken over by Benedictine monks in the Middle Ages, in whose care it remained until destroyed by Huguenot mobs. Today the hulking half arches and ruined walls are the only remnants of the temple, but are enough to give you an impression of the scale of the building in Roman times.

## The Maison Carrée

Following quai de la Fontaine east back to the centre brings you to the most famous sight of Nîmes, the **Maison Carrée** ("square house"), just down boulevard Daudet. Founded in 4 or 5 AD and dedicated to Augustus' adopted grandsons, this tiny but perfectly proportioned temple was once the centrepiece of the city's forum. Size, of course, is not everything, and as Henry James remarked, it is precisely because of its compactness that "it does not overwhelm you, you can conceive it." This is perhaps the world's best preserved Roman temple (rivalled only by Lebanon's Temple of Apollo at Baalbek), and can still boast all of its columns, an intact roof and *cella* (inner sanctum). If over the ages its functions – including use as a stable – haven't always done it justice, its aesthetic perfection has long drawn notable admirers. Colbert, Louis XIV's prime minister, wanted to carry it off lock and stock to Versailles, Thomas Jefferson modelled the Virginia Capital building on it, and Napoleon took it as inspiration for the Magdalene church in Paris. Today it houses a **museum** (daily: July & Aug 9am–noon & 2.30–7pm; Sept–June 9am–12.30pm & 2–6pm; free), which contains a small but somewhat overly-detailed exhibition on the building itself, and odds and ends of recovered Roman masonry. The Carré d'Art, facing the ancient temple, is home to Nîmes' Musée d'Art Contemporain (see p.216).

## Les Arènes

From the temple, follow boulevard Victor Hugo south, and just as you see the amphitheatre looming tantalizingly in front of you, turn right down rue Jean Reboul, which merges with rue Porte de France, passing through the **Roman gate** of the same name. It's worth pausing here to consider the immense size of the Roman city – the whole area between here and the Tour Magne was contained by its walls. Through the gate, the first left leads back towards Nîmes' coliseum, the entrance of which is on its northwest side. Although not the largest surviving Roman amphitheatre, **Les Arènes** (daily: July & Aug 9am–6.30pm; Sept–June 9am–noon & 2–5pm; closed during special events; 28F/€4.27) may well be the best preserved. Dating back to the first century, the 133-metre-long and 101-metre-wide oval surges 21 metres above the street, thanks to its uniquely intact upper galleries, and still holds the crowds of 20,000 spectators for which it was designed. An ingenious access system allows the public to enter and exit through the *vomitoria* – the great arched entryways which ring the building – quickly and with minimal jostling. Back before the stick-in-the-mud Christians banned gladiatorial matches in the fourth century, these entertainments, along with spectacles involving killing exotic animals, were the big draw. In the intervening centuries since the decline of these games the building has only managed to escape destruction thanks to its more or less continued use. With its occupation by the Visigoths it was used as a fortress, a role in which it remained through the twelfth century (in the east section, two contemporary windows remain). Thereafter it quickly filled up with houses, shops and churches, coming to constitute a veritable slum, which was only cleared out when restoration work began in 1809. Since the nineteenth century the amphitheatre has been used again for public spectacles, including bullfights. Once you have appreciated the grandness of its structure, however, the inside of the arena holds little interest; the long series of impressively vast but near-identical passages, stairways and bench-rows is a tribute to Roman engineering, but hides few surprises. Unfortunately, the concerts

## BULLFIGHTING AND TAUROMACHIE

Bulls have been raised in the Petite Camargue and the plains to its north for centuries, and **tauromachie** – the art of bull-handling – has come to represent, for the people of the ranch lands around St-Gilles, a measure of virility, testament to their proud rural roots. Its significance however, is also regionwide: in addition to the exciting action and dangerous elements of bull-handling – which naturally began to attract audiences – the growing cultural awareness of the mid-nineteenth century prompted intellectual Occitan patriots to find in it a further mark of the uniqueness of their local culture, thus sealing *tauromachie*'s transformation into a popular spectacle throughout Languedoc and Roussillon.

The traditions of the **bullfight**, which seem now to be so essential to the spirit of Gard, are in fact almost exclusively recent innovations. A *jeu taurin*, wherein ranch hands and sometimes other animals were pitted against bulls as entertainment, had developed by the Middle Ages, but it wasn't until the Iberian customs arrived, thanks to a visiting Spanish nobleman, that French *tauromachie* came into its own. The first real **corrida** (Spanish bullfight) in France was held in 1853 at Bayonne – it was a great success and soon spread throughout the Midi and into Provence. At Nîmes' Les Arènes the first official *corrida* was held in 1865, and by 1880 the spectacle could be seen across the south. Meanwhile, the local tradition, the **course** – in which men on foot would try to pull ornaments off the foreheads of charging bulls – had also been formalized, and achieved such popularity that when the government tried to ban it because of high fatalities, the population defiantly opposed the plan.

The standard Spanish-style *corrida* which can be seen at the *ferias* of Nîmes, Beaucaire, St-Gilles and Sommières is a highly ritualized **ceremony** – a fatal dance in which the bull is an unwitting but respected partner. In a typical afternoon, three matadors will dispose of six bulls, each of which will face a series of torments: first, after a few initial passes with the large cape (*capote*), the bull is subjected to the

and events held here often obscure the building with scaffolding and stage-works, and although the retractable cover which was added in the late 1980s makes winter-time shows possible, it frustrates efforts to imagine the building's ancient ambience. The best way to visit Les Arènes and appreciate a Roman-like atmosphere is to come for a **bullfight** (see box) during one of Nîmes' *ferias*.

## The Archeological Museum and Porte d'Auguste

Halfway along boulevard Amiral-Courbet, less than ten minutes' walk northeast from Les Arènes, sits the massive former Jesuit college, home to the collections of the **archeological museum** (Tues–Sun 11am–6pm; 28F/€4.27, including the natural history museum), as well as the natural history museum (see p.216). Disappointingly poor in Roman artefacts considering the city's ancient Latin glory – items are limited to a sizeable but visually monotonous collection of Latin epigraphy, and an assortment of household goods – it does have some fine Greek lacquerware and pre-Roman Etruscan. Continuing to place des Carmes, across which the Protestant Grand Temple and the Catholic church of St-Baudille contemplate each other uneasily, the excavated **Porte d'Auguste** can be found on the left – the surprisingly well-preserved triumphal entryway into the city, sunken by the rising ground level, was only discovered in the eighteenth century with the destruction of the medieval palace which had been built around it. It is through this gate that the **Via Domitia** entered Nîmes from the east: the larger central

long, barbed spear of the mounted *picadores*; next, the graceful *banderilleros* run at the bull and plant their colourful barbs in its shoulder; and finally, the matador executes a series of choreographed passes with his small red *mula* until, to the minor strains of a *paso doble*, the president of the *corrida* gives the order for the bullfighter to finish off his partner. Crowds at the event are extremely vocal and demonstrative: a poor matador and bull will be pelted with seat cushions, while a very successful matador will be greeted with cheers, showered with roses, rewarded with a gift of the bull's ears and tail and borne out of the ring on the shoulders of the crowd. The happiest ending, however, is the rare *indulto*, when the bull is also rewarded for his performance, and retired, living, to be used for breeding and allowed to die of contented old age.

The French *course* is quite distinct, although it has been permeated by an undeniable Spanish flavour. Less expensive and elaborate, it is more common in village *fêtes*, such as at **Uzès** or **Aigues-Morte**. The bulls (or cows) are first led to the ring in an *abrivado*, herded by a tumult of mounted *gardians* – if this takes place within a confined area, it is called an *encierro* (a "running" of the bulls). Once in the ring the animals are outfitted with a rosette and tassels suspended between their horns, and for fifteen minutes *raseteurs* (named after the hooked handgear they wear) provoke the animal into charging, attempting to snatch the rosette or tassels without getting trampled or gored. When all is complete, the bulls are herded out (the *bandido*) with great fanfare and frenzy and back to the pen.

Today *tauromachie* is more popular than ever; the *ferias* of Nîmes draw thousands of enthusiasts from all over France and the rest of Europe and are universally acknowledged as southern France's liveliest and most colourful festivities. And the practice has taken firm root even in the smallest of villages far from the *manades* of the plains – even if they can afford no more than an *encierro*, villagers pool their money in order to pay for some sort of taurine display, without which no *fête* would be seen as complete.

passages were for chariots and the smaller side entrances for pedestrians. A few paces southwest from here will lead you to place aux Herbes, in the heart of the old town, directly in front of the cathedral.

## The old town

With the core of the Roman city long buried and built over, and most of the medieval buildings destroyed in the course of the Wars of Religion, Nîmes' **old town** is for the most part a testament to the success of the local cloth-merchants of the seventeenth to nineteenth centuries – the builders of the grandiose *hôtels* which pepper the streets fanning out south and west from the **Cathédrale de Notre-Dame et St-Castors**. This church serves as a fitting transition point from Roman to early-modern Nîmes, set as it is on the foundations of the former Temple of Apollo. Of the original cathedral, founded in 1069, only the bell tower and the badly chipped friezes of the facade survived the Huguenots' wrath – the rest was rebuilt in the 1700s. The new building is rather nondescript and the drably remodelled interior is hardly worth a visit. On the south side of the square sits the seventeenth-century **bishops' palace**, now home to the **Musée de Vieux Nîmes** (daily 11am–6pm; 28F/€4.27), whose lively collection focuses on the city's artisanal and industrial past including, of course, the manufacture of denim, and will appeal to both adults and children. It is a well-organized exhibition, rounded out by a noteworthy furniture collection, which includes a nineteenth-century billiards table and sedan chairs. Heading south on rue des Marchands, you'll pass the plain facade of a medieval shop at no. 15 – a rare "commercial" survivor of the Middle Ages – before passing **Hôtel Régis**, a former merchants' house with a stately sixteenth-century courtyard in rue de Chapitre. The street ends at Grand Rue, where you'll be confronted by the clean Neoclassical lines of the former **Jesuits' Chapel** (Tues–Sun 11am–6pm; 28F/€4.27). Inside, there's a spacious and luxuriously appointed Baroque interior, now used for exhibitions and concerts. In rue des Greffes, to the south, sits the late-Rennaisance **Hôtel de Ville**, built in 1700 – watch for the stuffed crocodiles suspended above the staircase inside the entry hall, gifts to the city from contented (and rich) eighteenth-century burghers. West from here, the theme continues in place de la Marché, where a twentieth-century homage to the city's emblem has been paid in a **fountain** designed by Martiel Raysse and Silvio and Vito Tongiani. Just to the northwest, innocuous among the colourful boutiques and restaurants, sits the **Hôtel Bernis**, one of the town's earliest surviving mansions, its fifteenth-century facade studded by casement windows and concealing an atmospheric old courtyard with a well in the centre. Nearby, at 8 rue l'Aspic, you can see three early Christian sarcophagi incorporated into the walls of the **Meynier de Salinelles** mansion, as well as a splendid staircase leading up from its courtyard. Continuing up rue l'Aspic you reach the place de l'Horloge, whose solitary eighteenth-century **clock tower** is now crowded by the tables of café terraces; place aux Herbes is just to the east.

## The rest of the museums

In addition to those mentioned above, Nîmes has other museums which shouldn't be overlooked. For instance, the quirky **natural history museum** (Tues–Sun 11am–6pm; 28F/€4.27, including the archeological museum), which shares the same building as the archeological museum, holds a jumbled collection of Polynesian masks and spears, and a hotchpotch of stuffed animals, including a Royal Bengal Tiger. The museum resembles a large curio cabinet – a journey into the nineteenth-century European mind, which saw the world beyond its borders as a hunting ground for collectibles. South of the Roman gate, on rue Cité Foulc, the **Musée des Beaux-Arts** (daily 11am–6pm; 28F/€4.27) is worth a visit for the huge Roman mosaic, depicting the mythical "marriage of Admetus", which is its centrepiece, but the collection – mostly Flemish, Italian and French paintings of the sixteenth to eighteenth centuries – is endowed with works of surprising quality, including Rubens' uncharacteristically static *Portrait of a Monk*, and a fine example of the transition from medieval to humanist stylings in Giambono's *Mystical Marriage of St Catherine*. Opposite the Maison Carrée, and located in the Norman-Foster-designed Carré d'Art (see box), the two floors of the **Musée d'Art Contemporain** (Tues–Sun 11am–6pm; 28F/€4.27) contain an impressive survey of French and Western European art of the last four decades. Emphasis is on Gallic movements such as Nouveau Réalisme and Support-surfaces, but Mediterranean and northern European art is also strongly represented. Finally, should you be interested, the unusual **Galerie Taurine** (Tues–Sun 11am–6pm; free), across from the entrance to the Arènes, exhibits (and sells) bullfighting memorabilia, ranging from old promotional posters to full-blown matador suits.

## NIMES' AVANT-GARDE ARCHITECTURE

Since the mid-Eighties Nîmes has embarked on an audacious project of urban renewal, contracting high-flying architects from around the world to construct public housing developments, sport centres and civic spaces. These new buildings – Nîmes' modern pride – vary in originality and effect; you may judge them to be either wonders or monstrosities. Some of them you'll pass as you make the rounds in the centre, while the rest (which will really only be of interest to hard-core fans) are scattered around the southern edge of the city and are best visited either by bike or taxi.

The best work by far is Norman Foster's great **Carré d'Art** (1993), home to the modern-art gallery and city library just off boulevard Daudet. The building is a twentieth-century descendent of the Roman temple beside which it sits – four fine columns supporting the building's high portico with seeming effortlessness, either paying homage to or mocking the chunkier Ionic columns of the smaller Maison Carrée, reflected in the inscrutable glass face of Foster's building. Also in the old town are two remodelled urban *places*: Martiel Raysse's **la place d'Assas** (1989) and Philippe Starck's **Arbibus** (1987), both offering simple landscape architecture and decidedly underwhelming modern sculpture. The peripheral sites include the whale-like and rapidly ageing social housing development **Nemausus 1** (Jean Nouvel, 1987), its monstrous rejoinder, **Nemausus 2** (Alain Amedeo and Jacek Padlewski, 1989), and three sports complexes – **Stade des Costières** (Vittorio Gregotti and Marc Chausse, 1989), **Salle Omnisports** (Gregotti, 1993) and **Le Colisée** (Kisho Kurokawa, 1991) – which with their lunging surfaces of concrete and glass complete the discordant collection.

# Eating, drinking and entertainment

On the culinary front, Nîmes is a city of plenty, where three culinary traditions – Spanish, *gastronomique* and, of course, Gardois *terroir*, dominate the local **restaurant** *cartes*, with Indian and North African establishments adding a cosmopolitan flavour. The cuisine of Gard has a distinctly Mediterranean taste, with a strong current of olive and garlic, plus rosemary, basil, bay and mint, all of which sprout up in the *garrigues*. Look out for *boeuf à la Gardianne* (slow-cooked marinated beef), *soupe au pistou* (vegetable soup with pesto), and *brandade de morue* (cod and olive-oil purée); wash these down with the wines of the Costières, or with the famous Côtes-du-Rhône vintages.

**Bars** in Nîmes are smoking – literally. Over the course of an evening many establishments fill with the thick blue haze of Galloises and Gitanes; appropriately enough, given that the person who introduced the evil weed to France in the sixteenth century was the Nîmes native Jean Nicot (also the drug's namesake). But despite the newly opened university, Nîmes' bar scene is still quite sedate – nothing to compare with nearby Montpellier, and the **clubs**, as is frequently the case, are located in far-flung suburbs or out of town altogether, making them all but impossible to get to without a car. Nîmes has a **cinema**, Sémaphore, 25 rue Porte de France (☎04.66.67.83.11) showing films in v.o., but its high-brow cultural programme, possibly because of its proximity to more prestigious centres like Avignon and Montpellier, is pretty disappointing. That said, a steady stream of theatre groups and musicians, ranging from symphonies to rock and blues acts,

**THE FERIAS**

The most important dates on the Nîmes calendar are those of the **ferias**, lively street festivals featuring parties, music and *tauromachie*. The city is the French capital of the *corrida*, the Spanish tradition of bullfighting which the Occitans have striven to make their own, and during the three great annual *ferias* – **Primavera** (February), **Pentecôte** (seven weeks after Easter) and **des Vendanges** (mid-September), the best local and Spanish *toreadores* come to Les Arènes to practise the brutal pageantry of their art. During the *ferias*, particularly Pentecost, the centre of Nîmes becomes a massive round-the-clock party; the bars fill with boisterous revellers and the best hotels have already been booked a year in advance. If you plan to visit the city during one of the festivals, it is essential to make reservations for accommodation; for tickets to **bullfights** throughout the year, contact the Bureau de location des Arènes, at 1 rue Alexandre-Ducros (☎04.66.67.28.02).

do come to town – drawn primarily by the presence of an excellent venue in the Roman amphitheatre; groups who can't fill Les Arènes play on various smaller stages scattered about the town. For information and reservations for concerts and plays, contact the main tourist office and also check the annual *Guide Culturel* booklet for major shows. Of course, if Nîmes' nightlife is somewhat lacking in vibrancy, its famous **festivals**, the *ferias* (see below), more than make up for it.

## Restaurants

Many of the cheapest **restaurants**, including self-service cafés and cheap sandwich stands, can be found along the boulevard Amiral-Courbet, while the whole of the old town is thick with small restaurants and brasseries. When weather permits, these establishments lay out their patios, and you'll be threading through the tables which spread into the streets and squares.

**L'Ancien Théâtre**, 4 rue Racine (☎04.66.21.30.75). Just a 5min stroll west from the Maison Carrée, with zippy Mediterranean cuisine. Menus from 75F/€11.44. Closed Sat noon, Sun & early July.

**La Belle Respire**, 12 rue de l'Étoile (☎04.66.21.27.21). Located in the former quarters of one of Nîmes' most famous brothels, now a tastefully decorated restaurant serving deliciously prepared French cuisine, and a *carte* not overburdened by the usual Gardois fare. Prices around 140F/€21.35. Open until 11.30pm, closed Wed.

**La Bodega de Nîmes**, pl d'Assas (☎04.66.58.28.27). A relatively new place for Spanish food and tapas, with a good view of the Maison Carrée. A meal costs about 150F/€22.88.

**Le Chapon Fin**, pl Château-Falaise (☎04.66.67.34.73). A good no-nonsense family-run bistro featuring Gardois country cooking. One of the late-closing places in town (11.30pm). Menus from 75F/€11.44.

**Au Flan Coco**, 29 rue Mûrier-d'Espagne. A popular restaurant serving dishes prepared with market-fresh ingredients; it's particularly well known for its salads. Head for the patio in summer; otherwise there are two brightly decorated dining rooms. Expect to spend 80F/€12.20. Open Mon–Fri lunch & Sat dinner, closed Aug.

**Indien Punjab**, 8 bd Amiral-Courbet (☎04.66.76.01.21). Well-priced Tandoori restaurant open till midnight. Expect to spend around 80F/€12.20. Closed Mon midday.

**Le Jardin d'Hadrien**, 111 rue Enclos-Rey (☎04.66.21.86.65). Inventive cuisine based on local southeastern Gard tradition. Reasonable prices, too, with menus at 95–145F/€14.49–22.11. Closed Sun, Wed & part of Feb.

**Kebab**, 3 rue de Monnaie. Small Turkish place with great sandwiches and real Turkish coffee. Super-economical lunch specials for as little as 20F/€3.05.

**Le Magister**, 5 rue Nationale (☎04.66.76.11.00). Daring experimentation is the order of the day at this good *gastronomique* restaurant. Cod and salmon act as springboard for the most adventurous combinations, which blend tangy herbs with the sweetness of fruit. The 150F/€22.88 menu is a good bargain, and includes wine. Closed Sat noon & Sun, part of Feb, July & Aug.

**Ophélie**, 35 rue Fresque (☎04.61.21.00.19). An excellent choice, with good-value, quality food served in a seventeenth-century locale with romantic atmosphere. Open later than most. Menu at 140F/€21.35. Dinner only, closed Sun & Mon, part Feb & Aug.

**Le Paradis du Couvent**, 21 rue du Grand Couvent (☎04.66.76.26.30). Housed in a former convent, a large restaurant dishing out typical Provençal and Nîmoise cuisine. Open till midnight and you can eat from 55F/€8.39, so good value. Closed Mon out of season.

**Le P'tit Bec**, 87bis rue de la République (☎04.66.38.05.83). The best mid-range place for typical Gardoise cuisine, including the ever-present *bouef à la gardienne* and *brandade de morue*. Good menu options from 90F/€13.73, plus children's menus. Closed Sun eve & Mon.

**Simple Simon**, 11 rue Xavier Sigalon (☎04.66.76.01.21). Any restaurant in France daring to advertise English cuisine deserves credit. If you're tired of "under-cooked" meat, you can enjoy typically English dishes, such as fish-and-chips and pasties, here for 40–80F/€6.20–12.20. Closed Sun & Mon.

**La Truye qui Filhe**, 9 rue Fresque. Basic self-service place, incongruously tucked away in a fourteenth-century building. Fill up with *croque-monsieurs*, salads and the like from 50F/€7.63. Lunch only, closed Sun & Aug.

## Bars and cafés

Nîmes' two dominant types of drinking establishments are sedate neighbourhood **café-bars**, and louder and larger **music-bars**, which usually feature a DJ (or more rarely, unexceptional live music) on weekend nights. Smaller bars can be found scattered among the narrow streets of the town core, while the large, traditional-style café-bars are found on the wider streets such as boulevard Admiral-Courbet or Victor-Hugo, on either side of the old town.

**Café des Beaux-Arts**, pl aux Herbes. A cheerful and airy place with a good patio that's well located for people-watching, or simply for soaking up the ambience of the old medieval heart of Nîmes. Closed Sun.

**Café Carré d'Art**, bd Daudet. Great views of the city from inside the glassed-in interior or outside on the patio atop the museum of the same name. Open the same hours as the museum.

**La Casa Don Miguel**, 18 rue de l'Horloge. This popular and late-opening Spanish-style *bodega* is known for its cocktails and large variety of tapas. Closed Sun.

**Le Diagonal**, 41bis rue Émile-Jamais. Lively tapas bar which keeps hopping until 2am during the week, 3am Fri & Sat. Closed Mon & half of Aug.

**Le Grand Bourse**, 2 bd des Arènes. Solid, late-night bar and eatery. Menus from 85–100F/€12.96–15.25. Open daily till midnight.

**La Movida**, 2 la Placette. A Spanish bar with decent tapas and a gypsy/flamenco atmosphere that explodes during the *ferias*. Closed Sun & most of Aug.

**Café Napoléon**, top end of bd Victor Hugo. Famous old neighbourhood café – complete with faded wood décor, old cigar-chomping men in cardigans and unbeatable Gallic ambience. Great place for a refreshing mid-afternoon *pastis* break and right on the edge of the old town. Closed Sun.

**O'Flaherty's**, 26 bd Amiral-Courbet (☎04.66.67.22.63). British beer – seven kinds on tap – plus food and regular Thursday concerts of Irish, country and bluesgrass (except July & Aug). Open till 2–3am daily.

**Pub "Au Bureau"**, 24 bd Amiral Courbet (☎04.66.67.34.65). Massive bar and pool hall which also features live music on most weekends from Oct to May. Open late.

**Les Trois Maures**, 10 bd des Arènes. Fantastic old high-ceilinged bar beside the Arènes, festooned with bullfighting and rugby memorabilia and exceptionally busy during *ferias*. Open late. Closed Sun in July & Aug.

**Le Wine Bar**, 11 square de la Couronne (☎04.66.76.19.59). This is *the* place to begin your acquaintance with wines of Languedoc. All served up with traditional Gard cuisine. Closed Sun & Mon noon.

## Listings

**Airlines** Air France (☎08.02.80.28.02); Air Inter (☎04.66.70.70.70).

**Airport** The Aéroport International Garon (☎04.66.70.49.49).

**Banks and exchange** A number of banks have branches in the old town which offer currency exchange and ATMs.

**Bus departures** Intercity service leaves from the *gare routière* on bd Natoire (☎04.66.29.52.00; *www.stdgard.com*), connected by a footbridge to the gare SNCF. The main carriers are the SNCF and Cévennes Cars (☎04.66.29.27.29), although Sommières is served by Cariane Cars (☎04.66.38.13.98).

**Car rental** ADA, 6bis av Général Leclerc (☎04.66.84.25.60); Apex, 72 rue de la République (☎04.66.38.09.66); Astuce, at the *gare routière* (☎04.66.29.17.82); Avis, 1800 av du Maréchal Juin (☎04.66.29.05.33); Budget, 1800 av du Maréchal Juin (☎04.66.38.01.69); Europcar, 1bis rue de la République (☎04.66.21.31.35); National, 21 rue Notre Dame (☎04.66.21.03.62); Hertz, 5 bd de Prague (☎04.66.21.25.90). All except Astuce and Apex have airport offices as well.

**Children's activities** A good place to take the kids is Parc Aquatropic (☎04.66.38.31.00), a waterslide theme park near the Nîmes-Ouest *autoroute* exit, accessible by bus #D from outside the Halles shopping centre on bd Gambetta. Open summer only 9am–10pm.

**Hospital** Hôpital Gaston Doumerge, rue de la Biche (☎04.66.68.68.68).

**Internet access** Cyber Café Vauban, 34 rue Clérisseau (daily 10am–11pm).

**Laundry** There's a launderette on rue de Grand Couvent, at the corner of rue de Agau (daily 7am–9pm).

**Market** Farmers' market (Tues & Fri) and flea market (Mon morn) on av Jean-Jaurès; also general open-air market throughout the old town in July & Aug (Thurs 6–10pm).

**Police** *Mairie*, rue Hôtel de Ville (☎04.66.76.70.54).

**Taxi** TRAN (☎04.66.29.40.11). Their excursion to the Pont du Gard with a thirty-minute wait costs 250F/€38.13.

**Train information** (☎04.66.70.41.92).

# AROUND NÎMES

For such a small area, the southern portion of Gard contains a surprising number of draws for visitors. Just across the river Gardon to the north of Nîmes lies **Uzés**, the "First Duchy" of France, its castle still in the hands of a family which traces its roots back to Charlemagne. A few kilometres east of the city sits the **Pont du Gard**, perhaps the most famous of all Roman aqueducts, while along the Rhône, medieval **Beaucaire**'s castle and the uniquely sculpted facade of the church of **St-Gilles** deserve a visit. The southern edge of the *département*, sweeping west of here, is dominated by the westernmost branch of the swampy Rhône delta, the

**Petite Camargue** – an important way-station for migratory birds. On the west, the medieval walls of **Aigues-Mortes** are now besieged only by invading sun-seekers, crowding the beaches south of the town, around **Le Grau-du-Roi** and **Port-Camargue**. Upstream from Le Grau, on the Vidourle, **Sommières** and **Sauve** lie quietly languishing in forgotten obscurity, far from the bustle of the coast. Roman ruins pepper the entire area, including aqueducts, arches, and stretches of road still marked by milestones, and towns throughout the region share Nîmes' enthusiasm for the *corrida*; if possible trips should be planned to coincide with village *ferias*. The best time to visit the southern Gard is during the summer, when pleasure ports and beaches are busy, although inland towns follow a rhythm not so dependent on the sun. **Public transport** in the region is fairly good and, with the unfortunate exception of Uzès, the main towns are served by frequent bus and train routes. Distances, however, are not great and the generally even landscape make **cycling** and **hiking** good options.

# Uzès

Long disdained by the French literati as the proverbial "middle of nowhere", **UZÈS**, nestled among the rocky *garrigues* twenty kilometres north of Nîmes, has now been discovered. Like so many towns of the Gard, Uzès traces its history back to the time of the toga, when it served as an agricultural and local market centre, and it became the seat of a bishop as early as the fifth century. After the Counts of Toulouse lost the town to the French crown in 1229, their former under-lings, lords of Uzès, battled it out with the bishops for local control. These barons served the French kings well and were rewarded when the town was given the rank of the "First Duchy of France" in 1632 – the title had belonged to the Dukes of Montmorency until then, but they lost it as a consequence of Henri de Montmorency's failed revolt (see p.363). Like Nîmes, Uzès violently embraced Calvinism – becoming the fifth most important Huguenot centre in France – but once the movement was suppressed and the majority of Protestants fled, those "Catholics" that remained turned it into a wealthy silk town, which it remained for the next three hundred years. The early twentieth century brought depression and when the railway bypassed the town, the writing of Uzès' decline was on the wall. The history of the town's celebrities is also one of near misses: Guillaume de Grimoard, later to become Pope Urban V, was not from Uzès, but did live here for a while; the great seventeenth-century poet Jean Racine had an uncle from the town, and spent a year and a half here; while Charles Gide, father of Nobel-laureate author André, was a native – the junior Gide passed his childhood sum-mers here.

Today the town fairly packs out with tourists in summer months; each medieval stone arcade now conceals a bistro, and when the weather is good the restaurant patios which dominate the squares are frequented by buskers of surprising qual-ity. Saturday's traditional **market** is particularly lively, while gourmands will want to sample the **truffles** for which the town is renowned. If you're reliant on public transport and short on time the town is best visited on a day-trip that also takes in the **Pont du Gard**, 20km southwest; with only one bus daily to and from Uzès to Nîmes, and services to Remoulins (see p.225) far more frequent, heading for the aqueduct first gives you the most time in each spot.

# Arrival, information and accommodation

Uzès' **gare routière** (☎04.66.22.00.58) is located just west of the old town on Esplanade Maréchal de Lattre de Tassigny; from here it's a five-minute walk north along boulevard Gambetta to the **tourist office** (July & Aug Mon–Fri 9am–6pm, Sat 10am–noon & 2–5pm, Sun 10am–5pm; Sept–June Mon–Fri 9am–noon & 1.30–6pm, Sat 10am–1pm; ☎04.66.22.68.88, fax 04.66.25.95.19, *www.ville-uzes.fr*) in place Albert 1er, just north of the Duché. Web-surfers should head for the *Cyberland* **Internet** café on place Austerlitz (daily noon–2am), while **bikes** can be rented at Et Paysan on avenue General Vincent, one block west of the tourist office, which has free brochure of bike routes, including one to the Pont du Gard.

Most of the town's **hotels** reflect its noble past – which is to say, luxurious but pricey. The cheapest beds are found at the friendly *Hostellerie Provençal* (☎04.66.22.11.06; closed Sun & Mon eve Sept–June & Feb; ②) at 1 rue Grand Bourgade, near the church of St-Etienne. Next up is the attractively renovated *La Taverne* (☎04.66.22.13.10, fax 04.66.22.45.90, *www.logis-de-france.fr*; ③), behind the tourist office at 4 rue Xavier Sigalon. The only other option in town is the deluxe *General d'Entraigues*, 8 rue de la Calade (☎04.66.22.32.68, fax 04.66.22.57.01; ④), in a converted fifteenth-century mansion opposite the cathedral. And if you really want to treat yourself, the same owners also have rooms at the *Château d'Arpaillargues* (March–Oct; ☎04.66.22.14.48, fax 04.66.22.56.10; ⑥), a rural mansion converted into a hotel, located 4km northwest of town. Two **campsites** accommodate tenters in the warmer months – the municipal site (mid-June to mid-Sept; ☎04.66.22.11.79), set on the riverside 500m northeast of town on avenue Pascal, and *La Paillote* (mid-March to mid-Oct; ☎04.66.22.38.55), 500m along rue Xavier Sigalon. The local **gîte d'étape**, *L'Oregon* (☎04.66.22.16.25; April–Oct), is 1.5km north of Uzès, following avenue Pascal. It has one private room (②), in addition to its dorm (80F/€12.20) and guests have use of a kitchen.

# The Town

Uzès, the core of which can be walked in about an hour, is extremely easy to find your way around; the compact **old town** – shaped roughly like a kidney bean – is ringed by a broad one-way system. Within this perimeter the town is still dominated by the twelfth-century castle, **the Duché**, just south of the tourist office, while its other focal point, the place aux Herbes, lies a bit further southwest of the fortress. The **cathedral** sits overlooking the Alzon river on the eastern edge of the old town, as if pushed aside by the power of the town's dukes.

## The Duché

The old ducal castle of the de Cressol family, the **Duché** (daily: mid-June to mid-Sept 10am–6.30pm; mid-Sept to mid-June 10am–noon & 2–6pm; ☎04.66.22.18.96) is the centrepiece of Uzès, and the sight of its towering *donjon* topped by the family's red and yellow-banded pennant is a Hollywoodesque but authentic medieval tableau. The compact walled *enceinte* rises dramatically from amidst the old town's buildings, concealing a courtyard presided over by a majestically columned Renaissance facade, and a small garden, as well as the bulky and crude keep. Claiming roots which go back to Charlemagne and St Louis, the de Cressols are proud of their long lineage, and their motto *ferro non auro* – "by iron [ie the sword], not gold" – sets them apart from the later families who bought their way

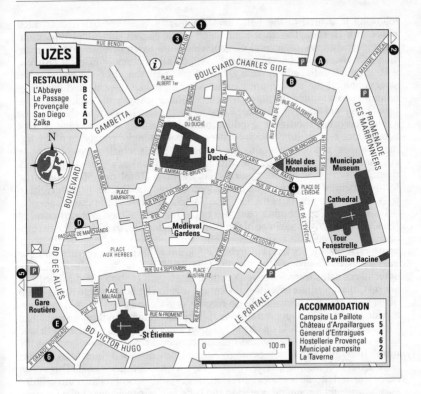

into the aristocracy. Their stay in Uzès has not been continuous, however, as the Revolution precipitated a hiatus which lasted until 1954. Among the most colourful of its members was the Duchess Anne (grandmother of the present Duke); monarchist, suffragette and enthusiastic hunter (she killed over 2000 animals), this energetic woman rode until the age of 87, and was France's first female driver (and the first to receive a speeding ticket). Despite the fact that it is still a part-time residence for the dukes, the castle can be visited on an entertaining hour-long **guided tour** (55F/€8.39; an English-language handout is provided), although given its price the budget-conscious may opt only to climb the tenth-century **Tour Bermonde** (25F/€3.81), from the top of which you can peek out between the battlements and admire fine views. The main tour through the family's apartments is entertaining and offers an intimate look at a disappearing aristocratic world, with personal effects set amongst the rare furnishings and ancient books. The visit wraps up in the castle's ancient cellars, where guests are invited to taste the Duke's own vintage (also on sale, of course) and buy grossly overpriced Provençal statuettes.

### The rest of the old town

The castle is far from Uzès' only attraction, and a wander through the dense and evocative alleys of the old town is a true pleasure. Leaving the Duché and following it around to the left, rue Dampmartin leads towards the arcaded **place aux Herbes**, the route punctuated by the carved stone doorframes and casement windows of several elegant sixteenth- to eighteenth-century mansions. Crossing the *place* towards the eighteenth-century St-Étienne **church**, with its thirteenth-century belfry, brings you past the old Gide house – the streets behind the church are pleasantly quiet, unlike the café and boutique-crammed area around the *place* to the west. Rue Foussat leads back up into the heart of the old town; on rue Port Royal, off to the left, look out for the entrance to the recreated **medieval garden** (daily: July & Aug 3–7pm; June & Sept 2–6pm; Oct 2–5pm; 10F/€1.53, children free) – set in the courtyard of the former bishops' palace, it contains the herbs and plants which were collected or cultivated in the area during the Middle Ages and makes a great stop for children. Further up, at the dour entrance to the plain **Hôtel des Monnaies** (the former bishops' mint), you can either loop back to the Duché, or turn right to pass the sumptuous Hôtel du baron de Castille to arrive at the cathedral.

Following the fate of other churches of the region, the medieval **cathedral** of Uzès fell victim to the violence of the Wars of Religion but, thankfully, the twelfth-century bell tower, the **Tour Fenestrelle**, survived. Rising 42m above the plaza on which it sits, the six levels of arched windows on this round structure – unique in France – recall strongly the "leaning tower" of Pisa. The new cathedral, on the other hand, dates from the seventeenth to nineteenth centuries and is hardly of interest, apart from its seventeenth-century organ. The broad verge to the south of the cathedral, the **promenade de Racine**, provides pleasant views of the countryside and river, and sports a curious eighteenth-century **pavilion** resembling a Victorian bandstand, built on one of the town wall's old towers. On the north side of the cathedral the sombre and hulking episcopal palace is now home to the **municipal museum** (Tues–Sun: July & Aug 10am–noon & 3–6pm; March–June, Sept & Oct 3–6pm; Nov, Dec & Feb 2–5pm; 10F/€1.53), which holds Polynesian relics carried home by local missionaries, some decent eighteenth-century portraiture, and a room dedicated to the Gide family, consisting of manuscripts, photographs, furniture and personal effects.

# Eating and drinking

Uzès' recent tourist boom has been good news for diners, as the town suffers from a surplus of **eating** establishments – stiff competition meaning good prices. Among the terraces which clutter the old town and line the ring road, a number of establishments stand out. The finest (and most expensive) dining is found at the restaurant of the *General d'Entraigues*, where menus are 125–200F/€19.06–30.50, and can be enjoyed on the panoramic terrace. For cheaper *terroir* cuisine, try *L'Abbaye*, 24 boulevard Charles-Gide (closed winter; ☎04.66.22.91.21) – a traditional family-run bistro with menus from 65F/€9.91. *San Diego* (closed Mon & Feb; ☎04.66.22.20.78) a few doors away at no. 16 is a better option both for its refreshing décor and generous servings; the plentiful menus here can be enjoyed from 77F/€11.74. The *Provençale*, on rue Grande Bourgade (☎04.66.22.11.06) has lunch menus featuring savoury dishes from neighbouring Provence from as low as 39F/€5.95, while vegetarians should head for *Zaïka* (☎04.66.03.27.37), an Indian restaurant on passage du Marchands. Couscous (55F/€8.39) is the speciality at *Le Passage*, 37 boulevard Gambetta, but also check out the four-course French menus from 65F/€9.91.

For a **drink**, try *Au Suisse d'Alger* on rue République, near place aux Herbes; it has a lively terrace and wine by the glass is very reasonably priced. Later in the evening *Bar l'Encas*, at the corner of Gambetta and République, is the place to head for – in addition to its pool table and good selection of beers, it has a terrace where off-duty buskers often sit down for an impromptu jam.

# The Pont du Gard and around

No one with even a passing interest in history or architecture should go through the Gard without seeing what is arguably the world's most famous Roman aqueduct, the **PONT DU GARD**, 20km to the northeast of Nîmes. But even if your interests lie elsewhere, the site merits a visit for its pleasant but stony river-beach and excellent **picnic** and **hiking** possibilities. While in the area, several of the hamlets nearby are worth checking out too, as is the **medieval bridge** of St-Nicholas, further up the Gardon river. The aqueduct can be visited as a day-trip from Nîmes and combined with a visit to Uzès but if you're planning an overnight sojourn, you can stay by the Pont itself, in the service town of **Remoulins**, 2km away or, particularly if you have some transport, in one of the hamlets which cluster between Uzès and Remoulins.

## The Pont du Gard

When the Romans needed to supply growing Nîmes with water, they found that the nearest suitable source was some 50km away on the Eure river, near Uzès. Despite the deep Gardon gorge which cut through the route, with Roman single-mindedness (and slave labour), they set about to construct a waterway. This remains nothing short of a technical marvel, descending only 17m in height along its course and bridging the Gardon with a monumental aqueduct, the **Pont du Gard**. Most likely constructed in the mid-first century, the Pont's three tiers of arches span an incredible 275m of length, carrying water 49m above the riverbed below. Pillaged for stone through the ages, and first used as a bridge in 1295, the

---

### A HIKE TO THE PONT DU GARD

The best way to get to the Pont du Gard and take in a bit of the countryside of the *garrigues* at the same time, is to **hike** from St-Bonnet-du-Gard. Buses don't pass through St-Bonnet, so if you don't have transport you'll have to begin by walking 3km southwest from Remoulins along the D86. As you pass the *mairie* in the centre of the village, turn off to the right to pick up the trail. From here, the GR6 leads through a level swath of vineyards before climbing the rise known as the "Falaises". At the top, the trail forks, and you can take either branch, proceeding through the low scrubby trees and past the remains of several Roman arches before reaching the Pont. The right branch, which is the GR6, is the more direct route, and takes you just to the east of the aqueduct itself. The left branch continues for 500m, passing a modern cistern, before ending in a T-junction. Turning right here, you will arrive at the top tier of the southern end of the Pont after 2km. If the passage is not closed for repairs, you'll then be able to traverse the aqueduct before descending.

aqueduct has suffered various misfortunes, including an earthquake of 1448, but there was enough of the structure remaining to begin a comprehensive restoration in the eighteenth century; when Rousseau passed by shortly after this work had been undertaken, the sight of the monument was enough to make him say he wished he'd been born a Roman. A visit here used to be a must for French journeymen masons on their traditional tour of the country, and many of them have left their names and home towns carved on the stonework. Among these the markings made by the original builders to facilitate construction can also still be found. For the moment, the top tier is under renovation (reopening has been continually postponed), and you can only cross the broad lower level. The best way to enjoy this ancient engineering wonder however, is to take it in from different perspectives, climbing up to the lookout areas at the top of either end, or viewing it upriver from the bed of the Gardon. Seen from here on a sunny day, the utilitarian but gracefully symmetrical beauty of the aqueduct's yellow-stone structure presents a striking contrast to the blue sky.

## Around the Pont du Gard

The Pont du Gard is a great place to cool down on a hot day (although the river slows to a trickle in August), and this part of the Eure is an easy stretch for **canoeing** and **kayaking** (see below). Two kilometres south of the aqueduct lies the **château de St-Privat**, the site where Richelieu signed the Peace of Alés with the Huguenots in 1629 (the lords of the castle, the Faret family, were Protestants) and famous for its elaborate formal garden, which dates back to 1644. One of the gardens' three sections, the "Avant-park", is home to the War Sacrifice Chapel, commissioned after World War I by then-owner Jacques Rouché; its walls are decorated with works of metaphysical allegory, mixing biblical figures with depictions of *poilus* (French common soldiers). Unfortunately the property can only be visited on a ninety-minute **guided tour** (July & Aug daily 3pm; May to mid-Nov Sat & Sun 3pm; 30F/€4.58) leaving from the Pont's tourist office (see below). Moving on from the aqueduct, the best way to leave is to hike along the Gardon gorge to the Pont St-Nicholas. The GR6 on the north bank and the AR6 on the south (passing St-Privat) lead to **Collias** 4km away, once a hippie Mecca, from where the GR6 can be followed upriver. Aside from the rugged beauty of the riverbed's red cliffs, watch out for the **Grotte de la Baume**, on the north bank after Collias, a cave with a medieval chapel set amongst what were once the rocky abodes of hermits. Finally, some 10km after Collias, you reach the ponderous and chunky thirteenth-century **Pont St-Nicholas**, now incorporated into the main Uzès–Nîmes highway. There are also some interesting hamlets along the Uzès–Remoulins road, the best of which (and also the one where the most buses stop) is **Vers**, only 4km north of the Pont, where you'll find bits of ruined arches and chunks of Roman road lying around town, and an eleventh-century church. Other nearby villages include **St-Hilaire** and **Castillon-du-Gard**, ancient and picturesque farming settlements which don't have any particular sights, but are worth wandering around.

## Practicalities

The Pont itself can be reached by **bus** direct from Nîmes (there is a stop on the south riverbank), or via Remoulins (a thirty-minute walk away), which is served by buses from Uzès and Nîmes. Those arriving by **car** can park in official spaces on either bank of the river or for free along the road before reaching the site. There is a **tourist office** (June–Sept daily 9am–noon & 2–6pm; ☎04.66.37.00.22) right by the aqueduct, just past the clutch of restaurants and shops on the south bank. For **canoe rental**, head to Kayak Vert (☎04.66.22.80.76, *Kayak.Vert@wanadoo.fr*, *www.canoe-france.com*) on the south shore, but if you're just going to splash around, keep your sandals on or buy some cheap plastic shoes to survive the pebbly bed of the Gardon. Remoulins has conveniences such as **banks** and **supermarkets**.

For **accommodation** right by the aqueduct, the cosy *Le Colombier* (☎04.66.37.05.28, fax 04.66.37.35.75, *www.logis-de-france.fr*; ③), on the right bank, offers facilities including parking, television and a restaurant. **Remoulins** itself has a surprising number of hotels, the best of which is the *Moderne*, at 8 avenue Perret-Geoffroy (closed early Nov; ☎04.66.37.20.13, fax 04.66.37.01.85, *hotelmoderne@wanadoo.fr*; ③), a mid-sized hotel with good amenities and helpful staff. Preferable to either of these however are the *L'Arceau* (closed late Nov to mid-Feb; ☎04.66.37.34.45, fax 04.66.37.33.90, *www.logis-de-france.fr*; ④) in **St Hilaire** and the *Gorges du Gardon* (closed Nov to mid-March; ☎04.66.22.80.54, fax 04.66.22.88.98, *www.logis-de-france.fr*; ③) in **Collias**, which offer similar amenities, but in more picturesque surroundings. Options in **Castillon** range from the humble and basic *Tuilleries* hotel (☎04.66.37.08.47, fax 04.66.37.02.43; ②) to the extremely luxurious *Vieux Castillon* (closed Jan to mid-Feb; ☎04.66.37.61.61, fax 04.66.37.28.17; ⑨). Also in Castillon, the restored farmhouse, *Mas de Raffin* (☎04.66.37.13.28; ④), provides rustic accommodation, but with all of the conveniences and English-speaking staff. In **Vers**, you can choose between the atmospheric *Vieux Moulin* (closed mid-Nov to mid-March; ☎04.66.37.14.35, fax 04.66.37.26.48; ⑤) close by the Roman bridge and the *Bégude St-Pierre* (☎04.66.63.63.63, fax 04.66.22.73.73; ⑧) a former seventeenth-century stage-post converted into a luxury hotel, located just outside the village. The Turions also have several well-appointed rooms at their farm (Easter–Oct; ☎04.66.37.18.11; ③) in the village, as well as providing the cheapest option in the region around the Pont with their three-room **gîte d'étape** located near the farm (open May–Sept; ☎06.86.90.44.84; 75F/€11.74). Those who hike on to the **Pont St-Nicholas** can stay at the modern *La Chaumière* (closed Oct–Mar; ☎04.66.22.16.06; ②), set right along the gorge's southern edge, some 500m east of the bridge.

There are four **campsites** in the area, all with cabins or trailers for rent. *La Sousta* (March–Nov; ☎04.66.37.12.80, *lasousta@aol.com*) has the widest range of facilities and lies on the south bank of the Gardon, right by the Pont. *La Soubeyranne* (April to mid-Sept; ☎04.66.37.03.21, *soubeyranne@wanadoo.fr*), on the other side of Remoulins, is more expensive but you may have little choice as campsites here often book up in high season. The *Gorges du Gardon* (mid-March to Sept; ☎04.66.22.81.81, fax 04.66.22.90.12) in Vers is the cheapest around, while *Le Barralet* (open April–Sept; ☎04.66.22.84.52, fax 04.66.22.89.17) in Collias wins out on both location and value – located on the riverside, it is cheap and far from the maddening crowds.

The most pleasant option for **eating** in the area is to have a **picnic** on the banks of the river. Each of the hotels noted above has a restaurant, most with *terroir* menus in the 90–150F/€13.73–22.88 price range – the most sophisticated is that of *La Bégude St-Pierre* in Vers (150–280F/€22.88–42.70 menus), whose *carte* features variations on local *terroir* themes (notable in the predominance of beef) as well as the surrounding country's best selection of wines. There's also *Le Clos de Vignes* (closed Mon & Tues midday & mid-Jan to mid-Feb; ☎04.66.37.02.26) in Castillon, which serves up good, inexpensive local food on two pleasantly situated terraces.

# Beaucaire and around

Located on the banks of the Rhône and crossed by the Roman Via Domitia, **BEAUCAIRE**'s success was grounded in its position as a crossroads, and as one of the region's main gateways – Provençal Tarascon lies just across the river. From the second century BC it was a Roman wine entrepôt known as Ugernum; when this disappeared along with the empire, the town was refounded in the tenth century, after which the Counts of Toulouse built the strong citadel which caps its hill. Under their patronage it throve, becoming an economic and cultural centre. But with the outbreak of the Albigensian crusade, Simon de Montfort seized the castle, and though Raymond VII of Toulouse eventually returned to the Catholic fold and to Beaucaire, accessing the walled town in 1216, Simon's men would not let him in to the castle. So, aided by the townsfolk, Raymond laid siege to the castle from within the town, while Simon, who had arrived in the meantime, laid siege to the town from without. Raymond prevailed in this strange double siege – a rare defeat for the fierce de Montfort – and the jubilant count granted the town the right to hold a yearly **trade fair** as a reward, which, bringing merchants from all over Europe, the Middle East and North Africa, survived the town's transition to the French crown in 1229 and continued to be held through the nineteenth century. Trade routes shifted, however, and by the time Richelieu ordered the castle torn down in 1632, Beaucaire was already a backwater.

Nowadays, the town presents a strange dichotomy. Although in summer, the tree-lined canal is alive with waterfront restaurants and the busy leisure of the boaters who ply the canals to Sète and Montpellier, the old town is a singularly decrepit area – a marginalized industrial neighbourhood which shows the stresses of high unemployment and unintegrated immigration. At night it takes on a fairly sinister aspect: dark and narrow streets and small deserted squares where care should be taken when walking; you should also avoid parking here. With all of this, Beaucaire doesn't necessarily merit making a special effort to visit, except perhaps during late-July's "Estival" festivities, but can be a rewarding stop for those passing through. This is particularly worth considering if you have your own transport, as the interesting **Roman** and **medieval** vestiges around the town are better reached by car, although **hiking** and **biking** are possible as well. The best time to visit Beaucaire is during June's traditional Fête du Drac or July's Estivales, a medieval pageant celebrating the town's once-famous fair.

## The Town

The limits of Beaucaire are roughly defined by the Sète canal on the south, the Rhône River on the east, and the castle-topped hill which rises sharply on the north side. Walking from the canal, there are only one or two sights as you make your way across the old town towards the castle. Just north of the tourist office sits the town's most noteworthy building, the Neoclassical **Hôtel de Ville**. This fine seventeenth-century edifice has a colonnaded facade and window casements lavishly carved in floral motifs; inside, the courtyard (Mon–Fri 10am–noon & 2–5pm) is girded by slender columns and dominated by a monumental staircase. Unfortunately the *hôtel*'s beauty is diminished by its surroundings; the scruffy and inhospitable place Georges-Clémenceau. On the south side squats the small nineteenth-century metal-and-glass **market**, whose picturesque quality is offset by the decaying shop fronts and miserable-looking bars neighbouring it. Beaucaire's main **church**, Notre-Dame de Pommiers, lying two streets beyond, has a plain facade which hides a gaudy and unexceptional late-Baroque marble interior. The church's real treasure is found on the building's exterior, which you will pass if you follow rue Charlier towards the castle – here, high up on the east wall, is the only remaining part of the original Romanesque structure: a remarkable low-relief frieze recounting scenes from the eve of the Crucifixion. Aside from these specific sights, you should also keep an eye out in Beaucaire for the seventeenth-century merchant's **mansions** which pop up en route to the castle, notably along rue de la République at the foot of the hill; the palace at no. 23, for example, has a strikingly elaborate facade, including caryatid columns on either side of the entrance. From the west end of rue de la République a stiff climb leads up the rise, dramatically crowned by the remains of the former keep.

Poised on a rocky promontory rising 35m above the Rhône, Beaucaire's **castle** provides dramatic views of the surrounding countryside, including one down over Tarascon's own castle. Fortunately, Richelieu did not manage to completely destroy the fortress. The fourteenth-century **curtain wall** survives, as do several towers, including the striking **Tour Polygonale**, shooting dramatically skyward out of the living rock of the hill. The castle now hosts an entertaining medieval **falconry** display, "Les Aigles", with hourly live demonstrations (daily: July & Aug 3–6pm; March–June 2–5pm; Sept–Nov 2.30–4.30pm, closed Wed off-season; 45F/€6.86) – the only way of visiting the castle ruins. On the other hand, the eighteenth-century listed **gardens** which fill the outer courtyard can be visited free of charge (daily: April–Oct 10am–noon & 2.15–6.45pm; Nov–March 10.15am–noon & 2–5.15pm; closed Wed off-season), and within these sits the municipal **Musée Auguste-Jacquet** (same hours; 13F/€1.98) – a conglomeration of small collections of medieval bits and bobs, local rocks and paraphernalia relating to Beaucaire's annual fair. On Friday nights during the summer the castle is the backdrop for the *son et lumière* "Raymond VII and the Siege of Beaucaire" (July & Aug daily 10pm), which floods the castle buildings in garish colour while recounting the town's moment of medieval glory.

## Practicalities

To get to Beaucaire by **train** you will arrive at Tarascon's **gare SNCF** (☎08.36.35.35.35) on boulevard Gustave-Desplaces, just across the Rhône. From here, you cross over the bridge, a ten-minute walk which brings you to the Rhône à Sète canal, or take a Nîmes-bound bus from the "Café de Fleurs" stop across from the station. Arriving by **bus** (information on ☎04.66.29.27.29), make sure to get off at "Passarelle" (the footbridge), which is the third stop coming from Nîmes, and the first from Tarascon. Those who come by **car** should be wary of the more isolated public parking spaces; it's safest to park outside the tourist office or on the far side of the canal. Beaucaire's friendly **tourist office**, 24 cours de Gambetta (Mon–Fri 9am–12.30pm & 2–6.30pm, Sat 9am–12.30pm & 3–6pm;

July & Aug also Sun 9am–noon; ☎04.66.59.26.57, fax 04.66.59.68.51, *beaucair @mnet.fr*) is on the north side of the canal, opposite the footbridge. Beaucaire's **pleasure port** offers everything from pedal-boats to yachts for rent, as well as cruises and custom trips down the Rhône into the bird-rich delta of the Camargue. One of the best itineraries is to the bird sanctuary at Pont de Gau, off the Petit Rhône. If you are looking to pick up a car in town, there are two **car rental** outfits: Avis, in the Total petrol station at 6 rue Général-de-Gaulle (☎04.66.59.29.89) and ADA, in the Le Mistral petrol station on route de Nîmes (☎04.66.59.37.77).

Beaucaire does not have the widest selection of **hotels**, but at least there is some range of price. At the lower end of the scale, the tiny and basic *Napoleon* at 4 place Frédéric Mistral (☎04.66.59.05.17; ②) reposes in the shadow of the *digue*, the massive flood dyke which protects the town from the Rhône. *Le Jardin d'Isis* (☎04.66.59.30.74; ③), no. 3 on the tree-lined boulevard Maréchal Foch, is more pleasant and only slightly more costly. Finally, for those willing to splash out, the three-star *Doctrinaires* (☎04.66.59.23.70, fax 04.66.59.22.26; ④) on Quai Général de Gaulle wins for comfort, atmosphere and location, set as it is in a seventeenth-century building overlooking the port. The 65-bed **HI hostel** is over in Tarascon at 39 boulevard Gambetta (closed mid-Nov to Feb; ☎04.90.91.04.08, *tarascon@fuaj.org*; 65F/€9.91), a ten-minute walk north of the Tarascon train station; it has dining facilities, a washing machine, but also a distressingly early 11pm curfew. The town's **campsite**, *Le Rhodanien* (June to mid-Sept; ☎04.66.59.25.50), lies on the north side of the castle by the fair ground and the bullring.

For **restaurants** the best deals are the *Brasserie du Midi* along the canal at 29 Quai de Gaulle (open daily; menus for 35–50F/€5.34–7.63) and, next door, *Le Soleil* (lunches from 55F/€8.39), both of which have traditional regional-based *cartes*. More interesting are the Portuguese *Churrasqueira*, no. 5 on Quai de Gaulle (closed Sun; lunch only, but dinners on Fri July & Aug; menus from 60–180F/€9.15–27.45), and *Ugernum Taverne* on place de la République (closed Sun), which has an eclectic menu (options from 60F/€9.15). For those looking for something more formal, the restaurant of the *Jardin d'Isis* (open until midnight) features Provençal fare for 100F/€15.25 and up, while the *Doctrinaires* (closed Sat midday) is as fancy as it gets here; service and atmosphere are good and there is a solid range of meat and fish options for up to 240F/€36.60.

# Around Beaucaire

Four kilometres northwest of Beaucaire, off the Remoulins road just before the dam on the Rhône, lies the turn-off for the **underground monastery of St-Roman** (July & Aug daily 10am–6.30pm; April–June & Sept daily 10am–6pm; Nov–March Sat & Sun 2–5pm; 20F/€3.05); to get there, follow the road 3km to the monastery car park, then walk 500m to the site itself. This incredible complex, founded in the fifth century, is one of the oldest monasteries in France. Later covered over by a castle which was subsequently destroyed, the huge abbey was not rediscovered until 1966. The subterranean main chapel – built to house the sacred remains of St Roman – still contains the impressive carved seat from which the abbots presided over their community until the sixteenth century. Inside you'll also find small tombs carved in the floor, and set with recesses in which oil-lamps were placed in honour of the dead. This church, the monks' cells and other chambers, were cut into the living rock of the hill in what must have been painstaking work. The terrace of the monastery offers a sweeping panorama of the Rhône, with the hills of Provence easily visible in the distance. Also worth a trip is a well-preserved eight-kilometre stretch of the **Via Domitia** leading west from Beaucaire, which still boasts three Roman **milestones**. One of the better ways to visit the site is to combine it with a visit to the recreated Roman winery of **Le Mas de Tourelles** (July & Aug Mon–Sat 10am–noon & 2–7pm; April–June & Sept–Nov Mon–Sat 2–6pm; Dec–March Sat 2–6pm; 27F/€4.12), 8km west of town on the D38 (no public transport). This is an entertaining stop, where you can see toga-clad types stomping, making wine with reconstructed first-century AD technology; you can taste the final result before drawing your own conclusions as to its "Roman" accuracy. From the vineyard it's a thirty-minute signposted walk north to the Roman road; when you reach it, turn right and you will arrive shortly at the milestones.

# St-Gilles and around

Twenty-six kilometres southwest of Beaucaire and 20km south of Nîmes lies the former pilgrims' stop of **St-Gilles**, another town whose candle blew out in the late Middle Ages, and whose only present attraction is the magnificent and fortunately preserved facade of its former **abbey-church** (a UNESCO World Heritage monument). St-Gilles is also a possible gateway to the vast and swampy Petite Camargue (see p.238) which surrounds it on the eastern and southern sides; moving away from town, the stony ground becomes increasingly sandy and marshy, and vineyards give way to flower farms, rice paddies and bull and horse ranches (*manades*), as the Rhône spills out to sea. The band of flat grape-growing land which stretches west from the town to the River Vidourle is punctuated by nondescript hamlets; it is here, near the town of **Vauvert**, that the famous **Perrier spring** and bottling plant sits – a site of modern Gallic pilgrimage.

## St-Gilles

Perched on the edge of the Camargue, quiet **ST-GILLES** – with its tiny, entirely residential old centre – is, like Beaucaire, a town rescued from complete oblivion only by its medieval monuments and the Rhône à Sète canal, each of which ensure a steady stream of passers by in summer months. The town takes its name from a legendary sixth-century hermit who converted the Visigothic king Wamba to Christianity. The ever-astute Cluniac monks promoted the cult of the saint in order to make the town (already on the Arles route to Santiago de Compostela) a lucrative stopping point early in the twelfth century – it was already a favourite of the Counts of Toulouse, and the crusader Raymond VI even preferred to be called "de St-Gilles". A good port and liberal market privileges further boosted prosperity and drew traders from around the Mediterranean, but within a few hundred years the unstoppable sands of the Rhône and the tide of the Reformation conspired to kill both the port and the pilgrim route. The Wars of Religion were especially bitter in St-Gilles – at one point a Protestant mob is said to have thrown the church's choristers down a well – and by the time the great **abbey-church** was virtually destroyed by Huguenot mobs in 1622, the town had already passed into history. Today the town's two principal roles have been revived: it has both a busy canalside **pleasure port**, and the pilgrim route to Compostela, which lives on as the GR653, coming into town from Arles and heading on west through the flat vineyards to Vauvert (see below) and on to Montpellier. The biggest festivities of St-Gilles take place in mid-August, with the Feria de la Pêche et de l'Abricot ("The Peach and Apricot Festival") featuring *abrivados, encierros* and full-blown *corridas*.

## The Town
The only part of St-Gilles which is likely to interest you is the **old town**, which lies on the eastern side of rue Gambetta, the main Arles–Montpellier road. Rue Gambetta ends at the tourist office, opposite which an arched passageway leads into the rue Porte des Marchaux, which takes you into the old centre and up to the **abbey-church**; as you round the last bend in the street and enter the compact place de la République, you'll be greeted by the stunning sight of its broad facade. Although the Religious Wars destroyed almost all of the church, fate spared the most interesting work of medieval art of the region: the great twelfth-century Romanesque **frieze** of the church's west entrance. Spreading between and over the three great doorways (reminiscent of a Roman triumphal arch), a series of bas-reliefs convey the story of Jesus' return to Jerusalem and subsequent cruci-fixion, representations of the Apostles, the three Marys and St Paul, and scenes based on the Old Testament and medieval iconography. These carvings are of superlative workmanship, a unique blend of Byzantine, Classical and medieval stylings setting them apart from the mass of contemporary work; they're best viewed (and photographed) in the afternoon, when the sunlight plays across the carvings. Aside from this entrance, two other interesting remains of the medieval church can be seen: the **choir** and the **crypt** (Mon–Sat: July & Aug 9am–noon & 3–7pm; June & Sept 9am–noon & 2–6pm; Oct–May 9am–noon & 2–5pm; 15F/€2.29 for both). Located behind the modern building, the ruins of the for-mer choir hint at the grandeur of the medieval church. On the north side lies the "vis", a twelfth-century stone **spiral staircase** which once climbed to the church's upper gallery: an architectural marvel – a massive self-supporting key-stone stairway – it was another mandatory stop on the traditional masons' tour of the country. From a gate on the south side of the church entrance, you can enter the massive vaulted eleventh-century crypt, which contains the **tombs** of St-Gilles and Pierre de Castelnau, and which is where services for the crowds of passing pilgrims were also held.

Opposite the church sits the **Maison Romane**, a restored medieval house in which it is claimed Gui Folques, who became Pope Clement IV in 1265, was born – it now houses a municipal **museum** of slight interest (Mon–Sat: July & Aug 9am–noon & 3–7pm; June & Sept 9am–noon & 2–6pm; Oct–Dec & Feb–May 9am–noon & 2–5pm, closed Jan; free) – mostly full of chunks of carved stone sal-vaged from the wrecked abbey-church as well as a dusty exhibition of stuffed birds. Before leaving St-Gilles, it is well worth taking a few minutes to wander around the narrow lanes and arch-covered streets of the old town – many of the tiny houses here retain their medieval details and it won't take long for you to dis-cover small doors set in slowly sagging walls, and half-open windows revealing pastel-toned plaster walls and ceiling beams within.

## Practicalities
St-Gilles' **gare routière** (☎04.66.87.31.32), 100m south of the tourist office and just north of the canal, is a fifteen-minute walk from the centre, to the northeast.

Arriving by **car**, stop in the free municipal car park on the west side of the old town – just off rue Gambetta. You'll find the **tourist office** at place Frédéric Mistral (July & Aug Mon–Sat 9am–noon & 3–7pm, Sun 10am–noon; Sept–June Mon–Sat 9am–noon & 2–5pm; ☎04.66.87.33.75 fax 04.66.87.16.28), at the northern end of rue Gambetta. The town's **hotels** all lie within a few minutes' walk of the *gare routière* and the canal. *Le Provence*, 7 rue Gambetta (☎04.66.87.31.38; ②) is the best budget option – a tiny hotel in a converted house, with simple but clean rooms. Only slightly more upmarket, the *Ste-Gillois* (☎04.66.87.33.69; ②) at 1 rue Nueve also does good-value half-pensions. For better amenities, head for *Le Cours*, 10 allée Griffeuille (closed late Dec to late Feb; ☎04.66.87.31.93, *www.logis-de-france.fr*; ③), or the three-star *Heracle*, 30 Quai du Canal (☎04.66.87.44.10, fax 04.66.87.13.65; closed Jan–Mar; ③). The **campsite**, *Chicanettes* (closed Nov–April; ☎04.66.87.28.32), is in town, just behind the public car park. For eating, St-Gilles offers a number of unremarkable but adequate *terroir* **restaurants** and pizzerias around the canal port, while those intent on dining well should head to the restaurant of *Le Cours*, where, for around 140F/€21.35, you can enjoy well-executed and imaginative cuisine in the recently renovated dining room – the local speciality is *taureau* (*bouef*) *à la gardianne*.

# Around St-Gilles

Although Aigues-Mortes is better situated for exploring the **Petite Camargue**, St-Gilles can also serve as a jumping-off point to the region by either boat or on horseback. The portion of the delta near St-Gilles is far from the coast, and comparatively dry and uniform: an expanse of salt marshes, with a bull or horse farm set wherever the land rises far enough above the water table. Several of the horse farms near St-Gilles offer half- and full-day **horseback** and **carriage tours** around their land, the cheapest of which is Manade Lebret (☎04.66.87.22.04), some 10km from St-Gilles (east on the N572 to the D37, and then south). Whether you approve of the *corrida* or not, a visit to a *manade* is an interesting experience – a chance to see the traditional lifestyle of the ranches of the delta, and witness the impressive equestrian skills of the *gardians* ("cowboys") who manage the herds. The tourist office in St-Gilles has a list of the twenty or so ranches in the area and can indicate which have English-speaking guides and which charge admission to visitors. If you choose to go by water, Crown Blue Line (☎04.66.87.22.66) in St-Gilles operates a boat rental service, and L'Isle de Stel (☎06.80.83.82.01) has a combination cruiseboat-bar which runs various itineraries along the network of canals and the Petit Rhône.

The flat band of plain between St-Gilles and the Vidourle river 20km to the west comprises a sort of transition zone between the salty swamps to the south and the rocky hills around Nîmes. A shadeless countryside of vineyards and indistinguishable hamlets, it is, however, home to one of France's proudest commercial institutions, the **Perrier spring and bottling plant**, located a few minutes' drive north of **Vauvert**, just before you reach the village of Vergèze. The source of France's second most famous bubbly stuff, the much-advertised **spring** (July & Aug Mon–Fri 9am–7pm, Sat & Sun 9.30am–7pm; Sept to mid-Dec & mid-Jan to June Mon–Fri 9am–6pm, Sat & Sun 1–7pm; ☎04.66.87.61.01) is a site venerated by the Gallic hordes who arrive daily, happily paying 30F/€4.58 a head to buoy along the two-hour tour, sharing vicariously in the glory of the water which has come to signify France abroad. The spring was known in Roman times, but subsequently languished in obscurity until 1894, when a certain Dr Perrier of Nîmes bought the property and set up the Perrier Spring Company in partnership with a young English aristocrat, who came up with the distinctive shape for the bottle. The **guided tour** includes a walk through the vast and modern bottling complex, a visit to the spring itself, and ends at the former owner's mansion, this last now the Perrier "museum" – a thinly disguised shop where you can pay ridiculously high prices for various bits of merchandise. Judging by the guest-book, the tour is a big domestic hit, but non-French – unless they are avid spring-water enthusiasts – are likely to regard the experience as time and money mis-spent.

If you head to the Perrier plant from Vauvert keep an eye out for the turrets of **Château du Candiac**, more or less at the halfway point, on the river bank off the right-hand side of the D56. It was here that the Marquis of Montcalm (1712–59), who unsuccessfully defended Quebec against the English general James Wolf, was born. Montcalm could not save the French colony from the invaders, and both he and his adversary died in the battle fought on the Plains of Abraham out-side the city.

# The Camarguaise coast

Lying 35km south of Nîmes, set amidst the flat swampy land of the westernmost reaches of the Rhône delta, sits **Aigues-Mortes**, its perfectly intact rectangular walls rising out of the plain around it like a storybook image of a medieval town. An ancient canal leads southwest to **Le Grau-du-Roi**, once a humble fishing town, now a teeming **summer resort**, exploiting the great unbroken band of dunes which stretch along the coast from the town's eastern limits all the way to the mouth of the Petit Rhône. **Port-Camargue**, a modern adjunct to Le Grau, is a purpose-built yachting complex – the biggest pleasure port on the whole of the Mediterranean. Heading east from Aigues-Mortes, you penetrate the heart of the **Petite Camargue**, the western portion of the Rhône delta, a ten-thousand hectare band of inhospitable terrain which forms a temporary home to a wide variety of migrating birds and, along the coast, crowds of summer-time sun bathers. Driving, cycling or horse-riding is the best way to explore the hinterland of the Carmargue.

## Aigues-Mortes

Originally intended to be France's principal Mediterranean port, **AIGUES-MORTES** was swallowed up in short order by the silt of the Rhône, which pushed the sea south and consigned the town to stagnation among the "dead waters" surrounding it. Founded by Louis IX in 1246, it was from here that the saint-king embarked on two of his expeditions: to Cyprus on the Seventh Crusade of 1248, and to Tunis in 1270, where he met his death. His son, Philip, gave the medieval town its present form – commissioning Genoan engineers to build walls in emulation of those of Damietta in Egypt, the site of Louis' early triumph. Local salt beds and trade privileges brought initial success, but by the end of the four-teenth century it had become a backwater, stranded by the waves of silt brought downriver by the Rhône. Aigues-Mortes' misfortune, however, has worked to our benefit, preserving the town's striking profile, which may have otherwise been built over and around. Today it is a mandatory photo-stop, and a tour of the **fortifications** and the grid of thirteenth-century streets is a pleasant way to pass an hour or so, combining well with a trip to the **beaches** to the south. If you have the fortune to visit during a festival, try to catch a bit of the *course camarguaise*; watching the crowds and the bulls beneath the medieval ramparts is a truly evocative sight.

## Arrival and accommodation

The **gare SNCF** (☎04.66.53.74.74), on the spur line which runs down from Nîmes to le-Grau-du-Roi, is on the route de Nîmes, about 100m north of the old town, while **buses** stop on avenue de la Liberté, across the canal from the *gare*. From either of these head south towards the massive Tour de Constance (see below) on the northwest corner of the old town. Drivers are directed by a signal system to free spaces in the **car park** along the east wall of the town. The **tourist office** (daily: July & Aug 9am–8pm; Sept–June 9am–noon & 2–6pm; ☎ & fax 04.66.53.73.00, *aigues-mortes@fnotsi.net*) is found just inside the Porte de la Gardette, one of the old town's five monumental gates, just east of the Tour de Constance on the north wall. **Bikes** can be picked up at Les Enganettes, 12 rue de Marceau (☎04.66.52.69.11).

If you are planning on staying in this area, you may want to choose between Aigues-Mortes and Le Grau (see p.236), which are only 8km apart. There are a number of **hotels** in and around Aigues-Mortes, but even so it is wise to book ahead in high season. Unfortunately those who do opt to stay here have to pay for the privilege – room prices are relatively high and do not offer great value for money. *L'Escale* (☎04.66.53.71.14, fax 04.66.53.76.74; ③), right by the Tour de Constance, is the best deal, with a traditional homely atmosphere, as well as a good restaurant. A little bit more expensive but with more amenities (TV and air conditioning), *Le Victoria* (☎04.66.51.14.20, fax 04.66.51.14.21; ④) is on the same square as the tourist office. Moving upscale, *Les Arcades*, 23 boulevard Gambetta (☎04.66.53.81.13, fax 04.66.53.75.46; ⑤) is a small, tastefully appointed hotel located in a beautiful old building; the rooms are not huge, but the service is attentive. Just outside the old-town walls, the *Tour de Constance* at 1 boulevard Diderot (closed Nov–Mar; ☎04.66.53.83.50; ②) lacks the ambience, but is economical and has larger rooms for families and groups. The **campsite**, *Le Petite Camargue* (late April to late Sept; ☎04.66.53.98.98) is a four-star super-site, a massive complex with a café-bar, laundry facilities and a gamut of other services, located 3km west of town.

## The Town

Aigues-Mortes' **old town**, where the sights, hotels and restaurants are concentrated, is laid out on a rectangular grid, girded by stout walls. Well maintained, its success as a day-trip and weekend destination has cluttered the streets with photo developing shops and souvenir boutiques, the regular street pattern adding to an air of artificiality and a certain too-clean tweeness. Henry James' observation of a hundred years past is equally valid today; Aigues-Mortes, he wrote, "can hardly be said to be alive; but it has been very neatly embalmed".

On the far side of the open *place* where the tourist office sits, looms the massive **Tour de Constance** (daily: Pentecost to mid-Sept 9.30am–8pm; mid-Sept to Pentecost 10am–5pm; 32F/€4.88), the main fortress of the town – once a lighthouse and for many years a prison for uncooperative nobles and stalwart

Huguenots. Protestant women were confined in the cells on the top floor, including the stoic Marie Durand, who spent almost forty years here in the eighteenth century, and whose graffiti remains etched in the stone to this day. It is also through the tower that you access the walk along the **town walls**, which provides sweeping views over the flat terrain of the delta, and allows a close-up look at the city's defences: arrow-slitted battlements, and stone ducts for pouring boiling oil on would-be attackers. Those on a budget, however, should almost certainly skip this steeply priced visit – a pleasant (and free) option is to walk across town from the Porte de la Gardette and take in the walls from the fields to the south. Looking back at the town from here, the tower which you see on the far left is "**the tower of the salted Bourguignons**"; the curious nickname dates back to an episode of the Hundred Years' War. When the town was seized in a raid by English-allied Burgundian forces in 1418, royalist Armagnacs came to try to retake the town. They were foiled by the strong fortifications, but one night a local citizen opened one of the smaller gates to let their forces in. Sneaking up on the sleeping Burgundian garrison, the Armagnacs slaughtered them before they knew what was happening, but rather than bury the bodies (no easy task in the fetid marshes surrounding the town), the victorious forces stuffed them into this tower, layering them with salt so they would not putrefy – leaving them, literally, in a pickle. There's little more to see in Aigues-Mortes, but the country **market**, held on Wednesday and Sunday mornings on the broad esplanade of avenue Frédéric-Mistral (75m north of the town walls), has excellent produce and prepared dishes, and you could do much worse than outfit a **picnic** and enjoy it with a bottle of the local *vin du sable*, "sand wine", on the grassy verge by the ramparts.

### Eating and drinking

On the **restaurant** front the old town fares quite respectably. Many establishments specialize in seafood, most in the 80–130F/€12.20–19.83 range. Other than these places and the hotel restaurants *La Galerie*, 10 place St-Louis (☎04.66.53.86.68), for seafood, and *La Goulue*, 2 rue Denfert-Rochereau (☎04.66.53.69.45; April–Sept), for *terroir*, are solid, inexpensive options. *Casa de Tora Luna*, 16 place St-Louis (☎04.66.53.68.75) is the local Spanish joint, with the requisite tapas and paella (menus from 80F/€12.20). Without a doubt, however, the culinary champion of Aigues-Mortes is the highly praised *Café de Bouzigues* at 7 rue Pasteur (☎04.66.53.93.95) – here (for only 68F/€10.37 at lunch) you can enjoy plentiful, elaborate menus on the cosy interior patio or in the comfortable dining room.

# Le Grau-du-Roi and Port Camargue

**LE GRAU-DU-ROI** and its sister **PORT CAMARGUE** are, between them, Aigues-Mortes' modern alter ego; the latter also a purpose-built port complex, but one dedicated to pacific hedonism rather than violent idealism. Le Grau (Occitan for "sand bar") has been a fishing village since the time of Henry IV in the sixteenth century, but it was only with the building of Port Camargue in 1969 that prosperity finally arrived. Now summer months fill the town with boaters from around the world, and sun-worshippers from France and abroad who seek out the duned expanses stretching off towards the mouth of the Rhône in the east. If on one hand the town resembles a package-tour nightmare, on the other, there's no shortage of bars, cheap food and beach-side fun. Off season, of course, it's another story entirely; things wind down quickly and, as happens in so many seaside towns, a certain air of cold desolation sets in.

Basically, the only two reasons to stay in Le Grau or Port Camargue are: the beach and the beach. West of the mouth of the canal which passes through Le Grau's centre, a narrow band of sand, hemmed in closely by road, leads 5km west to La Grande-Motte (see p.258), whose curious triangle-shaped buildings can easily be made out on a clear day. This is the most accessible swimming area, but the best **beaches** are east of town, once you pass the busy little bay between Le Grau and Port Camargue. Just beyond Pointe de l'Espiguette, the spur of land jutting westwards on the south edge of Port Camargue, is where the real beach starts – an uninterrupted swath of dunes stretching east to the lighthouse 5km distant and from there towards the horizon. Naturally the busiest area is around the **lighthouse** itself, which can be accessed by road from Le Grau, and where you will be charged a hefty 22F/3.36€ fee to park. The further east you go, the more the crowds thin out, and the more laid-back beach etiquette becomes. **Nudists** have staked their claim on one stretch of beach to the east of the lighthouse, and if you are prepared to go far away enough you can find seclusion even at the busiest time of year. The main attraction here aside from the beach is the **Seaquarium** (daily: July & Aug 10am–11pm; May, June & Sept 9.30am–7pm; Oct–April 10am–6pm; 43F/€6.56), one of the biggest indoor aquariums in Europe, located between the two towns in the Palais de Mer. The fairly steep admission price also gives access to the **Musée de Mer** ("The Sea Museum") in the same building, which features exhibits on local marine life and nautical history.

Apart from swimming there are facilities for a wide range of other water-related **activities** in Le Grau and Port Camargue, including outfits which rent sail-boards, sailboats, kayaks and jet-skis, many offering instruction (see below). For children, no less than three **water parks** have been set up around the towns. Summer months also provide an opportunity to enjoy regional diversions including *courses* and waterborne jousting competitions during the *fêtes* of mid-June and September.

## Practicalities

Both **buses** and **trains** approach the town along the narrow sandy spit leading from Aigues-Mortes and deposit passengers more or less smack in the middle of Le Grau, at the small **gare SNCF** (☎04.66.51.40.93) just off the canal on the east side. The large and efficient **tourist office**, 30 rue Rédarès (daily: July & Aug 9am–11.30pm; June & Sept 9am–8pm; Oct–May 9am–noon & 2–6pm; ☎04.66.51.67.79, fax 04.66.51.06.08, *www.ville-legrauduroi.fr*) is on the east side of Le Grau, five streets south from the train station. To rent **bicycles**, try Cyclo New Style, rue du Stade (☎04.66.53.08.06) or Loca Loisirs, avenue Jean Lasserre (☎04.66.53.45.12), while for **watersports** try Surf Loisirs on boulevard Front de Mer (☎04.66.52.40.01) or Société Nautique on Quai d'Escale (☎04.66.53.29.47); Espace Mer (☎04.66.51.75.25) in the Nouveau Port de pêche will handle your **diving** needs.

The dozen or so **hotels** which serve Le Grau and Port Camargue range from smaller and more attractive establishments in the old town to typical beach-side monsters. Surprisingly, prices tend to be fairly reasonable. In the **old town**, the least expensive choices are the small *Le Provençal*, 45 rue des Combattents

(☎04.66.51.41.68, fax 04.66.51.40.46; ②), and the basic *Quai d'Azur*, rue du Vidourle (March to mid-Nov; ☎04.66.51.41.94, fax 04.66.53.41.94; ②). The best of the smaller, old town hotels is the *Bellevue et d'Angleterre*, Quai Colbert (closed Jan; ☎04.66.51.40.75, fax 04.66.51.43.78; ④) which is a pleasant, airy and clean establishment with good views. In **Port Camargue** things tend to be more expensive, but have a greater amount of facilities. *Le Spinaker*, pointe de la Presqu'île (March–Oct; ☎04.66.53.24.91, fax 04.66.53.17.47; ⑥) is cosy and discreetly set in a green patch in the midst of the port, while *Oustau Camarguen*, 3 route des Marines (March–Nov; ☎04.66.51.51.65, fax 04.66.53.06.65; ⑥) is larger but has a more authentically maritime feel. **Campsites** abound, but three are set conveniently between Le Grau and Port Camargue, and all have excellent facilities: *Les Mouettes*, avenue Jean Jaurés (March–Sept; ☎ & fax 04.66.51.44.00) and *A.C.C.C.F*, route de l'Espiguette (March–Oct; ☎04.66.51.46.21) are both two-star rated, while *L'Eden*, on the same road (March–Oct; ☎04.66.51.49.81, fax 04.66.53.13.20) is a four-star, 400-pitch monster-site, which also rents chalets.

**Eating** in Le Grau and Port-Camargue means **seafood**, and it seems that on every corner there is a restaurant serving up the same bouillabaisse, *moules frites*, *coquiallages* and fish. Competition means prices are good, even if the product is often indistinguishable – most establishments have menus in the 80–150F/€12.20–22.88 range. The bargain places are *La Pichouline* on place de la Libération and *Le Provençal*, 45 rue des Combattents, which serve up lunch from 55F/€8.39. At the other end of the scale, *Le Spinaker*'s restaurant is recognized as the best eatery in the area, and menus are priced accordingly (185–395F/€28.21–60.24). Of the towns' many **bars**, the only one which stands out from the crowd is *Leon* at 2 avenue de la Gare, the home turf of the local bull-fighting aficionados association.

# The Petite Camargue

The **PETITE CAMARGUE**, which Lawrence Durrell called "Little Argentina", stretches east from Le Grau and Aigues-Mortes, an inhospitable expanse of marshes, crisscrossed by canals, and dominated by great saltwater *étangs* ("lagoons"). This is a lightly populated and unwelcoming area, with no villages to speak of, only isolated ranches, rice farms, and salt works. It is temporary home, however, to an incredible variety of **waterfowl** – some 400 different species – including a steady stream of migrating birds crossing the Mediterranean between Europe and Africa; look out especially for pink flamingos, herons, grand cormorants, and egrets. The delta is also where the Gard's strong traditions of horse-manship and *tauromachie* originate, on the great ranches where wild bulls are left to graze the salty scrub freely The *gardians*, whose simple huts dot the plain, have been the proud masters of the delta since at least 1512, when they established a formal confraternity. Riding their distinctively small "Camargue" ponies they pursue and corral the black bulls, rounding them up for branding in the springtime *ferrade*. The Camargue proper, which lies in Provence, has been incorporated since 1970 into a national park, but there is no visible characteristic which distinguishes the official parkland from the section of the delta near Aigues-Mortes and Le Grau.

Heading east from Aigues-Mortes into the Petite Camargue you pass the curious **Tour Carbonnière** on the left. Once the guard-post on the only land access to the medieval port-town, this 20m-high tower, perched on a rare mound of *terra firma* and pierced by a gate through which the road once led, is now a popular place for a picnic. Further along the same road lies the **House of the Fauna and Flora of the Camargue** (July & Aug 10am–noon & 2–7pm; otherwise by appointment only – ☎04.66.53.72.03; 30F/€4.58), a ghoulish stuffed collection of over 200 animals of the delta. Penetrating the heart of the area, the road rolls by a flat, unchanging landscape until you reach the bridge over the Petit Rhône. Heading in the other direction from Aigues-Mortes down to Le Grau you'll see the **salt-pans** of the Salins du Midi to the south – if you're interested in visiting these, a *petit train* (April–Oct; 50F/€7.63) does a 45-minute circuit of the area, with a guide explaining (in English) their history and the techniques of salt-harvesting; book the train at the tourist office in Aigues-Mortes (see p.235). Just past these salt works are the **Caves de Listel**, the wine *domaine* where locally produced "sand wine" can by sampled and purchased. On the far side of Le Grau, on the way to the lighthouse, you'll pass the **bird observatory**, a discreet cabin overlooking one of the shallow, salty *étangs*; early morning and evening in summer are the best times to look.

If you are exploring the Petite Camargue with your own vehicle, don't be tempted onto the unpaved roads and lanes leading out through the fields; quite often they are deceptively soft and you may find yourself walking back to civilization. The best ways to visit the more remote areas are either to sign up for one of the one-day "**safaris**" offered by travel agencies, or join a boat tour. Among outfits that can arrange organized visits are Cabane de Boucanet of Port Camargue (☎04.66.53.25.64), which sets up **horseback** rides, and Le Gitan in Le Grau (☎04.66.70.09.65, *francemarket.com/gitan*), which deals with **four-wheel drive** expeditions; Isle de Stel in Aigues-Mortes (April–Oct; ☎04.66.53.60.70) offers a half-day **boat** tour of the nearby *étangs* and canals.

# The Vidourle valley

West of Nîmes, the border of the Gard is marked by the **Vidourle valley**, which begins as a trickle on the southern edge of the Cévennes mountains at the northwest of the *département*. This is a quiet corner of Gard, relatively unexplored, and on the whole the villages here, some of which are impressively ancient, lack both the sights and amenities to draw travellers. Notable exceptions though are **Sommières**, where the breadth of the river is still spanned by a Roman bridge and watched over by the richly preserved castle of Villevieille; **Sauve**, an ancient hamlet which makes a convenient stopping-point en route from Nîmes to Ganges; and, further on, at the edge of the *départment*, just 15km from Ganges to the west (see p.241), **St-Hippolyte-du-Fort**.

## Sommières

**SOMMIÈRES**, the largest town along the Vidourle, lying halfway between Nîmes and Montpellier, is one point on the way west from Nîmes which definitely merits a stop. Its easy, unspoilt charm seduced the English author Laurence Durrell into spending the last 33 years of his life here, and prompted him to remark, in the *Spirit of Places*, that he had seen "nothing prettier". Walking through the old town or along the riverbank it's hard not to sympathize with

Durrell's judgement – Sommières remains a peaceful, idyllic village. Strongly Protestant, it was all but destroyed during the Wars of Religion as it repeatedly changed hands before being conquered personally by Louis XIII in 1622. Today Sommières makes a pleasant stop for a bite to eat and a wander around, and those looking for a few days of quiet relaxation could fare a lot worse than to spend some time here, away from the crowded beaches of Le Grau and the busy streets of Nîmes. April through to September is the season for *courses camarguaises*, held on Sunday afternoons.

The **Roman bridge** which spans the river remains an integral feature of Sommières, uniting the newer town on the west bank with the old town on the east. Something of a curiosity, it was built in the first century and originally consisted of seventeen arches, but half a dozen have been gradually covered over by the encroaching town. A testament to Roman engineering, it continued to carry all of the car and truck traffic passing through the town up until the recent opening of a new bypass. At the bridge's western end the walled old town is entered by passing through the **tour de l'horloge**, home to a ponderous seventeenth-century clock. From here you can descend to the left to the **bas marché** (low market), now the place des Docteurs M. et G. Dax, or proceed along the course of the old Roman road to the **haut marché** (high market), the place Jean-Jaurès – both arcaded *places* which still serve as marketplaces for local farmers. From the upper market, an alley leads to the steep stairs at the foot of the town's **castle**. Not much remains of this fortress, built in the tenth century and almost all but destroyed by Catholic forces in 1573, but you can climb to the top of the square **tower** (Mon–Fri 4–7pm, Sat & Sun 10am–noon & 4–7pm; 10F/€1.53) for a dramatic panorama of the Vidourle plain. Aside from the confines of the old *enceinte*, the Quai Griolet, between the town walls and the riverbank, makes for a particularly evocative stroll downriver, with the geese which mill about the small dam honking emphatically at each other and passers-by.

## Practicalities

**Buses** arriving in Sommières currently drop passengers off at the place de la République, along the northern wall of the old. The **tourist office** (July & Aug daily 9am–12.30pm & 3–7pm; Sept–June Tues–Sun 9am–12.30 & 2–6pm; ☎46.68.80.99.30, fax 04.68.80.06.95), on rue du Général-Bruyère, just west of the Place de la République, distributes a pamphlet detailing local walking routes. Of the two **hotels** in Sommières, the best value is the long-established *Le Commerce* (☎04.66.80.97.22, fax 04.66.80.32.64; ②), on quai Gaussorgues, while *Auberge du Pont Romain* (mid-Dec to mid-Jan & mid-March to mid-Nov; ☎04.66.80.00.58, fax 04.66.80.31.52; ④), is a snappy three-star affair in a renovated warehouse. But the best choices are the **chambres d'hôtes** *l'Orange* (☎04.66.77.79.94; ④), a seventeenth-century mansion tucked away in rue de Baumes, in the shadow of the castle, and Billy Gérard's cosy **gîte** at 8 rue Docteur Chrestien (☎04.66.80.35.66; ②). The **campsite** (☎04.66.80.33.49; Easter–Sept) is on rue Eugène Rouché, on the west bank of the Vidourle, heading north out of town. For **eating** *L'Olivette*, 11 rue Abbé Fabre (closed Tues; ☎04.66.80.97.71) is indisputably the best place in the area for exciting regional cuisine, with menus from 149F/€22.72, and you'll also find good *terroir* fare at *l'Estocade* on the same street (closed Mon–Fri eve Sept–June; ☎04.66.77.77.01; menus from 65F/€9.91). The restaurant of the *Commerce* (Mon–Fri lunch only, Sat & Sun lunch and dinner) has menus from as little as 60F/€9.15.

### Near Sommières: the Château de Villevieille

If you are passing Sommières you should not miss the opportunity to visit the **Château de Villevieille**, perched on the rise which dominates the old town. Villevieille itself is a beautiful little hamlet of stone-built houses, but the **castle** (April–Nov afternoons; Dec–March 2pm–nightfall; 30F/€4.57) is a must-see. Owned by the same family for some 750 years, it is one of the few noble castles to escape appropriation or destruction during the Revolution (due to the lord's friendship with Voltaire and Condorcet, who interceded on his behalf). Today it boasts a sumptuous interior; the furnishings, including sixteenth-century Flemish leather "wallpaper" and the first mirror in France are classed as national monuments, plus the beds in which three kings of France and Cardinal Richelieu slept are still in their respective rooms. One of the best things about the visit is that you're shown around by members of the family – an unassuming, friendly bunch who are disarmingly frank.

## Sauve

The first town of any interest on the road from Nîmes to Ganges is **SAUVE**, 40km to the west of the capital of Gard and 20km upriver from Sommières. It's a quiet little town, once fortified and still presided over by the castle which was centuries ago the summer retreat of the bishops of Maguelone, and although there are no monuments here, it is a particularly good example of a typical medieval-era town of the northern Gard. The **old town** is a maze of twisting alleys, some of which are covered, and the **view** from the other side of the bridge over the Vidourle is inspiring. In recent years it has been revived due to an influx of cosmopolitan urban refugees who have opened up interesting, ethnically flavoured eating establishments and now organize an annual African music festival in mid-July.

Sauve's only **bus** link is with Nîmes and Ganges: buses stop just off the main road, at the edge of the village. If you plan to stay, the small **tourist office** in place René Isouard (July & Aug Mon–Sat 10am–noon & 2–6pm, Sun 10am–noon; Sept–June Mon–Sat 10am–noon & 2–5pm; ☎04.66.77.57.51) can help find **accommodation**, and there is an agreeable *gîte*, *La Poussaranque* (☎04.66.77.51.97; ③), 2km east on the Nîmes road. There are two good **restaurants** in town: *Le Micocoulier* (July & Aug daily; Easter to Oct Mon & Thurs–Sun dinner only; ☎04.66.77.57.61; menu from 89F/€13.57), at 3 place Jean-Astruc, is a cosy little *auberge* serving up intriguing un-French food and lavish desserts, while *L'Auberge au Volet Verts*, 6 place Pascual-Vallongue (closed Tues & Oct; ☎04.66.77.53.28) is also open for lunch – a bargain at 60F/€9.15. You can stock up on supplies at Sauve's country **market**, held on Thursdays and Saturdays in the town centre.

## St-Hippolyte-du-Fort

Eight kilometres west of Sauve, across undulating farmland, **ST-HIPPOLYTE-DU-FORT** is the highest town on the Vidourle's course. Beyond lies Ganges, where the road dips into the Hérault valley, having crossed over into the *département* of the same name. St-Hippolyte, like so many old cloth towns of the Cévennes, switched over to silk production in the period before the Revolution, and prospered until a nineteenth-century epidemic wiped out the mulberry bushes on which the silkworms depended. Today the town is trying to generate interest as a tourist stop, encouraging its inhabitants to attach **sundials** to the fronts of their houses in order to develop a rather contrived identity. Some of the solar clocks are quite attractive, but most are unremarkable; the tourist office distributes a route map which takes you past all of them. Rather more interesting is the **silk museum** (daily: July & Aug 10am–7pm; April–June & Sept–Nov 10am–12.30pm & 2–6.30pm; 24F/€3.66) behind the old military school, a five-minute walk west of the main square, place de la Canourgue. In addition to reconstructed silk-weaving machinery, it houses an exhibition of live silk worms doing their stuff; the museum makes for a good stop for both adults and children. **Buses** roll through the town centre, stopping just before place de la Canourgue. The town's **tourist office** (Mon & Wed 3–6pm, Tues, Thurs & Fri also 9am–noon; ☎04.66.77.91.65, fax 04.66.77.25.36) is located within the courtyard of the same building as the silk museum. If you need to stay, you can choose between the **hotel** *Auberge Cigalois* (☎04.66.77.64.59, fax 04.66.77.25.08, *www.logis-de-france.fr*; ③), off the D999 a kilometre or so east of town, and two **campsites**: *Figaret* (☎04.66.77.26.34) and *de Graniers* (☎04.66.85.21.44). There are several **restaurants** and **cafés** around place de la Canourgue.

## travel details

### TRAINS

**Nîmes** to: Agde (10 daily; 1hr); Aigues-Mortes (6–12 daily; 50min); Alès (12 daily; 40min); Beaucaire (2 daily; 20min); Béziers (10 daily; 1hr 15min); Carcassonne (6 daily; 2hr 5min) ; Le Grau-du-Roi (6–12 daily; 55min); Lunel (10 daily; 20min); Montpellier (10 daily; 30min); Narbonne (11 daily; 1hr 30min); Paris (1 daily; 8hr); Perpignan (7 daily; 2hr 15min); Sète (9 daily; 50min); Tarascon/Beaucaire (18 daily; 12min); Toulouse (6 daily; 3hr 5min); Vauvert (6 daily; 25min); Vergèze (10 daily; 12min).

**Aigues-Mortes** to: Le Grau-du-Roi (6–12 daily; 5min); Nîmes (6–12 daily; 50min).

**Tarascon/Beaucaire** to: Nîmes (18 daily; 12min).

### BUSES

**Aigues-Mortes** to: Le Grau-du-Roi (5 daily; 10min); Montpellier (5 daily; 1hr 20min; increased service in summer); Stes-Maries-de-la-Mer (summer 1 daily; 30min).

**Beaucaire** to: Remoulins (2 daily; 45min); St-Gilles (2 daily; 30min).

**Nîmes** to: Aigues-Mortes (4 daily; 1hr 10min); Avignon (3 daily; 1hr 30min); Beaucaire (3 daily; 45min); Collias (3 daily; 1hr 5min); Ganges (4 daily; 1hr 15min); Le Grau-du-Roi (4–8 daily; 1hr 20min); Pont du Gard (7 daily; 50min); Remoulins (9 daily; 35–50min); St-Gilles (7 daily; 50min); Sauve (4–5 daily; 50min); Sommières (3 daily; 45min); Uzès (1 daily; 45min); Vauvert (4 daily; 35min); Villevieille (3 daily; 40min).

**St-Hippolyte** to: Ganges (3 daily; 40min); Montpellier (3 daily; 1hr 45min); Nîmes (4–5 daily; 1hr 5min); Quissac (3 daily; 10min); Sauve (3 daily; 16min).

**Sommières** to: Alès (1 daily; 55min); Montpellier (4 daily; 1hr 10min).

**Uzès** to: Avignon (8 daily; 1hr); Nîmes (1 daily; 45min); Pont du Gard (8 daily; 20min); Remoulins (8 daily; 25min); St-Hippolyte (2 daily; 25min); Vers (8 daily; 15min).

# CHAPTER FIVE

# MONTPELLIER AND AROUND

T ogether **Montpellier** and the surrounding country present the most varied and exciting region in Languedoc. The city is a capital in every sense of the word – a zesty centre of government, education, culture and economy for the whole of the Languedoc-Roussillon *région* and, best of all, it is minutes from the beach. And while it's true that Languedoc's **coast** may not be able to hold a candle to the likes of Provence's Côte d'Azur, if you can put up with the often-strong wind, its some forty kilometres of nearly uninterrupted sand bar – as well as providing ample opportunities for sun-soaking and watersports – means you can escape the crowds if you wish. Moreover, the seaside towns, although unavoidably busy in high season, have not sunk into the irretrievable triteness of their Provençal counterparts; the continuing role of **Palavas**, **Mèze** and **Sète** as fishing ports balances their beach town roles – endowing them with life and energy throughout the year. Just inland, **Pézenas** was the capital of Languedoc in the glory days of French Absolutism, and the many palaces which cram its old town preserve it as one of the most beautiful in the Southwest. The River Hérault gives its name to the *département* of which Montpellier is the administrative centre, and dominates its **interior**. Less travelled than the coast, its beautiful highlands are home to a wealth of natural wonders and historic sites. Dusty and provincial **Clermont-Hérault** acts as a gateway to the dramatically varied landscape at nearby **Lac Salagou**, while **Lodève** – still lorded over by its hulking medieval cathedral, is the best place to set off for the breathtaking **Cirque de Navacelles**. East of the cirque, Ganges sits on the banks of the Hérault at the point where the river completes its descent from the high Cévennes mountains to the north; just downstream you can visit one of France's most celebrated caverns, the **Grotte de Demoiselles**, before following dramatic gorges southwest past the ancient monastic centre of **St-Guilhem-de-Désert**, or bearing due south towards the towering **Pic-St-Loup**.

Getting around by **public transport** in the region around Montpellier is easy. The city sits on the main coastal rail artery, uniting it with Sète to the west and Nîmes to the east, while the area of greater Montpellier, the *agglomeration*, is served by the city's transport network (TAM), whose far-ranging buses reach Palavas and Maguelone on the coast. Inland, the lack of train lines is compensated by regular bus services connecting the bigger towns. Only the smaller villages, such as the hamlets around Lac Salagou and Navacelles, do not have useful bus services – to explore these you'll need a car or bike, or be prepared to hitchhike.

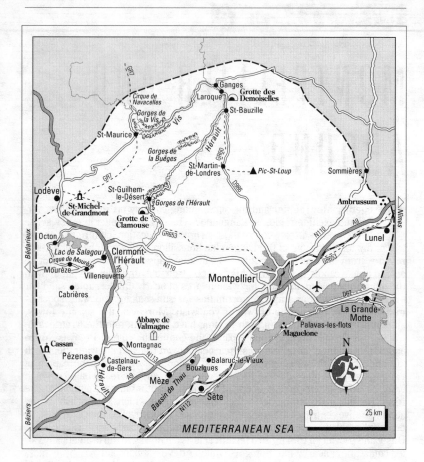

# Montpellier

**MONTPELLIER** is a great place. Home to a youthful and dynamic university culture, a host of artistic festivals and events, and a beautiful architectural fusion of the classical and the avant-garde, it is the most exciting city in Languedoc proper – it's even close enough to the Mediterranean to have the beach within reach of public transport. Since his first election in 1983, Mayor Georges Frêche has continued the successful policies of his socialist predecessors, pouring money heavily into the city's infrastructure and arts and drawing in investment – the effects of which are immediately obvious to the visitor. With fine museums, a charming old centre and a bouncy rhythm of life, you'll find that Montpellier offers an ideal place for either a longer, relaxing stay, or a whirlwind two-day tour of its highpoints, notably the **Musée Fabré** and the many Renaissance **mansions** of the old town.

Montpellier is a medieval city, and can't claim the same decorous Roman past of rival Nîmes. Starting off as market town for nearby **Maguelone** in the tenth century, in 1204 it was acquired by marriage by the Count-Kings of Barcelona, who favoured it as a residence – both Jaume I "the Conqueror" and his son Jaume II of Mallorca were born here. By the late thirteenth century it had become second only to Paris in size, thanks partly to its famous **university**, and a major centre for medicine, law and the arts. With Jaume I's divison of his realm, the city was incorporated into the kingdom of Mallorca until 1349, when Jaume II sold it – afflicted with plague, banditry and famine – to the French crown. In the era that followed the city was sustained by its university, through whose doors passed the pioneering Renaissance poet Petrarch and, later, the satirist Rabelais, who received his doctorate here in 1537. Despite the transfer of the bishopric of Maguelone here in 1537, Montpellier became strongly **Protestant** in the sixteenth and seventeenth centuries, losing many of its old church buildings in factionalist struggles, and was only saved from destruction at the hands of Louis XIII, who had personally waged war on the Huguenot stronghold in 1622, by an eleventh-hour truce. In a good position for trade and with a varied economic base, Montpellier managed to escape the post-Religious Wars depression which afflicted most of Languedoc, and the wealthy burghers vied with each other to build decadently outfitted **manors** in the surrounding vineyards. The city's leftist tradition began with a bang in 1789, and the revolutionary anthem known as "Le Marseillaise" was in fact first sung by a local medical student. Another wave of serious unrest came during the wine crisis of 1907, during which it was the strongest centre of popular agitation in reaction to plummeting grape prices (see p.366). The last shake-up was in 1962; with the dismantling of the Algerian colony, 13,000 French (*pieds-noirs*) and Maghrebi (*harki*) refugees arrived in the city, two groups whose integration into Montpellier society generated considerable friction, but whose presence brought a revitalizing dynamism to the city. Not long after this Montpellier became the official capital of the administrative *région* of Languedoc-Roussillon.

## Arrival, information and city transport

The city's **airport**, which has various car rental outlets, is 8km to the southeast of the centre, beside the Étang de Mauguio; from here buses run to the *gare routière* (hourly; 15min 25F/€3.81), or it will cost you 100–150F (€15.25–22.88) by taxi. The **gare SNCF** and **gare routière** are next to each other at the southern end of rue Maguelone – it's a five-minute walk along this street to the central place de la Comédie. The gare SNCF has a **left luggage** booth (7am–7pm). If you're driving, the simplest option for **parking** is to head for the "Comédie" car park, under the famous *place* – if however you want to avoid paying, you will be banished to the metered zones on the periphery of the old town. The main **tourist office**, which has **exchange** facilities (Mon–Fri 9am–6.30pm; July & Aug also Sat 9am–6pm) is on the northern edge of place de la Comédie (July & Aug Mon–Fri 9am–7.30pm, Sat 10am–6pm, Sun 10am–1pm & 2–5pm; Sept–June Mon–Fri 9am–6.30pm, Sat 10am–6pm, Sun 10am–1pm & 2–5pm; ☎04.67.60.60.60, fax 04.67.60.60.61, *www.ot-montpellier.fr*), while there are seasonal annexes at the gare SNCF (July & Aug Mon–Fri 9am–1pm & 3–7pm) and in the Antigone, at 78 avenue de Pirée (April–Oct Mon–Fri 9am–1pm & 2–6pm). All of these offices manage reservations for the official **guided tours** (Wed & Sat 3pm, prior reservation obligatory; 39F/€5.95), the advantage of which is that they allow you to visit certain normally

Most of the action in the Hérault *département* is centred on Montpellier, which is renowned for its cultural vitality, hosting a range of annual festivals. Also worth looking out for are the *fêtes* on the coast, which invariably feature the local tradition of water-jousting – throughout July and August in Palavas and Sète (see box on p.263) – as well as *tauromachie* (both Spanish and Camargue styles). The uplands of the Hérault valley also have a few small local festivals which you may have the good fortune of happening upon. Where no specific information number is given, contact the relevant tourist office for details.

### June

**Throughout June** Palavas: Maguelone music festival. Medieval and Baroque music concerts held several nights a week in the cathedral (☎04.67.60.90.92).

**Mid-June to mid-July** Montpellier: Le Printemps des Comédiens. Theatre, dance and music festival held in the grounds Château d'Ô, a mansion northwest of Montpellier (tram #1 to "Chateau d'Ô"; ☎04.67.01.04.04).

**Mid-June to mid-Aug** St-Guilhem: Musique Sacrée. Religious and Baroque music series, performed in the former abbey church (☎04.67.63.14.99).

**Late June to mid-July** Montpellier: Montpellier Danse. A three-week festival of traditional music and dance from around the world, held in the old Ursuline convent, the Comédie, Le Corum and other venues around town (☎04.67.60.83.60, *info@montpellierdanse .com*).

### July

**First weekend** Sète: Fête de la St-Pierre. Traditional fishermen's festival with a religious procession, street party and jousting.

**Second Sunday** Palavas: Fête de la Mer. Religious procession and blessing of fishing boats, followed by jousting,

off-limits sights, like the medieval mikvé (Jewish ritual bath) or the interior of the Arc de Triomf. For information on all sorts of practicalities and events, pick up the free student guide *L'Indic*, or the very comprehensive *Les Clés* (50F/€7.63) – again both available at the tourist offices.

The new star of the city's transport system (TAM; 27 rue Maguelone; ☎04.67.22.87.87) is its fleet of **trams**, which debuted in 2000 and has its hub at place de la Comédie. At present one line is in service, which runs a twisting course northwest to southeast across town. Coupled with **buses**, it makes an incredibly comprehensive network, the real advantage of the latter for visitors being that it runs out to Palavas on the coast. Both buses and trams operate from 5am to 1am, and **maps** and **passes** (one-day pass 20F/€3.05, weekly pass 63F/€9.61) are available at the TAM office above, although you can also buy tickets (valid for both; single 7F/€1.07, ten-trip ticket 53F/€8.08) from drivers and at tobacconists. Other green transport initiatives include the city's comprehensive **bike** path network, which has now topped 120km in length; bikes can be rented at Vill'a Vélo at the *gare routière* (☎04.67.92.92.67).

## Accommodation

With its roles as a student and administrative centre, Montpellier has abundant **hotel** facilities in all price ranges. Most accommodation is concentrated

fireworks and *tauromachie*. Also night-time *joutes* on July 14 (☎04.67.07.73.34, *www.palavaslesflots.com*).

**Mid-July** Mèze: Festival du Thau. A week-long "alternative", ska and World music festival on the banks of the Bassin du Thau, with three concerts per evening – all on the same ticket. Information on ☎04.67.18.92.80 (*www.festivaldethau.com*).

**Mid- to end-July** Montpellier: Le Festival de Radio-France et de Montpellier. Musical festival representing styles from classical to jazz, held at Le Corum and other venues. Half of the concerts are free (☎04.67.02.02.01).

**Mid- to end-July** Sète: Festival de Sète. Mediterranean-music festival featuring folk and pop music from African and European shores.

**July 21–23** St-Guilhem: Fête. Local *fête* of the town, featuring costumes, music and traditional market.

**Late July to early Aug** Sète: Fiesta Latina. Four-day celebration. Nightly performances of music and dance at the Théâtre de la Mer, as well as street-theatre and plenty of parties. Information on ☎06.67.74.48.44.

**Throughout July & Aug** Pézenas: Mirondela des Arts. International theatre festival with excellent quality performances held at the town's Théâtre de Verdure, in the old town's squares and other venues.

### August

**End Aug** Sète: Fête de St-Louis. One-day extravaganza of fireworks, street-parties, jousting and medieval pageantry.

### September and October

**Sept 29 to Oct 1** Palavas: Feria d'Automne. Local Camarguais-style festival, with horsemanship and *tauromachie* (☎06.61.46.68.85).

**Mid- to end-Oct** Montpellier: Festival du Cinéma Méditerranéen. Festival of feature-length films and shorts, with symposiums and awards (☎04.99.13.73.73).

in the compact grid of streets between the the *gares* and the place de la Comédie. You may be tempted to stick to this area for convenience, but there are options in the old town which are worth searching out, particularly in the area west of the central place des Martyrs-de-la-République. Note that hotels in Montpellier are obliged to charge a municipal booking tax of 1–5F/€0.15–0.76 (depending on the hotel's class), which is not included in published room rates.

Montpellier's **HI hostel** (☎04.67.60.32.22, fax 04.67.60.32.30; closed mid-Dec to mid-Jan; bus #6 "Ursulines"), fifteen minutes' walk from place Comédie, is in a renovated old building on impasse Petite Corraterie, off rue des Écoles Laïques at the northern boundary of the old town; the curfew is at 2am and it has amenities such as a bar and billiards room and a luggage check. Another option for low-budget accommodation is to contact L'Association des Residences Internationales (Mon–Fri 8am–noon & 1.30–5pm; ☎04.67.60.36.00, fax 04.67.60.36.58) at 2 rue Germain (just north of the Marché aux Fleurs), which administrates a network of over 600 rooms and apartments in the greater Montpellier area – a good option for medium to long stays and popular with students. The closest **campsite** to Montpellier is *L'Oasis Palavasienne* (☎04.67.15.11.61; April to mid-Oct), just south of town on the D21 (to Palavas; bus #28). There are also plenty in Palavas itself (see p.260).

## Hotels

**Le Chabaneau**, 7 pl Chabaneau (☎04.67.60.75.66). One of the best deals in town, this is a hip
place managed by young people with a good bar, on a quiet little square. Excellent weekly
rates too. ①.

**du Commerce**, 13 rue Maguelone (☎04.67.58.36.80, fax 04.67.58.10.64). Centrally located,
and well kept despite the ageing reception area. Good-sized rooms, some en suite with TV. ③.

**Edouard VII**, 10 rue Aristide-Ollivier (☎04.67.58.42.13, fax 04.67.58.93.66). Friendly place in
a great old nineteenth-century building with a striking facade and spacious interior. Every
room has en-suite shower, toilet and TV. ③.

**L'Escargot d'Or**, 14 rue Jules-Ferry (☎04.67.34.06.28). Good-value station-side choice with
en-suite bath, TV in every room, and a non-stop restaurant serving from 5am–1am. ③.

**des Étuves**, 24 rue des Étuves (☎04.67.60.78.19, fax 04.67.60.31.29,
*hoteldestuves@wanadoo.fr*). Simple, spotless rooms in the south of the old city, all with en-
suite bathrooms and TV. ②.

**Floride**, 1 rue François-Perier (☎04.67.65.73.30, fax 04.67.22.10.83). Friendly and clean, a
young travellers' favourite in a pleasant neighbourhood, even if the rooms are a bit small.
Some rooms with private bath, all with TV. ②.

**Le Guilhem**, 18 rue J-J-Rousseau (☎04.67.52.90.90, fax 04.67.60.67.67, *hotel-le-
guilhem@mnet.fr*). Beautifully restored sixteenth-century town house whose cheerful rooms
mostly overlook quiet gardens, and with a sunny breakfast terrace. ④.

**L'Hôtel**, 8 rue Jules-Ferry (☎04.99.13.33.44, fax 04.67.58.58.71, *www.interhotel.fr*). Newest
and best of the station-side hotels – modern, clean and soundproof, with good amenities.
Some rooms with bath. ③.

**Majestic**, 4 rue de Cheval-Blanc (☎04.67.66.26.85, fax 04.67.66.11.42). Very basic but clean,
quiet and central, with rooms with en-suite showers. ②.

**Le Mistral**, 25 rue Boussairolles (☎04.67.58.45.25, fax 04.67.58.23.95). Comfortable and
clean, a good option in the middle price range, offering satellite TV and garage parking
(30F/€4.58 extra). ③.

**New Hôtel du Midi**, 22 bd Victor-Hugo (☎04.67.92.69.61, fax 04.67.92.73.63, *www.
new-hotel.com*). A luxury option, but good value considering the level of service and the beauty of the building, right on the Comédie, in the old "Grand Hôtel du Midi" building. ⑥.

**du Palais**, 3 rue du Palais (☎04.67.60.47.38, fax 04.67.60.40.23). Tastefully renovated
eighteenth-century mansion on the west side of the old town, blending modern and antique
touches. Cosy rooms, most with en-suite facilities. ④.

**Royal Hôtel**, 8 rue Maguelone (☎04.67.92.13.336, fax 04.67.99.89.88, *www.hotel-centre-
ville.fr*). An ageing but well-maintained three-star hotel between the Comédie and the *gare*,
with old-world service and comfortable if not overly large rooms. ④.

**Sofitel**, 1 rue des Pertuisanes (☎04.67.99.72.72, fax 04.67.65.17.50,
*www.sofitel.montpellier.com*). Suitably futuristic design, with a somewhat cold predominance
of concrete over glass set in the city's flagship Antigone development. Four-star service and
amenities including a pool. ⑨.

**des Touristes**, 10 rue Baudin (☎04.67.58.42.37, fax 04.67.92.61.37). Friendly, inexpensive hotel with well-maintained if somewhat spartan rooms. ②.

# The Town

More or less everything you will want to see in Montpellier can be found in or on the edge of its compact and largely pedestrian **old town**, which spreads out north and west from the **place de la Comédie**, at the heart of the city. Bounded on the north by the boulevards Pasteur and Louis Blanc, on the east by the **Champ de Mars** park and on the west by the Jardin des Plantes and **place du Peyrou**, the terminus of the town's old aqueduct, the old centre is marked off into two unequal halves by the avenue made up of rues de la Loge and Foch. The north side was the most prosperous part, as the **mansions** which pepper it testify, and is also home to the city's old university buildings and **cathedral**. The crowded lanes of the south side were inhabited by the city's workers and artisans; its buildings are correspondingly less showy. East of the place de la Comédie you'll find the sprawling **Antigone** development, Montpellier's boldly designed modern quarter. Beyond the old town are mixed commercial and residential quarters, which provide interesting backdrops to stroll past, if lacking in significant sights, while further out still you'll find various **châteaux** ringing the town.

## The place de la Comédie and the Champs du Mars park

The **place de la Comédie** is a broad plaza which was opened up in the mid-nineteenth century with the inauguration of the then new **opera hall** at its southern end. Although superseded by the new Corum hall, the gaily domed building still hosts music and theatre performances. Today the *place* to its northeast is a busy crossroads for both pedestrians and trams, and is lined on each side by a series of old cafés and fast-food joints, although it retains its traditional role as morning marketplace (Mon–Sat 7.30am–1pm). At the northern end, the tourist office's pavilion marks the beginning of the **Champs du Mars**, a park with both a formal promenade and a network of paths and ponds which attract sunbathers and strollers in good weather. The main attraction in the vicinity of the park is the huge **Musée Fabré** (Tues–Fri 9am–5.30pm, Sat & Sun 9.30am–5pm; 25F/€3.81) situated halfway up its west side, and containing an immense collection of paintings – overwhelmingly French and post-eighteenth century in content and bridging a range of styles including the local "luminophile" movement of the early nineteenth century. Works by better known names include David's *Portrait of the Doctor, Alphonse Leroy* and Delacroix's *Fantasia*, as well as pieces by Dufy, Maillol and the local Frédéric Bazille. In addition to these, you'll find works by well-known foreign artists such as Reynolds, Zurbáran and Rubens. The museum also has a **pavilion** in the park opposite (same hours and ticket), which houses rotating exhibtions with an emphasis on French twentieth-century art, while to the south of this you'll find the small **Galerie Photo** (Tues–Sat 1–7pm; free) which hosts temporary exhibitions of contemporary photographers from around Europe. Across a small bridge by the pavilion you'll see the city's massive star-shaped seventeenth-century **citadel**, built in 1622 to guard the suspiciously Protestant-leaning town and now converted into a school. Finally, at the northern end of the park looms the concrete and pink granite **Le Corum** (July & Aug Sat & Sun 2–7pm; Sept–June Sat 2–7pm), designed by Claude Vasconi to house the city's new 2000-seat opera hall – the Opéra Berlioz – plus a convention centre and

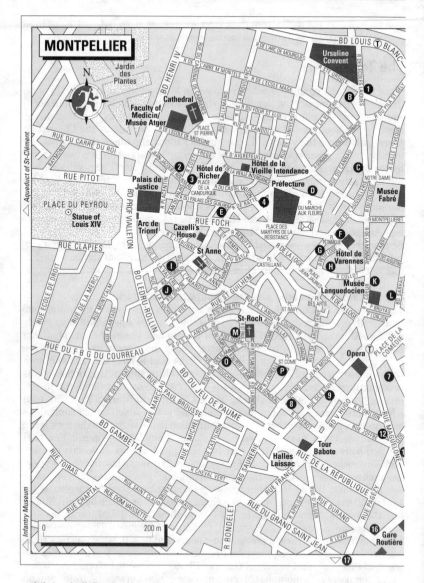

**MONTPELLIER**

Jardin des Plantes

Faculty of Medicin/ Musée Atger

Cathedral

Aqueduct of St-Clément

RUE DU CARRÉ DU ROI

RUE PITOT

PLACE DU PEYROU

Statue of Louis XIV

RUE CLAPIES

RUE ECOLE DE DROIT

RUE DE LA MERCI

Infantry Museum

BD LOUIS BLANC

Ursuline Convent

R DE L'ARC DE MOURGUES

R DE CANNAU

R DE L'ABBE M MONTELS

R DE L'ECOLE MAGE

R DE LA PROVIDENCE

R DE L'UNIVERSITE

PLACE ST PIERRE

RUE DE CANDOLLE

RUE DE RATTE

Hôtel de Richer

Hôtel de la Vieille Intendance

Préfecture

Palais de Justice

PLACE DE LA CANOURGUE

Arc de Triomf

Cazelli's House

St Anne

RUE FOCH

PLACE DES MARTYRS DE LA RESISTANCE

PLACE DU MARCHE AUX FLEURS

Musée Fabré

NOTRE DAME

Hôtel de Varennes

Musée Languedocien

St-Roch

Opera

PLACE DE LA COMÉDIE

RUE DU FBG DU COURREAU

BD DU JEU DE PAUME

BD GAMBETTA

RUE TOIRAS

Tour Babote

Halles Laissac

RUE DE LA RÉPUBLIQUE

RUE MAGUELONE

RUE DU GRAND SAINT JEAN

Gare Routière

0        200 m

exhibtion hall. During opening hours you can poke around the building and take in the sweeping **views** of the old city from its terrace.

Back at the place de la Comédie heading east brings you to the Triangle shopping centre, which marks the beginning of the Antigone development (see p.254); south down to the *gares* you'll find a bustling neighbourhood of shops and restaurants; while northwest from here is the core of the old town.

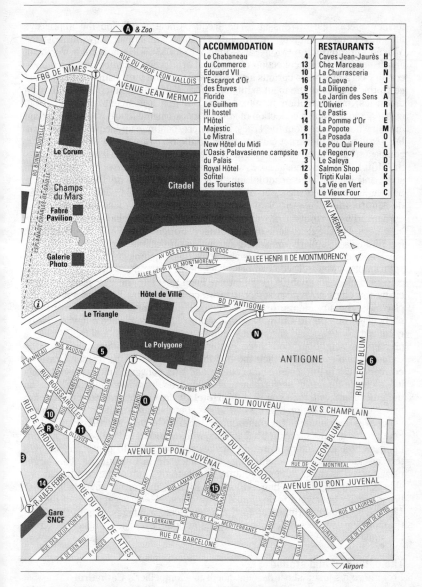

ACCOMMODATION

| | |
|---|---|
| Le Chabaneau | 4 |
| du Commerce | 13 |
| Edouard VII | 10 |
| l'Escargot d'Or | 16 |
| des Étuves | 9 |
| Floride | 15 |
| Le Guilhem | 2 |
| HI hostel | 1 |
| l'Hôtel | 14 |
| Majestic | 8 |
| Le Mistral | 11 |
| New Hôtel du Midi | 7 |
| L'Oasis Palavasienne campsite | 17 |
| du Palais | 3 |
| Royal Hôtel | 12 |
| Sofitel | 6 |
| des Touristes | 5 |

RESTAURANTS

| | |
|---|---|
| Caves Jean-Jaurès | H |
| Chez Marceau | B |
| La Churrasceria | N |
| La Cueva | J |
| La Diligence | F |
| Le Jardin des Sens | A |
| L'Olivier | R |
| Le Pastis | I |
| La Pomme d'Or | E |
| La Popote | M |
| La Posada | O |
| Le Pou Qui Pleure | L |
| Le Regency | Q |
| Le Saleya | D |
| Salmon Shop | G |
| Tripti Kulai | K |
| La Vie en Vert | P |
| Le Vieux Four | C |

## From place de la Comédie to place de la Canourgue

After the Musée Fabré, Montpellier's greatest attraction is its old town, richly adorned by elaborate mansion facades and home to a series of small museums. Simply strolling along the old streets is a pleasure and the following route is aimed to take you past the main sights. Starting on rue de la Loge, the city's main shopping street, leads you northwest into the old centre from in front of the former opera. Just off this at 7 rue Jacques-Coeur you'll find the impressive fifteenth-century facade of the Hôtel de Trésoriers de France, now home to the **Musée Languedocien** (Mon–Sat 2–5pm; 30F/€4.58). This museum is worthy of a visit not only for its collection of medieval artefacts, which include thirteenth-century ceramics and a curious lead baptismal font, but for the impressively vaulted Gothic interior of the main exhibition room. You'll also find luxurious Flemish tapestries, pre-Revolution furniture – including a seventeenth-century Italian celestial globe – and a collection of *faïence*, whose manufacture was an important industry here throughout the 1700s. From here, continue up Jacques-Coeur, turning left to follow the street curving round to the narrow place de Petrarque. This compact triangular *place* is closed in by a clutch of palaces, the largest of which is the **Hôtel de Varennes**, at no. 2, whose ground floor is almost entirely Gothic in style, and includes the beautiful fourteenth-century **salle de Petrarch**, a long hall vaulted with delicate stone ribs. On the first floor you'll find the city's **Musée de Montpellier** (Tues–Sat 9am–noon & 1.30–5pm; free), whose dull collection is dominated by portraits of city luminaries and assorted regalia of the town's public offices. On the next floor up, the **Musée Fougau** (Wed & Thurs 3–6.30pm; free) houses a similarly unexciting exhibition on traditional rural life, including nineteenth-century costume, tools and household implements.

From place Petrarch you can head back down to the main street via the lively café-lined place Jean-Jaurès, or follow rue Foch west into the wide *place* dominated by the city's *préfecture*, adjacent to which is a colourful market square, the place Marché aux Fleurs. Around here you'll find a concentration of mansions, particularly on **rue du Cannau**, whose string of facades, decked out with ornately carved doorways and casement windows, attest to the wealth of this street – a prestigious neighbourhood three centuries ago. If you continue north along Cannau you'll eventually reach the hulking stone mass of the former **Ursuline convent**, built in the seventeenth century and later converted into a prison; today it is a centre for dance performance. Heading west from Marché aux Fleurs, on the other hand, will take you past the **Hôtel de la Vieille Intendance**, the former governor's mansion at no. 9 on the street of the same name, a stately palace which was later home of the philosopher Auguste Comte and writer Paul Valéry. South of here, quiet place du Chabanneau, whose modest old houses box in a gurgling eighteenth-century **fountain**, makes a good place to pause and enjoy a terrace-side drink before continuing on to **place de la Canourgue**. This larger plaza served as the eighteenth-century adminstrative hub of the city. Its eastern side is dominated by the huge **Hôtel de Richer**, the former town hall, whose broad square courtyard is decorated in the finest Neoclassical pomp of the late 1700s. The square is ringed by further magnificent frontages; stop to check out the stone-carved faces which cap each window of the Hôtel de Cambacères across the square at no. 3.

## The cathedral and around

From here it's just a short descent north to Montpellier's **Cathedral** (Mon–Sat 9.30–noon & 2.30–7pm, Sun 9am–1pm), and the first thing you'll be struck by when you see it is its bizarre entrance, a porch flanked by two straight towers capped with high conical roofs. The effect, which resembles two old-fashioned rockets, smacks of a Viollent-le-Duc initiative but is, in fact, original – dating back to the church's fourteenth-century foundation. It is also the most interesting feature of the cathedral, whose dark and bare interior is not even worth poking your head inside. The cathedral has a covered cloister, which you can't enter, but can view from the back porch of the **Faculty of Medicin**, next door in rue de l'École du Médécin. The stately Neoclassical faculty building occupies the grounds of the now-vanished Benedictine monastery to which the cathedral once served as chapel. Passing through the main doors, flanked by bronzes of local medical giants Barthez and Lapeyronie, you'll find the interior is decorated with marble columns and rich low-relief detailing around the windows and ceilings. The porch is opposite the entrance, while up on the first floor, you'll find two noteworthy museums. The larger of these is the **Musée Atger** (Mon, Wed & Thurs 1.30–5.45pm; free), an art museum named after the local artist Xavier Atger, whose sketches make up the core of the collection, although you'll also discover contemporary southern French art, as well as paintings by noteworthy Flemish artists such as Rubens and Van Dyck. While on the first floor, the strong of stomach can also visit the **anatomy museum** (daily 2.30–5pm; free) a library of specimins, models and manuscripts relating to vivisection. At the end of rue de l'École de Medicine, which is lined with nineteenth-century university buildings, the **Jardin des Plantes** (July & Aug Mon–Sat 8.30–noon & 2–6pm; Sept–June 10am–5pm; free) marks the transition to the new town. Managed by the university's botany department, well-maintained paths lead among an impressive variety of plant specimens, from tropical to temperate. The garden dates back to 1593, when it was founded by order of the former Huguenot king, Henry IV, in order to cultivate and study homeopathic remedies.

## Place du Peyrou and south of rue Foch

Rising above the Jardin, on the western edge of the old *enceinte*, spreads the flat paved expanse of the **place du Peyrou**, flanked on either side by wide beds of colourful flowers. The plaza itself is dominated by a Roman-style equestrian statue of the "Emperor" Louis XIV – an 1838 replacement of the original statue of 1692, which was destroyed during the Revolution. The great bronze king is frozen in motionless stride towards the **Arc de Triomf**, opposite the eastern end of the park, at the head of rue Foch. The arch, designed on the ancient Roman model, consists of a single, free-standing entryway, whose sides are covered with low-relief sculptures celebrating the military victories of the "Sun King" over the Dutch and the Huguenots, the revocation of the Edict of Nantes, and the construction of the Canal du Midi. Behind Louis' statue, at the western end of the place du Peyrou, an octagonal, colonnaded pavilion marks the terminus of the 880m-long aqueduct of St-Clément, built in the late eighteenth century to carry water to the city from a nearby spring. The Neoclassical pavilion was the work of Jean Giral, the same architect who designed the Faculty of Medicine. From the two levels of terraces over which the pavilion stands, you can enjoy views over the city and a hazy panorama of the flat Languedocian littoral towards the distant Mont St-Loup.

From Peyrou, passing through the triumphal arch you'll come face to face with the striking Neoclassical **Palais de Justice**, whose Doric-columned facade is capped with an impressive tympanum in relief. From here, rue Foch sets out eastwards towards the *préfecture*, but before you reach it take a right into rue Petit Scel where, at no. 4, sits the former palace of Francese de Cazelli, a noblewoman named as governor of the coastal town of Leucate by the king in 1590 after she commanded its defence, refusing to surrender even in exchange for the life of her captured husband. The nearby plain stone nineteenth-century **church of St-Anne** is only really of interest for the occasional art exhibitions it houses; it's also the epi-centre of the "L'Isle aux Createurs", a collective of a dozen or so designers of dec-orative goods who have set up workshop-boutiques throughout the zone. South of the church on rue de l'Huile, you'll enter the city's old **artisanal quarter**, con-taining houses that survive from as early as the thirteenth century.

This neighbourhood is bounded on the east by rue St-Guilhem, a street of func-tional, quotidian shops, beyond which you'll find a successions of squares – good territory for restaurant-hunting. At the northernmost of these, place St-Ravy, are the scant remains of the **palace** of the Kings of Majorca and, crossing the colour-ful rue de l'Ancien Courrier, you'll pass the ruined church of St-Roch to arrive at a busy little bar-lined plaza at the end of rue Plan d'Agde. Just to the east, on the far side of the terrace-choked place St-Côme, squats the marvellous **hôtel** of the same name, girded by a double row of columns and capped by a low cupola. This edifice, built by Giral in the eighteenth century as an anatomical theatre, was donated to the city at the bequest of the Royal Surgeon François Gigot. Just to the south of it you'll come upon a final small *place*, set in the shadow of the **Tour de la Babote**, the only surviving portion of the town's twelfth-century defences. Crowned by an observatory in the 1700s it was also incorporated into the same semaphore system used at the Tour Chappe in Castelnaudary (see p.106).

## The Antigone

Cut off from the main part of the old city by the hideous sprawl of the Le Polygone shopping complex and defended on the north and south by a whizzing express-way, the **Antigone**, 21st-century Montpellier, is a world apart from that of the eighteenth. Laid out on an esplanade stretching east from the city for almost 2km, this self-contained and car-free development of residences, shops, services and restaurants is endowed with an uncompromising unity of form and design. The Catalan architect Ricard Bofill has created a massive low-rise building complex, drawing largely on Classical motifs, including smooth columns, triangular win-dow lintels and roof cornices reminiscent of ancient temples, but with a net effect that looks somehow futuristic–Georgian in result. The first section, the western-most part of the complex, was inaugurated in 1984, and the latest, a library designed by Paris-born architect Paul Chemetov, opened in late 2000. The whole thing, a striking if not entirely convincing Utopian landscape of broad cypress-lined courtyards, culminates in the monumental Esplanade de l'Europe on the bank of the River Lez, across which it gazes at the recently inaugurated Hôtel de Région, the governmental seat of Languedoc-Roussillon. It's an ambitious project, and you cannot deny it a certain graceful beauty, but it is somehow disappointing – perhaps it just needs some weathering to shake off the air of novelty. As a visi-tor to Montpellier, it would be a mistake not to see Antigone for yourself, but in the end it is nothing more than a suburb, and a quick walk through will likely exhaust your interest.

## Beyond the old town

Aside from those in old Montpellier and the Antigone, there are number of sights scattered around the city. Just to the southwest of the old town in the local mili-tary academy on avenue Lepic, you can visit an **infantry museum** (Mon & Wed–Sat 2–5.30pm; bus #7 from the *gare*; 25F/€3.81), which holds a collection of uniforms and memorabilia from over the last five centuries. To the north, you'll find the city's eighty-hectare **Parc Zoologique de Lunaret** (July & Aug

8am–7pm; Sept–June 8am–6pm; bus #9 to "René Bouginol"; free), a sprawling park with nearly 10km of paths leading through to where animals from around the world range about in spacious enclosures. The main attraction of Montpellier's hinterland however is the series of **follies** raised by the town's wealthiest citizens as summer houses in the 1700s. In a game of social one-upmanship, merchants and aristocrats vied to construct evermore luxurious estates, a few of which have been opened to the public, and are accessible by city transport. To the east of the centre, the eighteenth-century **Château de la Mogère** (June–Oct daily 2.30–6pm; Nov–May Sat & Sun 2.30–6pm; 30F/€4.58; tram #1 "Odysseum") is one of the most sumptuous of the mansions, and contains a considerable collection of period furniture and artwork, but perhaps the oldest and most elegant is the **Château de Flaugergues** (castle: July & Aug Tues–Sun 2.30–6pm; 40F/€6.10; grounds only: June–Sept Mon–Sat 2–6pm; bus #12 "Louis Lépine"), just to the north of la Mogère. Still lorded over by the original family which built the palace in 1696, the luxurious apartments, decked out with contemporary tapestries and *objets d'art*, and accompanying formal French gardens, sit amidst the vineyards of its *domaine*. The furthest out is former bishops' palace, the **Château de Lavérune**, arriving at which involves a considerable walk from the bus stop ("Les Bouisses", lines #4, #7 & La Ronde); it's worth it, however, to visit the **Hofer-Bufy museum** (Sat & Sun 3–7pm; 10F/€1.53), host to temporary painting exhibitions (check with the tourist office for the current programme).

# Eating, drinking and nightlife

No other city in Languedoc and Roussillon, with the possible exception of much-larger Toulouse, can compete with Montpellier in terms of either dining possibilities or cultural life. Cuisine in Montpellier is a combination of the bounty of the sea, the rich garden produce of the plain and the meats of the hills. Fish lovers should look out for the savoury, tomato-based seafood stew known as *tielle*, or crab-stuffed squid tails (*enornets farcis*) while *gâteau d'áubergine* (aubergine cake) makes a delicious meat-free option. Far from the *manades* of the Gard, pork makes a triumphant reappearance here as sausage, cured ham and paté, with duck and goose in strong supporting roles. In addition to its *terroir* options, the city has a wide range of ethnic **restaurants**, good *gastronomique* options, and a lively **café** culture, sustained by the university community.

The excellent **nightlife** in Montpellier, which has an incredible number of **bars**, **clubs** and **live music** options, is also thanks to the student population. You'll be able to find everything you need in the old town and its environs, but die-hard clubbers will want to head for the string of nightclubs (*boîtes de nuit*) on the route de Palavas in Lattes, from where you'll have to get a taxi home if you don't have transport. These are supplemented by a profusion of **café-littéraires** on a variety of themes (some permanent, some occasional); the restaurant *Le César*, 17 pl Nombre d'Or (☎04.67.20.27.02) holds two regular *café-littéraires* (both 6.30–8.30pm) – a general colloquium on the third Monday of each month, and a feminist one on the first Monday. **Concerts**, ranging from chamber music to classical as well as opera, are held at L'Opéra de la Comédie (☎04.67.60.19.99), the L'Opéra Berlioz in Le Corum (☎04.67.61.66.16), which also serves as a major venue for pop music, and at other venues – the tourist office has a complete list. The **theatre** scene thrives here too, with nearly a dozen regular stages scattered throughout town. Major performances are held at the Opéra, while you'll also find informal *café-théâtres*, like Le Cicrane on 9 rue St-Ursule (☎04.67.60.74.11). If you fancy the **cinema**, the Diagonal complex at place Pierre-Enaidel (☎04.67.58.44.74) is the place to head for.

Naturally, things tend to be quieter out of academic season, but there is still plenty to do, and the beaches and bars of Palavas are only a bus ride away.

## Restaurants

Practically every one of the squares of Montpellier's old town has a restaurant or two, so if you don't feel like searching out something special, you needn't do more than wander around and pick from among the many terraces.

**Caves Jean-Jaurès**, 3 rue Collot (☎04.67.66.08.09). Well-prepared local cooking served in a seventeenth-century *hôtel* just west of the Comédie. From 90F/€13.73.

**Chez Marceau**, 7 pl de la Chapelle Neuve (☎04.67.66.08.09). Excellent-value Languedocian cuisine (both inland and coastal varieties) with a wonderful shaded terrace. The *pâtés du canard* are particularly notable. Menus from 60F/€9.15. Closed Sun.

**La Churrascaria**, 17 pl du Nombre d'Or (☎04.67.22.10.75). Brazilian restaurant in the west of the Antigone, with a large terrace and small but cheerful dining room. Roast meat is the speciality, from 80F/€12.20. Closed Sun & Aug.

**La Cueva**, 18 rue St-Sépulcre (☎04.67.60.25.17). Tiny hole-in-the-wall Spanish place tucked away in the St-Anne district. Lively atmosphere and Iberian cuisine from 80F/€12.20. Closed Sat lunch & Sun.

**La Diligence**, 2 pl Pétrarque (☎04.67.66.12.21). Atmospheric vaulted medieval setting for innovative French dishes. Lunch menus from 85F/€12.96, or 145F/€22.11 in the evening, offering a good-value dip into the finest French cuisine. Closed Sat lunch & Sun.

**Le Jardin des Sens**, 11 av St-Lazaire (☎04.67.79.63.38). One of the highest-rated restaurants in Languedoc and universally acclaimed as Montpellier's best, just north of Le Corum. Excellent *terroir*-based creations in elegant surroundings. Menus 250–650F/€38.13–99.13. Closed Sun, Mon lunch & Jan.

**L'Olivier**, 12 rue Aristide-Olivier (☎04.67.92.86.28). Pretty little restaurant north of the station offering excellent-value traditional French cuisine. Menus at 165F/€25.16 and 200F/€30.50. Closed Sun, Mon and Aug.

**Le Pastis**, 3 rue Terral (☎04.67.02.78.59). Great southern French cooking in a fine old mansion. Strictly à la carte, from about 120F/€18.30. Closed lunch Mon & Sat and all day Sun.

**La Pomme d'Or**, 23 rue du Palais des Guilhem (☎04.67.52.82.62). Arty restaurant-bar with a predominantly gay clientele. Inventive menus in the 100F/€15.25 range. Closed Mon noon.

**La Popote**, 1 rue des Tessiers (☎04.67.66.05.77). Great-value Mediterranean food, in a cheerful setting with a streetside patio. Solid *plats du jour* at only 45F/€6.86. Open for lunch Tues–Sat, dinner Thurs–Sun.

**La Posada**, 20 rue du Petit-St-Jean (☎04.67.66.21.25). You'll need to book ahead for this popular restaurant with its well-priced Spanish and Mediterranean dishes, including paella and *moules à la crème de l'ail*. Menus from 50F/€7.63.

**Le Pou Qui Pleure**, 12 bd Sarrail (☎04.67.66.18.04). Transplanted Lyonnaise *bouchon* with an atmosphere of exuberant festivity. Expect to spend 100F/€15.25 or so. Open daily 8am–midnight.

**Le Regency**, 4 rue Cité-Benoît (☎04.67.64.42.69). Specialist in couscous and other dishes from the Maghrib, complete with traditional Moroccan décor and dances on Friday and Saturday evenings. From around 120F/€18.30. Closed Mon lunch time.

**Le Saleya**, pl du Marché aux Fleurs (☎04.67.60.53.92). In fine weather join the locals at the outdoor tables to feast on a daily selection of fish and regional fare for 70–100F/€10.67–15.25. Open for lunch mid-March to Oct, and also evenings June–Sept, depending on the weather.

**Salmon Shop**, 5 rue de la Petite-Loge. Novel "mountain cabin" interior offering oak-smoked salmon main courses in half-a-dozen guises at around 90F/€13.73. Just off place Jean-Jaurès. Closed Sun lunch time.

**Tripti Kulai**, 20 rue Jacques-Coeur. Quirky, friendly women-run vegetarian restaurant. Dishes with Oriental-influenced flair, including a good choice of salads, from 50F/€7.63. Closed Sun.

**La Vie en Vert**, 2 pl St-Côme. On fine days tables spill out of this tiny, vegetarian restaurant onto a pretty square. Menus at 69F/€10.52 and 85F/€12.96, or choose from a limited selection of nicely presented platters. Open for lunch only Mon–Sat.

**Le Vieux Four**, 59 rue de l'Aiguillerie (☎04.67.60.55.95). Meat eaters should head for this cosy, candlelit place specializing in *grillades au feu de bois* – meats roasted on an open spit. Menu at 98F/€14.95. Eves only.

## Cafés, bars and clubs

**Antidote**, pl de la Canourgue. Snappy bar which attracts the arty set. Techno-music dominates and there are occasional art exhibitions. Mon–Thurs till 1am, Fri & Sat 2am.

**Arts et Buffet**, pl St-Roch. Tucked behind the St Roch church, this delightful *salon du thé* is great for breakfast, a tea break or light meals of salads, home-made pies and cakes. Magazines and books available, some in English. Closed Mon & Tues.

**Café de la Mer**, 5 pl de Marché-aux-Fleurs. Popular gay-friendly establishment with a busy terrace. Mon–Sat 8am–1am, Sun 3pm–1am, open till 2am in July & August.

**Cargo**, pl Ste-Denis (☎04.67.92.56.05). Montpellier's best nightclub and live venue for blues, funk and soul. A ten-minute walk south of the old town. Tues–Sat 7pm–1am. Entry free or up to 30F/€4.58 on weekends, or for concerts or special events.

**Fitzparick's Irish Pub**, pl St-Côme. The name says it all. As Irish as you can hope for in the south of France. Daily noon–1am.

**JAM (Jazz Action Montpellier)**, 100 rue Ferdinan-Lesspes (☎04.67.58.30.30). Jazz bar, concert venue and home of the regular *café-littéraire* "Ethnologue" on the first Wed of month (8pm–midnight).

**Rockstore**, 20 rue Verdun. Legendary Montpellier club and concert venue. Can't miss the half-Cadillac protruding from the front of this former Calvinist temple. Free except for concerts. Mon–Sat 6pm–4am.

# Listings

**Airlines** Air France (☎04.67.22.65.05); Air Liberté (☎08.03.80.58.05); Air Littoral (☎08.03.83.48.34); British Airways (☎08.02.80.29.02); Buzz (☎01.55.17.42.42).

**Airport** Aéroport de Montpellier Méditerranée (☎04.67.20.85.00, *www.montpellier.aeroport.fr*).

**Banks** All major French banks are represented, most with branches in rue de la Loge, place Comédie or rue de Maguelone.

**Books** English books at: Book Shop, 4 rue de l'Université; Bill's Book Company, 44 rue de l'Université. Travel books at Les Cinq Continents, 20 rue Jacques-Coeur.

**Bus information** ☎04.67.92.01.43.

**Car rental** ADA, 58bis bd Clémenceau (☎04.67.07.96.47); Avis, 900 av Prés d'Arènes (☎04.67.92.51.92); Budget, at the gare SNCF (☎04.67.92.69.00); Europcar, 6 rue Jules-Ferry (☎04.67.06.89.00); Hertz, 18 rue J-Ferry (☎04.67.58.65.18); Rent-a-Car, 111 av de Palavas (☎04.67.22.42.52).

**Consulates** Britain, 64 rue Alcyone (by appointment only, ☎04.67.15.52.07).

**Cultural associations** Centre Culturel Juif, 5000 bd Antigone (☎04.67.15.08.76); Institut Franco-American, 55 rue du Mistral (☎04.67.20.05.09); Maison de Cambridge, 1 rue du Général-Riu (☎04.67.64.07.86).

**Internet access** There are lots of cybercafés around town; try Cybersurf, 22 pl du Millénaire in Antigone (Mon–Fri 8am–9pm, Sat & Sun 10am–6pm), or Planète Jeux, 33 rue Roucher (Mon–Sat 10am–1am, Sun 2pm–1am).

**Language courses** French courses are offered by several academies including: AICF, 3 rue Boussairolloes (☎04.67.34.07.79, *as.inter@wanadoo.fr*); École Méditerranée de Langue Française, 32 rue de l'Argenterie (☎04.67.66.14.51, *www.ecolemed.com*); and Langues Sans Frontières (☎04.67.91.31.60, *www.lsf.fr*).

**Laundry** 11 rue Serane (daily 7.30am–10pm).

**Markets** There are two main covered markets: Castellane, rue de la Loge; and Laissac, pl A. Laissac (both Mon–Sat 7.30am–1pm). There are also outdoor markets (Mon–Sat 7.30am–1pm) in bd des Arceaux (organic food), av de Heidelberg (flea market, also Sun), cours Gambetta (food and clothes) and pl de la Comédie (food and clothes).

**Medical emergencies** ☎04.67.22.81.67; Centre Hospitallier de Montpellier, 555 rte de Ganges (☎04.67.33.93.02) – take bus #16 from the *gare* to "Route de ganges" or the tram to "Hôpital Lapeyronie" and walk.

**Police** Hôtel de Ville ☎04.67.34.71.00.

**Swimming** Piscine Olympique d'Antigone, av Jacques-Quartier (☎04.67.15.63.00; tram to "Léon Blum").

**Taxis** Allo Taxi d'Oc ☎04.67.47.26.80; Taxi 2000 ☎04.67.03.45.45; Taxi à Montpellier ☎04.67.20.35.20; Taxi Bleu ou 5 ACTM ☎04.67.0.20.00.

**Train information** ☎04.99.74.15.10.

**Travel agencies** USIT Connect, 1 rue de l'Université (☎08.25.08.25.25, *www.usitconnect.fr*); Nouvelles Frontières, 4 rue Jeanne d'Arc (☎04.67.64.64.15).

**Youth information** CRIJ, 3 av Charles-Flahault (☎04.67.04.36.66). Youth information and a ride-sharing service, Allostop (☎04.67.04.28.28). Also Espace Montpellier Jeunesse, 6 rue Maguelone (Mon–Fri noon–6pm; ☎04.67.92.30.50).

# The coast: La Grande-Motte to Pézenas

From its narrowing point at Le-Grau-du-Roi, south of Nîmes, the Petite Camargue trails off westwards in fits and starts – a string of salty *étangs* and scrubby flats populated by birds and bulls respectively, passing close by Montpellier and continuing as far as Agde (see Chapter 6). The easternmost town along this stretch is **La Grande-Motte**, a bizarre 1960s planned resort handy for getting to the ruins of **Ambrussum** a few kilometres inland, where once the great Via Domitia carried goods from Cadiz, past Gibraltar, all the way to Rome. The other towns along this coast – **Palavas**, **Sète** and **Mèze** – have been fishing centres for generations, and their maritime heritage lives on in popular local traditions, such as the water-joust. Only **Maguelone**, once a bustling port, was unable to stand the test of the ages, and has been reduced to an ancient and romantically sited **cathedral**. Extremely popular and flooded with people in the summer months, all of these towns offer the makings of a good beach holiday, but they are far from being merely soulless seaside resorts. Finally, Languedoc's first modern capital, **Pézenas**, sits a few kilometres inland, now a town of beautifully preserved pre-Revolution palaces.

## La Grande-Motte and around

Separated by only a few kilometres of sandy beach from Le Grau-du-Roi to the east and less than 20km southeast of Montpellier's centre, **LA GRANDE-MOTTE** is undoubtedly the oddest resort town on the French Mediterranean. A

Canal du Midi, near Capestang

Sign advertising creperie, Carcassonne

Carrée d'Art, Nîmes

MICHAEL BUSSELLE

Boats on the beach, Collioure

B. ROBINSON/TRIP

Cathédrale St-Nazaire, Béziers

MICHAEL BUSSELLE

Pic-St-Loup, Hérault plain

B. SEACH/TRIP

St-Guilhem-le-Désert

Canalside buildings, Sète

Carcassonne

Parked car, Toulouse

Sixties-era beach-side version of Montpellier's Antigone development, this "futuristic" planned community, executed by Jean Balladur beginning in 1967, has aged about as gracefully as the beanbag chair and eight-track tape. The town consists of an immense array of weirdly shaped sand-coloured condos and apartment complexes with evocative names like "Le Calypso" and "Temple du Soleil", set on a long boardwalk. Traffic is banished to the background; you park (if you can find space) in the back streets, and reach the beach on foot. The strange aspect of the seafront is compounded by the absence of trees – nothing breaks up the pale beige landscape sandwiched between sea and sky – and, to cap it off, the proliferation of restaurants and shops on the promenade makes the whole place feel like an enormous shopping mall that just happens to have a beach. Aside from its peculiar looks though, the town is a run-of-the-mill family-holiday seaside resort, where apartments and hotels usually book for two- to four-week blocks. It's as good a place as any to stop for a swim, and if you want to spend a couple of days on the beach, you'll find all of the facilities and services you would expect.

## Practicalities

La Grande Motte's **tourist office** (July & Aug 9am–9pm; Sept–June 9am–12.30pm & 2–6pm; ☎04.67.56.42.00, fax 04.67.29.03.45, *www.ot-lagrandemotte.fr*) is on allée des Parcs, at the entrance to the town. **Buses** come in at the *gare routière*, located just to the east of the tourist office on avenue de Melguiel. The most appealing among the town's dozen or so near-identical **hotels** is the *Azur Bord du Mer* (☎04.67.56.56.00, fax 04.67.29.81.26; ④) – set out dramatically on the extremity of the town's quay it is no more expensive than the larger, uglier places stuck in the town itself. A cluster of seven **campsites** sits just west of the tourist office, among them *Louis Pibols* (☎04.67.56.50.08; April–Oct) and *Le Garden* (☎04.67.56.50.09; March–Oct) – both close to the beaches and with good facilities. The only **restaurant** which stands out above the uniform beachside fare is *Alexandre* (☎04.67.56.63.636; closed Sun eve & Mon) on esplanade de la Capitainerie, with good views of the port (menus from 140F/€21.35). **Bikes** and scooters can be rented at Bumpcycles (☎04.67.29.87.73), as well as at numerous other beachside outfits.

## Lunel and Ambrussum

Marking the northwestern extent of the Petit Camargue, **LUNEL** is just 14km north of La Grande Motte, on the western side of the Vidourle river. Aside from a few medieval buildings scattered about the decaying old town, the place is unforgivingly nondescript, and the only reason you should contemplate stopping here is to visit the nearby ruins of Roman Ambrussum, or to partake in the town's lively tradition of *tauromachie* – bullfights held occasionally from the spring to mid-autumn. If you're interest lies with the former, you'll most likely want to catch the first bus to Villetelle, which can drop you within a few kilometres (just before the A9 motorway; follow the sign-posted gravel road) of the Roman remains of **AMBRUSSUM**. This settlement (free entry) once commanded the bridge which carried the Via Domitia over the Vidourle, and which is now reduced to a couple of massive supports rising romantically out of the river. To get to the ruins climb the stairs on the hillside, to the old Roman **road**. Where this forks, taking the left will lead you past a series of indecipherable foundations and on to the remnants of the town's once formidable five-metre-thick walls. There are good **views** from up top, but the ruins themselves are disappointingly insubstantial. The visit is further frustrated by a total lack of informative plaques, but despite these short-comings the ruins are a popular spot – the riverside is quite beautiful, its trail makes for a pleasant walk, and the area is prime for picnicking.

A stop on the Montpellier–Nîmes line, Lunel's **gare SNCF** is on rue Verdun; from here it's a fifteen-minute walk south to the **tourist office** (July & Aug Mon–Sat 9am–7pm, Sun 9.30am–12.30pm; Sept–June Mon–Sat 9am–noon & 2–6pm, Sun 9.30am–12.30pm; ☎04.67.87.83.97, fax 04.67.71.26.67, *otlunel @capline.fr*) on cours Georges -Péri, beside the church in the old town. The summer-only (mid-June to mid-Sept) "Comet" **bus** service from La-Grande-Motte stops at the main roundabout by the rue République, which is also where you get the bus towards Abrussum. If you get stuck here for the night, *L'Embaracdere*, 273 avenue Victor-Hugo (☎04.67.71.10.45; ①) makes for cheap and adequate digs, and you can get a decent meal at *L'Auberge des Halles* (closed Sun eve, Mon & Feb; menus from 95F/€14.49) beside the tourist office. There are several **campsites** in the neighbourhood, including *Bon Port* on route de Camargue, just south of town (☎04.67.71.15.65; March–Oct).

# Palavas and Maguelone

**PALAVAS-LES-FLOTS** is Montpellier's own beach town, now absorbed into the metropolitan *agglomération* and even served by regular city buses. The town has been a popular seaside destination since almost a century ago, a fact attested to by the satirical caricatures of its inhabitants and visitors drawn by Montpellier artist Albert Dubout (1905–76). It's not as dismal as it seems, either, for once you penetrate the surrounding developments you'll find that the oldest part, where the banks of the canalized River Lez reach the sea, still retains the air of a pretty old fishing town. That said, Palavas is a busy, modern resort complete with all that that implies: restaurants of dubious quality, stores selling colourful junk, and crowds of people enjoying themselves swimming, sunbathing, sailing and cycling. Like so much of the coast the town is built on a sand-bar which encloses a series of *étangs*, the smallest of which, the Lac du Levant, on the north side of the old quarter, has a small eighteenth-century fort, La Redoubte, in the middle. Reached by a long causeway, the fort now houses the **Musée Albert Dubout** (July & Aug daily 4pm–midnight; April–June & Sept Wed–Sun 2–7pm; Feb, March, Oct & Nov Wed–Sun 2–6pm; Jan & Dec Sat & Sun 2–6pm; 30F/€4.58 including the Musée du Train), which holds works of the artist. Back on the mainland, a **Musée du Train** (same hours and ticket as Musée Dubout) houses the steam locomotive which used to run between here and Montpellier and was a favourite subject of Dubout (you'll see it in several of the works on display in the museum). The *étangs* themselves are replete with birdlife, and one of the few places on the French coast where you will see flamingos in their habitat; the tourist office can arrange **bird-watching** trips (Mon–Fri 9am–noon; 30F/€4.58).

The most interesting section of **beach** and the best for swimming and sunbathing lies west of the main town, past the campsite. You can get there by TAM bus or, if you drive, you will be obliged (mid-June to mid-Sept) to use the car park (25F/€3.81). From the parking area a narrow sand spit stretches west, separated from the *étang* behind by a shrubby embankment; the beach here is a popular gay spot and given over generally to nude (rather than topless) bathing. A road runs along the inland side of the embankment on which a free *petit train* runs every twenty minutes, ferrying people from their cars to the beach and on to the isthmus of **MAGUELONE** (TAM buses do the route out of season).

You wouldn't guess it, but the Romanesque **cathedral**, built in 1100s and dominating the green promontory today, was for centuries one of the most important churches in the medieval south of France. Before accumulating silt linked it to the mainland, Maguelone was an island most likely first settled by the Phoenicians. In the early eighth century the town here was taken by Muslim forces, but Charles Martel, court chamberlain and de facto ruler of France, pushed back the Muslim advance and destroyed the settlement in 737 to prevent its recapture and use as a forward base for further attacks. Refounded in 1030, the strongly-fortified church became an important religious centre and a place of refuge for bishops and popes in their quarrels with the nobility and kings of Europe. In 1096 Urban II proclaimed Maguelone as the second church after Rome – an indulgence which guaranteed the complete forgiveness of sins of whoever was buried there. Shortly thereafter the church was rebuilt in its present form. With the papal blessing and in its recovered role as port, the town throve from the Middle Ages until the Wars of Religion, when Louis XIII destroyed it for its unrepentant Protestantism. Nowadays all that remains is the ancient church. The building is still a place of worship, so you won't be able to enter it in beachwear, although you will be able to see its marble **portal**, with excellent mid-twelfth century low-relief carvings of apostles Peter and Paul. The **interior** (daily 10am–6.30pm; free), which has suffered total looting during through the ages, is dominated by a huge overhanging gallery. You'll find some ancient tombstones down by the altar, and from the gallery you can look down through the sluices over the entrance, which were intended to pour hot oil on the heads of attackers. The rest of the island presents a verdant idyll, and on the north shore, some restored fishermen's huts evoke the Maguelone of the early twentieth century, when the once glorious town had revived as poor fishing hamlet.

### Practicalities

TAM **buses** (line #28) from Montpellier circulate throughout the town. Palavas' **tourist office** (July & Aug daily 10am–8pm; April, May & Sept daily 9am–noon & 2–6pm; Oct–March Mon–Sat 9am–noon & 2–6pm; ☎04.67.07.73.34, fax 04.67.07.73.58, *www.palavaslesflots.com*) is in the unmistakable lighthouse building which towers above the port. For **accommodation**, try the comfortable beachside *Le Golfe* (☎04.67.74.01.87, fax 04.67.68.30.88; April–Sept; ④), just under 1km east of the tourist office, or the central *Flots Bleus*, at 21 quai Clémenceau (☎ & fax 04.67.74.01.73; ①), both of which are good value with excellent locations. There are several **campsites** around town, but the best situated is the beachside *Palavas Camping* (☎04.67.68.01.28; late-May to mid-Sept) at the westernmost part of town. You'll have no problem finding a **restaurant** here, most of which serve up the indisinguishable fare of seaside restaurants – grilled fish, *moules frites*, and steak and chips. The river-side *La Marine* (☎04.67.68.00.05) stands out for its original seafood creations (you'll spend 150F/€22.88 and upwards).

# Sète

Some 18km west along the marshy coast from Maguelone, and a twenty-minute ride by train or car from Montpellier, the cranes and winches of **SÈTE**'s busy port rise above the expanse of *étangs*. Entering town, you find yourself surrounded by grey warehouses, fenced-in storage yards and stacks of freight containers. This initial vision is somewhat disconcerting, but if you fight the impulse to turn back, you'll cross the wide Canal Maritime to arrive at the colourful old quarter, which straddles the westernmost of the two north–south canals, the Canal Royal. On the west bank of the canal, the land rises dramatically, hedging in the historical centre. This slope is the eastern side of the 175m-high rocky promontory, **Mont St-**

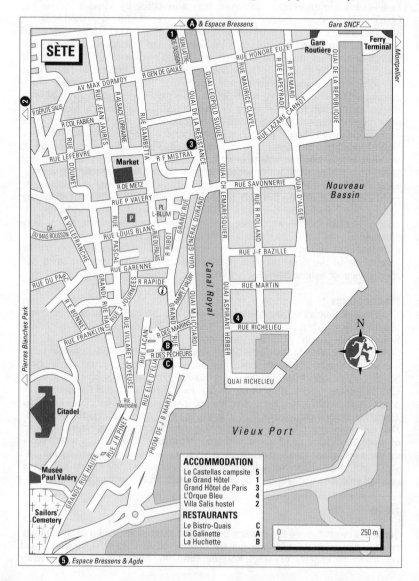

**ACCOMMODATION**

| Le Castellas campsite | 5 |
| Le Grand Hôtel | 1 |
| Grand Hôtel de Paris | 3 |
| L'Orque Bleu | 4 |
| Villa Salis hostel | 2 |

**RESTAURANTS**

| Le Bistro-Quais | C |
| La Galinette | A |
| La Huchette | B |

## WATER-JOUSTING

The beginnings of the curious Sètois sport of **water-jousting** have been lost in history, but the practice seems to have originated in the late seventeenth century, when Sète throve as a port thanks to its link to the Canal du Midi and the Canal à Rhône. The sport consists of two sleek boats, each manned by eight oarsmen, charging at each other on a near head-on course. On the stern of each boat a long raised tail supports the platform on which a jouster stands, dressed in white. The six remaining members of the team of seven jousters provide a counterweight on the platform, while the remaining crew, a coxswain and two musicians, keep the boat on course and in time. As the boats approach, the jousters steady their small shields, aim their long lances and attempt to strike their adversary from his mount. The spectacle is repeated seven times in each tournament or *joute*, and the winning team is the one who unseats its opponents the most times. There are about a dozen *sociétés des joutes* in Sète, and you can see them in action all through the summer in the town, and there are also local teams in other Langeudocian ports. The most important championships are held here on August 25, the *fête de St-Louis*.

**Clair**, whose presence has determined the growth of the town. As it expanded early this century, Sète grew as a long corniche completely circling the *mont*, until recently, when suburbs began to climb its steep slopes. The attractive town has a couple of small museums and a park, but primarily makes a good base for enjoying the 20km-long unbroken stretch of beach west towards Agde – it also has accommodation, excellent pleasure port facilities and lively nightlife in summer. It's also worth trying to aim your visit to coincide with one of the many times (frequently from late spring to early autumn) when **water-jousting** tournaments are held in the town's canals; the quaysides jam with people watching the boat-borne combatants, and afterwards the bars fill with boisterous revelry.

You're likely to spend most of your time in Sète along the Canal Royal, which is lined on the west side by restaurants and bars, or in the tight scrum of streets between the water and the hill. The closest of the two museums to the old quarter is the **Musée Paul Valéry** (Wed–Sun 10am–noon & 2–6pm; 10F/€1.53), southwest of the canal on rue François-Desnoyer, about a ten-minute walk west of the old port. This doubles as a municipal historical museum, whose collection focuses on the nautical traditions of the town – in which jousting figures prominently – and includes documents, models and paintings relating to the sport. Valéry's remains lie in the **sailors' cemetery** across the street from the museum, along with many Sètois fishermen who have lost their lives at sea. From this museum, or from the canal front you can take a long ride on bus #3 to the northwest side of Mont St-Clair. Here you'll find the **Espace Georges-Bressens** (Tues–Sun: July & Aug 10am–noon & 2–7pm; June & Sept 10am–noon & 2–6pm; 30F/€4.58 – French-only voice-recorded commentary), another local shrine. Bressens (1921–81) was perhaps France's most popular folk singer of the postwar era, a sort of Gallic Bob Dylan, whose simple guitar melodies served as platforms for irony-edged sentimental lyrics. Looking over the museum on a broad plateau on the west of Mont St-Clair, you'll find the park of **Pierres Blanches** (bus #5 from the Hôtel de Ville or the Valéry musuem), a scrubby habitat for lavender, thyme and rosemary, which provides impressive views over the shellfish beds of the Bassin du Thau to the north, particularly towards sunset. This is a also great spot for a picnic, but if you come without supplies you can get a snack at the small on-site café. Further east, at the summit of the *mont*, you'll find the nineteenth-century church of Notre-Dame-de-la-Salette (bus #5), built on the remains of a medieval fort; the church is nothing special but the **views** from here over the ports, old and new, are spectacular.

## Practicalities

Sète's **gare SNCF** (☎04.67.46.51.00) is on quai Maréchal-Joffre, on the north bank of the Canal Latéral; from here it's a forty-minute walk into town so your best bet is to take bus #3 to the "Les Pénitents" stop, near the tourist office. The **gare routière** is a little bit closer in, on quai de la République; from here it's a ten-minute walk west along rue Honoré Euze to the Canal Royal, and then another fifteen minutes south to the tourist office, or you can take bus #4 to the Hôtel de Ville, at the northern end of the old town. Across the Canal Maritime, to the east of the *gare routière*, you'll find the **ferry terminal**, Gare Maritime Orsetti (☎04.67.46.68.00; bus #4), which has regular departures for Mallorca and Morocco. The **tourist office** (July & Aug Mon–Sat 10am–1pm & 3–8pm, Sun 10am–1pm; Sept Mon–Fri 9.30am–noon & 2.30–6pm, Sat 9.30am–noon; Oct–June Mon, Wed & Fri 9.30am–noon & 2.30–6pm, Sat 9.30am–noon; ☎06.12.57.46.32, fax 04.67.46.17.54, *www.sete.org*) is at at 60 Grand'rue Mario Roustan. It has exchange facilities, and can also provide local bus tickets (6F/€0.92 for a single). You can get on the **Internet** at Le Cyber Snack, 10 avenue Victor-Hugo (Mon–Fri 9am–noon & 2–6pm) and rent **bikes** at Déferlantes, 6 quai Commandant Semary (☎04.67.74.82.30) or **scooters** at Cabello, 9 quai Vauban (☎04.67.74.50.29).

There's no shortage of **hotels** in town, starting with the ageing but funky *Grand Hôtel de Paris* (☎04.67.74.98.10; May–Sept; ②) at 2 rue Frédéric-Mistral; *Le Grand Hôtel* (☎04.67.74.71.77, fax 04.67.74.29.27, *www.sete-hotel.com*; ④), 17 quai de Lattre de Tassigny, alongside the northern part of the Canal Royal, is more elegant, but the best deal is *L'Orque Bleu* (☎04.67.74.72.13 ④), 10 quai Aspirant-Herber, at the same canal's southern end – try to get a quayside room in this converted nineteenth-century mansion as the views over the canal to the old town are great. The unhospitably basic **youth hostel**, *Villa Salis*, is on rue du Général-Revest (☎04.67.53.46.68, fax 04.67.51.34.01; closed late Dec; 80F/€12.20), a stiff half-hour walk west of the *gare routière* on the eastern slopes of the *mont*. The biggest and best **campsite** around is the mammoth *Le Castellas* complex (☎04.67.51.63.00; year round), 10km west on the RN112, although many people camp for free in the car parks along the road.

If you're at a loss to choose a place to eat, there's a barrage of **restaurants** along Quai Général-Duran, from the Pont de la Savonnerie right down to the pleasure port, all offering seafood in the 50–150F/€7.63–22.88 bracket. *La Huchette*, just south of the tourist office at 82 Grand'rue (☎04.67.74.40.24; closed Sun), offers some respite – a dark and cosy place offering tapas (three for 79F/€12.05), which also has a good cellar of regional wine, as does the equally tranquil *Le Bistro-Quais* (☎04.99.04.99.90; closed Sun eve), at no. 90 (menus from 90F/€13.73). For a more upscale seafood meal, you might head to *La Galinette*, 26 place des Mouettes (☎04.67.51.16.77; closed Sun eve, Fri lunch & Sat lunch out of season), on the north side of town (menus from 220F/€33.55). For **nightlife**, the bar *Grand de la Marine* at 90 quai Durand is a good place to start, while *La Bodega*, on 21 quai Noel-Guignon, is a cocktail bar with jazz, Latin and rock music (10pm–4am nightly).

# The Bassin de Thau and Mèze

North and west of Sète is the shallow expanse of the **Bassin de Thau**, which, at 20km long and some 6km wide, is one of the biggest salt lakes in Languedoc. From its northeastern end above Sète it accompanies the town's 14km stretch of beach southwest to Agde. Although there are no major sights on the length of road that runs from Sète around the eastern section of the *étang*, if you are going by car or bike there are a number of interesting little villages along the way. On the eastern bank of the Bassin, **Balaruc-le-Vieux**, an ancient fishing village, still retains its medieval walls and eleventh-century church, and close by on the north shore, the old town of **Bouzigues** looks out onto the oyster and mussel beds which crowd the lagoon – here you can visit the **Musée de l'Étang de Thau** (daily: June & Aug 10am–noon & 2–7pm; March–May, Sept & Oct 10am–noon & 2–6pm; Jan, Feb, Nov & Dec 10am–noon & 2–5pm; 20F/€3.05), whose array of imaginative multimedia displays explains the art of shellfish raising (including tanks with live specimens) as well as traditional fishing techniques. Non-French speakers will want to skip the video presentation, but the museum is worth a look if you are passing by.

**MÈZE**, a few kilometres to the west, is an ancient fishing hamlet whose old town is a dense maze of narrow streets flanked by low houses – the largest village on the Bassin de Thau's northern shore. As it isn't situated directly on the sea it gets relatively few visitors, and if nothing else provides some respite from the crowds of the coastal towns. It also has a surprising number of points of interest in and about town. The first of these is a three-hectare **Ecosite** (July & Aug daily 10am–7pm; 30F/€4.58), set up to preserve the habitat of the salt lagoon, with exhibitions on the flora and fauna of the *étang*, and on techniques of aquaculture (lagoon exploitation); you'll find this along the shore, 3km southwest of town. Also near Mèze, 5km north, just off the main road towards Pézenas, you'll find the **Musée-Parc La Plaine des Dinosaures** (daily: July & Aug 10am–7pm; April–June, Sept & Oct 2–6pm; Nov–March 2–5pm; 38F/€5.80) a musuem and excavation area established on the site of a major paleological find, including one of the biggest caches of dinosaur eggs yet discovered. Just to the east of town, on the road to Loupian, you can visit a recently excavated **Gallo-Roman villa** (mid-June to mid-Sept daily 10.30am–6.30pm; 30F/€4.58). Dating from the very tail end of the Roman period, it contains some impressive figurative and geometric mosaics. Finally, 12km north of Mèze along the D161 and a good detour on the way to Pézenas, the ruined Cistercian **abbey of Valmagne** (daily: mid-June to mid-Sept 10am–noon & 2.30–6.30pm; mid-Sept to mid-June 2–6pm; 38F/€5.80) sits in a romantic, wooded park, and is now used to host temporary art exhibitions and occasional concerts.

Mèze is the main service town for the Bassin de Thau; its **tourist office** (July & Aug Mon–Fri 9am–12.30pm & 2–8pm, Sat 9am–12.30pm & 2–7pm, Sun 9am–12.30pm; Sept–June Mon–Fri 9am–12.15pm & 1.30–8pm, Sat 9am–12.30pm; ☎04.67.43.93.08, fax 04.67.42.55.61, *www.ville-meze.fr*) is near the village centre on rue Massaloup. If you are looking to stay the town also has a good **hotel**, the economical *de Thau*, on rue de la Parée (☎04.67.43.83.83, fax 04.67.43.69.45; ③). You'll find a string of near-identical **restaurants** along the waterfront quai Descournut, all serving up shellfish fresh from the *bassin*: *Le Chabichou* or *Le Coquillou* are well regarded by locals, but any of them will do (menus from 70F/€10.68).

# Pézenas and around

PÉZENAS, about 54km southwest of Montpellier along the N113, and more or less halfway between Mèze and Béziers (see Chapter 6), is the last large inland settlement on the Hérault river, as it meanders south to Agde through the vineyards of the Languedoc plain. One of the most singularly beautiful towns in the French Southwest, endowed with an almost overwhelming concentration of grand architecture, it is also a centre for arts and crafts, and thus very popular – packing out with tourists in July and August. Although it had been an important market centre for centuries, Pézenas catapulted to glory when it became the seat of the Languedoc parliament and the residence of its governors in 1456, and reached its zenith in the late seventeenth century, when the Armand de Bourbon, prince of Conti and governor of Languedoc, made it a "second Versailles", drawing artists and writers of the stature of Molière to his court with his wealthy patronage – on and off the playwright spent a good four years here performing for the prince and garnering inspiration for the plays which would later make him famous. But with the prince's death in 1666, stagnation soon set in, and Pézenas reverted to the sleepy provincial town which – outside high season – it remains today.

## The Town

Pézenas' compact **old town** is set on the right bank of the Peyne river, occupying the area between the hill on which the town's castle once stood, and the village church. It is best accessed from the broad café-lined place 14 du Juillet, a lively square which now hosts the town's market and is set on the riverside just to the west of the *gare*. Entering from here, the first of the fine *hôtels* which you'll encounter is the **Hôtel Lacoste** (daily 10am–noon & 3–7pm; free), at 8 rue Oustrin, a fifteenth-century palace with a beautiful but compact vaulted courtyard framed by a monumental staircase; the mansion now houses temporary painting exhibitions. Continuing west, at place de Gambetta, you'll reach the tourist office, once the shop where Molière idled away his afternoons. Across the narrow, cobblestoned *place* stands the handsome sixteenth-century Council House, whose broad and square vaulted interior once held sessions of the Estates of Languedoc, but now houses the **Maison de Métiers des Arts** (daily 10am–noon & 3–7pm; July & Aug also Wed & Fri 8.30–11pm; free), a showcase for local crafts, including painting, decorative sculpture, stained-glass items and the like. From here wandering off in any direction will lead you to the carved stone facades of the wealthy merchants and nobles of Renaissance Pézenas; a glance up as you stroll around will almost certainly reveal a playful human face, a stately lion or regal sun carved out of a window casement or doorframe. If you head north from the square, down rue Alliés, you'll come upon the mansion housing the **Musée Vulliod-St-German** (Mon–Sat 10am–noon & 3–7pm, Sun 3–7pm; 15F/€2.29) – purportedly dedicated to the life and times of Molière, but in fact containing all manner of sixteenth- and seventeenth-century artefacts, from classically themed Aubusson tapestries to displays dedicated to the daily life of the humbler classes. The famous playwright is recalled in a room containing some of his papers and personal effects. Beyond this museum, you'll see the watchtower that forms the sole remnant of the medieval fortifications, while on the hill at the end of rue Béranger lie the ruins of the **castle** (closed) destroyed by Richelieu and dating back to as early as 1500 BC. At the foot of the castle's rise you'll find the small and rather dull **Musée de la Porte** (July & Aug

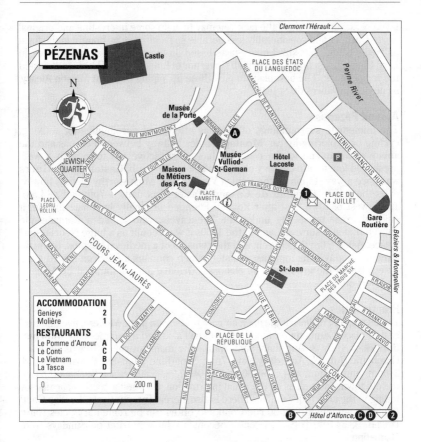

Mon–Fri 10am–12.30pm & 3.30–7pm, Sat & Sun 3.30–7pm; Sept–June Sun 2–6pm; free), celebrating the town's tradition of ironwork, most evident in the balustrades which can be seen around town. On the far side of the castle's base through rue Litanies, you'll enter the town's old **Jewish quarter**, marked off by gates, as was the custom – there's not much of interest here but heading east, between the gate of rue Juiverie and place Gambetta, you enter a warren of narrow streets jammed with magnificent *hôtels*; make sure you check out the doorway of the **Hôtel Grave** on rue de Château, the fifteenth-century **Hôtel de Jacques Coeur**, at 7 rue Émile Zola, and the impressive ironwork facade at 12 rue Sabatier. From the old Jewish quarter rue de la Foire eventually leads to the incongruously plain **church**, the Collegiate of St-Jean; passing this, head south down rue Conti, where, at no. 32 the **Hôtel d'Alfonce** (June–Sept Mon–Sat 10am–noon & 3–7pm; 10F/€1.52), contains a spacious courtyard girded by an ornately balustraded stone balcony; it was here that Molière's players put on performances during the winter of 1655–56.

If you like to shop while travelling, Pézenas will not disappoint, as two of every three frontages seems to house a store or workshop. Quality varies incredibly and if you persevere, amongst the tack you may turn up some interesting and original *objets*. Cheaper and considerably less durable souvenirs can be bought in the form of "petits pâtés", bite-sized mince-tarts based on the recipe of an Indian cook in Lord Clive's household – the British Governor of India holidayed here in 1768 and the recipe stuck. The best place to pick these up, piping hot, is at Maison Aleary, 9 rue de Chevaliers de St-Jean.

## Around Pézenas

The immediate surroundings of Pézenas offer good possibilities for walking, cycling or exploring by car. **Montagnac** lies halfway between Pézenas and the abbey of Valmagne to the east and has an attractive old town with a well-preserved fourteenth-century church, while to the south, **Castelnau-de-Guers** was once a way-station on the Roman Via Domitia. Most worthy of visit, however, is the priory, **Château de Cassan** (Easter–Sept daily 3–7pm; 30F/€4.58), 10km west of town, just after Roujan. Founded originally by Charlemagne, it enjoyed great prosperity under the Trencavels, who added a Romanesque church that still survives, and in the 1700s it was rebuilt as a huge Neoclassical palace. Aside from the church, and the remains of a medieval hospital, the main attraction today is its immense cloister, which contains a fine iron-forged staircase. Also on the grounds is an elaborate Oriental garden founded by Armand de Bourbon.

## Practicalities

**Buses** stop in Pézenas at the open-air *gare routière* on place Molière, five minutes' east of place Gambetta on foot; here you will also find a summer-only **information** kiosk (July & Aug daily 9am–7pm). The main **tourist office** is on place Gambetta (July & Aug daily 9am–7pm; Sept–June Mon–Sat 9.30am–noon & 2–6pm, Sun 2–5pm; ☎04.67.98.36.40, fax 04.67.98.96.80, *www.ville-Pézenas.fr*), in the old town – as well as all the usual information, they sell a good *Topoguide* for hiking in the area (30F/€4.58). There is also a great **Internet** café, Le Web Conti (daily 9am–midnight), at 30 rue Conti and **bikes** can be rented at Cycles Garin (☎04.67.98.34.04). The town centre becomes a busy **market** on Sundays from 10am–6pm.

There are two **hotels** in Pézenas, both of which have good amenities: *Genieys* (☎04.67.98.13.99, fax 04.67.98.04.80, *www.logis-de-france.fr*; ③) at 9 rue Aristide-Briand, near the end of rue Conti, and the splendid *Molière* (☎04.67.98.14.00, fax 04.67.98.98.28; ③), on place du 14 Juillet. If these are full, you can try *Les Rocailles* (☎04.67.24.00.27, fax 04.67.24.06.70, *www.logis-de-france.fr*; ③) on the N113 in Montagnac, and if you make the trip out to Cassan you can stay at the luxurious **gîte** *Domaine l'Eskillou* (☎ & fax 04.67.24.60.50; April–Sept; ③), whose price includes breakfast, in nearby Pouzelles. **Campsites** in the area include *Campotel* (☎04.67.98.04.02) and *St-Christol* (March–Sept; ☎04.67.98.09.00). **Restaurants** in Pézenas tend, somewhat surprisingly, to be unremarkable, falling into either the *terroir* or pizzeria bracket with menus for under 100F/€15.25; *Le Pomme d'Amour* (March–Dec) on rue Albert-Paul-Alliés and *Brasserie Molière* (in the hotel of the same name) fall into the first category, while *Le Conti*, 27 rue Conti (closed Sun) belongs to the second. International alternatives are *Le Vietnam* (closed Sat & Sun), at 11 rue Barbès, and the tapas bar *La Tasca* (closed Sun & Mon off-season), at 15 rue Anatole-France.

# Inland from Montpellier

The area **inland from Montpellier** is dominated by two rivers: the mighty Hérault, which cuts down southwest from the Cévennes mountains through the plains above the city, and the Vis, which runs along the northern rim of the *département* and into the Hérault at Ganges. Between them their underpopulated and lesser-travelled valleys – a world apart from the fishing towns and beaches of the coast – offer some remarkable scenery and attractions, and, taken in conjunction with a couple of absorbing towns, also form a naturally circuitous tour of the region by car, with plenty of hiking opportunities along the way.

The circuit starts with quiet **Clermont-l'Hérault**, poised on the eastern edge of the Haut Languedoc uplands 40km west of Montpellier, which provides access to the nearby reservoir **Lac Salagou** and an array of interesting sites: **Villeneuvette**, an old industrial centre, **Cabrières'** prehistoric copper mines, and the eerie landscape of **Cirque de Mourèze**. North of here is **Lodève**, an eminently explorable town which boxes in the Orb valley to the west and provides a good base for local excursions, as well as for the route eastwards across the high plateau des Garrigues to the beautiful **Cirque de Navacelles** in the Vis valley. From here you pass down through the Vis gorge to link up eventually with the Hérault just north of **Ganges**. On the southern border of the Cévennes, this area – with its gnarled olive trees and sturdy oaks – is a far cry from the Mediterranean scrub of the plains further south, a zone whose cloth industry was supported by the flocks of sheep which still roam its long valleys. Ganges provides easy access to the cavernous chambers of the **Grotte des Demoiselles**, which open up under the calcite plateau – you'll pass the *grotte* on either of two routes south to Montpellier. The first follows the **Hérault valley** itself, veering southwest to the deep Hérault gorge and the ancient hamlet and UNESCO World Heritage site of **St-Guilhem-le-Désert**, while the second, more direct route heads straight south via the **Pic-St-Loup**, standing sentinel above the coastal plain, and the old town of **St-Martin-de-Londres**.

## Clermont-l'Hérault, Lac Salagou and around

Some 40km west of Montpellier, a short distance from the banks of the River Hérault, lies quiet **CLERMONT-L'HÉRAULT**, a dull little cantonal capital whose only recommendation is as a jumping-off point for visiting the area around **Lac Salagou**. A brief walk around the town, with a stop to look at its thirteenth-century church, fortified in the fourteenth century to defend it against the English, more or less exhausts all the possibilities. Instead of sticking around, head west by car, foot or bike, towards **Villeneuvette**, 4km away. A model factory town founded by Colbert in the seventeenth century to produce high-quality wool for sale in the Mediterranean, Villeneuvette stayed in business until 1954 and still has 85 inhabitants. The walled-in compound is entered through a monumental gate bearing the legend *Honneur au Travail* ("honour to work"), and inside, a square, flanked by the church and *mairie*, opens onto neat rows of low, flower-bedecked workers' houses and the decaying factory. In its wooded surroundings, the little settlement presents a curious but enchanting idyll. A detour

5km south from Villeneuvette will take you to Cabrières, where you can visit the site of **copper mines** (April–Nov daily 10am–7pm; 30F/€4.58) that were exploited by the region's Neolithic inhabitants over 5000 years ago – the engaging hourlong tour takes you through 200m of galleries. On the other hand, heading northwest leads to the village of Moureze, located in the midst of an eerie zone of eroded dolomite known as the **Cirque de Moureze**, featuring a landscape consisting of an ancient seabed eroded by rainfall into a forest of rocky pinnacles. You can stroll though the myriad of paths which crisscross the area or enjoy an impressive panoramic view from the **Courtinales** (daily 9.30am–7.30pm; 25F/€3.81), a private park whose footpaths lead through a garden of local fauna and reconstructions of the prehistoric dwellings of the region – good fun for adults and children. Moureze was also the first town which the Resistance group, the Maquis Bir Hakeim, liberated from the Germans – a monument to them sits a kilometre or two south of the entrance to town. As you continue towards **Salasc**, a tiny crossroads hamlet 4km further west, the landscape becomes almost Martian, as the ground gives way to red iron-rich dunes. From Salasc, the road marked for Laiusson leads to the south shore of **LAC SALAGOU**, a reservoir whose shallow waters teem with bird life as well as fish and tiny crabs. The north shore, east of the larger village of **Octon**, is more developed and the landscape less striking. As the road follows the cliffs above the shore, it passes the ghost town of **Celles**, which was expropriated in the 1970s when the reservoir was built. The waters, however, never reached the hamlet, which now sits abandoned. After another eight kilometres of winding road, you'll join up with the busy Route National just north of Clermont.

## Practicalities

**Trains** and **buses** arrive in Clermont-l'Hérault at the **gare SNCF** on place Frédéric-Mistral, five minutes' walk south of the town centre. The **tourist office** (Mon–Sat 9am–noon & 2–6pm, Sun 10am–noon; ☎04.67.96.23.86, fax 04.67.96. 98.58, *www.ville-clermont-herault.fr*) for the *canton* is at 9 rue Gosse, between the station and the church. **Bikes** are available at Ozone (☎04.67.96.03.99), and other facilities in town include banks and laundry services. If you have to stay overnight in Clermont itself, the best bet is the basic but cheap **hotel** *Le Terminus* (☎04.67.88.45.00, fax 04.67.88.45.19, *www.logis-de-france.fr*, ③), 11 allées Salegro, by the station, but the Lac Salagou area offers better possibilities. Chief among these is Villeneuvette's *La Source* (☎04.67.96.05.07, fax 04.67.96.90.09, *www.logis-de-france.fr*; closed mid-Nov to mid-Dec & mid-Jan to mid-March; ④), a friendly place with great amenities and a good restaurant (menu from 100F/€15.25), while in Moureze *Les Hauts de Moureze* (☎04.67.94.04.84, fax 04.67.96.25.85; closed Nov–March; ④) is a comfortable inn with a rustic setting. Salasc has a **gîte**, the *Auberge Campagnard* (☎ & fax 04.67.96.15.62; ③ with breakfast), and at Octon you can stay or eat at the comfortable old *La Calade* (☎ & fax 04.67.96.19.21; March to mid-Dec; ③) in the village centre (lunch menu 73F/€11.13; closed Tues & Wed out of season). There's a **campsite**, *Les Rivières* (☎04.67.96.75.53; June to mid-Sept) just west of Clermont, and two on the lake: *Le Salagou* (☎04.67.96.13.13) at the eastern end, and the nudist *Village du Bosc* (☎04.67.44.13.99; May to mid-Sept) near Octon. A good choice of **restaurant** in Clermont is *L'Arlequin*, in place St-Paul, by the church (closed Sun & Mon; menus from 80F/€12.20), and in Moureze you'll find a couple of pizzerias by the entrance to Les Courtinales.

# Lodève and around

Located on the eastern spur of the massif that forms the bulk of the Parc de
Haut Languedoc, and just 10km north of Lac Salagou, **LODÈVE** is everything
which Clermont-l'Hérault is not – a pleasantly situated and friendly little town
with a couple of surprisingly good sights. Heading southwest from the *gare
routière*, you'll arrive in a few minutes at the greatest of these, the **Cathédrale
St-Fulchran**, built in the town's second great period of prosperity in the twelfth
and thirteenth centuries (the first was under Nero in the first century BC, when
it had been important enough to have an imperial Roman mint). The current
cathedral was raised on the riches of the woollen cloth industry that dominated
this area in the Middle Ages, and named in honour of a local tenth-century bishop. Although mostly late medieval, traces of an earlier cathedral's sixth-century
foundations can be seen, while the **cloisters** preserve part of the cathedral
building raised by the saint himself in the tenth century. The nave's dimensions
are impressive – 58m in length and 25m high – and its biggest bell weighs in at
2000 kilograms; in a small interior chapel opposite the door, you'll find where
the remains of the town's 84 bishops lie interred. Next door to the church, the
later **bishops' palace** has been converted into the *mairie*, and during business
hours you can peek in at the Italianate salons and staircases. From the cathedral, the old town spreads out east, bounded on three sides by a dramatic bend
in the Lergue river. Just south of the church you'll find the beautiful medieval
bridge, the **Pont de Montifort**, while in the centre of town, up nearby rue de
la République, is the surprisingly good **Musée Fleury** (Tues–Sun
9.30am–12.30pm & 2–6pm; 37F/€5.64), a gallery which draws the best fine-arts
exhibitions between Castres and Montpellier, as well as a good selection of
archeological finds and historical items dating from the prehistoric to the post-
Revolutionary. Just east of this museum, in the place du Marché, the old
nineteenth-century *halle* has been converted into the **Hôtel Dardé** (daily
9am–7pm; free), a showcase for local sculptor Paul Dardé (1888–1963).
Unfortunately, little survives of medieval Lodève, as the town was nearly razed
in retribution for its support of Montmorency's revolt. You can however get a
glimpse of the cloth-making industry (which died only in 1960) by visiting the
**Atelier National de Tissage de Tapis** (Tues–Thurs 2–6pm; 21F/€3.20; call
ahead ☎04.67.96.40.40) south of the old town, across the river – an exhibition of
looms and other machinery where you can see textiles being woven according
to traditional methods.

Lodève makes a pleasant base for exploring the surrounding area, including
the upper Orb valley to the west and Lac Salagou to the south, but the nearest
attraction is the **priory of St-Michel de Grandmont**, just 8km away, on a wooded rise to the east of town. The old monastery and its grounds can be visited as
part of a **guided tour** (July & Aug 10.30am, 3.15pm, 4pm & 5pm; June, Sept &
Oct 10.30am, 3.15pm & 4pm; Feb–May 3pm; Nov to mid-Dec Sat & Sun 3.15 &
4pm; 28F/€4.27), but you can also poke around the buildings on your own
(June–Oct 1–2.45pm; 20F/€3.05). Built in 1128, this was one of the first convents
of the extremely strict Grandmontine Order of hermits, whose alarming popularity with the faithful prompted the power-jealous John XXII to clamp down on them
in 1317. The buildings which remain today comprise one of their best preserved
houses, including a cloister, reception hall and an austere late thirteenth-century
church. The spacious **grounds** are well worth a visit, their shaded woods stocked

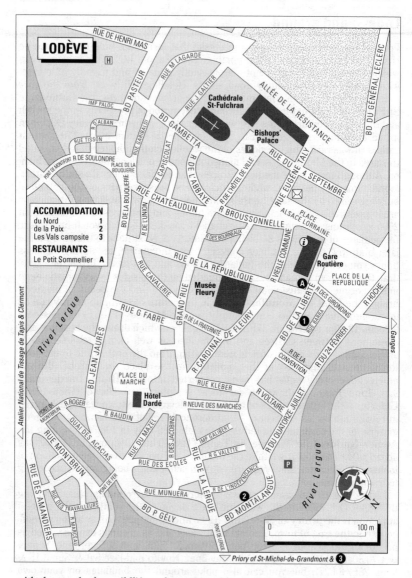

LODÈVE

**ACCOMMODATION**
du Nord 1
de la Paix 2
Les Vals campsite 3
**RESTAURANTS**
Le Petit Sommellier A

▽ Priory of St-Michel-de-Grandmont & ③

with deer and other wildlife and punctuated by prehistoric dolmens and menhirs (going back some 4000 years) as well as Visigothic sarcophagi.

## Practicalities

Lodève's **gare routière** (☎04.67.88.86.44) is on place de la République, right beside the town's **tourist office** (Mon–Fri 9am–noon & 2–6pm, Sat 9am–5pm &

July & Aug only also Sun 9.30am–1.30pm; ☎04.67.88.86.44, fax 04.67.44.07.56, *www.lodeve.com*). You can rent **bikes** at Club House (☎04.67.96.46.48). The best place to **stay** is the newly remodelled *Hôtel du Nord* (☎ & fax 04.67.44.10.08; ③) at 18 boulevard de la Liberté, just down from the post office. The young couple who run it are very welcoming and rooms range in size from singles to family-sized suites with kitchen. Another good choice is *de la Paix* (☎04.67.44.07.46, fax 04.67.44.30.47, *www.logis-de-france.fr*; closed Feb to mid-March; ④) on 11 boule-vard Montalangue, run by the same family for over a century. The nearest **camp-site** is *Les Vals* (☎04.67.44.36.57; closed Feb), just south of town. The *de la Paix* has one of the better **restaurants** (closed Sun & Mon Oct–April; menus from 85F/€12.96), with solid, home-cooked regional dishes, and *Le Petit Sommellier* (closed Mon; menus from 70F/€10.68), at 3 place de la République, is another good option. You can also pick up light meals at the *Café de la Bourse*, 1 avenue Fumel and *Le Grand Café du Nord*, in the hotel of the same name and there's a **snack bar** out at St-Michel. On Saturdays a large **market** is held throughout the centre of Lodève, while in the summer months (mid-June to mid-Sept), a *terroir*-produce market convenes on Tuesday, Wednesday and Thursday afternoons in the place de la République.

## North to Ganges via the Cirque de Navacelles

Taking the D25 eastwards from just north of Lodève, you'll climb 15km up the wooded Brèze valley before reaching an open plain stretching a similar distance to the hamlet of St-Maurice-Navacelles. Here the road drops into the Vis valley, descending with it all the way to Ganges (see below). If you turn off to the north at St-Maurice you'll come to the **CIRQUE DE NAVACELLES**, a breathtaking section of the valley where the river, carving down sharply through the sur-rounding plain, has doubled back on itself, leaving a small hillock stranded in the middle of the cirque all but surrounded by the river – at its base huddles the ancient hamlet of **Navacelles**. The cirque can also be reached by **hiking**; the GR653 east from Lodève links up with the GR7, which winds its way north, entering the Vis valley near St-Maurice before heading on into the Cévennes. Arriving by car, you'll first reach the belvedere on the south side of the cirque, from which you can contemplate the incredible sweep of the gorge and look down on the village 600m below. From the look-out point the road follows a dra-matic series of switchbacks descending to Navacelles itself – a tiny stone ham-let with a medieval bridge – before ascending to another look-out point on the north side. The **information centre** (daily 10am–noon & 2–6pm) for the cirque is located at the southern belvedere; it has a small exhibition explaining the formation of the curious canyon and conducts two- and three-hour walking tours (20F/€3.05, frequently English-language). A good alternative walk which you can easily manage without assistance is the spectacular 6km hike to the under-ground *source de la four*, along a trail leading west along the canyon floor from Navacelles itself. East of St-Maurice the road snakes down into the Vis gorges to cover the remaining 26km to Ganges. Contrasting with the open scrub around Navacelles, this section of the valley is a steep and lush canyon, whose tree-clad banks at times close off the sky above with thick boughs. As you con-tinue it gradually widens, passing occasional signs of life – riverside *relaises*, ancient bridges, and abandoned factories – before opening up abruptly when it reaches the Hérault at Ganges.

As you'd expect, services are rather minimal in this neck of the woods. Navacelles has one only **hotel**, *Auberge de la Cascade* (☎04.67.81.50.95, fax 04.67.81.53.45, *www.logis-de-france.fr*, ②), as well as the **gîtes** *Le Mas de Guilhou* (☎04.67.81.50.69; ①) and *Casa Lou Haîdouc* (☎04.67.81.51.54; ①). A CAP *gîte* at La Vacquerie, halfway between Lodève and St-Maurice (☎04.67.44.56.05; ①), provides shelter if you're hiking along the GR7. You can also stay at *Les Tilleuls* (☎04.67.44.61.60; ①) in St-Maurice itself, and there are other possibilities along the Vis gorge. The *Auberge* and the *gîtes* serve **meals**, as does the café *Baume Auriol* at the southern belvedere (*plat du jour* 50F/€7.63).

# Ganges and around

**GANGES**, the largest town on the upper Hérault valley, is primarily of interest as a transport hub and service centre for the more interesting places just to the south (which you can also access travelling along either of the two routes back to Montpellier– see opposite), and for the busy recreation industry which has grown up on the banks of the river. The town, like many villages of the Cévennes region to the north, enjoyed prosperity first as a wool then subsequently a silk centre, until the advent of synthetic fabrics and ravages of phylloxera disease in the late 1800s drove the industry under. It was also here in August 1944 that the local maquis managed to repulse a column of 3000 German troops after a fierce ten-hour battle. Nowadays there's little to see or do here, although a walk through the old quarter will take you past a few remaining medieval houses, a pretty eighteenth-century market square and an imposingly dour Huguenot temple. All in all, though, these do not suffice to dispel a certain lingering air of stagnation.

The **gare routière** is on rue Jules-Ferry, just west of the central Plan l'Ormeau, which is where you'll find the **tourist office** (Mon–Fri 10am–noon & 2–6pm, Sat 10am–noon; ☎04.67.73.00.56, fax 04.67.73.00.50). There are various banks with exchange services (look along rue F.-Mistral), and you can connect to the **Internet** at Médi@gora, beside the *gare routière*. L'Atelier (☎04.67.73.69.20), by the tourist office, rents **bikes**. Also on Plan l'Ormeau you'll find a **hotel**, the basic *de la Poste* (☎04.67.73.85.88, fax 04.67.73.83.79; closed Jan; ②), although you can also stay at the *Auberge du Pont Vieux* (☎04.67.73.62.79; ②), west of the centre on the route de Vigan. The municipal **campsite** (☎04.67.57.92.97), along the river at the southern end of town, has the only laundry. Of the local **restaurants**, the best is *Le Josyln' Melodie* (☎04.67.73.66.02; closed Wed), a homely little Lyonnais place on 4 place Fabre d'Olivet (menus 82F/€12.51), although *La Rose de Saigon* at 12 place des Halles (closed Tues) serves good Vietnamese cuisine (from 60F/€9.15). For something lighter try the creperie *La Luciole* next door at no. 11.

## Laroque, the Grotte des Demoiselles and St-Bauzille

A couple of kilometres south from Ganges, the first place you find is the hamlet of **LAROQUE**, attractively situated on a hillside along the Hérault river. It has a cheerful bank-side promenade, while narrow medieval streets zigzag up to the remains of its castle. At the entrance to the town there is a small twelfth-century church, while on the south side lie the ruins of a huge nineteenth-century textile plant. A few kilometres further south you'll come upon the area's biggest draw, the **GROTTE DES DEMOISELLES** (daily: July & Aug 9am–7pm; April–June & Sept 9am–noon & 2–6pm; Oct–March 9.30am–noon & 2–5pm; *www.Demoiselles .com*; 42F/€6.41), a little more than 2km east of the road. This incredibly vast cavern, discovered in 1770, stretches out below the plateau de Thaurac, the highland southeast of Ganges, and is famous for its huge stalactite and stalagmite formations. The **guided tour** (expect a long wait in high season) is made aboard an underground funicular (hourly; last departure 45min before closing), which lends the whole thing an amusement-park air, and though the cave is spectacular, it can be a bit of a let down after all the crowds and fuss. Just south of the grotto, **ST-BAUZILLE** is of note only as a stopping point in the vicinity of the cave and centre for river-oriented sports; it is a good place to shop for a canoe trip south.

Without a doubt, the nicest place to **stay** in this area is Laroque, where you can get a room or a meal (from 50F/€7.63) at the comfortable *Aux Trois Arches* (☎04.67.73.86.80; Apr–Oct; ②) on the main promenade. In a park on the northern edge of town, *Le Parc aux Cedres*, 120 avenue de l'Europe (☎04.67.73.82.63, fax 04.67.73.69.85, *www.logis-de-france.fr*; ④) also has a restaurant, while *Bar de Ramparts*, near the *Trois Arches*, has decent Belgian beers and home-made desserts. There is also a **campsite**, the two-star *Le Tivoli* (☎04.67.73.97.28; June–Aug), near the *Cedres*.

# South to Montpellier

Heading south from Ganges to Montpellier, you can choose between two routes, whose paths diverge at **St-Bauzille** (see above). The longer, more spectacular of the two leads down the Hérault gorge to the medieval abbey-town of St-Guilhem-le-Désert, emerging from the canyon shortly before Gignac, from where you either head 30km east to Montpellier or continue to Clermont-l'Hérault. Unfortunately only the St-Guilhem–Gignac leg of this route is served by buses, and then only in summer – if you do not have transport doing the whole thing will involve some walking or hitching. The other option is to head due south, a 40km route which takes you to St-Martin-de-Londres, from where you can hike to the Pic-St-Loup and surrounding sights. St-Martin is, in fact, only 6km from the banks of the Hérault, but is separated from the river by a series of low peaks – if you have a car or are willing to hitchhike or walk, you could link up the two routes by heading first to St-Martin and then doubling back on the treacherously winding D122 to the village of **Causse-de-la-Selle**, north of St-Guilhem on the valley route (a distance of 14km). Stopping at Causse also gives you the opportunity of making the trip to St-Guilhem by river raft (see below) – the most thrilling way to take in the gorges.

### Via St-Guilhem-le-Désert

The route from Ganges to St-Guilhem follows the course of the Hérault via the D4 on the river's right bank, which you access by crossing the bridge at St-Bauzille. After 15km the road cuts southwest across a plateau, passing the hamlet of Causse-de-la-Selle – the turn-off for St-Martin-de-Londres (see p.277) – before rejoining the river midway through the dramatic **Gorges de l'Hérault**. Hugging the western bank the road follows the tortuous canyon to reach the stunningly situated hamlet of **ST-GUILHEM-LE-DÉSERT**. There is no mistaking the great antiquity of this village, nestled in a steep and wooded ravine rising from the gorge, the reddish roofs of its medieval houses contrasting with the electric green of the surrounding trees. The town grew up around the abbey founded by Charlemagne's counsellor Guilhem, who returned from Rome in 800 with three pieces of wood said to be remnants of the Cross. Thanks to these relics the monastery and the village around it throve through the centuries that followed, both as a pilgrimage

in its own right, as well as a stopping point on the way to Santiago de
L. Today the immaculately preserved town, designated a UNESCO
itage site, is still presided over by the eleventh-century monastery
aily 8am–12.10pm & 2.30–6.20pm; free), at the upper end of the village,
by the obligatory car park (25F/€3.81). Crowned by a chunky fifteenth-century
bell tower, the church is the only surviving part of the once powerful monastic
house. Its magnificent entryway, flanked by columns pillaged from Roman ruins,
passes through a small vaulted narthex to enter the cavernous but plain nave, ending in a curiously oversized transept and apse. Inside the church you'll find the cas-
ket holding the remains of Guilhem (who was canonized after his death) and a reliquary holding one of the famous bits of wood. From the church you can climb
down to the **crypt**, which dates back to the eighth century, as well as the ruined
**cloister**, whose north and west galleries are still in place. There is also a small
**museum** here (July & Aug Mon–Thurs & Sat 11am–noon & 2–2.30pm, Sun
2–2.30pm; Sept–June Mon & Wed–Sat 2–5.30pm, Sun 2.30–5pm; 10F/€1.53) containing religious sculptures recovered from the destroyed abbey. The rest of the
village consists of low, ancient houses which follow the narrow lanes leading down
the ravine, interrupted by medieval pilgrims' fountains marked with the scallop-
shell symbol of St James. Looking back as you descend past the church, you'll be
treated to views of the church's impressive apsidal chapels.

On the other hand, a short one-hour **hike** leads up from the car park to the
ruins of a castle, from which you get the best **views** of the town. Just after this the
GR trail splits, with the GR74 climbing through a canyon towards Mont St-
Baudille, and the GR653 looping south before merging again with the GR74 to
proceeed west to Lodève. The tourist office (see below) can give you information
on the several AR trails which run through the hills hereabouts. Leaving St-
Guilhem by road, the D4 continues 4km further along the dramatic canyon,
passing the mouth of the **Grotte de Clamouse** (daily: July & Aug 10am–7pm;
June & Sept 10am–6pm; Feb–May & Oct 10am–5pm; Nov–Jan noon–5pm;
42F/€6.41), famous for its immense and delicate crystalline formations. Only
500m later the gorge abruptly opens up at the beginning of the low Languedocian
coastal plain; the transition is marked by a great medieval *pont du diable*, which
crosses the river above a gravelly bank now serving as a popular river-beach.
Shortly beyond, you pass the uninteresting hamlets of Aniane and Gignac, the latter of which serves as a bus interchange.

St-Guilhem's **tourist office** (July & Aug 9am–7pm; Sept–June 10.30am–
12.30pm & 2–7pm; ☎ & fax 04.67.57.44.32, *ot.st-guilhem@wanadoo.fr*) is at the foot
of the village, just above the main road; the office has an ATM, and you can also
buy a discount ticket (10F/€1.53) on local sights here. A number of **gîtes** in and
around St-Guilhem can put you up for the night, including the English-speaking
*Gîte de la Tour* (☎ & fax 04.67.57.34.00; ①) located in a medieval tower in the village, and the CAP *gîte* (☎04.67.52.72.11; ①), also in town. A dramatic approach to
the town can be made from the riverbank 3km east of Causse on the D122, from
where Canoë La Vallée de Moulins (☎04.67.73.12.45) runs **canoeing** excursions
downriver to St-Guilhem. St-Guilhem's **rafting centre** is at the bottom of the hill,
across the road (☎04.67.55.75.75).

## Via the Pic-St-Loup and St-Martin-de-Londres

Some 20km due south of St-Bauzille looms the great **Pic-St-Loup** (658m),
which, dominating the plain of Hérault, can be seen from Béziers almost to

Nîmes. **ST-MARTIN-DE-LONDRES**, 13km south from Ganges by road or hiking trail (the GR60, leaving St-Bauzille), makes the best base for hiking the remaining 10km to Pic's wooded summit – a site from which you can enjoy impressive panoramas, but which cannot be reached except by foot (car drivers can get as close as 4km by taking the D113 to the hamlet of Cazevielle). St-Martin is another town of great antiquity and, contrary to appearances, its name has nothing to do with English capital London; it is named after the Plaine du Londres (from the Celtic word for "swamp") in which the town is located. Testament to the town's history is the beautiful knot of buildings focused around the eleventh-century Romanesque **church**, founded by monks from nearby St-Guilhem. Its interior is plain, but is more than made up for by the three-lobed Byzantine-style exterior, which blends in harmoniously with the surrounding buildings. Elsewhere in the town you can see how the two concentric sets of walls and towers were swallowed up by houses over the centuries. If you're **hiking** into town, or if you're not up to tackling the Pic, about 2km north of St-Martin a leg of the GR60 leads off eastwards into the Ravin des Arcs, a high but narrow canyon which makes an excellent two-hour walking circuit; be sure to bring water along, as there is no potable source on the way – you can fill up at the public fountain in front of the tourist office (see below). Another option is the ninety-minute walk south of St-Martin (but also on the Montpellier bus route) to **Camous**, where you'll find a 5000-year-old unearthed **prehistoric village** (July to mid-Sept Tues, Wed & Fri–Sun 3.30–7pm; May & June Sat & Sun 2–6pm; mid-Sept to April Sun 2–6pm; 15F/€2.29).

St-Martin's **tourist office** (Mon–Sat 9am–noon & 2–7pm; ☎04.67.55.09.59, *www.tourismed.com*) is on the main road at the centre of town. For accommodation, there is the **gîte**, *La Bergerie du Bayle* (☎ & fax 04.67.55.72.16, *bayle @tourismed.com*; ①), which also does very affordable half-pensions. The **campsite**, *Pic de Loup* (☎04.67.55.00.53; April–Sept), is just east on the main road. A recommendable **restaurant** in St-Martin is *Les Muscardins* (☎04.67.55.75.90; closed Mon & Tues), which has superb *terroir* menus from 145F/€22.11 (weekdays) and 240F/€36.60 (weekends).

## travel details

### TRAINS

**Montpellier** to: Agde (12–20 daily; 30min); Béziers (12 daily; 37min); Carcassonne (4 daily; 1hr 30min); Lunel (3–8 daily; 15min); Narbonne (12 daily; 45min); Nîmes (14 daily; 22min); Paris (6–8 daily; 3hr 30min); Sète (12–20 daily; 17min); Toulouse (8 daily; 2hr 55min).

### BUSES

*Many bus routes in the interior run Mon–Sat only.*

**Montpellier** to: Bédarieux (2 daily; 2hr); Béziers (4–6 daily; 1hr 30min); Clermont-l'Hérault (4–12 daily; 40min); Ganges (4–5 daily; 1hr 15min); Gignac (for St-Guilhem; 3–6 daily; 40min); La Grande-Motte (8–12 daily; 1hr 5min); Grau-du-Roi (8–12 daily; 1hr 10min); Lodève (3–6 daily; 1hr 15min); Lunel (2–10 daily; 35min); Nîmes (2 daily; 50min); Palavas (local service); St-Bauzelle (4–5 daily; 1hr); St-Hippolyte (3 daily; 1 hr 45min); St-Martin-de-Londres (3–8 daily; 50min); St-Pons (2 daily; 2hr 20min); Sète (3–10 daily; 1hr 10min); Sommières (4–8 daily; 45min).

**Clermont-l'Hérault** to: Lodève (3–4 daily; 35min); Pézenas (3–4 daily; 55min).

**Ganges** to: Nîmes (3 daily; 1hr 15min); St-Hippolyte (3 daily; 40min); Sauve (3 daily; 54min); Quissac (3 daily; 50min).

**Gignac** (summer only) to: Pont du Diable (1–5 daily; 20min); St-Guilhem (1–5 daily; 35min).

**La Grande-Motte** to: Grau-du-Roi (4–10 daily; 10min); Grotte de Clamouse (1–5 daily; 25min); Lunel (summer only; 3 daily; 35min); Nîmes (4–10 daily; 40min).

**Lodève** to: Béziers (3–4 daily; 1hr 50min); Clermont-l'Hérault (3–4 daily; 45min); Pézenas (3–4 daily; 1 hr 20min).

**Lunel** to: Villetelle (for Ambrussum; Mon–Fri 4 daily; 20min).

**Pézenas** to: Béziers (6–8 daily; 32min); Clermont-l'Hérault (3–4 daily; 35min); Lodève (3–4 daily; 1hr 20min).

### FERRIES

**Sète** to: Palma de Mallorca (1–3 weekly); Tangiers (1–2 weekly).

# CHAPTER SIX

# NARBONNE, BÉZIERS AND AROUND

N arbonne and **Béziers** are the two provincial towns which dominate the flat expanse of marshy alluvial plain formed by the outpourings of the Hérault, Orb and Aude rivers, whose mouths all reach the Mediterranean within a 15km strip. The former town is the smaller, but generally livelier centre of the two, with a compact medieval core and vibrant nightlife, while the latter is an historically proud and defiant town, which, though somewhat more sedate these days, springs to life in the summer with its renowned *feria*. Narbonne, poised just north of the Étang de Bages' long expanse, is best situated for excursions into the **Corbières**, an isolated range of hills stretching south to Roussillon – once forming the Cathar heartland, they harbour the idyllic village of **Termes**, with its *château*, and the strikingly beautiful hamlet of **Lagrasse**. The River Aude, swinging sharp east at Carcassonne, makes its way along the northern edge of the Corbières, shadowed by the **Canal du Midi**, the incredible canal system which has dominated the whole of this area since the seventeenth century, and which links both Narbonne and Béziers. Following the course of the canal takes you past the various monuments of the **Minervois** – the region squeezed in-between the Corbières and Haut Languedoc – and attractive Languedocian scenery before it splits, with the Canal de la Robine heading south towards Narbonne and the main waterway meandering on, via Béziers, to the Bassin de Thau. Skirting Béziers, the **Orb valley** threads north along the border of the Parc Naturel de Haut Languedoc, passing a succession of villages which have survived the centuries thanks to the river's fertile banks. The coastal stretch curving between the two towns is, for the most part, an area of uninviting marsh, but at either end two chunks of terra firma, the Montagne St-Loup and de la Clape, provide anchors for a couple of old ports, **Agde** and **Gruissan**, each of which have modern beach-resort alter-egos. Despite the fact that if you're interested in sun and swimming you'll find prettier surroundings in the Côte Vermeille to the south, both of these old settlements are worth a visit for their gentle ambience – Agde from Béziers and Gruissan from Narbonne.

**Public transport** facilities in this region vary considerably. Narbonne is the point where the busy coastal rail line to Perpignan branches off from the main Toulouse–Marseille route, on which Béziers can be found. In the hinterland, you'll have to depend on bus services, which are fairly good for the major towns along the coast and the Orb valley. Out-of-the-way sites are more difficult, such as Minerve, which isn't served at all by public transport (although the narrow-gauge ATM train does approach it). But in any case – if you have time – the best way to

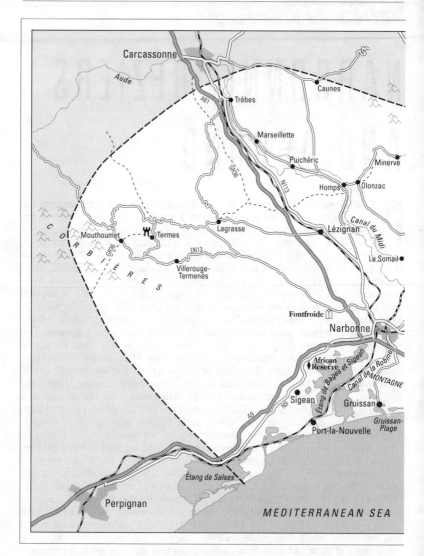

travel through the region is by canal – either by piloting a houseboat, or biking or hiking the towpath which accompanies the route.

# Narbonne and around

There's no mistaking **NARBONNE** as you approach it, its towering cathedral rising up over the rooftops and dominating the coastal plain for miles around.

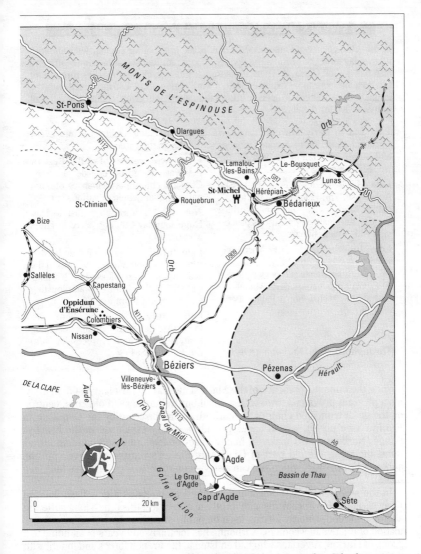

Once the capital of the Roman province of Narbonensis, it flourished as a port and communications centre from ancient times into the Middle Ages, and was home to an important Jewish university in the twelfth and thirteenth centuries. But in the mid-1300s things suddenly went awry: the Jews were expelled, the plague struck, the Black Prince burnt down the town, the dykes of the Aude burst and the port silted up, a series of disasters which brought ruin to the town's economy. A tentative prosperity returned only in the late 1800s with the birth of the modern wine industry, which continues to support the town. Today,

## FESTIVALS IN AND AROUND NARBONNE AND BÉZIERS

In this little corner of Languedoc Béziers is the hot spot for popular festivals, with its five-day *feria* the prime attraction. Narbonne, for its part, is big on theatre and also has a good Carnival. There are summer music cycles and parties throughout the area and, as can be expected from a wine region, local festivals timed with the grape harvest. Where no specific information number is given, contact the relevant tourist office for details.

**Late Jan to early March** Narbonne: Carnaval. A series of parades, dances and street entertainment held on the weekends leading up to Lent.

**Late April** Béziers: Fête de la Ste-Aphrodise. The Feast day of the town's patron saint, usually held on the third Sunday, and featuring a curious procession with a camel float.

**Late June to early July** Narbonne: Festival National de Théâtre Amateur. Free nightly theatrical performances (9.15pm) on the cours de la Madeleine and at the Archbishop's Palace (☎04.66.32.40.50).

**July**

**Throughout July** Narbonne: Orgues d'Été. Evening organ recitals every Sunday in the cathedral.

**First two weeks of July** Béziers: Festival de Musique de Béziers. Classical choral performances of international quality held in various venues.

**July 12–15** Narbonne: Bastille Day. Huge four-day outdoor party in cours Mirabeau.

**Late July** Cap d'Agde: Fête de la Mer. After an open-air mass for victims of the sea, the boats are blessed in this festival, which also features water-jousting and general celebration.

**Late July** Gruissan: Fête des Pêcheurs. Sea-faring rituals, including boat blessings and a procession with the statue of St Peter.

despite the ominous presence of the Malvesi nuclear power plant just 5km away, it's a pleasant provincial town with a small but well-preserved old core, centred on the great truncated choir of the **cathedral**, and bisected by the **Canal de la Robine** (see p.299), whose banks provide a grassy esplanade in the heart of things. Narbonne also makes a handy base for exploring surrounding attractions, including the old port of **Gruissan**, Sigean's **nature reserve**, and the abbey of **Fontfroide**, which you can also visit en route to the Corbières hills (see p.293).

In the summer of 1991 Narbonne acquired notoriety as a new flash point in France's continuing problems with its ethnic minorities, this time a long-suffering and disregarded minority forcing itself on public attention. Among its mixed population of relative newcomers, Narbonne has for thirty-odd years been home to a group of **Harkis**, Algerians who had enlisted in the French forces and fought with them against their own people in the Algerian war of independence in the late 1950s. After the war they were settled in France for their own protection, and since then have received little or no help. In 1991 the Harki's children, now French citizens, broke out in open protest, angry at finding themselves still last in the pecking order in spite of their parents' sacrifice. Since then, the discontent has rumbled on, its most recent manifestation being a sit-in outside the *mairie* during the winter of 1997.

### July and August

**Throughout July & Aug** Bédarieux: Soirées Musicals. Evening performances of music (from medieval to jazz to reggae) and comedy, which are usually free, in the place Nouvel.

**Throughout July & Aug** Lamalou-les-Bains: Festival National d'Operettes. Operetta troupes from around France perform in the Lamalou's casino (☎04.67.95.70.91, *perso.wanadoo.fr /operettes.lamalou*).

**Throughout July & Aug** Villerouge-Termènes: Fête Médiéval (☎04. 68.70.06.24). Medieval market, fair and events held in even-numbered years.

**Mid-July to mid-Aug** Orb valley: Festival de la Vallée de l'Orb. Choral music and folk activities related to wine, held in town squares and churches throughout the region. Information on ☎04.67.89.65.32.

**Late July to early Aug** Sigean: Musical (☎04.68.40.40.95). Street festival featuring music, theatre and children's activities.

### August

**Aug 5 & 6** Narbonne: Fête du Commerce et du Vin. Wine festival.

**Aug 10 & 11** Narbonne: La Via Mercaderia. Medieval street market and fair.

**Mid-Aug** Béziers: La Feria. Four-day festival with street entertainment, fireworks, music and a daily Spanish-style *corrida*.

**Aug 25–28** Narbonne: Semaine Bavaroise. Narbonne's summer version of the Munich Oktoberfest, with plenty of lager and lederhosen.

**Throughout Sept** Narbonne: Orgues d'Été. September's version of the July series of recitals.

**Late Oct** Béziers: Les Primeurs d'Oc. The best of the local wine festivals, with wine contests, music and traditional activities.

## Arrival, information and accommodation

Narbonne's **gare SNCF** is situated at the eastern end of the railyard running along the northern edge of the city centre, at the head of the RN9 as it leaves town. It has **left luggage** facilities; enquire at the information desk. From here it's about a fifteen-minute walk to the place de l'Hôtel de Ville in the centre, or a short hop on buses #1, #2 or the Petit Bus. Just to the west, on the far side of the freight terminal, you'll find the **gare routière**. If you're **driving** into town, you can park just about anywhere you find a spot – most plazas and streets have meter-parking. The town's main **tourist office** (April–Sept daily 9.30am–12.15pm & 2–6pm; Oct–March Tues–Sun 10am–noon & 2–5pm; ☎04.68.65.15.60, fax 04.68.65.59.12, *www.Mairie-Narbonne.fr*) is on tiny place Roger-Salengro, just to the north of the cathedral, but there is also canalside **information kiosk** on quai Victor-Hugo (June–Sept Mon–Sat 10am–7pm; Nov–May 8am–noon & 2–6pm) at the southern end of the centre. Information on festivals and events can be picked up in the free fortnightly events magazine, *Olé!*, which also covers the surrounding area.

Narbonne has an efficient municipal **bus** system. You can buy single tickets (5.80F/€0.88) from drivers and ten-trip TICTEN passes (42F/€6.40) at tobacconists. If you want to rent a **bike** try Cycles Cancel, 50 boulevard Frédéric-Mistral (☎04.68.65.12.26).

You can find reasonable **accommodation** in Narbonne. In addition to a fair number of hotels, whose prices are relatively good compared with many other cities in the South of France, there's a hostel and a couple of decent campsites. The two main concentrations of accommodation are in the immediate vicinity of the gare SNCF and along the Canal du Robine, which flows through the centre.

## Hotels

**Alsace**, 2 av Carnot (☎04.68.32.01.86, fax 04.68.90.43.81). Just across from the station, this small old-fashioned two-star is clean, but the rooms are on the small side. ③.

**La Dorade**, 44 rue Jean-Jaurès (☎04.68.32.65.95, fax 04.68.65.81.62). Founded as a hotel in 1648 and a traditional favourite of visiting nobility, this beautiful building was entirely renovated in 1990. Great location, facing out onto the canal, and excellent service; amenities include TV and garage. ③.

**de France**, 6 rue Rossini (☎04.68.32.09.75, fax 04.68.65.50.30, *hotelfrance@bigfoot.com*). Just south of the old town, steps from the covered market and the canal, this quiet nineteenth-century establishment has TV in the rooms, parking facilities, and is wheelchair accessible. ③.

**de la Gare**, 7 av Pierre-Sémard (☎04.68.32.10.54). This stationside hotel is a bit run down, but does the trick if you're looking for cheap, basic accommodation. ①.

**Grand Hôtel du Languedoc**, 22 bd Gambetta (☎04.68.65.14.74, fax 04.68.65.81.48). Another attractive old building – a nineteenth-century house – which has been converted into an unremarkable but comfortable hotel. Located on the ring road, a five-minute walk south of the cathedral. ③.

**de Paris**, 2 rue du Lion d'Or (☎04.68.32.08.68). Small old-town hotel which is probably the best bargain option in town; more expensive rooms have TV and en-suite bath. ①.

**Le Regent**, 5 rue Mosaïque/13 rue Suffren (☎04.68.32.02.41, fax 04.68.65.50.43). Reasonable accommodation in the quieter and newer part of the city centre, 2min south of boulevard Gambetta. Rooms also have TV. ③.

**La Résidence**, 6 rue 1er du Mai (☎04.68.32.19.41, fax 04.68.65.18.48). Another early nineteenth-century converted house, with a great location on a quiet street near the Pont Voltaire. Comfortable rooms, and comes with AC, a garage and lift, but you pay for the privileges. ④.

**Will's**, 23 av Pierre-Sémard (☎04.68.90.44.50, fax 04.68.32.26.28). Friendly place and a travellers' standby, which accepts pets and has amenities like TV and cable, but fills up quickly. Right by the train station. ③.

## Hostel and campsites

**Les Floralys**, rte de Gruissan (☎04.68.32.65.65, fax 04.68.96.94.73). This is the closest campsite to town, located 3km from the centre on the road heading south towards the coast. It is a small, thirty-pitch site with good services (including laundry and restaurant), open all year round.

**MJC Centre International de Séjour**, pl Salengro (☎04.68.32.01.00, fax 04.68.65.80.20). Modern hostel right by the tourist office, with dorm (66F/€10.07) and – limited – private room (③) accommodation. Nice lounge with TV and a simple restaurant.

**Roches Grises**, RN9 (☎ & fax 04.68.41.75.41). This large two-star campsite is 4km out along the main Perpignan-bound road (bus #3; "Roches Grises"). A year-round site with all of the amenities.

# The Town

If Narbonne's name lends itself to a certain sense of grandeur, you'll be shocked by its diminutive size. The whole of the **old town** – which is where all the sights are – fits snugly into a 1km-by-750m rectangle, bisected north–south by the **Canal de la Robine**. Of the two halves it is the eastern that holds the main draws, with the **archbishops' palace**, its **museums** and the **cathedral** dominating affairs, plus a number of medieval attractions on their periphery. If you get time the western side of the canal, though less salubrious than its eastern counterpart, also harbours a couple of interesting sights.

## The Archbishops' Palace

The broad square of the place de l'Hôtel de Ville, in whose centre you'll find a recently uncovered section of the Roman Via Domitia, is marked on its southern side by the grand old Aux Dames de France department store, while the entire north side is taken up by the great facade of the **Archbishops' Palace**, peppered by pointed ogival windows and decorated with Gothic-looking vegetal flourishes. But while you marvel at its medieval beauty, it is worth bearing in mind that what you are looking at is in fact one of Viollet-le-Duc's imaginative repair jobs (see p.123), an ersatz bit of medievalia. Now the town hall, the palace consists of a rambling complex, incorporating the city's two major museums, plus the entrance to the cathedral (see below). Passing through the main doors of the palace, which are directly on the square, on the left you'll find the entrance to the towering **donjon** (Mon–Fri 9am–noon & 2–6pm; 15F/€2.29) commissioned in the late thirteenth century by the town's lord and archbishop, Gilles Aycelin. This ponderous 42-metre tall defensive tower is a fine example of late thirteenth-century military architecture – its splayed-out base, which was constructed over the remains of the previous Roman wall, was designed to prevent battering and better withstand attempts to undermine the keep. There's not much to see inside, but from the top (after managing a 162-step key-stone staircase) you can enjoy excellent **views** of the cathedral and the surrounding countryside. Back at the main entrance heading straight ahead leads you out into a broad courtyard, occasionally the scene for concerts and exhibitions, and from here you can access the two museums: the **art and history museum** and **archeological museum**.

### THE ART AND HISTORY MUSEUM

On the left you'll see the entrance to the **art and history museum** (April–Sept daily 9.30am–12.15pm & 2–6pm; Oct–March Tues–Sun 10am–noon & 2–5pm; three-day combined ticket with archeological museum and Horreum 30F/€4.58), which is located on the upper floors of the palace. The collection, featuring scores of canvases of mediocre seventeenth-century portraiture and landscape, plus some early modern pottery and faïence, is on the whole less than stunning, and at times you'll find it more rewarding to take in the luxurious

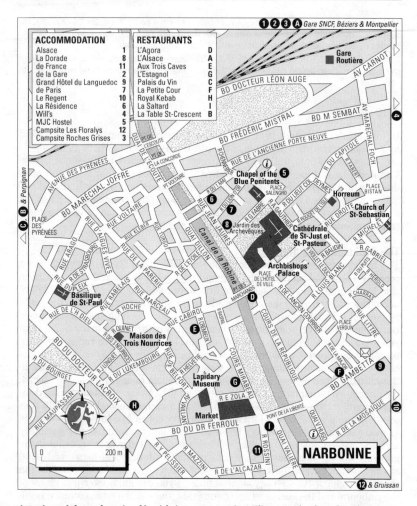

**ACCOMMODATION**

| | |
|---|---|
| Alsace | 1 |
| La Dorade | 8 |
| de France | 11 |
| de la Gare | 2 |
| Grand Hôtel du Languedoc | 9 |
| de Paris | 7 |
| Le Regent | 10 |
| La Résidence | 6 |
| Will's | 4 |
| MJC Hostel | 5 |
| Campsite Les Floralys | 12 |
| Campsite Roches Grises | 3 |

**RESTAURANTS**

| | |
|---|---|
| L'Agora | D |
| L'Alsace | A |
| Aux Trois Caves | E |
| L'Estagnol | G |
| Palais du Vin | C |
| La Petite Cour | F |
| Royal Kebab | H |
| La Saltard | I |
| La Table St-Crescent | B |

**NARBONNE**

interior of the palace itself, with its *artenesado* ceilings and other details; rooms to look out for in particular are the audience hall, the king's chamber – with seventeenth-century painted walls – and the grand salon. That said, however, a smattering of medieval pieces certainly warrant attention, and the museum's highlight, the **Orientalist collection** in the salle Hippolyte Lazerges, alone almost justifies the admission price. Here some thirty-odd works, dating from the seventeenth to twentieth centuries, reflect the European fascination with the world of the desert: paintings depicting sultry Berber girls staring enigmatically at the viewer, or eyes flashing from under turbans, as bearded men pose with cruel-looking swords on horse or camel-back. On your way out, poke your head in the **Hall of the Synods**, accessed from the same grand staircase as the museum. Built by one of the archbishops in 1628, it was used for clerical meetings and sittings of the Parlement of Languedoc and is decorated with impressive Aubusson tapestries.

*THE ARCHEOLOGICAL MUSEUM*
A much better collection can be found just across the courtyard at the **archeological museum** (same hours and ticket as the art and history museum). This museum, which strikes a good balance between the artefact and explanation, starts with the Neolithic period, represented by various skull parts and a series of footprints preserved in solidified muck, and follows with Bronze Age finds (the usual broaches and weapons) from the *oppida* of the region. The mainstay of the exhibition, however, is its **Roman collection**, whose strong maritime streak reflects the important role which Narbonne played as a major port of Roman Gaul. Various stone carvings illustrate ships of the period, and there's a towering 3.5-metre wood-and-lead ship's **anchor** on display. Combined with the seafaring items is a collection of first-century BC **Roman paintings** – the best of its kind in France. Most of the pieces came from a villa in the northern part of the Roman town and include elaborate borders, depictions of country scenes and "portraits" of gods. The collection winds up with an impressively large mosaic from the same period as the paintings, and a number of paleo-Christian sarcophagi.

## The Cathédral de St-Just et St-Pasteur
From the archeological museum a narrow alley, the passage de l'Ancre, leads further into the complex, towards the entrance to the **Cathédral de St-Just et St-Pasteur** (April–Sept 9.30am–12.15pm & 2–6pm; Oct–March 10am–noon & 2–5pm). Christianity in the city dates back at least to the time when Constantine the Great proclaimed it the Empire's official religion in 328 AD; as a provincial capital Narbonne became seat of an archbishop, and a cathedral was raised. Its exterior is pure Gothic – the tall and narrow core of the building, dominated by expanses of stained-glass window, is braced by sturdy buttresses, from which delicate-looking flying buttresses launch up to support the highest points on the walls. The building which you see today is the fourth to sit on this site, and was begun in 1272. With the completion of the hulking 49-metre choir some fifty years later, construction of the nave, which was meant to extend westwards, was held up after the first couple of stages, because extending it would have involved knocking down the old Roman defensive wall – still very useful in those uncertain times. Thus, as with Toulouse's cathedral, the project was never completed, leaving the church with its strikingly odd form. As you climb the short flight of stairs from the street you'll arrive first at the compact **cloister**, from where you'll get a good view of the seemingly delicate array of buttresses which support the light Gothic-style walls. A door on the west side of the cloister leads to the formal-style **Jardin des Archevêques**, with even better views, and around to the so-called **Cour St-Eutrope**, which is in fact the sealed-off stub of the aborted nave. The entrance to the church itself can be found on the north side of the cloister.

On entering, the first thing that will strike you is the tremendous space inside the unfinished building – its soaring ceiling the third highest for a French cathedral. Along with the upward dynamic of the design, the predominance of stained glass over stone on the walls is a hallmark of high Gothic style – some of the windows date from the original construction. The centre of the church is taken up by elaborate eighteenth-century **choir stalls**, presided over by a massive **organ** of the same era. Facing it is the high altar, and behind this a series of chapels hung with fine Gobelin and Aubusson tapestries. Directly behind the altar a badly damaged but nevertheless beautiful fourteenth-century stone **retable** illustrates themes of the Redemption with exceptionally carved and incredibly kinetic high-relief figures. From the southernmost of the chapels, a spiral stair leads up to the beehive-shaped chamber housing the cathedral's **treasury** (15F/€2.29), the centrepiece of which is a sumptuous fifteenth-century tapestry depicting the Holy Trinity, personified as three kings. On your way out of the church complex, after descending the stairs from the cloister, take a peek in the cathedral's gift shop (same hours as the church), not so much for the stuff on sale, but because it is housed in the elegant **Salle au Pilier**, an airy fourteenth-century chamber whose Gothic vaulting is supported by a single delicate pillar, and in which you'll find carvings dating back to the Visigoths of the sixth century.

## Around the palace and cathedral

It's worth taking the time to explore the lesser sights found in the vicinity of the palace and cathedral. First among these is the small **chapel of the Blue Penitents**, just steps from the tourist office on the west side of place Salengro, in the heart of the "quartier de Europe", as this part of the old town is called. Originally founded in 1149 for the Hospitaller Knights, the chapel has suffered a bout of Baroque, and its interior (hours vary) is a bland white with pale blue detailings, but you can still recognize the fine Romanesque features of its doorway. South of the square two small streets lead directly away from the massive east wall of the cathedral and into a compact **medieval neighbourhood** which was once the *quartier* of the choristers and other functionaries of the great church: rue de Lieutenant-Colonel-Deymes and the next street along, rue Rouget de l'Isle, both contain houses with distinctly medieval windows and doors. On the latter street, at no. 7, is the **Horreum** (April–Sept daily 9.30am–12.15pm & 2–6pm; Oct–March Tues–Sun 10am–noon & 2–5pm; three-day combined ticket with art and history and archeological museums 30F/€4.58). Despite Narbonne's importance in Roman times, this is the only structure in the city which has survived from that era – in fact it had disappeared and was not rediscovered until 1838, when the building covering it was demolished. It's name means "granary" in Latin, and that's precisely what it was: an underground grain store which was most likely attached to a market building or depot above the ground. Its 40m-by-50m area is divided into a series of small storage chambers leading off a rectangular passage. There's not much to see inside, apart from some ancient graffiti, but it does make for an interesting visit.

From the Horreum, head east to the bend in rue Maréchal, where an ancient Roman **stela** sits in the courtyard of the grandiose Hôtel de Poulhariez (now apartments). Following this street further will take you to place Bistan, where you'll see the meagre remains of the Roman forum and capitol, while the once graceful yet flamboyant Gothic **church of St-Sébastian** rises up in rue Michelet, just to the south of the square. From the *place*, atmospheric rue Droite traces the route of both the Roman and medieval main street west back to the place de l'Hotel de Ville.

## West of the canal de la Robine

Narbonne's old town extends over the Canal de la Robine to the west, but in the Middle Ages, as today, this neighbourhood on the far side is a humbler section of town. The narrow lanes and crooked streets are home to the city's marginalized

North African community, and the plethora of police who comb it are testament to the social problems which grip the area. Even so, it is eminently explorable; there are fewer shops and restaurants here, and the tiny windows of the ageing buildings hang with laundry, but the main reason for visiting is to see the two parish churches which share this side of the river. The first is the **Basilique de St-Paul** on rue Dupleix, which you can reach by crossing the canal at Pont Voltaire and proceeding south. It's a tall thirteenth-century construction, chipped and battered on the outside over the years, but inside possessing a pleasant mixture of Romanesque and Gothic. The main attraction is the **crypt** (Mon–Sat 9am–noon & 2–6pm; free); built over a paleo-Christian necropolis and dating back to the fourth century, it is where the town's first bishop was buried. Also scattered about the low-ceilinged room are various amphora, sarcophagi and a small mosaic.

Leaving the crypt, around the far side of the church, pick up rue de l'Hôtel Dieu, at the corner of which, with rue Quinet, you'll find the magnificent sixteenth-century facade of the **Maison de Trois Nourrices**. Taking the next left will lead you to place and rue Belfort, and another crop of medieval dwellings, while at the end of the street, a car-filled *place* opens up in front of the former abbey church of Notre-Dame-de-la-Mourguié. Currently undergoing a prolonged restoration, it will eventually reopen as the town's **lapidary museum** (July & Aug daily 9.30am–12.15pm & 2–6pm; 30F/€4.58), with a large, but monotonous collection of over 1000 statues, inscriptions, tombstones and sarcophagi, most dating back to the days of Roman glory. The town's beautifully restored nineteenth-century **covered market** (daily 7am–1pm) is right beside the church on the banks of the canal, while along its south side runs the boulevard du Dr-Ferroul, whose stately facades braced by elaborate wrought-iron balustrades testify to the wealth which the wine industry brought in the late 1800s.

## Eating, drinking and nightlife

Narbonne is definitely not the culinary capital of the Southwest, but you won't starve. There are a couple of **restaurants** which stand out, as well as an array of unexceptional brasseries and bistros, where you can eat for under 100F/€15.25. The best places to browse are along the cours de la République on the southern portion of the canal, where you'll also find lots of informal snack places, and the boulevard Gambetta which runs off it to the east.

The **nightlife** situation is quite the opposite, with a profusion of energetic bars and clubs – curious in a town so quiet and lacking a university. A good place for an early evening **drink** is *Café le Soleil Noir* in place de l'Hôtel de la Ville (open till 2am in July & Aug, otherwise till 9pm), a small corner café with sleek décor, a mixed crowd and good sandwiches. Livelier late-night venues include *Le Cyrano*, 26 boulevard Gambetta, a bar with pool table, or *Le Galion* on avenue Anatole France (nightly 9pm–2am) which has different nightly themes and dancing. The coolest places are the cocktail bars *Why Not Café* and *Le Bal Masqué*, at no. 4 and no. 6 rue Marcelin-Coural, respectively. The former (Mon–Sat until 2am) has live music and DJs with a predominantly Sixties playlist, while the latter (daily till 2am) has better musical variety (including salsa on Fridays), with live bands occasionally playing on Thursday nights. Another **club** option is *Le Talgo*, at 8 avenue des Pyrénées (Tues–Sun 6pm–2am). If you're in the mood for a quieter drink, head to the pub *Chez Fred*, in the beautiful old *Hôtel Dorade* (June–Sept 5pm–1am).

Narbonne does have a reasonable **theatre**, le théâtre-scène Nationale de Narbonne, 2 avenue Domitius (Mon–Fri 12.30–6.30pm & Sat 3–6pm; ☎04.68.90. 90.20, *www.narbonne.com/letheatre*; bus #2 to "MI Juin"), but otherwise the city's cultural programme is nothing to write home about.

## Restaurants

**L'Agora**, 9 pl de l'Hôtel de la Ville (☎04.68.90.10.70). Despite the Roman name, this is a *terroir* which specializes in foie gras and *magret en confit*, as well as doing a fine line in tapas. Menus from 59F/€9.

**L'Alsace**, 2 av Pierre-Sémard (☎04.68.65.10.24). Just opposite the train station, this is Narbonne's best restaurant, hands down, featuring *terroir* and northeastern French dishes. Great décor, mammoth servings and menus from 110F/€16.78. Open Mon & Wed–Sun.

**Aux Trois Caves**, 4 rue Benjamin-Crémieux (☎04.68.65.28.60). Quirky place whose modern decorative touches clash incongruously with their surroundings. Inventive dishes based on local standbys are served in an excavated Roman cellar. Expect to spend 120–240F/€18.30–36.30.

**L'Estagnol**, cours Mirabeau (☎04.68.65.09.27). On the market-side of the canal, this good no-frills *terroir* restaurant also has a good fish selection. Good menus in the 100F/€15.25 range; less at lunch time. Closed Sun.

**Palais du Vin Domaine de St-Crescent le Viel**, rte de Perpignan (☎04.68.41.47.20). A *terroir* restaurant, with menus starting around 100F/€15.25, that's part of the local vintners' complex – a showroom for over 2500 regional wine growers. *La Table St-Crescent*, below, is part of the same complex; to arrive, walk 30min west of the town centre or take bus #3 to "St-Crescent".

**La Petite Cour**, 22 bd Gambetta (☎04.68.90.48.03). Fish and seafood is the order of the day in this high-ceilinged room decked with seascape murals, with a good choice of lunch-time menus around 75F/€11.44, or at 125F/€19.06 in the evening.

**Royal Kebab**, 14 bd Docteur-Lacroix. The town's Turkish *table*, with all the usual suspects: shish and doner kebabs, salads and sweets.

**La Saltard**, 1 rue Rossini. A big, brightly lit brasserie, diagonally opposite the old *halles*. Simple but plentiful menus and good, lively atmosphere from 70F/€10.68.

**La Table St-Crescent**, Domaine St-Crescent-le-Vieil (☎04.68.41.37.37). It's worth the effort to get to this excellent *gastronomique* located in an ancient eighth-century oratory, amongst vineyards and olive groves. Expect to spend about 240F/€36.60 per person. Closed Sun eve & Mon.

# Listings

**Banks and exchange** Several major French banks are represented in Narbonne; all have ATMs and most will change money during normal banking hours. Try the Caisse d'Epargne in bd Dr-Ferroul, beside the indoor market, or the Crédit Lyonaisse opposite the *passarelle* in cours de la République.

**Boat tours and rental** For canal trips Berges de la Robine, cours de la République (☎06.11.73.87.97) rents electric boats by the hour (from 120F/€18.30), while Connoisseurs Cruisers, promenade des Barques (☎04.68.65.14.55) is the best place for houseboats.

**Car rental** ADA, 12 av des Pyrénées (☎04.68.42.44.81); Avis, 21 bd Marcel-Sembat (☎04.68.32.43.36); Europcar, 52 bd Frédéric-Mistral (☎04.68.32.34.54); Locabest, 2 rue Romain (☎04.68.65.35.50).

**Hospital** Centre Hospitalier de Narbonne, bd Docteur-Lacroix (☎04.68.41.00.00; bus #1, #2 or #3 to "Hôpital").

**Internet access** Versus, nos. 73 & 82 rue Droite (Mon–Thurs 10am–8pm, Fri 10am–midnight, Sat 2pm–midnight, Sun 2–8pm, *www.versus.com*).

**Laundry** Launderettes at 24 av des Pyrénées; 25 bd Docteur-Ferroul; 3 av Karl-Marx.

**Pharmacy** Pharmacie de l'Hôtel de la Ville, pl de l'Hôtel de la Ville. For night-time and weekend, check the notice on the pharmacy door.

**Police** Gendarmerie, rue Anatole-France (☎04.68.90.38.50).

**Rugby** Local team RCNM play at the Parc des Sports et de l'Amitié, southeast of the old town (bus #3 to "Parc des Sports"; ☎04.68.41.76.93).

**Swimming** Éspace Liberté, rte de Perpignan (☎04.68.42.17.89; bus #3 to Roches Grises or Hautes de Narbonne).

**Taxi** ☎04.68.32.03.00.

**Train departures** All trains leave from the main gare SNCF (☎04.68.80.77.74), except the ATM service to Sallèles and Bize (see p.300), which leaves from a separate station on the place de la Constituante, just off the place des Pyrénées; the fare from Narbonne to Bize is 58F/€8.85.

# Gruissan and Gruissan-Plage

Some 20km southeast of Narbonne, the quiet fishing town of **GRUISSAN** cuts a striking figure from the distance, with its circular streets huddled around an ancient tower, filling a dramatic-looking promontory in the inland *étang* which bears its name. When you approach, you'll find to your surprise that there is very little sign of life among the fading colours of its houses or even around the ruins of the **watchtower** (free entry) – development has turned its back on the town, which basically consists of an array of low-roofed houses. The "action" is to be found on the town's long shore, partly in a smattering of bars and restaurants, but mainly in the daily business of the fishermen, tending to their boats or bringing in the catch. The salty Étang du Grazier separates Gruissan from the narrow spit of sands marking the Mediterranean's shore. Here, a concrete expanse of low-rise hotels has choked the banks of the inlet, and spreads north to the equally vacuous development of **GRUISSAN-PLAGE**. Apart from the traditional array of beachside activities and sights for which the towns are admirably equipped, there is virtually nothing to see or do on this stretch of the coast. When you tire of wandering Gruissan's near-deserted streets, you can head to the tourist office, which distributes a series of **biking** and **walking** itineraries in the low but rugged mountain of La Clape, separating Narbonne from the coast. The most popular of these is the one- to three-hour **excursion** (depending on whether you start from town, or a car park up the hill) to the local sailor's graveyard, and hill-top chapel, Notre-Dame-des-Auzils. The landscape along the way is archetypically Mediterranean, with scrubby pines and slender cypress trees sprouting up between the red stones and, from the top, you'll enjoy a panoramic view: the slender band of yellow sand set against the turquoise sea to the east, the vineyards and *châteaux* of the La Clape *appellation* to the west.

Arriving by **bus** in Gruissan, you'll be left by the new **tourist office** (July & Aug daily 9am–1pm & 3–7pm; Sept–June Mon–Sat 9.30am–noon & 2–6pm; ☎04.68.49.09.00, fax 04.68.49.33.12, *www.ville-gruissan.fr*), located on boulevard Pech-Maynaud, between the old and new towns. Given the town's proximity to Narbonne, there's really no reason to spend the night here, but if you are intent on a bout of beach-side hedonism, you'll find a selection of near-identical modern two- and three-star **hotels** ready to serve you. Right on the beachfront, *Le Tahiti* (☎04.68.49.22.28, fax 04.68.49.52.95, *www.logis-de-france.fr*, ③) is a reasonable choice with good amenities, while closer to the old town the *Port* (☎04.68.49.07.33, fax 04.68.49.52.41, *www.logis-de-france.com*; ⑤) is a good if slightly expensive option. Among the several **campsites** in the area, the best deal is the municipal site (☎04.68.49.07.22, *camping@ville-gruissan.fr*; June–Sept), on route des Salins. If you're looking for a **meal** in town, well-priced seafood and fish can be enjoyed at *L'Estangol*, on avenue de Narbonne (☎04.68.49.01.27; April–Sept) whose patio dining area has good views (menus from 90F/€13.73), and *Le Lamparo* (☎04.68.49.93.65; closed Sun & Mon out of season) in old Gruissan, at 4 rue Amiral-Courbet (mini-menu from 85F/€12.96). **Bikes** can be rented from Luc Mallien on rue de la Croix Blanche (☎04.68.49.49.52; April–Sept).

## South to Sigean

Heading south from Narbonne, the road hugs the base of the rising hills, separated from the sea by a wide buffer – a series of salty *étangs* – and accompanied by a landscape characterized by scrubby trees, red soil, and an impossibly blue sky in summer. Travelling by rail south from Narbonne provides a different perspective, as the line threads the marshy spits connecting the saltpans and lagoons; on board you'll feel no hint of the steady and unforgiving wind which lashes in from the east. There's little along the coast to detain you until you arrive at **SIGEAN**, just north of which is a large **African nature reserve** (daily 9am–9pm; 98F/€14.95). This immense drive-through park (no motorcycles) recreates several equatorial habitats, including brushland, savannah and plain, and lazing around you'll see lions, giraffes, rhinos and hippos, as well as graceful oryx and springboks. There is also a bear area and a bird reserve, while chimpanzees are exiled to their own island at the southern end of the park. For those without cars, a series of footpaths have been laid out among the habitats in a limited area of the park. Sigean itself is nothing special, although it does have a small **archeological museum** by the tourist office (mid-June to mid-Sept daily 10am–noon & 2–5pm; 20F/€3.05), holding artefacts recovered from the nearby *oppidum*; the remains of this hill-top settlement, just outside of town and dating back to the sixth century BC, can also be visited (no public transport; same ticket).

**Buses** from Narbonne, Perpignan and Port-la-Nouvelle stop right in the centre of Sigean, near the **tourist office** (July & Aug Mon–Sat 9.45–11.45am & 4–7pm; Sept–June Tues & Wed 10am–noon; ☎04.68.48.14.81, fax 04.68.48.87.89, *www.sigean.org*) on place de la Libération. Accommodation hereabouts is limited to two **campsites**: the municipal site, at the Étang Boyé (☎04.68.48.43.68; July & Aug), a few minutes' walk from the town centre, and *La Grange Neuve* (☎04.68.48.58.70), near the reserve.To eat, head to the **restaurant** *Le Ste-Anne* on 3 avenue Michel-de-l'Hospital (closed Mon; menu 72F/€10.98). Or, if you are just passing town, you might pause for a drink in the wonderful old glassed-in *Café La Rotunda*, at the centre of town on the main street.

# The Corbières

To journey into the heart of the hilly **Corbières** region, which fans out southwest of Narbonne, bordered to the west by the upper Aude valley and to south by the Fenouillèdes hills of northern Roussillon, is to enter a world distinct from the coastal plain. As the land rises the roads narrow, twisting and writhing up into the forests of the low mountains, tenaciously following the streambeds which cut into the slopes. Once the heart of Cathar territory, this district has suffered centuries of abandonment and neglect, and many hamlets lack even a café or a proper payphone, let alone a restaurant or hotel. For all of this, it is a splendid place to drive through – offering the ancient monasteries of **Fontfroide** and **Lagrasse**, and the Cathar sites of **Villerouge-Termenès** and **Termes**. Without your own transport the Corbières is difficult to access, the only bus route following the D613 from Narbonne.

# Fontfroide

Passing through the rocky *garrigues* west of Narbonne, 22km out of town the D613 leads you past the narrow turning off to the **Monastery of Fontfroide**. Following this road south for four kilometres you'll come across the stout walls of the ancient Cistercian foundation, tucked inside a shallow valley, hidden amongst cypress groves. Founded in the late eleventh century by a Count of Narbonne, it saw its greatest prosperity in the two subsequent centuries, after which, like so many monastic centres, it began to decline. The monastery's best-known abbot was Jacques Fournier, who as Bishop of Foix commanded the Inquisition which investigated the Cathars of Montaillou (see p.140), and went on in 1337 to be elected pope as Benedict XII. In private hands for the last hundred years or so, the abbey can only be visited as part of a one-hour **guided tour** (daily, every 45min except 1pm & 3.15pm: 10am–5.30pm; 37F/€5.64). It's best to come early in the morning or late in the day in order to avoid crowds; but be warned, this is a popular stop on bus tours, and in high season is frequently too busy to be enjoyable.

The visit starts in the open courtyard, the Cour d'Honneur, built by the sixteenth-century abbots. From here you are led to the refined beauty of the **cloister** – originally built in the 1200s, but added to as late as the seventeenth century. Off the east side of the cloister you enter the marvellously vaulted **chapterhouse**, and then the **church**, a simple twelfth-century Romanesque basilica, on the south side of which is an interesting ossuary, the salle des Morts, which contains a fifteenth-century crucifixion scene. After a visit to the storage **cellars** which, going back a thousand years, are the oldest surviving part of the monastery, the tour concludes with the monks' living quarters above. Afterwards, you can wander freely around the paths which lead through the surrounding groves and gardens.

There's no accommodation at Fontfroide, so if you are travelling by **bus** you'll want to make sure you are back at the main road in order to catch the last one back to Narbonne or further on up into the hills. There is, however, an excellent **restaurant** at the monastery, *La Bergerie* (closed Dec–Feb). This establishment is divided into two parts: the less expensive lunch-time dining room, which serves traditional but well-executed dishes (menus from 90F/€13.73), and the evening-only *gastronomique*, where you should be prepared to spend 200F/€30.50 or more (closed Mon).

# Villerouge-Termenès and Termes

If you continue west from Fontfroide along the D613, you'll arrive at St-Laurent-de-la-Cabrerisse, where the road forks right for Lagrasse (see p.295), and left towards the hills. Following this second route will lead you into some of the wildest back-country of the region, where forested uplands are capped by the tumbled remains of nameless castles. The road first climbs to the 404-metre-high Col de Villerouge, and as you round the top, you'll get a startling view of the castle and village below. **VILLEROUGE-TERMENÈS** is dominated by the tall keep of its impressively restored **castle** (July & Aug daily 9am–8pm; May, June & Sept daily 10am–6pm; April & Oct daily 10am–5pm; March & Nov Sat, Sun & school holidays 10am–5pm; 25F/€3.81). The earlier Cathar fort was destroyed in the wake of its conquest by Crusaders in 1210 and the present structure, dating from the 1300s, was designed not to protect but to dominate the inhabitants of the surrounding hills. A visit to the castle involves an engaging audiovisual show which recaps the history of the area and recounts the tale of Guilhem Bélibaste, the Cathar *parfait* who was burned at the stake here in 1321. Afterwards it's worth taking a walk through the village huddled around the castle; the town was almost certainly fortified in the twelfth century, but the walls which are visible today were built to fend off the English and their allies during the Hundred Years' War. South of the *enceinte* you'll find the **church** of St-Étienne, which houses an immense sixteenth-century retable.

Leaving Villerouge, another steep ascent takes you to the **Col de Bedos** (485m), where a narrow paved road veers off to the right. Carefully following this relentless succession of hairpin curves will take you over hill and into valley until at last you make a sharp descent to **TERMES**. Little more than a cluster of ancient houses set on cramped but orderly streets, this extraordinarily beautiful hamlet would be worth a visit even if it weren't for its famous castle. Trees crowd over the narrow stream, breached by a centuries-old stone bridge, and above the sharply rising slopes are covered by a blanket of beech, ash and stunted oak. The only thing which ruins the effect is the modern reception centre across the river, which is the point at which you begin the arduous ascent to the ruins of the **castle** (July & Aug daily 9am–8pm; May, June & Sept daily 10am–6pm; April & Oct daily 10am–5pm; March & Nov Sat, Sun & school holidays 10am–5pm; 20F/€3.05). You wouldn't know it from either the ruins or the village, but this castle was dominated by one of the greatest feudal domains of Languedoc. Ruled by an unrepentant heretic lord, Raymond, it was a prime target for de Montfort, who besieged it for four months, sapping its walls, and firing on it with artillery, until the disease-ravaged garrison could resist no more. After it was taken the castle continued to be used, and was not destroyed until the seventeenth century, when Richelieu systematically cleared the land of possible points of resistance to central rule. Clambering among the remains of the two concentric sets of walls, you'll find the chapel and enjoy breathtaking **views** over the hills around. From Termes, you have two options: continue on for another twenty hair-raising kilometres to reach the main road heading north to Lagrasse, or double back the way you came, and descend the Col de Bedos to **MOUTHOUMET**. This sleepy village serves as the end for the bus line which runs up from Narbonne and, if nothing else, makes a welcome stop on the GR36 as it winds its way south from Termes to Peyrepertuse, or on the west towards Arques and Rennes-le-Château.

## Practicalities

Services are extremely thin on the ground in this neck of the woods. **Accommodation** is especially rare; aside from Madame Lefranc's **gîte** (☎04.68.70.00.42 or 04.68.48.85.95, fax 04.68.48.46.20; ③) in Villerouge, all you'll find is an unofficial **campsite** on the riverside outside Termes, just before you enter town. Eating is a little better: in Villerouge you can enjoy a lively meal in the castle's *Rôtisserie Medieval* (☎04.68.70.06.06; closed Sun eve & Mon except hols) for about 175F/€26.69, while in Mouthoumet on the "main square" you'll find the *Auberge du Terroir* (closed Mon), a homely little place which has excellent salads, and menus from 69F/€10.52 (wine included).

# Lagrasse

Just over halfway from Narbonne to Carcassonne and separated from the Aude valley by the low ridge of the Montagne d'Alaric, **LAGRASSE** is the largest and most beautiful village of the Corbières highlands. A compact walled hamlet set idyllically where the Orbieu opens up in a broad hollow, it hugs the right bank of the shallow river, while the magnificent abbey squats on the far side. Delightfully, but surprisingly, Lagrasse does not seem to have been discovered yet by the tourist industry; the grid of streets in the old town are almost strictly residential, and you'll hardly see a postcard stand or gift shop. It's a real pleasure to wander the cobbled lanes down to the arcaded *place* and its ancient **covered market**, with flowers cascading from the windows of the houses which hem the streets and crowd around the fort-like **church**. Much of the old *enceinte* is intact, and as you cross the eleventh-century bridge, try to crane over its protective walls to look at the town's riverside fortifications, now pierced by the scores of windows of the houses built against them – an especially evocative sight at dusk. Its only about a five-minute walk from the far side to the **abbey of Ste-Marie d'Orbieu** (daily: May–Sept 10.30am–12.30pm & 2–6.30pm; Oct–April 2–5pm; 35F/€5.34). This is one of the region's oldest monastic houses, founded when it was a dangerous underpopulated frontier of the eighth-century Carolingian empire. Cultivating the extensive lands with which they had been endowed, the monks slowly increased the monastery's wealth until its golden age in the fourteenth century, which saw the building of the town's walls and market. The complex is now a pastiche of styles, with components dating from the tenth to eighteenth centuries. The abbot's Renaissance **palace** and cloister both date from the monastery's second great period of revival – just before the storm of Revolution swept it away, while the old Romanesque-style **cloister**, like the bulk of the **abbey church**, dates to the thirteenth century, although it has suffered substantial remodellings. You'll also get a look at the monks' cavernous **dormitory**, and have the chance to climb the Gothic-tinged fifteenth-century **clock tower**, from whose heights you'll enjoy impressive vistas of the town and valley. Leaving the abbey, continue along the riverside to a low dam bridging the river – you can walk across here and re-enter the town.

Heading on from Lagrasse towards Carcassonne, the most scenic route takes you west through the Gorges d'Alsou.

### Practicalities

Lagrasse's services and shops are mostly strung along the length of the tree-lined boulevard de la Promenade; the **tourist office** (July & Aug daily 10am–12.30pm & 2–6pm; ☎04.68.43.11.56, fax 04.68.43.16.34, *www.lagrasse.com*) is at no. 6. Further along at no. 9, you'll find the friendly *Auberge St Hubert* (☎04.68.43.15.22, fax 04.68.43.16.56, *www.logis-de-france.fr*; closed part Feb, & Sun & Mon Sept–Easter; ③), which also has a pleasant restaurant (menu from 75F/€11.44). Otherwise, there are **chambres d'hôtes** in the old town at *Les Trois Grâces*, 5 rue de Quai (☎ & fax 04.68.43.18.17; closed Jan & Feb, and Wed & Thurs; also serve meals; ③), and a **gîte** (☎04.68.78.30.81; ①) in the hamlet of Villemagne, at the top of the Alsou gorge. The most interesting restaurant in town is *Les Temps de Courges* (☎04.68.43.10.18; closed Wed & Thurs lunch) at 3 rue des Mazels, where you can order vegetarian or meat dishes and dine on a cosy little terrace (menu at 150F/€22.88). Otherwise there are a string of family-run establishments on the boulevard de la Promenade, including *Le Petit Saint* and *L'Affenage*, both of which have basic *terroir* menus for under 100F/€15.25 and offer the possibility of eating on street-side terraces.

# Along the Canal du Midi east from Carcassonne

Heading east from Carcassonne, the **Canal du Midi** (see pp.110–111) follows the course of the lower Aude valley, past the shady port at **Trèbes**, and on into the wine country of the **Minervois**, bounded by Haut Languedoc to the north and the hills of the Corbières to the south. Here the small port of **Homps** provides a jumping-off point for the old Cathar stronghold of **Minerve** and the monastery at **Caunes**, while bustling **Lézignan** is a hub for non-fluvial transport. Just after the old way-station of Le Somail the canal splits; the offshoot **Canal de la Robine** glides past the ancient wine centre of **Sallèles**, and on through Narbonne to reach the sea near Gruissan, while the main channel edges on to pass the magnificent **Oppidum d'Ensérune**, before reaching Béziers and, eventually, Agde (see p.305). As with the western leg of the canal system, you needn't commit yourself to boating to enjoy this archetypal southern French landscape, since the two paths which run along its length make for excellent **biking** and **walking**.

## Trèbes and Puichéric

The first and prettiest port of call along the eastern stretch of the Canal du Midi is **TRÈBES**, just a few kilometres east of Carcassonne. The canal makes a broad curve here, following the wide meander of the Aude; arriving at Trèbes, two canal bridges, the second designed by the military architect Vauban in 1686, carry the watercourse over the Frequel and Orbiel rivers. Aside from being an attractive town with a canal port overlooked by the town walls at its western end, Trèbes is home to the remarkable **church of St-Étienne** (July & Aug Mon–Fri 10am–noon & 3–7pm; free), the wooden-beamed ceiling of which, dating back to the early fourteenth century, has over 350 individual faces painted on the ends of its roof supports, including caricatures of various professions and social classes, exotic foreigners and grotesques. For boaters the town is a well-equipped stage-post, just as it was in the seventeenth century, with mooring facilities and a range of services.

From Trèbes, the canal meanders east to **Puichéric**. This Cathar town survived the Crusade, but was put to the torch by the Black Prince a century later. There's not much to see, as its medieval castle is now private, but it makes a good accommodation stop for cyclists and walkers.

Trèbes' **tourist office** is by the former canal *auberge*, on rue Pierre-Loti (July & Aug daily 10am–12.30pm & 2–8pm; June & Sept Mon–Sat 10am–12.30pm &

2–7.30pm, Sun 10am–12.30pm; May Mon–Sat 10am–noon & 2–7pm; April & Oct Mon–Sat 3–7pm; ☎ & fax 04.68.78.89.50, *www.mairie-trebes.fr*). Two decent **hotels** can be found in the nearby commercial zone Sautès Le Bas, *La Gentilhommière* (☎04.68.78.74.74, fax 04.68.78.65.80; ③) and the *Andalousie* (☎04.68.78.88.48, fax 04.68.78.63.48; ①). The town's **campsite**, on chemin de la Lande on the west side of Trèbes (☎04.68.78.61.75), is open from May to October. At Puichéric, you can stay the night and eat (menu at 140F/€21.35) at the well-equipped **chambres d'hôtes**, *Château de St-Aunay* (☎04.68.43.72.20, fax 04.68.43.76.72; mid-April to mid-Oct; ③), by the castle. There are a number of inexpensive **restaurants** in Trèbes, including *Les 3 B*, on avenue Pasteur, and *Le Relais de Capuchins*, at 34 rte de Narbonne – either of which can set you up with a 55F/€8.39 midday menu. For **boat rental** see the port office (☎04.68.78.83.08) or Connoisseur Cruisers (☎04.68.78.73.75).

# The Minervois

As the canal arcs northward it passes **HOMPS**, a town which suffered destruction in the Crusade and the Wars of Religion, but revived with the construction of the waterway. It is the main port of the **Minervois** region, a sun-bleached wine-producing territory stretching from the north bank of the Aude up to the hills of Haut Languedoc. The principal town of the Minervois, **Olonzac**, lies just 2km north of the canal, linked to Homps by the D910 and a convenient stop on the road to the former Cathar stronghold of **MINERVE**, which lies a further 15km north. A tiny medieval hamlet, located at the cirque where the deep gorge of the River Cesse doubles back on itself, Minerve's main attraction is its stunningly dramatic location – only a single pile of stones remains of its **fortress**, which resisted Simon de Montfort for five months in 1210. When it was taken, 140 Cathars who refused to recant their beliefs voluntarily jumped into the fire which the Crusaders had pre-pared for them. Neither of the town's museums merit much attention: the **arche-ological museum** (daily 10am–6.30pm; 10F/€1.53), with its shambolic collection set in dusty fly-specked display cases, is quite a specimen itself, while the **Musée Hurepel** (April–Sept daily 11am–12.30pm & 2–6pm; 15F/€2.29) is nothing more than a thinly disguised shop, where you can pay to see a series of dioramas recounting the Cathar saga. A visit to the town is best spent hiking the path through the **canyon** which surrounds it, and where you can walk in natural tun-nels bored through the cliffs. It's best to avoid Minerve in high season and at weekends, when the volume of visitors threatens to obliterate its charms.

If you have a car, you might want to drive 20km west of Olonzac (or alterna-tively a short drive from Carcassonne) to the far western edge of the Minervois, where you'll find the town of **CAUNES-MINERVOIS**, the centre of which is dominated by its rambling **abbey** (July & Aug daily 10am–7pm; April–June & Sept daily 10am–noon & 2–6pm; Oct–March Sat & Sun 10am–noon & 2–5pm; 20F/€3.05), notable not only for its thirteenth-century church but also for the abbots' mansions, which were constructed through to the sixteenth century. Caunes is famous for its marble quarries, which supplied stone for many of the churches throughout the region.

## Practicalities

There are **tourist offices** in the centre of Olonzac, at 3 place de la Mairie (July & Aug daily 9am–noon & 2–6pm; ☎04.68.91.34.95, fax 04.68.91.21.08), and behind the church in Minerve, at 2 rue des Martyrs (July & Aug daily 10am–noon & 2–6pm; ☎04.68.91.81.43). Comfortable **hotels** in the region include the *Hôtel du Parc* on avenue de Homps in Olonzac (☎04.68.91.24.77; ③) and *d'Alibert* in the place de la Mairie at Caunes (☎04.68.78.00.54; closed Sun & Mon in low season & late Dec to Feb; ④), which also has a good restaurant. In Minerve you can choose between the overpriced **chambres d'hôtes** *Ulysse Martin* at 23 Grand Rue (☎04.68.91.22.97; ⑤) or the better *Relais Chantovent* (☎04.68.91.14.18, fax 04.68.91.81.99; closed mid-Dec to mid-March; ③), which is also a decent place in town to get a meal (menus from 100F/€15.25). Caunes also has a municipal **campsite** (☎04.68.78.07.83; June–Aug). You can **eat** in Olonzac at the simple *Du Minervois*, rue des Écoles (☎04.68.91.20.73; closed Sun & Mon) but a better option is to head for the *Auberge de l'Arbousier* in Homps (☎04.68.91.11.24; closed Wed, Sun eve & Mon in summer), which has *terroir* menus from 85F/€12.96. Justfun (☎04.68.91.56.22) in Olonzac rents **bikes**, while for boats and cruises, contact Camargue Plaisance (☎04.68.91.25.99) or Luc Lines (☎04.68.91.24.00) in Homps' port.

## Lézignan-Corbières and Le Somail

Veering south and east after Homps, the Canal du Midi enters a particularly beautiful stretch, passing a series of castles as the landscape settles into a vine-covered plain. Some 5km south of the canal sits **LÉZIGNAN-CORBIÈRES**, the capital of the rugged region rising gradually to the south. Lézignan has been in the business of wine production since the time of the Romans and today it remains a small but bustling centre of the viticulture industry. There's no overwhelming reason to visit the town, although if you are dependent on public transport you may find yourself stopping here to change buses or grab a train. While here, you can stop in at the **Musée de la Vigne et du Vin** (daily 9am–noon & 2–7pm; 25F/€3.81) right by the gare SNCF (see below), whose interesting exhibition focuses directly on the modern wine business that has brought prosperity to the countryside since the nineteenth century.

This leg of the canal continues, over the canal bridge of Répudre – France's first, and an invention of Riquet himself – and on to **LE SOMAIL**, the last port before the Canal de la Robine splits off from the waterway and heads south towards Narbonne. As a whole, the town, mired among modern housing developments on a broad expanse of flat land, looks unpromising as you approach, but the area along the canal which formed the seventeenth-century port is a world apart. Here a single-arched stone **bridge** dating to the 1700s spans the canal, still attached to the old post-house *auberge* on the east bank and a small **chapel** on the west. There's little to do here aside from enjoy a drink or meal and soak up the canalside ambience before moving on, although if you're not in a hurry you might take a look at the private **hat museum** (June–Sept daily 9am–noon & 2–7pm; Oct–May Mon–Sat 2–6pm, Sun 2.30–8pm; 20F/€3.05) located at the south end of town, where you'll find more than six thousand hats on display from around the world.

In Lézignan-Corbières **buses** will let you off as they pass through the town's centre and **trains** stop at the **gare SNCF**, 3 rue Turgot. There's also a **tourist office** (July & Aug Mon–Sat 9am–9pm, Sun 10am–noon; Sept–June Mon–Fri 10am–noon & 3–6pm; ☎04.68.27.05.42, fax 04.68.27.05.42, *tourisme-lezignan @wanadoo.fr*) at 9 Cours de la République, on the southern side of the ring road which skirts its old town. You'll find a good selection of shops and services in Lézignan, plus a number of **hotels** should you need to stay the night, the best of which is the *Tassigny* on rond-point de Lattre-de-Tassigny (☎04.68.27.11.51, fax 04.68.27.67.31, *www.logis-de-france.fr*, ③), which has clean rooms and good amenities. You can also get a bed at the local MJC hostel, 25 rue Marat (☎04.68.27.03.34; 60F/€9.15), while Lézignan's **campsite**, *La Pinède* (☎04.68.46.25.08; March–Oct) is on the main road on the eastern edge of town. In Le Somail, there is a small canal **information office** (☎06.84.81.96.20) by the old bridge, around which you'll find **accommodation** options. The friendly bar and restaurant *L'O à la Bouche* (☎04.68.46.30.57; April–Oct) on the west side of the old bridge offers **rooms** (②) in addition to *terroir* cuisine (menus from 85F/€12.96; off-season Sat & Sun only), while the old canal *auberge* on the east side also offers **chambres d'hôtes** (☎04.68.46.16.02; ③). Slightly more sophisticated meals can be enjoyed at the neighbouring *Auberge Lou Somaillou* (☎04.68.46.19.41; March–Nov), which has a comfortable dining room and a canalside terrace (98–200F/€14.95–30.50 menus). If you're tempted to continue from Le Somail by **boat**, Minervois Cruisers (☎04.68.46.28.52) can help you out, while land-lubbers can find **bikes** at Plancade (☎04.68.27.29.13), at 33 avenue Président-Wilson in Lézignan.

# Routes from Le Somail

From Le Somail you have a choice of two routes: the first follows the subsidiary canal, the Canal de la Robine, on a course through the southern portion of the alluvial plain, passing the old wine town of **Sallèles**, while the second stays with the main Canal du Midi heading east to Agde and the northern section of the plain, via the ancient **Oppidum d'Ensérune**.

## Along the Canal de la Robine

The **CANAL DE LA ROBINE**'s short trajectory carries it almost directly south, crossing the course of the wide, but here tame Aude, and continuing through Narbonne before penetrating the marshy extent of the Étang de Bages et de Sigean. After Narbonne there are two legs; the longer traces the same spit of land as the railway, skirting the bird-lovers' paradise of Île de Ste-Lucie, before arriving at Port-la-Nouvelle and the sea, while the shorter cuts east past the vineyards of La Clape, passing Gruissan (see p.291) and the saltpans of St-Martin before reaching the Mediterranean.

The only major port of call on the Canal de la Robine is **SALLÈLES**, a few kilometres before the canal merges with the Aude. Like Lézignan, Sallèles is a wine town of great antiquity, whose vintages graced the tables of Rome more than two thousand years ago. Bearing testimony to this are the Roman pottery works which have been discovered in the town, now incorporated into the **Amphoralis** museum on Sallèles' northern edge (July–Sept Tues–Sun 10am–noon & 3–7pm; Oct–June Tues–Fri 2–6pm, Sat & Sun 10am–noon & 2–6pm; 25F/€3.81). Named after the distinctively tapered vessels (*amphorae*) it's a well laid out and entertaining museum, which includes the excavation site itself. The walk out to the museum from the tourist office is interesting too, thanks to the series of six sets of **locks** which grace the part of the canal running alongside. While you are in town, you might also head to the rather less imaginative **Musée de Vieux Sallèles** (Sat & Sun 2.30–6.30pm; 20F/€3.05) in the centre, a rather traditional small-town French museum with extensive but familiar collections of tools relating to traditional crafts, viticulture and nineteenth-century life. The old town itself, a tight knot of narrow lanes, is also a good place to stretch your legs.

Finally, at Sallèles' canalside station, you can also hop on board the narrow-gauge **Autorail Touristique de Minervois** (ATM; ☎04.68.27.05.94, *www.multimania.com/autor*), a 1950s-era tourist train which uses the old line connecting Narbonne with Bize-Minervois, some 25km west of Minerve. The ATM runs on Sundays and the occasional Saturday (late-April to late-Aug), and the fare for the half-trip leg from Sallèles to Bize is 35F/€5.34. At Bize, the end of the line, you'll find the *Buvette de Cabezac*, a bar-restaurant and shop.

Sallèle's canalside **tourist office** (Mon–Fri 10.30am–12.30pm & 4–6.30pm; ☎04.68.46.81.46) is just southeast of the centre at 2 quai de Lorraine, and the only place to stay in the village is the municipal **campsite**, *Les Sablous* (☎04.68.33.61.30; mid-June to mid-Sept), a ten-minute walk from the centre on the east side of the canal. You'll find a couple of **cafés** along the main road where you can get a meal.

### East towards Agde

East of Le Somail the canal enters the most picturesque stretch of the whole waterway, snaking through rugged landscape, low and rocky vine-clad hills whose only reminder of civilization is an occasional bell tower. Sixteen kilometres after the Robine it passes under the old hill-top town of **Capestang**, whose small castle is capped by a distinctive tower. After cutting through the equally ancient hamlet of Poilhes, some 5km beyond, it enters a long tunnel, eventually arriving at **Colombiers**, a tiny village which merits a stop if only because it is the closest town to the exceptional excavations of the **OPPIDUM D'ENSÉRUNE**, which lies just 2km to the west.

Set on a long ridge towering over the surrounding plains, the site of this *oppidum* (Latin for "town", referring generally to pre-Roman hill-top settlements) has attracted settlers for over 2500 years. Even before Hannibal and the Romans took it over in turn it was an important centre for trade, maintaining commercial ties with Greece, while under the latter it served as one of the postal way-stations on the busy Via Domitia. The site itself, a rocky spur crowned with cypress and brambles, is characteristically Mediterranean, and climbing to the top, looking north, you'll get a view of a strange array of fields, resembling a spoked wheel. This was once the *étang* of Montady, one of the many salt lagoons of the lowlands, drained and cultivated in the thirteenth century. The **excavations** (June–Aug daily 9.30am–7.30pm; April, May & Sept daily 9.30am–6.30pm; Oct–March Mon & Wed–Sun 9.30am–5pm; 30F/€4.58) of the ancient ruins, covering most of the hill top, are impressive, with remains of defensive walls, villas, and a large array of cisterns and sunken grain stores. The small site **museum** inside the grounds holds a collection of statuary found here, including small devotional peices and larger civic portraits. If you have the time, **NISSAN-LEZ-ENSÉRUNE**, the largest town near the ancient settlement – just 4km to the south on the main road – is also worth a look. Its thirteenth-century Gothic **church** contains inscriptions in Occitan and some fine medieval statuary, and it also has a small **museum** (Mon & Wed–Sun: July & Aug 9.30am–7pm; April–June, Sept & Oct 10am–1.30pm & 2–5.30pm; Nov–Feb 1.30–5.30pm; 25F/€3.81), housing Roman finds from the surrounding area. At the roadside leaving town you'll see an extremely ornate country cemetery, with several impressive mausoleums.

As it arrives at the foot of Béziers' ridge, the canal descends another set of multiple locks, the **neuf écluses**. Billed as a tourist attraction, and endowed with footpaths and snack bars, the lock complex draws families and tour groups, who dutifully stand around watching the boats make their slow descent – altogether about as exciting as watching someone take the lift. Only 5km later, tiny **Villeneuve-lès-Béziers** is the last mooring point on the Canal du Midi before it follows a flat and featureless course to Agde (see p.305) and empties into the Bassin de Thau. From this lagoon you can reach the sea or connect with the other great inland waterway of Languedoc, the Canal du Rhône à Sète, which carries on past the Petite Camargue into Provence.

The only **tourist office** around the *oppidum* is at Nissan, in place Rene-Dez (Mon–Sat 9am–noon & 2–5.30pm; ☎ & fax 04.67.37.14.12), while Villeneuve, on the eastern side of Béziers, also has a tourist office in rue de la Fontaine (daily 9am–noon & 2–6pm; ☎04.67.39.48.83, fax 04.67.39.48.83). Nissan also has the best choice of **hotel**, the *Résidence* (☎04.67.35.00.63, fax 04.67.37.68.63; closed Nov & Dec; ③) set in an old mansion at 35 avenue de la Cave, while other local options include the two-star *Franche Comté*, 39 cours Belfort (☎04.67.93.31.21; ③) in Capestang, the well-sited *Via Domitia* (☎04.67.35.62.63, fax 04.67.35.62.00; ③) in Colombiers, and *Las Cigalas* (☎04.67.39.45.28, fax 04.67.39.39.61; ③) at no. 28 in Villeneuve's boulevard Gambetta. You'll find municipal **campsites** at Capestang (☎04.67.49.85.95; July & Aug), Colombiers (☎04.67.37.05.26) and Villeneuve (☎04.67.39.36.09; March–Oct). The only **restaurant** hereabouts which stands out is Poilhes' *La Tour Sarrazine*, 27 boulevard du Canal (☎04.67.93.41.31; closed Sun eve & Mon), which serves imaginative *terroir*-based cuisine in a cosy old house (menus from 140F/€21.35). Villeneuve's country market is held on Tuesdays and Sundays, and you can rent **boats** from Rive de France (☎04.67.37.14.23) at Colombiers.

# Béziers and around

**BÉZIERS**, just inland from the mouth of the Orb river and dominating the strip of plain between the coast and Haut Languedoc, could be held up as a metaphor for Languedoc – it is a town with a long and proud past, and a history of independent spirit, which it has more than once paid for in blood. Like neighbouring Narbonne, Béziers was already a sizeable settlement when the Romans took it over in the second century BC; under *pax romana* it throve, and through the Middle Ages it was the seat of a bishop and prosperous market town. The last great event here was the attack it suffered in the Albigensian Crusade, and since then it has been something of a sleepy bywater – Paul Riquet, the genius behind the Canal du Midi, is the town's biggest claim to fame. Still, its former grandeur is evident from afar – as you approach, its great **cathedral** towers over the Orb river, high up on a dramatic ridge – but as you enter the city, its dusty streets and deteriorating shop fronts betray the slump into which the town has settled in the last century or so. Nevertheless, the town's **old quarter** makes for a pleasant amble and Béziers is also home to two great Languedocian adopted traditions: English **rugby**, and the Spanish **corrida**, both of which it follows with a passion. The best time to visit is during the mid-August **feria**, a raucous four-day party which you will enjoy even if you don't find bullfighting to your tastes. The town is also a useful staging point for excursions up the **Orb valley** (see p.307) towards Haut Languedoc, or down to **Agde** and the coast.

## Arrival, information and accommodation

If you arrive at the **gare SNCF** on boulevard de Verdun, about fifteen minutes' walk southeast of the old town, the best way into the centre is through the land-scaped gardens of the Plateau des Poètes, opposite the *gare* entrance, and up allées Paul-Riquet to place de la Victoire. The **gare routière** is on place Général de Gaulle, just to the east of Victoire, while the **tourist office** is at 5 place Jean-Jaurès (July & Aug Mon–Sat 9am–7pm, Sun 10am–noon; Sept–June Mon–Sat 9am–noon & 2–6.30pm; ☎04.67.76.47.00, fax 04.67.76.50.80, *www.ville-beziers.fr*), which opens up off allées Paul-Riquet just north of place Garibaldi. If you are **driving**, there is no need to park in the underground garage at place Garibaldi – there's plenty of metered street parking in and around the town centre. You can rent **bikes** at La Maison du Canal (☎04.67.62.18.18) beside the Port Neuf, south of the gare SNCF. For a central place to **stay**, the best option is the welcoming *Angleterre*, 22 place Jean-Jaurès (☎04.67.28.48.42; ②), while other good alternatives are *Hôtel des Poètes*, 80 allées Paul-Riquet (☎04.67.76.38.66, fax 04.67.76.25.88; ③), at the south-ern end overlooking the gardens, the smarter *Hôtel du Théâtre*, 13 rue Coquille (☎04.67.49.13.43, fax 04.67.49.31.58; ③), right beside the municipal theatre, and the town's de luxe option, *Hôtel Imperator* (☎04.67.49.02.25, fax 04.67.28.92.30 ④), at 28 allées Paul-Riquet, which is a notch above the rest but won't break the bank. There's no **campsite** in Béziers, but you can head to nearby Villeneuve-lès-Béziers (see above) or 6km east to Clariac (☎04.67.76.78.97; March–Oct).

## The Town

Béziers' vaguely semicircular **old town** snuggles into a gentle meander of the Orb, which, along with the canal – the Ruisseau de Bagnols – bounds it on three sides. The eastern limit is marked by Allées Paul-Riquet, which has a broad pedestrian concourse running down its centre. From place Jean-Jaurès, which opens up off Allées Riquet, you can descend rue due la Citadelle to place Gabriel Péri, the old town's centre.

### The Cathédrale St-Nazaire

Béziers' main attraction is undoubtedly the majestic Romanesque **Cathédrale St-Nazaire** (free entry), about five minutes' walk west from place Péri on the west-ern rim, just off place de la Révolution. Constructed in the thirteenth century, the cathedral's marriage of style and function is immediately apparent from its west face, which has a great rosette window flanked by two fortified towers. From the entrance here, the first part of the cathedral you enter is the cloister. Walking around its low and austere gallery, you can see a collection of old funerary stones, including one with Hebrew characters, while on its east side a stairway descends into the airy gardens, the **Jardin de l'Évêché**, built off the south side of the great church, or you can enter the cathedral itself. The voluminous, predominantly unadorned **interior** is dominated by an outrageous Baroque retable – a gaudy starburst of saints and cherubs which clashes with the sobriety of the building. The high point of the visit though is the dizzying climb to the **upper galleries** (free) – a rare opportunity to get a pigeon's eye view of the cathedral's interior. Ascending the well-worn and narrow keystone staircase you'll traverse a small landing before continuing up to the top – here, walking around the balconies which circle the pinnacles affords spectacular **views**. Staring nearly straight down

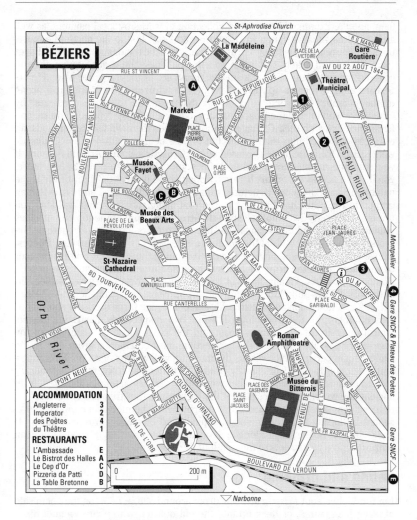

△ St-Aphrodise Church

**BÉZIERS**

La Madéleine

PLACE DE LA VICTOIRE

Gare Routière

R G MANDEL

AV DU 22 AOÛT 1944

RUE PORTE OLIVIER

R CLAIR

R TRENCAVEL

R C PERET

RUE ST VINCENT

R P RIQUET

Théâtre Municipal

R BUGUAL

RUE DE LA TOUR

DE PAUL

**Ⓐ**

RUE DE LA RÉPUBLIQUE

RUE ETIENNE FORCADEL

RUE EN-VERT

R CARLES

RUE MAIRAN

**❶**

**Market**

PLACE PIERRE SEMARD

ALLÉES PAUL RIQUET

**❷**

COLLEGE

R FLOURENS

RUE DU 4 SEPTEMBRE

RUE PAUL PELISSON

**Musée Fayet**

PLACE G PÉRI

R DU GAL CROZAT

R DES BALANCES

**Ⓒ** **Ⓑ**

RUE BOUDARD

R CAPUS

VIENNET

AVENUE ALPHONSE MAS

R MONTMORENCY

R DE LA CITADELLE

**Ⓓ**

**Musée des Beaux Arts**

LA JUIVERIE

RUE DE BONSI

R ESTÈVE

PLACE DE LA RÉVOLUTION

R ARGENTIER

R MASSOL

PLACE JEAN-JAURÈS

**+** FRIEND SQ

RUE FABREGAT

RUE DE BONSI

**St-Nazaire Cathedral**

BD TOURVENTOUSE

PLACE CANTERELLETTES

R DU DR BOURGUET

RUE JEAN JAURES

**ⓘ**

AV DU M JOFFRE

**❸**

Orb

RUE CANTERELLES

R DES ARENES

RUE DU COQ

PLACE GARIBALDI

R DE L'ABREUVOIR

R DU PUITS DES ARÈNES

River

PONT VIEUX

RUE DE L'ORB

R SAINT JACQUES

R GAVEAU

AVENUE GAMBETTA

PONT NEUF

AVENUE COLONEL D'ORNANO

R DES CASERNES

RUE SAINT JACQUES

**Roman Amphitheatre**

RAMPE DU 96e

AVENUE DE LA MARNE

RUE DE L'HORTET

RUE DU MIDI

▷ Montpellier

▷ Gare SNCF & Plateau des Poètes

R DE LA MAILLE

**Musée du Biterrois**

N

QUAI DE L'ORB

R G MARGUERITE

PLACE SAINT JACQUES

PLACE DES CASEMES

RUE FR RASPAIL

Gare SNCF ▷

**ACCOMMODATION**
Angleterre       **3**
Imperator        **2**
des Poètes      **4**
du Théâtre      **1**

**RESTAURANTS**
L'Ambassade          **E**
Le Bistrot des Halles   **A**
Le Cep d'Or            **C**
Pizzeria da Patti      **D**
La Table Bretonne    **B**

0                  200 m

BOULEVARD DE VERDUN

**Ⓔ**

▽ Narbonne

over the cliffs on which the cathedral stands, you'll see the evocative eleventh-century *pont vieux* as it crosses the Orb below and, beyond to the west, the whole of the Bitterois plain stretching off into a haze – on a clear day you might make out the form of Le Canigou on the horizon. Take care when climbing the stairs and circulating up top, particularly if you are travelling with children – the only protective fencing here is the old stone balustrade.

## The rest of the old town

Leaving the cathedral, walk to the far end of the pleasant place de la Révolution, where republican protesters were fired upon in 1851, and you'll find the Hôtel Fabrégat, a mansion which houses the **Musée des Beaux Arts** (Tues–Fri

9am–noon & 2–6pm; 15F/€2.29), a collection of works by local painters, as well as better known artists such as Delacroix and Dufy. Just to the north, the museum's sculpture annex is lodged in another aristocratic residence, the **Hôtel Fayet** (same hours and ticket). Continuing north, you'll pass the beautiful wrought-iron covered market (Tues–Sun 7.30am–12.30pm), set in the attractive place Pierre-Sémard and, further on up rue Paul Riquet, the **church of la Madeleine**, scene of the infamous massacre of 1209. In that year the town was besieged by Crusaders who invited the local Catholics to leave, but they refused to do so, preferring to stick with their Cathar neighbours. When the town fell, seven thousand refugees crammed into the church, but none – neither Catholics nor Cathars – were spared from the flames ordered by the Crusade's leader, Arnaud-Amaury. If you continue north from the church for some 250m up to place St-Aphrodise, you'll come across the **church** (briefly open some days at 5.30pm) of the same name – an incredibly old structure, with a tenth-century nave and Gallo-Roman crypt. On the other hand turning to the east along rue Trencavel will lead you towards the pretty Art Nouveau-style **théâtre municipal** at the top end of allées Paul-Riquet, a broad, leafy esplanade lined with cafés, crêpes stalls and restaurants. The boulevard ends at the gorgeous little park of the **Plateau des Poètes**, whose ponds, palms and lime trees were laid out in the so-called English manner by the same team, the brothers Denis et Eugène Bülher, who created the Bois de Boulogne in Paris. Finally, west of this, you'll find the impressive **Musée du Biterrois** (Tues–Sun: July & Aug 9am–7pm; Sept–June 9am–noon & 2–6pm; 15F/€2.29), housed in an old barracks, and containing three sections: natural history, ethnography and archeology. The first two, respectively illustrating the biological diversity of the marshy coast and the rural and craft traditions of the region, are passable. But it is the last section, most of which is given over to the Gallo-Roman period, which makes the museum well worthy of a stop. This important collection ranges from locally produced pottery and ceramics, to funerary monuments and milestones. There are also various artefacts dredged from ancient shipwrecks off the coast, but the highlight is the "treasure of Béziers" – a rich cache of silver platters found in a nearby field. The medieval period is represented by locally sculpted medieval capitals and bas-reliefs. You can finish off your visit to Béziers by taking a look at the remains of a modest Roman **amphitheatre** two streets to the north of the museum.

# Eating and drinking

For **food**, check out *Pizzeria da Patti* (from around 50F/€7.63), on the north side of place Jean-Jaurès, or head up into the old quarter, where rue Viennet has a good choice of restaurants. Two specific places to try here are the elegant *Le Cep d'Or*, at no. 7, serving mostly seafood (menus from 78F/€11.90; closed Sun eve & Mon), and *La Table Bretonne*, at no. 21, a homely crêperie in the shadow of the cathedral where you can eat well for around 60F/€9.15 (closed Mon). *L'Ambassade* (☎04.67.76.06.24; closed Sun & Mon), at 22 boulevard de Verdun is one of the town's best places (menus from 145F/€22.11), while *Le Bistrot des Halles*, further north on place de la Madeleine behind the market square, is popular for its varied, well-priced menus (from 90F/€13.73; closed Sun & Mon). A good **café** is *La Bourse* at the corner of place Jean-Jaurès and allées Riquet, while a livelier time can be enjoyed at two tapas bars, *Charlie & Carlos* and *Le Mondial*, which square off at the corner of rues Boieldieu and Solferino.

# Listings

**Banks** All major French banks are represented here, and most have offices in allées Riquet or place Jean-Jaurès. On the former you'll find BNP at no. 34, Banque Populaire du Midi at no. 39, and Crédit Lyonnais at no. 16.

**Boat rental** At Béziers' port: Amica Tours (☎04.67.62.18.18) and Béziers Croisières (☎04.67.49.08.23); the latter also runs canal trips.

**Bus information** ☎04.67.28.23.85.

**Car rental** Avis, 18 bd Verdun (☎04.67.28.75.44); Europcar, 70 allées Paul-Riquet (☎04.67.72.09.99).

**Internet access** Cyberia, 7 rue St-Ferignon (☎04.67.72.99.91).

**Police** pl Général-de-Gaulle.

**Rugby** Béziers has one of the star rugby clubs in France, A.S.B.H., based at the Stade de la Méditerranée in the eastern suburbs (☎04.67.11.03.76).

**Taxis** ☎04.67.35.00.85

**Train information** ☎08.36.35.35.35

# Agde and the coast

Just 12km east of Béziers, **AGDE** is one of the most unspoilt towns on the Languedocian coast, thanks to the few kilometres which separate it from the sea. It boomed as port 2500 years ago under the Phoenicians and on through the Middle Ages, until competition from neighbouring towns and the silting up of the Hérault pushed the seashore from its walls. Today, its compact old town has resisted intensive development and remains a quiet respite from the crowds – the best time to arrive is on one of Agde's market days: Thursday for produce and Wednesday and Saturday for the flea market. Set along the now canalized river, it is dominated by the twelfth-century fortified **cathedral**, St-Étienne, on its south bank, whose appearance is more castle than church, its three-metre-thick walls and hot-oil sluices having formed the strongpoint of the town's defences. A series of *places* follows the riverside from east to west: the lively Jean-Jaurès, with its sidewalk cafés; Picheire, where you'll find the small porticoed medieval **market**; and de la Marine, a grittily authentic fishermen's quarter. Heading south from place de la Marine, the residential rue Poissonerie is a step back in time – a neighbourhood of fishermen's families living in modest and ancient row houses. Following it to the end, you'll arrive at the old convent housing the **Musée Agathois** (July & Aug daily 10am–noon & 2–6pm; Sept–June Mon & Wed–Sun same times; 15F/€2.29), one of the better of the region's "local" museums, with exhibitions on life in the area from the prehistoric era to the present day; relics of the town's seafaring past range from ancient Greek *amphorae* to nineteenth-century navigational instruments. Continuing on, you'll pass the new market building, and the **church of St-André**, occupying a site on which there's been a church since as far back as 506 AD, when an episcopal council was held here. Just south opens up the wide tree-lined La Promenade, with its multitude of terraced bars, while close by, rue de l'Amour and rue Jean-Roger are lined with tacky souvenir shops.

## Cap d'Agde and le Grau d'Agde

**CAP D'AGDE**, Agde's evil twin, lies to the south of Mont St-Loup on the seashore 7km away from Agde. A sprawling modern resort, its only redemption is the abundance of colourful plants and flowers which line its broad streets, only partially concealing the sea of cream-coloured holiday villas behind. The Cap has everything you would want for a beach holiday – nightclubs, watersports and restaurants, although here you will pay dearly for them. If you're just passing through though a worthwhile stop is the **Musée de l'Éphèbe** (July & Aug daily 9am–12.30pm & 2.30–6.30pm; Sept–June Wed–Sat 9am–noon & 2–6pm, Sun 2–6pm; 15F/€2.29), in the central Parc de la Clape, which holds a collection of Greek and Roman relics retrieved from the sea bed, including the beautiful little Hellenistic bronze statuette known as the Éphèbe d'Agde, until recently one of the treasures of the Louvre. There is also an **aquarium**, at 11 rue des Deux-Frères (daily: July & Aug 10am–11pm; Sept–June 2–7pm; 37F/€5.64), though it's not as good as that at Grau-du-Roi (see p.236), and a huge Aqualand **amusement park** (mid-June to mid-Sept daily 10am–7pm; 90F/€13.73) on the west end of town. **Fort de Brescou**, which, dating back to 1680, served for centuries as a prison, lies just offshore and can be reached by ferries departing from the ports at either Cap d'Agde or le Grau d'Agde (Mon, Tues & Thurs–Sun 10.30am, 2.30pm & 6.30pm; 35F/€5.34). The grim fortress, which evokes Marseille's famous Château d'If – of *Man in the Iron Mask* fame – can be visited on a **guided tour** (timed with boat arrivals in July & Aug; 15F/€2.29), or you can simply scamper about the rocky seagull-infested island for free.

If you fancy a dip, the best **beaches** are on the west side of the cape stretching over towards La Guirandette; there's also a huge, self-contained **nudist colony** here on the east side – to drive through will cost you 50F per car, plus 13F for each passenger. Nearby **GRAU d'AGDE** is the beach-town antithesis of the Cap: a dispersed settlement of weathered houses and ageing bungalows, a sort of dissipating suburb which distils into an old fishing town as you reach the lighthouse-capped wavebreak.

## Practicalities

**Trains** and **buses** arrive in Agde just across the river from the old town. To continue south to the Cap you can take a municipal bus (3F/€0.46) from the *gare* or use the superb network of cycle paths – once there you'll realise it's no place to walk, and end up using one of the two *petits* trains which circulate around the town (10–15F/€1.53–2.29) or the various **water taxis**. Agde's **tourist office** (July & Aug daily 9am–7pm; Sept–June Mon–Sat 9am–noon & 2–6pm; ☎04.67.94.29.68, fax 04.67.94.03.50) is on place Molière, near the main roundabout; it is here that you can leave on a two-hour **guided tour** of the town (in English Tues & Thurs 10am; 25F/€3.81). In Cap d'Agde, you'll find the **tourist office** (daily: July & Aug 8.30am–8pm; May, June & Sept 9am–7pm; Oct–April 9am–noon & 2–7pm; ☎04.67.01.04.04, fax 04.67.26.22.99, *www.capdagde.com*) on the huge roundabout which marks the centre of the settlement.

The best **hotel** in Agde is the Dutch-run *La Galoite* (☎04.67.21.30.28, fax 04.67.94.41.33, *www.laGaliote.fr*; ③), located in the old bishops' palace on place Jean-Jaurès, while a close second is *Le Donjon* (☎04.67.94.12.32, fax 04.67.94.34.54; ④) on the same square. Some of the cheapest but still decent digs can be had at the *Hôtel des Arcades* (☎04.67.94.21.64; ③) in an old convent at 16 rue Louis-Bages. One reasonably priced option at the Cap is *La Voile d'Or* on place de Globe (☎04.67.01.04.11, fax 04.67.01.04.20; ④), while Grau has the seaside *El Rancho* (☎04.67.94.24.35, fax 04.67.94.85.47, *www.logis-de-france.fr*; ③). There are no fewer than 24 **campsites** in the area – you might start with *Sud*

*Loisirs* (☎04.67.21.09.10) near Agde, or *La Clape* (☎04.67.26.41.32; March–Oct) at the Cap, while the naturist centre also has a site (☎04.67.01.06.36) and a hotel (☎04.67.26.71.70; ⑦). The area's best **restaurant** is *La Tramissière* (☎04.67.94.20.87; closed Jan to mid-March & frequently Sun & Mon; bus #275 from the main road through town), a *gastronomique* halfway between Agde and Grau on the far bank of the Hérault (165F/€25.16 and up), while a good choice at the Cap is the seafood specialist, *Le Brasero*, Port Richelieu II (☎04.67.26.24.75; menus from 85F/€12.96). In Agde itself, you could do worse than *Casa Pépé* (☎04.67.21.17.67), a popular seafood place with a small terrace, at 26 rue Jean-Roger, and there are also a number of places right on the quayside or in rue Chassefière, which runs along it. Also in Agde, you'll find an **Internet** connection at Globe Trotter, 4 place de la Marine, and **bike rental** at La Cadotière, 1 place Jean-Jaurès (☎04.76.94.26.20), while Les Bateaux du Soleil (☎04.67.94.08.79) at the port offers canal and river trips.

# The Orb valley

The **River Orb** winds a twisting path down from its source in the hills of Haut Languedoc north of Béziers, descending some 120km through the highlands and across the broad coastal plain to skirt the city before emptying into the Golfe du Lion. Heading up its valley from Béziers provides rapid access from the coast to the lesser-travelled uplands of Haut Languedoc. Just after **Roquebrun**, a centre both for viticulture and rafting, the valley delves into the rugged uplands, wheeling off to the east to pass the old spa town of **Lamalou-les-Bains** and **Hérépian** – both good bases for walks into the Parc Naturel de Haut Languedoc – and following the park's edge round until the land opens up into a compact but fertile plane around **Bédarieux** – another possible departure point for exploring the highlands. Heading further north into the **upper valley** you eventually reach a series of tiny hamlets high up at the river's origins.

## Roquebrun

Journeying 21km upriver from Béziers the D14 joins the course of the Orb at Cessenon, just before it ascends into the rugged uplands. The border of the Parc du Haut Languedoc (see p.189) has recently been pulled south to incorporate the area around **ROQUEBRUN**, less than 10km further along. This old town, clumped on a hillside beneath the ruins of its medieval tower, is located in an exceptionally mild microclimate, making the valley floor, which is still wide here, an idea place for vine cultivation – indeed the town has produced several award-winning vintages, which you can sample and buy at the various *domaines* scattered around the valley. The good weather also makes possible the town's **Jardin Méditerranéen** (daily: July & Aug 9am–7pm; mid-Feb to June & Sept to mid-Nov 9am–noon & 1.30–5.30pm; 15F/€2.29), a collection of exotic, primarily arid-climate plants from around the world, while in winter the valley around the town bursts into colour with the blooming of mimosas. After Roquebrun the valley begins to meander drunkenly, reeling between the ever-higher peaks which gird it until, at last, you reach the mill at **Terassac** 14km on, where the Jaur and the Héric join the Orb; here the river course takes an abrupt swing to the east on towards Lamalou. The mill is also the place to rent **canoes** (☎04.67.97.74.64) for the exciting rafting journey downstream to Roquebrun, the terminus for this and trips from higher up in the hills.

There is a small **tourist office** (July & Aug Mon–Sat 10am–1pm & 3–7pm; Sept–June Mon–Fri 9am–noon & 2–6pm; ☎ & fax 04.67.89.79.97) in Roquebrun, while for **accommodation** here, you can choose between the *Campotel* **campsite** (☎04.67.89.61.99; ③) or the Anglo-run **gîte** *Les Mimosas* (☎04.67.89.61.36, *latouche.les-mimosas.fr*; ④) on avenue Orangers, which also does meals (155F/ €23.64).

## Lamalou-les-Bains and Hérépian

**LAMALOU-LES-BAINS** lies just a kilometre north of the river course, built on the hot springs which have brought it prosperity for the last thousand years. In the late nineteenth and early twentieth century it came into fashion, and notables such as the writers Alphonse Daudet and André Gide came to enjoy its curative waters. Today it is still a popular therapeutic spot, and the more or less constant parade of ailing people moving among its faded *fin-de-siècle* mansions gives it the strange air of a large outdoor hospital. The town is most useful as a stop-over for hikers making their way through the hills, but there is also a beautiful old parish church here, **St-Pierre-de-Rhèdes**, which dates back to the spa's earliest beginnings. The church's pastiche of stylistic touches, overlaying its basic Romanesque form, results from immigrants to the region, including Mozarabs from Spain, who left Christian inscriptions written in Arabic.

Only a few kilometres upstream, **HÉRÉPIAN**, has a much more salubrious air, a pleasant workaday town, with only the most basic of services. While here you can visit the Bruneau-Garnier **bell foundry** (daily: July & Aug 10am–noon & 2–7pm; April–June & Sept 10am–noon & 2–6pm; Oct–March 10am–noon & 2–7pm; 25F/€3.81) – one of the last in France still functioning – or you might hike up to the ruins of the **Castle of St-Michel**, 300m above the riverbed on the slopes of the **Pic de la Coquillade**. The trail head begins on the south bank, just west of the hamlet of Les Aires, and the gruelling 6km will take you first to the extensive ruins of the castle, which was founded in 990, and on to the summit, where you'll find a small chapel.

Lamalou's **tourist office** on avenue Dr-Ménard (June–Sept Mon–Fri 9am–noon & 2.30–6.30pm, Sat 9am–noon & 2–5pm, Sun 10am–noon; Oct–May Mon–Fri 9.30am–noon & 2.30–6pm, Sat 9am–noon; ☎04.67.95.70.91, fax 04.67.95.64.52, *omt.Lamalou@wanadoo.fr*) has information on nearby towns and also sells SNCF bus tickets. There is no shortage of accommodation here and the **hotels** *De la Paix l'Arbousier*, 18 rue A-Daudet (☎04.67.95.63.11, fax 04.67.95.67.78, *www.logis-de-france.fr*; ③) and *Galimar*, 17 boulevard St-Michel (☎04.67.95.22.99, fax 04.67.95.23.64; ②) are both good deals. Both of these establishments have good **restaurants**, and there are many others to choose from around town. Lamalou is also a good centre for serivces; there are several banks, a laundry and even a car rental office here.

## Bédarieux

Continuing from Hérépian, the valley broadens suddenly, forming a wide pocket of flat land dominated by **BÉDARIEUX**, the biggest place north of Béziers on the course of the Orb. The town is something of a transport hub and, as an administrative centre, is also busy, but for all that you are not likely to want to stay too long. Bédarieux's one tourist attraction is the predictably mediocre **Maison des Arts** (Wed–Sun 3–6pm; 20F/€3.05) on avenue Abbé Taroux, whose collection is dominated by local painter Pierre-Auguste Cot. Otherwise, the tourist office can set you up with detailed information on **walks** in the local countryside (5F/€0.76 for their booklet). One of the better short ones is the trail, through vines and bulrushes, to the twelfth-century pre-Romanesque **chapel** of St-Raphaël, on the far bank of the river, while a more challenging option is the ascent of the Pic de Tanajo (518m) to the southwest.

Bédarieux's **gare SNCF** (☎04.67.95.02.92), which is also where **buses** call in, is a good twenty-minute hike north of the old centre, where you'll find the regional **tourist office** (Mon, Tues, Thurs & Fri 9am–12.30pm & 2–7.30pm, Sat 9am–12.30pm; ☎04.67.95.08.79, fax 04.67.95.39.69, *francis.ot@libertysurf.fr*), on place aux Herbes. There are two reasonable **hotels** in town: the *Moderne*, at 112 avenue Jean-Jaurès (☎04.67.95.01.52; ③) and the aptly named *Central*, 3 place aux Herbes (☎04.67.95.06.76; ②). The municipal **campsite** (☎04.67.23.30.19) is on the south bank of the Orb, just west of town. The best restaurant deal is *Le Rapier*, by the Hôtel de Ville on rue de la République, where you can get a four-course meal including dessert, coffee and wine for 65F/€9.91. If you have come without a vehicle to explore the uplands of the Orb and the Parc Naturel you can rent a **car** at Wallgren, 4 rue de la République (☎04.67.23.18.23), while Passion Sauvage (☎04.67.23.69.33) will rent **bikes**. There are markets in the town's *places* on Monday and Saturday mornings.

## The upper Orb valley

Moving north, the valley continues to rise, before petering out to little more than a brook as it reaches its sources in the Monts d'Orb. Proceeding from Bédarieux, you should take the turn-off 6km north of town and ascend to the tiny medieval hamlet of **Boussagues**, an extremely well-preserved walled town, replete with church, fountain and *donjon*, and which is surprisingly unvisited; the only service you'll find here is a (frequently closed) café. The ruins of its castles, on the hill above, are little more than foundations overgrown by vine and bramble, but the views they provide are great. **Hikers** on the GR7 will pass by Boussagues as they make their way between Lamalous and Lodève. **Le-Bousquet**, 10km further up the valley, has a strange air, as if everyone is waiting for something to happen – nothing ever does, however, and aside from taking a fleeting look at the old quarter gathered in a mound on the right bank, there is no reason to stay. **Lunas**, just a few kilometres further (and on the GR653) makes a much more pleasant option. Here the river glides past the walls of a pitched-roof *château*; you'll find an old bridge and a church which, it is claimed, dates back to the fifth century – nothing particularly stunning, but, with the low, forest-clad hills rising on either side of the river valley, an attractive and peaceful scene, and a good stop before braving the spectacular mountain road which leads east along the steep ridge to Lodève (see p.271).

If you make a stop in Le-Bousquet, you can stay at the small and homely *Hôtel Berthomieu* (☎04.67.23.80.45; closed Jan & weekends in winter; ②), whose restaurant has basic home-cooked meals from 62F/€9.46. At Lunas you can stay in the **hotel**, *Auberge Gourmand* (☎04.67.23.81.41; ②) whose restaurant (closed Fri–Sun in winter) has menus from 63 to 230F/€9.61 to 35.08, wine included. A more unique choice and a great bargain, however, is to take one of the simple rooms in the castle, *Le Château* (☎04.67.23.87.99; ①) which also has a **bar** (till 1am) and an excellent restaurant (menus from 95F/€14.49). There are seasonal (June–Sept) **campsites** here (☎04.67.23.77.62) and at Le-Bousquet (☎04.67.23.80.89).

## travel details

### TRAINS

**Narbonne** to: Agde (12 daily; 34min); Béziers (15 daily; 22min); Carcassonne (14 daily; 35min); Cerbère (10 daily; 1hr 25min); Lézignan (14 daily; 12min); Montpellier (12 daily; 45min); Nîmes (14 daily; 1hr 15min); Paris (5–6 daily; 6hr); Perpignan (12 daily; 45min); Port-la-Nouvelle (10 daily; 15min); Salses (10 daily; 30min); Sète (12 daily; 43min); Toulouse (14 daily; 1hr 30min).

**Béziers** to: Paris (1 daily; 12hr).

### BUSES

*Most lines listed below have no Sunday service.*

**Agde** to: Cap d'Agde (20 daily; 15min).

**Bédarieux** to: Castres (2 daily; 2hr); Lamalou-les-Bains (5 daily; 20min); St-Pons (5 daily; 1hr 20min).

**Béziers** to: Castres (2 daily; 2hr 30min); Colombiers (6 daily; 23min); Montpellier (4–6 daily; 1hr 30min); Narbonne (2 daily; 55min); Nissan-les-Ensérune (6 daily; 35min); Pézenas (6–8 daily; 32min); St-Pons (5 daily; 1 hr 20min).

**Carcassonne** to: Caunes-Minervois (1–4 daily; 30min).

**Narbonne** to: Bize (1–2 daily; 40min); Gruissan (3–5 daily; 20min); Mouthoumet (1–2 daily; 2hr 5min); Perpignan (1 daily; 2hr); Sallèles (1–3 daily; 30min); Salses (1 daily; 1hr 55min); Sigean (3–6 daily; 40min); Sigean Reserve (6 daily; 25min); St-Julien/Fontfroide (2–5 daily; 40min); Villerouge-Termenès (1–3 daily; 1hr 40min).

**Port-la-Nouvelle** to: Sigean (3 daily; 10min).

# CHAPTER SEVEN

# ROUSSILLON

**R**oussillon, bordered by the Mediterranean to the east, the hills of the Corbières along the north, and the upper Aude and Ariège valleys to the west, is France's southernmost region, sometimes known as French Catalonia; the peaks of the eastern section of the Pyrenees, which it shares with Spain, mark its southern limit. Although absorbed by France some three and a half centuries ago, and now known officially as the *département* of Pyrénées-Orientales, it hasn't entirely lost its Catalan flavour: in the mountains there are many people whose language of choice is Catalan, and even in the larger towns you'll find the survival of customs such as the *sardana* dance or Paschal rituals. You'll also register a definite shift towards the use of traditional Catalan ingredients and recipes in the region's *terroir* cuisine. But despite these particularities, and recent efforts by Catalan speakers to broaden the currency of the language, Roussillon is fundamentally French in cultural orientation, and unlike other French regions, such as Corsica, it has no significant separatist movement or regionalist political party – most likely your only encounter with the language will be overhearing the conversation of the many visitors from Catalonia proper to the region. Traditionally a poor and neglected area, its people have historically lived off fishing on the coast; agriculture, herding and lumber in the hills; and, of course, smuggling, which, with the region's frontier position and the inhospitality of its landscape, until recently provided a meagre source of income. In the last decade or so though, Roussillon's mild climate has provoked its resurgence as a retirement spot for Northern French, viewed by some of the local inhabitants with a jaundiced eye as "foreign" encroachers.

Roussillon is a beautiful region, marked by the variety and contrasts of its landscape. North of the cosmopolitan main city, **Perpignan**, a marshy coastline hems in the **Fenouillèdes** hills stretching up to the northeast corner of the *département* – home to the easternmost Cathar castles and a number of prehistoric caves. Southwest from the capital you can follow the course of Roussillon's jugular, the River **Têt**, up the valley to **Canigou**, the peak which still symbolizes all of Catalonia, and the scene of a patriotic torchlight procession on midsummer's eve. Roussillon's mountains begin with the Canigou massif and include the zones of the **upper Têt** – shadowed by the spectacular route of the *Train Jaune* – the **Capcir** plateau, stretching up to the Aude, the **Cerdagne**, tucked away in the far southeast corner of the *département* and, north of that, the forbidding **Carlit massif**; all of these regions offer excellent **hiking** and **skiing** amidst superb scenery. There are also many architectural treasures worth seeking out here, in particular the sturdy Romanesque **monasteries** which cropped up along this length of the Pyrenees in the eleventh and twelfth centuries. The **Tech valley** runs a vaguely parallel course to the Têt, leading up from the plains south of Perpignan and along the Spanish border; a favourite zone with refugees from Franco's repression, its villages are some of the most traditionally Catalan in the

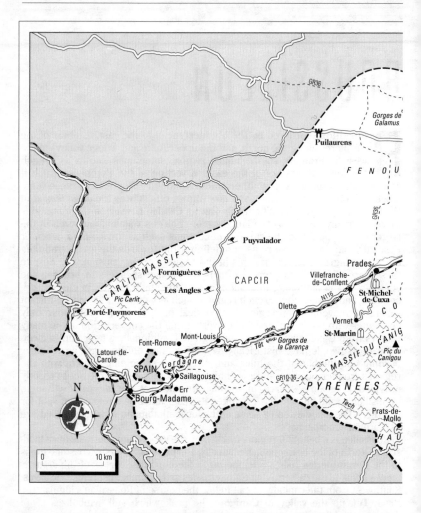

whole region. Finally, the rugged **Côte Vermeille**, the seashore to the north of the frontier, is ideal for swimming and relaxing, its rocky harbours, cut out of wind-blown precipitous hills, forming a mirror image of Catalan Empurdà on the far side of the Pyrenees.

Despite its relative lack of development, Roussillon is fairly easy to get around, as long you stick to the main **transport** routes, which run along the coast, and up the major valleys – the Têt, Tech, and rivers of the Fenouillet. Travelling between the valleys is more problematic, and unless you have your own transport you'll have to resort to hiking or hitching. The main road and rail links to Spain head south from Perpignan, the latter passing through the towns of the Côte Vermeille.

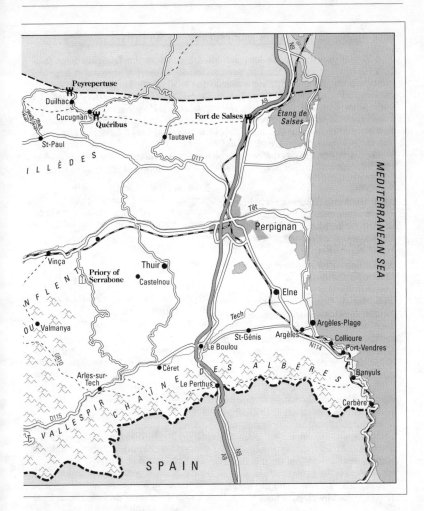

# Perpignan and around

**PERPIGNAN**, the capital of Roussillon, is the most multinational city in the Southwest. A substantial part of its population is descended from Spanish Catalans who poured across the border in the final days of the Spanish Civil War, desperate to avoid reprisals at the hands of Franco's Castilian and Moroccan troops. There's also a sizeable Romany contingent, and some of the suburbs were settled by French colonists who fled the upheavals associated with the Maghrebi independence movements of the 1950s and 1960s. Finally, a run-down zone in the centre has become the quarter for recent arrivals from

## ROUSSILLON'S FESTIVALS AND TRADITIONS

The Roussillonaise seem to have inherited a penchant for **festivals** from their Spanish cousins south of the Pyrenees, as just about every village has at least one cheerfully energetic celebration – usually the local saint's day, or *festa major* (*fête majeur*, in French). It is in these that the region's Catalan and Spanish character come to the fore, with *sardanas, corridas de toros*, and Holy Week processions. The last of these, a solemn barefoot march by taper-carrying and hooded penitents, is best seen in places like Collioure, Arles-sur-Tech and Céret. Lest you forget that you are in France, there are also mid-October grape-harvest festivals in the wine-producing regions, two of the best of which are at Banyuls and Elne. Where no specific information number is given, contact the relevant tourist office for details.

### February

**First weekend** Arles-sur-Tech: Fête de l'Ours. This ancient festival rooted in prehistoric magical and hunting traditions marks the time when bears come out of hibernation.

**End Feb** Prats-de-Mollo: Fête de l'Ours. Similar festival to Arles'.

**Feb–March** Perpignan: Carnaval. Pre-Lenten celebration held approximately four weeks before Easter, including much drinking and dancing. As in Catalonia and Spain many party-goers dress up in elaborate and outrageous costumes.

**April 23** Perpignan: San Jordi. Festival of Catalonia's patron saint, St George. Also the birthday of Cervantes and Shakespeare, now declared International Day of the Book; the – slightly sexist – custom on this day is for the men to present their sweethearts with a red rose, and the women to reciprocate by giving a book.

**Mid-May** Céret: Grand Fête de la Cerise. "Festival of the Cherry", held over several days; Céret is the cherry capital of the Pyrenees, and it celebrates the traditional source of its prosperity with music, dance and bullfights.

### June

**June 23** Têt valley: Nit de Sant-Jaume. On the eve of St John's Day people come from all over Catalonia for the torchlight pilgrimage from the Castillet in Perpignan to the peak of El Canigó – one of the symbols of the Catalan nation.

**End June** Arles-sur-Tech: Fete de St-Éloi. This three-day festival culminates in the Sunday morning blessing of the mules – traditionally indispensable here, as the only transport over the surrounding mountains.

### July and August

**Second weekend in July** Céret: Feria de Céret (☎04.68.87.47.47). A month-long festival featuring regular bullfights, as well as runnings-of-the-bulls. Also a Flamenco programme around the middle of the month.

**July14–21** Perpignan: Día de Sant-Jaume. The second biggest Catalan

Morocco and Algeria, who moved here fleeing unstable and repressive political regimes or simply in search of a brighter economic future. The melting-pot atmosphere of the city makes it difficult for a distinctly Catalan atmosphere to coalesce, but the people are nonetheless happy to set themselves apart from the rest of their countrymen by promoting this identity – even if their own spoken Catalan is frequently nonexistent or limited to a few phrases pronounced with a distinctly Gallic accent. Unfortunately, though, Perpignan is far from a model of tolerance – Le Pen's Front National party and its derivatives have done well

holiday kicks off a week of medieval pageantry in Perpignan, with a medieval-style market held in the place de la Loge and around the cathedral on July 14 itself.

**Mid-July** Prades: Ciné-Recontres (☎04.68.05.20.47). A week-long film festival with an international but essentially retrospective programme.

**July 28–30** Arles-sur-Tech: Festa Major. Typically boisterous Catalan festival, featuring processions and loaded with medieval traditions.

**Throughout July** Perpignan: Estivales (☎04.68.35.01.77, *www.estivales.com*). Music and dance festival featuring international acts; the varied programme tends to have a heavy Spanish influence.

**Mid-July to late Aug** Perpignan: Les Jeudis de Perpignan. Thursday evening street market throughout the old town, also featuring street performers and live music in many bars and squares.

**End July to mid-Aug** Prades: Festival Pablo Casals. A world-famous classical music festival. Over 25 concerts with soloists and groups from around the world, and a programme which ranges from Bach to Ravel. The venues include the monastery at Cuxac and other regional churches. Information on ☎04.68.96.33.07 (*pro.wanadoo.fr /festival.casals*).

**Aug 16** Collioure: Festa Major. The town's saint, Vincent, is feted in the finest Catalan and Spanish styles, with merrymaking, fireworks, dancing and a *corrida*. It's a very popular event, and you must book ahead with the

town's tourist office if you want to see the *corrida*.

**Penultimate weekend in Aug** Céret: International Sardana Festival (☎04.68.87.46.49). Extending over three days, this involves renditions and contests of the traditional dance, held in the town's streets, as well as a market, and evening concerts and dancing.

### September

**First week** Elne: Festival de Musique en Catalogne Romane. A classical music festival featuring mostly French artists, held in the medieval cathedral.

**First weekend** Arles: Fête Médiéval. A rollicking medieval festival complete with dancing bears and fire-eaters.

**Late Sept** Céret: Méditerranéennes de Céret (☎01.44.79.00.36, *Azimuthprod @wanadoo.fr*). Huge three-day Latin and Mediterranean music festival, which draws crowds in excess of 12,000.

**First two weeks** Perpignan: Visa pour l'Image (*www.visapourlimage.com*). International festival of photojournalism held at the Palais de Congrès, with seminars, exhibitions and screenings of journalistic photos by leading photographers and rising stars.

### October

**Last two weekends** Perpignan: Jazzebre (☎04.68.51.13.14). Eclectic programme ranging from mainstream jazz to klezmer, performed by musicians and groups from around the world.

here at the polls, peddling a racist vision of white French nationals "swamped" by outsiders.

Perpignan has had a quiet history. Too far from the sea to serve as a port itself, it was a sizeable if unremarkable town until the thirteenth century, when it began to boom as a cloth-making centre. Jaume II of Mallorca and Roussillon enhanced this prosperity in 1276, when he made the town his alternative mainland capital (Montpellier being the other, and Palma de Mallorca the king's principal residence). When that kingdom evaporated in 1344, however, the city was absorbed by the Catalan-Aragonese Crown, whose own main capital, Barcelona, in near proximity, brought an end to Perpignan's elevated status. In the centuries that followed it was the object of repeated campaigns of conquest by France, finally becoming French territory with 1649's Treaty of the Pyrenees. Aside from taking in the pleasant Mediterranean ambience of the place there are a number of interesting monuments and museums worth seeking out here, and the one sight that shouldn't be missed is the **Palais des Rois**, in the south of the old town. In addition, Perpignan is the principal transport hub of the region and serves as a handy base for exploring nearby **Salses**, as well **Tautavel** on the way into the Fenouillèdes (see p.326), plus the beaches of the Côte Vermeille.

## Arrival, information and city transport

Perpignan's small **airport**, Perpignan-Rivesaltes, 6km north of town, handles daily flights to and from Paris, Montpellier, Lyon and Strasbourg, as well as services from London in summer; its meagre facilities include shops, a bar and restaurant, and car rental offices (see "Listings"). An airport **navette** (28F/€4.27) makes the twenty-minute trip into the centre up to eight times daily, stopping at the gare SNCF, place de Catalogne, and the *gare routière*; a **taxi** into the centre will cost around three times the bus fare.

Perpignan's **gare SNCF**, at the west end of avenue Général-de-Gaulle, was once dubbed "the centre of the world" by Salvador Dalí – hence the milestone atop an arch near the entrance which announces "Centre du Monde: 0.0km". To get into the heart of the city from here, walk along the avenue, over place de Catalogne, and cross the River Basse at **place Arago**, close by the *quartier de piétonnes* (pedestrian zone) – a twenty-minute walk. If you arrive by local or long-distance bus or airport *navette*, you'll be dropped at the **gare routière** just off avenue du Général-Leclerc near Pont Arago, a short distance northwest of place de la Résistance. If you're arriving by **car**, follow signs for the "Centre" to get to the old town. There are car parks – that of the Palais des Rois is a good option – but also free and metered street parking on most roads outside the pedestrian area; avoid leaving your car in the seedier areas of the old town.

The **municipal tourist office** (mid-June to mid-Sept Mon–Sat 9am–7pm, Sun 10am–noon & 2–5pm; mid-Sept to mid-June Mon–Fri 9am–6pm, Sat 9am–noon & 2–6pm; ☎04.68.66.30.30, fax 04.68.66.30.26, *www.little-france.com /perpignan*) is in the Palais des Congrès, the white building at the eastern end of the leafy Promenade des Platanes which runs parallel to boulevard Wilson – they can supply you with the free monthly *Perpignan Mag*, which will keep you abreast of cultural events in the city. There's also a well-stocked **regional tourist office** (Mon 2–6pm, Tues–Fri 9am–12.30pm & 2–6pm; ☎04.68.34.29.94, fax 04.68.34.71.01, *www.cg66.fr*) on the quai de Lattre-de-Tassigny, near the main post office.

As far as city transport goes, your feet are the best bet in the old town, or you can rent **bikes** at Cycles Mercier, 20 avenue Gilbert Brutus (☎04.68.85.27.1) or Eurobike, 1 rue Fontaine-St-Martin (☎04.68.54.59.83). Alternatively there are plenty of **city buses**; the CTP kiosk in place Peri, near the *Palmarium* café, supplies information and tickets (a single costs 6.50F/€1, also available from drivers).

# Accommodation

Accommodation is plentiful in Perpignan, with a selection of establishments in all price and luxury ranges, although the most common are small and serviceable, few-frills hotels. For a start there's a range of reasonable **hotels** strung along the lively avenue Général-de-Gaulle beginning just as you leave the train station. This is a fair distance from the old town though, so if you prefer to be more central there are some good options there, particularly around the place de la Loge or along the promenade de Platanes. Perpignan also caters well for the budget-conscious traveller, with a few **hostels** and **campsites**.

## Hotels and B&B

**Avenir**, 11 rue de l'Avenir (☎04.68.34.20.30, fax 04.68.34.15.63). Unprepossessing, simple comfort near the train station, with a wide range of rooms from singles to a family room; also has secure parking. ③.

**La Cigale**, 78 bd Jean-Bourrat (☎04.68.50.20.14, fax 04.68.66.90.40.22). Renovated and comfortable hotel at the far end of the promenade de Platanes, near the Church of St-Jacques. Good facilities and service. ③.

**Domaine de Mas Boloux**, chemin du Pou de les Colobres (☎04.68.08.17.70, fax 04.68.08.17.71). Well-appointed B&B with five rooms, sitting room and garden. ④.

**des Expéditeurs**, 19 av du Général Leclerc (☎04.68.35.15.80). On a rather desolate stretch near the *gare routière*, this small place is by far the cheapest in town. Also has a good restaurant (see p.324). ①.

**L'Express**, 3 av Général-de-Gaulle (☎04.68.34.89.96). One of the small, old hotels near the station. The rooms do not rise much above functional but they do all have TV. ②.

**de la Loge**, 1 rue Fabriques-Nabot (☎04.68.34.41.02, fax 04.68.34.25.13). Beautifully decorated old hotel in a quiet old-town alley off place de la Loge. Overall the best choice for location, economy and service. ④.

**Le Mediterranée**, 62bis av Général-de-Gaulle (☎04.68.34.87.48, fax 04.68.34.51.12.24; *www.hotel-mediterranee.com*). Hip new hotel near the station which is very popular with the backpacking crowd. The building isn't the most modern or in the best repair and the service relaxed to say the least, but its bar, cybercafé and laid-back atmosphere more than make up. ①.

**Mercure**, 5bis cours Palmarole (☎04.68.35.67.66, fax 04.68.35.58.13). Ideal for families, this distinctive-looking hotel has five suites in addition to its well-outfitted rooms. Just within the confines of the old town, north of the tourist office. ④.

**Le Metropole**, 3 rue des Cardeurs (☎04.68.34.43.34). Basic and very cheap, this is another backpacker haunt in a narrow, bistro-lined street just to the east of the Loge. ①.

**Poste et Perdrix**, 6 rue Fabriques-Nabot (☎04.68.34.42.53, fax 04.68.34.58.20). Central, beautiful old nineteenth-century hotel with period details. One of the better deals around. Closed Jan–March. ③.

---

### ACCOMMODATION PRICE CODES

All the hotels and guesthouses listed in this book have been price-coded according to the following scale. The prices quoted are for the cheapest available double room in high season.

| | | |
|---|---|---|
| ① Under 160F/€24 | ④ 300–400F/€46–61 | ⑦ 600–700F/€91–107 |
| ② 160–220F/€24–34 | ⑤ 400–500F/€61–76 | ⑧ 700–800F/€107–122 |
| ③ 220–300F/€34–46 | ⑥ 500–600F/€76–91 | ⑨ Over 800F/€122 |

**Regina**, 4 pl Arago (☎04.68.34.28.80, fax 04.68.34.92.61). Cosy, old-fashioned hotel on Perpignan's best square, with simple but comfortable rooms, some of which have TV. ③.

**Terminus**, 2 av Général-de-Gaulle (☎04.68.34.32.54, fax 04.68.35.48.16). Old but well-maintained station-side hotel, which has rooms with and without private baths and TV. ③.

**Windsor**, 8 bd Wilson (☎04.68.51.18.65, fax 04.68.51.01.00, *www.inter-hotel.com*). Large, modern hotel with balconied rooms, well located between the Castillet and the tourist office. All the mod cons, including AC. ⑤

## Youth hostels and campsites

**Camping la Garrigole**, 2 rue Maurice Lévy (☎04.68.54.66.10). Small and basic but shady campsite 5km to the northwest of the city. Bus #19 will drop you off nearby. Open all year.

**Centre du Parc Ducup**, rte de Prades (☎04.68.68.32.40). Large park-side hostel run by the local Catholic diocese, some 5km north of the city centre, which can provide dorm beds (165F/€25.16) or full pensions. No membership necessary, but no cheaper than a hotel. On the bus #19 route.

**HI Hostel**, av de la Grand-Bretagne (☎04.68.34.63.32, fax 04.68.51.16.02). Modern, well-run hostel beside a park, fifteen minutes' walk from the centre, between the *gare routière* and the gare SNCF, but with a noisy road running behind it. Curfews 11am–4pm & 11pm. Closed mid-Dec to mid-Jan. Dorm beds 48F/€7.32.

**Roussillon Camping Catalan**, rte de Bompas (☎04.68.62.16.92). Large two-star site, 8km northeast of the city, with shop, swimming pool and laundry service. Also rents caravans and is wheelchair accessible. No service by municipal bus. March–Oct.

# The City

Perpignan's medieval walls, though spared by Richelieu, were demolished early this century to allow for expansion, and replaced by wide boulevards. This, in fact, maintained the separation of the city's older districts from the new, and it's still easy and enjoyable to get around the compact **old town** on foot. The overriding impression is favourable: the Mediterranean is perceptible to the east, the River Têt skirts the town to the north, while the narrow River Basse threads through the centre, dispensing welcome greenery along its banks. Most of the city's sights are concentrated in the dense clutch of pedestrian streets northeast of riverside **place Arago**, and stretching towards the geographical centre of the old town, while between **place de la Loge** and place Rigaud just to the east, you could be on the Left Bank in Paris, the old streets now a maze of chic boutiques. On the north side of the pedestrian area you'll find the **cathedral**, from where you can follow the course of the old walls, through the Romany and **Maghrebi quarter** to the church of St-Jacques, marking the eastern limit of old Perpignan. To the south of this the land rises towards the massive **Palais des Rois de Majorque**, crowning the hill which dominated the southern quarter of the medieval town. In the **new town**, to the west of the River La Basse, you won't find many sights, but the avenues leading west towards the train station make for excellent hotel and restaurant hunting.

## Place Arago to Le Castillet

The heart of the city is café-lined **place Arago**, on the flower-decked bank of the canalized La Basse river. From here you can head south along rues Proted'Assaut and Maréchal Foch to bring you to a tiny old thirteenth-century *faubourg*, whose quiet grid of streets contains well-restored houses and the odd café; Maréchal Foch itself contains a small **Musée d'Algérie Française** (Wed

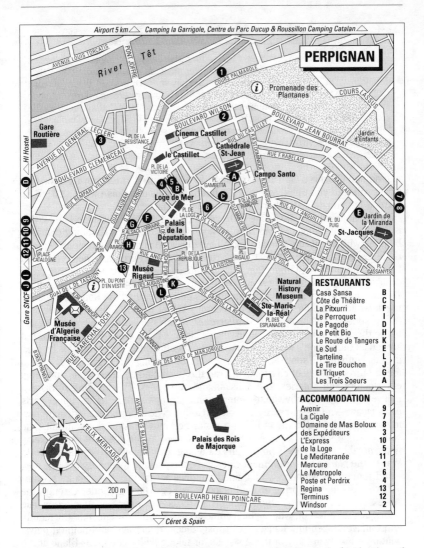

Airport 5 km △  Camping la Garrigole, Centre du Parc Ducup & Roussillon Camping Catalan △

## PERPIGNAN

River Têt

PONT JOFFRE

AVENUE LOUIS TORCATIS

COURS PALMAROLE

(i) Promenade des
Plantanes

COURS LASSUS

BOULEVARD WILSON

❶ Mercure

❷ Windsor

BOULEVARD JEAN BOURRAT

Jardin
d'Enfants

Gare
Routière

HI Hostel

AVENUE DU GENERAL LECLERC

❸ Poste et Perdrix

PL DE LA
RESISTANCE

Cinema Castillet

Cathédrale
St-Jean

RUE F RABELAIS

le Castillet

BOULEVARD CLEMENCEAU

RUE REMPART VILLENEUVE

PL DE LA
VICTOIRE

❹ ❺ B
Loge de Mer

PL
GAMBETTA

Ⓐ Campo Santo

RUE FRABELAIS

QUAI VAUBAN

G F

RUE DU CASTILLET

Ⓒ

RUE DE LA REV
FRANCAISE

RUE DE L'ANGUILLE

PL DU
PUIG

Ⓔ Jardin de
la Miranda

R ALSACE LORRAINE

Palais
de la
Députation

PL DE
LA LOGE

❻

RUE DE L'ARGENTERE

St-Jacques

H

PL
ARAGO

RUE ANGE

RIGAUD

RUE ZOLA

PL
CASSANYES

PL
PERI

PL
CATALOGNE

❶❷❶❶❾

❿

PL DE LA
REPUBLIQUE

R DE LA FUSTERIE

❶❸ Musée
Rigaud

QUAI DE TASSIGNY

(i)

PL DU PONT
D'EN VESTIT

R DES AUGUSTINS

K

RUE PETITE LA REAL

L

Natural
History
Museum

## RESTAURANTS

| | |
|---|---|
| Casa Sansa | B |
| Côte de Théâtre | C |
| La Pitxurri | F |
| Le Perroquet | I |
| Le Pagode | D |
| Le Petit Bio | H |
| Le Route de Tangers | K |
| Le Sud | E |
| Tarteline | L |
| Le Tire Bouchon | J |
| El Triquet | G |
| Les Trois Soeurs | A |

Gare SNCF

J

Musée
d'Algerie
Française

RUE MARECHAL FOCH

RUE GRANDE

PETITE LA REAL

RUE DE LA MONNAIE

Ste-Marie-
la-Réal

PL DES
ESPLANADES

## ACCOMMODATION

| | |
|---|---|
| Avenir | 9 |
| La Cigale | 7 |
| Domaine de Mas Boloux | 8 |
| des Expéditeurs | 3 |
| L'Express | 10 |
| de la Loge | 5 |
| Le Mediteranée | 11 |
| Mercure | 1 |
| Le Metropole | 6 |
| Poste et Perdrix | 4 |
| Regina | 13 |
| Terminus | 12 |
| Windsor | 2 |

BD LES PYRENES

BD FELIX MERCADER

AVENUE DES BALEARS

RUE DES ROIS DE MAJORQUE

LA MINAIE

N

**Palais des Rois
de Majorque**

0        200 m

BOULEVARD HENRI POINCARE

▽ Céret & Spain

3–6pm; free), at 52 rue Maréchal Foch, commemorating France's domination of North Africa with bitter nostalgia. But you'll most likely prefer to dive directly east into Perpignan's historical centre. Heading from the *place* along rue Ange, you'll find the **Musée Rigaud** (Wed–Sun noon–7pm; 25F/€3.81) on the the right at no. 16. This musuem is housed in a seventeenth-century palace, originally the work-shop of local artist Hyacinthe Rigaud, a favourite of Louis XIV, and it later served as studio and living space for Picasso, Dufy and Cocteau. Today it holds a good collection of modern art, including works by Maillol, Alechinsky and the afore-mentioned artists. Just beyond the museum, rue Ange crosses the evocatively

---

### MUSEUM DISCOUNT PASSES

For 40F/€6.10 you can purchase a **Passeport Musées** for Perpignan, which gives you free access to four of the city's pay-to-enter museums – not including the Palais des Rois. The Palais is included however in the **"Intersite"** discount card (25F/€3.81), which gives you reductions of fifteen to fifty percent on the entrance fees to 23 museums and monuments in Pyrénées-Orientales, including those on the coast and the most important fortresses and churches of the Tech and Conflent valleys. Both passes are available at participating museums and monuments, as well as tourist offices throughout the *département*.

named rue Cloche d'Or ("the street of the Golden Bell"); turning right on this street will lead you uphill towards the hulking Palais des Rois (see p.322), while turning left you delve further into the medieval quarter.

At the nothern end of Cloche d'Or, you'll pass through place Jean-Jaurès; this is the centre of the pedestrian zone, now serving as the city's shopping district – bustling with life during the day, and all but deserted at night. Next along is **place de la Loge**, the centre of activity in fourteenth-century Perpignan: here you'll find three of the city's most important administrative buildings, lumped together on its eastern side. The first of these is the fifteenth-century Gothic-style **Palais de la Députation**, where the Catalan count-kings once convened the Roussillon parliament, while next door, the sixteenth-century **Hôtel de Ville** is worth a peek for the Aristide Maillol bronze, *La Méditerranée*, which sits in the courtyard. The last of the three great buildings is Roussillon's famous **Loge de Mer**; built in 1397, it served as the region's stock exchange – the meeting-place and court for its merchants. High on the south wall you'll see a blazon bearing three arms, which stand for the three classes of city folk who ran the town council: merchants and drapers, doctors and notaries, and artisans and gardeners. The building remains a marvel, with a gracefully vaulted interior and gargoyles adorning the upper parts of its facade – a fine and rare example of Gothic civic architecture – despite having suffered the ignomiry of being transformed into a fast-food restaurant. The square which spreads around la Loge long served as the scene of grisly executions, notably of the rebels housed in Le Castillet (see below), while during World War II, the *place's* busy pavement cafés were the place to meet *passeurs*, the men – and sometimes women – who guided refugees across the Pyrenees into Spain.

If you feel like exploring around place de la Loge, take a wander through the series of ancient lanes which run off towards the river, including tiny rue Fabriques d'En Nabot, where you'll come across a number of notable thirteenth- and fourteenth-century houses, with magnificent doorways, and pointed ogival windows. Following any of these streets, or taking wider rue Louis-Blanc at the north end of place de la Loge, will lead you to Perpignan's distinctive red-brick **Le Castillet**, the lone surviving tower of the old town walls. Also known as the Casa Païral ("The House of the Ancestors"), it now houses a **museum** celebrating Roussillonaise rural culture (Mon & Wed–Sun: mid-June to mid-Sept 9.30am–7pm; mid-Sept to mid-June 6am–6pm; 25F/€3.81) and in particular commemorating the anti-French rebellions of 1661–74, when the tower held captured Catalan insurgents. The place de Verdun, on the south side of Le Castillet, is the setting for summer evening performances of the *sardana*, the perplexingly insipid Catalan folk dance. Nearby, at 1 boulevard Wilson, is the battered but splendidly ornate **Cinema Castillet**, the oldest cinema in France, now converted into an eight-screen complex.

## The cathedral and east

Two hundred metres east of Le Castillet, but most easily accessed from the north end of place de la Loge, you'll find another ancient square, place Gambetta, scene of the town's open-air market since the Middle Ages. On its eastern end towers the **Cathédrale St-Jean** (Mon & Wed–Sat 10am–noon & 2–5pm, Tues & Sun 2–5pm; free), commissioned in 1324 and elevated to cathedral status in 1602, when the diocese of Elne was transferred to Perpignan. Next door, its predecessor, the impressive Romanesque St-Jean le Vieux (currently closed for renovations), is linked to the cathedral by mammoth buttresses. The cathedral's striking exterior sports bands of river stones sandwiched by brick, while inside there's a majestically columned nave, whose side chapels, though badly damaged, retain some elaborate sixteenth- and seventeenth-century retables. Leaving through the south transept, poke your head in the **chapel** on the left, which is presided over by an excellent fourteenth-century polychrome crucifixion, known as the *Dévot Christ*, and most likely the work of a Rhineland sculptor. Past the chapel, on the left, is the entrance to the **Campo Santo**, one of France's oldest cemeteries, going back some 600 years (same hours as cathedral) – it is now used for occasional concerts.

On the far side of Campo Santo, the lively rue de la Revolution Française, populated by arty cafés and hip bars, runs east to the *place* of the same name. From here you can turn right to ascend into the slums of old Perpignan, which spread south from here almost as far as the great palace, and east to place Cassanyes, at the former limits of the city walls. Inhabited almost exclusively by recent arrivals from North Africa, with a Romany enclave centred on **place du Puig** (pronounced "pooch"), this can be an intimidating district; the cramped quarters are littered with refuse and hung with washing, a stereotype of immigrant poverty. But it's worth persevering – the various squares dotted around are rich with history, such as the innocuously named place Fountaine-Neuve, which dates back

---

### THE CAGANER AND CAGA-TIO

Among the many Catalan folkloric customs which have survived centuries of French domination are two rather strange practices associated with **Christmas**. Like the Provençals, the Roussillonaise are known for their elaborate Nativity scenes (*pessebres*), populated by hordes of figurines. However, if you look carefully at the Catalan version, among the various shepherds, angel choirs, and wise men you'll note a small figure, usually dressed in rural garb and sporting a traditional Catalan red cap. This is the **caganer**, a crouching figure, poised with pants around his ankles, in some stage of the act of defecation. Similarly, although Catalan children customarily receive presents on the Epiphany (Jan 6), the **caga-tio** (literally, the "shitting uncle") ensures that they don't go completely empty handed at Christmas. It consists of a log with a painted-on face, draped with a red cloth at its posterior end. As children gather round the caga-tio, beating it with sticks and singing a song invoking bowel movement, to the delight of all the blanket is withdrawn to reveal the sweets which it has apparently "excreted". You can purchase your own *caganers* and *caga-tios* at Perpignan's Christmas market, held in front of the cathedral during the four weeks of Advent.

some 700 years, to the time when the "new well" after which it is named was dug here. If its interminable renovations have finally been concluded, you might also stop at Perpignan's **natural history museum**, at 12 Fontaine Neuve (Mon & Wed–Sun: July & Aug noon–7pm; Sept–June 11am–5.30pm; 25F/€3.81), which holds the usual stuffed specimens of local fauna, as well as a prized Egyptian mummy. Northeast of place Fontaine-Neuve and just east of place du Puig is the fourteenth-century **church of St-Jacques** (Mon & Sun 2–6pm, Tues–Sat 10am–noon & 2–6pm), the nucleus of Perpignan's oldest parish, originally founded by Jaume I in honour of his patron saint (Jacques being French for Jaume) a hundred years earlier. The king was also a donor to the confraternity of Sanch – a parish-based social organization typical of the Middle Ages, dedicated to the Holy Blood of Christ ("sanch" means "blood" in old Catalan). On the Maundy Thursday of each year, they hold a Spanish-style procession of Penitents, who walk from the church through the town hooded (so as not to take pride in their piety) and barefooted, carrying heavy candles or crosses. Behind the church, the **Jardin de la Miranda** (daily: July & Aug 8am–noon & 2.30–6.30pm; Sept–June 8am–noon & 2.30–5.30pm), built on a section of the city's old fortifications, provides an airy respite for the inhabitants of this quarter. If you want to avoid the seedy part of the old town, the church and garden can also be reached from place de la Révolution Française, by heading north and following rue Pierre Ronsard, in the shadow of the city's remaining **walls**, or, further north still, alongside the **square Bir Hakeim**, and the adjacent Jardin d'Enfants, a grassy, tree-lined park crisscrossed by paths and complete with the usual assortment of children's rides, bandstands and *buvettes*.

## The Palais des Rois de Majorque

Perpignan's most famous sight, and the kernel around which it grew, is the massive **Palais des Rois de Majorque** (daily: June–Sept 10am–6pm; Oct–May 9am–5pm; 20F/€3.05) on the southern fringe of the old city; the entrance is on the west side of the complex in rue des Archers, around fifteen minutes' walk from place de la Loge, and slightly longer from the church of St-Jacques.

The history of Perpignan is more or less synonymous with that of the palace, originally built in the late thirteenth century as a residence for Jaume I of Mallorca, son of Jaume I (The Conqueror), Count of Barcelona and King of Aragón and Valencia, who conquered Mallorca from the Muslims. At his death "The Conqueror" divided his kingdom between his two sons: to the elder, Pere II, went the titles of King of Aragón and Valencia and Count of Barcelona, but only a portion of the actual kingdom; the remainder, including Roussillon and Mallorca, went to the younger Jaume. The two branches of the family were immediately at each other's throats, and stayed that way until Roussillon was reunited with Aragón and Catalonia in the early fourteenth century by the powerful Pere III. Having passed to the French, then back to the Catalans, Perpignan changed hands for the last time in 1642, a couple of years after France had occupied Roussillon in the wake of the revolt of the Catalans against the Hapsburg rulers of Madrid; in September, after a siege that was at times commanded personally by Louis XIII and Richelieu, Perpignan fell. Vauban, military engineer to Louis XIV, constructed the imposing outer walls in the fit of over-enthusiastic fortification that followed consolidation of French sovereignty accorded by the 1659 Treaty of the Pyrenees.

After ascending an impressive zigzagging ramp, large enough for several cavalry to ride abreast, you enter a grassy park, with the square thirteenth-century

**castle** ahead of you, standing incongruously with its curious stone and mortar construction. Passing into the splendid two-storey **courtyard**, whose upper level opens into graceful Gothic galleries on the east and west sides, you ascend the stairs to the former kings' apartments, now a boutique for Roussillon vintages. Across from these you'll find the unsullied but sparsely furnished queens' apartments, which have delicately vaulted period ceilings and windows. Between the two sets of royal apartments are the so-called king's and queen's **chapels**, one the upper floor and one on the lower, and both with interesting details in Gothic style, from carved corbels to fading frescoes. The palace frequently holds temporary exhibitions on local history and culture (included in admission).

### The new town

Although the far bank of the Basse opposite place d'Arago did fall within the boundaries of the medieval ramparts, its character resembles more that of the new town which grew up around it. There's little in the way of specific sights here, but a stroll through the series of attractive nineteenth-century-styled *places* – Gabrielle Péri, Bardou-Job and Jean-Payra – is pleasant. The last of these leads into the large place de Catalogne, dominated on its east side by the beautiful and derelict Aux Dames de France department store. From here, avenue du Général-de-Gaulle heads due west to the *gare*, the main artery of a surprisingly lively neighbourhood, with workaday shops, grungy bars and tattoo salons, as well as many good hotels and restaurants. Running north from the place de Catalogne, the busy cours Lazare-Escarguel leads to avenue de Grand Bretagne, where, at no. 42, you'll find the **Musée Numismatique Joseph-Puig** (Tues–Sat 9am–noon & 2–6pm; 25F/€3.81), an impressive early twentieth-century mansion, with some 1500 coins on display, ranging from ancient small change to monies of medieval France, Aragon and the Catalan lands. The prize of the collection is the "treasure of Bompas", a Gallo-Roman coin hoard discovered by a local farmer.

# Eating, drinking and nightlife

Don't dally when pondering **dinner**: most of Perpignan's restaurant shutters seem to roll down at 10pm sharp, though you can get served later at several brasseries which stay open till midnight, including the popular *Arago* and *Café Vienne* in the palm-shaded place Arago – this and avenue de Général-de-Gaulle are the places to head for if you don't feel like wasting a lot of time looking around. For a fix of Asian or North African food, head for the eastern side of the old town, particularly rue Llucia, where modest establishments serve up stir-fries and couscous/*tajine* dishes – you'll find food like this in very few other places along the Pyrenees.

Perpignan is not great for **nightlife**, but it has plenty of **cafés**. Start on place de la Loge – call in at *Brasserie de la Loge* or *Grande Café de la Bourse* – and place de Verdun, where the *Grande Café de la Poste*, shaded by huge plane trees, is the best. *Café la Paix* in place Arago is another popular choice but best of all is the huge, airy *Palmarium*, on the opposite side overlooking the River Basse, a downbeat, self-service place, where you can linger for hours over a coffee. In July and August the town comes alive on Thursday nights with a **street festival** featuring markets and music. Otherwise there are **bars** scattered throughout town: *Casa Nova*, at 8 rue de la Fusterie, features Afro-Cuban sounds; the Spanish *bar musical*, *La Movida*, 45 avenue Général-Leclerc; while *O'Shannon* at 3 rue de l'Incindie is the local headquarters for stout. Most of Perpignan's **discos** are on the fringes of town, but in the centre you can dance at *Napoli*, 3 place Catalogne and the *Uba Club*, 5 boulevard Mercader (both open Wed–Sat 11pm–3am).

## Restaurants

**Casa Sansa**, 2 rue Fabriques-Nadal (☎04.68.34.21.84). Catalan cuisine served up in this comfortable establishment in one of the old town's most beautiful streets. Wheelchair accessible. Closed Sun. Menus from 49–300F/€7.47–45.75.

**Côte du Théâtre**, 7 rue du Théâtre (☎04.68.34.60.00). One of Perpignan's best choices, serving food that's a splendid synthesis of local trends and *gastronomique* flair. Closed Sun and Mon lunch. Menu from 148F/€ 22.57.

**des Expéditeurs**, 19 av Général Leclerc. Good quality and cheap, if unsophisticated, local cuisine, in the hotel of the same name. Menus from 65F/€9.91. Closed Sat eve & Sun.

**Le Pagode**, 6 cours Lazare Escarguel (☎04.68.33.40.38). Just a few minutes north of place de Catalogne, this superb Vietnamese restaurant may be your last taste of sophistication if you are journeying on into the mountains. Savoury menus from 98F/€14.95.

**Le Perroquet**, 1 av Charles-de-Gaulle (☎04.68.34.34.36). Very close to the station on the north side of the street, with a good choice of Catalan specialities; menus from 55F/€8.39. Closed Wed Sept–April.

**Le Petit Bio**, 1 rue d'Iéna (☎04.68.51.11.00). The city's only organic food stop, open for lunch only, with a wide selection of dishes ranging from salads and quiches, to more substantial pasta meals (11am–3pm). Menus from 40F/€6.10.

**La Pitxurri**, 7 rue de la Poissonerie (☎04.68.51.25.35). Basque specialities here, heavy on fish (lots of cod) and seafood, and elaborate Basque-style tapas. Menu from 80F/€12.20.

**Le Route de Tanger**, 1 rue du Four St-Jean (☎04.68.51.07.57). Welcoming Moroccan restaurant with the traditional *tajines* and couscous as well as more adventurous fusion recipes. Closed Sun & Mon lunch. Menu 79F/€12.05.

**Le Sud**, 12 rue Bausil (☎04.68.34.55.71). Eclectic and delicious Mediterranean cuisine served up in the heart of Perpignan's Romany quarter. No menu, and à la carte at about 160F/€24.40.

**Tarteline**, 10 rue Petite la Monnaie. Good stop for delicious home-made quiches and tarts, to eat in or take away. Open lunch time only Mon–Fri (except hols). Menu at 50F/€7.63.

**Le Tire Bouchon**, 20 av Général-de-Gaulle (☎04.68.34.31.91). A small family-run brasserie, the best of those in the vicinity of the station. Closed Sun. Menu at 70F/€10.68.

**El Triquet**, 9 rue Lazare (☎04.68.35.19.18). Friendly Spanish-run eatery specializing in Catalan cuisine as well as tapas. Menus from 70F/€10.68.

**Les Trois Soeurs**, 2 rue Fontfroide (☎04.68.51.22.33). Elaborate seafood creations hold centre-stage at this cheery establishment near the cathedral. Lunch menu from 80F/€12.20.

# Listings

**Airlines** Air Liberté (☎08.03.80.58.05, *www.air-liberté.fr*).

**Airport** Aéroport de Perpignan Rivesaltes (☎04.68.52.60.70, *aeroport@perpignan.cci.fr*).

**Banks and exchange** All major French and some Spanish banks have offices in the centre, many along bd Clémenceau, and quai Vauban – most have ATMs. Change du Castillet, 6 rue Grande des Fabriques and Tabac de la Loge, 1 place de la Loge, exchange currency at weekends.

**Bus departures** At the *gare routière* (☎04.68.35.29.02) you can get a tourist pass (150F/€22.88) giving eight days' unlimited bus travel around the Pyrénées-Orientales *département* – take a passport-sized photo and your passport.

**Car rental** Access, 6 rue Elisée Reclus (☎04.68.67.44.47); Avis, 13 bd du Conflent (☎04.68.34.26.71); Budget, 9 av Général de Gaulle (☎04.68.56.95.95); Europcar, 28 av Général de Gaulle (☎04.68.34.65.03); Leclerc, 27 av Général de Gaulle (☎04.68.34.77.74); Sixt, 48 av Général de Gaulle (☎04.68.35.62.84). Europcar, Budget and Avis also have offices at the airport.

**Cinemas** Rive Gauche, 29 quai Vauban (☎04.68.51.13.84) has four screens, with some VO.

**Consulate** British Consulate, 28 rue Guy-de-Chauliac (☎04.68.54.92.03).

**Internet access** *Le Mediterranée*, 62bis av Général-de-Gaulle, or Arena Games, 9 rue de Docteur Pous (daily 3pm–midnight; *arena.games@altranet.fr*).

**Laundry** Laverie Foch, 23 rue Maréchal Foch (daily 9am–7pm); Laverie St-Jean, 3 rue Cité E. Bartisol, near Campo Santo (daily 7.30am–7pm).

**Markets** General market in pl de la République (Mon 7am–1pm, Tues–Sat 7am–12.30pm & 4.30–7.30pm), plus antiques in promenade des Platanes (Sat 8am–6pm) and organic food in pl Rigaud (Sat 8am–noon). The most colourful market takes place on Saturday and Sunday mornings in the tree-shaded place Cassanyes, with a mixture of French, Arab and African traders selling cheap clothes, crafts and all sorts of local produce.

**Medical** Centre Hospitalier, av du Languedoc (☎04.68.61.66.33), on the north side of the city, reached via avenue Maréchal-Joffre.

**Police** av de Gran Bretagne (☎04.68.35.70.00), and allée Marc Pierre (☎04.68.66.30.70).

**Rugby** Perpignan's Rugby à XV team, USAP, has long held a place in France's First Division, and has won the championship four times. It plays at Stade Aimé Giral on allées Aimé-Gira; for ticket information call ☎04.68.61.18.18, or go to *www.usap.fr*. The rugby à XIII team, XIII Catalan, plays at stade Jean-Laffon, on av des Sports (☎04.68.55.13.13).

**Swimming** Champs de Mars, rue Paul Valéry (Mon & Sat 12.15–1.30pm, Tues, Thurs & Fri 6.30–8pm; 13F/€1.98).

**Taxis** ☎04.68.35.35.15 or 04.68.67.62.60. There are also taxi stands at pl de Verdun, at the gare SNCF and on pl Arago.

**Train information** ☎04.68.51.93.39.

**Travel agency** Nouvelles Frontières, 40 bd Clémenceau (☎04.68.35.50.55).

**Youth information** Bureau d'Information Jeunesse, 35 quai Vauban (☎04.68.34.56.56).

# North of Perpignan: Salses and the coast

The main attraction heading north from Perpignan towards Narbonne along the N9 is the enormous stronghold of **Salses-le-Château**, built to dominate the strategic strip of land between the Étang de Leucate and the uplands of the Corbières. The **fortress** (daily: July & Aug 9.30am–7pm; June & Sept 9.30am–6.30pm; April, May & Oct 9.30am–12.30pm & 2–6pm; Nov–March 10am–noon & 2–5pm; 32F/€4.88), constructed by the Spanish in the fifteenth century to guard the northern border of Roussillon from French attack, is a curious structure – set low within a deep moat, like a cannon-age fortress, but with the basic design and overall squareness of a medieval castle, it represents an intermediary stage in the evolution from early to modern fort. Salses withstood four sieges before it was taken by the French in 1642; with the shift of the frontier south to the mountains, the fortress was first abandoned and then later used as a prison until being declared a monument in 1886. Back in the village, which lies to the east of the castle, you can also visit the **Musée Catalan d'Histoire** (Tues–Sat 9.30am–12.30pm & 2.30–7.30pm; free), which has a small collection of arms as well as archeological relics going back to the Roman period, when the Via Domitia passed through town.

The narrow strip of sand which hedges in the Étang de Leucate to the north-east of Salses is buried under a holiday conurbation but **wind-surfers** may be attracted to this part of the coast for the relentless winds which pelt the lagoon. The northern end of the *étang* has parking along the spit and is the best place to get in the water.

At only 15km from Perpignan Salses' is a fairly easy **bike** ride (wind permitting), but it also has a **gare SNCF**, just west of the fortress, while **buses** stop at the place de la République, where you will find a small **tourist office** (July & Aug daily 9am–7pm; Sept–June Mon–Fri 9am–6pm, Sat 10am–5pm; ☎ & fax 04.68.38.66.13). There is no accommodation in town except for the **campsite** *La Pinede* (☎04.68.38.68.44; July–Sept), on the far side of the *autoroute* (follow rue Jean-Jaurés, and then route d'Opoule). The **restaurant** situation is pretty grim here too, with the only good choice the medieval farm house *Auberge de Vespeille*, also on route d'Opoule (☎04.68.64.19.51) which has an open-hearthed fire in its rustic dining room.

# The Fenouillèdes

Stretching out to the northwest of Perpignan, the **Fenouillèdes** is the range of scrubby limestone hills which marked the inland border between France and Spain until the Treaty of the Pyrenees gave Roussillon to France in 1659. It is a rich area to discover, with highlights including the caves at **Tautavel**, where some of Europe's earliest hominids have been discovered, and several Cathar castles, the most famous being **Quéribus** and **Peyrepertuse**. Further west, you can explore the dramatic **Gorges de Galamus** and continue on to another Cathar stronghold at **Puilaurens**. The main artery through the Fenouillèdes is the D117, running westward from Perpignan to Quillan (see p.326); all the sights can be accessed from various points along this road, whether you're driving or reliant on the bus. If you have time to take the hills in by foot however, head out on the **Sentier Cathare**, which leads west into the Pays de Sault (see p.133), or the **Tour du Fenouillèdes**, a seven-day circuit that links the main sights of the region (for information on this the regional tourist office in Perpignan, or visit their Web site – see p.316).

## Tautavel

In 1971 archeologists working at the Caune de l'Arago, a cave near the village of **TAUTAVEL**, 20km northeast of Perpignan on the edge of the Fenouillèdes, discovered the front part of a skull of *Homo erectus* – an evolutionary midpoint between the African *Homo habilis* and modern *Homo sapiens* – dating back to half a million years ago, a period from which scarcely any other human remains have been found in Europe. The reconstructed skull, with its enormous cranial ridge and low eye sockets, is displayed in Tautavel's **Musée de la Préhistoire** (daily: July & Aug 9am–9pm; April–June & Sept 10am–7pm; Jan–March & Oct–Dec 10am–12.30pm & 2–6pm; 45F/€6.86), centrepiece of a small but extremely moving exhibition which includes stone tools, animal bones and casts from the floor of the cave. The cave itself (July & Aug daily 10am–noon & 12.30–5.30pm; visits in other seasons by arrangement with the museum) is situated in a low hill on the opposite side of the Verdouble valley. All of the finds – some 250,000 objects –

have been removed, but it's exciting to stand where primordial hunters dwelt half a million years ago. Nearby **Estagel**, 7km south on the main road and bus route, makes the best base in the Tautavel area. The *Charmotel les Graves*, 9 boulevard Jean Jaurès (☎04.68.29.00.84, fax 04.68.29.30.26, *www.logis-de-france.fr*, ②) is the best place to stay; the municipal **campsite** is on avenue du Docteur Cortade, on the west side of town.

# Quéribus and Peyrepertuse

The Cathar stronghold of **Quéribus**, the easternmost of "mother" Carcassonne's five "sons" is a short detour off the D117, from the turn-off at Maury, 10km beyond Estagel – if you don't have transport of your own the Perpignan–Quillan bus stops in Maury, from where it's a steep two-hour uphill walk. Visible on its turret of bare rock long before you reach it, the castle turns out to be much bigger than it looks, since much of the **interior** (July & Aug daily 10am–7pm; May, June & Sept daily 10am–7pm; April & Oct daily 10am–6pm; Feb, March, Nov & Dec Sat, Sun & school hols 10am–5pm; 25F/€3.81) is below ground level. A single stairway links all the various structures, including the so-called **salle de palmier** in the polygonal keep, where the vaulted ceiling is supported by a graceful pillar sprouting a canopy of intersecting ribs.

Quéribus was constructed at the end of the tenth century, and belonged successively to the count-kings of Barcelona and Aragón and the counts of Fenouillèdes. After the fall of Montségur in 1244 it became the refuge of some of the last surviving Cathars (see p.361), an affront that King Louis IX decided to erase. His opportunity came in 1255, when the local lord who sponsored the Cathars, Chabert de Barbaira, was captured by royal forces and forced to cede this and other castles as his ransom. But unlike at Montségur the Cathar garrison here had time to escape, probably south across the mountains.

Another of the five "sons" of Carcassonne, **Peyrepertuse** (daily: July & Aug 9am–8pm; April–June & Sept 10am–7pm; Nov–March 10am–6pm; 20F/€3.05), 4km west of Cucugnan, is the largest and one of the best preserved of the so-called Cathar castles. Its age and history is nearly identical to that of Quéribus, with Paris assuming definitive control here by treaty with Catalonia-Aragon in 1258. As well as the ten-minute drive along the D14 from Cucagnan, you can approach the *château* on **foot** via the Sentier Cathare, or along the GR36 from Rouffiac (see below). The setting of the castle, draped the length of a jagged ridge with sheer drops at most points, is its most impressive feature. No single architectural feature amongst various cisterns, chapels and towers claims attention, but from the highest **Chapelle San Jordi** there are sweeping views east to the Mediterranean and Perpignan, with Quéribus in-between on its rock stalk.

### Practicalities

Both of the castles are isolated. The closest amenities to Quéribus are 3km west, in **Cucugnan**, which has crumbled vestiges of its own castle and vineyards all around. You can **stay** at the *Auberge du Vigneron* in the village centre (☎04.68.45.40.84, fax 04.68.45.01.52; closed mid-Feb to mid-March; ③), but you might prefer to **eat** at the *Auberge de Cucugnan* (reserve on ☎04.68.45.03.00), well signposted one street higher, where ample four-course menus start at about 100F/€15.25 (including house wine) and *cargolades* (Catalan barbecues) are a feature of the interior garden.

Near Peyrepetuse, the village of **Duilhac** coils picturesquely at the eastern foot of the castle ridge. Here you'll find a shop and bakery, plus both a *gîte d'étape* (☎04.68.45.01.74; closed Jan; ①) in the centre and the comfortable, stone-clad *Auberge du Vieux Moulin* (☎04.68.45.02.17; ③), on the northerly through road. But better accommodation can be found in **Rouffiac des Corbières**, 3km north, where the *Auberge de Peyrepertuse* on the main through road (☎04.68.45.40.40; ②) serves hearty food and offers excellent en-suite rooms. Otherwise there's a **gîte** (☎04.68.45.01.74; ①) and a **campsite** in the hamlet.

## The Gorges de Galamus and Puilaurens

From Rouffiac the D14 winds westwards to the **Gorges de Galamus**, a short but impressive limestone *défilé* worn through the ridge by the River Agly, although most visitors enter the gorge at its downstream end, 3km out of St-Paul-de-Fenouille. At this end there's a fee car park and the start of a path to the exquisitely sited **Ermitage de St-Antoine**, about halfway down the gorge's east flank (daily 10am–6pm) – a huge, sanctified grotto thrusting deep into the cliff, from which a steep path, culminating in a rock ladder, drops down to pools below. The river is deep enough for swimming, and the gorge also a popular **rafting** venue (see below). Some 18km west of St-Paul along the D117, at Lapradelle, you'll find the turn-off for the castle at **Puilaurens** (daily: July & Aug 9am–8pm; April–June & Sept 10am–7pm; Nov–March 10am–6pm; 20F/€3.05), another of Carcassonne's "sons", perched majestically on a 700-metre-high ridge. Built originally by the Visigoths, Puilaurens was enlarged not long before its captured lord, the Cathar Chabert de Barbaira, turned it to Crusader forces as a condition of his release. You enter from the west, via a stepped maze of *chicanes* or staggered low walls; much of the interior is dilapidated, but make sure you catch the view east over pined hills from outside the southeastern gate, and the point on the **western donjon** complex where you're allowed briefly on the curtain wall to take in the vista in the opposite direction.

**St-Paul-de-Fenouillet** has little to offer aside from its role as staging point for **buses** west, and two **hotels**: *Le Châtelet*, on the main road (☎04.68.59.01.20, fax 04.68.59.01.29, *chatelet.rauss@wanadoo.fr*; ④), and the more upmarket *Relais des Corbières* (☎04.68.59.23.89, fax 04.68.59.03.40, *www.logis-de-france.fr*; ⑥), which has a restaurant. At **Lapradelle**, the *Hôtel Viaduc* – named after the disused rail viaduct opposite – has better food than promised from its appearance (menus from 62F/€9.46) and can also serve as a stopover, with private rooms at *gîte* prices (☎04.58.20.53.01; ①). If you're interested in taking a **rafting** trip down the gorges de Galamus, contact Sud Rafting (call ahead; ☎04.68.20.53.73), whose office is situated 16km west of St-Paul at the crossroads near Axat. It offers canyoning through Galamus, as well as rafting and hydrospeed trips through the Aude gorges.

# The lower Têt valley

From Perpignan the Têt valley (also known as the Conflent), provides a fast if initially not very scenic route southwest into the Pyrenees. The **lower Têt valley** is that stretch running up to the peak of Canigou, and its most interesting parts are found some 30km west of Perpignan, where **Ille-sur-Têt** provides a jumping-off point for the spectacular rock formations of **Les Orgues** to the north and, just west, the narrow Boulés gorge climbs south to the region of Les Aspres, within whose wooded isolation you'll find the magnificent Romanesque **priory of Serrabone**. Further west along the Têt valley, you'll come to **Prades**, a good access point for the Canigou mountain and, skirting the north side of the the famous massif, you reach **Villefranche-de-Conflent**, which marks the transition to the upper valley, covered on p.331. Both regular trains and buses run along this part of the valley.

# Upstream towards Prades

Heading out of Perpignan along the N116, a detour southwards from the river's course at St-Féliu will take you 6km south to **THUIR**, although if you are driving or cycling you can reach it more directly by taking the D612. This town is known chiefly as the main producer of the red aperitif wine called Byrrh (pronounced "beer"), and you can visit the winery at 6 boulevard Violet (July & Aug daily 10–11.45am & 2–6.45pm; April–June & Sept Mon–Sat 9–11.45am & 2.30–5.45pm; Oct Mon–Fri 9–11.45am & 2.30–5.45pm; Nov–March by appointment only; free) and taste the sweet ferment, which is aged in what is claimed to be the world's biggest oak vat. From Thuir you can head directly to Ille-sur-Têt along the D615 or go via **CASTELNOU**, a lovely stone village 4km west from Thuir, which is more worthy of the effort; it has a tenth-century **castle** (daily: mid-June to mid-Sept 10am–8pm; March to mid-June & mid-Sept to Nov 11am–7pm; Jan, Feb, Nov & Dec 11am–6pm; 28F/€4.27), with good views and a restaurant (roughly 90F/€13.73). The hamlet reeks of medieval ambience, and has a well-preserved gate and walls. Back at the riverside, and 12km beyond Castelnou, **ILLE-SUR-TÊT** has an attractive medieval quarter of narrow alleys, within which a well-run **Centre d'Art Sacré** (mid-June to Sept daily 10am–noon & 2–7pm; Oct to mid-June Tues–Fri 10am–noon & 3–6pm, Sat & Sun 3–6pm; 20F/€3.05) is housed in the seventeenth-century Hospice d'Illà – the local headquarters of the medieval Hospitaller Knights – and hosts temporary exhibitions of local religious art. More remarkable are the clay cliffs just across the River Têt, a kilometre or so on the road north towards Sournia, and which the elements have eroded into extraordinary figures known as **Les Orgues** ("the Organs"), so called because of their resemblance to the pipes of the church instrument. Rising dramatically up from a deep tributary of the Têt, they can be explored by a series of footpaths laid out within the gorge (July & Aug daily 9.30am–9.30pm; mid- to end-June & Sept daily 9.30am–7.30pm; March to mid-June Sat & Sun 10am–5pm; 20F/€3.05).

## The priory of Serrabone
But the most compelling stop en route to Prades involves a detour south from Bouleternère, 5km after Ille-sur-Têt, up a perilous 8km track to Roussillon's celebrated **priory of Serrabone** (daily except public holidays 10am–6pm; 10F/€1.53). The location of the simple church, set as it is on a high hill top, backed against a precipitous and wooded drop, is impressive, and its exterior blends with the surrounding rocky landscape; in the grounds around the priory, a botanical garden has been set up to showcase the region's diverse flora. The building's modest facade conceals a strange cloistered gallery, which looks out on the hills, and leads inside to the church's equally curious interior. Here, the almost windowless nave is dominated by an exquisitely decorated tribune of rose

marble – a curious "indoor" cloister, reminiscent of some Spanish *mozarab* churches. Excavated columns found here suggest that much of the original priory – founded in the twelfth century – was as elaborate as the tribune. From the foot of the hill on which the priory sits, the road continues 5km south to the village of Boulés d'Amont. From here a harrowing 9km drive brings you to the chapel of **La Trinité**, just before the Col Xatard (752m). Superb ironwork adorns the outside of the door, and inside there's a *Christ en Majesté* – a Gothic-styled sculpture in which a regally robed Christ reposes impassively on the Cross. If you're **hiking**, you can get to Serrabonne and La Trinité by taking a trail from Vinça, 6km beyond Bouletenère on the N116.

### Practicalities

Ille's gare SNCF is a five-minute walk south of the town centre, which is where you will find the town's **tourist office** (July & Aug Mon–Fri 9am–noon & 2–7pm, Sat & Sun 9am–noon & 2–6pm; Sept–June Mon–Fri 9am–noon & 2–6pm, Sat 9am–noon; ☎04.68.84.02.62, fax 04.68.84.16.20, *office-tourisme.ille@wanadoo.fr*) in quare de la Poste. There's little by way of services in this neck of the woods, and if you decide to stay in Ille, the only **hotel** is the noisy and uninviting *Hôtel du Midi* on the main avenue Pasteur (☎ & fax 04.68.84.19.60; ④). The best **restaurant** hereabouts is *Le Patio* (☎04.68.53.23.30; closed part Oct & part Jan), just up the street from Castelnau's old gate, which offers Catalan cuisine in a relaxed, intimate atmosphere at 98–130F/€14.95–19.83.

## Prades and around

Midway along the Têt valley, **PRADES** is by far its biggest town. Distinctively pink with its marble masonry and pavements, it is the birthplace of Thomas Merton, the twentieth-century Catholic mystic who eventually settled in a Trappist monastery in Kentucky. But it is best known for hosting the annual summer music festival founded in 1950 by the Catalan cellist **Pablo Casals** (or Pau Casals in Catalan). In exile from Franco's Spain, Casals spent the second half of his life here, composing such works as the oratorio *The Crib* and the popular *Song of the Birds*. A one-room **Casals Museum** (summer Mon–Sat 9am–noon & 2–6pm, winter Mon–Fri 9am–noon & 2–5pm; free), in the same building as the municipal tourist office (see below), commemorates the virtuoso, who died in 1973, two years before the Spanish dictator. In the main place de la République, you'll find the **church of St-Pierre**, which contains a huge and sumptuous seventeenth-century retable, a masterpiece by the Catalan sculptor Josep Sunyer. Prades is in fact conspicuously Catalan in feel, hosting a summertime Catalan university (☎04.68.96.10.84) and having established the first Catalan-language primary school in France. On Tuesdays there is an excellent **market** in the square and surrounding streets.

Much of the music festival takes place at the restored ninth-century Benedictine monastery of **St-Michel-de-Cuxa** (May–Sept Mon–Sat 9.30–11.50am & 2–6pm, Sun 2–6pm; Oct–April Mon–Sat 9.30–11.50am & 2–5pm, Sun 2–5pm; 20F/€3.05), whose single ponderous square tower suddenly appears above a copse of poplars 3km south of the town, on the orchard-lined road to Taurinya. St-Michel reached its peak in the eleventh century and then went into slow decline: closed and abandoned in 1790, much of its stone was pillaged during the Revolution, some of it eventually finding its way – like many other

Romanesque fragments from the region – to the Cloisters Museum in New York. Today the highlights of a visit include a subterranean crypt consisting of a circular chapel dating back to the monastery's foundation, and the remains of the broad cloister, whose columns are capped by fine twelfth-century detailings. The church, accessed from a tiny door off the cloister, contains a puzzling mishmash of features, superimposed during the renovations which followed the building's construction.

### Practicalities

The **gare SNCF** is at the southern edge of Prades, about ten minutes' walk from the centre; **buses** set you down on avenue Général de Gaulle (RN116), which is the main road through the centre of town. The **tourist office** (July & Aug Mon–Sat 9am–12.30pm & 2–7pm, Sun 9am–noon; Sept–June Mon–Fri 9am–noon & 2–5pm; ☎04.68.05.41.02, fax 04.68.05.21.79, *www.prades.com*), at 4 rue Victor-Hugo, is a mine of information about everything from *chambres d'hôtes* and changing money to walking trails, biking trails and climbing the Pic du Canigou. The **music festival office** is next door (☎04.68.96.33.07). You can **rent bikes** at Cycles Cerda, 114 avenue Général de Gaulle, or Michel Flament, 8 rue Arago.

For cheap and reasonable **accommodation** you can't beat the faded elegance of the white-painted, simply furnished *Hostalrich*, at 156 avenue Général de Gaulle (☎04.68.96.05.38, fax 04.68.96.00.73; ①), still run by a family who were friends of Casals; its spacious restaurant, with a 70F/€10.68 menu, also offers the best value in town. The best alternative is *Les Glycines* at no. 129 on the same street (☎04.68.96.51.65, fax 04.68.96.45.57; ④) – more expensive, but spotlessly clean and friendly. The beautifully sited municipal **campsite** (☎04.68.96.29.83; closed Nov–March) in the valley just east of the town centre off chemin du Gaz also has chalets for rent. **Eating** out in Prades offers a slightly better choice than accommodation: apart from the reliable *Hostalrich*, you could try *El Patio*, at 19 place de la République (closed Wed), which serves both traditional and Andalucian-style food for about 120F/€18.30 per person. **Café** life is centred on the place de la République, where the *Café de France* has a reputation for the best *plats du jour*.

# Villefranche-de-Conflent and around

Beyond Prades the Têt valley narrows dramatically, becoming a gorge 6km further on, where the high walls of **VILLEFRANCHE-DE-CONFLENT** almost block the way. As there's almost no construction outside the walls, externally at least the town looks much as it did three hundred years ago: an elongated, two-street place squeezed between the palisade just to the south and the river. Within the ramparts, the historic atmosphere is strongest along the bank of the Têt, by the thirteenth-century church of **St-Pierre**; the best view is from the far side, from where the weathered red-tiled roofs and the tower of the twelfth-century church of **St-Jacques** peer over the ramparts. But more satisfying, perhaps, than any man-made constructions are the vast **cave** complexes (see below) which riddle the strata below and around the town.

Villefranche dates from 1092, when Guillaume Raymond, Count of Cerdagne, granted the charter for the town, meant as a strategic bulwark against the counts of Roussillon. Some remnants from that period still stand, notably the **Tour d'en Solenell** on the little square known as the **Placette**. In 1654 Villefranche – then controlled by Spain – was besieged by Louis XIV's troops, and fell after eight days' fighting. After the Treaty of the Pyrenees confirmed their annexation of Roussillon, the French rebuilt the Spanish fortifications, according to plans drawn up by Vauban.

As you walk the immense and maze-like **ramparts** (daily: July & Aug 10am–8pm; June & Sept 10am–7pm; April, May, Sept & Oct 10am–noon & 2–6pm; Feb, March, Nov & Dec 2–5pm; 20F/€3.05), their vulnerability to attack from the surrounding heights is obvious – a defensive weakness that Vauban remedied by adding various bastions and building the upper fort now known as **Fort Liberia** (daily: June–Sept 9am–8pm; Oct–May 10am–6pm; 30F/€4.58), rising high above the main town on the steep northern bank of the Têt. Reached by a 734-step underground staircase or a much gentler trail (or by minibus from outside Porte de France, near the Prades–Vernet road – look for signs for "Navette Liberia"), the castle has seen more service as a prison than as a fortress, whose interns have included a group of seventeenth-century noblewomen of the court of Versailles, locked up in isolation and silence for over thirty years, on allegations of witchcraft and poisoning.

### The caves

The most celebrated incident in Villefranche's history was the 1674 revolt against French rule, which culminated in the betrayal of the rebellion's leader, Charles de Llar, and his co-conspirators by Llar's own daughter, Inès. His hiding place was the **Cova Bastéra** (daily: July & Aug 10am–8pm; Sept–June 10am–noon & 2–6pm; 30F/€4.58), a cave which he could enter and exit from within the walls of the town – today the entrance is just west of the town walls on the N116. If you plan on visiting the cave, consider buying a combined ticket, also good for the limestone formations of the **Grottes des Canalettes** (daily 10am–6pm; guided tour 45min; 35F/€5.34), 1km along the road south towards Vernet-les-Bains. The most spectacular caves, however, are the adjoining **Grottes des Grandes Canalettes**, which require a separate ticket (mid-June to mid-Sept daily 10am–6pm; April to mid-June & mid-Sept to Nov daily 10am–noon & 2–5.30pm; Dec–Feb Sun 2–5pm or by appointment ☎04.68.96.23.11; guided tour approx 1hr; 30F/€4.58). Entry is via a 160-metre passageway, hollowed out by water over the past four hundred million years; the water dripping down the sides is now directed over moulds to create limestone images for sale at the shop. Beyond a door you then enter a succession of huge chambers crammed with stalactites, stalagmites, pillars and tiny feathery formations.

### Practicalities

Main-line trains from Perpignan terminate in Villefranche, at the **gare SNCF** (☎04.68.96.56.62), 400m north of the town; for onward *Train Jaune* services (see p.336), simply change platforms. The **tourist office** (Feb–Dec daily 10am–12.30 & 2–5.30; ☎04.68.96.22.96, fax 04.68.96.23.93) runs a booth at the entrance to the ramparts. There are two **hotels**, *Le Vauban* in place de l'Église (☎04.68.96.18.03; closed Oct–March; ②) in the centre of town, and the magnificent old *Auberge du Cédre* (☎04.68.96.05.05; closed Nov–April; ③) situated just east of the old walls. There is also **gîte** accommodation (contact the *mairie*, ☎04.68.96.10.78). Of the **restaurants**, the most interesting is the *Calypso* (some vegetarian dishes) in rue St-Pierre, the alley leading down to the Pont St-Pierre (and on to Fort Liberia).

# The Pic du Canigou and around

Rising to a height of 2785m between the Tech and Têt valleys, **Pic du Canigou** (*Canigó* in Catalan) is the great landmark of Catalonia, dominating the whole of the Roussillon lowlands. Situated well inside French territory, the mountain became a symbol for Catalonia's lost independence in the course of the nineteenth-century literary renaissance, and came to symbolize Catalan cultural unity, endorsed today by the small flags and other patriotic paraphernalia festooned from its summit cross. Before modern geographic surveys had covered the whole of the Pyrenees, the Canigou was thought erroneously to be the range's highest peak – it does, however, overshadow the rest of the **Canigou Massif**, wedged between the two rivers. The massif has been protected as a nature reserve and the peak (when not clouded) affords breathtaking views; if you're intent on reaching the summit, you must **hike**, and the most direct route is from the **Chalet des Cortalets** (2150m) on the peak's northeastern slopes – you can get to this by vehicle or on foot. There are, however, other, more challenging hikes up to the peak either from the Tech valley to the south or from the amenable village of **Vernet-les-Bains** on its northwestern slopes; if you choose to take on these trails or explore the massif further you should purchase either the 1:50,000 "Canigou/Vallespir/Fenouillèdes" *carte de randonnée* published by IGN, or the TOP 25 1:25,000 **map** (no. 2349ET "Massif du Canigou"), readily available at shops in the area. Vernet is also the place from which to access the key sight around Canigou – the **monastery of St-Martin-du-Canigou**, easily reachable by car. For all route information, contact the regional tourist office in Perpignan (see p.316), or visit their Web site. Before setting out to the summit, either by car or foot, be sure to check the weather conditions. In general the best time of year to hike up is the autumn, when there is no snow on the summit (as in late spring); summer is not the best of times to make the ascent, as the heat can be uncomfortable and humidity reduces visibility from the top.

## To the summit via the Chalet des Cortalets

To get to the chalet you can either come from the east or the north. The easternmost route is the quiet and impressively steep (but not difficult) approach from **Valmanya**, which you can drive or **hike** to (along the GR36) from Vinça – some 20km to the north. From the village, a narrow road climbs a further 5km west, before petering out – you must then use the GR36 to complete the remaining 8km to the Chalet. Approaching from the north, there is a jeep track from near **Prades**. A scenic but busy alternative, this route provides the gentlest ascent to *Chalet des Cortalets* and is the one used by **jeep-taxis** (roughly 150F/€22.88 per person) from Prades; booking offices in the town include Amalric Sports Shop (☎04.68.96.26.47) and La Bohec (☎04.68.05.20.48). If you're **driving**, take the D35 out of the south side of Prades to Villerach (8km; signposted as "Clara-Villerach"), from where an unpaved *route forestière* dirt track rises to the Chalet – an hour's drive. This is a superb approach, often running close to the River Llech, each turn revealing a new arrangement of rock, water, sky and forest. An ordinary car can easily get as far as the ruined hut at Prat Cabrera (1650m), an hour's walk from the *Chalet des Cortalets*, and – with extra care and ideal conditions – all the way to Cortalets.

A *maquisard* hideout in the last war, and consequently heavily shelled by occupation forces, the restored **Chalet des Cortalets** (May–Oct; other times emergency shelter only; ☎04.68.96.36.19; ①) is now run by the Club Alpin Français. There are double rooms as well as dorm beds (55F/€8.39), while **meals** in the bar-restaurant cost about 70F/€10.68. The smaller shelter adjacent, with no bunk linen provided, costs half as much as the dorms. Be warned that the main lodge can get overcrowded, and the tracks bring up jeeps full of revellers – as opposed to walkers – at weekends to picnic at the tables around the little lake, ten minutes' walk west of the refuge. **Tents** are tolerated on the lake shore, and next to another smaller pond closer to *Cortalets*.

### The summit

The normal, well-marked **hike to the summit** goes past the larger lake, with its fine view up into the summit cirque, then climbs south along the ridge connecting with the **Pic Joffre**, which often teems with izards at sunset. It takes about ninety minutes and provides only a slight sense of exposure as you reach the wrought-iron summit cross and *table d'orientation*. Even though it's the process of getting to the top that makes Canigou so memorable – rather than the experience of standing on the peak – the views encompassing everything from Andorra to the sea are wonderful.

At midsummer (technically June 21 but in Catalonia observed on the eve of June 23–24, the Festa de Sant Joan), the refuge and the peak are both spots to avoid or gravitate towards depending on your temperament: seemingly half the population of Catalonia descends for merrymaking and the kindling of the traditional bonfire which is then relayed to light numerous others in Catalan villages on both sides of the frontier. Even at other times there is often a patriotic Catalan or two prepared to bivouac the night beside the peak's highest cairn.

## Vernet-les-Bains and St-Martin-du-Canigou

The biggest village on the Canigou's slopes and the major stop en route to the famous abbey of St-Martin is the pleasant if slightly stuffy spa town of **VERNET-LES-BAINS**, whose easiest approach is via the D116 for 10km south from Villefranche. English visitors like Rudyard Kipling made the place fashionable during the last century and a waterfall, 3km out of town on a well-marked track, is even called the **Cascade des Anglaises**. Along with the thermal paraphernalia of plunge-pools and institutional adjoining therapy wings – first installed in 1377 – a range of more contemporary pastimes is now offered (mountain biking, canyoning, hydrospeed and caving), though the baths are still the focus of activity. Often overlooked, the old quarter's warren of alleys is capped by the ninth-century but much-restored double church of **Notre Dame del Puig/St-Saturnin**, which incorporates remaining bits of a castle. You can also visit the town's **geological museum** (June–Sept daily 10am–12.30pm & 2.30–6.30pm; April, May & Oct Wed–Sun 10am–noon & 2–6pm; 20F/€3.05) in Parc du Casino, which has a collection of local silex and other fossils.

From Vernet-les-Bains a paved road and a footpath lead 2.5km south to **Casteil**, an appealing, quiet hamlet, close by the **monastery of St-Martin-du-Canigou**, a ubiquitous sight on local book covers, postcards and posters. Access to the monastery is only by a thirty-minute climb up the continuation of the footpath, or by jeep transport from Casteil along a steep, narrow road. Inaccessibility helps protect the place from the worst tour-bus excesses – as does its continuing use by an active religious community. Built from tan stone and roofed with grey slates, the monastery ranks as one of the most gorgeous monuments in the eastern Pyrenees, and the surrounding woods of sweet chestnut, beech and aspen form an unimprovable backdrop to the pinnacle of rock on which it stands. Founded in 1001 by Count Guifred de Cerdagne, it was severely damaged by an earthquake in the fifteenth century and thoroughly pillaged after abandonment in 1782. Restored through the twentieth century, the glory of the place resides in its **cloister capitals**, reassembled in unity by a bishop of Perpignan. The monastery is now occupied by an unusual mixed order of monks and nuns, called the "Beatitudes", with a sprinkling of lay workers. Ordinarily, visitors are allowed only on silent **guided tours** (departures daily, every hour: June to mid-Sept 10am–noon & 2–5pm; mid-Sept to May 10am–noon & 2.30–4.30pm; 20F/€3.05). Descending from the rear of the complex, you can take an alternative marked footpath for half an hour back to Casteil via the entrance to the **Gorges du Cady**, where the river falls 500m over a distance of 3km, making this a popular spot for **canyoning**.

### Practicalities

The **tourist office** is quite central, on place de la Mairie, near the corner of boulevard Lambert-Violet and rue du Canigou (Mon–Fri 9am–noon & 2–6pm; ☎04.68.05.55.35, fax 04.68.05.60.33), close by where buses will drop you. **Jeep-taxis** up Canigou (same price as from Prades) and to the monastery can be arranged through Taurigna (☎04.68.05.54.39). Vernet has three two-star **hotels**, each offering a range of amenities and all good value: *Eden*, 2 promenade du Cady (☎04.68.05.54.09, fax 04.58.05.60.50, *www.logis-de-france.fr*, ④), the *Moderne*, 7 avenue des Thermes (☎04.68.05.52.17, fax 04.68.05.66.64; ④), and the *Princess*, rue de Lavandiers (☎04.68.05.56.22, fax 04.58.05.62.45, *www.logis-de-france.fr*, ④). You'll also find a *gîte d'étape* in chemin St-Saturnin, on the left bank of the Cady next to the municipal pool (☎04.68.05.51.30; ①). There are plenty of **campsites** too: the nearest are *Les Cerisiers* (☎04.68.05.60.38), on the same side of the river as the *gîte*, and *Dels Bosc*, 1km north on the Villefranche road (☎04.68.05.51.62). **Eating**, you can easily spend a fortune in the elegant surroundings of *Le Cortal* (closed Mon and in Oct & Nov), up in the old quarter behind the church at rue de Château. Down in the modern town, the best place is *L'Escapade* on avenue des Thermes.

At Casteil, you can eat and stay at either *Relais St Martin* (☎04.68.05.56.76; ①), or the more picturesque two-star *Molière* (☎04.68.05.50.97, fax 04.68.05.55.11; ③), with a delightful summer restaurant in the apple orchard. There's also a *gîte d'étape* (☎04.68.05.51.30; ①) and a **campsite**, *Camping St-Martin*, with a swimming pool.

# The upper Têt and the Capcir

The lower Têt finishes at Villefranche-de-Conflent, above which the shaggy flanks of the **upper Têt** close dramatically around the narrow-gauge *Train Jaune* rail line and N116, which forge their separate ways along the river up to **Mont-Louis**, at the top of the Têt. En route, interspersed with abandonded villages colonized by hippies and New Age travellers, are a number of small hamlets, on the valley floor or perched just above, which make serviceable bases for excursions into the

---

**THE TRAIN JAUNE**

The best way to move up the Têt valley and on into the Cerdagne is on the **Train Jaune**, once an essential local service, but now more of a fun ride – during summer some carriages are open-air. Built in the early twentieth century, the railway climbs for 63km from Villefranche (427m) up to Latour-de-Carol (1231m), where it connects with the Transpyrenean railway (Toulouse–Barcelona). Tourism saved the scenic narrow-gauge line from closure early in the 1970s, but its future remains uncertain. As it is, return tickets are valid for only 24 hours, with **fares** double those of French main-line services; as an example, Villefranche to Mont-Louis and back (the most popular stretch) will cost at least 98F/€14.95.

From late May through to September there are four to six **departures** a day in each direction; the first train of the day leaves Latour-de-Carol soon after 8am, and takes two and a half hours to reach Villefranche. For the rest of the year service is cut to two round trips. Since most of the line is single track, there are often delays caused by long halts at Mont-Louis or Font-Romeu to allow the uphill train to pass, the first of these leaving Villefranche well before 8am. The train is scheduled to stop only at certain stations, and if you want to alight at one of the smaller, unstaffed stations (designated *arrêts facultatifs* on carriage placards) you have to notify the driver in advance. Similarly, to get on at such stations, you have to flag the train down.

For **information** on timetables and prices contact the following stations: Villefranche-Vernet-Fuilla (☎04.68.96.56.62); Mont-Louis (☎04.68.04.23.27); Font-Romeu (☎04.68.30.03.12); Bourg-Madame (☎04.68.04.53.29); or Latour-de-Carol (☎04.68.04.80.62). You can also call the main information number (☎04.68.96.56.62) or look up their Web site *www.ter.sncf.fr/trjaune*.

---

hills. Of these, the hot springs and no-nonsense **Carança gorge** near **Thuès** is one of the most accessible and rewarding. North of Mont-Louis a sedimentary plateau called the **Capcir** spreads towards the gorges of the upper Aude. Bare and extremely flat, dominated in the centre by the large artificial lakes of Matemale and Puyvalador, it is cradled by densely wooded slopes that sweep up to Pic Madrès and the Carlit Massif, with only the pistes of the **ski resorts** Les Angles, Formiguères and Puyvalador interrupting the trees – one of the harshest winter climates in southern France also makes this excellent **cross-country skiing** terrain. The Capcir woodlands, with its sprinkling of *gîtes* and hotels, provide ample opportunities for **hiking** during warmer months, well within the capabilities of a novice walker; contact the Randonnées Pyrénéennes organization for information on trails in the area and longer circuits like the four-day **La Tour du Capcir**. In July and August, and during ski season, all the main Capcir villages and resorts are served by a taxi-bus, which departs from the Mont-Louis/La Cabanasse train station.

## The Carança gorge area

At **NYER**, less than an hour from Villefranche on the *Train Jaune*, the road south from the station to the village climbs on into the impressive Gorges de Nyer, but you're probably better off staying on the train until **THUÈS-CARANÇA**, four minutes above the small spa of Thuès-les-Bains and the gateway for the even more spectacular **Gorges de Carança**. The gorge is clearly signposted from the train station and from Thuès village, and more notices at its mouth (over which the *Train Jaune* clatters on a bridge) advise you of entry at your own risk. After a short walk from the car park, the path divides: the left-hand path (signposted for Roc Madrieu) climbs steeply up the wooded side of the valley, while the right-hand path (over a small bridge) follows the more spectacular corniche route; the two paths converge at the *pont des singes* (suspension bridge). The first ninety minutes of corniche walkway are the most amazing, poised over sheer four-hundred-metre drops – not for the vertigo-prone. Next are a series of nerve-wracking catwalks, ladders and wobbly metal suspension bridges, these last not advisable for heavily laden walkers. If you want to **hike** further, beyond the narrows the route becomes a shady streamside trail on the west bank; soon the countryside opens out, and you should reach **Ras de Carança** (1830m), with its summer-staffed refuge, in about four to five hours – here you can join up with the GR10-36 (see below).

As you would expect there is little by way of services in this rugged and under-populated stretch, but you'll find enough **accommodation** to make even an overnight visit possible. At Nyer, you'll find a **campsite**, *La Catalane* (☎04.68.97.07.63), and you can eat at *Castel Val*, a gourmet restaurant featuring trout and quail for 90–120F/€13.70–18.30, but more enticing is Thuès-entre-Valls' delightful **gîte-campsite**, *Mas de Bordes* (☎04.68.97.05.00, fax 04.68.97.11.51; ①), next to the church. This restored farm is part of a 300-hectare property which includes its own outdoor hot springs, a remote log cabin and a meadow for pitching tents. The place is always mobbed during July and August, when you must ring ahead, but it's worth trying to fit it into your plans for a night or two. Good *table d'hôte* suppers are provided for about 80F/€12.20, a blessing since the village itself is not up to much at all.

## Mont-Louis and around

Approaching Mont-Louis, the *Train Jaune* passes over the 150-metre-long **Pont Gisclard** suspension bridge, which carries the track 80m above the river; it was designed early this century by the mathematician and engineer Albert Gisclard, who was tragically killed by a runaway train on the very day of the official bridge trials in 1909. Soon after you'll find the turn off for **PLANÈS**, whose peculiar triangular church was once thought to be an adapted Muslim structure. To get to Mont-Louis from here you can get back on the train (stop at La Cabanasse) or **hike** 4km down the GR10-36, which passes through the hamlet. At 1600m, the garrison town of **MONT-LOUIS** is the highest on the Têt, only 14km southeast of the river's source, the Lac des Bouillouses. Known as the gateway to the Cerdagne, Mont-Louis is the quintessential work of Louis XIV's military engineer Vauban, and its massive moat-ringed **ramparts**, built between 1679 and 1682, represent a glorious but failed effort to close off the Spanish frontier. Though promoted as a resort, Mont-Louis is still essentially a military town (now a commando training centre), and apart from the walls, its only other attraction is the world's first **solar oven** *(four solaire)*, built in 1949 and now open for one-hour **guided tours** (daily: summer 10am–6.30pm; winter 10am–12.30pm & 2–6pm; 30F/€4.58); the huge mirror for the *four* stands in the moat, just to the left of the main gate (Porte de France).

In Mont-Louis there's a **tourist office** in rue du Marché (July & Aug daily 9.30am–noon & 2–7pm; Sept–June Tues–Sat 10am–noon & 2–6pm; ☎04.68.04. 21.97), while the best deal for **accommodation** is the attractively furnished *La*

*Taverne*, in rue Victor Hugo (☎04.68.04.23.67, fax 04.68.04.13.35, *www.logis-de-france.fr*; ④)), which has excellent-value menus (from 68F/€10.37) and delicious pizzas from a wood-fired oven. If this is full, try the *Bernagie*, 10 rue Victor (☎04.68.04.23.67, fax 04.68.04.13.35, *www.bernagie.fr*; ③) whose restaurant does Catalan cuisine. The closest **campsite**, *Pla de Barres* (☎04.68.04.21.18; mid-June to mid-Sept), lies 3km west along the road towards Lac des Bouillouses. *Lou Roubaillou*, a celebrated **restaurant** in rue des Écoles Laïques, offers mushrooms, boar and duck among other local delicacies (menus 125–195F/€19.06–29.74). Near Planès, there's a *gîte d'étape* (☎04.68.04.21.40; ①) at *La Cassagne* farm, along the GR10-36 towards Mont-Louis.

## The Capcir ski resorts

All of the Capcir **ski resorts** lie on, or just off, the D118 road served by the taxi-bus. Nearest to Mont-Louis, **LES ANGLES** is also the area's largest, with 40km of pistes – half of them red, with the top run at 2100m. Chalets predominate rather than high-rises, but the old village has still been almost completely swamped. **FORMIGUÈRES**, 6km further north, is far more attractive with its shops (some selling outdoor gear), cafés and creperies giving it the feel of a county town. Its **church of Ste-Marie** features an unusual triangular facade culminating in the belfry; inside is a masterful, seventeenth-century *majestat* or clothed figure of Christ, typical of the Catalan regions. The pistes here total just 20km, with no really tough runs, but a good-value seasonal pass is available through the local tourist office (see below). Moreover, standing at the heart of 100km of marked trails, Formiguères is the perfect place to start your **cross-country skiing** career; this sort of skiing requires no lessons – experience teaches you how to avoid falling over – and equipment rental can cost less than half downhill piste rates. The ski station at **PUYVALADOR**, at the north end of the Capcir plateau, is 5km west of its namesake reservoir and village (which has no amenities). It was created in 1982, with 20km of pistes, and has a top station of 2380m.

The area's only **tourist office** (July & Aug 8.30am–12.30pm & 2.30–6.30pm; Sept–June 9am–noon & 3–6pm ☎04.68.04.47.35, fax 04.68.04.43.51) is in Formiguères, which also has two **hotels**: the one-star *Picheyre* behind the church (☎04.68.04.40.07, fax 04.68.30.99.03, *hotel-picheyre@wanadoo.fr*; closed late April, May & Nov; ②) and the fancier *Auberge de la Tutte*, on the road out of town by the junction for Les Angles (☎04.68.04.40.21; ③). The *Picheyre*'s **restaurant** is old-fashioned if dull, but good value at 75F/€11.44. In Angles you can choose between five hotels, least expensive being *Le Coq d'Or*, place du Coq d'Or (☎04.68.04.42.17, fax 04.68.04.44.84; ④). The Bureau Montagne in Angles (☎04.68.04.34.30) is a multidisciplinary sports outfitter for summertime **activities** such as horse-riding, mountain-biking and canyoning. Close to Puyvalador (which has no independent services) you'll find the excellent *Al Cortal* **restaurant** (eve only during ski season; also lunch time in summer; weekends only otherwise), with slightly pricey four-course menus for 140F/€21.35.

## The Cerdagne and the Carlit Massif

The French **Cerdagne** is half of the ancient Catalan county of La Cerdanya, lopped in two by the Treaty of the Pyrenees. It is the highest point of the Segre watershed which descends south to Catalan Lleida, and the sunniest area in the French Pyrenees, the ripe colours of summer grain and hay on its treeless, rolling hills reinforcing this impression. Due to a technicality in the treaty, the Cerdagne consists of the hamlets and countryside surrounding the sizeable Spanish enclave of Llívia. To its northeast the ski-centre of **Font-Romeu** is the biggest town in the region. To the south, **Saillagouse**, **Err**, and **Bourg-Madame** ring the island of Spanish territory and can be traced west to **Latour-de-Carol**, which marks the terminus and frontier-crossing of the railway which ascends the Ariège valley from Toulouse; north of Latour is the excellent ski-station of **Porté-Puymorens**. The granite ridges of the lake-spangled **Carlit Massif**, the last truly alpine region of the Pyrenees, occupy a compact area just north of the Cerdagne and offer one of the most challenging regions for serious **hiking**. As with the upper Têt valley, the *Train Jaune* provides the best access to the entire area.

# Font-Romeu and around

Sprawling at the foot of Roc de la Calme, at the southeast corner of the Carlit Massif, **FONT-ROMEU** is one of the most famous ski resorts in the Pyrenees. Its reputation though is somewhat unjustified – a triumph of marketing over reality – since the much touted *Cité Préolympique* was nothing more than an altitude training camp for the 1968 Mexico summer games. Its top station is a mere 2200m, with a maximum vertical descent of just 500m, and out of thirty pistes only five are challenging to the good skier – it does however have good cross-country skiing; more than 80km of marked trails. The nearby Superbolquère, better known as **Pyrénées 2000**, is no higher than Font-Romeu and of an ugliness exceeded only by other purpose-built French winter resorts.

Aside from the kind of hedonism associated with the worst of ski-resort life, the town is known for its famous Virgin statue, a source of devotion and the origin of the Font-Romeu's name, meaning "pilgrim's spring" in Catalan. The legend tells of a cowherd uncovering a buried figure of the Virgin – a recurring motif through out upland Catalonia – having been led to the spot by a bull. The statue is now housed in the **Ermitage**, just a stroll from the main town, off avenue Emmanuel Brousse (early July to early Sept daily 10am–noon & 3–6pm), much altered since its fourteenth-century construction. The Catalan artist Josep Sunyer sculpted the retable in 1707, and five years later created a flamboyantly Baroque "bedroom" for the Virgin, known as the *camaril*. On September 8 the Virgin is taken down the hill to **ODEILLO**, returning on Trinity Sunday. Odeillo has the only other "sight" of the immediate area – the **Four Solaire**, or solar power station (daily: July & Aug 10am–6pm; Sept–June 10am–12.30pm & 2–6pm; 30F/€4.58). It no longer functions as a generator, but rather as a museum and PR exercise, with occasional full-moon-powered demonstrations on summer evenings.

### Practicalities

The *Train Jaune* **station** is at Via, from where it's a fairly steep two-kilometre walk north to Font-Romeu, passing Odeillo about halfway. **Accommodation** in Font-Romeu tends to be expensive, but with eighteen thousand beds you should be able to find something. For a list of holiday apartments ask at the **tourist office** (daily 9am–12.30pm & 2–6.30pm; ☎04.68.30.68.30, fax 04.68.30.29.70, *www .font-romeu-station.com*) near the top of avenue Emmanuel Brousse. In the central

area, the *L'Homme des Neiges*, avenue Emmanuel Brousse (☎04.68.30.07.76; ③),
has kitchenettes instead of a restaurant. Among **hotels**, the two-star *Le Regina*, on
the same street (☎04.68.30.03.81, fax 04.68.30.12.00; ⑤), is also open year round,
while west of town the *Hôtel Y Sem Bé* (☎04.68.30.00.54, fax 04.68.30.25.42; ⑤)
enjoys views over much of the Cerdagne and its **restaurant**, *L'Equirol*, is an excellent if pricey option for a Catalan meal (menus from 140F/€21.35).

# West to Porté-Puymorens

Beyond Odeillo, the *Train Jaune* winds its way across the wide open plain to the
south side of the Cerdagne, to depopulated **SAILLAGOUSE** (1320m), also along
the N116, and a base for the glorious 12km round-trip **hike** through the **Gorges
du Sègre**. The road snakes southeast from the village, passing through the
extremely picturesque hamlet of **LLÓ**, before continuing up the gorge as a *route
forestière*. The next *Train Jaune* stop is on the north edge of **ERR**, a tiny village at
the foot of heavily wooded Puigmal – and another place with a "found Virgin" legend. The twelfth-century effigy is housed in the **Chapelle de la Vierge**, considerably enlarged in the eighteenth century. Separated from it by the cemetery is
the church of **St-Genis**, which an almost indecipherable inscription says is the
burial place of Bishop Radulf of Urgell, a close relative of Guifré el Pelós of Ripoll
(known in English as "Wilfred the Hairy" and hailed as the first of the line of the
great Catalan count-kings). Skirting the Spanish enclave of Llívia, the *Train Jaune*
reaches the frontier at **BOURG-MADAME**, which in 1815 changed its name
from Les Guinguettes d'Hix in honour of the wife of the Duc d'Angoulême, bear-
er of the title "Madame Royale". It had grown from insignificance to a major
bazaar over the course of the eighteenth century, both as a smuggler's entrepôt
and legitimate competitor to Puigcerdà across the Spanish border. But since the
renaming it hasn't amounted to much, and is visibly depressed and fading, its
vitality sapped by its more favoured neighbour. From Bourg-Madame, the *Train
Jaune* continues fifteen minutes on to the end of the line, the Gare Internationale
of **LATOUR-DE-CAROL/ENVEITG**, the interchange for trains south towards
Barcelona and north towards Toulouse. The *gare* lies between the two villages,
though it's actually much closer (700m) to Enveitg, the larger place. Finally, north
of Latour-de-Carol on the N20 or by train, on the western slopes of the Carlit
Massif, the ski station above the village of **PORTÉ-PUYMORENS** is probably
the best the French Catalan Pyrenees has to offer. For although the nearby Col
de Puymorens marks the shift from the arid Cerdagne to the damp Ariège, a lot
of snow often falls on the Cerdan side and stays there, protected from the worst
of the wind. The seventeen runs here are fairly evenly distributed amongst all difficulties, with top points at a respectable 2400m and 2500m. There are also 25km
of trails for *ski de fond*, a snowboarders' "surf park", and a whole gamut of non-ski
leisure facilities (horse-riding, bike trails and fitness). The village itself has a nice
valley setting, off the main road, and horse-riding facilities.

### Practicalities

**Saillagouse**'s *Train Jaune* station is actually across the river, about a fifteen-
minute walk, from the town's *mairie*, where you'll find a small **tourist office** (July
& Aug daily 10am–noon & 3–7pm: ☎04.68.04.72.89, fax 04.68.04.05.57). You can
stay at the **youth hostel**, on the edge of the village (☎04.68.04.71.69; 60F/€9.15),
or the *Hôtel Planes*, place de Cerdagne (☎04.68.04.72.08, fax 04.68.04.75.93,

*www.hotelplanes@logis-de-France-66.com*; ④), or one of two **campsites**, *Le Sègre* (☎04.68.04.74.72) and *Le Cerdan* (☎04.68.04.70.46; closed Nov). In Lló, the only option is the three-star *Auberge Atalaya* (☎04.68.04.70.04, fax 04.68.04.01.29; ⑦), providing expensive accommodation and more affordable high-quality meals, and in **Err**, you can stay the night at a *gîte d'étape* (☎04.68.04.74.20; ①). Bustling **Bourg-Madame**'s cheapest option is the two-star *Celisol* (☎04.68.04.53.70; ③), though you've a choice of **campsites**, both open year round: *Le Sègre* on route de Toulouse (☎04.68.04.65.87), and the *Caravaneige Mas Piques* (☎04.68.04.62.11). Because it's on the main road between Spain and the Ariège, **Latour-de-Carol/Enveitg** has some very tacky **hotels** which can get away with charging too much. It's best to stay at Enveitg's *Hôtel Transpyrénéen* (☎04.68.04.81.05, fax 04.68.04.83.75, *www.logis-de-france.fr*, ④), between the Enveitg village centre and the station. You can **camp** at either the riverside *Municipal de l'Oratory* in Latour-de-Carol (☎04.68.04.83.70) or the more expensive *Caravaneige Le Robinson* in Enveitg (☎04.68.04.80.38). At **Porté-Puymorens**, which has a small gare SNCF, developments are in the works, but for the moment accommodation can be found at *Hôtel Restaurant du Col* (☎04.68.04.82.06, fax 04.68.04.87.22; ④) down in the village. The valley-bottom **campsite** – *La Rivière* (☎04.68.04.82.20) – is open all year, but you'd have to be a polar bear to stay in winter.

# The Carlit Massif

Being easy of access, the mountains of the **Carlit Massif** are popular, and the lakes – even where not dammed – are sometimes a little overly manicured, but still provide opportunities for several days of **trekking**. Three major walking routes which range in difficulty from moderate to extreme – the **HRP**, the north–south **GR7** and the trans-Pyrenean **GR10** – as well as marked secondary trails, cross the massif, while segments of the GR7 and GR10 comprise sections of the less demanding **Tour du Carlit**, aimed at hikers of medium experience. For all of these explorations you'll want the IGN 1:50,000 *Carte de Randonnées no. 7*, "Cerdagne-Capcir"; the IGN TOP 25 no. 2249 ET is also well worth having. The ascent of **Pic Carlit** (2921m) itself is within the capabilities of any reasonably fit person, especially from Lac des Bouillouses, accessible either by car or foot, on its eastern slopes.

## Climbing Pic Carlit

A quick approach to the summit can be made from Mont-Louis on the **east** side, up the very narrow but paved D60 road. On a fine summer day, expect hundreds of cars at the **Lac des Bouillouses** parking area 13km along, with an even greater number of trippers milling about – definitely not virgin wilderness, and with family groups crammed four to a vehicle, you've little chance of hitching a lift. For purist hikers who don't mind a long slog, the **GR10** out of Bolquère, two stops west of Mont-Louis on the *Train Jaune*, climbs gently through woods to the **Col del Pam** (2005m), where it links with the HRP coming from Font-Romeu, both continuing past ski lifts and pistes to Lac des Bouillouses (5hr from either town).

There's plenty of **accommodation** and **food** at the Bouillouses lake, actually a huge reservoir dating from the early 1900s. The CAF-run *Refuge des Bouillouses* (formerly *Combaleran*; ☎04.68.04.20.76; dorm beds 43–75F/€5.56–11.44, doubles with half-pension ④), the cheapest option, stands east of the dam wall at just under 2000m. Tucked inconspicuously behind this is the smallish, privately managed *Auberge du Carlit* (☎04.68.04.22.23; ③, as well as dorms at 75F/€11.44), with menus at 75–95F/€11.44–14.49. Just above the west end of the dam at 2050m looms the gigantic *Refuge Le Bones Hores* (☎04.68.04.24.22, fax 04.68.04.13.63; obligatory half-board ⑥), popular with families.

From next to *Le Bones Hores*, where a placard informs fishermen which lakes are legally open, you get on the **HRP**, whose course is scantily waymarked with faded paint splodges but deeply grooved into the terrain. You arc up gently through the woods, between **Étang Noir** and **Étang Vive**, reached twenty minutes along; the next natural lake, **Dougues**, is a mere 45 minutes above the dam, and thus a hugely popular outing. However the crowds do thin somewhat as you press on past the necklace of smaller lakes – Casteilla, Trébens and Soubirans – under the shadow of **Touzal Colomé** (2804m), and finally up the ridge that leads to the summit from the east. This is a superb climb, with the tarns glinting in the sun, the grass green in June but usually a faded ochre by August, and the scree-strewn pyramid of Carlit overhead. There and back from Lac des Bouillouses is at most six-and-a-half hours, a day's walk in good conditions – though rather ominously there are green sheds by most of the lakes, for sheltering from foul weather which is often not long in appearing. If – as so many do – you just want to take in the lakes, it's only a three-hour round trip from the dam to the highest one, Soubirans, at 2320m.

# The Tech valley and the Albères

Running more or less parallel to the Têt valley, but roughly 30km further south, the **Tech valley** (or Vallespir) is the southernmost in France, endowed with exceptional sunshine (300 days a year) and relatively low rainfall which nurtures a flora that includes oranges, cacti and bougainvillaea – as well as dense forest on the higher, wetter slopes. Heading up the valley will take you through the Hispanified art-centre, **Céret**, and on to **Arles-sur-Tech**, the gateway to the exciting **Gorges de la Fou**. Further upstream, the upper Tech is dominated by **Prats-de-Mollo**, where the main road departs from the river to reach the Spanish frontier. The northern face of the Pyrenees, rising out of the sea at the rugged Côte Vermeille and bordered by the Tech to the north, is known as the **Albères**. Here, a myriad of paths – a traditional route of shepherds, refugees and smugglers – cross the frontier into Spain, which is officially marked by the village of **Le Perthus**. Access into both regions from Perpignan by car or bus is via **Le Boulou**, where the N9 splits to head straight south for Le Perthus, and west to shadow the Tech valley as the N115.

## South to Le Perthus

Aside from being the cork capital of France, **LE BOULOU**, 20km south of Perpignan, is basically a nondescript traffic interchange. A few minutes' ride south from here, where the Tech cuts by on its way to the sea, you can visit the remarkable **chapel of St-Martin-de-Fenollar** (mid-June to mid-Sept daily 10.30am–noon & 3.30–7pm; mid-Sept to mid-June Mon & Wed–Sun 2–5pm; 15F/€2.29). Its twelfth-century frescoes are the best Romanesque wall paintings in Roussillon, and their clarity and simplicity of line may well have been influential on Picasso, who sometimes stayed in nearby Céret. Nine kilometres further south, **LE PERTHUS** was marked in history on the night of February 5, 1939, when a column of twenty thousand Spanish Republicans arrived at the border post to seek sanctuary in France. Nowadays consumer armies descend here every day, disgorging from coaches to spend their money on foodstuffs, booze and perfume, or to cross the border to fill up their tanks in Spain. The main landmark is **Fort de Bellegarde** (July–Sept daily 10.30am–12.30pm & 2.30–6.30pm; Oct–June phone for details – ☎04.68.83.60.15; 15F/€2.29) which looms on a peak above the town. Built in the sixteenth century and later reinforced by Vauban, it comprises two rows of dilapidated buildings and the deepest well in Europe (63m) within an enclosure of mighty walls, and gives superb views south into Spain and north across Roussillon. In Roman times the Via Domitia crossed the Albères 2km to the west at the **Col de Panissars**, accessible by the narrow road which continues past Fort Bellegard, and is probably the way that Hannibal came in 218 BC. When Pompey returned victorious from Spain a century and a half later, he ordered a triumphal monument to be built at the *col*, and the excavated base of this edifice is now visible through a cordon of barbed wire.

With its proximity to Perpignan, the coast and more interesting Céret, there is little impetus to overnight in the Albères, but if you do need to **stay** your only choice is *Chez Grand-Mère* in Le Perthus, at the summit of the main road (☎04.68.83.60.96; ④ with obligatory half-pension), although there is a *gîte* (☎04.68.83.62.20; ①) 5km east of town in l'Albère.

# Céret

Just 10km or so upstream along the Tech from Le Boulou lies the cherry capital, **CÉRET**, a friendly and bustling place with a shady old town of narrow and winding streets, still dominated by its much built-into medieval fortifications. The best time to visit is during any of the town's famous **festivals** (see p.314), which have a markedly Catalan and Spanish flavour, including *sardanas* and *corridas* held in the arena to the north of town – but you'll have to plan ahead, as accommodation sells out well in advance. At the entrance to the town, a single-arched **Pont du Diable** was said to have been built by the Devil in 1321 in return for the soul of the first Cérétan to cross. The engineer who made the bargain duly sent a cat over first, but the trick backfired as none of the locals would then risk the Devil's vengeance by using the bridge themselves. Like Prades on the Têt, Céret was a place of refuge for escapees from Franco's fascist regime, with many artists passing through or staying here. At that point, the town was already a creative colony, having been a temporary home to luminaries such as Pablo Picasso, Marc Chagall and a clutch of Catalan and French artists, including Pierre Brune, who in 1950 opened the **Musée d'Art Moderne** at 8 boulevard Maréchal Joffre (mid-June to mid-Sept daily 10am–7pm; May to mid-June & mid-Sept to Oct daily 10am–6pm; Nov–March Mon & Wed–Sun 10am–6pm; 35F/€5.34). This museum's small but varied collection includes works by the Fauvists, Cubists and Surrealists, as well as works by recent artists such as Tàpies, but the highlight is a series of painted bowls with bull motifs by Picasso. Other sights in the town include the small **archeological museum** (irregular hours; 10F/€1.53) tucked behind one of the old gates, the **war memorial** by Aristide Maillol, in the old town and the **monument** to the composer Déodat de Sévérac by the Catalan sculptor Manolo in avenue Clémenceau.

## Practicalities

The **tourist office** (July & Aug Mon–Sat 9am–12.30pm & 2–7pm, Sun 10am–
12.30pm; Sept–May Mon–Fri 10am–noon & 2–5pm, Sat 10am–noon; ☎04.68.
87.00.53, fax 04.68.87.00.56, *www.ot-ceret.fr*) is at the top of avenue Clémenceau,
on the corner of boulevard Maréchal Joffre. The most central **accommodation**
is provided by the atmospheric one-star *Vidal*, housed in the old bishop's palace,
off place Soutine (☎04.68.87.00.85, fax 04.68.87.62.33; ③). Opposite stands the
two-star *Arcades* (☎04.68.87.12.30, fax 04.68.87.49.44; ④), and you might also try
the *Pyrénées* on rue de la République (☎04.68.87.11.02, fax 04.68.87.31.66; ②). All
these places have a variety of rooms available, with and without bath. There are
several local **campsites**, two of them on route de Maureillas: *Les Cerisiers*
(☎04.68.87.00.08; year round) and *Les Deux Rivières*.

When it comes to **eating**, you should perhaps forgo the hotel kitchens in favour
of the good bistro-creperie, *Le Pied dans le Plat* (closed Sun), and an adjacent
pizzeria, both on place des Neuf-Jets, with outdoor seating. Social life at the *Grand
Café* in boulevard Maréchal Joffre is perhaps not what it was when the "bande
Picasso" hung out there, but it's still a good place to sit outside with a glass of
wine and a plate of *frites*; there are more **cafés** around the corner by the Porte de
France. Saturdays see a morning farmers' **market** along the old walls, the street
stalls groaning with local produce.

# Arles-sur-Tech and around

Continuing upstream from Céret, the next town which merits a visit is **ARLES-
SUR-TECH**, which is known for having preserved the curious folk traditions of
the eastern Pyrenees – if you can manage it, try to make it for one of the several
festivals that are celebrated throughout the year (see pp.314–315). The heart of
the town is formed by its compact medieval quarter, centred on the eleventh-century **abbey-church of Ste-Marie** (July & Aug Mon–Fri 8am–noon & 2–7pm, Sat
2–7pm; March–June, Sept–Nov Mon–Fri 10am–noon & 2–6pm; Dec–Feb by
appointment only; 20F/€3.05). Before passing through the main door built into
its impressive facade, check out the grilled-off marble block just to the left. This
is the *saint Tombe*, a fourth-century sarcophagus, revered for the pure water
which it miraculously issues, and which plays a key part in the town's ancient religious rituals. The interior of the church has a number of good **chapels** as well as
an elegant thirteenth-century **cloister**.

From Arles, you can **hike** up the northbound GR10 towards the Canigou, but
a less ambitious and more attractive option is the nearby **Gorges de la Fou**,
(☎04.68.39.16.21; Easter to Oct daily 10am–6pm, closed during bad weather;
30F/€4.58), one of the great – if touristy – spectacles of the eastern Pyrenees.
It can be reached by taking the Corsavy road from Arles, or by ascending the
trail leading off the D115, 3km west of Arles. You need at least an hour to cover
the 1500m of metal walkway to the end and back, squeezing between 200-
metre-high walls, so close together that they have trapped falling rocks. In
places, water erosion has made the walls as smooth as plaster, and the force of
the torrent during storms in 1988 was sufficient to sweep part of the walk away
– when storms threaten, the route is closed. If you have transport, you should
consider leaving the main road at Arles, and continuing past the top end of the
Gorges de Fou trail to Corsavy and on to **MONTFERRER**, which – with its
ruined castle and Romanesque church – is one of the most attractive

settlements in the upper Tech. Set amongst dense forest and crags, with sweeping views east to the opposite side of the valley, it enjoys its status as the truffle capital of Roussillon.

South of the main road a tortuous sideroad ascends through forests of sweet chestnut to the village of **ST-LAURENT-DE-CERDANS**, an important junction on the World War II refugee route to Spain. Here the local history museum, **Musée d'Arts et Traditions Populaire** (daily: July & Aug 10am–noon & 3–7pm; May, June & Sept 10am–noon & 3–6pm; 10F/€1.53), preserves rural arts such as the manufacture of espadrilles, the traditional esparto woven shoes favoured by refugee guides (*passeurs*). Further on at tiny **COUSTOUGES**, the spine of the Albères rises northeastwards to the highest point of the chain at **Roc de France** (1450m).

### Practicalities

**Buses** stop in Arles a short walk from the **tourist office** (Mon–Sat 9am–noon & 2–6pm; ☎ & fax 04.68.39.11.99), in rue Barjou at the top of the town, which has suggestions for walks and trails around Arles, plus a map for 25F/€3.81, and also stocks a list of *chambres d'hôtes*, invaluable in hotel-poor Arles. The place to **stay** in town is the comfortable two-star *Les Glycines*, 7 rue du Jeu-de-Paume (☎04.68.39.10.09, fax 04.68.39.83.02, *www.logis-de-france.fr*; ④), which also has the best **restaurant** in town, with a shaded terrace and Catalan specialities (menus 105–165F/€16.01–25.16). Among **campsites**, the scenic *Riuferrer* (☎04.68.39.11.06; open all year), is on the west side of town, near the mouth of the Freixe stream; *Le Vallespir* (☎04.68.39.90.00; closed Nov–March) lies on the road to Amélie-les-Bains; or there's the naturist camp *Le Ventous* (☎04.68.87.83.38, *www.perso.club-internet.fr/le vento*; June to mid-Sept) on the road to Prats-de-Mollo. Between St-Laurent and Coustouges you can stay at the very comfortable but pricey *Domaine de Falgos* (☎04.68.39.51.42, fax 04.68.39.52.30, *www.silencehotel.com*; closed Jan & Feb; ⑦), converted from an old barn. Arles' alternatives for **eating** – other than *Les Glycines* – are *La Treille* (☎04.68.39.89.59; Sept–May closed Mon) at the beginning of boulevard Riuferrer, with a pleasant vine-shaded terrace (70F/€10.68 menu) or the grill-bar at the Musée Jean Cordomi (March–Dec 10am–10pm), opposite the *mairie*.

## Prats-de-Molló

From Arles, the road climbs 19km to the medieval city of **PRATS-DE-MOLLÓ**. The present road follows the path of a former railway (the station houses can be seen along the way), since the old road, with houses and bridges, was washed away in the disastrous floods of October 1940. In the seventeenth century, when the Treaty of the Pyrenees subjected this area to the outrageous tax policies of Louis XIV, Prats-de-Molló and a number of other towns and villages revolted against the French Crown. Living at the far end of what was then a densely wooded valley, the rebels probably felt themselves invulnerable when they murdered the king's tax collectors. And indeed they held off two battalions before the forces of Maréchal de Noailles made a surprise attack over the western flanks of Canigou to put down the insurrection. **Fort Lagarde** (daily: April–June 2–6pm; July & Aug 10am–7pm; Sept–March 2–5pm; 20F/€3.05), which dominates the town from above, was built in 1680 under the direction of Vauban, as much to subdue the local population as to

keep the Spanish at bay; the town walls, raised on fourteenth-century foundations, are another Vauban relic from this period. To make the 25-minute climb
up to the fort, head for Porte de la Fabrique on the north side of town, then
either follow the footpath which winds up the hill from behind the church or
take the covered walk which starts in a ruined building to the right of the
cemetery entrance. The fort itself has been beautifully restored, and there are
superb views all round from the ramparts. An extra attraction here is the
**Visite-Spectacle** on summer afternoons, when horsemen dressed as cavaliers
recreate eighteenth-century cavalry training, with trick riding, sword fights
and the firing of muskets and cannons (Mon–Fri & Sun: July & Aug 2.30pm &
4pm; June 3.30pm; 42F/€6.41).

With Canigou at its back and the River Tech in front, picturesque Prats-de-
Molló has now become a tourist attraction but is still surprisingly unspoilt – particularly the old *ville haute* within the city wall, with its steep, cobbled streets and
ancient fortified church. In summer, the pedestrianized streets buzz with activity;
the rest of the year the hotels are locked up, and the locals pass the time at *boules*
under the plane trees of El Firal, the huge square outside the walls, where markets and fairs have been held since 1308.

### Practicalities

The **tourist office** in place le Firal (July & Aug daily 9am–12.30pm & 1.30–6.30pm;
April, May, Sept & Oct Mon–Sat 9am–noon & 2–6pm; Jan–March, Nov & Dec
Mon–Fri 9am–noon & 2–6pm; ☎04.68.39.70.83, fax 04.68.39.74.51, *www.
pratsdemollolapreste.com*) has a wealth of information, including maps and advice
for walking in the Haut-Vallespir. The only one-star **hotel** is the chintzy *Ausseil*,
place Joseph Trinxeria (☎04.68.39.70.36; ②); among two-stars, both the family-ori-
ented *Le Relais*, no. 3 on the same *place* (☎04.68.39.71.30, *lerelais.aol.com*; ②) and
the friendly *Bellevue* overlooking place le Firal (☎04.68.39.72.48, fax 04.68.39.78.04,
*www.logis-de-france.fr*; closed Nov–March; ③) serve reasonable meals, *Le Relais* at
tables outside in the square. You can also stay at the **gîtes** *Chalet de Conques*
(☎04.68.39.23.49; ①) or *Notre Dame de Coral* (☎ & fax 04.68.39.75.00; ①), and
there's plenty of local **camping**, too. The two sites with the longest seasons are *St
Martin* (☎04.68.39.77.40; all year) and *Can Nadal* (☎04.68.39.77.89; March–Nov)
about 1km along the road towards La Preste.

# The Côte Vermeille

When the nineteenth-century Fauvists discovered the **Côte Vermeille**, which
extends southeast from Argelès-sur-Mer to the Spanish border, they found natural inspiration for their revolutionary use of colour: the sunsets (from which the
coast earned its name) are a gentle red, the sea is turquoise and, as Matisse
wrote, "no sky is more blue than that at Collioure". **Elne**, inland, and once
Roussillon's main town, is the gateway to the coast, and proceeding south you'll
pass the broad beaches of **Argelès**, before reaching the characteristically rocky
coves of **Collioure**, **Banyuls**, and **Cerbère**. The beauty of this stretch of coastline has inevitably been exploited, but cut up along the trails into the hills at the
back of the resorts and you'll often be on your own. Public transport along the
coast is good, with a regular train and bus service connecting all the major points
of call.

# Elne

Standing on a hill just 6km from the sea, the first stop on the coastal transport line is **ELNE**, an ancient fortified town which was once the capital of Roussillon. Despite the heavy beach-bound traffic whizzing past on the main road, the old town, inside the sixteenth-century ramparts, is eerily quiet after dark. Its one great attraction worth visiting is the former **cathedral of Ste-Eulalie** (June–Sept daily 9.30am–6.45pm; April & May daily 9.30am–5.45pm; Oct daily 9.30am–noon & 2–5.45pm; Nov–March Mon & Wed–Sun 10am–noon & 2–4.45pm; 27F/€4.12), the seat of Roussillon's bishops until their transfer to Perpignan in 1602. The **cloister**, built from Céret marble, is the highlight: one intact side of twelfth-century Romanesque pillars and capitals, immaculately carved with motifs such as foliage, lions, goats and biblical figures, is complemented on the other sides by fourteenth-century Gothic work. A small museum in the twelfth-century St-Laurent chapel, which you access from the cloister, is mainly given over to exhibits found in the excavations of Roman villas around Elne. Opposite the cathedral, at 3 rue Balaguer, is the **Musée Terrus** (same times and ticket as the cathedral), dedicated to the landscape painter Etienne Terrus (1857–1922), a contemporary of the Fauvists and friend of sculptor Aristide Maillol (whose bust of Terrus stands on the Plateau des Garaffes, nearby); the *salon de thé*, on the first floor, has a panoramic view.

### Practicalities

The **gare SNCF** (☎04.68.22.06.15), on the main line from Perpignan to the Côte Vermeille, lies about ten minutes' walk west of the old town; **buses** stop at the parking place in the centre, near the cathedral. The **tourist office** is at 2 rue du Docteur Bolte (July & Aug Mon–Fri 9.30am–noon & 2–6pm, Sat 9.30am–noon; June & Sept Mon–Fri 9.30am–noon & 2–5pm, Sat 9.30am–noon; Oct–May Mon–Fri 9.30am–noon & 2–5pm; ☎04.68.22.05.07, fax 04.68.37.95.05, *www.ot-elne.fr*), between the post office and Hôtel de Ville. Of the three **hotels**, the modest *Cara Sol*, in boulevard Illibéris on the edge of the old town (☎04.68.22.10.42; ②), offers the best value and the location, with great views from the front rooms over the Tech valley, the Albères and Canigou. More upmarket is the two-star *Le Weekend*, 31 avenue Paul Reig (☎04.68.22.06.68, fax 04.68.22.17.16, *www.logis-de-france.fr*, ④), just off centre on the Argelès road, with a celebrated garden **restaurant** (menus 90–120F/€13.73–18.30); less well situated is *Le Carrefour*, at no. 1 (☎04.68.22.06.08; ③), on a small but busy crossroads. There are two municipal **campsites** (June to late Sept): *Les Padraguets* (☎04.68.22.21.59) on the Argelès road and *Al Mouly* (☎04.68.22.08.46) on boulevard d'Archimède, in the direction of St-Cyprien.

# Argelès-sur-Mer and around

Poised on the northern edge of the Côte Vermeille, **ARGELÈS-SUR-MER** has the last wide, sandy beach on the coast. At the end of the Spanish Civil War thousands of refugees lived in camps here, their numbers including the Republican poet Antonio Machado, who failed to survive the first harsh winter. Not surprisingly, given camp conditions, nearly ten thousand of the inmates volunteered to serve in the French army upon the 1939 outbreak of hostilities. Nowadays, more than any other resort on this section of coast, this is a mass-tourist town, wooing its visitors with holiday essentials like mini-golf, gambling tables and beauty contests.

The town itself is divided in two: the old **Argelès-Ville**, a little inland, and the new **Argelès-Plage**, which receives an annual inundation of up to three hundred thousand French, Belgian, Dutch and English visitors. Plage Nord and Plage des Pins are **beaches** of the smooth, sandy and potentially windblown variety, whereas **Le Racou** – the first bay of the Côte Vermeille – is more intimate and offers a taste of mountain coastline. The only cultural attraction is the old town's **Casa de les Albères**, in place des Castellans, a small museum of local art and traditions, mostly agricultural tools and implements (June–Sept Mon–Fri 9am–noon & 3–6pm, Sat 9am–noon; 10F/€1.53).

Some 10km due west of Argelès, **ST-GENIS-DES-FONTAINES** was once home to an ancient **Benedictine** abbey. Most of this has disappeared, but the two-metre lintel over the doorway of the church, dating from 1020, is one of the earliest examples of Romanesque sculpture in France. When the church is open (June–Sept Mon–Fri 10am–noon & 3–7pm, Sat & Sun 9am–noon & 3–7pm; Oct–May daily 9.30am–noon & 2–5pm; 10F/€1.53) you can visit its fine twelfth-century Romanesque cloister, whose single row of short columns supports semicircular arches of multicoloured marble, and has capitals carved with engaging primitive figures: half-human and half-beasts, fantastic creatures, and Christ crucified.

## Practicalities

The **gare SNCF** is a few minutes' walk west of the centre of the old town, while **buses** stop opposite the Hôtel de Ville. An hourly bus service (10F/€1.53) runs in summer between the station, the old town and Plage-Nord. There is a summer-only **tourist office** in the old town (July & Aug Mon–Sat 9.30am–12.30pm & 2.30–6.30pm; ☎04.68.95.81.55, fax 04.68.95.16.01), by the Hôtel de Ville on allée Ferdinand-Buisson; Argelès-Plage has its own office (summer daily 8.30am–8pm; winter Mon–Fri 9am–noon & 2–6pm, Sat 9am–noon; ☎04.68.81.15.85, fax 04.68.95.16.01, *www.argeles-sur-mer.com*), in place de l'Europe, on the corner of avenue des Platanes and avenue des Mimosas.

**Accommodation** can be difficult to find in midsummer, especially for a short stay. If you're looking for a hotel in Argelès-Ville, try the long-established one-star *Le Soubirana*, 58 route Nationale (☎04.68.81.01.44; ②), or the two-star *Clair Logis*, 78 route de Collioure (☎04.68.81.03.27, fax 04.68.95.93.01; ③). Among dozens of hotels in Argelès-Plage, the two-star *Les Mimosas*, 51 avenue des Mimosas (☎04.68.81.14.77, fax 04.68.81.50.96; ④), and *Al Pescadou*, rue des Aloes (☎04.68.81.31.12; ③), are reasonably priced and well situated. There should never be a problem finding a spot for your tent, as there are more than fifty **campsites** in the neighbourhood: *Calanque de l'Ouille* (☎04.68.81.12.79; April–Sept) and *Mini Camping* (☎04.68.81.08.72; April–Sept) are two desirable seafront establishments in the direction of Collioure. The **food** situation in Argelès is a little on the bleak side, rarely rising above mediocre beach-town fare. One of the few places that manages to stand out is *Amadeus* (☎04.68.81.12.38; closed Mon April–Nov & all Jan) on avenue des Platanes (by Argelès-Plage's tourist office), which offers reasonable Catalan dishes, with menus from 80F/€12.20.

# Collioure

Eleven kilometres down the coast from Argelès-sur-Mer, **COLLIOURE**, a true Côte Vermeille town, which to a certain extent still banks on its maritime and artistic past, sits nestled in a picturesque cove. Established as a trading port by the Phoenicians and ancient Greeks, Collioure was later occupied by Romans, Visigoths and Arabs. Altogether, the place has been the focus of nearly a dozen territorial squabbles, including four invasions by the French and two by the Spanish. The sixteenth-century **Fort St Elme** overlooking the town from the south (now privately owned), and the seventeenth-century **Fort Miradou** to the north (still used by the military), are reminders of this turbulent past. In the early 1900s, invaders of a different sort came; the group of painters – including Matisse and Derain – known as the **Fauvists** (*les Fauves*) made Collioure their summer base. Some of their original work adorns the bar at *Les Templiers* (see below); you can also follow the "Chemin du Fauvisme" around the town, a trail of twenty reproductions of paintings by Matisse and Derain placed on the sites where they were painted (a map is available from the tourist office). Collioure's **Musée d'Art Moderne** (July & Aug daily 10am–noon & 2–6pm; Sept–June Mon & Wed–Sun same times; 12F/€1.83), housed in the beautiful Villa Pams on the edge of the town in route de Port-Vendres, has a small permanent collection, which includes Picasso's poster *Hommage à Antonio Machado*, remembering the Republican poet and martyr, who is buried in the town, and temporary exhibitions by artists associated with the region.

The artistic tradition of Collioure survives today, albeit with less distinction; the forest of easels that occupies the promenade in summer produces mainly tourist souvenirs, but there are also a few serious commercial galleries. Many of these are in the old quarter of the town, the **Mouré**, whose steep, narrow streets are lined by pastel-tinted houses and assorted shops and cafés. Lateen-rigged fishing boats might be moored in the **harbour** itself, or drawn up on the palm-lined beach; those no longer used by fishermen are now beautifully restored and sailed as pleasure vessels by their new owners. The **château-royal** (daily: July & Aug 10am–6pm; Sept–June 9am–5pm; 20F/€3.05), the imposing fortress which dominates the harbour, was founded by the Templars in the twelfth century, rebuilt and used as a summer residence by the kings of Mallorca and Aragón two hundred years later, and modernized by Vauban after the Treaty of the Pyrenees. The impressive ramparts and some of the well-restored rooms provide terrific settings for seasonal exhibitions of sculptures and paintings, and displays relating to local subjects like quilting and cork production, with great views over the harbour, town and vine-covered hills beyond; the beautiful courtyard at the heart of the castle is used for summer concerts.

At the opposite end of the harbour, the **church of Notre-Dame-des-Anges** was erected in the seventeenth century, replacing the ancient Ste-Marie, razed on the orders of Vauban. The distinctive round bell tower – once doubling as the lighthouse – onto which it was grafted has been damaged many times by storm and war: the base dates from the thirteenth century, the middle from the fourteenth to seventeenth centuries, and the bell chamber from the nineteenth. It's worth taking a look inside (daily 8am–noon & 2–5.30pm) to see the magnificent gilt retable, carved and painted in three tiers, another work by Joseph Sunyer. Beyond the church, the tiny **Chapelle-St-Vincent** stands above the sea on a rocky peninsula, with the south-facing St Vincent beach on one side and the Plage Nord on the other.

## Practicalities

Collioure's **gare SNCF** is less than ten minutes' walk west of the centre, along avenue Aristide Maillol; **buses** stop at the central car park, off avenue Général de

Gaulle. The very helpful **tourist office** is just behind the harbour in place du 18 Juin (July & Aug daily 9am–8pm; Sept–June Mon–Sat 9am–noon & 2–6.30pm; ☎04.68.82.15.47, fax 04.68.82.46.29, *www.little-france.com/collioure*) and there is also an information kiosk (July–Sept Mon–Sat 9am–5pm) in the small tower by the beach on the other side of the castle. The quieter Plage Boutigue, southeast of the harbour, has some desirable seaview **hotels**, including the attractively furnished *Le Boramar* (☎04.68.82.07.06; closed Nov–April; ③) and the nearby, year-round *Triton*, 1 rue Jean-Bart (☎04.68.98.39.39, fax 04.68.82.11.32; ③). The most unusual accommodation is *Hostellerie des Templiers*, 12 quai de l'Amirauté (☎04.68.98.31.10, fax 04.68.98.01.24; ⑤), in which the individually decorated rooms, staircases and dining rooms are filled with original artworks; reservations here are essential. There are three summer-only **campsites** to the north of the town, near the coast: the *Criques de Porteils* (☎04.68.81.12.73), on the Argelès road; *Les Amandiers* (☎04.68.81.14.69), in the sheltered bay known as L'Ouille; and, the best of the bunch, *La Girelle*, plage d'Ouille (☎04.68.81.25.56). For **eating**, there's a great choice of very reasonable creperies, sandwich bars and pizza-pasta places around the old Mouré quarter, but it's worth the premium to sit at a table on the fashionable rue Camille Pelletan, by the harbour, to watch the world go by – the most atmospheric is *Les Templiers*, a café-bar well known to the Fauvists, and now filled with drawings and paintings donated by Matisse, Maillol, Picasso and Dufy, among many other artists. While in town, try to sample the famous salted anchovies, a local standby and an important component in Roussillonaise cookery. **Markets** (Wed & Sun morning) are held in place du Général Leclerc.

## Port-Vendres

The next settlement southeast, **PORT-VENDRES**, a five-minute ride from Collioure), is marred by the busy main road, but for a genuine, unsophisticated fishing port, this is your best (indeed only) choice on the Côte Vermeille – though you probably won't want to stay longer than it takes to have a look around the port and tuck into a fish lunch, or to watch the fish auctions which take place at the far end of the port every weekday evening (usually 5–7pm). A huge fish-processing factory dominates one side of the harbour, while sardine- and tuna-fishing boats are moored under the Maillol-designed war memorial opposite, with nets and other paraphernalia piled along the harbour wall. Salt has taken its toll on Maillol's work, and the uncharacteristically draped figures have lost limbs, noses and various other features.

To the Romans the town was Portus Veneris (Port of Venus), a place of strategic trading importance. By the Middle Ages its significance was diminishing in direct relation to the rising star of neighbouring Collioure, but by the eighteenth century it had recovered somewhat through the business of shipping Roussillon wines. In 1830 it became the primary port for dispatching soldiers and supplies to the French colony in Algeria, a link that lasted for more than a century.

## Banyuls-sur-Mer to the Spanish border

As the road crosses the Col du Père Carnère and drops down towards the Plage des Elmes, the once-elegant wine town of **BANYULS-SUR-MER**, 6km south of Port-Vendres, comes into view, with dry-stone walls and orderly rows of vines stretching into the hills behind it. Banyuls is famous for its dessert wine, which the French tend to drink as an aperitif; if you fancy a tipple, try a **guided tour** of one of the larger cellars, such as the Cellier des Templiers in route du Mas-Reig (April–Oct daily 9am–7pm; Nov–March Mon–Sat 9am–noon & 2–6pm; free). Less fashionable than Collioure, Banyuls is still a lively and popular seaside resort. It's marred by the busy road which runs along the seafront, and the wide, stony main beach is less attractive than some of the smaller bays to the north and south, but the whole town comes alive in the evenings when everyone gets together to promenade along the seafront, play *boules* or eat out at one of the many beach cafés and seafood restaurants.

You shouldn't leave Banyuls without visiting the **Laboratoire Arago**, the large white building overlooking the port. Run by the marine biology and land ecology department of the Sorbonne, its **aquarium** (daily: July & Aug 9am–noon & 2–10pm; Sept–June 9am–noon & 2–6.30pm; 24F/€3.66) comprises over forty tanks of fascinating local specimens, including seahorses, bright red starfish and wicked-looking eels, and is supplemented by a comprehensive display of local birds. The coastal waters of this area, rich in marine life due to the Pyrenees' steep underwater descent, were the first *réserve marine* to be declared in France, indeed throughout the Mediterranean. If you have the necessary qualifications you can **dive** within the reserve area by contacting Plongez Rederis Club, operating from the port (☎04.68.88.31.66 or 04.68.92.02.01).

## Practicalities

The **gare SNCF** lies at the very western edge of town, while **buses** stop on the coastal boulevard. The **tourist office** is on the seafront, opposite the *mairie* (July & Aug daily 9.30am–12.30pm & 2.30–7pm; Sept–June Tues–Sat 9.30am–12.30pm & 2–6.30pm; ☎04.68.88.31.58, fax 04.68.88.36.84). Recommendable one-star **hotels**, open all year, include the quaint and unpretentious *Hôtel Canal*, 9 rue Dugommier (☎04.68.88.00.75; ②), the slightly smarter *Le Manoir*, 20 rue de Maréchal-Joffre (☎04.68.88.32.98; closed Nov & Dec; ④), and its neighbour *Sant Sebastien* (☎04.68.88.34.90, fax 04.68.88.11.71; ②), all in the quieter back streets. For a reasonably priced hotel on the seafront, try *La Pergola*, 5 avenue du Fontaulé (☎04.68.88.02.10, fax 04.68.88.55.45; closed Nov & Dec; ④), near the port, where most of the rooms have a balcony and seaview; they also have a good restaurant (menus from 90F/€13.73). **Camping** is at the *Camping du Stade*, rue Jean Boin (☎04.68.88.31.70), or the cheaper *Camping Municipal La Pinede* nearby, on route du Mas-Reig (☎04.68.88.32.13).

Banyuls has a good choice of **restaurants** specializing in fresh seafood. The most expensive, with starched tablecloths and live lobster tanks – among which *Le Sardinal*, 4bis place Paul Reig, is reckoned the best – are lined up opposite the seafront, but there are several less expensive choices: the best is *Les Canadells*, just off the main boulevard at 4 avenue du Général de Gaulle, with excellent menus (from 78F/€11.90) and specializing in *zarzuela*. Nearby rue St-Pierre is home to a number of restaurants, including *Chez Rosa*, at no. 22, *Casa Miguel*, which has Spanish and Catalan specialities at no. 3, and the livelier *La Paillotte*.

## Maillol's tomb

The four-kilometre **hike** from Banyuls to **Maillol's tomb** and house makes a pleasant excursion up into the vine-clad Albères. Sculptor **Aristide Maillol** (1861–1944) was a Banyuls native famous for fleshy nude sculptures. He is buried at his farm, La Baillaurie, now restored as the **Musée Maillol** (daily: May–Sept 10am–noon & 4–7pm; Oct–April 10am–noon & 2–5pm; 20F/€3.05); his tomb is topped by his *La Pensée*. To arrive, walk the length of avenue Général de Gaulle, until you pass under a bridge. Shortly afterwards, where the road curves around to the right, take the left-hand road, following the line of a river: signs from here point to the "Musée et Tombeau de Maillol". The round trip takes about two-and-a-half hours.

## Cerbère

The Côte Vermeille comes to an end at **CERBÈRE**. The harbour is quite pretty and the mountain backdrop is impressive, but the beach is negligible. Depending on the service, train passengers have to change either here or on the Spanish side of the border at the much nicer Port Bou (see opposite), where the rail line changes track size. In Cerbère, you can **stay** and **eat** at *La Dorade* on the harbour (☎04.68.88.41.93; ③) or tent down at the palm- and cactus-fringed *Camping del Sorell* (☎04.68.88.41.64; June–Sept).

## travel details

### TRAINS

Note that the *Train Jaune* (see p.336) also runs a service up the Tech valley.

**Perpignan** to: Argelès (12–14 daily; 20min); Banyuls-sur-Mer (12–14 daily; 40min); Carcassonne (5 daily; 1hr 30min); Cerbère (12–14 daily; 50min); Collioure (12–14 daily; 23min); Elne (12–14 daily; 10min); Ille-sur-Têt (6–8 daily; 25min); Montpellier (10 daily; 1hr 30min); Narbonne (12–14 daily; 40min); Nîmes (10 daily; 2hr 10min); Prades (6–8 daily; 45min); Salses (12–14 daily; 15min); Toulouse (1 daily; 1hr 40min); Villefranche-de-Conflent (4–6 daily; 40min).

**Villefranche** to: Font-Romeu (3–6 daily; 1hr 20min); Ille-sur-Têt (5–7 daily; 35min); Latour-de-Carol (2–4 daily; 2hr 20min); Mont-Louis (2–4 daily; 1hr); Perpignan (5–7 daily; 45min); Prades/Molitg (5–7 daily; 20min).

### BUSES

**Perpignan** to: Argelès (8 or more daily; 30min); Arles-sur-Tech (6–8 daily; 1hr 15min); Axat (2 daily, 1hr 40min); Banyuls-sur-Mer (3–5 daily; 1hr 10min); Céret (12 daily; 55min); Collioure (4–6 daily; 45min); Elne (Mon–Sat 2–5 daily; 35min); Font-Romeu (1 daily; 2hr 30min); Latour-de-Carol (3 daily; 3hr); Le Perthus (4 or 5 daily; 45min); Mont-Louis (4 daily; 2hr 15min); Narbonne (daily; 1hr 55min); Port-Vendres (3–6 daily; 55min); Prades (3–7 daily; 1hr); Prats-de-Molló (5 daily; 1hr 40min); Quillan (2–5 daily; 1hr 30min); St-Génis (Mon–Sat 4 daily; 45min); St-Laurent-de-Cerdans (3 daily; 1hr 45min); St-Paul-le-Fenouillet (2–4 daily; 1hr); Salses (Mon–Sat 4 daily; 15min); Tautavel (1–3 daily; 30–40min); Thuir (3–5 daily; 25min); Vernet (4 daily; 1hr 30min); Villefranche-le-Conflent (7 daily; 1hr 15min).

**Argelès** to: Céret (1–4 daily; 1hr); St-Genis (Wed 2 daily; 22min).

**Arles-sur-Tech** to: Coustouges (1 daily; 40min); Prats-de-Molló (3–5 daily; 15min).

**Mont-Louis** to: Formiguères (2–4 daily; 30min)

**Villefranche-de-Conflent** to: Prades (7 daily; 10min); Vernet-les-Bains (7 daily; 10min).

# PART THREE

# CONTEXTS

# THE HISTORICAL FRAMEWORK

The two areas of Occitan Languedoc and Catalan Roussillon, in addition to having their own cultural particularities, present strong historical differences. Languedoc was traditionally ruled by a native aristocracy, while Roussillon fell into the ambit of Catalonia, fated to become part of modern Spain. Even before they were integrated into the nation-state of France, though, their geographical proximity ensured that their pasts had parallels and connections; each enjoyed its "golden age" in the Middle Ages, which may account for the nostalgia with which the inhabitants regard these periods, and their shared borders saw considerable movement and contact.

## PREHISTORY

The earliest traces of the human occupation of Languedoc and Roussillon date back to the early **Paleolithic era** (Stone Age): the cranial remains of the slight but upright *homo erectus*, discovered in the 1970s at Tautavel, near Perpignan, date back nearly half a million years. These early ancestors, who do not appear to have harnessed fire, hunted with the aid of simple stone weapons and tools and lived off the abundant (and dangerous) fauna of the region,

which included wolves, hippos, rhinos, wild sheep and goats, and the ferocious cave bear, whose claw marks are still visible on cave walls in the region (for example at Limousis, in the Montagne Noire). As the evolutionary tree branched off, taller and smarter **Neanderthal** humans appeared, dominating the local scene during the mid-Paleolithic era (approximately 150,000–35,000 BC). With a better tool-making capability than *homo erectus*, the Neanderthals were able to pursue the mammoth and elephants of the Languedocian plain, and the remains of burial places scattered about the Pyrenean foothills dating from this time point to the beginnings of culture and religion.

It was not until the late Paleolithic era that **modern humans** (*homo sapiens*) came to dominate the area, thriving especially in the Magdelanian period, some 14,000 years ago, which followed the last retreat of the glaciers. The earliest **cave paintings** of the Ariège valley (at Niaux and Mas d'Azil) date from this period and show the preoccupation of this early people with the hunt. In addition to cave art, they fashioned the small corpulent "Venus" statuettes which are generally considered to relate to fertility rites.

With the invention of the harpoon, the development of fishing began to draw people towards the coasts of modern Roussillon. Nevertheless, the mid-altitude caves remained the favoured habitat into the Mesolothic and Neolithic (new Stone Age) periods, which lasted here until about 1500 BC. Several important innovations occurred in the Neolithic era: **agriculture** and **animal husbandry** came into being in the fifth-millennium BC, as did the use of grain storage facilities. **Mining** and smelting were developed for the crude utilization of metals, and better management of fire also permitted the manufacture of ceramics. Technical improvements encouraged specialization and this, in turn, trade, which seems to have first arisen among the lowland settlements of the Narbonnais plain. It was also in the last millennium of the Stone Age that the **dolmens** (Megalithic henges) and **tumuli** (burial mounds) which dot the mid-level Pyrenees and Haut Languedoc appeared.

## THE BRONZE AGE

The Bronze Age in Languedoc and Roussillon was one of great movement and change.

Around 800 BC the **Celts** arrived and began displacing the indigenous peoples, and an area roughly analogous with modern Languedoc – stretching from Nîmes in the east past Toulouse in the west – came under the hegemony of the Volcae, one of several large Celtic tribal groups who dominated the South of France. Meanwhile, **Phoenicians** and **Greeks** began to arrive on the region's shores. They set up outposts (such as Maguelone and Port-Vendres) and began to trade with natives, who lived for the most part in fortified hill-top towns now known as **oppida** (plural of the Latin *oppidum*, or "town"), like the settlement of Enserune. As archeological finds have confirmed, the native tribes were not uncivilized "barbarians" as Romans were later wont to claim, but participants in complex, technologically capable societies linked to extensive trade networks. Their rich culture is evinced by the objects which have survived them: skilfully worked bronze weapons and jewellery. Although perhaps not comparable with contemporary civilizations of the eastern Mediterranean, they had their own diversified agricultural and craft-based economies and stratified social structures. Their one weakness was that they were not oriented towards the sea and so needed intermediaries like the Phoenicians to reach foreign markets.

## THE ROMANS

In the fourth-century BC, the **Romans** embarked on a series of campaigns of conquest which brought the whole Iberian peninsula and the bulk of Greek possessions under its power and set it against the **Carthaginians**, heirs of Phoenicia in the western Mediterranean. The Romans were the ultimate victors, and the futile rumble of **Hannibal**'s elephants across the length of Languedoc in 218 BC presaged the beginning of a long colonial period in southern France. A few decades later the **Via Domitia**, the Rome–Cadiz superhighway, was built along the Languedoc coast, facilitating Roman military and economic expansion, and the Roman city of Narbo was founded – by about 70 BC all of what is now France south of Lyon and Toulouse constituted Narbonnensian Gaul. With the completion of the conquest by **Julius Caesar** and his successor the Emperor **Augustus**, the zone was elevated to the rank of an Imperial Province, and severed (in 27 BC), so

that Narbonne became the capital of the lands from the Rhône to the Pyrenees.

Enjoying the benefits of *pax Romana*, the region enjoyed an easy prosperity under the first emperors. Trade (wine was a big export) flourished and there were major settlements at Baeterra (Béziers) and Nemauses (Nîmes). Nîmes became the region's most important city under Antoninus Pius in the mid-second century – an emperor who lavished favours on his home town. During this period, Roman organizational infrastructure and slave labour permitted the elaboration of architectural projects of a scale and complexity which were not to be duplicated for fifteen hundred years. This is particularly true in the case of public civic architecture, such as Nîmes' huge amphitheatre, **Les Arènes**, the nearby aqueduct, the **Pont du Gard**, and the **bridge** at Sommières. Religious buildings, the finest surviving example of which is Nîmes' **Maison Carrée**, were constructed based on Greek styles – temples usually consisting of a *cella* or inner sanctum (the abode of the god), ringed by a colonnade of columns which were topped by decorative capitals. Less grandiose remains of civic and residential structures can be found at Mèze and Enserune, along the length of the Via Domitia. The cities and settlements of Roman Languedoc-Roussillon have yielded a wealth of intricate mosaics and Roman-style civic and religious statuary.

But there were rocky times ahead for the empire, as the expansion on which its prosperity had depended slowed. Domestic economic crises were compounded by the growing threat of neighbouring powers: Persia in the east, and "barbarians" in North Africa and northwest Europe. While the frontiers under attack by **Franks** and **Goths** were far from Languedoc, the disruption of the empire's stability had economic repercussions which reached Narbonensis. The growing dissatisfaction and malaise in the empire encouraged a certain trend towards new religions such as the Mithra cult and **Christianity**, which spread rapidly through urban Languedoc. The latter was seen as a threat to the imperial order and a series of emperors set about trying to quash it. The most fierce persecutions, which saw Christians submitted to all manner of brutal public tortures and executions, were carried out under Valerian and Diocletian between 257 and 311 – many of the area's martyred saints date from this era.

When **Constantine the Great** came to the throne in 324, he proclaimed Christianity a tolerated religion and it quickly took hold in the towns and cities of Languedoc. With the capital of the Empire now in far off Constantinople, the bishops, who were appointed in each Roman town after 391, helped hold together the decaying fabric of administration. In the new contracting, Christianized empire, Nîmes and Narbonne waned as Roman cities in Provence, like Arles, came to the forefront. But great changes were afoot, and as central power declined, people left the cities, taking refuge in smaller fortified towns and villas, and frequently trading off their liberty for the protection of a powerful patron. Imperial policy in the east was to deflect the waves of semi-nomadic steppe peoples westward, a tactic which saved the core of the empire, but brought about its disappearance in the west.

## AFTER THE ROMANS

In the fifth century wave after wave of these small but aggressive invading bands passed through Languedoc and Roussillon, first the Suevi, then the Vandals and finally the **Visigoths**. It was the last of these who set up a durable kingdom, which in its greatest extent covered the southwest of France and most of Iberia. Their first capital was **Tolosa** – modern Toulouse – and they initially ruled as Roman Imperial governors. At this time, however, a rival group, the **Franks**, had coalesced in the Low countries and, led by King Clovis (482–511), drove southwards, incorporating Toulouse into the kingdom of Aquitaine. Most of Languedoc and Roussillon, however, known then as **Septimania** (after its seven great cities: Narbonne, Agde, Béziers, Maguelone, Lodève, Nîmes and Uzès), remained under the Visigoths.

The weak and conflictive Visigothic kingdom was dealt a death blow by **Muslim armies**, which arrived in Spain around 711. Wiping out the nobility in a single battle, they quickly conquered most of Iberia, and small raiding parties crossed the Pyrenees, taking Toulouse and Septimania in the 720s. The most northern of these groups was turned back near Poitiers by Charles Martel in 732. Numerically too few to hang on to such an extensive area, the Muslims occupied the towns, exacting tribute and using them as raiding bases. In the years that

followed the battle of Poitiers the Muslims were turned out of Toulouse, Carcassonne and eventually their coastal enclaves – it was to prevent their return that Martel destroyed the town of Maguelone (see p.261) – until one by one these fell to the Franks. This long campaign was carried out under the leadership of **Pepin the Short**, the first Carolingian king (751–68), and it was his successor, **Charlemagne** (Charles the Great), who pushed Muslim power back over the Pyrenees. Languedoc was absorbed into the **Frankish Empire** and Roussillon became part of the semi-autonomous frontier region known as the **Spanish Marches**. After the decline of Roman power in the West, the Empire continued in the East, but despite the fact that Constantinople was now its capital its rulers continued to bear the title of Emperor of Rome. During Charlemagne's era it so happened that it was a woman, Irene, who was in power; seeing an opportunity to enhance his prestige – given that no one actually held the title of Emperor – Charlemagne journeyed to Rome and had the Pope crown him as "Holy Roman Emperor" in 800. Thus his dominions, which covered almost all of Western Europe, came to be known as the **Holy Roman Empire**, and the papacy, which up till then had been little more than an ordinary bishopric, gained justification for its later claims to be the power which could (or not) crown emperors.

## THE COUNTS AND FEUDALISM

Despite his centralizing policies, Charlemagne followed Germanic custom, separating his kingdom among his heirs, and Languedoc fell into the **Kingdom of the Western Franks**, more or less contiguous with modern France. When its second king, Louis the Stammerer, died heirless in 879 the kingdom rapidly disintegrated, leaving power in the hands of local **counts**, although nominally Charlemagne's other descendants held the highest authorities. Among the local nobility, one family, the **"Raymonds"** or "dynasty of St-Gilles", eventually came to dominate. They had ruled Toulouse since 840, thanks to a grant by Pepin II, and by the late 900s, they were to all intents and purposes independent rulers. As such, they began to expand, absorbing neighbouring territories, such as Albi, or co-opting other lesser noble lines, such as the **Trencavels** of Carcassonne, as vassals. **Raymond IV** ruled a realm which stretched from Toulouse to the banks of the Rhône; it was he who adopted the surname of "St-Gilles", in honour of his favourite possession. Meanwhile, the most powerful lord of the Spanish March, **Guifré el Pelós** ("Wilfred the Hairy"), count of the Cerdagne, Girona and Barcelona, was granted independence from the Empire. Roussillon, then dominated by Elne, came under his power; it is at this point that Languedoc and Roussillon's histories as separate regions begin – over the course of the centuries that followed their paths would be linked, but not united again until Louis XIV's formal annexation of Roussillon in the 1600s.

In these early medieval centuries, what little industry and urban life existed under the Romans all but disappeared. Western Europe became overwhelmingly agrarian, developing an economy of near subsistence in which the noble class siphoned off the meagre surplus and provided military protection to the masses. Local magnates depended on military strength to maintain their power and protect their subjects, obtaining warriors by granting lands in exchange for loyalty, and **feudal** structures developed. Religion too was a largely private and local affair: the nobles built churches and monasteries and put them under the charge of their friends and relatives, who lived comfortably off the income from these posts. The common folk continued to depend as much on traditional pre-Christian beliefs and magic – just as well, since most local priests knew no more than a smattering of Church Latin and were not particularly exemplary in their moral life. Learned culture too all but vanished with the disappearance of towns, and was maintained only by the monks who lived in isolated communities – fortresses of faith, hidden in isolated valleys and on remote mountainsides.

## TWELFTH-CENTURY REVIVAL

In the twelfth century the picture began to change rapidly. A shift away from subsistence, possibly as the result of climatic change and aided by improvements in agricultural technology, allowed the population to grow, while under the counts the region began to enjoy a stability which stimulated **trade** and **industry**. People started to move around Europe looking for better opportunities; towns expanded, shaking Toulouse and the cities of Septimania back to

life. The agrarian social structures which had developed in the previous period were not suitable to town life, and the counts, anxious to promote economic growth, recognized that by extending liberties and privileges to the burghers, their own position could be improved. Oligarchic **town councils** such as the **Capitolo** in Toulouse were formed, sharing in or taking over urban administration and further stimulating growth.

Changes were afoot in the Church as well: the papacy was in the process of becoming a geopolitical power, initiating a level of bureaucracy and organization which would give them control of the resources and policies of local churches – traditionally the turf of the nobles. Some efforts were made to improve the priesthood too – to ensure that priests were educated and lived, at least in appearance, morally upright lives. On the popular level, **pilgrimage** played an important role, carrying ordinary believers across Europe, to Rome or Santiago de Compostela – along the way they visited local churches such as that at St-Gilles and came in contact with a larger Christian world. A wave of reformation also swept over the **monasteries**, where the degenerate and locally independent Benedictines were replaced by new, pious and strict orders, most importantly the Cistercians, who were controlled by a strong central organization.

With all of this new wealth, secular and religious culture began to revive. Great churches were raised in the towns, and old cathedrals were replaced by new, more grandiose and elaborate structures. The courts of the counts' palaces became the focus of a new culture as well, one which sought refinement in elaborate manners, rich clothes and imported luxuries – **courtly traditions**. The most visible manifestation of the new culture was the tradition of courtly love and the **troubadours**. These singing poets – the first of whom is said to have been the Guilhem de Peitieu, count of Poitiers and father of Eleanor of Aquitaine, Queen of England – composed odes of yearning, unrequited love to anonymous "dark ladies". Their language of choice was not Latin, which had previously been the only voice of culture, but the local vernaculars, Occitan and Catalan. It was also in this era that the rites and rituals associated with feudalism, such as heraldry and the tournament, began to be formalized –

precisely when the feudal world began to decline.

However, with this period of revival came a greater demand for fulfilment, directed at the Church from just about every corner. The newly wealthy and increasingly literate craftsmen, the **burghers**, who had no role to play in the warrior-aristocratic culture of the court – wanted a level of political power and social prestige which reflected their economic standing and, better educated, began to look for more satisfying theological answers than the still feudal-oriented Church could provide. Town life generated new social problems, particularly among the urban poor, which the Church – effectively a social welfare organization in the countryside – was not equipped to address. The peasants too were dissatisfied; although increasingly interested in Christianity, a shortage of priests meant they were frustrated by a lack of pastoral care. In short, the Church was seen as **corrupt** by everyone but the nobility, a situation aggravated by the taxes which people were forced to pay to support it. In addition, Latin, once the only accepted sacred language – preserving the mystery of the Church – now acted to cut off the faith from the common folk.

Although their religious consciousness was high, as local nobles, such as the Crusader Raymond of St-Gilles, distinguished themselves by reclaiming the Holy Land from the Muslim "infidels", the upper classes in Languedoc began to find themselves turning against the Church too, but for a different reason: the nobility considered it their natural privilege to control local institutions, including bishoprics, parishes and monasteries and, unconcerned by the theological preferences of their subjects as long as they continued to pay their taxes, resented papal expansionism as a threat to their own power.

In the meantime, neighbouring Roussillon, though it went through most of the same social and economic processes as Languedoc, followed a distinctive political and religious course. In the centuries following Guifré el Pelós, his descendants, the **Counts of Barcelona** had been struggling to gain supremacy over their various rival counts in Catalonia, who did not want to recognize them as superior. They were aided in this campaign in 1142 when Ramon Berenguer IV married the princess of Aragon, obtaining the title of king of

Aragon for his heirs. Thus Barcelona became the capital of a multinational monarchy and its rulers, the count-kings, were to become one of the great powers of the medieval Mediterranean. Linked by ties of marriage to noble houses in Languedoc and further east in Provence, they angled for political expansion, and for a time their holdings included Montpellier and various parts east of the Rhône. Indeed the Counts of Toulouse became their vassals – although this represented a formality and amounted to a pact of mutual assistance rather than a recognition of the count-kings' authority.

## CATHARISM AND THE ALBIGENSIAN CRUSADES

In the climate of dissatisfaction with the Church popular **heresies** began to spring up, led by men who preached to the people in their own language and led lives of austerity and poverty, in emulation of the Apostles and in contrast to the wealthy and aloof Catholic clergy. The Church tried at first to quash the problem with force, but then, co-opting the impulses which drove the heretics, licensed two new groups, the Dominican and Franciscan preaching friars who – in contrast to isolated monks – were to minister and preach among the common people. But the damage had already been done and the most successful of the new heresies, **Catharism** (see pp.138–139), had become firmly ingrained. This religion was a variant of ancient mid-Eastern beliefs combined with Christianity, a dualistic creed which portrayed the material world as evil and the spiritual world as good. It resonated among the common folk (who appreciated its populism) and nobles (who wanted to set themselves apart from the influence of Rome and its northern French political allies), and a shadow counter-Church began to organize itself, holding its first Council at St-Félix in 1167. In most of the major towns of Languedoc, and the countryside around Toulouse and south of the Aude this new Church gained a strong presence. Here, the nobility, including the Counts of Toulouse, the Trencavels of Carcassonne and a whole array of minor barons remained Catholic themselves, but gave free reign to Cathar preachers to spread their religious message. As Roussillon did not develop an urban society as quickly as Languedoc and the count-kings' had a more favourable political attitude to the papacy, Catharism was discouraged from gaining a strong hold here. Preachers and refugees did arrive in Catalan lands, but they could not live openly in their faith, for fear of persecution.

By the end of the 1100s the Catholic Church had become a powerful corporation, and it was not about to brook the loss of Languedoc to the heretic Cathars – or **Albigensians**, as they are commonly known. When persuasion failed to convert the heretics or influence the Cathar-protecting lords of Languedoc, and excommunication had little effect, the papacy turned to military force. Although it hardly had a formal army, the papacy could count on the support of powerful multinational monastic organizations such as the Cistercian Order, whose headquarters, Cîteaux, was in Northern France, and which was dominated by noble families from the north. These same families, which had been united under the Capetian kings of France, began to look with hungry eyes at the extensive but fragmented lands of the counts to the south. Papal efforts to bring the Cathars back into the fold began as early as 1150, and in 1204 **Raymond IV** of Toulouse was excommunicated for refusing to persecute his Cathar subjects. However, the Albigensians and their lords would not cave in – the papal legate Pierre de Castelnau was murdered at a parley in 1208 – and **Pope Innocent III** called a Crusade, providing the northern nobles with the ideological justification to wage war on Languedoc. They were joined by knights from across Christendom, drawn by the allure of religious redemption and loot.

The campaign was led initially by **Arnaud Amaury**, abbot of Cîteaux, whose campaigns carried him rapidly across the littoral from Nîmes, which gave up without a fight, to Béziers. Here, faced by the refusal of the town's Catholics to give up their Cathar neighbours, he ordered the wholesale slaughter of the town's occupants; some 20,000 are said to have perished.

At about this time, the ageing Crusader **Simon de Montfort** set his sights on the Cathar lands and, taking up leadership of military operation, embarked on a campaign marked by its terror and efficiency. Carcassonne was taken, and with it **Count Raymond VI**; thereafter Cathar towns and fortresses were besieged one by one, including Lastours,

Minerve, Hautpoul, Lavaur, Termes and Puivert. Almost without exception they fell or surrendered, and the unfortunate defenders were executed or mutilated and sent on as blunt warning to the next victims; the only survivors were those on the inaccessible southern border: Quérigut, Peyrepertuse, and Montségur.

After a brief exile in England **Raymond VII** returned to lead a counterattack, calling on the aid of various allies, including his liege-lord **Pere el Catòlic**, count-king of Catalonia-Aragon. Fresh from a decisive victory against Spanish Muslims, Pere went into the field at Muret (14km south of Toulouse) in 1213, but was singled out and killed by de Montfort's men, dealing a grievous blow to Raymond's forces.

It took five more years of fighting to turn the tide against the northern forces, who were deprived of their leader de Montfort (who had assumed the title of Count of Toulouse), when his head was smashed in by a missile outside the walls of Toulouse. His son Arnaud attempted to carry on the campaign, but could not sustain his position and returned back to his lands in the north, carrying with him his father's dead body and broken dreams. After this long, drawn out battle, Raymond had no choice but to make **peace** with the papacy in order to recover his lands, reaffirming his Catholicism and recovering his scarred and battered territories. These he began immediately to fortify, founding strategic strongholds such as Cordes-sur-Ciel.

However, despite Raymond's concessions and preparations Occitan **independence** was not to last – by the mid-1220s the French king, **Louis VIII**, swelled by victories over the English Crown, turned his own sights south, proclaiming a fresh Crusade against the Occitan Cathars, who continued to live discreetly in Raymond's lands, or openly under the defiant and unconquered barons of the south. This time the exhausted forces of the counts and local nobility could not respond, and after a brief campaign much of Languedoc came under the direct power of the king of France. Louis VIII's aggressive policy was followed up by his heir, Louis IX (later St Louis), who came to the throne in 1226 and finished off the job. With the counts out of the way, the papacy sent in the **Inquisition**, led by the Dominican Order. Their job was to investigate and root out heretics, employing torture if necessary, and urging them to recant before turning them over to the king's forces to execute. Needless to say, they were not popular among the local citizenry, and it was greeted with some relief when a band of renegade Cathars sallied out of their stronghold at Montségur in 1242 to **massacre** a band of Inquisitors. The royal reaction was immediate: an army of six thousand was assembled and laid siege to the fortress. Six months later, when it fell, the garrison of two hundred were burnt alive. Subsequent mopping-up operations finished with the surrenders of Puilaurens and Quéribus in 1256. Catharism had disappeared as a political force and, confined to secrecy and isolation, was hunted into extinction over the next century.

But royal policy was not wholly destructive in Languedoc, as its aim was not to lay waste to the region but to extinguish possible sources of rebellion and resistance. From the time of de Montfort's death, the kings had worked to rehabilitate the area, particularly through the founding of royal **bastides**, such as Revel and Réalmont. These planned and usually fortified towns were set up by royal charter. Ruled by a council they answered directly to the king rather than to an intermediary noble, and were given privileges such as the right to hold a market. Thus, they strengthened the royal position and, with their liberties and self-determination, helped to boost the economy.

On the fringes of Languedoc, mountainous **Foix**, like Toulouse, had been an independent county since about the time of the Carolingian disintegration. Over the following centuries, it remained isolated, even more than Roussillon, from the modernizing trends which were shaping Languedoc. That said, the Counts of Foix were sworn enemies of the French Crown and allied themselves with the Raymonds during the Albigensian Crusade; in the campaigns that followed, the county managed to escape more or less unscathed, and when the French Crown threatened in the 1270s, the ruling house eluded their control by forging a marriage alliance with the neighbouring kingdom of Béarn.

Except for the loss in battle of the count-king Pere, **Roussillon**, too, all but escaped the effects of the Albigensian Crusades. The death of Pere, and the period of uncertainty that followed, when his five-year-old son, Jaume, was made king, entailed the end of any Catalan-Aragonese pretensions in Provence, as the French Crown had a long breathing period in which to consolidate its power there. Roussillon, however, remained for the moment firmly in the Catalan-Aragonese ambit, and its nobility was drawn towards the campaigns of conquest which the count-kings carried out against their Muslim neighbours (Valencia, Mallorca and Menorca), Sardinia and Sicily. When **Jaume the Conqueror** died after a 63-year reign he divided his kingdom between his elder son Pere (who received the mainland holdings south of the Pyrenees) and Jaume, who became **King of Mallorca** and Count of Roussillon and Montpellier. Perpignan served as his mainland capital. The kings of Mallorca allied with the French against their Barcelona-based rivals, and in the 1280s Roussillon served as the springboard for the French invasion of Catalonia, launched in retribution for Catalan seizure of French-ruled Sicily.

## THE HUNDRED YEARS' WAR

Under **Philip the Bel** (1285–1314) France became a superpower. The astute king managed his treasury well, disbanded and appropriated the funds of the wealthy Knights Templar and brought the papacy under his ominous protection in Avignon.

But the royal domination of Languedoc brought only short-lived peace and prosperity to the region. Philip died childless, and Edward III of England, who had married Philip's daughter, claimed the throne. Edward's family, the Plantagenets, were French in origin, and the language and culture of their court was northern French, but the prospect of Edward taking the throne was highly undesireable to a large section of the French nobility, who stood to see themselves marginalized by such a turn of events. So they invoked the ancient French Salic Law, which forbade succession to the throne through the female line, and resisted the English claim. These were the circumstances which provoked the series of wars which came to be known as the **Hundred Years' War** – essentially a struggle between two French royal houses.

England took the early advantage, defeating the French at Crécy in 1346 and capturing the French king shortly after. Meanwhile, the king's son, Edward, the Prince of Wales (known as the **Black Prince**), was unleashed on Aquitaine and ravaged the Aude valley. These military campaigns coincided with a series of disasters, including **crop failures**, the arrival of the **Black Death** and the Jacquerie peasant uprising. In 1360 a **truce** was called and part of western Languedoc remained under English control until nine years later, when **Charles V** began a campaign which all but expelled the English from France.

Unfortunately Charles' successor, **Charles VI**, was considered mentally unfit to rule, and a struggle ensued between the dukes of Burgundy and Orléans, who had been entrusted with the care of the realm. The English intervened on the side of the Burgundians, against the Duke of Orléans and his Armagnac allies, and began to reconquer the country. After a series of defeats, including Agincourt in 1415, all seemed lost for the French crown. It was then that **Joan of Arc** appeared, and helped to turn the tide against the invaders. Five years later, Charles VII entered Toulouse in triumph, once again master of Languedoc, and although the reconquest of the former royal territories dragged out over the length of the fifteenth century, France emerged from the struggle as a unified, powerful nation-state.

In this protracted period of **crisis**, the people of Languedoc coped as best they could. Population decreased, agriculture suffered and traditional industries, such as leather-working, which accounted for the prosperity of the Tarn region, were almost extinguished. However, in the mid-fifteenth century it was discovered that a local plant, **woad**, could be made to yield a fine blue dye, *pastel* – a high-priced luxury commodity much in demand by the fabric industry of the day – provoking an economic renaissance which lasted for over a century. Toulouse, still ruled over by a council of burghers, took the lead in this industry. Fortunes were made, fine palaces were raised, and the city's famous university was founded, turning Toulouse into a centre of culture. On the Occitan coast, Montpellier (which had been bought by the French crown in 1349) was also driven by the growing textile industry and set up its own prestigious university.

As had happened with the Albigensian Crusade, Catalonia was not involved directly in the Hundred Years' War, but did have to contend with France's relentless efforts to chip away at its holdings north of the Pyrenees, Cerdanya and Rosilló (the **Cerdagne** and **Roussillon**), and through the fourteenth and fifteenth

centuries, they were shifted back and forth between the two powers. In 1462, when **Louis XI** mounted a military campaign against Roussillon – seizing it in response to the Catalan-Aragonese capture of French-dominated Naples, Catalonia was on the verge of a major realignment. The marriage of Ferran (Ferdinand) of Aragon and Isabel of Castile in 1469 laid the foundations for the creation of Spain, and the ultimate submission of Catalonia and its dependencies to Madrid; it thus became a secondary concern, and Roussillon was set further on the periphery.

## THE RISE OF PROTESTANTISM AND THE WARS OF RELIGION

Despite the peace which came with re-establishment of a strong monarchy in France under **François I** (1515–47), there was much dissatisfaction in Languedoc and Roussillon. This resentment took two forms: that towards the Church on the part of the people, and that towards the Crown and the northern nobility on the part of local lords and magnates. As had happened in the Cathar period the interests of these two groups coincided, and even more so after 1483, when the Crown gained direct control over the church in France. So social and political discontent once again was voiced on religious terms – this time the revolutionary movement was **Protestantism**.

The new faith first arrived in Haut Languedoc close on the heels of **Martin Luther**'s defiance of Church authority in 1519. However, French Protestantism, or the **Huguenot** movement (named after an obscure Swiss political event), tended to follow the teachings of **John Calvin** (Jean Cauvin), which had a clearer political message. Calvin had studied theology at the conservative University of Paris and had been swept up in the wave of reforming theology which very quickly provoked a clampdown by the religious and royal authorities. He fled into exile in Geneva, which became a hotbed for the Protestant creed that he formulated. His beliefs focused on the omnipotence of God, denying hierarchies and earthly elites and concentrating on hard work and pastoralism – a recipe for success among the artisanal classes – and it spread like wildfire in Paris and through Occitania.

By 1559 **Calvanism** was established as a religion and organization in France, and had the support of some of the kingdom's greatest noble houses, despite the persecution which had been carried out by François I's son Henri II. When Henri died (in an accident allegedly presaged by Nostradamus), the succession of two weak child kings gave the rival **noble factions** led by the Protestant Bourbons and the Catholic Guises the opportunity to battle for control of the realm. Forty years of bloody and relentless civil war followed, of which the most famous episode is 1572's **St Bartholemew's Day massacre**, in which the Protestant elite, who had come to Paris for a royal wedding, were ambushed. A nationwide campaign against Protestants ensued, during which some 20,000 were killed. The violence was not all one-sided, however: the Calvinists committed atrocities as well, among them the murder of Nîmes' Catholic clergy in 1567's **Michelade massacre**.

The wars were concluded by the victory of Henri, King of Béarn (or Navarre), the leader of the Protestant faction. It was, however, politically impossible for him to become king as a Huguenot, so having decided that "Paris is worth a Mass", he converted and was crowned as **Henri IV** of France in 1593. Thanks to his ascension, Foix was incorporated in the French Crown. Six years later he proclaimed the **Edict of Nantes**, which granted political and religious freedom and the right to maintain certain fortified strongholds.

Although most of Languedoc had been ruled by the Catholic Guises, its population was strongly Protestant. Castres became a "protected zone" for Huguenots, and home to one of the four **courts** empowered to mediate legal disputes between Catholics and Protestants. In Nîmes, some three quarters of the population converted to Calvinism, while Montpellier was home to the Protestant Theological Institute. In the East most of the towns – mainly herding and textile centres – were firmly Huguenot but, despite regional imbalances, the new pluralistic French society seemed to function well.

## THE AGE OF ABSOLUTISM

The liberal vision of Henri was not to last, however. When he was assassinated by a Catholic reactionary, his year-old son **Louis XIII** came to the throne under the strict control of his staunchly Catholic mother, Marie de Medici. In 1624, that supreme Machiavellian **Cardinal Richelieu** managed to wrest control from the queen. Richelieu made it his mission to establish France as an absolutist Catholic state, and for almost two decades he was the sole power behind the Crown. He immediately set about stripping the towns and cities of their defensive walls (to prevent revolt) and then began reducing Protestant strongholds. He also adopted an aggressive foreign policy, attacking France's neighbours, and taking Roussillon. But his heavy-handedness provoked reaction at home. In 1622 the Protestant Duke de Rohan raised a **revolt** in the Cévennes (just north of the Hérault) and although after seven years of fighting he was forced to make a settlement with Richelieu, which stripped the Huguenots of political power, he maintained their freedom to worship.

Heavily Protestant Languedoc was not pacified, however, and shortly thereafter its royal governor, Henry, **Duke of Montmorency**, raised a revolt against Richelieu which spanned the region from Nîmes to Toulouse. He was no match for the cardinal, who defeated him in battle at Castelnaudary in 1632 and led him off to be beheaded on the Place du Capitoule in Toulouse. The vindictive Richelieu then exacted revenge on Henry's heirs by transferring the title of First Duchy of France to the loyally Catholic Dukes of Uzès.

In 1643, the "Sun King" and supreme absolutist **Louis XIV** came to the throne. Continuing the centralizing policies initiated by Richelieu, he hamstrung the French nobility by obliging them to take up residence at his palace in Versailles and to participate in its expensive and regimented court life. His megalomaniac tendencies ("I am the state") led him to embark on a series of costly and ultimately disastrous military adventures, the successful episodes of which are recorded on the Roman-style monuments, such as the equestrian statue and triumphal arch of Montpellier, which he erected to commemorate his grandeur. He waged **war** in Flanders, Germany and Spain, managing to secure the permanent annexation of La Cerdagne and Roussillon with the **Treaty of the Pyrenees** in 1659.

The able management of his successive prime ministers, Mazarin and Colbert, managed to preserve the kingdom from financial ruin, and it was Colbert who gave the green light to Riquet's visionary project of linking the Atlantic and Mediterranean by canal. The main channel of the **Canal du Midi**, which stretched from Toulouse to Agde, was opened in 1666, provoking an economic recovery in the region, which had languished in depression since the wane in demand for local dye (thanks to the discovery of cheaper alternatives in the Indies); the canal allowed locally grown grain to be shipped to distant markets. But on the whole, Louis' reign was not a happy one for Languedoc and Roussillon. In 1674, the **Catalans** rose up against French rule, which they found even more oppressive than that of the Spanish Habsburgs, against whom they had risen a generation earlier. The **uprising** was brutally crushed, and its leaders imprisoned and executed in Perpignan.

A decade later, Louis moved against the Protestants by issuing a **Revocation of the Edict of Nantes** (1685), which deprived the Huguenots of their rights and outlawed their religion. Half a million Protestants chose to flee the country, including many merchants and textile workers, dealing a grievous blow to the industry on which the prosperity of eastern Languedoc depended. Those who remained were subjected to **oppression**; they were spied on and hounded, forced to carry on their services in secret and brook the humiliation of having soldiers billeted in their homes. Intransigent Protestants were imprisoned, among them Marie Durand, locked up for over thirty years in a tower in Aigues-Mortes. Some feigned conversion, some were deported to the colonies, and others fled to the "desert" – the wild and isolated hills of the Cévennes. It was here that they rose again in protest, in what is known as the **Camisard revolt**. The spark came in July 1702 when the parish priest of Chayla arrested and detained a small group of fugitive Protestants. A group of villagers stormed the castle to free them and in the course of the struggle the priest was killed. Knowing that retribution would be swift and cruel, Protestants across the Cévennes (mostly refugees from Languedoc proper) began a guerrilla war which pitted their forces, numbering between three and five thousand, against some 30,000 royal troops. The shirts they wore as a sign of recognition earned them the popular name of Camisards (from *chemise*, French for "shirt"). Battles raged across the region, with one of the greatest confrontations taking place

at **St-Hippolyte**. The guerrillas and civilian population took refuge where they could, hiding in the remote hills or in caverns, like the Grotte des Demoiselles, south of Ganges.

In the course of the struggle two leaders emerged: the aristocratic **Jean Cavalier**, and the commoner **Roland**. Unable to conclude the struggle militarily, the French commander Villars began to negotiate with Cavalier at Nîmes, offering him the rank of colonel, command of a Protestant legion which would fight for the French abroad, and a hefty annual salary in exchange for submission. Cavalier accepted, greatly harming the uprising. The former leader left France and served the English, eventually being named governor of Jersey. Roland continued the struggle, but later the same year was killed in battle, bringing an end to the revolt.

In the century or so that the episode of the Camisards Languedoc had been tamed into discontented submission by France, ruled by the princes of Conti, members of the ruling Bourbon family, since the defeat of Montmorency. Pézenas, which had been the region's capital since the 1450s, became a paler southern Versailles, especially in the 1650s when **Armand de Bourbon** lavished the town with his patronage, playing host for a time to the playwright Molière and his company.

The absorption of Roussillon, while it aggrandized France, struck a blow against the towns of the Aude valley, which up to then had enjoyed a trade-based prosperity thanks to their position on the Spanish frontier. As part of Madrid's empire, in which Church institutions like the Inquisition kept a very tight lid on any potential sources of dissent or heterodoxy, Protestantism was basically unknown in Roussillon during its efflorescence, and by the time of the region's annexation, it was virtually a spent force.

## THE REVOLUTION

Languedoc and Roussillon were not the only areas which chafed against the Sun King's absolutism. As the **economic crisis** deepened, taxes were driven up, forcing the masses of the kingdom, the *sans-culottes* ("trouserless"), into an ever more desperate state of poverty. A series of bad harvests compounded the problem, and indebted smallholders had their lands repossessed and were reduced to penury and near servitude. In order to gather the revenue which was necessary to maintain the court, fund expensive military adventures and service the spiralling national debt, **tax-farming** was resorted to. Speculators paid the Crown a set sum upfront and then were free to extract as much as they could from the area under their control. This excluded most of the nobility, many of whom enjoyed hereditary exemptions, and the largest single land-holder, the Church, which paid no royal taxes and continued to collect its own. At the same time, the Crown's growing obsession with control bred a fear of rebellion, which became self-fulfilling. Law was completely subverted to royal authority, and suspected troublemakers were imprisoned indefinitely without charges, by writ of the feared letters of cachet, or orders of detention.

These **dictatorial** tendencies worsened over the course of the eighteenth century, as Louis XIV's successors continued his absolutist style of ruling and his disastrous policy of foreign intervention. **Louis XV** (1715–74) carried France into the Polish and Austrian Wars of Succession and the Seven Years' War, as a result of which the kingdom lost all of its colonies. Ironically the king also encouraged the incredible literary and philosophical blossoming, in which Voltaire and Rousseau figured among others, that laid the philosophical foundations for the Revolution which was shortly to follow.

Poor grain harvests continued after Louis XV's death in 1774, provoking riots and unrest. Royal finance ministers attempted to institute reforms, but to little avail. In Languedoc, the new king Louis XVI's conciliatory policies were chiefly noted in the form of the **Edict of Toleration** (1787), which was aimed at diffusing the rebelliousness of the Protestants by restoring their rights and liberties. The situation was such that the king was forced in 1789 to summon the Estates General (the equivalent of Parliament) for the first time in nearly two centuries. The newly consisted Third Estate, made up of commoners, who for the first time joined the nobility and clergy in governing, called for the formation of a National Assembly.

When in the months that followed the country rose in **revolution**, Languedoc and Roussillon were solidly Jacobin (revolutionary). Even Montpellier, at that time a wealthy bastion of Catholicism and cotton-lords, could not resist. In 1791, the French Republic was declared and as southern troop levies marched towards the capital a young medical student from Montpellier composed the "War Song of the Army of the Rhine", better known as **La Marseillaise**, which was adopted eventually as the national anthem. The Revolution was a focus for the discontentment of diverse groups in the south: the Protestants, the poor, the Occitans and the local magnates, all of whom had a bone to pick with Paris or the monarchy. But although the monarchy fell, Paris persevered, emerging as the capital of a sharply centralized and thoroughly French state.

The short and bloody revolutionary experiment was centred in Paris, and Languedoc felt its influence chiefly in the administrative novelties which were introduced, the most durable of which was the division of the region (as with the rest of country) into administrative **départements**. The rationalist (and centralist) policies of the new government ensured a break with historical traditions in defining these areas. They were based on geography, for the most part on the major river valleys. Roussillon became the culturally neutral Pyrénées-Orientales.

## THE NAPOLEONIC ERA AND THE NINETEENTH-CENTURY REPUBLICS

The rise of revolutionary France did not, however, bring about a change in foreign policy, which remained aggressive. The **armies** of the Republic, among whose leaders figured a young **Napoleon Bonaparte**, lashed out against neighbours on all sides. Back at home, power had devolved to a five-member **Directory**, whose heavy-handed governing was met with growing resentment by the populace. When Bonaparte returned from his defeat by the British in Egypt, he set a coup d'état in motion, which saw him elevated initially, in 1799, to First Consul, and subsequently, to **Emperor**. His campaign of European domination brought him up against practically every other power in Europe and, after initial successes in Germany and Spain, his campaign in Russia brought about the decimation of his Grand Army and his ultimate ruin.

Although most of the Napoleonic Wars took place on foreign soil, Languedoc was to feel the sting of the Emperor's defeat. **Wellington**'s British expeditionary force, which had been sent to aid Spain and Portugal, pushed its way across the peninsula and dealt the French a severe defeat at Toulouse in 1814.

For the next forty years France and Languedoc returned to monarchy, with the reigns first of the Bourbons **Louis XVIII** (1814–24) and **Charles X** (1824–30), and then the Orléans-king **Louis-Phillipe** (1830–48). The Bourbons, who had obviously learnt nothing from previous experience, immediately embarked on a heavy-handed Catholic-oriented policy, and were brought down by popular revolution in 1830. The throne was then taken by Louis-Philippe, the candidate of the middle class elite, a commercial nobility no less despised than their aristocratic forbears. He was unseated in the **revolution of 1848**, European Socialism's *annus mirabilus*, which saw uprisings in capitals across the continent. But the Second Republic quickly gave way to the **Second Empire**, when Bonaparte's crafty nephew gained the throne as **Napoleon III** in 1852. Protests followed his seizure of power, such as those in Béziers, where troops opened fire on a crowd of Republican demonstrators led by the town mayor. As a tactician Napoleon III proved as unsuccessful as his namesake, first embroiling the country in the bitter Crimean War, and then in 1870 provoking the ignominious **Franco-Prussian War**, which saw his own capture and the subsequent German siege of Paris.

Although Roussillon continued to drift in agrarian poverty, Languedoc weathered all these events with some measure of good fortune. While the bulk of the population suffered in poverty, the **textile industry**, based on wool and cotton and later on silk, boomed. The herds of the uplands of the Cévennes and Haut Languedoc were the chief source of raw material, and the fast-flowing rivers provided the energy to run the newly mechanized factories. All along the fringe of the mountains, towns which had up to then been insignificant villages – Castres, Mazamet, Ganges, St-Hippolyte – enjoyed unprecedented good fortune. As coal was discovered, new industries, such as **mining** and **glassmaking** (at Albi and Carmaux), sprang up, and when the railways arrived in the middle of the century, the towns along their route benefited additionally from better access to distribution networks. Of course this good fortune tended to remain in the hands of a

relative few – the factory owners and merchants – and this fact contributed to the popularity of egalitarian and **socialist ideologies** among the masses of the region.

The era of the **Third Republic**, which followed France's defeat at the hands of the Prussians, was one of introspection, not least because of the massive war indemnities which the state was forced to pay. Socialists were scapegoated and there were mass executions at the hands of the new reactionary regime; in excess of 20,000 were killed in Paris alone. Nor was all well in Languedoc and Roussillon, as outside the industrial areas the people of the countryside still eked out only the most meagre of livings. Many left, frequently for Paris, compounding the capital's social and economic problems. The new, modern **wine industry** which had developed along the littoral provided a seasonal source of income for many, and stimulated related industries, such as bottle-, cork- and barrel-making, but in 1875 the vineyards were decimated by phylloxera. This was followed by a second epidemic which attacked mulberry trees, the silkworm's staple food, precipitating a crisis in the silk industry.

A marked tendency towards the Left continued to colour local politics, partially fuelled by a resentment towards remote and indifferent Paris. These political trends were personified in **Jean Jaurès**. Born in Castres, he was drawn to Paris as a brilliant student but later returned to his home region of the Tarn. Here he entered politics and embarked on a series of labour-orientated campaigns, helping to organize miners' unions, and setting up co-operative, worker-run factories. He joined other liberals in defending **Alfred Dreyfus**, a Jewish army officer wrongly convicted of espionage in 1898, founded the communist newspaper *L'Humanité* in 1904, and a new socialist party in 1905. Speaking out against the anti-German nationalist hysteria which gripped the country in the years leading up to World War I, he paid with his life, assassinated by a nationalist in 1914.

However, popular politics in Languedoc and Roussillon were not cut strictly across ideological lines, as the cross-class solidarity of the **wine revolts** would show. As the wine industry recovered in the last years of the nineteenth century from the blow dealt by disease, it received further setbacks. A series of abundant harvests drove down the price of grapes, and the combination of competition from cheap Algerian vintages and a law permitting sugar to be added during fermentation (reducing the amount of grape pulp required) decreased demand. Wages plummeted and unemployment rose. Led by the innkeeper, Marcellin Albert, half a million protesters turned out in Montpellier in 1907, and similar numbers rose up in other wine towns, like Béziers and Narbonne. People across the class spectrum depended on the wine industry, so the uprising had the character of a regional revolt. The interior minister, Georges Clémenceau, responded by sending in the troops, but the locally levied 17th Infantry Regiment sympathized with their countrymen and mutinied. They were packed off to Tunisia in short order, and troops from the north were sent in to quell the "Midi madness". In the confrontations between army and civilians, shots were fired and there were some casualties, but the episode served to instigate the creation of a regional wine board to manage prices and quality and bring stability to the industry.

## THE TWO WORLD WARS

In 1914 the diplomatic strain between Europe's uniformly conservative powers finally snapped, and the **assassination** of the Austrian Archduke Ferdinand at the hands of a Serbian nationalist in Sarajevo led to a diplomatic chain reaction which brought about **World War I**. The French were particularly anxious for revenge for their recent defeat at the hands of Prussia, which deprived them of the Rhenish provinces of Alsace and Lorraine. After an initial German advance, both sides settled in for a drawn-out campaign of near-static trench warfare, along a 400km front stretching roughly from the Swiss border to Ostend, that was to last four years.

The two sides ground away at each other in the first modern mechanized war – over its course the front shifted almost imperceptibly, but an exhausted Germany surrendered in 1918. France paid a high price for its eventual victory – almost one and half million dead. Although none of the fighting took place in Languedoc and Roussillon the **cenotaphs** which mark the centre of each hamlet and village bear dramatic testimony to the price which they paid in the struggle.

Languedoc and Roussillon limped through the 1920s and 1930s, suffering along with the rest of Europe in the postwar **flu epidemic** (which claimed more lives than the war) and the **Great Depression**. Weak postwar democracies arose in Italy and Germany and were quickly replaced by dictatorial Fascist regimes, and a prelude of the struggle to come took place in Spain, where General Franco's attempted coup set in motion a civil war in 1936. The bitter struggle, from which France – as did the rest of the Allies – remained aloof and uncommitted, lasted until 1939. As Fascist troops took over Catalonia and the Basque Country, tens of thousands of **refugees** poured over the border, the Catalans arriving initially in Roussillon.

A few months later German soldiers poured over the Polish border, initiating **World War II**. The following year they circumvented France's defensive white elephant, the Maginot line, and arrived in Paris in June. For the first time in seven hundred years Languedoc and Roussillon found themselves independent of Paris as they were incorporated into the puppet **Vichy Republic**, which enjoyed a fictitious independence under the World War I hero, **Henri Pétain**. He collaborated with the **Nazis**, facilitating the repression of their opponents, the deportation of "undesirable elements" and the wholesale transportation of southern French citizens to labour camps and factories in Germany.

In 1942 the Germans decided to dispense with even the illusion of autonomy in the south and brought the whole region under their direct control. Repression was intensified, but the local guerrilla **Resistance**, the *maquis*, benefited from a stiffened resolve on the part of the populace. Across France as a whole there were about as many active collaborators to Nazi rule as resistors, but Resistance activity in Languedoc and Roussillon was considerable, the efforts of local companies like the famed Maquis Bir Hakeim of Haut Languedoc, or of individuals like Jean Mance of Béziers, who founded the National Committee for Resistance, proving a significant element in the war. In their mountain redoubts in the Pyrenees and Cévennes and in the hills of Haut Languedoc they sustained German air attacks and pacification missions, while the civilian population suffered direct reprisals for their collusion with the rebels. In the Cerdagne and Roussillon clandestine *passeurs*, motivated by either ideals or profit, helped to slip people and contraband back and forth over the frontier with neutral Spain.

From 1943 on the disasters of the Russian campaign focused German manpower in the East, and with the **allied invasions** of Italy in 1943 and Normandy in 1944, the undergunned maquis finally had a chance, and began to mount an open military campaign. The first towns which they managed to recover were mere mountain hamlets, like Mourèze, near Clermont-l'Hérault, but when the Germans sent a column of 3000 troops to retake the upper Hérault, they were fended off after a fierce day-long battle with the local Resistance. Memorial plaques which pepper the streets of Toulouse and other major towns recall the *maquis* who fell in the widespread **streetfighting** of 1944. By the end of that year France had been liberated.

### RECENT HISTORY

In the postwar **Fourth Republic** France endeavoured to recover from the damage wrought by four years of occupation and two invasions. The colonial age of Europe was coming to an end and for France this signalled nationalist revolts in Indochina and Algeria. In Languedoc and Roussillon the wine industry recovered and mining continued, but with the advent of cheaper synthetic fibres, the textile industry all but disappeared. **Poverty** and **depopulation** continued and served to channel political consciousness ever more to the Left.

Former general and self-proclaimed liberator of France **Charles de Gaulle**'s conservative **Fifth Republic**, which came in 1958 on the heels of France's entry into the new European Common Market, gradually became something of a dictatorship. In the south, certain progressive economic policies were embarked upon, including the construction of **reservoirs** and **hydroelectric facilities** and the articulation of a regionwide irrigation plan.

Meanwhile in **Algeria** native unrest led to open rebellion, and when de Gaulle reacted by announcing the abandonment of the **colony**, the French population who had ruled it since 1830 felt betrayed and carried out a brief armed resistance. With the **Accord of Évian** (1962) they agreed to be settled, along with the **Harkis** – their native Algerian allies – in Languedoc. The influx of this population – a largely educated and skilled workforce – gave new life to the cities of the coast (notably

Montpellier, Narbonne and Perpignan), although the welcome which the Harkis received was hardly warm. Forty years later they continue to protest the official neglect to which they have been subject.

The **Student Revolution** of 1968 presaged the departure of de Gaulle, who resigned in 1969 after a failed attempt to widen his already broad powers by popular referendum. The unrest of that summer also heralded an era of openly **left-wing politics** in Languedoc and Roussillon. In the elections of the years that followed Languedoc voted massively in favour of the socialists and communists, encouraged by the areas' traditional economic marginalism and an antipathy to the conservative north.

The nation, however, remained under **conservative rule** through the presidencies of Georges Pompidou (1969–74) and Valéry Giscard d'Estaing (1974–81). In this era of baby boom and general prosperity, the infrastructure of Languedoc and Roussillon was improved by the construction of *autoroutes* and the improvement of roads. The **tourist industry** also received stimulus through the revitalization of the abandoned Canal du Midi and the creation of regional parks, such as that of Haut Languedoc. The area still retains a shadow of its former textile industry, but manufacturing has been dominated in the west by the high profile **aviation industry** based in Toulouse. The city had been a pioneer of flight since before the days of St-Exupéry, and served as a hub for Africa and South America between the wars. It was here that the Concorde was first put to test, and the European joint venture Airbus Industries was founded.

Despite these recent successes, the region remains underpopulated and relatively poor, and *départements* like the Aude, Ariège and significant parts of the Hérault are now actively stimulating tourism as way of bringing investment and employment.

As the French population ages, waves of northern retirees are heading south to the affordable property and agreeable climes of Languedoc and Roussillon – a trend which is seen with a jaundiced eye by many natives, who perceive in it a modern reprise to the invasions of the past. Some also see the massive influx of North African immigrants from France's former colonies and protectorates as an invasion, and this has served to divert part of the traditional extreme Left vote, paradoxically, to the **extreme Right**. The 1995 municipal elections gave a surprisingly high return to the parties of the far Right, dominated then by Jean Le Pen's racist **Front National**. It is not without irony that Roussillon's "Perpignan la Catalane" should be ruled by an extremist French mayor. On the *région* level the Right scored well in the 1998 elections; the UDF–FDR coalition's (President Chirac's power base) 22 seats added to the FN's thirteen made for a narrow majority over the 31 seats won by the socialists and resurgent communists.

As parties gear up for the 2002 elections, it appears that the region will return to its traditional socialist orientation. The FN has suffered a series of setbacks and divisions in the years after the 1998 elections and has now splintered, while in late 2000, the **Chirac government** was discredited by an influence-peddling **scandal** involving government contracts which seemed to point at the president's office.

Unlike some of France's other regions, such as Corsica, Alsace, the Pays Basque and Brittany, the issues of a distinctive language and identity do not seem to have made their way into the political dialogue of either Languedoc or Roussillon. For all the resentment which these regions may feel towards Paris, and despite the survival or revival of their native tongues, there is no doubt among the people of the region that their future lies with France.

# BOOKS

Publishers are detailed below in the form of British publisher; American publisher, where both exist. Where books are published in one country only, UK or US follows the publisher's name. Where the publisher is the same in both the UK and US only one name is given. Abbreviations: o/p (out of print); UP (University Press).

## HISTORY

### GENERAL

**Alfred Cobban**, *A History of Modern France* (3 vols: 1715–99, 1799–1871 and 1871–1962, Penguin; Viking). Complete and very readable account of the main political, social and economic strands in French history from the death of Louis XIV to mid-de Gaulle.

**Colin Jones**, *The Cambridge Illustrated History of France* (CUP, o/p). A political and social history of France from prehistoric times to the mid-1990s, concentrating on issues of regionalism, gender, race and class. Good illustrations and a friendly, non-academic writing style.

### THE MIDDLE AGES

**Richard Barber**, *Edward, Prince of Wales and Aquitaine* (Boydell Press; University of Rochester Press). A weighty, academic read, but perhaps the best of the biographies on the Black Prince, including much on his campaigns in Languedoc.

**Natalie Zemon Davis**, *The Return of Martin Guerre* (Harvard UP). A vivid account of peasant life in the sixteenth century and a perplexing and titillating hoax in the Pyrenean village of Artigat. Better than the movie and the musical. Not within the strict geographic bounds of this Guide, but culturally very much so.

**Emmanuel Le Roy Ladurie**, *Montaillou* (Penguin; Random House). Village gossip of who's sleeping with whom, tales of trips to Spain and details of work, all extracted by the Inquisition from Cathar peasants of the eastern Pyrenees in the fourteenth century, and stored away until recently in the Vatican archives. Though academic and heavy-going in places, most of this book reads like a novel.

**J.R. Maddicott**, *Simon De Montfort* (Cambridge UP). An academic but readable treatment of this complex and problematic figure – carefully balancing de Montfort's senses of piety and ambition.

**Stephen O'Shea**, *The Perfect Heresy* (Walker & Co). Lively but partisan non-academic account of the history of the Cathar Church and faith and the Catholic campaign mounted to wipe it out.

**Jonathan Sumption**, *The Albigensian Crusade* (Faber & Faber). Concise but readable account of the Albigensian Crusades from the beginnings of the Cathar movement through to the fall of Montségur

### THE WARS OF RELIGION

**Joseph and Francis Bergin**, *The Rise of Richelieu* (Manchester UP). An interesting look at Richelieu's rise to power, presenting the cardinal as a complex Machiavellian figure, who was not without his convictions.

**Willert Paul Ferdinand**, *Henry of Navarre and the Huguenots in France* (AMS Press, o/p). Ageing but interesting study of the French Protestant movement, focusing on the figure of Henry IV.

**Mack Holt**, *The French Wars of Religion, 1562–1629* (Cambridge UP). A recent survey of the whole period of the Wars of Religion, available in paperback as part of the New Approaches to European History series.

**Abraham Lavander**, *French Huguenots* (Peter Lang, US, o/p). Readable academic account focusing on the social history of the French Protestant movement and its oppression.

**James Valone**, *Huguenot Politics, 1601–1622* (Edwin Mellen). Recently published, exacting study of the Huguenot situation during the reign of the former Protestant Henry IV.

## EIGHTEENTH AND NINETEENTH CENTURIES

**Anthony Crubaugh**, *Balancing the Scales of Justice: Local Courts and Rural Society in Southwest France, 1750–1800* (Pennsylvania State University, US). Engaging new academic study of local court documents, revealing the subtleties of peasant life in Languedoc in the era of the Revolution.

**Norman Hampson**, *A Social History of the French Revolution* (Routledge, Kegan & Paul). An analysis that concentrates on the personalities involved. Its particular interest lies in the attention it gives to the *sans-culottes*, the ordinary poor of Paris.

**Christopher Hibbert**, *The Days of the French Revolution* (Quill). Well-paced and entertaining narrative treatment by a master historian.

**Peter McPhee**, *A Social History of France, 1780–1880* (Routledge, o/p). A scholarly work arguing that historians have underestimated the fundamental differences between how people lived and thought in 1880 compared with the time of the 1789 Revolution. He goes into such subjects as relations between men and women, education and reading material, the and culture, and changes in the physical environment.

**J.M. Thompson**, *The French Revolution* (Blackwell). A detailed and passionate account, first published in 1943, but still the classic account in English.

## TWENTIETH CENTURY

**H.R. Kedward**, *In Search of the Maquis: Rural Resistance in South France 1942–44* (OUP o/p). Written in a slightly dry style, but full of fascinating detail about the brave and often mortal struggle of the countless ordinary people across France who fought to drive the Germans from their country.

**Barbara Tuchman**, *The Proud Tower* (Papermac; Ballantine). A portrait of England, France, the US, Germany and Russia in the years 1890–1914. Written in Tuchman's inimitable and readable style, it includes a superb chapter on the extraordinary passions and enmities aroused by the Dreyfus Affair which rocked French society between 1894 and 1899 and on

the different currents in the rising socialist movement in the run-up to World War I, centring on the life of Jean Jaurès.

**Paul Webster**, *Pétain's Crime: The Full Story of French Collaboration in the Holocaust* (Papermac; IR Dee). The fascinating and alarming story of the Vichy regime's more than willing collaboration with the Holocaust and the bravery of those, especially the communist resistance in occupied France, who attempted to prevent it.

**Alexander Worth**, *France 1940–55* (Beacon Press, US, o/p). Extremely good and emotionally engaged portrayal of the taboo Occupation period in French history, followed by the Cold War and colonial struggle years in which the same political tensions and heart-searchings were at play.

## SOCIETY AND POLITICS

**N.A. Addinall** (ed), *French Political Parties: A Documentary Guide* (U of Wales Press, UK). Clear and concise textbook introduction to the constitution and political parties of the Fifth Republic; quotations and source materials are not translated but this need not deter non-French speakers.

**Bernard Henri-Lévy**, *Adventures on the Freedom Road: The French Intellectuals in the 20th Century* (Harvill). Huge, clever and complex essays by the contemporary philosopher-celebrity, mercilessly analysing the response of all the great French thinkers, of Left and Right, to the key events of the century. Easy to dip into, surprisingly readable, and very provocative.

**Ian Ousby**, *Occupation: The Ordeal of France 1940–1945* (John Murray, UK). Non-academic book which reflects the recent trend to deflate the myth of massive resistance to the Nazis. Examines the development of the Resistance and the counterweight of collaboration.

**David Thomson**, *Democracy in France Since 1870* (Cassell, UK, o/p). An inquiry into why a country with such a strong socialist tradition should have had so many reactionary governments.

**Harold R. Weinstein**, *Jean Jaurès: A Study of Patriotism in the French Socialist Movement* (Octagon, US, o/p). First published in the 1930s this ageing but eminently readable study looks not only at the figure of Jaurès, but locates him in the wider context of late nineteenth-century French socialism.

## ART AND ARCHITECTURE

**John Berger**, *The Success and Failure of Picasso* (Penguin, o/p, Vintage). The success is self-explanatory; the failure (and the tragedy) lies in Picasso's poverty of subject matter – or so Berger argues in this brief and highly persuasive book. Perhaps the best one-volume study of Picasso in English.

**David J. Brown**, *Bridges Across Time* (Mitchell Beazley, UK, o/p). A very beautiful book about both the technical and aesthetic aspects of bridge building; not exclusively about France, but includes many French bridges from the Roman Pont-du-Gard to the Pont d'Avignon,.

**Kenneth J. Comant**, *Carolingian and Romanesque Architecture, 800–1200* (Yale UP). Good European study with a focus on Cluny and the St-Jacques pilgrim route, which includes good sections on the sections through Languedoc.

**Julia Bloch Frey**, *Toulouse-Lautrec: A Life* (Trafalgar Square, UK). An intimate look at the life of the painter, with special emphasis on his friends, family, and artistic contemporaries.

**Walter F. Friedlaender**, *David to Delacroix* (Harvard UP, o/p). Respected survey of French art from the late seventeenth to late nineteenth centuries, from Neoclassicism through to Romanticism, and including figures who were influential in Languedoc and Roussillon.

**John Golding**, *Cubism: A History and an Analysis 1907–1914* (Faber & Faber; Harvard UP). Excellent work on the formative stages of Cubism, particularly relevant to a journey to Céret.

**Edward Lucie-Smith**, *A Concise History of French Painting* (Thames & Hudson, US, o/p). If you're after an art reference book, this will do as well as any . . . though there are of course hundreds of books on particular French art movements.

**Sarah Whitfield**, *Fauvism* (Thames & Hudson). A survey of the movement, accompanied by colour plates, emphasizing the major figure of Matisse, but with good material on Maillol and lesser known artists.

## TRAVEL BOOKS AND GUIDES

**Sabine Baring-Gould**, *In Troubadour-Land: A Ramble in Provence and Languedoc* (W.H. Allen,

o/p). A very British, late nineteenth-century aristocratic ramble through the French south, offering a very interesting perspective of the region under the Third Republic.

**James Bromwich**, *The Roman Remains of Southern France* (Routledge). The only comprehensive guide on the subject – detailed, well illustrated and approachable. In addition to accounts of the famous sites, it will lead you off the map to little-known discoveries.

**Glynn Christian**, *Edible France* (Grub Street; Interlink). A guide to food rather than restaurants, concentrating on regional produce, local specialities, markets and the best shops for buying goodies to bring back home.

**Cicerone Walking Guides**, (Cicerone, UK). Neat, durable guides, with detailed route descriptions. Titles include *The Way of St James* (GR65); *The Pyrenean Trail* (GR10); and *Walks and Climbs in the Pyrenees*.

**Mary Davis**, *The Green Guide to France* (Green Print, UK). Definitely not the Michelin version, this is a resource guide to French national parks and wildlife reserves, vegetarian restaurants, communes and the like.

**Nina Epton**, *The Valley of the Pyrene* (Cassell, o/p). Lively Fifties-era memoir of a tour through the Ariège, peppered with entertaining anecdotes.

**Footpaths of Europe** *Walking the Pyrenees* (Robertson McCarta, UK, o/p). Route guide covering the system of GR footpaths, illustrated with 1:50,000 colour survey maps. It is an English version of the Pyrenees *Topoguide des Sentiers de Grande Randonnée* (CNSGR, Paris), which is widely available in France and not hard to follow for anyone with a working knowledge of French.

**Mark Hampshell**, *Live and Work in France* (Vacation Work, UK, o/p). An invaluable guide for anyone considering residence or work in France; packed with ideas and advice on job hunting, bureaucracy, tax, health, etc.

**Rion Klawinski**, *Chasing the Heretics: A Modern Journey through Languedoc* (Ruminator, US). A traveller's account of the Cathar heresy and the Albigensian Crusade, arranged in a guide-book format. A good handbook for those who want to make a Cathar-themed trip.

**Carol Pineau and Maureen Kelly**, *Working in France* (AL Books, US, o/p). A practical guide, aimed at American readers, on how to get jobs in France, highlighting the cultural differences that affect interviews and business practice.

**Kev Reynolds**, *Walks and Climbs in the Pyrenees* (Cicerone Press, UK). The classic English guide for walking in the Pyrenees.

**John Sturrock**, *The French Pyrenees* (Faber & Faber, o/p). Well-written travelogue emphasizing the history of the French side of the range. Covers the mountains from coast to coast, but has significant sections covering the Ariège and Roussillon.

# OCCITAN AND CATALAN

By the time the Roman Empire in the West disintegrated, Latin had become the language of daily speech in nearly all of what is now France. Over the course of the following centuries, spoken Latin began to evolve into local variants and eventually into new Romance languages, from Spanish to Romanian. In the south of France (and in part of modern Italy) **Occitan** (pronounced ok-si-tan) or the **Langue d'Oc** developed – so-called for the word for "yes", which set it apart from the northern French Langue d'Oïl. Occitan itself had discrete regional variants, chief among them Provençal in the east (including Nîmes), Limousin in the north, Gascon in the west (including the Ariège) and Languedocien, from the Corbières to the Camargue. In northeast Spain and across the present-day border into southern France emerged the **Catalan** language, which bears similarities to both Occitan and Castilian Spanish. Ironically, the name Catalan derives from the same root as the name of its chief rival language, Castilian, both terms referring to the castles which covered the landscapes of each region.

## OCCITAN LANGUAGE AND CULTURE

Around the turn of the first millennium, a distinct Occitan literary language emerged, thanks to the wealth of the southern counts and their patronage of **troubadours**. These poets composed and performed works which were sung accompanied by music, for which they were also known as *jongleurs* or "players" [of instruments]. The themes of their works varied from popular or religiously toned epics, like the *Chanson de Roland*, to portrayals of courtly love, considered to be the most elegant of subjects. Across these could be found recurring motifs, including righteous battle (for example, against the infidel), unrequited love, and above all the glorification of good manners, sophistication and virtues, such as knightly loyalty or pious chastity. The poetry of courtly love was not erotic in nature; the idea was that the poet should be recognized as honourable by the noble woman (or man) who was the object of the work. The genre was so idealized that the great troubadour Jaufré Rudel claimed to have fallen in love with the Countess of Tripoli without having ever laid eyes on her. Troubadours were not merely court entertainers, as many were noblemen themselves, and the first is said to have been the powerful duke, William IX of Aquitaine, father of Eleanor of Aquitaine, later Queen of England. But the bulk of them were not wealthy, and they practised their art as a way of ingratiating themselves with a noble house, and entering its service, much as a knight would.

The Albigensian Crusades of the thirteenth century brought about the end of many of the native ruling families in Languedoc and brought an influx of northern nobles. Naturally, these were French in cultural orientation rather than Occitan, and the literature of the language declined as sources of patronage dried up and it waned as an administrative language. Occitan literature persevered in prose, which emphasized secular and narrative themes. The decline of the language was met with some alarm, and in 1323 a group of poets from Toulouse determined to save the poetic tradition of the troubadours by instituting the **Jocs Florals** (floral games) – a sort of poetic Olympics in which winners were awarded gilded flowers. The tradition has continued since that time, held annually on May 3, although in 1694, Louis XIV Frenchified it and established in Toulouse a society called the Académie des Jeux Floraux, which administers the games to this day. With the establishment of the Jocs Florals, Occitan survived as a literary language for a time, but with the increasing centralization of the realm devolved once again into an unwritten language of common speech. In 1539 on the eve of the Wars of Religion, François I declared at Villers-Cotterêts that French – the dialect of the **Langue d'Oïl** which was spoken in the area around Paris – was to be the only language of administration in his realms.

As the language of education and administration, French thus displaced Occitan, which was – and sometimes still is – referred to insultingly by Francophones as *patois* ("the dialect"). It was not until the mid-nineteenth century that it was revived in literature, in an intellectual environment which saw subject peoples across Europe establish or re-establish literatures for their own languages. The major figure in the new Occitan literature was **Frédéric Mistral**, the venerated Provençal poet and cultural messiah. Born in 1830, Mistral spent a lifetime working to revive and modernize Provençal Occitan as a written and spoken language, producing countless works of literature and grammar, and campaigning in favour of Occitan folk practices, such as *tauromachie*. His efforts were recognized on an international level when he received a Nobel Prize in 1904. Meanwhile philologists strove to standardize the language, which had degenerated into countless local variants as a result of its submission to French.

Nevertheless, reform was slow. Although it may have been the common language of the villages and fields through the middle of the twentieth century, the relentlessly centralist policies of the state and the greater diffusion of French-language education and literacy conspired against Occitan's revival. In Toulouse, the **Escola Occitana** (1919) and the **Institut d'Études Occitanes** (1945) were founded to promote and modernize the language, but it was not until 1951 that it was permitted to teach Occitan in schools, and only in 1969 that it was officially ranked by educational authorities as a language.

Ironically, the only area which has Occitan as an official and dominant language is Spain's **Vall d'Aran**, a tiny valley high in the Pyrenees to the southwest of Toulouse. **Aranese**, as the seven thousand or so inhabitants call the language, is in fact the Gascon dialect of the Langue d'Oc. In Languedoc proper efforts continue to revive the language, but since the 1920s the number of speakers has decreased from ten to two million – an optimistic estimate which sets the proportion of Occitan speakers as fourteen percent of the whole of Languedoc. (By contrast, in Corsica some fifty percent of the populace speak native Corse.) Nevertheless there are Occitan-language newspapers (like the weekly *La Setmana*), radio stations (*Ràdio País*) and television broadcasts, and bilingual public schools have been established in Albi, Toulouse, Monestiès and St-Sulpice. As a visitor you're not likely to encounter Occitan either spoken or written, apart from the Occitan street signs which are frequently set alongside their French counterparts.

Although readership is limited, authors such as **Max Roqueta**, **Bernat Maciet** and **Marcèla Delpastre** have begun to publish novels in Occitan, theatre companies tour performing original and traditional works, and musical groups of the 1970s and 80s, like Massilia and the Fabulous Troubadours created the modern Occitan musical style called **nòva cançon**, which blends traditional melodies and instruments with modern styles, and still has a hardcore following today. For the most part, however, Occitan musicians have adopted other genres, from jazz, blues and folk, to rap and punk fusions (here known as *ragga-aïoli*), and of course regional and linguistic identity do not necessarily coincide – Toulouse's **Zebda**, a strongly regional-minded group whose mix of politics and music is reminiscent of America's Rage Against the Machine, sings exclusively in French.

Although Languedoc is rich with customs and traditions which set it apart from the rest of France, such as water-jousting and *tauromachie*, it is thoroughly subsumed in the French identity. There is no independence movement here such as exists in Corsica, the Basque Country or Brittany, and regional identity is vague, focusing with romantic nostalgia on episodes of northern French oppression such as the Albigensian Crusades and the Wars of Religion. Bernat Lubat, a renowned Occitan jazz musician, expresses an opinion on the subject of regional independence which is representative of the overwhelming majority of the area's inhabitants: "The desire for independence seems to me neither interesting, nor realistic, nor even poetic."

## STUDYING OCCITAN

**Occitan language courses** are offered across the region for example at the University of Toulouse and at smaller centres in Carcassonne and Béziers – and in Paris. For information about courses and Occitan culture in general, contact the Centre Interrégional de Développement de l'Occitan (CIR-DOC), place du 14 Juillet, Espace du Guesclin, BP 180 34502 Béziers Cedex (☎04.67.11.85.10, *www.cirdoc.org*).

## CATALAN LANGUAGE AND CULTURE

Most of the ten million or so Catalan speakers live in Spain, in a band of territory stretching south from the Pyrenees to Valencia, and in the Balearic Islands. The 120,000 Catalan speakers of France live in the *département* of Pyrénées-Orientales, which incorporates the Catalan cultural regions of **La Cerdanya** and **Rosselló**, and has its capital at Perpignan (Perpinyà in Catalan). Here they represent 34 percent of the population, although only half of that figure claim a high proficiency level.

The **Cerdagne** and **Roussillon**, traditionally part of the realms of the Counts of Barcelona, were long-disputed in border wars waged with the French. The French Crown took permanent control of the territory in the 1620s under Richelieu, but the land was not formally ceded by Spain until 1649's Treaty of the Pyrenees, negotiated by Louis XIV. Curiously, a fine reading of the text of the treaty allowed Spain to maintain control of the town of Llivia, which has remained a Spanish enclave, a few kilometres inside the French border, to this day.

Catalan, like Occitan, was a language of the troubadours of the Middle Ages, and had a healthy tradition of narrative literature before Spanish or English. One of the most famous early Catalan works is the autobiographical *Llibre de feyts* (Book of Deeds), written in the thirteenth century by the great count-king, **Jaume I the Conqueror**, son of Pere el Catòlic. Through the Middle Ages, Catalan culture flourished thanks to the powerful maritime dominion of Barcelona. The count-king Joan I (1387–96) instituted a Catalan version of the **Jocs Florals**, in imitation of the Occitan contest (but winners were given a real, rather than a golden flower). But as happened to Occitan, the domination of powerful "foreign" administration – in this case, the Hapsburgs of Madrid – contributed to the marginalization of the language, and literary usage declined after the fifteenth century. This process was exacerbated in Roussillon by the French takeover in the seventeenth century. Like Occitan, Catalan was proscribed from official use, and denigrated to the status of a peasant *patois*.

The wave of regional and national consciousness which swept through Europe in the mid-nineteenth century washed over Catalonia as well, where the linguistic renaissance was spearheaded by the philologist **Pompeu Fabra**, who set about standardizing the Catalan grammar, and writers, such as the poet **Manuel Milà i Fontanals**. In 1859 the Jocs Florals were resumed. With the victory of strongly Castile-centric Franco in the Spanish Civil War, a wave of Catalan refugees washed over the border into France, giving the native language and culture an additional boost in Roussillon and the Cerdagne. Catalan was proscribed under the Fascist dictatorship in Spain, but the post-war period in France signalled a liberalization of language laws and the admission of Catalan to the public school curriculum.

Today, however, while there is a lively literary, television and cinema culture in Catalonia proper, in Roussillon it is almost nonexistent. Some Catalan folkloric customs have survived the centuries of French domination and still contribute to the distinct flavour of Roussillon. Among these are the distinctive **Christmas customs** (see box on p.321), and the penitents' processions of **Setmana Santa** (Holy Week). A recent addition is the **sardana**, brought to Roussillon by the refugees of 1939, and a symbol of Catalan nationalism. It is a popular dance, in which participants, frequently wearing the traditional woven *espardinya* shoes, form a circle linking hands and do a slow hopping dance to the minor strains of an eleven-piece *colbla* (orchestra). Each dancer places some object (frequently a handbag) in the centre, which is said to symbolize sharing; and the dance is undemanding enough that young and old alike can participate (you'll find information on where and when you can see the *sardana* in Chapter 7).

The sizeable independence movement in Spanish Catalonia advocates the unification of all of the *Països Catalans*, including Roussillon and the Cerdagne, as a separate state. Indeed, the most potent symbol of Catalan identity, towering **Mont Canigou** (*El Canigó* in Catalan), sits in French territory, in-between Prades and the border. An imposing mountain casting its shadow over all of Roussillon, it had long been venerated by the region's inhabitants when a monastery was founded on its slopes by the grandson of Guifré el Pelós in 1001. Over the centuries its symbolism intensified, and for Catalans it became their sacred mountain, celebrated in literature through to Jacint Verdaguer's epic *Canigó* of the late nineteenth century. To this day it is the site of a yearly mid-summer torchlight pilgrimage to celebrate the *día de Sant Joan* (St John's Day) on June 24. The traditional pagan solstice holiday, celebrated here, as in many societies, by raising a great fire, stands as a Catalan "national" holiday, celebrated both in Spanish and French Catalonia. But aside from annoying graffiti on buildings and road signs, there is little evidence of nationalist fervour on the French side. Although Catalan speakers of Roussillon, and even many non-speakers, delight in the distinctiveness which the region's diluted Catalan identity gives them, they tend to recall the revolts against the French merely for their

**STUDYING CATALAN**

Naturally, the best place to **study Catalan** is in Catalonia proper, but if you are determined to do so in Roussillon, your best option is to take a course at **Céret's** Catalan summer university (☎04.68.96.10.84).

sense of rose-tinted nostalgia. The region is culturally very much closer to Paris than Barcelona – convincing confirmation of its predominantly French sensibility can be found in the election in 1995 of the extreme right-wing mayor of Perpignan, Jean-Paul Alduy of the Nouvelle UDF.

# LANGUAGE

Although Occitan is still spoken among some older rural folk and by recent students of the language, it serves little purpose for a visitor. Catalan, while more current, is nevertheless a second language throughout Roussillon and the Cerdagne. As a foreigner speaking French you will be understood by all and you will not offend anyone's regional sensibilities.

French can be a deceptively familiar language because of the number of words and structures it shares with English. Despite this, it's far from easy, though the bare essentials are not difficult to learn and can make all the difference. Even just saying "Bonjour Madame/Monsieur" and then gesticulating will usually get you a smile and helpful service. People working in tourist offices, hotels and so on, almost always speak English and tend to use it when you're struggling to speak French – be grateful, not insulted.

Of the **phrasebooks** and **dictionaries** available the *Rough Guide French Dictionary Phrasebook* is a handy and comprehensive companion, with both English–French and French–English sections, along with cultural tips for tricky situations and a menu reader. There's also the *French and English Slang*

*Dictionary* (Harrap/Prentice Hall) and *Dictionary of Modern Colloquial French* (Routledge) – both volumes are a bit large to carry, but they are the key to all you ever wanted to understand about the French vernacular.

## FRENCH PRONUNCIATION

One easy rule to remember is that **consonants** at the ends of words are usually silent. *Pas plus tard* (not later) is thus pronounced "pa-plu-tarr". But when the following word begins with a vowel, you run the two together: *pas après* (not after) becomes "pazaprey".

**Vowels** are the hardest sounds to get right. Roughly:

| | |
|---|---|
| *a* | as in h**a**t |
| *e* | as in g**e**t |
| *é* | between g**e**t and g**a**te |
| *è* | between g**e**t and g**u**t |
| *eu* | like the **u** in h**u**rt |
| *i* | as in mach**i**ne |
| *o* | as in h**o**t |
| *o, au* | as in **o**ver |
| *ou* | as in f**oo**d |
| *u* | as in a pursed-lip version of **u**se |

More awkward are the **combinations** *in/im, en/em, an/am, on/om, un/um* at the ends of words, or followed by consonants other than *n* or *m*. Again, roughly:

*in/im* like the **an** in **an**xious
*an/am, en/em* like the **don** in **Don**caster when said with a nasal accent
*on/om* like the **don** in **Don**caster said by someone with a heavy cold
*un/um* like the **u** in **u**nderstand

**Consonants** are much as in English, except that: *ch* is always "sh", *c* is "s", *h* is silent, *th* is the same as "t", *ll* is like the "y" in yes, *w* is "v", and *r* is growled (or rolled).

## FRENCH WORDS AND PHRASES

### BASIC WORDS AND PHRASES

French nouns are divided into masculine and feminine. This causes difficulties with adjectives, whose endings have to change to suit the gender of the nouns they qualify. If you know some grammar, you will know what to do. If not, stick to the masculine form, which is the simplest – it's what we have done in this glossary.

| | | | |
|---|---|---|---|
| today | *aujourd'hui* | that one | *celà* |
| yesterday | *hier* | open | *ouvert* |
| tomorrow | *demain* | closed | *fermé* |
| in the morning | *le matin* | big | *grand* |
| in the afternoon | *l'après-midi* | small | *petit* |
| in the evening | *le soir* | more | *plus* |
| now | *maintenant* | less | *moins* |
| later | *plus tard* | a little | *un peu* |
| at one o'clock | *à une heure* | a lot | *beaucoup* |
| at three o'clock | *à trois heures* | cheap | *bon marché* |
| at ten-thirty | *à dix heures et demie* | expensive | *cher* |
| at midday | *à midi* | good | *bon* |
| man | *un homme* | bad | *mauvais* |
| woman | *une femme* | hot | *chaud* |
| here | *ici* | cold | *froid* |
| there | *là* | with | *avec* |
| this one | *ceci* | without | *sans* |

### NUMBERS

| | | | | | |
|---|---|---|---|---|---|
| 1 | *un* | 15 | *quinze* | 80 | *quatre-vingts* |
| 2 | *deux* | 16 | *seize* | 90 | *quatre-vingt-dix* |
| 3 | *trois* | 17 | *dix-sept* | 95 | *quatre-vingt-quinze* |
| 4 | *quatre* | 18 | *dix-huit* | 100 | *cent* |
| 5 | *cinq* | 19 | *dix-neuf* | 101 | *cent-et-un* |
| 6 | *six* | 20 | *vingt* | 200 | *deux cents* |
| 7 | *sept* | 21 | *vingt-et-un* | 300 | *trois cents* |
| 8 | *huit* | 22 | *vingt-deux* | 500 | *cinq cents* |
| 9 | *neuf* | 30 | *trente* | 1000 | *mille* |
| 10 | *dix* | 40 | *quarante* | 2000 | *deux milles* |
| 11 | *onze* | 50 | *cinquante* | 5000 | *cinq milles* |
| 12 | *douze* | 60 | *soixante* | 1,000,000 | *un million* |
| 13 | *treize* | 70 | *soixante-dix* | | |
| 14 | *quatorze* | 75 | *soixante-quinze* | | |

### DAYS AND DATES

| | | | | | |
|---|---|---|---|---|---|
| January | *janvier* | October | *octobre* | Friday | *vendredi* |
| February | *février* | November | *novembre* | Saturday | *samedi* |
| March | *mars* | December | *décembre* | | |
| April | *avril* | | | August 1 | *le premier août* |
| May | *mai* | Sunday | *dimanche* | March 2 | *le deux mars* |
| June | *juin* | Monday | *lundi* | July 14 | *le quatorze juillet* |
| July | *juillet* | Tuesday | *mardi* | November 23 | *le vingt-trois* |
| August | *août* | Wednesday | *mercredi* | | *novembre* |
| September | *septembre* | Thursday | *jeudi* | 2002 | *deux mille deux* |

*Box continues on next page. . .*

*. . .Box continued from previous page*

## TALKING TO PEOPLE

When addressing people you should always use *Monsieur* for a man, *Madame* for a woman, *Mademoiselle* for a young woman or girl. Plain *bonjour* by itself is not enough. This isn't as formal as it seems, and it has its uses when you've forgotten someone's name or want to attract someone's attention.

| | | | |
|---|---|---|---|
| Excuse me | *Pardon* | OK/agreed | *d'accord* |
| Do you speak English? | *Parlez-vous anglais?* | please | *s'il vous plaît* |
| How do you say it in French? | *Comment ça se dit en français?* | thank you | *merci* |
| | | hello | *bonjour* |
| What's your name? | *Comment vous appelez-vous?* | goodbye | *au revoir* |
| | | good morning/ afternoon | *bonjour* |
| My name is . . . | *Je m'appelle . . .* | good evening | *bonsoir* |
| | | good night | *bonne nuit* |
| I'm English/Irish/Scottish/Welsh/American/ Australian/ Canadian/a New Zealander | | How are you? | *Comment allez-vous?/ Ça va?* |
| *Je suis anglais[e]/irlandais[e]/écossais[e]/ gallois[e]/américain[e]/australien[ne]/ canadien[ne]/néo-zélandais[e]* | | Fine, thanks | *Très bien, merci* |
| | | I don't know | *Je ne sais pas* |
| | | Let's go | *Allons-y* |
| | | See you tomorrow | *Á demain* |
| yes | *oui* | See you soon | *Á bientôt* |
| no | *non* | Sorry | *Pardon, Madame/ Je m'excuse* |
| I understand | *Je comprends* | | |
| I don't understand | *Je ne comprends pas* | Leave me alone (aggressive) | *Fichez-moi la paix!* |
| Can you speak slower? | *S'il vous plaît, parlez moins vite* | Please help me | *Aidez-moi, s'il vous plaît* |

## FINDING THE WAY

| | | | |
|---|---|---|---|
| bus | *autobus/bus/car* | on foot | *à pied* |
| bus station | *gare routière* | Where are you going? | *Vous allez où?* |
| bus stop | *arrêt* | I'm going to . . . | *Je vais à . . .* |
| car | *voiture* | I want to get off at . . . | *Je voudrais descendre à . . .* |
| train/taxi/ferry | *train/taxi/ferry* | | |
| boat | *bâteau* | the road to . . . | *la route pour . . .* |
| plane | *avion* | near | *près/pas loin* |
| train station | *gare (SNCF)* | far | *loin* |
| platform | *quai* | left | *à gauche* |
| What time does it leave? | *Il part à quelle heure?* | right | *à droite* |
| | | straight on | *tout droit* |
| What time does it arrive? | *Il arrive à quelle heure?* | on the other side of | *à l'autre côté de* |
| | | on the corner of | *à l'angle de* |
| a ticket to . . . | *un billet pour . . .* | next to | *à côté de* |
| single ticket | *aller simple* | behind | *derrière* |
| return ticket | *aller retour* | in front of | *devant* |
| validate your ticket | *compostez votre billet* | before | *avant* |
| valid for | *valable pour* | after | *après* |
| ticket office | *vente de billets* | under | *sous* |
| how many kilometres? | *combien de kilomètres?* | to cross | *traverser* |
| how many hours? | *combien d'heures?* | bridge | *pont* |
| hitchhiking | *autostop* | | |

## QUESTIONS AND REQUESTS

The simplest way of asking a question is to start with *s'il vous plaît* (please), then name the thing you want in an interrogative tone of voice. For example:

| | | | |
|---|---|---|---|
| Where is there a bakery? | *S'il vous plaît, la boulangerie?* | Question words: | |
| Which way is it to the Eiffel Tower? | *S'il vous plaît, la route pour la tour Eiffel?* | where? | *où?* |
| | | how? | *comment?* |
| | | how many/ how much? | *combien?* |
| Similarly with requests: | | when? | *quand?* |
| | | why? | *pourquoi?* |
| Can we have a room for two? | *S'il vous plaît, une chambre pour deux?* | at what time? | *à quelle heure?* |
| Can I have a kilo of oranges? | *S'il vous plaît, un kilo d'oranges?* | what is/which is? | *quel est?* |

## ACCOMMODATION

| | | | |
|---|---|---|---|
| a room for one/ two people | *une chambre pour une/ deux personnes* | sheets | *draps* |
| a double bed | *un lit double* | blankets | *couvertures* |
| a room with a shower | *une chambre avec douche* | quiet | *calme* |
| a room with a bath | *une chambre avec salle de bain* | noisy | *bruyant* |
| | | hot water | *eau chaude* |
| for one/two/three nights | *pour une/deux/trois nuits* | cold water | *eau froide* |
| Can I see it? | *Je peux la voir?* | Is breakfast included? | *Est-ce que le petit déjeuner est compris?* |
| a room on the courtyard | *une chambre sur la cour* | I would like breakfast | *Je voudrais prendre le petit déjeuner* |
| a room over the street | *une chambre sur la rue* | I don't want breakfast | *Je ne veux pas de petit déjeuner* |
| first floor | *premier étage* | | |
| second floor | *deuxième étage* | Can we camp here? | *On peut camper ici?* |
| with a view | *avec vue* | campsite | *un camping/terrain de camping* |
| key | *clef* | | |
| to iron | *repasser* | tent | *une tente* |
| do laundry | *faire la lessive* | tent space | *un emplacement* |
| | | youth hostel | *auberge de jeunesse* |

## CARS

| | | | |
|---|---|---|---|
| service station | *garage* | put air in the tyres | *gonfler les pneus* |
| service | *service* | battery | *batterie* |
| to park the car | *garer la voiture* | the battery is dead | *la batterie est morte* |
| car park | *un parking* | plugs | *bougies* |
| no parking | *défense de stationner/ stationnement interdit* | to break down | *tomber en panne* |
| | | gas can | *bidon* |
| gas station | *poste d'essence* | insurance | *assurance* |
| fuel | *essence* | green card | *carte verte* |
| (to) fill it up | *faire le plein* | traffic lights | *feux* |
| oil | *huile* | red light | *feu rouge* |
| air line | *ligne à air* | green light | *feu vert* |

*Box continues on next page. . .*

*. . .Box continued from previous page*

## HEALTH MATTERS

| | | | |
|---|---|---|---|
| doctor | *médecin* | stomach ache | *mal à l'estomac* |
| I don't feel well | *Je ne me sens pas bien* | period | *règles* |
| medicines | *médicaments* | pain | *douleur* |
| prescription | *ordonnance* | it hurts | *ça fait mal* |
| I feel sick | *Je suis malade* | chemist | *pharmacie* |
| I have a headache | *J'ai mal à la tête* | hospital | *hôpital* |

## OTHER NEEDS

| | | | |
|---|---|---|---|
| bakery | *boulangerie* | bank | *banque* |
| food shop | *alimentation* | money | *argent* |
| supermarket | *supermarché* | toilets | *toilettes* |
| to eat | *manger* | police | *police* |
| to drink | *boire* | telephone | *téléphone* |
| camping gas | *camping gaz* | cinema | *cinéma* |
| tobacconist | *tabac* | theatre | *théâtre* |
| stamps | *timbres* | to reserve/book | *réserver* |

# GLOSSARY

## FRENCH TERMS

**ABBAYE** Abbey.

**AUBERGE DE JEUNESSE** Youth hostel.

**BASILIQUE** Basilica.

**BASSIN** Reservoir.

**BASTIDE** Planned, usually fortified town of the thirteenth century, typically laid out on a grid in a square or octagonal area.

**CANTON** District.

**CHÂTEAU** Fort, castle, mansion or country house.

**CITÉ** Citadel: the fortified section (usually the oldest, and highest part) of a town.

**CLOCHÉ** Bell tower.

**COL** Pass.

**COLOMBIER** Dovecote.

**DÉCOUVERTE** Open pit mine.

**DEFILÉ** Narrow gorge, canyon.

**DÉPARTEMENT** Administrative area, similar to an English county, within a *région*.

**DOMAINE** Estate.

**DONJON** Castle keep.

**ÉCLUSE** Canal lock.

**ÉGLISE** Church.

**ENCEINTE** Area falling within the walls of a castle or town, or the defensive enclosure itself.

**ÉVÊCHE** Palace or property pertaining to a bishop, or archbishop (archevêché).

**FAUBOURG** Extramural suburb, usually referring to late medieval town extensions built outside the walls of the original enceinte.

**FÊTE** Festival.

**GARE** Station.

**GARE ROUTIÈRE** Bus station.

**GROTTE** Cave.

**HALLES** Market building.

**HORLOGE** Clock.

**HÔTEL DE VILLE** Town or city hall.

**HÔTEL PARTICULIER** Private mansion or palace.

**MAIRIE** Office of the mayor: town hall.

**MONASTÈRE** Monastery.

**MUSÉE** Museum.

**NAVETTE** Shuttle service.

**PAYS** Country, land.

**PIC** Peak.

**PLACE** Square.

**PONT** Bridge.

**PONT DU DIABLE** Arched medieval bridge.

**PONT VIEUX** Old bridge.

**PORTE** Gateway.

**PRÉFECTURE** Main office, headquarters.

**PRISE DE L'EAU** Dam.

**RÉGION** Administrative region.

**TERROIR** Literally meaning "soil", refers to traditional peasant cooking, using local ingredients.

**TOUR** Tower.

**USINE** Factory, workshop.

**VILLE BASSE** Lower town.

## ARTISTIC, ARCHITECTURAL AND ARCHEOLOGICAL TERMS

**AMBULATORY** Passage round the outer edge of a church's choir.

**APSE** Semicircular termination at the east end of a church.

**ART DECO** Geometrical style of art and architecture popular in the 1930s.

**ART NOUVEAU** Ornamental style of art and architecture which developed in the late nineteenth century, emphasizing decorative detail, and avoiding straight clean lines.

**BAROQUE** High Renaissance period of art and architecture, distinguished by extreme ornateness, exuberance and complex spatial arrangement of interiors.

**CAROLINGIAN** Dynasty founded by Pepin the Short; mid-eighth to early tenth centuries. Also refers to art, sculpture, etc of the time.

**CARYATID** A sculptured female figure used as a column.

**CHAPTERHOUSE** Room in a monastery or church where the clergy met daily to discuss business and administrative affairs.

**CHEVET** East end of a church.

**CLASSICAL** Architectural style incorporating Greek and Roman elements: pillars, domes, colonnades, etc, at its height in France in the seventeenth century and revived in the nineteenth century as Neoclassicism.

**CLERESTORY** Upper storey of a church, incorporating the windows.

**CRENELLATION** Battlements along the top edge of a wall or tower.

**CURTAIN WALL** Straight upright medieval defensive wall.

**DOLMEN** Neolithic stone formation, frequently consisting of a henge.

**FAUVISM** Artistic school of early twentieth-century France characterized by vivid colour.

**FOLLY** Overly ostentatious rural dwellings of seventeenth- to nineteenth-century aristocracy.

**FRESCO** Wall painting – durable through application to wet plaster.

**FRIEZE** A sculpted decorative band, typically along the upper or lower limit of a wall, and usually in low relief.

**GOTHIC** Architectural style of the thirteenth to sixteenth centuries, characterized by pointed arches, rib vaulting, flying buttresses and a general emphasis on verticality.

**IMPRESSIONISM** Late nineteenth-century French style of painting which emphasized the perception of objects through the effect of light, rather than shape.

**MAJESTÉ** Romanesque and early Gothic sculptures of Christ on the Cross (*majestat* in Catalan).

**MEROVINGIAN** Dynasty ruling France and parts of Germany from the sixth to mid-eighth centuries. Also refers to art, etc of the period.

**MOZARAB** Arab- and North African-influenced art and architectural style from Spain, brought to France around 900–1100 by Christians.

**NARTHEX** Entrance hall of church.

**NAVE** Main body of a church.

**NYMPHAEUM** A Roman or Greek shrine to a nymph, typically located at a fountain head or spring.

**OPPIDUM** Pre-Roman hill-top settlement.

**OPUS MIXTUM** Roman building technique consisting of interspersed layers of stone and brick.

**ORIENTALISM** The study of Eastern and, particularly, Middle Eastern peoples from a Western and usually heavily romanticized perspective, in the late seventeenth to eighteenth centuries.

**REFECTORY** The dining room of a monastery.

**RELIEF** The three-dimensional quality of a sculpture; its depth.

**RENAISSANCE** Artistic/architectural style developed in fifteenth-century Italy and imported to France in the sixteenth century.

**RETABLE** Altarpiece.

**ROMANESQUE** Early medieval architectural style distinguished by squat, rounded forms and naive sculpture.

**ROOD SCREEN** Barrier set in some churches between the area of the altar and choir and the rest of the nave (where the main congregation gathers).

**STUCCO** Plaster used to embellish ceilings, etc.

**TRANSEPT** Transverse arms of a church.

**TRIBUNE** Apse containing a bishop's throne; a gallery or raised area in a church.

**TROMPE L'OEIL** A decorative technique popular in the Baroque, wherein a two-dimensional painting gives the impression of being a three-dimensional object.

**TUMULUS** A Neolithic burial mound, frequently concealing a dolmen.

**TYMPANUM** A sculpted panel above a church door.

**VAULT** An arched ceiling or roof.

**VOUSSOIR** Sculpted rings in the arch over a church door.

# INDEX

# Stay in touch with us!

**ROUGHNEWS is Rough Guides' free newsletter. In three issues a year we give you news, travel issues, music reviews, readers' letters and the latest dispatches from authors on the road.**

---

I would like to receive ROUGHNEWS: please put me on your free mailing list.

NAME . . . . . . . . . . . . . . . . . . . . . . . . . . . . . . . . . . . . . . . . . . . . . . . . . . . . . . . . . . . . . . . . . . . . . .

ADDRESS . . . . . . . . . . . . . . . . . . . . . . . . . . . . . . . . . . . . . . . . . . . . . . . . . . . . . . . . . . . . . . . . . . .

Please clip or photocopy and send to: Rough Guides, 62–70 Shorts Gardens, London WC2H 9AH, England or Rough Guides, 375 Hudson Street, New York, NY 10014, USA.

# ROUGH GUIDES: Travel

Alaska
Amsterdam
Andalucia
Argentina
Australia
Austria

Bali & Lombok
Barcelona
Belgium &
 Luxembourg
Belize
Berlin
Brazil
Britain
Brittany &
 Normandy
Bulgaria
California
Canada
Central America
Chile
China
Corsica
Costa Rica
Crete
Croatia
Cuba
Cyprus
Czech & Slovak
 Republics

Dodecanese &
 the East Aegean
Devon &
 Cornwall
Dominican
 Republic
Dordogne & the
 Lot
Ecuador
Egypt
England
Europe
Florida
France
French Hotels &
 Restaurants
 1999
Germany
Goa
Greece
Greek Islands
Guatemala
Hawaii
Holland
Hong Kong &
 Macau
Hungary

Iceland
India
Indonesia
Ionian Islands
Ireland

Israel & the
 Palestinian
 Territories
Italy
Jamaica
Japan
Jordan
Kenya
Lake District
Languedoc &
 Roussillon
Laos
London
Los Angeles
Malaysia,
 Singapore &
 Brunei
Mallorca &
 Menorca
Maya World
Mexico
Morocco
Moscow
Nepal
New England
New York
New Zealand
Norway
Pacific
 Northwest
Paris
Peru
Poland
Portugal
Prague
Provence & the
 Côte d'Azur
The Pyrenees
Romania
St Petersburg
San Francisco

Sardinia
Scandinavia
Scotland
Scottish
 highlands and
 Islands
Sicily
Singapore
South Africa
South India
Southeast Asia
Southwest USA
Spain
Sweden
Switzerland
Syria

Thailand
Trinidad &
 Tobago
Tunisia
Turkey
Tuscany &
 Umbria
USA
Venice
Vienna
Vietnam
Wales
Washington DC
West Africa
Zimbabwe &
 Botswana

## AVAILABLE AT ALL GOOD BOOKSHOPS

# ROUGH GUIDES: Mini Guides, Travel Specials and Phrasebooks

## MINI GUIDES

Antigua
Bangkok
Barbados
Beijing
Big Island of Hawaii
Boston
Brussels
Budapest
Cape Town
Copenhagen
Dublin
Edinburgh

Florence
Honolulu
Ibiza & Formentera
Jerusalem
Las Vegas
Lisbon
London Restaurants
Madeira
Madrid
Malta & Gozo
Maui
Melbourne
Menorca

Montreal
New Orleans

Paris
Rome
Seattle
St Lucia
Sydney
Tenerife
Tokyo
Toronto
Vancouver

## TRAVEL SPECIALS

First-Time Asia
First-Time Europe
Women Travel

## PHRASEBOOKS

Czech
Dutch
Egyptian Arabic
European
French
German
Greek

Hindi & Urdu
Hungarian
Indonesian
Italian
Japanese
Mandarin
  Chinese
Mexican
  Spanish
Polish
Portuguese
Russian
Spanish
Swahili
Thai
Turkish
Vietnamese

AVAILABLE AT ALL GOOD BOOKSHOPS

Will you have enough stories to tell your grandchildren?

©2000 Yahoo! Inc.

Yahoo! Travel

Do You Yahoo!?